Léon Degrelle in Exile (1945–1994)

# LÉON DEGRELLE IN EXILE

# (1945–1994)

*— José Luis Jerez Riesco —*

*Translated by Jason Rogers*

ANTELOPE HILL PUBLISHING

To Léon Degrelle, a leader of Europe.

To the Legion of the Fallen and the Martyrs who, defending the traditional culture and civilization of the West, fought heroically in the cause of the social revolution to achieve the dream of a national European reality.

And to all those who today, with bravery and honor, sacrifice their lives in defense of the superior ideal to confront the "selected and chosen" worshipers of the insatiable god Moloch.

*José Luis Jerez Riesco*

*José Luis Jerez Riesco with Léon Degrelle in Madrid, 1972*

# Contents

## II. The Great Fugitive of Injustice (1946–1951)

## V. Settling in the Watchtower of La Cabaña (Fuengirola) (1963–1985)

## VI. Residential Move to the Boardwalk City of Melilla, Number 23, Malaga Capital (1986–1994)

# Translator's Foreword

Translating José Luis Jerez Riesco's book *Léon Degrelle en el Exilio, 1945–1994 (Léon Degrelle in Exile, 1945–1994)*, originally published in Spanish by Ediciones Wanderwöguel, has been both a pleasure and an education.

*Léon Degrelle in Exile* is one of those unique books that are only possible because of unique people: Waffen SS General Léon Degrelle was that unique person whose life was almost cut short on numerous occasions. Riesco's book will take you briefly through his early life, touching upon many of his exploits during the war, and then will focus on his exile in Spain. The entire story of how General Degrelle managed to get to Spain is an adventure in itself! The book is also unique in that we hear so much of Degrelle's voice, a voice that was *supposed* to be snuffed out by his enemies, but who failed repeatedly. Their failures allow us—students of history, lovers of truth, or simply the open-minded man—to hear the other side.

The importance of the book you now have lies in the fact that it challenges so much of what we think we know about the events of the Second World War. Most of our history, our understanding of the Second World War, especially in the United States and Western Europe, is told through the lens of "Holocaust" history; this colors everything we think we know about those crucial years in the twentieth century. The demonization of the Waffen SS, the "crime" of National Socialism, the "evil intent" of everyone who happened to be on the opposing side, etc....these things are taken for granted and opposing views are rarely encountered in mainstream publications. *Léon Degrelle in Exile* is that opposing voice. You will hear a strikingly different version of events, why men fought for the Axis powers, why they volunteered for the Waffen SS, what the goals of the war were, etc. Through Riesco's presentation of actual legal history, you will witness a very different side to the judicial process in Allied "justice," particularly in Belgium.

For the student of Léon Degrelle, this current volume represents a rich, detailed biography of his life in Spain, including many personal notes and letters, his personal struggles, his successes, his lawsuits, the assassination and kidnapping attempts, his deep, Catholic piety, and his ferocious bravery. The reader will learn how much other people came to know and love Degrelle as a person.

## A Few Notes on the Translation

The author of *Léon Degrelle en el Exilio, 1945–1994* is a Spanish attorney, and his writing style combines erudite, professional Spanish and legal Spanish (which is heavily influenced by Latin and just as frustrating as English "legalese"), along with a flair for lionizing his beloved subject Degrelle. This English edition generally attempts to capture his style, when possible, although in some places I have chosen to simplify for the sake of readability.

The reader should know that the author José Luis Jerez Riesco was a personal friend and disciple of Degrelle, which is why the author was uniquely privileged to obtain many personal cards and letters, which are included in this volume. Those cards and letters, most of which were originally written in French (Degrelle was a Belgian Walloon), exist primarily in physical form, so they are not yet available in digital or soft copy. After much thought and deliberation, we have decided to produce the English translation of those letters from their Spanish versions (originally translated by the author), and not directly from the French; tracking down all the original physical copies, digitizing them, collecting them in a single volume, and translating from the French would have delayed the publication of this work for quite some time.

Additionally, this volume contains a number Spanish political materials, diplomatic cables, and personal letters never before translated into English. These give a particularly rich look at the details and communications surrounding Degrelle's life.

**Republican**: *Republicano* in the Spanish context refers to that liberal, democratic government—aligned with communists—against whom the Spanish nationalists were fighting in the civil war. The term comes from the establishment of the Second Republic in 1931. In the Spanish context, this word does not refer to a politically "conservative" party, as is the case in the United States.

*Juntas de Ofensiva Nacional Sindicalista* (Councils of National Syndicalist Offensive), abbreviated as JONS, was a nationalist and fascist group that began in the early 1930s. Its followers were referred to as *jonsistas*. In 1934, this organization merged with the *Falange Española* (Spanish Phalanx) to become *Falange Española de las Juntas de Ofensiva Nacional Sindicalista* (*FE de las JONS*). The Carlists were monarchists, whose support for the Spanish monarchy distinguished them from the more fascist-oriented Falange and JONS. Francisco Franco's uniting of these right-wing, conservative groups is, in part, what allowed the nationalist forces to present a solid front against the liberal, anti-Catholic Republicans.

The author uses the term ***Anglo-Saxon*** to refer broadly to the English-speaking powers, namely Great Britain and the United States. It can be used to refer generally to politics, culture, or tendencies among these powers. I highlight this term because although its use is common, especially among French and Spanish authors, it does not generally refer to the meaning most common for American readers; that is, the historical Anglo-Saxon kingdoms and peoples of early England. Similarly, the author uses the term "England" to refer broadly to the government of Great Britain. I have maintained the author's choice of "England" in this regard most of the time, changing it to "Britain" only when I feared the less accurate term might jeopardize a larger point in the text.

In discussing the life of Degrelle or his activity in his homeland of Belgium, the terms "Walloon" and "Flemish" appear with some regularity, and they refer to the French-speaking (*wallon*) and the Flemish-speaking (*vlaams*) parts of Belgium, respectively. Degrelle hailed from the Walloon area as did many of the men who made up the SS Division Wallonia.

All footnotes have been provided by me, unless otherwise indicated.

*Jason Rogers*

*Crash landing on the beach of San Sebastián, Spain of the bomber Heinkel 111, which was transporting Léon Degrelle from Norway, May 8th, 1945*

# I

## Arrival in Spanish Territory: Convalescence in the General Mola Military Hospital, San Sebastián

## (1945–1946)

### The Incredible Aerial Feat of the Flight from Oslo to San Sebastián

The storm of the Second World War had exhausted its gunpowder, thunder, and shrapnel in the early days of May 1945. On May 7th, Germany, exhausted and bloodied, signed its surrender in the conflict. Adolf Hitler had resisted like a titan. Embraced until his last breath by the Hitler Youth, and surrounded by the cry of his people, he held the place of honor until the final moment defending the chancellery. After his death, the unmistakable Wagnerian chords and musical notes of "Twilight of the Gods" were heard on radio broadcasts of the Third Reich. The Europe of traditional, noble, and eternal values had been, on this occasion, ransacked by the machinations of the secular enemies of her immemorial culture. The spirit of struggle and combat of the European nationalist youth ceded to overwhelming and disproportionate forces. From the East, they faced a sweeping pincer of enslaving, malignant, bestial, and merciless Soviet communism, and on their western flank, they were met by greedy, usurious, and wild capitalism. An allied clamp gripped Europe, suffocating what it surrounded, bombing and destroying with blood and fire. Since then, it has grabbed all humanity with the communist-capitalist pliers that forcefully squeeze, with the same perfidious and hidden claws of the insatiable who, behind the scenes, manage the levers of power for the exclusive profit and benefit of their greedy and cursed people.

The Belgian general of the Waffen SS, Léon Degrelle, the legendary hero of that contest between life and death, was in Oslo and was surprised by the end of that storm of steel in that hyperborean landscape of great cliffs and abrupt coast. As the drama ended, his instinctive impulse, and as a first initiative, was to try to get onto a submarine that was anchored in the Norwegian fjords to transport him to Japan, the land of the rising sun. Japan had not yet surrendered. He wanted to go there in order to continue the struggle without surrender, like a samurai, until the final sunset. He was only able to locate in the vicinity of his position a small, anchored submarine. It was a single-seat submersible with reduced autonomy and meager operational range. At that point, there was no warship out at sea, so Degrelle had to give up the idea of joining the Japanese Army to continue the fight.

It was of paramount importance not to fall into the hands of the communists. The Soviets would have treated him—as Degrelle was already known as an elite fighter and a living legend—as coveted prey, as a prized war trophy, which would lead to his martyrdom in the midst of that witches' coven, that vodka-soaked vortex, represented by a human horde of incontinence.

If he had to die in the final siege, Degrelle was fully determined to do so with weapon in hand. He would fight to the point of exhaustion for the cause of the ideal, as did the glorious knights of old who were devoted to their noble causes.

On May 7th, the day of the cessation of hostilities, Léon Degrelle, as we have already pointed out, found himself in good battle morale in the Norwegian boreal lands, ready to reform a combat group, however small it might be. Dr. Josef Terboven, the German governor in Norway, communicated to him that neighboring Sweden was not prepared to grant him asylum, so it would be fruitless and suicidal to head east, where he would most likely be arrested and handed over to the new and brutal masters of the situation.

He left that day from the hotel where he was staying in Oslo and made his way to the airport in a small Volkswagen convertible. He was accompanied by a handful of young comrades in arms. All of them were properly uniformed, as if they were to participate in a triumphal parade. They wore their respective dress uniforms with their numerous decorations, won with much effort and sacrifice. They shone clearly on their chests, decorations they proudly displayed on that day after the armistice. They crossed the half-empty streets of Oslo under an open sky, about eight hours after the cease-fire that occurred with the signing of the inevitable surrender. The car, which was moving slowly with the convertible top down, was, in addition to General Degrelle, occupied by the German driver, Albert Durigen, and his liaison officer, Robert du Welz. Du Welz would pass away in Spain in 1979. The other companions, of German nationality, had been waiting for him next to the plane which was going to transport the uncompromising commander.

It was just about midnight when Degrelle, in the company of his five air adventure comrades, climbed inside the small machine. The plane, parked on the runway, had belonged to the German minister Albert Speer. It was recently abandoned by its usual crew at the Oslo airfield. The Reich Minister of Armaments had decided at the last minute not to travel with him to Iceland to seek shelter there, at the ends of the earth, in his retreat. He preferred to remain at the Schleswig-Holstein headquarters where Admiral Dönitz was located. The plane was an H-23 type Heinkel 111, with TQ+MU encryption, a former bomber specially adapted for transport of up to ten passengers.

The commissioner of the German Third Reich in Norway, Joseph Terboven, had previously authorized its availability and use. The airman was Albert Durigen, who would emigrate from Spain to Argentina in 1947. He initially worked in the Ministry of Agriculture and Livestock and would become a famous pilot for the civil aviation flag company Aerolíneas Argentinas. Durigen set out to fly the plane, taking off from an improvised runway without proper air navigation conditions. The operational range and flight autonomy of the plane was not designed to cover the distance of the 2,300 kilometers (1,429 miles) that separated the passengers from their starting point to the unbelievable goal that was to be achieved: Spain. More than ever, it would be necessary to take the risk. "Take the bull by the horns and go!" as the squadron motto of the Spanish ace pilot, Joaquín García Morato, proclaimed. Ironically, the street where Léon Degrelle lived in Madrid would share the name of that famous Spanish pilot.

On board this unique aircraft, accompanying General Degrelle on his last campaign flight, was his faithful assistant and inseparable friend, Captain Robert du Welz, one of the first rexists[1] to join the legion of Belgian volunteers that left Brussels as part of the first contingent headed for the Eastern Front on August 8th, 1941. Durigen was assisted by the rest of the crew, composed of a German mechanic and two German co-pilots: Georg Kubel, Gerhard Stride, and Benno Epner. They were all perfectly and impeccably dressed in their uniforms, military insignia, and decorations, their corresponding ranks achieved with pride and courage in the service of the Third Reich's disciplined, fierce, and admired army. Degrelle was wearing his *Ritterkreuz* (Knight's Cross) around his neck.

"We took off from an improvised runway, without lighting or signals. God help us! There were five of us" Degrelle remembered later.

Embarking on this high-risk flight was important. It was a gamble for life, surrounded, once again, by the dizzying specter of death. The die was cast.

The cartography available on board the plane at the time of takeoff was practically zero. They had only a worn, large-scale, detailed map of Norway and a

---

[1] The rexists, or the Rex Party, was Léon Degrelle's politically right-wing party in Belgium. The Rex Party will be further defined and clarified in subsequent chapters.

tiny, folded sheet, little larger than the size of a leaflet, torn from a pocket diary, with the silhouette of Europe in miniature. The navigation plan was traced along the following route: from Oslo, the nose of the plane was oriented towards England and, upon reaching that coastline, the plane would change course, pointing its trajectory towards the south of the European continent, thus pretending to be a British or American flight from Britain. The stratagem did not have the fully desired effect. The Dutch, when discovering the twin-engine flight on radar, lit up the sky with searchlights, casting luminous beams everywhere, trying incessantly to confirm the identity of the crew and the flight order. Confronted with radio silence and no response from those veritable knights of the air, the dry and rapid bursts of deadly, long-range artillery came with persistent repetition from the coastal anti-aircraft defenses.

Miraculously, the plane emerged undamaged and continued on its solitary journey through the European night sky. The plane's tail was painted with an easily recognizable and prominent swastika. It dodged, like lightning bolts, from the anti-aircraft batteries that tried to bring down the plane every time the rumble of its motors was heard in the darkness of the night sky. It was the grand finale, the end of the party, the great *mascletá*, the climax, a chaotic, infernal storm, and, at the same time, the apocalypse.

The plane skirted the turbulence from the anti-aircraft fire and passed through the airspace of the old and wounded European continent at an altitude of 4,000 meters (13,123 feet) before first flying over Brussels in a sentimental farewell. Their lives flashed in front of their eyes and danced in their minds like fire, that eschatological vision that is felt at glimpsing the moment of death. Later, they skirted the periphery of Paris, crossing over France to its southwest limit; in a few hours they reached Bordeaux, already having spent the last reserve liter of fuel. They were beginning to lose altitude in Biarritz, where the plane, driven by inertia, was gliding forward in non-motorized flight. Their resolute intention was to reach the Iberian Peninsula and land at any airport that could be located within their view. They were prepared to quickly remove the military clothing they were wearing, replacing it with the civilian clothing they carried in their rucksacks. Then, they would blow the plane up with the two or three bombs they carried. Screened by the smoke and confusion, and being protected by the element of surprise, they would put an end to the operation and slip into Spain undetected. Once on dry land, they aimed to board a merchant ship that would bring them closer to their ultimate goal of Japan. They would arrive, in whatever way possible, either as stowaways or as part of the merchant crew, to join the last resistance, the last focal point of the great battle, without surrender.

Years later, Léon Degrelle, the protagonist of that feat, would comment to the journalist, Wim Dannau, that:

*The adventure of San Sebastián was an impossible mission. The impossibility was overcome because anything for me was preferable to capitulation. I preferred death a thousand times, being killed in flight, crashing against the ground, dying at sea, rather than perishing as a victim of injustice.*

Degrelle made it very clear, with that unprecedented aerial adventure, that he preferred to die rather than surrender. Moreover, he had also calculated the intoxicating euphoria that news of the German surrender would have produced among the Allied troops. It would make that first night of "victory" an inebriated celebration, with alcohol and collective hangovers shared among the jubilant hosts, and who knows what else. Degrelle was not going to be present to find out!

## On Spanish Soil

At 6:40 a.m. on May 8th, the plane's fuel tank was totally empty. Yet somehow it was still pushed along by the sea breezes like the last, desperate gasps of a breathless agony, its tail wind tossing the plane about like a tree leaf in autumn. The plane gradually lost altitude until it crashed into the bay of La Concha de San Sebastián, into the middle of the beautiful cove over which the verdant mountains Igueldo and Urgull keep watch, those giant sentinels of the secluded island of Santa Clara. It was quite fortunate for their survival that the water was at low tide.

The impact on the beach was hard, violent, and brutal. That inevitable emergency landing with the plane's abrupt and spasmodic movements, uncontrolled because of the lack of fuel and the loss of altitude, was increasingly jolting in the midst of those turbulent waters of the Cantabrian Sea. The friction of the fuselage, with the landing gear pulled up—the twin-engines sliding over the wet sand at low tide, the propellers already split by the collision of smacking the sea water—served as the brake on their improvised aquatic runway. The remains of the Heinkel 111 aircraft slid down the fine sands of La Concha beach, and due to the semicircular shape of that haven, the plane re-submerged in the water as it came to a halt, as if being buried in a glorious twilight baptism.

The remains of the Heinkel 111 were rescued and taken at first to Lasarte airport, and then later, before being scrapped, to a hangar in Logroño.

Léon Degrelle's body was completely broken, like a cup of fine porcelain having fallen sharply to the ground. His bones were fractured by the shock of the plane slamming into the water and the sand. Fire from the immolating plane quickly began to spread, igniting the rest of the combustible material. His upper humerus and left shoulder had four fractures. One of his legs was also fractured due to the violent impact. It was a brutal set of injuries, but Degrelle was alive.

Léon always considered the miracle of his surviving that accident an act of divine protection. During his extended stay in the hospital, he distributed as many icon cards as he could of Saint Michael the Archangel, on which, together with the litanies, he had the following text of thanksgiving printed:

> *In memory of May 8th, 1945, thanks to a constant divine protection from the "terrible judgment" of merciless enemies, I descended at 6:40 a.m. onto the beach of La Concha de San Sebastián, in the midst of the great roar of my plane, which shook land and sea, and survived.*

First a passer-by saw them, and then an ambulance came to the aid of the wrecked aircraft. Degrelle's crippled body was transported to Navy Command, located near of the beach, where Colonel Espinosa de los Monteros, after the usual, mandatory military identifications, asked him some preliminary questions. From there, he was immediately transferred to the General Mola Military Hospital in the city of Donostiarra for surgery. His entry was under precautionary measures, with his admission to the military medical compound kept classified.

His field assistant, Robert du Welz, also survived the crash landing, as did Albert Durigen who, at the time of rescue, was still trapped in the cabin, caught by the aircraft's controls. Only one of the German crew perished in the crash landing.

Navy Command communicated the incident to its corresponding minister in Madrid in a dispatch, in which Léon Degrelle was already identified as a survivor of that suicidal expedition. The cable was intercepted by British intelligence services who now had news of their arrival on the Spanish coast. For his part, the British Deputy Consul in the city of Donostiarra immediately confirmed the news that reached him of the whereabouts of the rexist chief and his companions. A Belgian business manager in Madrid, Jacques de Thier, who had been there in a diplomatic role since September 1944, was informed by telephone of the event by the Spanish authorities around 8:00 a.m. Upon receiving the unexpected news, Thier was shocked and surprised. He was immediately called to jointly analyze the situation by the Under-Secretary for Foreign Affairs, Cristóbal del Castillo. Castillo, lacking an exact knowledge of the actual events early on, told Thier that the damaged aircraft would be repaired. Once ready and refueled, the Spanish government would hand it over, along with those people who arrived in it, to a United Nations representative to take charge. From there, and depending on the circumstances, the UN could make them available to the Belgian authorities or to whomever they deemed appropriate. Upon later confirming the impossibility of recovering the aircraft, the Spanish official suggested the possibility of forming a commission, with representatives from Belgium, the United States, and England, to make an allied and joint determination on the situation. It was even hypothesized that a ship, anchored in the vicinity of the Cantabrian Sea, might be allowed to pick up Degrelle at a decided hour, or even, if feasible, deliver him to the Rock of Gibraltar.

As hard as it may seem, the crash landing was actually a stroke of luck. If Léon Degrelle had been uninjured during the crash, it is possible that the Spanish authorities, in order to avoid complications in those crucial moments, might have asked him to leave Spain immediately. Léon Degrelle was totally immobilized by his multiple fractures and severe trauma, and this is what saved him. His short-term misfortune was really a long-term blessing.

Everything seemed to indicate that, had it not been for the aviation accident and its subsequent consequences, the fate of Degrelle would have been the same as French Minister Pierre Laval. Laval had flown to a Barcelona airport a week earlier, on May 2nd. He was arrested and detained in the Montjuich Fortress on the orders of Spanish Foreign Minister José Félix de Lequerica. On the same day as Laval's arrest, Marcel Deat and French Minister Abel Bonnard had also been arrested in a precautionary and preventive manner. At the same time, another compatriot of Degrelle, the Chief Propaganda Officer of the Rexist Party in La Louvière and Director of Passive Defense in Soignies, Albert Emile Laurens Druart, who had entered Spain through the border crossing at La Junquera, was intercepted and held in the town of Figueras on April 9th, 1945.

On May 8th, the guard officer in the garrison of San Sebastián was the young and handsome lieutenant, Antonio Vallejo Zaldo. Zaldo was a great patriot and a seasoned warrior. He had fought for God and for Spain as a provisional ensign during the crusade of Spanish liberation.[2] Later, he fought against Bolshevism as a Blue Division[3] volunteer on the steppes of Russia.

---

[2] Reference to the Spanish Civil War.

[3] *La División Azul* (The Blue Division) was a full-strength division of four regiments largely made up of Spanish volunteers. This unit served on the Eastern Front. Organized in 1941 shortly after Germany's invasion of Soviet Russia, the division was integrated into the German Wehrmacht as its 250th Infantry Division. Like many volunteers from across Europe, whether serving with the Wehrmacht or with the Waffen SS, this military service was seen primarily through the lens of anti-communist sentiment.

Initially there was a rumor, which spread quickly throughout the city, that the plane stranded on La Concha beach could be the arrival of Adolf Hitler himself in Spain, chosen as his land of asylum. The word circulated—wide and fanciful—throughout the day through all the cafes, shops, and gossip holes of the Donostiarra capital.

## Admission to the General Mola Hospital

In the emergency ward of the General Mola Military Hospital, in San Sebastián, five fractures were found in Léon Degrelle's body. He had a broken foot and several injuries to the left shoulder, with a fracture to the top of the humerus bone of the arm, requiring the physicians to immobilize both limbs. For several months his body would have to remain completely immobilized in his narrow room, so he asked the nursing staff to place him against the other wall, in front of a collection of iron tubes that were painted like a map of Europe. It was a precious and priceless icon.

His medical team stipulated that, given his delicate condition, rest should be scrupulously observed. Any movement or displacement of the patient was prohibited, regardless of what civil or military authorities might advise or use to try to evacuate the warrior. The doctor's orders on this issue were quite clear and unambiguous. Violating such an order would be tantamount to a premeditated crime and would be subject to serious repercussions, including criminal penalties.

The plaster and metal gadgets used to reset and mend Degrelle's crippled and bruised body, including a sling arm, weighed more than 5 kilos (11 pounds). Degrelle had to endure both the injuries and the extra weight with fortitude, serenity, and stoicism. In fact, that terrible, almost fatal, tragedy brought the mythological hero of the Second World War to the threshold of death and then rebirth, just like a Phoenix. He would emerge to a new and complicated life of exile.

The victory of the soul had survived the defeat of the body. As Blas Piñar[4] wrote in his memoirs, "…only a man strong of body and soul could survive the tragedy and the fractures and injuries of that very forced and dangerous landing."

Léon Degrelle had to accept an uncomfortable hospitalization in a small room at General Mola Military Hospital. It was furnished austerely with an iron bed, over which a crucifix hung, a white wooden table, and two chairs. The walls were

---

[4] Blas Piñar López was a right-wing attorney and politician who served in the Franco regime as the director of the Institute of Hispanic Culture, a court prosecutor, and a national councilor. After Franco's death, he remained active in right-wing politics. Piñar and Degrelle were friends.

painted in limestone white, decorated only with some personal mementos affixed with push pins: photos of his wife and children, geographical maps and photos of fighting from an illustrated magazine, and some literary inscriptions, such as this verse from Racine:

> *Quoiqu'à peine à mes maux je puisse résister,*
> *J'aime mieux les souffrir que de les mérite.*[5]

In solitude, between those four white walls with only a single window to the outside world that allowed a view to a distant railway, Léon would spend sixteen uninterrupted months of his life.

## Harassment Begins

On May 21st, just two weeks after he was admitted to the hospital with multiple injuries, the British government sent a communication to its Ambassador in Spain, letting him know that he was prohibited from intervening in handing over Léon Degrelle to his country of origin. Degrelle was not considered a war criminal, and therefore the situation was an internal, bilateral issue between the Belgian and Spanish governments. The government of "His Gracious Majesty," however, stated that the Spanish government should proceed with Degrelle's surrender and expulsion, considering him an "*undesirable alien.*" The United States government had also not blacklisted Léon Degrelle.

One of the first letters that Léon Degrelle sent during his convalescence was a month into his hospitalization. He wrote to Pierre Daye on June 7th to bring him up to date on the situation. He was one of Degrelle's comrades at the very beginning of the Rexist Movement, a national deputy and Director of the Belgian-German Chamber of Commerce. Daye was one of the first to take the lead in joining the detachment sent from Brussels on August 8th, 1941, to fight against Bolshevism.

Pierre Daye, in the spring of 1944, had made a trip to Barcelona to have an interview with General Moscardó[6] and decided then to settle definitively in Spain. He then moved to Madrid, where he proceeded to request the political and legal

---

[5] The following verse is not from Racine, but rather from Pierre Corneille's *Horace*. The lines are Camille's response to Julie in Act I, Scene Two: "*Although hardly can I resist my troubles, I would rather suffer them than deserve them.*" [translator's translation].

[6] José Moscardó Ituarte was a military hero from the Spanish Civil War, for which he was promoted to general, and continued to serve under Franco. By late 1944, Moscardó held command in Barcelona.

protection of the Spanish authorities. Among those who endorsed his request for political asylum was the academic, Eugenio D'Ors, and the journalist, Manuel Aznar. The Spanish government, which initially showed itself receptive, subsequently denied his asylum claim when, in the midst of a purging campaign, it became known that Daye had been sentenced to capital punishment *in absentia* in Belgium on December 18th, 1946, for his political alignment with the Third Reich during the war. This motivated his expatriation to Argentina.

For historical reasons, the content of this letter is interesting because in it Degrelle describes, in great detail, his last days of the war before his arrival in Spain. The letter, although extensive, is worth relating in full:

*My dear Pierre,*

*I miss you a lot! What has been going on with you? When are you going to decide to come to San Sebastián to see your old friend of yesteryear? I am sure that, being so eloquent, you will not refuse the invitation to come and tell me good morning! I will stay here for a few months to mend my broken bones! On the x-ray this morning it was noticed that there were two more fractures, just in the back where the left arm and shoulder come together. Result: I am going to have half of my body in a cast. This is not fun. I cannot imagine that I will be better before the end of August, at the soonest.*

*Not having any news is killing me. You must have Spanish and French newspapers, magazines, books. Through our friend, Espinosa de los Monteros, get me a package with some reading material. I know you are a maniac collector, so I would be very grateful to you for this favor!*

*As for my family, I live in terrible anguish. You know that two days after my crash here, Hayoit de Termicourt committed the shameful act, in his spite, of having my old father and old mother arrested and imprisoned! They are seventy-eight years old with twenty-eight grandchildren! Dad has grown quite old and is no longer in a position to dress himself! As for my mother, as you know her evangelical sweetness well, she has been dying of heart disease as of last February. She is kept alive only by injections. I cannot think, without bursting into tears, of the crucifixion that these poor people are going through. According to what I have read in a small French newspaper from the Pyrenees region, everyone in the Degrelle family, including poor Jeanne Raty, whose state of health you know well, and her two daughters, has been detained. Two little girls!*

*I wonder how far this shamefulness will go?*

*As for poor Marie-Paule [Degrelle's wife] who has had great courage and mastery, I know absolutely nothing of what has happened to her, or our five small* children, one of them a baby of only eight months! She was hidden in a forest, and in her three-line telegram she says nothing about it. What a tragedy! How can we be reunited one day? Are the International Red Cross or the Vatican going to deal with all these tragedies?

I could bring Marie-Paule and the children here, assuming they are at liberty, but how? With whose help?

Let us not forget that there is going to be a horrible famine as has never been seen...

How many events since our separation! At the time of the Allies' arrival in Belgium, I was fighting in Estonia, a very exciting country of lakes, fir trees, heather. I was able to safeguard—for a short time perhaps—the old university town of Dorpat, thus winning my oak leaves. Then it was the offensive of the Ardennes. You see our joy! Christmas at home! We were in our beautiful Ardennes, covered in snow, with its violet valleys, its old shelters with turrets, the immense panoramas of the plain of Houffalize. We spent Christmas Eve and New Year's Eve among all the brave farmers who had given us an unforgettable welcome. Then came the methodical and relentless crushing. Everything was reduced to ashes. La Roche, Houffalize, Saint Vith were nothing more than horrible mountains of rubble. Nothing could escape. This was our return home.

Soon we were again assigned to the Russian front. In the Ardennes, we had not played any military role, at any time. In Pomerania, in front of Stargard, it was another matter. The power of the Soviets was fabulous. To the assault of each village, they used huge 20-20-40 tanks![7] We had four hundred-fifty deaths and seven hundred injured (out of the one thousand four hundred men we had fighting) in five weeks! It was absolutely horrific. Poor Meseta died with his usual heroism by a horrible grenade explosion that got him in the stomach. Four times in a week, I was made prisoner, virtually prisoner. Every time they took me prisoner, I slipped away like a snake. The nights were grandiose, all the villages burning in the snow, while the Russian tanks roared at point blank with their headlights on! We spent thirty-five days pulling back 30 kilometers (17 miles)! The heroism of the German Army was an indescribable thing, but in the last three days of the battle of Altdam, in front of Stettin, there were only one thousand men left among the three divisions!

We had a month of respite behind the Oder. We had gathered all the remaining forces, about two thousand men, of whom six hundred fifty were from the shock troops.

---

[7] While the "20-20-40" designation is unclear, Degrelle may be referring to the Russian T-40, which featured a 20 mm TNSh autocannon.

On April 20th, the Russians crossed the river. We threw our six hundred fifty men against the attack: on five occasions they repelled the Russians several kilometers back, but in the end the fighting was already a mêlée, and we only had thirty-five men left! Poor Albert Verpoorten had his two arms blown off and his head opened! We had a family of four brothers, all four of whom died.[8]

What could we do? The secret orders I received as a division commander prohibited me from firing more than one shot per piece of artillery per day and from firing more than two grenades per grenade launcher! Our ammunition was depleted. You know our Walloons. They were there to the end in everything.

The whole army withdrew in the direction of the English, who were, despite everything, two days behind everybody!

I was only able to escape by a real miracle. The night of May 1st to May 2nd, I had been called by Himmler; my division and that of the Flemish (which I was also commanding towards the end!) had to position themselves behind Lübeck. I had just enough time to get my little off-road vehicle between the Russians and the English. Shortly thereafter, the path was cut off. It was a good mess; I could not regroup with the rest of the legion, which was otherwise completely dispersed. I only had a handful of men left, who had already reached Lübeck. A last anti-Bolshevik front remained, that of northern Norway. I decided to reconstitute a combat unit there, all the more so because I had news that other Walloons were trying to reach Denmark by sea. I arrived in Copenhagen, after a thousand adventures, just to fall into a full-blown revolution. I spent fourteen hours in the midst of a triumphant mob. One of my two assistant officers was engulfed by the tide of people. Thanks to the unprecedented self-confidence and help of a German, I was able to cross the whole city at the peak of the tide. I jumped on a small warship and after seeing the English deboard a plane right under my nose in Copenhagen, I arrived in Oslo on Sunday.

The next day, in Oslo I witnessed another surrender again at 2:00 p.m. We spent some incredible hours. Finally, at 10:00pm, a German deputy aviation officer, whom I knew nothing about, offered me the chance of flying overnight to Spain. The airfield had not yet been taken. A private plane was in a hangar. The plane's aviator had explained to him that he should go to Trondheim. We slid into the plane like "stoemelings."[9] At 11:30 p.m., without a navigation chart, the adventure began. To have stayed longer in the city of Oslo would have risked our

---

[8] A note in the Spanish version identifies these men as the Neuteleer brothers, but this has not been confirmed.

[9] [Dutch for silly, naïve, or dummy.]

being taken by the partisans. To wait till the next day would have made us prisoners of an English airborne division. We had to try our luck!

What an adventure! First, we took a long trip across the North Sea, then we had to reach Holland. Soon I could see, in horror, a beacon of light that was glaring behind us, then it passed beneath us, until it was ahead of us. Ground lights were lit. We were questioned by radio: "Who are you?" We were going to set off alarms across Europe while they were celebrating victory! What excitement! We were signaling all over the arrival of enemy fighter planes!

At full speed, we flew over Antwerp, shining in the dark of night. Oh! My heart broke as we flew over my homeland! Antwerp was there, Brussels was there, the forest of Cambre, my house! I also thought of all my enemies, over which I was passing! Then it was Lille! Then Paris, dazzling, with trails of light everywhere trying to catch us with a hit! The farther south we headed, the more normal our flight became. Who could imagine, on this festive evening, a German plane flying over Orléans or Angoulême?

We were more concerned about which course to take than the aircraft's range, with a maximum fuel capacity for 2,100 kilometers (1,305 miles). A straight line from Oslo to the Pyrenees, however, is already 2,150 kilometers (1,336 miles). There was a terrible risk of running out of fuel before we made it to salvation!

The gasoline was coming to an end. We looked at the night. There were cities, we imagined, near the border. Some vehicles were driving around. Suddenly I noticed a shimmering river, powerful, like the arm of a giant. I was sure of what I saw: it was the mouth of the Gironde. We were on the right track, but the fuel was rapidly burning up. Failures were multiplying. The plane was slowing down, increasingly descending towards the waves below. Those were horrible moments.

We put on the life jackets. We followed the coast. We saw Arcachon, reflecting in the twilight, then the large hydroplane harbor, and then the endless, completely dark landmass. Behind it was the glare of the sea. Oh! When will this landmass end! I was looking for the lights of Biarritz, but there was nothing! We were quickly losing altitude; we were almost flush with the waves. The dawn slowly gave out a little light. I guessed, more than distinguished, the Pyrenees and their humps. They were too pretty. Blue, black, with a slight pale pink shade against the background of dawn. We were going to go under when dawn broke. The pilot turned on the red lights of the landing gear. To think that Spain was ahead: we could even make out a lighthouse! Already two French motorboats were going out to sea to fish. With an astonishing slowness, the plane gasped, driven by its dry engines: still six kilometers to go, five, four, one…, we now saw dark green rocks. The pilot then jumped for joy. Landing here meant a crash landing. He put the plane almost vertical, and *gulping the last few drops of gasoline, our plane sputtered over the cliffs and roofs. Ahead of us we had a narrow strip of sand between the rocky mounds of the inlet. To attempt a normal landing here would risk crashing against the rocks. The landing gear did not activate, and the plane lurched, sliding across the sand without wheels! Obviously, we had to capsize, but that would be less terrible than getting crushed! At the end of 20 meters (66 feet), the right motor fell off, followed by a dizzying fall. I was tossed around like a ball in the fuselage. We had penetrated the sea, which flooded the plane, but we were alive! I was able to see two agitated policemen with tri-colored hats on shore! We were in Spain!*

*I have not yet told you that with me came a colleague of ours, dear Robert du Welz, who held the rank of captain and who had made the decision not to abandon me at that time. He was able to be taken out perfectly, without any fractures.*

*As for me, my left foot is broken, but I can stand pretty well. I got three fractures right at the point where the left arm fits into the shoulder, although it is not just the arm in a plaster cast, but my entire trunk on the left side. I assure you that two and a half months for such a convalescence is not too exciting!*

*That is why you must come and visit me. If times are difficult for you, I will cover the price of your trip, my old comrade. I do really want to see you and hear you. Besides, you are an old observer of human nature, and you should not doubt that I too, for the last few months, have not been staring at my shoes. If I had an American publisher, I could give him a book that would be different from the stupidities that are spoken around me. I have had views from all sides over the past few weeks. I am shocked to see that no one has yet spoken of certain formidable things that happened in the end. I wonder if, finally, I am the only one who knows them.*

*In any case, I have lived, I can tell you, a fabulous epic and I believe that no one has been better able than I to observe the double aspect, both political and military, of this fabulous tragedy.*

*As far as I am concerned, it is necessary to remain strictly in my capacity as a senior officer.*

*I have not been a head of government, nor a minister. I have been a soldier against Bolshevism, that is it! I have earned all my promotions (I was promoted to general just this year) solely on my war merits. I am in possession of the Iron Cross with Oak Leaves, the German Gold Cross, and the Gold Medal of the Wounded (which is awarded to those who have been wounded at least five times). Moreover, and this proves my role as a true combatant, I have received from the Führer the Golden Badge for Close Combat, which is granted after having participated in at least fifty hand-to-hand battles. This is the highest decoration of the infantry, and*

*I was the first officer of the whole German Army to receive it. There are only about eighty soldiers who have earned it, and no foreigner except me.*

*I say this to you so that, if you have the opportunity, you can speak on the true and entire military role I had during the war.*

*As far as my family is concerned, just look around. In time, it will be necessary to find a Spanish or English person who, with the necessary documents, could go to lend a hand to my wife and children. In terms of this, it is a simple humanitarian case: a woman and five young children, from eight months old to eleven years old.*

*For my parents, just an intervention from someone high up and the Red Cross, the Vatican, or England—they were arrested in the English zone—could, I think, put an end to this shamefulness. If my mother stays in jail, she will almost certainly die there this year. To think that they should celebrate their golden anniversary on June 12th!*

*Now, my dear Pierre, I conclude:*

1) *Come. Insist that our friend, Lequerica, obtain permission for you to make a friendly visit to a seriously injured person.*

2) *Through our friends, the Espinosa de los Monteros family, send me some periodicals, newspapers, and current books.*

*If you have accurate news about my family, please let me know what is going on.*

*Obviously, these months here are complicated months. You are a good man and a true friend. Remember the time you came to look for me in Carcassonne and to feed my heart with your friendship?*

*To our French friends send my best wishes. Robert du Welz will tell you a thousand affectionate things. For my part, my dear old Pierre, I embrace you with heartfelt emotion.*

The Spanish government would refuse the request for extradition, although it tried to find the best way to resolve the case. This in no way facilitated the normalization of full relations with the Allies, the new masters of Europe, given that Franco's regime had been stigmatized by the victors. Discussions on May 30th between the Belgian representative, Jacques de Thier, and the Spanish undersecretary, Cristóbal del Castillo, led to the possibility of surrendering Degrelle on the condition that he not be considered by his claimants as a "war criminal" and, of course, that the surrender would not in any way result in his execution. Another possibility that was raised in those tedious talks concerning extradition was a pure and simple expulsion from Spanish territory, putting Degrelle somewhere on the border, maybe even the border of the British enclave on Gibraltar, although this possibility was not considered by Britain.

Belgian representation at the San Francisco Conference, which took place from April 25th to June 26th, was headed by its Foreign Minister, Paul-Henry Spaak, a corrupt politician linked to freemasonry and an enemy of Léon. In order to extort the Spanish government, Spaak presented the proposal that no government, thinking primarily of Spain, which had risen to power with the help of the Axis, should be admitted to the United Nations.

Despite threats and diplomatic tensions, on June 30th the Spanish government refused to hand Degrelle over to French police, as the Belgians had hoped. It still did not, however recognize him as a political refugee and continued to consider a consensual handover to the United Nations.

## The Personal Diary

When Degrelle was healthy enough to write, he kept a personal diary in which he would write down his inner thoughts. Some paragraphs from his notes are provided below:

*We all carry our cross. It must be carried with a proud smile, so we know we are stronger than suffering and also so that those who wounded us know their arrows reached us in vain.*

*The only true joys are not those given to us by others, but those of which we are the bearers, those which our faith creates, which nourish our dynamism! The rest comes, moreover, like foam on the sea, bright on the crest of the waves, agitated but for an instant, on the edge of the sand, only to suddenly die or withdraw with the tide. That is the happiness that others bring us.*

*The joy that arises from our passion for life and from our will is similar to the great force that roars and rolls at the bottom of the seas, which leaps towards its meeting with the sun, being renewed every second.*

*It is necessary, hitched to a boat, to watch the mighty sea throw its waves like giant leopard skins, and then to spread out, flexible and shiny, and straighten like a silver fire or like a great sheaf of white flowers. Without ceasing, this life returns, springing forth again; it is known that nothing, until the end of the world, will stop this impulse.*

*Thus, must our hearts be strong, impetuous, yet similar to this wonderful rhythmic, orderly force, undertaken as an eternal song.*

*Next to the long voluptuousness of solitary domination, which is human melancholy, it flowers without vigor, with muted colors, on which the weak breezes float!*

*Melancholy is the disease of the defeated.*

*Joy is the fire of untamed colors, and no mishap can quench or suffocate these fiery colors!*

*Joy passes like the wind, real like the wind, but also fast and untrappable like the wind! When the song of the breeze comes, it has already disappeared forever.*

*It is necessary, however, to love happiness, as the song of the wind is loved, however fleeting it may be, as the colors of evening are loved even though you know they will die…*

*For the great winds are reborn and sing again and, every day, the colors climb again the great mast of the risen sun.*

*When you watch the sea descending on the sands, and returning to the deep shadows of the horizon, know that it will return, in a great resurgence, a few hours later, white, flashing in the sun, bold and strong, as if the waves were the first to assault the world!*

*My imagination searches in the void, just as the arms of a blind man are disoriented. My soul was like a bird, struck by the winds, that has lost its course.*

## The Case of René Lagrou

In Girona, on June 30th, 1945, the Spanish police questioned the Belgian leader, René Lagrou. He had been arrested for clandestinely having crossed the Spanish French border, accompanied by his secretary, Cornélie Jeanne Simone LeClercq. When asked by the acting officials about the issue he was being charged with and for which he had been arrested, he declared that he was coming to seek asylum and political refuge in Spain because he faced a death sentence, which could not be appealed. It had been handed down without any procedural guarantee by a war council held in Antwerp on January 24th, 1945. The court had been composed of communist elements and members of the resistance in his country and this death penalty was imposed on him for the sole and exclusive reason of having fought alongside the German Army.

René Lagrou was a member of the board of directors of the *Vlaamsch Nationaal Verbond* (Flemish National Front) party. He was also the author of an interesting eye-witness account of his political and military experiences during the early days of the war when he was deported in France. The book, entitled *Wij Verdachten* (*We*

*Suspects*) had been published in Brussels in 1940. Like his compatriot Léon Degrelle, he had departed, on May 10th, 1941, as a volunteer to fight on the Eastern Front in the European crusade against Bolshevism.

After the Allied occupation of Belgium, he first traveled to Vienna and later to Berlin and Soldau, where he attempted to restore a government in exile. When Berlin fell to the Allies, he managed to pass into France via a Swiss route, with false documentation, arriving in Perpignan, where he remained hidden for a month and maintained contacts with Jan Brans, José Verdeyen, and Antoine Vandervost.

The civil governor of Girona, in view of the result of the interrogation, placed Lagrou and his secretary at the disposal of the chief of police in Barcelona, in compliance with instructions received from the Ministry of Foreign Affairs and the Directorate General for Security. Both were held in the Montjuic Fortress while seeking a way out of their irregular situation. During their prison stay, they met with the French Minister, Pierre Laval.

With the help of the monks at the Monastery of Montserrat, René Lagrou was able to first escape and then flee to South America. He would return to Belgium in 1960 to reunite with his family.

## The First Kidnapping Attempt

In July, Belgian Intelligence Services faced Spanish demands for full guarantees for the handover of Degrelle. The Spanish government was reluctant to extradite Degrelle to the new socialist-communist authorities in Belgium. Belgian agents then launched a plan to kidnap the patient hospitalized in San Sebastián. The goal was to take him using a commando unit comprised of former communist members of the resistance, led by Commander Ides Floor. Others among the team were André Hautain, André Wodon, and Dr. Pierre Houssa. They had settled in the neighboring French city of Biarritz to carry out the terrorist action. They were willing to bribe Basque criminals with large sums of money, amounting to one hundred thousand pesetas, a fortune in those times of scarcity, to drive their coveted prey to the border.

The Belgian agents in charge of carrying out the mission also contacted the junior hospital staff, guards, and nurses, hinting at the possibility of a worthwhile reward if they agreed to facilitate things. The police discovered the team's intentions, and the plan was derailed. This was how news of the foiled kidnapping attempt made it into the media, both into the French newspaper, *Le Monde,* and into the Belgian newspaper, *Le Soir,* on July 31st. This was a serious warning to the wardens guarding the convalescent that they needed to redouble their efforts. The Spanish authorities, intending to disseminate false information, let the word out that Degrelle was to be transferred very soon to Montjuic in Barcelona. They tried to pull attention away from Degrelle's actual location to make it difficult for any future kidnapping attempts to be carried out, or to have them be entirely impossible.

### "In Evil Days"

In August 1945, Léon Degrelle left us a relic and a poetic testimony in a beautiful eight-page poem, entitled *"Aux Mauvais Jours"* ("In Evil Days") written in the hospital of San Sebastián. It would then be printed as a small booklet, published in January 1951, in celebration of the arrival of the new year.

Those were difficult times. Therefore, in an expression of farewell and inner depth, the poem conveys the lyrical evocation of the voice of a body bidding farewell, of a flame that seems to be extinguishing:

*Is it over? Is the sweet perfume of roses extinguished?*
*The sea breeze dying down,*
*The time when the water comes back to the edge ending,*
*The sky being eclipsed, the horizon of things is finished?...*

*Will my eyes not see the blue morning firmament again,*
*Nor the sun hiding in its sunset in the depth of the forest?*
*Will the whiteness of the roads no longer be followed with the eye,*
*Should they leave the sight of light jumping in the waves,*
*Give up the meatiness of gladiolas and jasmine,*
*To the sweetness of ashen afternoons, with rosy mixtures,*
*To the quick, brief impulse of a roosting sparrow,*
*To the full-throated songs, in the shelter of a garden?...*

*One would have to interrupt the coming of dreams!*
*The light of heaven that follows death.*
*On the red fallen leaves of sleepless nights,*
*On the gray reeds lying on the edge*
*Of the ponds, on the scintillation of the sand,*
*Where the sea rushes, sings, and dies!*
*I should kill in advance*

*My fiery look that advances*
*In life like a lantern,*
*Being no more than trivial litter,*
*Who knows nothing more than nocturnal lights,*
*Of the greenery of fields, of the blackness of waters,*
*Of the golden or red roundness of warm fruits,*
*Of the nightingale closing the fainting daytime*
*For its trill that peeps the clearing of the groves…*

*I should stir in my distressed soul*
*The pleasure that I will have tomorrow when I see the sky,*
*Following its nuanced movement in the winds,*
*To lose myself in its immaterial journey*
*Among the grays, the greens, the reds, the oranges.*
*I should say: "Let us go, it is over, this evening I put in order*
*My memories so pure of lines, of colors.*
*And march towards the death drowning my heart…"*

*I should give up the beautiful monotonous songs.*
*When rain has filled the forests in fall*
*I should forget the chirping of the birds,*
*The mysterious noise of sneaky animals*
*Scurrying, in the evening, under the shelter of branches.*
*To forget that there are nightingales that trill,*
*That the storms sing for strong men.*
*Nor to know that human voices are*
*More tender than the canticle of the Sirens.*
*I should abdicate, to penetrate into death*
*Without seeing anything, nor with quivering lips.*
*To moan no more about impotence and fever,*
*To listen no more to a song, a word, a cry of love.*
*To die without tomorrow, less happy than the days*
*Stabbed every evening, then magnificent rebirth.*
*To lose everything, abandon everything, be a tragic defeat*
*That no longer hears, that no longer sees, suddenly no longer feels his heavy arms*
*And limpid hands downcast*
*Along a body of fire that becomes cold and empty…*

*Do not you hear, O Fate, on the night you laugh,*
*My life screaming, to escape my dying youth?*
*I say, do not you hear, then, that a heart is stabbed?*


## In Holy Brotherhood with His Falangist Comrades

Degrelle had a state of mythical aura about him, an aura due to his warrior exploits and his relevant political and moral decorations—the best service record of a volunteer during the Second World War, Knight of the Iron Cross with Oak Leaves—and because of the destruction and physical injuries sustained from the plane crash on the beach of La Concha in San Sebastián. With that aura, Degrelle arrived in Spain seeking to meet his comrades of the Holy Brotherhood of the Spanish Falange, of which Léon was in possession of card number one of the Falange Exterior.[10] José Antonio Primo de Rivera had granted it to him in 1934 and which accredited him as Old Guard, the old shirt with that constellation of stars, of that movement of poets and heralds of the new Spain that its founding martyr launched on October 29th, 1933 at the Teatro de la Comedia in Madrid.

Among those who welcomed him from the beginning, with the hospitality of the Spanish nobility, was the Toledano and great friend of José Antonio, José Finat y Escrivá de Romaní, Count of Mayalde. He was a liaison and a man utterly trusted by José Antonio when he was held in the prison of Alicante on the eve of his murder. José Antonio entrusted him with carrying his messages to General Mola, the "Director," in Pamplona. The Count of Mayalde had been for some years, during the Second World War, Spanish Ambassador to Berlin. He knew well the service record and behavior of his extraordinary comrade Léon Degrelle.

Degrelle was also greeted with open arms by General Agustín Muñoz Grandes, First Commander-in-Chief of the glorious Blue Division, his comrade in arms on the Eastern Front. Like Degrelle, Grandes had been personally distinguished and decorated by Hitler for courage and valor with the Iron Cross with Oak Leaves.

José Antonio and Léon Degrelle were, arguably, twin souls. You cannot understand Degrelle's personality without highlighting his poetic soul. Above all, he was a poet. Even politics was for him a great poem that he tried to compose "not with vowels and consonants, but with the flesh, heart, sorrows, and hopes of a people." He spoke, wrote, and thought like a genuine poet. Both Degrelle and José

---

[10] *El Servicio Exterior de Falange*, or *Falange Exterior* for short, was the organization charged with coordinating the activities of various groups and delegations associated with the Falange outside Spanish territory.

Antonio were imbued with a primordial and undeniable poetry. They were bards of politics and poets of Christendom, who raised the flag, holding it upright to defend it joyfully and poetically because they were persuaded that people with a mission could only be seduced by minstrels. "In the face of the poetry that destroys," they both opposed "the poetry of promises" with a strong voice and military tenacity, with a marshal air, a warrior spirit, and a soul of monastic stoicism.

Degrelle would be recognized and awarded the medal of the Old Guard of the Falange, created by the Decree of March 10th, 1942. It was published in the movement's bulletin, number 129, to attest to the spirit and seniority of the founders previously affiliated with the Falangist squads prior to the elections of February 16th, 1936, of the national-syndicalist revolution in Spain. The record for the award of the medal as a member of honor of the Falange Exterior bears the number 35.214.

His mystical temperament and his artist's sensitivity were intermingled. Politics was only of interest to him as a "higher projection of the peoples' calling." Politics was framed fully within the concept of beauty. "Politics is the supreme art," he exclaimed in the Donostiarra hospital, "it is the masterpiece created not with any color that the artist transforms, but with all the enormous power of beings, which he transfigures."

For Degrelle, the scale of art's value started with architecture, then ascended to painting, poetry, music, and at the top, politics.

Degrelle was also captivated by music at the hospital in San Sebastián. For whole weeks at a time, he delighted in listening to Wagner's work, in enjoying Beethoven, and in having Mozart accompany his dreams.

This was not the first time Léon Degrelle set foot on Spanish soil, although it was the first time he did so to maintain his freedom. In his childhood, he had come to Spain on vacation. Later, he would return in the period of Primo de Rivera's dictatorship. He returned once again, under President Manuel Azaña Díaz. It was on this visit that a little-known event happened to him. Next to the city of San Sebastián, there was a large wooden cross on which the following inscription had been roughly engraved with a field knife: "Erected by the Belgians." It was a cross that had been knocked down by leftists, cursing it and ripping it out of its placement. A group of Belgians, among whom was Léon Degrelle, were passing through the place while fleeing from the authorities towards the border. Seeing the rustic and simple monument pulled down into a ditch, they proceeded to raise the giant crucifix. Léon Degrelle, with that handful of rexists, raised the cross again towards the sky of the Basque provinces. They jumped back into the old Ford they were driving and sped to the Irún border with Azaña's police right on their heels.

It is no surprise that on the front page of the Madrid daily *Informaciones,* dated June 15th, 1936, a portrait of Léon Degrelle appears with the heading: "What the Rex Movement's Leader is Like: There is Something Spanish about León Degrelle."

Léon Degrelle was an expert on the history of both Spain and Belgium, and, in particular, of the so-called "Spanish Period" in Flanders. He deeply admired Emperor Charles I of Spain and Charles V of Germany, as well as Philip II, the prudent king under whom Spain and Belgium had shared crown and scepter. He shared with comrade Jean Denis his reflection that "our people were great when Spain was great, and this was not a casual coincidence, but a true alignment of destiny."

Additionally, many Spaniards fought under the flag of Burgundy towards the end of the war, during 1944 and 1945. They were the volunteers who remained fighting with their European comrades after the withdrawal of the Blue Division. Many of them did so in the Twenty-Eighth SS Division Freiwilligen-Grenadier-Wallonien, which was then commanded by Waffen SS Lieutenant Colonel Léon Degrelle in the final months of the conflict, when the fighting was hardest and most intense. First Lieutenant Luis García Valdajos, a twenty-six-year-old Falangist from Valladolid, who joined the unit in November 1944, served under Léon's command. Valdajos had recruited a handful of Spaniards and, forming an almost independent nucleus with nearly a hundred strange and defiant men, were concentrated in the Walloon barracks in Breslau. They fought against communism in Pomerania for more than a month, side by side, in the battle of Arnswalde. Up until Stetin, new Spaniards were arriving and joining until the Third Company was completed. This company's sections were headed by Sergeants La Fuente, Lorenzo Ocaña, and Abel Ardoz, and they were led by acting Company Commander Pedro Zabala. In the general retreat to the Reich's capital, a heroic handful of Spaniards were also fighting among the ruins, defending the chancellery with honor and courage together with Miguel Ezquerra's group. The bond that united Degrelle with Spain was almost one of blood.

## Diplomatic Crossroads

In his book, *Un Diplomate au XXe Siècle* (*A Diplomat in the Twentieth Century*), Belgian Ambassador Jacques de Thier has written that "…the arrival of Degrelle in Spain would come to greatly complicate and delay the normalization of diplomatic relations between Spain and Belgium."

The victors immediately requested the surrender of Léon Degrelle. They were full of hatred and thirsty for open vengeance against the man who had set up a communion of ideals among the Belgian youth and who held the line of battle, together with his European comrades, in order to crusade against Bolshevism on the Eastern Front. Léon Degrelle, without being heard in court, had been unjustly sentenced to death *in absentia* and without appeal. Degrelle was on their priority list, so his extradition was immediately requested. Jointly supporting his repatriation to Belgium were both the United States and England,[11] albeit indirectly because he was not considered a war criminal.

Due to Christian and humanitarian sensibilities, Spanish authorities did not approve the initial claim, nor did they agree to the surrender of the war hero, that brave and decorated warrior who was on their soil recuperating from serious injuries in one of their military hospitals. The resentment and attitude evidenced by the new Belgian authorities was miserable and dishonorable. They held a seething and unconditional hatred of him throughout his long exile, and it even lasted beyond Degrelle's death.

## The Vicious Persecution against the Degrelle Family

There was much animosity and worldly wickedness directed at the Degrelle family by the new masonic leaders who rose to power in Belgium, and by the Jews, those eternally cruel merchants who follow false idols and golden calves, who established themselves so selfishly in the bastions of world politics (the true victors of the Second World War). While Léon was fighting on the front, they assassinated his brother Édouard, a pharmacist in his hometown, with five cowardly bullets on July 8th, 1944. His widow, Ghislaine Marchand, Léon Degrelle's sister-in-law, was then arrested by the partisans.

The purge in Belgium after the war was particularly inhuman; it was bloodthirsty oppression. It seemed like a group of unscrupulous murderers had taken complete control of the country.

Degrelle's elderly mother was arrested towards the end of May 1945, imprisoned and subjected to suffering and innumerable humiliations for the terrible crime of "motherhood." After years of captivity in the prison infirmary, she died.

---

[11] The author routinely uses "*Inglés*" and "*Inglaterra*" ("English" and "England") to refer to what is more accurately—especially when discussing government and politics—British and Great Britain. Since this inaccurate use happens to be very common in American English as well, I have retained the author's preference in this translation most of the time.

His father, who was of advanced age, was locked in a gloomy dungeon at the Saint Gilles Prison in Belgium, where he was mercilessly allowed to die, accused of the crime of "fatherhood."

Degrelle's wife, Marie-Paule Lemay, a French national, had moved to Germany in August 1944 with their five children. When the Allied troops invaded, she and her terrified young children abandoned the village of Oexter and, making their way through Austria, headed toward Switzerland, a country she considered a more neutral, safe place for her family. At first, she settled in a refugee camp, but she was recognized and handed over to the Belgian communists. They did not regard the neutrality of the Swiss territory where she was located, or her French nationality, or the children's status as minors. She was arrested and sent to Forest Prison on June 22nd, 1945. An irregular political process under the War Council was held in Brussels on May 16th, 1946. In this judicial proceeding, Marie-Paule received a (predetermined) sentence of ten years imprisonment, with a fine of two million Belgian francs for the new and unprecedented criminal offense of "being married." Her political participation had been non-existent, with her merely being the honorary president of "Solidarity," a charity and social aid association for women and children in need. She spent six years in prison. She was released on the first day of September 1950, seriously ill and at risk of death. Since Marie-Paule was of French nationality and was not even an activist in the Rexist Movement, there were no sufficient grounds for condemning her to ten years forced labor.

The children were interned, despite their tender age, far from their mother. Their youngest daughter, Marie Christine, only eight months old, was, for a few weeks, the youngest girl in history to ever be imprisoned. They were kept in the juvenile correction center of Uccle-Stalle, where children were deprived of their liberty and suffered mistreatment, and in some cases, death. Léon Degrelle would know nothing of his children's whereabouts for fourteen long years.

His sister, Jeanne, who had been the General Inspector of the Walloon Women's organization, the women's section of the Rexist Movement, was sentenced to two years in prison by the War Council.

His brother-in-law, Charles Raty, Jeanne's husband and the brother of the famous painter, Albert Raty, had worked as a simple chief accountant. He was mercilessly butchered in Saint Gilles Prison; a warden found him in a pool of blood one morning. Neighboring cellmates had shouted for help, but no officers answered the desperate calls. Their two daughters, Suzanne and Marie, were also innocent victims of persecution, suffering unjustified condemnation.

Léon's other sisters were arrested and held for several months without charge and without trial, deprived of liberty without ever hearing a verdict. A policy of persecuting and destroying family members was implemented against Léon and those closest to him.

Repression and extermination touched any member of his family who had any relationship with Degrelle, either directly or politically. This was in response to his powers of oratory and his proven intelligence, vigor, faith, and courage in bravely confronting the enemies of God and of humanity in a social, national, and revolutionary mission.

Even the birthplace of Léon Degrelle was ordered to be destroyed. It was reduced to rubble and deliberately razed by people who hated Degrelle, in order to erase all memory and vestige of the home of his birth. A court building was built on its site years later.

Even his residence in Drève de Lorraine, a former hunting lodge used at one time by Emperor Charles V, was vandalized. It had been exquisitely decorated by his wife. Léon treasured its incunabula,[12] its Napoleonic swords, its old Flemish tableaux, its tapestries, the gallery of the glories of greater Burgundy, and its ten thousand ancient maps from the sixteenth and seventeenth centuries, all colored by hand. Everything in it was destroyed or looted with greed, hate, and most importantly, revenge.

When Degrelle became aware that his elderly mother had been arrested and found herself between bars, incarcerated in Belgium, he entered a state of great dismay. Yet, the feeling that overwhelmed him also redeemed him by pushing him to write poetry, putting the longing of his early years spent at her side in his childhood and adolescence in his hometown of Bouillon to tearful rhymes. It was a way of communicating telepathically and spiritually with his most beloved person. These poems made up twelve songs collected in two thousand verses, marked both by the pain of the situation and at the same time by the sweetness of his memories. He titled the collection *La Chanson Ardennaise* (*Song of the Ardennes*). They represent a sequence inspired by the land of his birth, the scene of his first frolics and youthful antics, and by the arms of his mother, who always welcomed him with her warm smile. The work was published in Paris in 1951 under the publishing label, Oak Leaves.

## His Writings from the Hospital

In the hospital, completely immobilized, his thoughts turned into dreams and ideals that seemed unattainable and even impossible to realize. These inner fantasies

---

[12] Books printed before 1501.

were collected within intimate poems, which he wrote in July 1945. His tone was one of farewell, diminished in the prime of his life, a fruitful life. He later compiled this collection under the title, *L'Ombre des Soirs* (*The Shadow of Evenings*), which was published in Seville in 1952 as a tribute to his veteran comrades. He also produced the unpublished verses in a book titled, *Les Îles Blanches* (*The White Islands*).

It was also then that he began to recall, with freshness, spontaneity, and truthfulness, the most shocking moments of his experiences on the Eastern Front. He began his draft of *To the Caucasus on Foot*, the first notes of which he had taken down in the record-keeping diary he carried with him to the front. He recorded what happened after each day's long walk. *Encircled in Ukraine* and *Agony in the Baltic* also emerged, later serving as notes and drafts of his original sources, for his great epic work, *The Russia Campaign*.

## The Traumatic Repression of the Victors

The repression carried out in Belgium after the Second World War was brutal and merciless. Sanctions, purges, and victims were counted by the thousands. Even the notion of the "uncivil" was created to refer to any Belgian citizen who could have been Germanophile or a supporter of Germany during the war, or often simply anti-communist. A special law, called the Article 123 Series, was passed after "liberation," prohibiting the "uncivil" from assuming any public offices and from working in a wide range of jobs and professions.

As Eduardo Núñez Barrado referenced on January 19th, 1945, in the magazine, *La Voz del Pueblo*, the military auditor of Brussels informed the public that anyone who helped the "uncivil" could be handed a sentence ranging from fifteen to twenty years in prison. In May 1945, the Bruges Bar Association reported that its members, as a result of the threats they received from the socialist and communist extremists who made the laws in Belgium, were ordered to cease representing any of the "uncivil."

The Belgian state ordered the arrest of twenty-eight thousand entrepreneurs —almost all of Belgium's employers—for "economic cooperation" with Germany. Some fifteen thousand people were killed and using the lowest figure given by Robert Poulet, another two hundred thirty-one thousand people were declared "uncivil," of which seventy thousand were imprisoned. Additionally, seventy-five thousand three hundred ninety-one "dossiers" were opened for "economic collaboration."

Even more odious, Núñez continues to point out, was the repression used against the many thousands of Belgian (Flemish and Walloon) volunteers who fought in Russia against Bolshevism.

Towards the end of May 1945, some three thousand Belgian workers returned who had voluntarily left to work, as wage laborers, for the Germans. They returned on a Belgian ship that had picked them up in Odessa, Ukraine. Those volunteer workers, who believed that they were returning from exile, had no time to even get off the boat. In Paris the *Le Monde* reported, on May 25th, 1945, that "The crowd, in Ostend, took hold of them and threw them into the water. They swam towards the shore. The crowd pushed them back. They all drowned." That was the morality and the new law exercised by the victors.

As for those who, with arms in hand, had opposed communism, they were seen, simply and cruelly, as "traitors" to Belgium.

Some of Léon's comrades, however, managed to reach the Spanish border in search of asylum, as was the case of Louis Eugène Esther Rignard who had been a volunteer of the Walloon Legion. After being wounded on the Eastern Front, he was evacuated to Belgium, where he served as delegate on the Committee for Assistance to the Families of Veterans. He was arrested in La Junquera on October 21st, 1945, for illegal entry into Spanish territory. He immediately requested political asylum due to the persecution in Belgium against activists of the Rexist Movement. On March 1st, 1946, the rexist activist, Émile Victor Balieu, a former combatant of the Walloon Legion who had been injured in April 1945 and evacuated to the Sonneborg hospital in Denmark, arrived at the same border post as Rignard. He was later interned by the English in a concentration camp for being a "collaborationist." He managed to escape on July 2nd, 1945. On August 5th, 1947, the driver for the Chief of Staff of the Walloon Legion, Théodore Duchateau Dessart, was arrested in La Junquera. He had reached the Spanish border post after two years of painful captivity in a Belgian concentration camp from which he was able to miraculously flee.

The reflections that Degrelle left us within his writing during those tedious hours of his mandatory rest at General Mola Military Hospital in San Sebastián leave us with no doubt:

> *History weighs the merit of men. Above all earthly imperfections, we unreservedly sacrificed our youth. We fought for Europe, her faith, and her culture. With sincerity and selflessness, we remained faithful until the end. Sooner or later, Europe and the world must recognize the justice of our cause and the purity of our*

*dedication. Hatred dies. It chokes in its foolishness and vileness. Everything great is eternal.*

## The Dual Solution: Laval-Degrelle

Léon Degrelle remained bedridden and immobilized at the General Mola Military Hospital under the categorical indication and unambiguous orders of the doctors who treated him there.

At the end of July 1945, an ambulance was sent to the hospital to evacuate him to Barcelona. The idea was to board him on the same plane on July 31st that would take Pierre Laval to France. The Spanish authorities decided to hand over Laval as a result of an agreement with the Allies who ensured a fair trial, with full guarantees for the former Vichy Chief of Government under General Philippe Pétain. Laval had also previously been Minister of War (1925), Minister of Justice (1926) and Prime Minister on two occasions (1931–1932 and 1935). As soon as he was in the hands of the Allies, however, in spite of the self-righteous commitments and false promises, they failed to comply and unilaterally broke all the agreements reached with the government in Madrid. Laval was murdered after an absurd and theatrical show trial. Spain also sought a means of ending, once and for all, the issue concerning Degrelle's handover, of putting an end to the incessant foreign pressure, specifically from the new Belgian authorities.

The ambulance that was sent returned to Barcelona empty. The doctors opposed the patient transfer because they suspected that if Léon were discharged, he might possibly arrive in Barcelona dismembered, seriously injured, or even dead. The firm stance of his doctor saved him from certain death from the butchers of Europe who were waiting with sharpened knives.

On July 22nd, 1944, a dinner was held at the home of the Third Reich Ambassador in Paris, Otto Abet. It was attended by Pierre Laval and Franco's Ambassador to the Vichy Government, José Félix de Lequerica. Léon Degrelle was there and personally heard Lequerica, in an after-dinner conversation, say affectionately to Laval, "Mr. Prime Minister, if you come across some misfortune one day, be sure that Spain will always be a second homeland for you!" One should understand that Pierre Laval enjoyed a very special status and significance among the Spanish. When Laval was Chair of the Committee on Foreign Affairs in the French Senate, it was he who made France's diplomatic recognition of General Franco's regime possible. The government of the French Republic, at his proposal, sent as the new French Ambassador to Spain the most glorious and famous of her soldiers, the old Marshal Philippe Pétain. Pétain had been entrusted with the defense of Verdun (1916) in the First World War, succeeding Nivelle the following year as Commander-in-Chief. Such was the prestige of Marshal Pétain in the Gallic country that, in 1940, concluding his diplomatic mission in Spain, he assumed the position of Head of State. If Pierre Laval chose Spain for his political exile after the occupation of his homeland by the Anglo-Americans, who had offered it up on a platter to Jews and partisans under the baton of Charles de Gaulle, it was because he had considered the words and promise expressed by Spanish Ambassador Lequerica. Lequerica subsequently became Minister for Foreign Affairs.

Laval relocated to Barcelona with his wife at the end of April 1945, after the world watched with horror the embarrassing spectacle put on by the partisans in Italy. Benito Mussolini was not only murdered, but also mocked by being hung upside down at a gas station in Milan. It was an act as savage as it was despicable, and it was carried out with total impunity by terrorist partisans.

Lequerica, despite his promises, had planned a clever diplomatic two-for-one, simultaneously handing Degrelle and Laval over to the Allies on the same flight, which would depart on July 31st, 1945, from the Prat Airport in Barcelona. It flew to Linz, an area under American control. As soon as the plane carrying Laval arrived at the airport, the Allied troops handed Laval over to the French authorities. They locked him in Fresnes Prison and later executed him. Since Degrelle's doctors refused to release him from the hospital, he was not on the plane with Laval. Lequerica and his associates could not execute their larger plan. The patient was "totally immovable," under strict and final medical judgment.  It was this providential act that kept Degrelle from death yet again.

Laval's death by firing squad in France, carried out on October 15th, 1945, was in complete violation of each and every procedural guarantee given to the Spanish government (in the sense that if he were handed over, he would not be executed). The resulting effect protected Degrelle and kept him on Spanish soil. In matters of justice or humanitarian affairs, Spain could no longer trust the victorious "democratic" forces, who had proved unable to fulfill their international commitments or keep their word. In addition, they had proceeded with absolute violation against the principles of international law and with cruelty against the great French politician. His killing, rather than being just an execution, was nothing more than a vile state-sanctioned murder, led by the euphoria of bloodletting and purging that was unleashed against the defeated.

Lequerica had actually been considered to be too Germanophile for the Allies, and had been dismissed as minister on July 21st, 1945, ten days before Laval was sent to France. He was succeeded in office by Alberto Martín Artajo, one of the leaders of Catholic Action, who had studied at the Jesuit University in Deusto.

Artajo had not opposed the deportation of Laval arranged by his predecessor, but later, knowing the results of the handover, he bitterly and deeply regretted it.

Degrelle at first considered General Franco's ministerial replacement of Lequerica with Martín Artajo a positive development, since Artajo had six family members in the Jesuit Order. He believed that this affinity with Catholicism would improve his own political/legal situation.

An unfounded rumor that Degrelle was preparing to leave Spain was disseminated in some circles, echoed on August 5th by the newspaper, *La Libre Belgique,* which had picked up the news from radio broadcasts aired on Radio France.

### The Belgian Government Formally Requests Extradition

The execution of Pierre Laval in France shocked the Spanish government, as it had not, under any circumstances, expected or imagined such an outcome. The Spanish Under Secretary for Foreign Affairs confirmed to Belgian Chargé d'Affaires Jacques de Thier that Degrelle could not be sent using the same procedure as Pierre Laval. The plane Degrelle used to get to Spain had been totally destroyed. Moreover, the behavior of French authorities in relation to Laval caused the Degrelle case to be postponed indefinitely. No determination was made by the new Spanish Foreign Minister, considering he did not want to be handing men over to death sentences. It was assumed this would be the case with Degrelle. This was repugnant to the conscience of those responsible for the ministerial portfolio. This did not mean that they were considering protecting Degrelle; rather, once he resumed health, they would arrest him and then adopt, at the appropriate time, whatever relevant measures were needed to settle this contentious bilateral issue.

In light of diplomatic evasions by the Spanish authorities for the voluntary surrender of Léon Degrelle, Belgium proceeded to officially request the extradition of Degrelle on August 2nd, 1945. Since the Belgian government was aware that its application was unworkable because it was politically motivated, it invented a series of allegations based on fictitious and imaginary common crimes so that their extradition request could be taken into consideration. These crimes were not backed by evidence but were said to have theoretically taken place during the Ardennes offensive in the later part of the war.

On August 16th, in the face of this false legal fraud concocted by the Belgian government, Léon Degrelle drafted a memorandum in which he strongly opposed the extradition request, both for himself and his colleagues. They had arrived jointly in Spain on board the German Heinkel aircraft on May 8th and requested care and assistance from the Spanish authorities until the end of September. In his writing, he put forward three concrete proposals or alternatives to the Spanish government to help them find the best solution to resolve the issue of official extradition by Belgium:

1) To be released discreetly and live under an assumed name in a friendly house, in a Spanish province;
2) To spend a few months participating in monastic life with the Augustinian monks of the Royal Monastery of San Lorenzo de El Escorial or any other monastery, preferably the El Escorial because of its extraordinary library, and world-famous thirteenth to fifteenth century manuscripts. They would serve him, during the period of cloistering, as an invaluable object of study; or
3) To enlist in the Spanish Legion, as a *novio de la muerte*.[13]

In Belgium, the press jumped the gun and reported the imminent arrival of Degrelle back to his country. Even the false news that extradition had been granted and authorized by the government in Madrid was published in those days. The dark desire of the socialist and communist Belgian government forced them into a delirium, and they tried to confuse public opinion as a result.

The international arrest and surrender order launched by Belgium against Degrelle desperately sought support and endorsement from its allies England and the United States, in order to fulfill their desire for persecution. The official request arrived in Spain on August 21st, the same date that Minister of Foreign Affairs, Martín Artajo, permitted a hearing with the Belgian businessman, Jacques de Thier. The Minister made him see the difficulty of the hand over, and the dishonor in granting the request.

The Belgian publication *Pourquoi Pas?* on September 7th, 1945, reported that:

*Degrelle will soon be delivered by Franco into Anglo-American custody, who, in turn, will deliver him to Belgium…that is because Franco has realized that the wind has changed direction, that the "big players" are impatient, that the time has come to release some ballast, and the ballast that he has decided to throw away immediately is Degrelle, in person, without delay.*

---

[13] [Spanish for "bridegroom of death," it is both the name of the regimental hymn and a nickname for Spain's Foreign Legion, an elite light infantry unit.]

On November 7th Thier sent a telegram to his government informing them that the Spanish Foreign Minister had told him that after the execution of Laval, he considered it unlikely that Degrelle would be handed over to those Spain believed would certainly execute him as well. Therefore, in order to keep up the pressure, Thier insisted that Belgium should not re-establish full diplomatic relations at the highest level with Spain until the Degrelle case had been resolved.

There were difficult legal acts that made the fulfillment of the Belgian demand unfeasible. Degrelle never received, nor had he ever thought to apply for, German nationality, which would have weakened the Allies' position in prosecuting his honorable conduct. Furthermore, paradoxically, Belgium had deprived Degrelle of his Belgian nationality, and therefore, in Spain, his legal status was technically, "stateless." Consequently, Belgium's request was invalid, regardless of whether the alleged crimes were all political offenses, for the extradition of a citizen born on its soil whose nationality was now not recognized by Belgium. Even if they undertook legal proceedings of forced repatriation, in principle and by the extradition agreement signed between Spain and Belgium, the Belgian demand for Degrelle's extradition was without standing and outside the realm of possibility.

On the first day of December 1945, coincidentally, the rexist activist, Georges Jean Bouvier, crossed the Spanish border. He declared in the Espollá border post that he had arrived in Spain "to work, and at the same time present himself to Mr. Degrelle, head of the Belgian legion, residing in Madrid."

## The Second Attempted Kidnapping by Colonel Lovinfosse

Staying at the General Mola Hospital was actually a pretty well-kept secret. Degrelle remained guarded day and night by a detachment of twenty soldiers, headed by an army officer. One of those soldiers of the guard was Jamie de Mora y Aragón who got along with Degrelle from the first moment. Interestingly, his sister Fabiola would marry King Baudouin years later and become queen. Overall, soldiers conducted themselves as if they were at a high-risk guard post. Degrelle's convalescence was under a regimen of incommunicado, so the distinguished patient was not permitted to receive visits from abroad and his communication by mail was intercepted as well.

As it was a military hospital, everything around him had a sober and Spartan air. The room was small, with a window where sunlight entered in for a few hours. The bed was made of iron pipes. The slatted, metallic mesh had small tensioners at the ends that were crimped to nickel-plated support beams. Above the headboard hung an icon of Christ standing out on the whitewashed wall of the room. He had a sink with a tap that dripped with incessant monotony. There were some family photos attached with push pins, and a map of Europe. Russia was well visible, and he could retrace his memory of those intense and historical moments lived in the heat of battle for the West and for Christianity.

During his extended stay in the hospital, a second and well-planned kidnapping attempt was carried out in January 1946 by the Belgian authorities. The idea was to have Degrelle expeditiously liquidated without having to submit to legal or diplomatic explanations. Colonel George de Lovinfosse, the planner of the kidnapping, wrote about this in his memoir entitled *Au Service de Leurs Majestés (At the Service of Their Majesties)*, recalling, "I had the opportunity to go and kidnap Degrelle in San Sebastián."

Colonel Lovinfosse was born in Brussels on September 19th, 1895 and died in 1986. He volunteered in the First World War, was wounded twice, and finished the conflict with eight awards won at the front. During the Second World War, he was wounded again in 1940. He exiled himself to England, where he served in the Home Guard and later in the Special Operations Executive (S.O.E.). He reached the rank of major in the British Army, in charge of special operations. He later served as a commander in the French Army paratroopers and was finally elevated to the rank of colonel and major A.R.A. in the Belgian Army. He was entrusted, in September 1944, with liaison relations between the communists of the Belgian resistance and the Anglo-American occupation armies. Later in charge of espionage services, he ended the war in Germany running intelligence missions.

During the war, as Chief of Information Services in Belgium, Lovinfosse received a letter from a good friend of his, a Belgian Merchant residing in Spain. This friend was motivated by his desire to see his impressive earnings increased on the basis of lucrative profits that could be secured with the signing of a trade agreement in process between Belgium and Spain. This was delayed *sine die*[14] by the pending political-diplomatic dispute, so that the signing of the trade agreement was now conditional upon the surrender of Léon Degrelle. In his communication, this merchant friend told Lovinfosse, motivated by his own interest, that the Spanish Army wanted to get Degrelle out of Spain. Now was the time to act without delay, proposing that he relocate to San Sebastián, where he assured Lovinfosse that everything would be sorted out easily.

On January 2nd, 1946, Colonel Lovinfosse went to the private residence of Belgian Prime Minister Achille Van Acker for a meeting. He was accompanied by

---

[14] [French for indefinitely, with no appointed date.]

Paul Stasse, legal adviser to the partisans. Although in bed with the flu, the Prime Minister received them in order to authorize the kidnapping of Léon Degrelle. He gave Lovinfosse written instructions, with a manuscript text on official paper from the Cabinet of the Prime Minister, signed by his own hand. It stated: "To the Belgian and Allied authorities: Render all help to Major Lovinfosse, who will travel to France to carry out a mission." As they left, he said, "Thank you. Good health and good luck."

Colonel George de Lovinfosse, the most decorated résistant in his country, mercenary in the service of foreign armies—England and France—would rely on the complicity of French secret agents of the Greyhound Network in order to accomplish the kidnapping of Degrelle eight months after the war's end.

On January 2nd, after his visit with the Belgian Prime Minister, who with his authorization and related instructions had approved the criminal plan, Lovinfosse went to meet another secret agent, a fellow thug in the resistance named André Hautain, who would accompany him on the dark mission he intended to carry out. The next day, both made their way to Paris. Without wasting time, they went to the police station on rue des Saussaies, where they met with the Director of French Information Services, Commissioner Duval. They requested logistical support, plus the necessary cooperation from the French security and espionage services, all of which was assured. While there, Commissioner Duval also called Morel, a representative of intelligence services in Hendaye, to give them the required coverage and support.

The order to carry out the kidnapping, drafted by the Chief of General Information Services, which was subsequently called into question, stated:

> *Render all necessary assistance to Major Lovinfosse to cross the border with Léon Degrelle. You will accompany the vehicle of Major Lovinfosse, in which the prisoner shall be located, with a car from your service. Your mission will end at the Franco-Belgian border.*

This was also agreed to by Belgian Prime Minister Van Acker, and the execution of this sinister and cowardly plan was to be undertaken, without further delay, in the month of January 1946.

The preparations for the kidnapping were made down to the last detail, even the hood that they were going to put over Léon's head at the appropriate time had been prepared. The only thing left to do was to carry out the diabolical plan.

The attempted kidnapping seemed to pose little risk, given that it had been approved by such high-level officials. In early January 1946, the Belgian colonel arrived in the Pyrenees. The plan was for Degrelle to be transferred to a hospital in Pamplona. Along the way, at an agreed point near the town of Lecumberri, the drivers would pretend to have engine failure, causing them to stop the vehicle. The hijackers, already waiting, would immediately rush the vehicle, grab Degrelle, cover his head with the hood, and, in collusion with the French agents and police, transport him to Belgium without obstacles or impediments. He would then be ruthlessly eliminated.

French security was officially notified from Paris and had placed their vehicles and best agents from Bordeaux at the disposal of Colonel Lovinfosse. The kidnappers arrived in Hendaye on January 4th, and they immediately contacted Agent Morel from the Directorate of Territorial Surveillance (DTS). Morel provided them with the vehicle to carry out the operation. After crossing the border over the international bridge in Irún, on January 5th, Colonel Lovinfosse held a meeting with a Spanish security agent. The agent informed him:

> *We are fed up. Degrelle will be transferred within three days from the General Mola Hospital to the Pamplona prison. In this way, he will be out from under military responsibility and jurisdiction and his file will be the Ministry of Interior's responsibility. This is only a provisional expedition. If during the course of the journey you want to take him with you, that will not inconvenience me in the least; quite the contrary. We will follow the road in the direction of Toulouse. Two kilometers (1.2 miles) before entering Lecumberri, we will stop the van. There he will be defenseless. That will be the time for you to intervene. You will then leave Spain via Saint Jean-Pied de Port, where you will find the route clear.*

After this brief interview, Lovinfosse immediately returned to Hendaye to finalize the preparations. On Saturday, January 6th, they were all fully operational. They preselected a "station" to stop the prison van in which Degrelle would travel handcuffed. The moment they stopped the van, Degrelle would be captured and moved across the agreed-upon border, with the help of the French DTS. Those in Spain who were willing to collaborate and carry out Degrelle's abduction and drive him to the nearby French border, had agreed to do the job for the price of two hundred thousand pesetas, a real fortune at the time.

Mr. Morel of the Special Commissariat of Hendaye (France) provided safe travel order three hundred seven for permission to drive through "all prohibited areas," valid from January 5th to January 15th, 1946. The vehicle being driven by the Belgian agent, Hautain, in which Lovinfosse was traveling, was an Auto-Union, registration number 31.275. Two days later they would cross the Belgian border and kill Degrelle.

At the last minute, it seems that the preparations of that despicable plan were leaked and picked up by Spanish intelligence services. Taking this development into consideration, which would entail greater risk if the plan was carried out, the Belgian Foreign Minister, Henry Spaak, had to halt and postpone the kidnapping for a more opportune time. The postponement was set and planned to take place on Monday, January 8th. On the night of January 7th, the same colonel of the Spanish Information Service who had previously had a meeting with Lovinfosse, requested another urgent interview. Lovinfosse traveled to their meeting place in Irún. The following confidential information was transmitted to him:

> *Inside developments do not allow tomorrow's operation to take place. Nothing has changed for the moment, but you will have to wait a week or two. You must return to Brussels. When the action is operational, I will communicate to you by telegram.*

Lovinfosse, potential kidnapper in the making, reported the incident to his superiors, and returned provisionally to Brussels. On February 10th, he finally received the expected communication from San Sebastián with the following code: "The package is now ready. We look forward to seeing you."

It was the agreed upon signal to try again. They rushed back to Spain. During this interval, Lovinfosse had prepared a report for Prime Minister Van Acker, informing him of all the details. Before leaving, he again requested confirmation of the written order from January 2nd. He was received on this occasion by Roger Roch, Head of the Prime Minister's Cabinet, who asked him: "Are you the one who has requested an order to carry out a mission from the Prime Minister?" Lovinfosse answered "Yes, and as a matter of urgency, as Degrelle could escape if we do not act quickly." Roch replied, "This issue is now the responsibility of Foreign Minister Paul Henry Spaak, and he does not want Degrelle to return to Belgium at all. Therefore, you must refrain from intervening and have the counter-order transmitted."

Meanwhile, oblivious to the plot, Degrelle was artistically contemplating Velázquez's painting *The Surrender of Breda*, also known as *The Lances*, which is exhibited at the Prado Museum in Madrid. In this work, our distinguished painter has shown, with masterful stroke, the generosity of the victors toward the defeated in the Siege of Breda, concluding with the victory of the Spanish legions on May 25th, 1635. This has been reflected in the elegant gesture, the placid countenance, and honorable conduct of the characters in the work when collecting the symbolic keys of the conquered city from the vanquished.

All the Belgian and French documents relating to the case were subsequently published by Colonel Lovinfosse himself. They were as overwhelming as they were indisputable: a Belgian Prime Minister, a Belgian Colonel, and French Security planned to carry out the completely illegal kidnapping of Degrelle inside a foreign country. This can simply be called multinational democratic state terrorism.

Thirty years later, on his birthday on June 15th, 1976, on a postcard-sized portrait of himself, Degrelle wrote the following to the person who once tried to violently kidnap and execute him:

> *To my dear and glorious friend-adversary, Colonel George de Lovinfosse, who so magnificently honored our country, with the friendly talent of a "front-line" fighter, who, too, fought passionately for his homeland; kind greetings from Léon Degrelle.*

It was a gesture of forgiveness and magnanimity.

Colonel Lovinfosse was embarrassed by this action towards the end of his life. In his memoirs, published six years later in the *La Libre Belgique*, he wrote the following: "I realized that Degrelle had not committed any crimes and that I would never again do an operation like that. We must leave Degrelle in peace." He further confirmed his repentance and change of heart when, reflecting over time, he again published in *La Libre Belgique*, on December 18th, 1974, the following: "Thirty years later, I am happy that the mission failed." On another occasion, he gave public testimony regarding his admiration for the valor and courage shown at all times by Degrelle, his former "prey" and political adversary.

## Diplomatic Pressure for Surrender

On January 12th, 1946, at a press conference with foreign correspondents in Spain, Foreign Minister Martín Artajo informed them that the Degrelle case was pending the mandatory opinion of the Council of State, and it was they who decided on the legality or extradition in progress.

Six days later, another meeting took place between Foreign Minister Artajo and the British Ambassador Victor Mallet. On this occasion, Artajo rebuked the English diplomat on behalf of the Spanish government, concerning the execrable execution of former French President, Pierre Laval, after a trial devoid of the most elementary guarantees. The promises of normalization of relations with France had been frustrated by his death. Mallet understood that this humiliating elimination of Laval was now an insurmountable obstacle for those who hoped to have Degrelle extradited. He informed his government of this in a report sent on April 15th, 1946, in which he stated: "The Spanish government does not intend to repeat the unfortunate experience suffered during the Laval case."

The pressure, threats, and blackmail exerted on the Spanish government to proceed with the surrender of the "badly wounded prey" were incessant. Belgium did not tire in its obsessive endeavor. On January 30th, Belgium again raised the issue of Degrelle at a United Nations session, through its representative Dehousse. He stated that "traitors, collaborators, and all those who had carried arms against his country, could not be regarded as refugees, and should, therefore, be handed over and punished." He demanded an international position be taken.

General Franco was also pressured on all sides. Had he not had the strong humanitarian and clinical arguments for the repeated refusal to hand over the wounded Degrelle, it would have been very difficult to safeguard him on the basis of only State reasons.

In San Sebastián on March 1st, 1946, the General Military Governor of Gipuzkoa, Pedro Pimentel, addressed a letter to his ranking superior, the Captain General[15] of the Sixth Military Region, Juan Yagüe Blanco, who was based in Burgos. Pimentel made him aware of the shortage of troops in the area and informed him that "…in this Plaza the following services have to be set up: an official guard of twenty men for Degrelle…"

---

[15] Captain General is the equivalent of an American General of the United States Army (five-star) and is the highest rank in the Spanish Army, although in this situation the author identifies Blanco as a general with regional command.

In the same month, Jacques de Thier, with his usual monomania, returned to his charge of urging the Spanish government to resolve the extradition case.

On March 23rd, the Council of State finally issued its report with an unfavorable opinion on the extradition of Degrelle under the Extradition Treaty. The treaty had been signed by Belgium and Spain on June 17th, 1870 and was still applicable. The third article did not offer the least interpretative legal doubt in establishing that "Extradition will never be granted for crimes or infractions of a political nature." This same article was also being used contrarily by Belgian authorities in order to *not* hand over numerous communists and republicans to Spain. In many cases, they had committed violent crimes, and had criminal cases pending in Spain. The Council of State recognized Degrelle as a political refugee. The resolution was communicated by Director General for Foreign Affairs García Olay on April 9th, 1946, to Jacques de Thier, stating that "…it is repugnant to make the death of Degrelle the price for restoration of friendly relations between the two countries."

The General Military Governor of Gipuzkoa, Pedro Pimentel, sent a brief to the hospital for Degrelle to sign and return, requesting him to voluntarily agree, once he was fully recovered, to depart Spain's national territory. This is why under the circumstances, and facing an eventual, forced deportation, Degrelle considered a possible exile to Ireland, even though that would have had its own additional risks, difficulties, and uncertainties. Degrelle never signed that document. When his health improved, he remained hospitalized as a temporary detainee.

Meanwhile, in the Belgian Chamber of Deputies, during its session on May 2nd, 1946, socialist MEP Piérard called on his government to take vigorous measures to resolve the issue of Degrelle's extradition definitively, even if it meant rupturing diplomatic relations and contacts if Spain's refusal persisted. Belgian Foreign Minister Henri Spaak took the opportunity in Parliament the following day to launch a hysterical diatribe against the Spanish government, whom he accused of "…digging an ever-deepening chasm between Belgium and Spain," and threatened to bring the matter to the United Nations Security Council, confirming that no bilateral trade agreement would be signed as long as the issue of extradition went unresolved.

Degrelle then wrote a letter to General Franco, referring to the fact that the Great Mufti of Jerusalem had been freed by the Allies themselves, and saying to him, "Let us see if the blood of a Christian is worth less than the Arabs' oil!" Léon had officially visited the front during the Spanish Civil War, having been invited by the Falange who named him a guest of honor, and he had the opportunity to meet Franco personally at his campaign headquarters during the visit.

## The First Press Interview

On May 8th, 1946, Léon Degrelle, with the authorization of Minister of Foreign Affairs Martín Artajo, was allowed three hours of free conversation, the first exclusive interview since his exile began at General Mola Hospital. He was dressed in the only clothes he had, which was his German Army uniform, the same one he was wearing at the time of the crash landing. His uniform was the only belonging he kept in the closet of his tiny room. The interview took place with Belgian Captain Robert-André Francote, who was the Madrid correspondent for *Associated Press* and a correspondent for the daily *Le Peuple*. Degrelle frankly told him that "...freely and spontaneously it was his desire to surrender to Belgian justice whenever he was given assurance that he would be given a fair trial."

Robert-André Francote had been a Belgian correspondent for *Associated Press* during the Second World War. He served in the Belgian forces at the rank of captain. Later in England, he carried out the duties of war correspondent with G.I.s in the United States Army. He was also sympathetic to socialist ideas. That was the only exclusive interview that Léon gave to a journalist during that long period of hospitalization. The Duchess of Valencia recalled how at dusk, when Captain Francote had finished doing the interview, and he was back at the Hôtel de Londres where he was staying, the journalist shook his head from side to side, walking slowly, and repeating, "What a pity that Degrelle did not fight on our side!"

Degrelle gave Francote a written and signed proposal, which was published on the front page of *Le Peuple* (*The People*) on June 12th, 1946. It was entitled, "I Offer My Head, Exclaims SS Officer Léon Degrelle: Statements to Our Special Envoy on the Last Moments of Nazi Germany." It laid out the basic conditions for his voluntary surrender:

1) *That the Belgian government grant total amnesty to my brave officers and soldiers of the Eastern Front. They may have been wrong (I alone assume full responsibility for their error), but they were certainly brave, pure, and righteous. It is shameful to persecute them. May Belgium cleanse itself of future reproaches by recognizing these true heroes and granting them freedom.*

2) *That I be allowed to assume my own defense of my ideals, of my cause, and of my head in a completely free way before an impartial criminal hearing, assisted, if possible, by Allied observers. That press and radio outlets be allowed ample presence at the oral hearing of the trial and to ensure that said hearing be published in bulletins so that the whole country can be made aware. If I*

> *have been wrong, I will apologize. I ask for nothing more than that the truth*
> *be completely exposed to the light.*
>
> *Do my enemies fear that?*
>
> *Finally, a soldier's request: I ask to appear and die, if necessary, wearing my*
> *glorious uniform, with the Belgian insignia, with which I fought on the front, and*
> *wearing my decorations won in combat.*
>
> *My soldiers died like this. I want to fight and fall exactly as they did.*
>
> *These are my very sincere conditions, and they are, moreover, entirely logical.*
> *I want them to be publicly and solemnly made known and accepted. With these in*
> *place, I would then ask the Spanish government to authorize me to return to my*
> *country. If not, I am still young, and like truth, I can wait.*

With regard to the conditions set out by Degrelle to appear freely, voluntarily, and spontaneously before the Belgian Court of Justice, the first ennobled him all the more. With the second demand, that a minimum guarantee of procedure be ensured based on the impartiality of the judge, he tried to prevent the court room from becoming a *cheka*,[16] or parody place to commit a crime in the name of "the victors' justice." His understandable and logical claims were not met by the Belgian authorities with approval. They were driven only by their eagerness for revenge and repression, without restraint and without meaning. In short, the only thing Léon aspired to in this sense, reasonably and with the absolute conviction of innocence, was to undergo an honest and decent trial, in full public view, with the possibility of expressing himself freely, with radio broadcasts of the oral hearing and media broadcasts of its sessions. The Belgian government never intended that he should be tried and brought to justice. They only aspired to kill him in the name of "freedom and democracy."

Captain Robert-André Francote published his extensive report in *Le Peuple*, in the June 9th, 10th, and 11th, 1946 editions. It was entitled: "In the Slum of Spain: The Sensational Interview with SS Officer Léon Degrelle."

Thirty-six years after that interview from Madrid on December 5th, 1979, Léon Degrelle sent him the following handwritten message:

---

[16] *Cheka* (from Russian Чека́) is taken from the initials of the unit's Russian name; it refers to the first secret police units set up in 1917 that enjoyed broad discretion over the life and death of their detainees.

*To my dear and admirable friend "on the other bank," Robert Francote, in memory (unforgettable memory!) of his visit to me in the Military Hospital of San Sebastián, where I discovered the generosity of his heart. With faithful affection, Léon Degrelle.*

## Blackmail by the Belgian Government:
## The Degrelle Case Is Brought to the United Nations

It should be remembered that Léon, upon his arrival in Spain, had absolutely no money, not a peseta to his name. During the first winter he spent at the General Mola Hospital in the capital of Guipuzcoa province, a friendly doctor gave him a coat so that he could withstand the low temperatures and the prevailing cold. In order to be able to clean his military trousers, the only ones he had, he had to save money by selling his cigarette ration to other patients in the ward who smoked. The wounded were entitled to three cigarettes per week. It took several weeks to save up the pesetas needed,

The Belgian government now tried to blackmail the Spanish government in order to obtain the surrender of Degrelle. On May 6th, 1946, they presented a more forceful, new turn in the "international screw": they laid a protest against Spain before the United Nations Security Council, addressed to the Secretary General of the Organization, on the basis of an obstruction of Belgian justice by the political asylum granted to Léon Degrelle by the Spanish authorities. The note sent by Spaak to the U.N. read as follows:

> *The government of General Franco has seriously injured the sense of justice of the Belgian people and caused a great malaise between the two countries and their respective governments.*
>
> *The attitude of the Spanish government towards Degrelle is a blatant act that aims to make Spain a refuge for former Axis agents and their cronies. The Belgian government considers the collusion of the Spanish government with these elements as an attempt to create a dangerous nest of agitation, whose actions are directed against the war's victorious nations.*

The Spanish government reacted that same day by giving Foreign Minister Artajo instructions for his Brussels Chargé d'Affaires Aguirre de Cárcer to inform the Belgian government that progress between the two government administrations could only be achieved under three basic conditions: 1) withdrawal of the complaint made to the Security Council against Spain; 2) the formal and unequivocal promise that the trial of Léon Degrelle would be held with due legal guarantees; and 3) a declaration that the solution of the Degrelle case would help restore normal diplomatic relations.

The first of the conditions was feasible and perhaps could be agreed to by the Belgian government. The second, however, that of holding a trial with due process of law, the Belgian government was not prepared to commit to. The whole point was to push through an obviously unjust verdict without a trial and simply have Degrelle executed.

Belgian Foreign Minister Spaak considered the three conditions proposed by his Spanish counterpart unacceptable. Artajo, for his part, confronted with the Belgian refusal, upbraided him for "…wanting the Spanish government to bow to its threats and that such an attitude is not acceptable."

On May 13th, at 4:30 p.m., the Spanish Chargé d'Affaires in Belgium, Gullón, sent a confidential and encrypted communiqué to the Foreign Minister Artajo, in which he informed him of the result of his interview with the Belgian representative in Madrid, writing:

> That this conversation, held with the Belgian Chargé d'Affaires, had been transmitted by him to the Belgian Ministry of Foreign Trade, perhaps too laconically, as I thought, and had produced a painful impression. This Minister of Foreign Trade considers it difficult to withdraw the complaint in the Degrelle case from the UN Security Council without being able to provide said agency with reliable evidence that its grounds for complaint no longer exist. Given that this evidence does not exist, this would present Belgium as lacking seriousness and because after a year of requests, Spain has not specifically determined the date or mode of delivery. The Minister of Foreign Trade considers it an attack on Belgian national dignity and democracy to demand, as a precondition, the obligation to give Degrelle procedural and legal guarantees because these already exist in the Belgian Constitution and it is offensive to call them into question. He insisted that his statements in the Chamber of Deputies were not the product of personal feelings; rather, it reflects Belgium's unanimous feeling of the apparent lack of Spanish understanding and Spain's delay in resolving the matter. This has the appearance of wanting to be left pending after being continuously evaded for a year. In this long conversation, I have maintained the attitude of our government, explaining the procedures followed and the jurisdictional channels through which it went and, at the same time, highlighting our good will. I think I have dissipated the acrimonious ambiance that existed after receiving the telegram of Monsieur Thier. In this case, however, the unanimity of the Belgian people and the history of this

*Minister of Foreign Trade, of whom V.E. is aware, should not be forgotten on this matter, about which I have also repeatedly reported. Gullón.*

The Spanish representative's report was received the following day and read at 1:30 p.m. by Artajo, who personally decrypted its contents, and followed the topic as a matter of priority.

While Artajo was dealing with the situation of his representative in Brussels at the Ministry of Foreign Affairs, Léon Degrelle sent the following letter to the Spanish Head of State, Francisco Franco:

*San Sebastián, May 14th, 1946*

*Your Excellency,*

*I know that you are a tough and upright man, who is not afraid of truth and whom foreign pressure does not intimidate. Of course, you know, abominable pressures are exerted to obtain my extradition, or rather, my life. Whether I lose my life or not is all the same to me. I was on the front for four years. I know I can look death in the face.*

*I do not want to allow myself to be dishonored by evil accusers, who can forgive neither my Catholic faith nor my successes with the working masses, nor my fight against Bolshevism. They know that if I survive, I will triumph. That is why I must die…*

*How do we deal with these abominable campaigns that concern Spain because of my faults?*

1) *Hand me over to the left-wing government in Brussels? It is preferable to kill me in the hallway of the San Sebastián hospital.*

2) *Give me to the Anglo-Americans? If I am guaranteed full justice, then I accept, but they will not guarantee it. Moreover, what would the basis be for this Allied legal process? I have never been at war with the Anglo-Americans. I have never been a German official. So, in what capacity could I be given to them? Or under what capacity would they judge me? This process makes no sense.*

3) *Judge me in Madrid? Here we can do something outstanding, to show that Spain is not afraid of the truth, or the light, or of publicity. It is necessary that you yourselves, the Spanish government, announce the creation of an International Tribunal to judge my case in Madrid. The U.N., Allies, and neutrals must be invited to send judges. The doors to the press must be opened completely. We have to take the offensive. For a year now, you have been on the defensive.*

4)   *I, an old soldier, have seen a hundred times that being on the defensive leads to defeat. Spain has everything in its favor to win internationally by opening this process as widely as possible. I am in the right. I have absolutely nothing to repent for. I would fight like a lion. My enemies would be ridiculed. You will see, it will be a great triumph. As a result, the bad faith of these campaigns against Spain, which are a pack of lies, will be demonstrated.*

*I am enclosing the draft which I have included in my "Letter to the Generalissimo." If you, "the strong man of Spain," understand me and support me, then everything is possible.*

On May 24th, the Spanish government made a new effort in its approach to the crisis by sending a new proposal to Belgium, a statement that would be jointly signed by both governments. The proposal contained the following points:

1)   *The Spanish government has informed the Belgian government that giving continuity to the request of the British and American authorities, it intends to include Degrelle and Lagrou among a group of German military personnel for an upcoming repatriation.*

2)   *The Belgian government shall notify the U.N. of the communication received from the Spanish government.*

3)   *Degrelle and Lagrou will subsequently be delivered by the Allied authorities to the Belgian authorities to be tried in the Belgian courts, in accordance with their legal system.*

4)   *This procedure will resolve the Degrelle case and contribute to the improvement of relations between the two countries.*

A week later, Brussels declined the Spanish initiative to sign the joint communiqué of the terms proposed by Spain.

In the negotiations for the delivery of Degrelle, the British and American embassies suggested to the Spanish government the possibility of his surrender not directly to Belgium where certain death was expected but to a territory under the jurisdiction of any of its flags, where the trial could take place with certain guarantees. They did not, however definitively rule out the subsequent surrender to the Belgian authorities after a trial. They suggested, and there was a pre-agreement with a declaration of intent, that Degrelle could board the U.S. vessel *Marine Perch*, which would dock in the port of Bilbao on a stopover to Germany to pick up several returnees. On June 6th, 1946, Degrelle would be under surveillance during the voyage by a squad of American soldiers. Finally, despite progress in their efforts, the surrender did not occur, as the Belgian government obstinately kept its protest before the United Nations Security Council and did not yield in its insistence on sentencing without trial.

On June 6th, Martín Artajo informed British Ambassador Victor Mallet that Degrelle would soon leave Spanish territory of his own will. Before this passage could happen, and without any new developments concerning the transfer of Degrelle to a third country, the American embassy again called for his extradition or expulsion on July 1st. Only a few days earlier, the same issue had been discussed in the British Parliament.

Faced with a dilemma, the Spanish Foreign Minister intended to consider the beginning of official proceedings for an expulsion order. This was confirmed by the Military Governor of Gipuzkoa, General Pedro Pimentel, to the Belgian consul in San Sebastián, Pierre de San. On July 5th, Pimentel assured him that the Spanish government would shortly decide to grant a peremptory period to Degrelle during which he must inexorably depart from Spanish territory.

The bulletin of *Noticias Confidenciales*, in the morning edition of July 26th, quoted Reuters News Agency, from Brussels, concerning Spain, which tersely referred to the following:

*The Belgian press reports today in Madrid that the extradition of Léon Degrelle, a former Belgian Rexist leader, is expected soon. Degrelle was sentenced to death in absentia in December 1944 and fled to Spain after the collapse of Germany.*

## Beginning to Think about Escape

In light of the gravity of the situation, and the insistence, pressure, and blackmail that the Belgian, English, and American governments were exerting against Madrid, Degrelle's Spanish friends and comrades planned his escape from the hospital. They relied on the cooperation of the nuns of the hospital, especially Sister Isabel, who had been leaving the window to the street open for several nights. This would make it relatively easy for Degrelle to escape.

During this time, a former Blue Division officer was waiting every night under the window for Degrelle. Just 50 meters (164 feet) away, there was a parked car with a driver inside ready to take off immediately. He even managed to get inside the hospital to offer his services to Léon, who immediately refused and told him: "I do not want to get a Spanish soldier shot who would be fulfilling his duty by detaining me." He also added:

*Moreover, they can leave all the doors open that they want because I am not ready to leave. To flee would mean that I am running from a fight in court, an admission that I am guilty of the filth that they accuse me of. I will not leave.*

At some point, some time ago, he had also considered the possibility of going to Ireland, or, perhaps, to a South American country that was reluctant to see refugees extradited, like what French Prime Minister Pierre Laval had been offered the previous year. Unfortunately, he preferred to return to France, where he hoped to confidently prove his innocence during a trial. As Degrelle well remembered, when Laval had been handed over by Spanish authorities, despite the conditional promise of remission, he was murdered without a second thought.

Léon refused to escape per the plan drawn up by his Spanish friends and comrades, along with a nucleus of rexist officers pledged and sworn to liberate their leader. Some of them were already clandestinely located in San Sebastián to carry out the escape. They did as much as they could, overcoming unimaginable obstacles, to give faith and witness of fidelity and to try and forge an open path toward South America as a last resort and alternative solution.

The Germans had also been concerned about Léon's fate while he was hospitalized. A captain of the former National Socialist Intelligence Services managed to meet with him, disguised as a priest wearing a cassock. He offered to prepare, if necessary, an emergency escape, but Degrelle insisted on his pledge to stay, saying "leaving would be admitting guilt."

## Visits at the Hospital

Degrelle, with few exceptions, was permanently guarded and not allowed visitors. Only doctors and medical staff had direct access to his room. One notable exception was his extraordinary comrade Narciso Perales, an old guard of the Sevillian Falange. Since he was a doctor, Perales was given full access to Degrelle. Of the women nurses and health personnel at the hospital, it is worth mentioning that Marichu de Aguirre was a nurse of the Women's Section of the Falange. She was the rector at the University of Deusto. As a trustworthy comrade, she continually found ways for Degrelle to leave the hospital intermittently until the end of his stay there. She even tasted his food, for safety reasons, before serving him. On one occasion, she took the train from Bilbao to see her uncle the rector, who, at her pleading and instance, traveled by train to Madrid with the intention of presenting himself in the official office of his former pupil and now Minister of

Foreign Affairs, Alberto Martín Artajo. When he met with Artajo, he said: "Alberto, if you hand over León Degrelle—who cannot defend himself, and you know it very well—you will be collaborating in murder and committing a mortal sin!" Those words profoundly impacted the deeply religious foreign minister, touching upon the conscience of his Catholic morality.

Marichu de Aguirre also served as a liaison for Degrelle and handled his correspondence with the outside world. Degrelle entrusted her with the letters and messages that he needed to get to his contacts, and she, as an act of loyal service, fulfilled this confidential and responsible mission with diligence and pleasure.

He was also visited by military chaplains who came to comfort patients during their recovery. Even several nuns were authorized to see Degrelle, in particular Sister Isabel, who visited him regularly. The nuns who assisted at the hospital got along well with Degrelle. They offered to help in case Degrelle needed to escape in the event of imminent danger. They even managed to drill a large hole in the partition of the room, camouflaged behind a map, where he might eventually escape, and even had an emergency shelter prepared for him behind the sacrosanct enclosure of their convent.

The Duchess of Valencia, Luisa Narváez, was another woman interested in trying to save him at all costs. She had obtained a special visit pass, and during her visits, she did not hesitate to warn him, "Attention, be prepared. You will not be handed over to the Belgian police, but at some time or another, you can be taken to the French border." León answered, "What can I do? Ever since I arrived, there has been a sentinel that protects and watches me."

Luisa María Narváez Macías was the Duchess of Valencia, goddaughter of King Alfonso XIII. She was known in political circles as the "Red Duchess" because of her ideological and social positions as a radical and a revolutionary. She met León Degrelle at the palatial home of the Foreign Delegate of the Spanish Falange in Avila, on February 5th, 1939, during his official visit as Director of the Rexist Party to see the Spanish battle fronts. Degrelle had travelled from Toledo to Avila, arriving at sunset. On his way through the city of Santa Teresa, León spent the night in the home of Luisa's parents, the Duke and Duchess of Valencia. Luisa served as an interpreter during his brief stay in the city and in their home. The Duke of Valencia, who offered him his generous hospitality, showed him the palace and gave him a detailed explanation of the historical treasures that the mansion held. The young Belgian leader impressed everyone. As a reminder of that magical evening, the Duke of Valencia gave his guest of honor the sword wielded by the first Duke. With this symbolic gesture, he recognized Degrelle as the contemporary "bearer of the sword." This unique historical piece constantly accompanied Léon, who always kept it in a prominent place in his work cabinet.

Luisa, the future Duchess of Valencia, was captivated by that young man who stayed in her family's house during his visit to the front lines. She continued to follow the vicissitudes of the young, tumultuous fascist leader through the newspapers and magazines that published reports from the eastern front. She was reminded of him one day while watching documentary footage in which Hitler was shown awarding Degrelle the Iron Cross with Oak Leaves at the cinema. She even saw, in 1944, towards the end of the conflict, a large photograph of Léon on the front page of the prestigious magazine *Signal*.

In May 1945, six years after their first meeting in 1939, when Léon Degrelle's plane crashed into the Bay of La Concha in San Sebastián, and he was hospitalized at General Mola Hospital, the Duchess heard on the Radio Paris broadcast, "that Degrelle had fallen from the sky in Spain, on the coast of Gipuzkoa." She immediately wrote to the Spanish authorities to get news and details of the accident and to obtain, through sheer tenacity, a special authorization to be able to visit him in his hospital room. It was during those repeated visits that she was able to collect the testimony of the hero who made such an impact on the spirit and heart of the young Spanish aristocrat. At that time, she was cultivating activist groups associated with the *Avanzadillas Monárquicas*,[17] who worked for the cause of restoring the Chameleon King, Don Juan de Borbón, to the throne. Despite her role in these organizations, she was never linked with fascism or any fascist governments.

In September 1945, in an audacious move, Luisa once presented herself to the Council of Ministers and warned that if they decided to hand over Léon Degrelle she would return and shoot all the ministers. She was sentenced to eight months in prison.

The Spanish press kept silent about the presence of León Degrelle in Spain, but both international radio broadcasts and newspapers devoted extensive comments and reports on this subject.

In 1950, Luisa decided to publish an account of what she had heard and gathered directly from Degrelle about his career and his adventures.

---

[17] *Avanzadillas Monárquicas* (monarchist outposts) one of the pro-monarchist factions during the Spanish Civil War that backed the restoration of the Bourbons to the throne and that remained active during Franco's regime. The organization was actually created and directed by Duchess María Luisa Narváez, according to *ABC*, April 11th, 2015 (itself a monarchist-supporting newspaper) and *La Vanguardia*, December 26th, 2018.

Writing just a little pamphlet was not the objective; it was in fact, a whole book. Whoever reads it can testify that half of the book is directly from Léon Degrelle's own words. In referring to her work, he states in an excerpt:

> *I do not deny it. Hundreds of my personal quotes are published between quotation marks!*
>
> *My interlocutor brought together, even in Belgium, twenty more interviews, numerous texts from memoirs of contemporaries, and reports on the issue, such as that of Robert Brasillach.*
>
> *In this way, the "puzzle" was created and completed that allowed the Duchess of Valencia to "offer" to the larger public my adventures in that book in which Lucien Rebatet, the famous French fascist writer, has said "that you could think up ten novels and fifteen films.*

Léon added:

> *I do not believe in congratulating anyone* [the victors], *neither for the expansion of communism throughout the rest of Europe, nor for its survival in the USSR. In sixty years, communism has proved to be an immense failure, intellectually and morally, destroying the personal characteristics of man.*
>
> *Only one country had sufficient strength, like that of Bonaparte's France or the Führer's Germany, to make a great continental unification into a reality.*
>
> *It is precisely in this explosion, that of the USSR itself, that I want to believe. In the midst of the French Revolution, who could have thought in those times of criminal terror, that a Bonaparte would soon emerge? That he would rebuild, with an iron fist, the France that was falling to the bottom of the abyss? A few years later, it would be this Bonaparte who was on the point of creating a united Europe!*
>
> *At first, like Napoleon, who was but a Corsican, Hitler was but a southern German, born in Austrian territory.*
>
> *Later he was a German of the Reich. Then of the Great Reich, that unification of all Germans. Then, finally, he wanted to unify all Europeans.*

In 1961, Degrelle published the first edition of *Degrelle M'a Dit*,[18] under the pseudonym, "The Duchess of Valencia." This was something unusual for Degrelle, who was used to writing under his own name. He had to write this work in the third person and with this pseudonym because it would have been banned in French and

---

[18] [French for *Degrelle Told Me.*]

Belgian markets and subjected to relentless state repression and censorship. Using this subterfuge, the work was published in Paris through the Moret publishing house. It was able to reach the public, including Belgian readers. To make the ruse more credible, Degrelle even included a photograph of "the author," that beautiful and rebellious woman.

In this book he announced that the future political struggle would pass through pro-European activism:

> *The action that might interest me now goes beyond the narrow national entities. A powerful Europe must be forged, in which today's countries will have the role that the old, unified provinces had within European countries from the Renaissance to the nineteenth century. In the face of an immense world that threatens or wants to defeat her, this Europe must unify, or she will die.*

In 1977, Éditions du Baucens publishing house, published a new, generously illustrated second edition of *Degrelle M'a Dit*. The prologue to the book was even signed by the Duchess of Valencia.

The work was a huge success. The copies sold numbered into the tens of thousands. In the second edition, Degrelle added an additional chapter, signing his own name to it.

On the cover of the new edition appeared a photograph taken at dawn in Crete, with the first rays of sun rising and highlighting the silhouette of Mount Isa. On the back, two well-illustrated photographs were published: one of Léon Degrelle dressed in the uniform of the Spanish Falange, with his German decorations on his chest. The picture was taken at his house, La Carlina, in 1961. The second was a photograph of the beautiful and sensual Duchess of Valencia.

The 1977 edition also included a new epilogue, signed by Léon Degrelle, dated June 15th, (his birthday). He dedicated it to Alain-Valéry Aelberts and Jean-Jacques Auquier and began with these words:

> *More than a quarter of a century has passed since the Duchess of Valencia opened to the public the tableau of my life and of my struggle during the fifteen months I spent, between 1945 and 1946, in a small room of the Mola Hospital, in San Sebastián.*

In the extensive final chapter, he analyzes both the shortcomings of democracy and the achievements made by the fascism under Mussolini during the interwar period. The Duce managed to lift Italy to its feet during that time. The same happened with the social revolution carried out by German National Socialism. The German people were awakened from their lethargy, produced by the "sleeping pill" administered to them by the international banking elite. This put the nation at the head of the most advanced and developed peoples on earth. After a thorough analysis of what the joint victory of American capitalism and Soviet communism—the union of those holding the puppet strings behind the scenes—meant for Europe, the epilogue ends with the following:

*We lost all of that on May 8th, 1945.*

*More than thirty years of exile has only increased the pain I feel of not being able, with Hitler and with our millions of comrades, to give Europe that real gift. Instead, we have to suffer from the spectacle of the decrepitude of a West that was, for centuries, the very heart of humanity.*

*The two great "democracies," one as falsely democratic as the other; one being nothing more than a dictatorship of money, the other being nothing more than a proletarian dictatorship. They have struck Europe twice. America has poisoned Europe's soul with its mercantile materialism; the USSR has robbed half of her territory, increasing its pressure every year thanks to the endless diplomatic insanity of Americans. Now all of that has spread everywhere.*

*So, I truly prefer, a thousand times over, to have been among those who lost, but who held on to a great dream, then to have been on the side of these fanatical democracies, which after provoking the Second World War, finally left on the charred land of their victory a Europe in decline.*

*Trapped in my exile, I have been persecuted with a savage blood lust by the victors, jumping from refuge to refuge, forced nonstop, and by whatever means necessary, to survive. Six times I have been the target of kidnapping attempts. I have often had brushes with death. Condemned exclusively for political reasons—the evidence presented has repeatedly shown that all the accusations of war crimes leveled against me were nothing but lies—I still hope for the smallest gesture that would allow me to believe in a vague amnesty.*

*As far as my own country, I can only remember my murdered brother, my elderly parents who painfully died in atrocious prisons, and all the other members of my family who were overwhelmed by the worst persecutions. All in the name of democracy, of course, AND in the name of human rights!*

*What does adversity matter! At least I will have lived nobly, trying to straighten out the destiny of my homeland before 1940, fighting for its survival after invasion, for its resurrection and for the restoration of its historical borders, all of which would have been the glorious fruit of our suffering on the Eastern Front.*

*I would have lived for Europe as if, from our epic, I would have gone beyond everything the great builders of old could have dreamed of for her.*

*One man's misfortune is just an episode. Besides, I am not unfortunate. I am satisfied and happy with my life. Tomorrow, if destiny comes to meet me again, I shall start again. I will keep up the same hard fight. I will go still further, if possible.*

*What counts in me is having possessed what is essential: the passion of that which is great, of the pure, of the beautiful, of the just, and of having projected it widely and fraternally among men.*

*In the shadows of my unending exile, I keep in my soul all the vibrant light that illuminated my childhood, my youth, my political conquests, my battles as a soldier. I will have no other wish, at my death, than to claim, as Goethe did, "Mehr licht! Mehr licht!" ("More light! More light!"). The light of every day of my life will be there.*

## Mystical Writings during His Mandatory Rest

Doctors, nurses, nuns, priests, and the Duchess of Valencia were all the bearers of messages from his friends confirming that everything was ready and available for an escape, and that he could disappear without a trace. They believed it was urgent for Degrelle to decide whether or not to leave the hospital secretly, since any delay brought with it incredible risks. Léon was not yet persuaded to escape, so he continually told the messengers, "To leave would be to capitulate."

Since he would not leave the hospital by means of escape, Degrelle spend much of his time writing. He had considerable experience with the craft. In his youth, he had taken charge of the magazine, *L'Avant Garde* (1927), also collaborating with *Le XXe Siècle* (1929) for larger reports. He directed the weekly *Soirées* (1931), dedicated to the world of art, cinema, and fashion. He founded the weekly *Rex* (1932), for political and societal information, and the magazine *Vlan*, for general information; in 1933 he participated in starting up *Foyer* and in 1936 he inaugurated and managed *Le Pays Réel*, a daily newspaper of general information. The monthly *National-Socialism* appeared between 1942 and 1944. Writing was in Degrelle's blood.

In 1946, during his endless days of convalescence, he would write about, comment upon, and translate the poems of Saint Teresa of Avila. Poetry was the transcription of his inner life, of his state of mind, his yearnings, and also his demons. He began to incorporate the poetic works of Saint Teresa into his everyday vernacular. The preface of the collection of her poems was dated June 28th, 1946, in which Degrelle stated:

> *I have guessed, much more than translated, these "poems" by Saint Teresa of Jesus.*
>
> *I am not a philosopher, a philologist, or a Puritan. Strange as it may seem, I do not even really know the Spanish language.*
>
> *Beyond the words of the great mystic, there was the canticle. I have felt this song, which has shaken me. I wanted to reproduce this great cry of a soul.*
>
> *As I write these poems, I face death before me. It is she who suggests to me to prefer the heart's impulse to the rest: in poetry, as in everything, only love counts.*
>
> *L.D.*

When this inner and inspired version of her poetry was finished, he gathered them into two books: *Je Te Bénis, O Belle Mort*, a mystical exaltation and inner reading that would see publication in 1951, and *Pastorales*, where the soul is serene in the lap of quiet life. [19]

Curiously, Léon Degrelle had not written a single verse since his adolescence. Direct action, rallies, and politics had totally consumed him. Now, in a most natural way, he returned to meet Polymnia,[20] causing him to pluck the most sensitive strings of his heart and create a myriad of poetic verse.

He wrote tirelessly. As stated previously, during ten endless days, he translated the verses of his native land into twelve great poems. His source of inspiration was the memories of his childhood: the valleys, the forests, the customs of his people, and the landscape, which he kept as a spiritual treasure nestled in his heart. He titled them *La Chanson Ardennaise* (*Song of the Ardennes*), later published in 1951. He also compiled the books *Les Îles Blanches* and *L'Ombre des Soirs*, in which he reveals, with sincere and beautiful words, his passion for life, his joy of living, his struggle as a gentleman of faith and of the ideal, and his passion for all that is noble and beautiful.

His poetic tone was vibrant, of bugles and light. He did not allow himself to be overcome at any time by nostalgia, infirmity, or melancholy, nor did he allow himself to fall into sadness and despair, even when facing his own mortality. For Degrelle, "melancholy is the disease of the defeated." Despite various earthly defeats, he always optimistically retorted, "Yes, but only *temporarily* defeated."

---

[19] [French *For I Bless you, Oh Beautiful Death* and *Pastoral*, respectively.]

[20] [Polymnia – Πολύμνια in Greek – was the muse of sacred hymns, poetry, and eloquence in Greek mythology.]

In his notebook, which he jealously guarded in the drawer of his hospital room table, he pointed out: "It is necessary, however, to love happiness, as the sound of the sea is loved, fleeting as it may be; as the evening colors are loved, even though it is known that they are going to perish…"

Degrelle anxiously wanted to recover quickly so he could fully dedicate himself to writing of the meritorious deeds of his volunteers on the Eastern Front. He wrote quickly, paragraph after paragraph, in a clear hand, with few mistakes or corrections. From time to time, he repeated an idea that was becoming firm in his mind and in his warrior-like will: "I am not willing to buckle or capitulate."

.

*Léon Degrelle and Otto Skorzeny in Spain*

# II

# *The Great Fugitive of Injustice*

# *(1946–1951)*

## Léon Degrelle's "Double"

The Falangist doctor Narciso Perales had designed a detailed plan to extract Léon Degrelle from the medical ward of General Mola Hospital, where he had been recovering for sixteen months. The stealthy escape depended on the invaluable help of the worthy comrade of the Falangist Women's Section, Marichu de Aguirre; on the help of his good friend José Finat y Escrivá de Romaní, Count of Mayalde, and his distinguished wife Casilda, Duchess of Pastrana; and upon the "approval" of the nun who attended him, Sister Isabel. Ramón Serrano Suñer, brother-in-law of General Franco, also collaborated in the secretive hospital escape, although he later recognized that "…it would not have been easy at that time without Franco's quiet approval," and therefore, "everything was prepared in agreement with him."

The Spanish government knew perfectly well that Léon Degrelle was absolutely innocent of the false accusations looming over him by the irascible fury of the "victors." They were convinced that they could in no way allow the Laval case to be repeated, but the international pressure that they received demanding Degrelle's head was becoming untenable. The Belgians were making a lot of international noise, attacking Spain and demanding the surrender of Léon Degrelle without further excuses or pretexts. The Belgian Prime Minister, Henry Spaak, a known freemason, missed no opportunity to speak in Parliament about Spain's grievous offences of being Degrelle's land of asylum, shelter, and protection. Spaak's intentions were clear: to eliminate the political fugitive quickly and expeditiously, to silence Degrelle forever for the simple fact that he fought against communism with the heroic forces of the Axis and his indomitable Walloon volunteers on the Eastern Front. This meant the death penalty *in absentia*, an unappealable sentence. All simply for being an exceptional political figure, a great motivator of crowds, and a providential popular and revolutionary leader of the future Europe.

Léon Degrelle had been sentenced to death by firing squad, on December 27th, 1944. At that time, he was on the Eastern Front fighting like a wild boar for Europe's freedom and to keep Western culture out of the claws of Marxism. The trial was held without his presence, without defense, and without any legal guarantees. The allegations made against him, in a devious and cowardly manner, were as follows:

1) *Carrying arms against Belgium;*
2) *Helping the enemies of the State by contributing soldiers, money, and food;*
3) *Participating with the enemy in the transformation of legal institutions or organizations, breaking, in time of war, the fidelity of the citizens towards the king and the state, and directing propaganda against resistance to the enemy and its allies;*
4) *Conspiring to incite civil war;*
5) *Directing armed troops and enlisted soldiers;*
6) *Leading armed units; and*
7) *Creating private militias or other private organizations.*

The brief, laconic, and terrible sentence of Judge Couturier, stated:

*Since 1941, Léon Degrelle has been recruiting men for a combatant legion, instituting the Walloon Guards, who exercise surveillance functions, which are, in principle, entrusted to the army. He has provided both men and labor, having created a Women's Battalion of the Red Cross and an Agricultural Service designed to send Belgians to East Prussia.*

*He has favored the politics of the enemy, putting his party at the service of National Socialist policies since January 1st, 1941.*

*In May 1941, he signed an agreement with the VNV to have the country divided into two distinct communities. Later, he addressed the question of the Walloon region's integration into the Reich, a region he has said to be of Germanic origin; of the annexation by Germany of Belgium or of a part of Belgium; and of the Walloon Guard and the Légion Wallonie to be able to carry out the National Socialist revolution.*

*Léon Degrelle is sentenced to death by firing squad at Saint-Gilles.*

*Within six months, if there is no opposition to the trial, Degrelle will be deprived of Belgian nationality.*

Degrelle was accused of preparing civil war, when in reality, civil war was being organized and promoted precisely by the Belgian communist-leaning "resistance."

Léon Degrelle was never charged with "war crimes" of any kind, not even by the Soviet madmen against whom he fought on the Eastern Front most of the time he served during the armed conflict (1940–1945). Léon Degrelle was an exemplary soldier and a courageous warrior.

In August 1946, in view of the untenable and implacable situation and of pressure of all kinds exerted at the international level, the Spanish authorities granted Léon Degrelle eight days to leave Spanish territory. This was more of a simulation. Franco worked, in this case, in a *gallego* way,[21] so his resolution was ambiguous: "Well, Degrelle will be officially expelled, but not actually expelled." They decided to stage a guarded escort and expulsion from Spanish territory along a Portuguese border with a "Léon Degrelle" double. Thus, the requirements and formalities would be technically fulfilled.

Léon Degrelle had already recovered from his serious injuries by August. In view of the urgent requests for surrender and extradition, the "expulsion" of a Degrelle double from Spanish territory was made in order to give satisfaction to the Belgian, British, and American governments, who tenaciously insisted upon apprehension. The simulated itinerary was to travel by rail, from San Sebastián to Salamanca, and from there toward Ciudad Rodrigo until they arrived at the Spanish-Portuguese border of Fuentes de Oñoro, bordering Vilar Formoso on the Portuguese side. State security forces dropped "Degrelle" off, and in this way, the Spanish government, at least "officially," illustrated that Degrelle was no longer on Spanish soil.

### The Escape is Carried Out

On August 21st, Degrelle's escape from the hospital finally took place. It happened to be his eldest daughter Chantal's birthday. The escape required overcoming a number of seemingly insurmountable difficulties. Under pressure from the Allied authorities, the guards monitoring the hospital grounds had been reinforced, with forty men taking turns day and night to guard Degrelle. Even the

---

[21] *Gallego* normally refers to the region and local language in Galicia, in northwestern Spain. Here the idiomatic expression means to do something openly so as to achieve the opposite of what was anticipated.

window of his room, which faced the street, had been shuttered to avoid any attempt of escape.

Despite the strong security measures in place, Degrelle maintained permanent contact with the Spanish comrades willing to assist him. Twice a day, the nurse, Marichu de Aguirre and Sister Isabel, accompanied by two soldiers and the watch officer, entered his room to serve him food. Léon took advantage of these essential visits to request from nurse Aguirre the purchase of some basic toiletries and personal hygiene products, like toothpaste, a bottle of aspirin, and other hygiene-sanitary items, for which he gave them the appropriate peseta bills to pay the amount of the order. Inside the bills he would fold a note with instructions to be sent to his contacts outside. What Degrelle did not suspect was that an employee of the post office on Calle de San Martín, in San Sebastián, had control of his daily mail. He passed the information to the Deputy Consul of Belgium, who paid him handsomely for violating this private correspondence.

The departure from the hospital was to be executed during the night. Degrelle occupied a room located on the third floor of the building about 12 meters (39 feet) above the inner courtyard. Before leaving, in case of misfortune, he had written his will and indicated the prayers that should be offered for the eternal rest of his soul at his burial. He thought about getting out using the lighting wires, whose cables ran outside the walls of his room. When Degrelle told his friends that a decision was made, one of them, a soldier, feigned illness to gain access to the interior of the building. Once he was inside and cross-checked Degrelle's plan, he considered it unfeasible. During this time, the Spanish government's change of criteria also happened, decreeing Degrelle's expulsion but not his extradition. This made things easier. It was enough to lure his persecutors with false clues, such as the idea that Degrelle would leave by way of the French border. The direction taken by the agent who impersonated Degrelle on August 21st, 1946, was exactly the opposite in the direction of Portugal.

That same day, at 9:00 a.m., the civil and military governors of the province of Gipuzkoa arrived at General Mola Hospital. Degrelle received them lying in his bed. They were tasked with delivering the government's expulsion order that Degrelle was to comply with within eight days. They told him that he would be taken by the relevant authorities to a border post of his choosing. He signed only the notification document, but not the consent form. He was also informed that he had to vacate the hospital immediately, but that a room was reserved for him at the Maria Cristina Hotel.

Situated behind the governors, Marichu de Aguirre just smiled with a look of complicity. She was carrying a bottle of aspirins containing a message from the outside with only one line: "Get down as quickly as possible. There is a taxi waiting for you." The two governors, having fulfilled their official assignment, kindly took their leave of Léon.

Degrelle's influential, loyal friends and Falangist comrades managed to have a like-minded man appointed as watch officer on the same day, who was amenable to helping them pull off the plan successfully. To make it easier for Degrelle to escape in a nearby car, the officer would, at some point, receive an outside telephone call that would apparently distract him from his duties. The false "Degrelle," of striking physical resemblance to Léon, remained in the hospital waiting for events to unfold, while the real Degrelle left unnoticed. The false Degrelle then took a train in the direction of the Portuguese border.

His friends had arrived to pick him up at the agreed upon time. As the governors walked out of the main entrance of the building, surrounded by all the associated pomp and protocol, Degrelle was crossing to the side door, thus avoiding an encounter with journalists and agents ready to shadow him and stick to him like glue for the next eight days. The escape operation was mounted by José Finat y Escrivá de Romani, Count of Mayalde, and by his wife Casilda, the Duchess of Pastrana. Franco was not unaware of the plans, and neither was the Minister of the Interior, Blas Pérez González. Dr. Narciso Perales, Alberto Martín Artajo, Ramón Serrano Suñer, and Maillán were also collaborators. The previous afternoon, they had gathered at the Palacio de El Pardo to prepare the necessary papers to allow Degrelle to remain in Spain discreetly. It was then that Franco put in over twenty thousand pesetas of his personal money to be sent to Degrelle, who was penniless. Spanish passport number 597/46 was provided to him under the name "Enrique Durand." It showed his place of birth as Warsaw, Poland, on March 14th, 1907, and indicated that he was a merchant. Later, Léon wrote on the back cover, "This is the passport with which I left San Sebastián on August 21st, 1946. It was provided to me by the Minister of the Interior (governing). I had personally sent him the photo. The fingerprints are fakes."

He was also provided, on August 20th, with a safe passage permission so that he could travel throughout Spanish territory without problems. It was valid for three months and was issued by the Secretary General of the Directorate General for Security, with the same affiliation as the passport. In it appeared the following:

*Don Enrique Durand, resident of Madrid, is authorized to travel throughout the national territory using whatever means he deems necessary, having in the present document the validity of SAFE PASSAGE for a period of three months. Madrid, August 20th, 1946. The Secretary General.*

On the same page of that document under the signature of the Secretary General of the Directorate General for Security and the official seal of the bureau that issued the document, Degrelle later hand wrote the following text:

> *The safe passage permit that was handed to me by the Minister of the Interior (governing) on August 21st, 1946. It should be emphasized that it is authorized for three months, whereas, theoretically, I should have left Spain within eight days of the notification of my expulsion order. If they had really wanted me to leave the country, a safe passage permit would have been issued for eight days, not three months. At the same time, they handed me the sum of twenty thousand pesetas on behalf of the Minister.*

This comment and note ends with, as an authentication, the signature of Léon Degrelle.

Degrelle took his documents and quickly departed in the car waiting for him outside the hospital. They drove to the outskirts of the city of San Sebastián, where Casilda and Jose were waiting for him. They transferred him to their own car, and drove without delay, to his new destination in Madrid.

Degrelle had been firm with his friends in his appreciation for their help when he sent them his determined personal resolution:

> *I do not go to the slaughterhouse. I do not give myself up. I am not going to Portugal because there President Salazar will have the same problems, the same difficulties as General Franco, and furthermore the Portuguese police will turn me over. I stay here, even if I am thrown into the road, or in a ditch. I will hide as I can, but I will stay here.*

### An Impenetrable Hideout in Madrid's Salamanca District

In the capital of Spain, he was put up in a safe house, an apartment kept by Dr. Narciso Perales, in cooperation with Serrano Suñer. It was located on Calle Goya, in the heart of Madrid's Salamanca neighborhood, although the documentation provided to Degrelle gave his address as 57 Calle Escosura. In this apartment lived an elderly couple, who had a son who was also a fellow doctor and friend of Perales. The safe haven was a veritable hovel, whose window overlooked an elevator shaft. He was warned, "Here, your room does not even look out on the balcony." Years later, Degrelle remembered:

*I lived in the maid's room. No light, no ventilation. The man in the house weighed about 130 kilos (287 lbs.) It was unbelievably hot, even during the middle of the night. I remember going to bed every night with a large chamber pot. I produced four liters (1 gallon) every night.*

Contact with the outside filtered out through his hosts' son, the doctor. He spoke directly with Dr. Perales, who, in turn, informed Serrano Suñer and the Count of Mayalde, his main supporters.

Everything had been laid out to perfection. He was out of the reach of his tenacious persecutors. He was provided with false documentation under the name of "Enrique Durand," a Polish national. Only a small group was aware of this documentation, including Minister of the Interior, Blas Pérez, and Francisco Franco himself.

On his first Christmas outside the hospital, although stuck within his small room, he received a couple of bottles of champagne and some nougat from his comrades. The secrecy and total discretion surrounding Degrelle was such that even the Spanish Foreign Minister, Alberto Martín Artajo, when asked about the whereabouts of Degrelle, was convinced that he had escaped and taken refuge in America, and even provided an official note stating that he was no longer on Spanish territory.

For a year and a half, he did not see the sky of Madrid; trapped between the four narrow walls of that tiny room, and visible only by the light of a fifteen-watt lamp placed on a bedside table, he wrote unceasingly. He wrote out his political narratives and military memoirs along with his thoughts on other issues, which he would later compile in three thick volumes.

He disappeared like Knight Lohengrin[22] and like him, he would emerge no more until the Holy Grail demanded it.

A year and a half locked in that dark little bedroom, without being able to do any kind of exercise, and without news from his family, only that they were all imprisoned in Belgium, was difficult at first. At that time, Degrelle learned from the Madrid daily newspaper, *Informaciones*, about the tragic death of his father and mother inside the Belgian penitentiary where they had been so unjustly and inhumanly detained.

---

[22] Knight Lohengrin is a character in German literature. He is a knight of the Holy Grail, who is sent to rescue a maiden who can never ask his identity.

## The False News of His Move to Portugal Is Disseminated

The day after his departure from General Mola Hospital in San Sebastián, on August 22nd, 1946, the Spanish press published that Léon Degrelle had been expelled from the country. The Ministry of Foreign Affairs, in a brief note, leaked the confirmation of the news to the media. For more than two weeks, Americans tracked the borders. They later searched all the ships that had sailed from Portugal within those dates and even forced a Spanish ship, the *Monte Ayala*, to return to Lisbon in order to search it thoroughly. All vessels, regardless of the flag they sailed under, were stopped and inspected. The Allies tried desperately to intercept Degrelle, having sought his capture for a year and a half, pressured as they were by Belgian freemasons and international Jewry. It was unbearable for them that this man should be alive, this man whom Hitler had praised on February 23rd, 1944, while placing the *Ritterkreuz* around his neck. He told Degrelle fondly that, "if I had had a son, I would have liked him to be like you."

*Adolf Hitler decorates Léon Degrelle*

According to Carlos Eduardo de Soveral, after the war in Portugal, it was Sebastián Cardoso who spoke to the *Mocidade Portuguesa*[23] about Belgian Rexism and its chief founder. There was speculation that the criticism published on the literary page of the Portuguese weekly, *A Nação*, which was directed by Miguel Trigueiros in 1946, regarding the piece "*Limite*" by Eduardo Bastos, as well as the commentary on "*Poetry, Poetics, and Poemática*," might have been penned by Léon Degrelle himself. This turned out to be false.

Although the news of Degrelle's "departure" from Spanish territory had been published in the Spanish press, and was confirmed by the Foreign Ministry on August 27th, English Ambassador Victor Mallet sent a note to London, questioning the veracity of such information:

> *Far from having left Spain, he has either escaped or has been hidden by some friends. If he has really left the country, it is absurd that they give us no details. They instead refuse to give further explanations in this regard unless they are personally corroborated by the Foreign Minister himself.*

During that time, the Western press was tirelessly trying to sniff out his whereabouts and ceaselessly publishing sensational news. Degrelle was believed to be a refugee in Colombia, in Uruguay, or in Ecuador, or on board a sailboat with the bow pointed toward Dublin, or in Lisbon waiting for a ship with passage to Buenos Aires, etc. All the rumors were absurd, and no one suspected the secure hide out where he was actually hidden in Madrid. Some people speculated that another of his potential destinations might be Spanish Morocco.

### The "Degrelle Affair" Brought to the Council of Ministers

On August 29th and 30th, 1946, a Council of Ministers was held in La Coruña, chaired by General Franco. The government discussed the "Degrelle case," among other issues on the agenda. On this subject, the Minister of the Interior reported on the expulsion and departure of Degrelle from the Spanish territory. Due to the unjust allegations against the Spanish nation, and in order to dispense with malevolent interpretations, which were all seeking pretext, the Council of Ministers agreed to publish the following official note on this subject:

---

[23] [Portuguese for Portuguese Youth. The *Mocidade Portuguesa* was a right-wing youth movement started in 1936 under Prime Minister Salazar.]

Since the arrival on national territory of Léon Degrelle, due to the special circumstances of international order during which they occurred, and the passionate hour in which Europe has lived, the Spanish government, serving the general interests of the nation, decided to deny formal authorization to the Belgian exile to reside in Spanish territory after his hospitalization for injuries sustained during his landing in Spain.

His extradition has been demanded by the Belgian government, on the grounds of the international agreements concerning this matter. The question of legality was submitted to the Spanish Council of State and its report was contrary to the claims of that government, considering that, under the terms of the provisions of the Spanish-Belgian Convention on Extradition of Offenders of June 17th, 1870 and the supplementary declaration of January 28th, 1876, those accused of political offenses were exempted from extradition, at the discretion of the requested country to determine whether the offenses on which the extradition request is based are or are not covered by the provisions. In the opinion of the Council of State, the facts alleged against Léon Degrelle are of a political nature. Concerning those facts which can be regarded as common or political offenses, it is the motive of the fact that decides. According to this high reporting body, it is clear that in the case of Mr. Degrelle the request was politically motivated.

In the face of the persistent requests of the Belgian government, the Spanish government informed them of the formal obstacles to extradition, which, moreover, would have had to comply with the terms of the "humanitarian clause" that is traditionally used in these cases. This would prevent the execution of the prisoner, which is a guarantee the Belgian government has not offered.

The Spanish government, in making these facts public, must state the following:

1) That since the extradition of Léon Degrelle is not appropriate, no international norm, nor any Spanish law, obliges the Spanish government to surrender him or to take part in his persecution, which, moreover, would be contrary to traditional Spanish honor and opposed to the state of her public opinion.

2) That the mere expulsion of said foreigner from Spanish territory, in accordance with the repeated request of England and the United States of America, has been decreed in use of a strict right of sovereignty and in response to the good will of Spain toward these countries, and her traditional friendship with the Belgian nation.

3) That international obligations being by nature reciprocal, Spain is obliged to draw attention to the fact that, in contrast to her clear and loyal conduct, in the Degrelle case as in other similar cases, the tolerance or inhibition of the

*governments of other countries to allow common criminals from our war to circulate freely on foreign lands. They are allowed to carry out public acts of political belligerence and conduct activities in the countries that house them, where they promote campaigns of agitation and propaganda, and even subversive and revolutionary aggressions paid for with the gold plundered from the official treasury and from the private wealth of our nation.*

4)    *Having fulfilled at all times the Spanish government's duties of friendship and good relations with the Belgian nation, it is pleased to reiterate at this time its feelings of sympathy and affection toward that people, as was revealed during the time of war and in their moments of misfortune; and it would strongly regret that any kind of political passion could disfigure before any part of the Belgian people the noble conduct that the Spanish nation and her government have maintained for them at all times.*

## Exonerated by the War Crimes Commission

From a strictly legal point of view, extradition was impossible. As previously stated, Spain had signed a treaty with Belgium in 1870 which expressly stated that everything pertaining to extradition claims on political exiles was excluded. To overcome this technicality, the Belgian authorities demanded Degrelle, not as a political prisoner, but as a "war criminal." Everyone was aware that Degrelle had never committed a "war crime," in Belgium or elsewhere. Facing such a slanderous accusation, Degrelle called for the establishment of an international tribunal to judge his case where he could defend himself against such allegations, proving his innocence triumphantly, with logic and justice on his side.

The Allied War Crimes Commission was, the highest court to qualify such cases. Typically, when collecting testimonies, it tended to visit the site where there had been the slightest suspicion of such reprehensible acts having taken place. The commission issued a comprehensive official report regarding the Degrelle case. This was then published by the Belgian government, who removed the name of Léon Degrelle from the report evidencing the political manipulation and false and spurious accusations used by the government to claim Degrelle, thus contradicting the War Crimes Commission itself.

Degrelle recognized that "Franco agreed to expulsion, with the assumption that I would not be expelled." As previously mentioned, Degrelle was helped by the Count of Mayalde, a Falangista from Toledo—and a good friend of José Antonio Primo de Rivera, as well as the Mayor of Madrid—and by his wife, the Duchess of

Pastrana, in finding his first secret refuge carrying false documentation under the name of "Enrique Durand." Franco gifted Degrelle the sum of twenty thousand pesetas so he could cover his basic needs.

## Tribulations and Misconceptions:
## The Ambassador of the United States Issues a Statement

On August 30th, 1946, a Portuguese newspaper *República,* cited two dispatches—one in New York and the other in Madrid—from the United Press news agency, in which they observed that the Argentine government had announced that they would not allow Degrelle to enter the Argentine Republic. This was in reference to the rumor that his whereabouts were unknown and that he could have left Spain in a fishing boat, possibly headed for South America.

A spokesman for the Spanish Ministry of Foreign Affairs confirmed that Degrelle was not on board the *Monte Ayala*, a ship docked in the port of Vigo with provenance from Santander from where it had departed on August 22nd for Buenos Aires. The British Consul in Vigo suspected he was aboard this ship carrying false documentation and disguised among the passengers. So obsessive was their harassment, that on the ship's next stopover in the port of Lisbon, the Portuguese police, whose agents were accompanied by British representatives, carried out a thorough investigation on board the vessel, but Degrelle was not found. Interestingly, one of the five companions who had made the famous and perilous flight from Norway to Spain in May 1945 with Léon Degrelle was on board the ship. As no one had claimed him or laid any charges against him, however, he was released, allowing him to continue his voyage.

By that time, there also appeared some chatter in various Spanish newspapers, that Degrelle had been seen and recognized in Portugal, but this was not truly confirmed. The Spanish government was thus trying to remove, or at least decrease, the pressure it was receiving on the issue.

When the Americans, despite their own intense search efforts, realized that Degrelle was nowhere to be found, their ambassador appeared before Franco at his summer residence in Pazo de Meirás, all but demanding explanations. After a few tense moments, Franco, with a quiet voice, told the Ambassador, "If you want to see the reports, they happen to be here on my desk." He let him peruse the false reports of the invented Degrelle, along with the telegrams from his escorts sent from all the railway stations along the route. The reports even detailed what he was eating, when he urinated, etc. In the "dossier" containing the telegrams that the

American Ambassador was able to view, there were also messages sent by the police who held "Degrelle" that stated: "The prisoner arrived well"; "The prisoner came out at the appointed place in the province of Salamanca"; "The prisoner was picked up by a Portuguese lieutenant colonel..." Franco's strategy of showing the U.S. diplomat the "dossier" worked effectively. The Ambassador left the meeting, fully reassured by the documentation he had seen. Meanwhile, the real Degrelle lay quietly in his dark, narrow room, busily writing books, one after the other, his mind absorbed by recollection and reflection.

### The Belgian Government is Suspicious of the Expulsion

The Belgian government's response to Spain on the Degrelle case came quickly, and it was reported in the Belgian newspapers on September 4th, 1946. This information was also fully reflected in the Information Bulletin number 98, dated September 13th, 1946, which was published biweekly by the British Embassy in Madrid. In summary, the Belgian government estimated that the conditions under which Degrelle was intended to have left Spain indicated that there had been "...true complicity between the government of Madrid and the Belgian citizen," basing that accusation on four elements:

1) *That when the Chargé d'Affaires of Belgium was told on August 22nd that Degrelle had been expelled, he, according to the official explanations given later, had already left Spain.*

2) *That Degrelle, who was under an alleged supervised freedom and properly guarded, was actually released on the morning of August 21st.*

3) *That he was released on August 21st, after a fifteen month stay, supposedly under guard. Degrelle was able to leave Spain on the night of August 21st–22nd. No one can believe that such a departure could have been made within such a period of time without the help of the Spanish authorities.*

4) *When asked by the Belgian government about the conditions of Degrelle's disappearance, the Spanish government refuses to provide the requested information, arguing that no legal text obliges it to do so. In doing so, the Spanish government clearly shows that on political, criminal, and moral grounds it sympathizes with the "traitor" Degrelle against Belgium, and that it intends to help him, to every extent possible, to evade the justice of his homeland.*

The Belgian government, moreover, threatened that:

> [A]gainst such actions the Belgian government has submitted a strong note of protest in Madrid and intends to bring the incident to the United Nations, for it considers that in the way the Spanish government works, there is evidence of the Spanish government's will to protect and aid those who were agents and accomplices of the Axis.

## The Case is Again Submitted to the United Nations

Belgium carried out its threats and filed a new protest against Spain before the United Nations Security Council on September 9th, 1946.

On Wednesday, September 11th, the daily *Nouvelle République* collected a supposed text given by Léon Degrelle to the civil governor of San Sebastián: "I will not be shot so soon." The newspaper also reported, notably, that "…officially expelled…he remains hidden in Spain, under the protection of the Falange."

The sadness experienced in those days by Degrelle was great. He meditated in silence. "My greatest suffering," he insisted, "is that because of me Spain might be struck or wounded." He again offered to return voluntarily to Belgium, on the condition that he be given a fair trial, that this trial should be public knowledge, and that his statements should be transmitted over the air waves. The press recognized his required conditions to present himself, which were very reasonable. The Belgian government responded to him in silence, its desire only to capture Degrelle in order to eliminate him at the first opportunity and silence him forever with impunity.

In September 1946, the British Ambassador sent London a note indicating his confirmation of the scant sympathy that Spanish Foreign Minister Alberto Martín Artajo felt for Degrelle. It was therefore likely that the Expulsion Order issued on August 21st, giving him an eight-day deadline in which to comply, had been executed. According to the note by the Ambassador to the Minister himself: "The Order of Expulsion was fulfilled that same night (that of August 21st) and Mr. Artajo, looking me in the eye, assured me that he [Degrelle] had really left Spain." Perhaps Martín Artajo really was convinced of this, giving credence to Franco's method of not letting the left hand know what the right hand was doing.

Degrelle later commented:

> If I had been a scoundrel, as my enemies were claiming, then broadcasting the court proceedings by radio would only have contributed to demolishing me definitively before the public. The Belgian regime enjoyed the totality of the press. I could not

*count on the smallest newsletter anymore. So, what are they afraid of, when they were going to have, as the icing on top, the great pleasure of executing me?*

It occurred to Degrelle that he should probably surrender himself to the United Nations in New York, drawing up an extensive letter to that end which he sent to the General Secretary.

Some of the more significant paragraphs are translated here for the first time in the Castilian language[24]:

*Ladies and Gentlemen:*

*It has been two years since the Second World War came to an end, but the spiritual conflict, you know as well as I, is more bitter and fiercer than ever. The world is poisoned by hatred. This hatred engenders a thousand injustices. These injustices prepare new hatreds that, sooner or later, become polarized.*

*1) Averting Crime or Fanaticism?*

*Before, the defeated were respected. Today, whatever may have been the motive for their acts, they are trampled, dragged through mud and blood, unceremoniously thrown into prisons, and have faced firing squads or the gallows.*

*Let true war criminals whoever that may be—be punished, fair enough! Mercy and justice are by no means contradictory virtues. The criminal must pay for his crimes. Furthermore, the example of punishment is a useful warning: it can prevent further wrongs. Conceived in this way, it is in fact an act of mercy and not a failure to do mercy.*

*Who can be made to believe today that only criminals are punished? That only the prevention of crime guides countless vigilante acts?*

*Having professed political opinions different from those of the victor, or risking life to defend, on the Eastern Front, a perfectly honorable civilization, is enough to be spectacularly labeled a "war criminal." Even if crimes do not exist, suspicions are sufficient enough to become truths that then expand, unnoticed, to the four corners of the world, calling for blood and revenge.*

*2) Collaboration and Patriotism*

*I will cite my case, ladies and gentlemen, as it has been widely heard and because I am able to speak about it with precision.*

---

[24] The following text of Degrelle's letter to the U.N., according to the author in his 2000 Spanish edition, had been translated into Spanish for the first time. This translator, likewise, is unaware if the letter has ever seen an English translation from the French; this English text is translated from the Spanish.

*I was the victim, in 1944, of a death sentence, nothing more than a political sentence. A condemnation for a certain way of service to the homeland, nothing more.*

*For me and for millions of Europeans like me who were absolutely free of any connection with the Reich before the Second World War, love for one's homeland in the autumn of 1940—while our countries were occupied, and while the Third Reich's dominance in Europe seemed a definitive, irrevocable fact—I told myself, consisted in saving it from prostration and obtaining for it, at the same time, a place in keeping with its genius, its honor and its economic possibilities in the huge European complex that had been created. It was not a question of betrayal. It was a question of service; service according to the needs of the moment, to a homeland overwhelmed by misfortune and which we could not leave lying on the ground.*

*This was what Pétain thought, what Leopold III thought, what millions of honest people thought; loyal citizens who were motivated by nothing more than patriotism.*

*I wanted—many had wanted—to take advantage of the situation, to create an atmosphere of respect and greatness around my homeland. Knowing the importance that the German people attached to military courage, I set out with thousands of Belgian volunteers to conquer, in the snows of the Eastern Front, the supplementary rights to the idea that ensured the resurrection and development of my country.*

*This campaign was terribly hard, as you all well know. We fought for four years. We fought nobly. Even if, to your understanding, we were wrong, our consciences, at least, were clean and we risked our lives for our ideal.*

3) *Is Losing Sufficient to be Considered Wrong?*

*We lost. This is obvious. Is it enough to have lost to be wrong?*

*Germany might well have won the war, not only in 1940, but even much later.*

*If the new weapons of the Reich had come out in time, if Hitler had definitively ensured the unification of the European continent, then our political lucidity and our soldiers' self-denial would have been glorified! Fighting as equals on the front, in suffering and in glory, we would have been able, on behalf of our people, to speak as equals to the German victors when it came to the reorganization of Europe.*

*Other Belgians, other Frenchmen, other Europeans had bet on the Allies' victory, and wore Allied uniforms in the R.A.F. and in commando units. Patriotism just as vibrant as ours, so we would like to believe, had led them to their decision. Would they have been considered and automatically labeled miserable traitors if the fate of the war had turned out differently than they had anticipated?*

*Let us be sensible and frank. There were idealists on both sides. The result of the war, a purely material result, has elevated one side to the clouds and thrown the other to the ground. The opposite could also have occurred: the Reich could have invented the atomic bomb first; Hitler could have reigned over the ruins instead of Mister Churchill.*

*The question, therefore, is not whether some have collaborated with the Reich, victor in 1940 (the "bad guys"), or whether others have collaborated with Mister Churchill, candidate-winner of 1944 (the "good guys"), but if the motivation for these collaborations was clean, selfless, free from any pre-war ties, vigilant for Europe, stimulated only by passionate love for the homeland, and love for thy neighbor.*

*All post-war political processes have ignored this essential consideration. That is why everyone is misrepresented and will be reviewed one day, whether by courts more sensitive to the law, or by history, the true court of men, of states, and of nations.*

*Having served my people with tenacity, having lived and fought for nothing other than their well-being and their greatness, I look forward with calmness and faith to the hour of serenity, objectivity, and the preeminence of the spirit over hatred and over material incidents.*

4) *Abuse of the "War Criminals" Label*

*Ladies and gentlemen, this is not just about political processes. The victors of 1945 know very well that sooner or later, the future, devoid of the wild post-war passions, will review today's furious judgments and will restore balance. To counter the progress of these inevitable revisions, some have striven to find other reasons for crushing, staining, and dishonoring their victims.*

*This was the epidemic of "war crimes."*

*Whether or not these crimes were ever committed does not matter. From the moment one is politically defeated, he is instantly transformed into a vulgar and abominable criminal! By this procedure Europe has become a huge aquarium of pseudo "war criminals" floating in a bath of blood…*

*It is absolutely pointless at this time to attempt to justify oneself before the courts of exception, which are sectarian and trample on the most elementary guarantees of justice. They sabotage the hearings of the proceedings under way, prohibit the accused from arguing a normal defense, and turn the sessions of the court into clamorous pre-election meetings. The scandal of the Laval trial was not an isolated event. Thousands of identical scandals dishonor contemporary justice. You all know it very well.*

*Why these excesses? Because they judge with hatred and not with evidence, only to massacre and kill the defeated.*

*The arguments put forward, the evidence submitted, are of no importance. What counts is the verdict, the physical liquidation of political adversaries by riddling them with bullets or by hanging them with ropes. The rest of the trial only comes into play as an accessory, true or false, distorted or invented.*

5) *How "War Criminals" are Made*

*Allow me to return to my personal case, ladies and gentlemen, as it perhaps illustrates a method and time accurately.*

*My death sentence has been exclusively political. The inability of my adversaries to obtain my extradition has led them—they who are more cruel than ingenious—to turn the political man and soldier who I was, and whom they condemned to death as such, into "the war criminal Degrelle." No Belgian court or any foreign court, had ever described me in this manner before.*

*What "war crimes," indeed, could I have committed? None, ladies and gentlemen, not one! I have never committed any war crime of any kind, neither directly or indirectly, nor even suggested by council; neither in Belgium, nor in the Soviet Union, or anywhere! Is there evidence against me? Let it be well understood that there is none! My official persecutor, Mr. Spaak, Belgian Foreign Minister and President of the United Nations has never dared to present in public, under his personal responsibility, a valid charge of war crimes against me, either based on a specific fact, or on direct testimony, or with serious evidence, however limited it might be. The anonymous slander published in this regard in some sensationalist newspapers is nothing more than miserable gossip, which has no legal basis. These are odious and ridiculous assumptions that no conscientious man would take seriously, either in the U.N. Tribunal or elsewhere.*

*This does not prevent me, in the eyes of millions of men subjected without opposition to this diabolical campaign of lies, even if it seems impossible, from being turned into a "war criminal" by the verdict of the press. Press agency articles, thousands of newspaper reports, and radio broadcasts repeat this fragment of categorical phrasing whenever they receive it: "Léon Degrelle: war criminal!" None of them knows anything, obviously. No one has studied anything about the "dossier." No one has asked anything. No one has any kind of precision. Slander, accepted with enthusiasm, makes the world turn, and penetrates everyone's mind! The "criminal" who has committed no crime becomes a cornered beast, already listed among the infamous, while every country's police rush to capture him!*

*This is my case. This is the case for many others.*

*Are these superficial acts not simply criminal, ladies and gentlemen? Here is the real crime: to slander, to spread slander, to sow hatred, to turn men into sport for human hunting, against whom the slightest valid proof of guilt has not been presented! In these post-war times, a claim, dictated by political hatred, is enough to dreadfully unleash the most blind fury against an innocent man who, beset on a thousand sides, does not even have the possibility of defending himself.*

*Is this justice, ladies and gentlemen? Is it for these witch hunts that so many men have died? Do you think that it is by such methods that peace will be restored among people? Do you not feel that such a confusion between the unjust and the just, that such a tyranny of hate, in which anything goes, will not provoke, on the contrary, sooner or later, a terrible reaction?*

6) *Thousands of Innocent People Can be Thrown into Despair and the Ground Can be Set for a Reaction Whose Magnitude is Impossible to Foretell*

*If all justice is denied to the thousands of defeated but innocent idealists, if they can neither defend themselves nor clear their names, if they are exiled from life and are desperate, do you believe that they are going to give in and submit to a society made unnatural? Through blows of intolerance and injustice, a true army of despair is being prepared in Europe. They see right to the truth refused to them, cornered, and persecuted everywhere, and will explode when the occasion presents itself.*

*Who can foresee, ladies and gentlemen, what the future will be, what the weapons of tomorrow will be? Who will dare to say that clever men, overwhelmed men, or simply men flouted by these blind persecutions, will not invent, or are not already inventing, the deadly means that will allow desperate minorities tomorrow to seize the justice that is denied to them by the hateful and frantic majorities?*

*Hatred begets hatred.*

*Violence calls for violence.*

*Injustice opens the door to other injustices, crime to other crimes, fanaticism to more fanaticism.*

*Really, ladies and gentlemen! Are people going to continue to hate like this? Does the universe want to completely kill itself? Have anger and intolerance finally conquered the world? Will the United Nations go down in history with the name of "United Hatreds?"*

7) *Impossibility of Improving Local Injustices in the Short Term*

*I confess to you bluntly: I do not believe that it is possible to change at present whatever is now poisoning the atmosphere at the "national" level, given the thousands of collaboration trials and so-called "war crimes."*

*The suffering of the storm and the occupation is still too raw to allow souls to find again, in such a short time, the necessary thoughtfulness and objectivity in these different states, where justice considers consciences as well as facts.*

*It is therefore necessary to look further than in these hell-fire courts.*

8) *The Need to Create an International Jurisdiction*

*In the present state of things, ladies and gentlemen, you alone are able to help pacify the universe. You have, together with so many others, tried to constitute an international body that should theoretically help to bring men together. Weak or strong, your organization has at least one quality: it exists. At the present time, it alone can try to channel the crazy passions that are shaking the world and to initiate an effort to make available to men a supra-national justice, devoid of personal resentments, of local prejudice, and of political party anger.*

*The United Nations is empowered to create an international tribunal, which, at the request of the accused as well as the accusers, would put an end to these so-called "war crime" cases by defining what the "war crimes" are, the classification of which today is abandoned to any particular fanaticism.*

*The U.N. has every interest, ladies and gentlemen, to have the hotbeds of agitation shut down in the world, that thousands of the "outlaws" might re-enter the normal sphere of humanity, to find either freedom if they are innocent, or punishment if they are guilty.*

9) *First Field of Action: "Political Criminals" and "War Criminals" Currently in Hiding*

*In order to avoid, at first, a torrential bottleneck, this International Tribunal could begin work on a limited objective: to resolve, at their request, cases of individuals convicted of "political crimes" or "war crimes," and who hide in a world turned into a true international resistance movement, provided—let it be understood—that these individuals agree to physically appear before the Tribunal.*

*Obviously, this International Court should be free of any political fanaticism, composed of judges currently selected among the jurists of recognized prestige in the neutral countries, and among the great moral and spiritual bodies of humanity. It should offer, to those who submit themselves willingly, the necessary guarantees for the exercise of a full defense. Being regulated, your moral position would be extremely strong.*

*If those convicted or accused of war crimes who are in hiding today, voluntarily present themselves to your jurisdiction, you will have lanced a serious abscess. You will have drained the anarchy of men who are being crushed at the moment, but who could, tomorrow, their patience being exhausted, provoke extremely dangerous reactions.*

*If, on the contrary, they do not risk standing before impartial judges, then they themselves will be admitting their guilt, losing the prestige of martyrdom that they acquire from the current persecution.*

*The deeds imputed to these people generally have an international aspect, and the secrecy of these deeds is clearly international. Your jurisdiction would, therefore, be perfectly suited to judge them. Nothing would prevent you, on one hand, from sending the accused to national police after the trial if their material and moral guilt were proven and established.*

*On the other, if they were declared innocent, but because of the intolerance of our time, a return to their homeland was momentarily impossible, they could, at least, live normally in other countries, as citizens of the universe.*

10) *Second Field of Action: The "Political Criminals" and the "War Criminals" Currently Imprisoned*

*This court could then expand its scope of action, becoming the court of appeal for persons convicted and imprisoned in their own countries for the above-mentioned crimes, but who are considered innocent.*

*You all know, as well as I, ladies and gentlemen, that thousands of politically motivated sentences, carried out in "national" courts since 1944, have been given through incoherence, agitation, and passion, and should be reviewed.*

*As long as thousands of innocent people are deprived of their liberty, resentment will continue.*

*Here too, a serene solution is needed that only an international court can offer, independent of any fanaticism, which judges a man on the scale of man.*

*The creation of "international organizations," such as the United Nations, necessarily implies delegations of power on the part of each State. The law is eminently supra-national in nature. Why refuse to grant in your favor what you are prepared to grant, for example, in the field of armaments?*

11) *Third Field of Action: Cases of War Crimes Committed on Both Sides*

*A third objective could and should be, sooner or later, assigned to your international jurisdiction. Appeals would not need to be received in this case, but rather complaints could also be received.*

*No one among you, ladies and gentlemen, would imagine that crime, on a regular basis, goes only in one direction. War crimes have been committed on both sides of the war. Military triumph is not sufficient to be considered, automatically, a fleur-de-lys, an angel, a paragon of virtue.*

*If justice is not only an adjustment of accounts imposed by victors upon the defeated and an instrument of revenge and oppression in the service of the strong, if any crime must be punished, as crime, then it matters that the victims, whoever they may be, can be heard and can go before an international court, file their complaints against criminals, as criminals, whatever their nationality may be. Ladies and gentlemen, ensuring thus the creation and development of a higher court—strong, morally harmonious, balanced, moderate, serene—you will be able to seriously lessen the fearsome tension that threatens the world today, and especially Europe.*

*12) World Amnesty for "Small" Political Convictions*

*Your deed would be complete if, alongside the creation of this international court, you added, through recommendation or otherwise, a global amnesty in favor of "small" politically motivated convictions. There are hundreds of thousands imprisoned for nonsense charges or imprisoned for nothing. They have suffered frighteningly. There is enough pain in the world; let peace be more than a brutal sign of victory, let it mark an impulse of hearts toward understanding!*

*Ladies and gentlemen, if hate is bad business, then goodness, on the contrary, is good business, a business that is profitable. I do not just ask you to be human. I ask you not only to respond to the great calls for fraternity of all the world's religions. I ask you to be lucid. To indefinitely prolong today's crazy blind hatreds, to unceasingly feed them, is to prepare relentless, mathematically certain reactions for tomorrow, of which nothing is known, in the current state of scientific research, what frightening aspect they could take.*

*I cannot believe, ladies and gentlemen, that there is no righteous heart in your assembly to heed this call and believe in its sincerity.*

*13) Treaties Are Not Enough*

*I speak to you on behalf of the defeated, on behalf of the persecuted, on behalf of the innocent who are suffering today in countless prisons.*

*To prove my good faith to you, I am willing to hand myself over to your tribunal if you decide to open the doors of the UN courageously to truth and true justice. I would hand myself over to you with joy, to encourage and incentivize others, to eliminate the seeds of new conflicts in Europe, in order to help bring about the return of a true peace in the hearts of people, without which all your treaties will be nothing more than words, traps, or pretexts, despite their stamps, seals, and signatures.*

*May God enlighten you, ladies and gentlemen, who, for many, will create the slow and difficult peace. Or perhaps because of your lack of faith, far-sightedness, and psychology, you will lead us all towards new abominations tomorrow, even more cruel than yesterday's.*

*Ladies and gentlemen, I extend my greeting to you as a free man!*

*Léon Degrelle*

In a broad statement by the Belgian government in which they threatened and accused the Spanish government, reference was made to the fact that Degrelle entered Spain wearing a German officer's uniform. The traditional, chivalrous feelings of the Spaniards could not be applied to those who had worn the uniform of the Wehrmacht, and even less so to the facilitation of his clandestine departure. They blamed the government of Madrid, which for almost fifteen months "…has given León Degrelle asylum, refusing to extradite him, refusing to expel him, refusing to hand him over to the governments of Britain and the United States, who have claimed him."

The conclusion to this statement ends by saying "Today, the Spanish government, having allowed preparations, directly or indirectly, for the escape of Degrelle, with its refusal to answer the questions that have been addressed to it, still does its utmost to save him."

Given the chivalrous and humanitarian attitude of the Spanish government, Belgium carried out its threat to bring the Degrelle case to the UN for the second time. In September 1946, *The Times* in London published a telegram in which the Madrid government provided facilities for a military observer who could investigate the "Degrelle case" and prove that he was not in Spain. The telegram flatly rejected the statement from the Belgian government that had been presented to the General Assembly of the United Nations and confirmed once again that Degrelle "…left Spanish territory last August, by virtue of the order of expulsion, and that his departure was not carried out by boat or by plane." The Spanish note stated that the government of Madrid "…knew the residence of Degrelle but did not make it public as a courtesy to the country that hosted him and so as not to create a conflict between that country and Belgium." The telegram reproduced in *The Times* ended by saying that foreign press correspondents had been carrying out feverish investigations for two days across Spain to discover Degrelle's whereabouts.

## Press Campaign and Harassment from Non-Government Actors

The Belgian press maintained its defamation efforts nonstop, continually publishing new and increasingly sensational media pieces. In September 1946, the newspaper *La Cité Nouvelle* dedicated a series of five articles under the heading "*The Crimes of Degrelle*," with high profile headlines and seven columns. The Belgian government, in their paranoia, even sent an emissary to Madrid; the unpresentable billionaire Marquet—a corrupt politician who later became the owner of Madrid's luxury hotels, the Ritz and the Palace—who conveyed to Franco the desirability of handing over Degrelle to his detractors, to certain death for being a "war criminal." This pressure caused the Spanish leader to hesitate slightly, wavering between protecting an innocent man or surrendering him to be charged for some alleged crimes, although they were completely unfounded.

In their obsessive harassment, the new moguls of Belgian power sent a note, dated October 9th, 1946, "…concerning Spain's alleged help in the disappearance of the Belgian traitor, Léon Degrelle," through the Belgian Embassy in Washington. It was addressed to the Secretary General of the United Nations, Trygve Lie, requesting that, through his mediation, he have the note presented to the Security Council.

The note stated:

> Despite all the requests filed, the Spanish government does not want to give details about the disappearance of Degrelle and refuses to say by which border and by what means Degrelle left Spain, thus justifying the hypothesis that the former Belgian rexist has not left the country and is hidden somewhere with the consent of the Spanish authorities.
>
> This persistent silence of the Spanish government can only be seen as complicity with the Belgian traitor. It reveals that the Spanish government is trying to protect Degrelle's escape and to prevent the criminal, as much as possible, from being detained by Belgian police.
>
> The aid publicly and officially rendered to Degrelle provides another example of the friendship that Franco's government offers to those who stood alongside Nazi Germany during the war and their desire to help them escape the fate they deserve for political, as well as common crimes, they committed.
>
> The Belgian government believes the complicity of the Spanish government with traitors such as Degrelle, who was an agent of the Axis powers, likely to create great disturbances in Europe and threaten the security of victorious democratic nations.

On February 10th, 1947, Spain's Chargé d'Affairs in Belgium, Mr. Gullón, sent a "confidential and reserved" communiqué to the Spanish Minister of Foreign Affairs, in which he transmits:

> Have received telegram V.E. number eight. Just been informed of confidentially secret meeting of Liberal Party on the 8th, at which a report on Spain was verbally presented. Talking points were hearty defense of our correctness. Explanation of Spanish character and its fair reaction to UN indiscreet interferences that

*strengthens Spanish regime. Attacks Mr. Spaak's attitude in UN, completely unjustified on part of Belgium. Damage that this can do to Belgian interests and need to normalize relations between both countries is of vital economic importance to Belgium. Said thesis was approved by all those gathered who are also willing to see it voiced without it becoming public for the time being because of complicated internal political situation. If occasion presents itself soon, they will present in Parliament in a skillful speech showing their discontent without provoking crisis. Mr. Spaak, for the moment, considered dangerous because of his international situation and current need of his services in UN. According to Gullón interview, delicate point is Degrelle question, which continues to unite all right- and left-wing voters and that if able to resolve, would facilitate swift favorable action. Concerning all above communication, am asked by President of Senate for silence and absolute discretion, since these were secret deliberations that, if disclosed, would jeopardize own situation and their party's situation at present time. He assures me his action has been effective and he is persisting with determination and waiting for satisfactory results. His always enthusiastic defense of Spanish cause continues these days and will have interview with highest political personalities in country. I have expressed to him the deepest gratitude of the Spanish government and my own, as this will benefit both countries.*

*Gullón*

From time to time, the press would publish some news of the finding of Degrelle. They found him everywhere and nowhere at the same time. Reality was quite different. Léon stayed invisible, guarded from eyes and ears, in the houses and places provided by his friends and comrades of the Spanish Falange.

## The First Work Permit

On November 21st, 1947, the Spanish Foreign Labor Division issued employment card number 20.969, corresponding to file number 28.164, on behalf of "Enrique Durand," Degrelle's new alias. He was authorized to work in Madrid in the Enrique Durán[25] Company as an art expert, with a salary of twelve thousand pesetas per year. It stated that "the holder of this card is authorized to work in the destination and locality determined until July 7th, 1948, without being exempted

---

[25] The names "Durand" and "Durán" are written distinctly in the Spanish original.

from compliance with the police requirements." The card was signed by the head of the Foreign Labor Division.

This was the first time Léon Degrelle had been given the necessary administrative documents and permissions to gain access to the labor market, opening up a world of new opportunities and enabling him to conceive of an industrious future. The employment card identified art as his professional qualification, the activity and skill he most loved. This was not only because of the studies and courses on that subject he had studied in his younger years when he was a student at the Catholic University of Leuven; in reality, art was for Léon the sublimation of the human being, the absolute creative power that differentiated humanity as superior entities from those of nature, and because in art lie the purest and most genuine essences of primordial sensitivity.

## The Wild Belgian Purge Strikes Degrelle's Soul

Meanwhile, in Belgium, in 1946-1947, in the midst of a massive purge, likened to a Luciferian bacchanal gorging on innocent blood, many hundreds of nationalist leaders and activists were shot, including José Streel, Victor Vandevelde, and Victor Matthys.

José Streel[26] was a Doctor of Philosophy and was one of the ideologues of the Rexist Movement. He had worked as editor-in-chief for the weekly *Rex* and served as head of rex's political service during the first stage of the German occupation. He was shot on February 21st, 1946, after a farce of a trial. It was Victor Matthys who coined the slogan, *Rex Vaincra!* (Rex will be victorious!) and was the organizer of the active propaganda cadres. In 1941, after Degrelle's departure with the Walloon Legion toward the Eastern Front, he provisionally assumed the head of Rex on an interim basis. For Degrelle, his temporary successor was like a younger brother whom he held in great esteem, appreciating his enormous capacity to work and whom he considered "his oldest and most faithful partner." Sentenced to death at the War Council held in Charleroi on July 4th, 1946, he was executed in November 1947 along with twenty-six other comrades.

Historian Xavier Casals Meseguer reminds us in his book, *Ultrapatriotas*, that the end of the war left twenty-six thousand political prisoners in Wallonia and

---

[26] Lucien Alphonse Joseph Streel, commonly known as José Streel, authored the influential *La Révolution du Vingtième Siècle* (*The Revolution of the Twentieth Century*), important for fascist—specifically rexist—philosophy. Published in 1942 in Brussels by NSE, a new edition of this work was published by Déterna in 2010 as *La Révolution du XXème Siècle* (*The Revolution of the Twentieth Century*).

seventeen thousand in Flanders; three hundred forty-six thousand two hundred eighty-three cases of collaborationism were tried, of which fifty-seven thousand corresponded to persons who were found guilty of collaboration—who were designated as "uncivic"—and one thousand two hundred forty-seven death sentences were handed down.

Sequestered in his claustrophobic living space in Madrid, Léon Degrelle sent his mother the following letter in 1947:

*My dearest Mother:*

*It is your birthday, which is more poignant to us than ever before, after these terrible anguishes where your grave illness has melted our hearts. Oh! When will I know that you are better, that you are getting along? When can I let go of this burden that weighs me down, that crushes my soul! Every hour, I pray for you! I pray to Saint Rita of Cascia, the "patroness for impossible causes." It is to her that I pray, especially for me. It is she who has heard my "impossible cause!" I have also entrusted your situation to her, dear mother, in these days when you, in such a saintly way, offer up for me your sufferings and your dangers. This absolute love that you give me is, I know very well, what protects me every day.[27] You have obtained extraordinary miracles from heaven. How would I have survived without your prayers, without your suffering! You are my mother in two ways: the one who has given me life and the one who has saved my life. I am your affectionate child, with such vibrant fervor! There are no two mothers like you: so fervent, so tender, so absolutely generous, so good despite the years and the trials! You have retained a wonderfully sharp intelligence, weighing everything, foreseeing everything, giving all. Your own writing (your letter dated August 6th of last year), is prodigious, clean, alive, without amendment, as if you were twenty-five!*

*I am proud to have such a young mother, and so confident as well, for your extraordinary vitality will shield you from whatever blows may come. On the other hand, everything moves fast, the wheel turns. A year or two more and I will have been right; life will again become human, and I will be in your arms, crying with joy.*

*I have absolute confidence. The hardest thing has already passed. Dangers are already being mitigated. Time is approaching with great steps, where I will be able to have an almost normal status, where contact will be possible again, without*

---

[27] *Offering up for me your sufferings* refers to the Catholic teaching that for the Christian, suffering itself can be a form of salvation, a saving grace, inasmuch as this suffering is united to the suffering of Christ. In pious practice, one can "offer up" his suffering to God—much like prayer—for the benefit of others.

*complications and without risks. I have had time to write the great books of my life, to meditate, to take a long retreat, all this together with the Sacred Heart.*[28]

*You should never worry about me; I am doing very well. My health is great. I have never been as fit as I am now, despite so many mishaps. I have faithful friends who look out for my safety and no evil can happen to me. My three war books will be published in America with large print runs. You will see, they will cause a stir. I have also written two voluminous political books on collaboration. In August and September, I hope to write a third.*

*Next, I will write about my beginnings, but above all, I am overwhelmed with happy sighs by my love for my mother. A dozen times, here and there, behind some excited, active lines, you reappear everywhere.*

*This great work will take me at least another six months, but it will be magnificent, and you will see how many things you will carry in your heart.*

*I hope you can read my three books about the frontlines soon, although the others (my memories) will interest you more. In short, this life as a soldier was a great life, and you will find it active and noble in these books.*

*Outside my intellectual work, I pray, and I think about you. I am with you all the time, with you first, dear mother; with father so brave, so courageous, despite all the evil that has been done to him; with Marie-Paule, of whom I am so happy to know that she persists with encouragement (rather, my union of souls and my faith in the future); and with my dear little children, whose separation is so cruel to me, a wound, the pain of every day. All the others abound in my tenderness. Mary, my dear godmother, all of them at home, my dear nieces and nephews, the whole family. Many greetings, from me to Uncle Paul and Father Louis, who is so wonderful. Tell him, if he does not know, that I saved Léon Laloix's life, in 1944, when I was taken on the bridge at Dinant. Without my intervention, he would have been lost. What Louis does is very nice. Above all, care must be taken for the souls of the little ones, in case the grandmother has already had enough with her own children; the temptations of fourteen- and fifteen-year-old children and having raised them in a sad atmosphere that marked them for their whole life. A catastrophe in this regard would be about as hard as death. May Louis do everything for this: faith, fresh piety, affection, healthy joy. Let him repeat a little, sometimes, that they have a father who loves them dearly, who thinks of them without ceasing, prays for them without ceasing, and suffers for them by being so distant from them...*

---

[28] This is one of the most well-known and widely practiced Catholic devotions. The heart of Jesus is seen as a symbol of God's endless and fervent love for mankind.

*Dear mother, let me extend my cordial greetings from Saint Mary. Remember the last year! What a path traveled! How the Holy Virgin has helped us! For you, above all, my dear mother, my saintly mother, my most tender affection, my most fervent kisses. Share them with father and everyone!*

*I ask for your blessing. I am, always, your big boy! I love you!*

On May 30th, 1947, Léon Degrelle's elderly father was sentenced in Arlon to eight years imprisonment. He arrived at the tribunal session accompanied by his daughter, Suzanne. He would die in the "democratic" dungeons for the "flagrant crime" of having been the progenitor of the exceptional Léon Degrelle. He died a few weeks after his wife, who was also imprisoned. The body of Léon's father was shown, completely naked, to his children, in deplorable conditions, in the Belgian prison of Saint-Gilles on March 11th, 1948. His attorney had requested clemency on February 7th, 1948, even petitioning Prince Charles of Belgium, but it was of no use. They asked for forgiveness of his faults, as well as a reduction or the commutation of the sentence. The lawyer's request did not receive a reply, or even an acknowledgment of it having been received. His daughter Louise Degrelle,[29] when visiting her father, asked one of the jailers for a glass of water to alleviate the suffocating heat. He agreed to do so for fifty Belgian francs, but she was not able to bring another glass to her father who was being deprived of water. Another prison guard offered to bring a glass to the prisoner if he was compensated with another fifty francs!

Some news was able to get through to Degrelle while he was in hiding, but it was always bad news that wrenched and tore at his heart. It was there that he learned that his wife, Marie-Paule, had been sentenced to ten years in prison, although she never had a political role or any part in Rex. She had remained completely removed from active politics and always lived surrounded by her five young children. The health of their firstborn, for years, required special, time-consuming care.

Later, he also learned of the death of his mother, news that caused him infinite pain, for he had a true devotion for his parents, above all for his mother. Léon's elderly mother was arrested in 1945 and imprisoned in the worst conditions imaginable; she died in prison on October 28th, 1947.

It was a tragic blow. As soon as he learned of the death of his mother, he sent his father the following letter:

---

[29] Louise Degrelle was born in Bouillon on July 20th, 1907 and died in Brussels on March 10th, 1999.

*My poor, dear father,*

*With such a loving and trembling heart, I am the cause of your terrible ordeal. What a blow to your heart, already so upset! Our dear mother! You too, you even said, "Our dear mother!" Our sweet mother, our pious mother! I imagine your pain, separated from her so cruelly during her last days! Poor father! Poor father!*

*You know how tenderly we love you, how we all marshal our love to try to comfort you while she is on her path to heaven...*

*There, she will meet our dear grandfathers and grandmothers and her two very beloved Edouards. Together, they await us. They will help us, and dear Father, one day we will meet them! Our dear mother has now escaped from the wild hatred of men! God loves her and fills her with blessings! Our dear mother is in heaven, glowing, triumphant, comforted by her wonderful virtues. I know, dear father, with what admirable courage you accept God's designs. He has taken mother to give her the highest happiness. Father, dear father, my filial love is close to you every second. Courage! Trust in God, the complete love, the love that our dear mother has received...I embrace you, my dear, poor father, and love you stronger, more tenderly, more filially than ever.*

He also wrote, with the ink of grief and mourning, to one of his sisters on the occasion of the cruel and inhuman death of his mother:

*What a pain, what a heartbreaking pain this new misfortune...mother is dead! I find myself here in my black hole, shedding all my tears. She has died without me being able to give her my love for the last time. She has died overwhelmed by all the evils my life has brought upon those who loved me. Ah! What a torment it is to think about this, about this terrible blow that father's latest arrest brought to mother, guilty only of having given me life. To have loved my parents so much and finally to see it come to this, that mother died because of me, that father suffers cruelly because of me. Nothing can quiet my grief. I feel like I will carry this burden in my heart until death!*

In another letter, from October 1947, addressed to his sisters, he told them:

*Torn apart, I read the terrible news...what pain! I cry, I have cried for days, not knowing how to do anything but weep, completely abandoned by everything, so tragically alone in my despair and grief! Mother, our mother! Every day I embraced her picture, speaking to her with so much love! [...]*

*I have now lost my mother, I have only a terrible wound in my heart, and tears that roll down my cheeks. I am at the end of the world, without a home, without my dear little children, and now without mother. I will no longer be able to see her again. I will not be able to hold her close to my chest. That hope is what has kept me alive. I was clinging to life so I could one day give our mother the joy of standing in front of her, of embracing each other, crying with heartfelt emotion and joy after these terrible years of trials, but it is over. You have at least seen her, our dear mother, motionless and cold; you will have been able to kiss her cold face for the last time. For me, I did not know anything about mother until a few weeks after her death. I will never ever feel her loving look, her sweet hands, her love that responded so well to my own. I only cry and weep, in shock, with a torn heart, a heart that can no longer be consoled, that will carry with itself its pain until the day when I meet her again above. Oh, if I did not have my duty and my home, what a relief it would be for me to go to death! To the death that would free me from this world of weakness and revenge that knows no more than to persecute, to hate, to soil, to cause suffering...*

*Mother has again found her parents, her two Edouards. She will be angelically happy, filled by God's goodness. For me, "her big man," so alone, so unfortunate here, what a pity! My tears fall without ceasing. I cannot take it anymore. Thank you for your tenderness. I love you all, with all my soul and I embrace you.*

These sorrows and the absolute enclosed isolation took a terrible toll on his weakened health. Degrelle, whose strength and robustness were incredible, who seemed impervious to fatigue, immune to all danger, always awake and cheerful, broke down. He completely lost his appetite, began to feel stomach pains and dropped in weight.

After she was transferred through several prisons in Brussels—Liege, Namur, and Arlon—his mother's death, for the terrible crime of "motherhood," shattered Degrelle. He bore immense grief over the news about his father, imprisoned in Saint-Gilles; the sentencing of his wife to ten years imprisonment for the crime of "marriage"; the indiscriminate and mass arrests of his old comrades; the murder of his brother Edouard on July 8th, 1944, a pharmacist in his hometown; the murder of his brother-in-law in Saint-Gilles prison; the demolition of his home; and the separation of his children. Had it not been for his moral fortitude in the face of these trials, an acute depression or a general collapse would have taken hold and caused irreparable damage.

On learning of the death of his elderly father in March 1948, he sent the following letter to his sister Suzanne:

*My dear and brave Mémère,*

*Here I am, in the distance. I share with you the heartbreaking sufferings with which heaven has overwhelmed us. Poor dear father, such a good father! His painful, tragic end has plunged me into the abyss of sorrow. He, so affectionate, so kind to everyone, so always willing to help. How much hate and weakness there is in this world, abandoned to anger and base instincts!*

*At least he has now met with our saintly mother again. United as they had always been, this separation would have been for him a constant affliction…*

*My pain has been consoled a little by the news of the happy birth of your little child. You are lucky! If you knew with what melancholy I thought of my dismembered country, from which I was parted cruelly without the least reference. They want me to be killed in the hearts of my children. This tragedy undermines me, corrodes my heart and body.*

*I will do my best, on this great holiday, to send someone to look for the oldest kids at least. I have sent a note to let my mother-in-law, Mrs. Lemay, know in advance, but will they allow it? I do not quite understand what inhuman obstacle has been put between me and my children. I get emotional and weep every time I think of our poor mother, who was allowed to die without receiving a single visit, or even a letter, from my dear children for the last few weeks. I will try to get them to come for at least two weeks, even though the luck of seeing them visit me is practically nonexistent…What do they mean by this? They should realize that one day I might get angry, and besides, I am not a man who will let someone take away my children!*

*All these concerns, which you know well my brave Mémère, have produced in me an unpleasant ulcer that puts my stomach into a figure eight…*

*I often think of you, of the fate of all. Now, I do not believe in a new, and immediate global brawl. Stalin is an old cunning lizard, biding his time and he will not prematurely risk his loot to reach for European and Asian fruit that will eventually fall into his hands. Do not be disturbed. If one day this goes all wrong, arrive as soon as possible with M., who will lead you in the best conditions. The foreigner is always a foreigner, and exile is only a solution when no other exists. Pray for me, that this blow stops until everything returns (this is unavoidable) and until triumph. This will come about, but it is necessary for God to help me, and also your affection and the vigorous hearts of my dear little children.*

Moreover, the Spanish Embassy in Brussels once again reiterated for the announcement and official confirmation that Léon Degrelle had been expelled from Spain, leaving the country on August 23rd, 1946. The announcement followed a publication in the general Belgian newspapers insisting that the head of the Rexist Movement, who had been sentenced to death *in absentia*, was still being protected by the Spanish authorities. In its denial of this, the Spanish Embassy took the opportunity to invite the Belgian state security police to send a research group to Spain to ensure, beyond suspicion, that the highly sought-after Belgian political leader had left the country without a trace. They also added that if he returned to Spain illegally, he would be handed over to Belgian authorities immediately.

## Quitting His Dark Shelter

The shadow of death was cast upon Léon Degrelle in his dark confinement. For a man like him—young, active, fiery in his physiology, with an extreme need to externalize himself—this gloomy life, as if buried underground, was extremely painful. Cultured conversation was not remotely possible with his village-minded hosts. They were good people, but absolutely illiterate and short on intelligence, whose concerns were limited to the price of groceries and cinema billboards. Degrelle would pace along the narrow corridor that surrounded his opaque room. It overlooked an inner courtyard where light only indirectly penetrated the living room, as his "gracious host" had an irrational horror of the sun, of dust, and of any book, paper, or newspaper.

In those circumstances, Léon Degrelle could only throw himself into his work, convinced that it could give him a reason to live apart from the liberation of his thought. He wrote unceasingly, transcribing his memories into masterful works such as *La Cohue de 1940* (*The Mob of 1940*), *With Hitler the European*, and *The Great Strangle*.[30]

In 1948, Léon Degrelle wrote a letter to his war comrades:

*Dear Comrades,*

*From the bottom of my distant lair, I live in communion with you daily. I know your sufferings, the bitterness of your scandalous imprisonment and the forced labor you have been subjected to for three years; you, bravest of the brave, bearers of such a hard-won glory for the sake of your country, in the terrible fighting in the East.*

*Soon, the pages upon which I record your deeds, describing your fabulous epic, will appear throughout the world. Reading them, they will see what you are worth,*

---

[30] Oddly, in Riesco's book, these last two titles are given not in their French forms but in the Spanish: *Con Hitler el Europeo* and *El Gran Estrangulamiento*. This translator has not been able to ascertain the original French titles, or whether they were ever published in English.

*what you accomplished, and will end up doing right by you. One day you will leave prison with your head held high, honored by your people, who will understand that you have not only been implacable heroes, but also the most clairvoyant and most selfless of the forerunners.*

*Comrades! In spite of your misery, do not let yourselves be tempted or manipulated by those who have scorned you, by this ignoble capitalist society which, after having so shamefully left you to suffer at the end of the war in 1945, would like to tear you up, abusing the laxity motivated by your sorrows, the signatures that, meanwhile, serve nothing, save to make believe that you admit that you were wrong. No, comrades, you were not in the wrong! Only you have been right, right in everything! Right in your resistance against Bolshevism, right in your willingness to build a social and brotherly Europe. It is these unclean bourgeois who have been wrong, trusting their Bolshevik friends; wrong by turning stupidly to the slimy dictatorships who are themselves censored by the plutocratic mafias in London and New York. Healing will not come to the world from these cowards, nor from these corrupt bankers willing to throw the universe into a third massacre to further increase their material power!*

*The health of the world and of all European patrias will never come from Asian Bolshevism. There, you will never fall into the traps that they set for you! Remember what you have seen in Russia! Also remember the monstrous terrorism that the Soviet scoundrels carried out in Belgium against your families during the war, massacring hundreds of women and children of so many of our brave comrades! Bolshevism is slavery, it is abject, it is crushing! Down with communism, and hyper-capitalism! Tomorrow, as yesterday, there will be no healing but in our ideal: the conjunction of patriotism and socialism within a young and united Europe!*

*Comrades do not let this trial overcome you! From the outside I prepare—hard and powerful—the great reconquest of tomorrow! There will be surprises, returning to denounce them. I am alive! Others live too! Europe, annihilated by "democratic" victors, is ripe for resurrection. Saviors and guides are awaited, and they shall come! God has saved you to accomplish this great task.*

*Comrades! In May 1945, I should have died. You know that I stayed to the last minute with the last squad of legionaries. I did not leave the last area of combat until the night of May 7th into May 8th when the war had just ended a few hours prior. It was a real miracle that I could escape from my bitter enemies there. Since then, I have offered my head to them ten times in exchange for your release, yours, my dear brothers, my brave comrades. You know it! Although they have silenced my voice as much as they have been able, news of my offers of surrender must have come to you in the foreign press. They have not accepted my head, because they feared the revelations I would make before I died; revelations that would have made the entire regime in power fall into confusion: ministers, high clergy, freemasonry, parties, plutocrats.*

*My revelations, as you can well imagine will come out either way, despite the monstrous blackmail to keep me quiet, despite the abominable fate inflicted on my unfortunate parents, murdered over a slow fire, in the hope that their martyrdom would reduce me to silence. They died blessing me and encouraging me for my cause, for our cause. No threat or pain has been able to bring me down! Nothing—as I well know, my brave comrades—will beat you! The hour of reckoning will come! The hour of resurrection will come! It will come soon. One day, we will find ourselves face to face again, exulting with joy over the reunion, triumphant to see our ideal victorious at the end! Yes, it is necessary to persevere in faith! Yes, above all it is necessary to keep your soul fierce, your head high!*

*We were right. We are right. We will be right.*

*We are beaten in our prisons and in exile. Let us remember Gromovoja-Balka, Cherjakov, Cherkassy, our glorious cities! There too everything seemed lost, but every time your fiery heroism swept everything out, transfigured everything, saved everything! Heroes like you are invincible!*

*Comrades, we will see each other AND we will win!*

*Let us all come together in victory!*

*Léon Degrelle*

In those days Gaston Lucien Dewageneire, a former comrade of Léon, entered Spain secretly at La Junquera border post and was detained on May 28th, 1948. Gaston had worked as a liaison for the German Labor Front in Berlin from 1940 to 1943, moving on to Belgium to work in youth organizations. After the war, he was imprisoned and released three months after his arrest. In 1947, a new trial was opened against him. In the face of political harassment, he decided to take the path of freedom. When questioned by the police in Spain, he said that "he was arriving as a political refugee and that he did not know anyone in this country, although he was a personal friend of Léon Degrelle, having been active in his party since 1934."

Degrelle's life of seclusion and shadow in 1946 proved unbearable. The loneliness in Degrelle's heart, the absolute deprivation of all contact with the living world, was a painful and extreme test. He had nothing around him that could spiritually comfort him, nor did he find much moral relief. For a man who had been passionately loved and followed, who had commanded and directed thousands of men, who was delighted with the spectacle given to him by the world, who loved beauty—his beatitude—in all her forms, who was excited about a flower or the light of heaven, this hidden life was an ordeal, a perpetual tension. He had nothing beautiful or nice to behold in his surroundings. No light filtered through any of the slits in his tiny, sad room. His hosts, grumpy and greedy, did not open the windows for fear of dust. They only minimally aired the rooms to cut down on drafts and to air out the stale pantry. There was frustration and tension on either side. The months spent in this debilitating darkness were actually the most painful months of Degrelle's life. His whole being called out for sun, for action, for life!

## The Wounds of His Body and Soul Are Reopened

In the days after receiving the news of the horrendous death of his beloved parents in the dungeons of the masonic "democracy" in Belgium, he suffered such an emotional crisis that the scar of one of the surgical operations he received during the war, coupled with the injuries sustained in his crash landing in Spain, opened from his neck to his stomach. The incessant hemorrhages began. The wound was opening more and more, and his weight became dangerously low. In a short time, he lost almost 35 kilograms (roughly 77 pounds). The pain of exile and the lack of news about his five children, also contributed to his emotional stress and the reopening of the scar produced by shrapnel from the Eastern Front. It was lodged in the cavity of his perforated stomach, and as a result he suffered from painful ulcers.

He decided to risk leaving his confinement to go to the sunny Malaga coast, an idea that he had felt he had to attempt, given that death was likely the only other option. The day came when he could stand it no longer in that gloomy and miserable confinement. It was like being under house arrest, with no hope of it ever ending. He had to get out.

He contacted the Falangist writer Víctor de la Serna and José Antonio's cousin, Sancho Dávila, with whom he had become friends, to assist him in getting to Malaga. He traveled to the south of the peninsula and landed on the luminous Costa del Sol.

He initially went to La Carihuela, in the province of Malaga, a corner of the coast that was then only a small coastal fishing port. There, for 30 pesetas a day, he could eat and sleep. "I was there for two months, ready to die, just going swimming in the evenings," he would recall later.

## A Providential Encounter

To bring them up to date on the situation, Léon wrote a letter to his sisters, in which, despite all the moral and physical suffering he endured, he still managed to evoke a fighting spirit. He stated:

*In an hour, I will be taken to a clinic and tomorrow I will be holding my belly open again. It is necessary to go through with this. I am losing two pounds a week. I have become as thin as I was in my school days. They believe I have an ulcer in the cardia, just in the triangle of the ribs, in the upper part. In any case (especially this), it causes me a lot of pain. As for my back, on the left, I have an unbearable burning....*

*Thank God, I do not feel worried in the least. I have suffered so much being separated from my children (that is what has led me to the mood I find myself in, along with the death of father and mother) that life and death have become indifferent to me.*

*It is true that precautions must be taken and relegated to the entire bourgeois vocabulary of "prudence," "reflection," and other constipated words. This should not prevent you from getting a picture of my children, even if that was the case, especially when you know that they are going to open me up on an operating table. No, not even this little joy in my suffering have they wanted to give me. I find it horrible. It hit me hard when I learned that Marie-Paule had left afterward, with the sledgehammer, saying that this was a joke. Tell her with what love I am her calvary, I share her sufferings, I await her liberation and her coming. Besides, there is no other solution, and this is not a child's game. She and the little ones only have to let themselves be brought here, everything else will be prepared.*

*As for throwing myself into heartfelt tears and other antics, let it be known once and for all that I do not regret anything (but only of having temporarily lost). I have offered my life to a magnificent ideal and will continue to fight for it until my last breath. Let this be crystal clear. Having said that, nothing prevents us from having a few years of family life in peace, in a small, quiet corner, if our dear Soviet friends want to leave our good theorists of prudence and comfort in peace! I agree to a truce, but not forever. No, I do not want to mortgage myself out; that would be a betrayal. Whoever loves me must follow me in spite of everything!*

One fine day in September 1948, a man came to greet him, who turned out to be José Antonio Girón de Velasco, the Minister of Labor. Prior to this meeting, a German citizen, Johan Hoffman, Consul of Germany in Malaga, had recognized

Degrelle and told Girón de Velasco, a *jonsista*[31] from Valladolid. De Velasco was the chief of the centuria[32] who took the heights of the Leones de Castilla after the outbreak of the National Uprising of July 18th, 1936. A captain through field promotion during the Crusade of Liberation, he became the Falange Minister of Labor, a responsibility for which he was appointed by Franco when he had just turned twenty-eight. When he saw Léon in such a bad state of health, with continuous bleeding, he lifted him up, light as a feather, and took Degrelle in his car to Madrid. He was transferred to the hospital on calle Eloy Gonzalo, where he was immediately examined in the surgery room.

The famous and distinguished Falangist physician, Dr. Lafuente Chaos, was a good friend of Girón de Velasco, and he performed the critical surgery on Degrelle's damaged stomach.

It was a difficult and extremely delicate operation. The shrapnel had shifted an organ out of place, and the metal shard was still embedded close to the heart, but Dr. Chaos was successful.

Later and whenever the occasion presented itself, Léon Degrelle did not hesitate to point out, "Girón saved my life." After the surgery, the director of the hospital ordered his transfer to one of the recovery rooms in the medical center. Unfortunately, the nurse in charge of the transfer discovered Degrelle's true identity and his stay there was compromised. He was then rushed, under great secrecy, to the house of a humble family whose young son had died as an early volunteer enlisted in the Blue Division. Being carried up the narrow staircase of the building's five floors on a stretcher was very complicated and required too much effort for a patient who had just come out of surgery. The new stitches came loose and the wound reopened. His new living quarters were then transformed into an "emergency hospital" for the post-operative period; the wound was again sutured so it would heal properly and quickly.

During this time in 1948, in a letter to his sister Louise-Marie, he said:

*How do I find myself? Physically, I have been dealt a blow. Hemorrhages still persist, with some frequency, especially when I am too sad. Morally, I feel very abandoned. The story of the children kills me. Additionally, I used to feel like I could carry the world under my arms and now I am wasting away with useless, empty arms.*

---

[31] *Jonista*, a member of JONS, or *Juntas de Ofensiva Nacional-Sindicalista*, which merged with the Spanish Falange.

[32] *Centuria* in the Falange's organization was a unit similar to an army company; the *jefe*, or chief, of the *centuria* was the head of that unit.

*All in all, I am still fighting. I have a small chapel whose presence alone gives me strength. Every day, I say the fervent prayers to God we said as children. Who knows, maybe at the end of the madness of our ruined times, some possibility or another might allow us to recreate greatness, nobility, and beauty. In any case, I will be prepared to deal with these current times.*

*Give your daughters my best. They are so wonderful! They would love taking a walk around here. I will try to see your face and your heart in theirs...*

In writing to his doctor, he confessed:

*All these days here have been regrettable. Yesterday, my right side, in the back, was just a sheet of fire. This morning, as was predictable, a new hemorrhage. So, will I throw myself out of the window, me, so strong in the face of this weakness? Me, a conqueror, before this surrender of my own body? I feel like I will not recover. It is the soul that is sick. The soul loaded down with so many painful events, by all my great dreams that have died. I was made, so I used to feel, to change the world, to convey to it a great ideal. Instead, I will die of having turned this immense and devouring fire against me. This is what consumes me, excessively, made by the universe and resting upon the poor heart of a defeated giant. Even this word "giant" will make you smile, but it is true. I believed I was born for an epoch and felt I had the right to look, with the eyes of a teacher upon a people made to receive my faith and be transfigured by it. We can take care of it, with attention, with tenderness, but my great dreams of yesterday, who will resurrect them? This not being able to act breaks me down...*

Knowing the gravity of his health, he made a desperate attempt, in vain, to see his children, at least the two older ones, before undergoing the decisive, risky operation. He wrote sad, melancholy poems,[33] with profound feeling:

*Mes amours! L'avez-vous renié, votre nom ?*
*Tendu trop haut, comme la fleur du liseron*
*Qui se pâme et se meurt sur sa tige trop frêle.*

---

[33] The poems are given in Riesco's work in the original French, untranslated. The translator includes here the original French, as well as his own translation of these verses in English.

*My dears ! Have you forgotten your name?*
*Stretched too high, like the flower of the morning glory*
*That fades and dies on a stem too frail.*

Or, when he remembered with yearning:

*On vous appelait les Infantes*
*O mes enfants, perdus là-haut.*
*Dans je ne sais quel triste hameau*
*Où vous suit mon âme dolente.*


*They called you princesses*
*Oh, my children, lost up there.*
*In which sad hamlet I know not*
*Where my sorrowful soul follows you.*

In some note he left lying around he had written:

*My evils are different from those of the body. [The doctors] have opened my chest.*
*They were mistaken; it is the heart that is sick and that needed to be opened for me.*
*There is the wound that unjust gods and blind luck have opened in me. The ulcer—*
*or cancer—is in the soul, this soul of mine that had dreamed of casting to men a*
*great song and yet its voice has been silenced and insulted.*

Two months after the first surgery, a second operation was required to close up the
wounds of the esophagus that had reopened, also the result of shrapnel received in
the Caucasus. The second operation was also successful.

Also in 1948, he wrote a heartfelt letter to his cousin, Louis, the priest, in
which he confessed:

*My dear Louis,*
*From my bed in the hospital, I am dictating these lines to answer your*
*affectionate initiatives.*
*Thank you for all you are doing for Marie-Paule and the kids.*
*I have understood very well that I cannot expect any visit and I have put myself*
*in the hands of the surgeons, offering up my suffering for my children, whom I may*
*not be able to see again. Although I admit, in a certain way, the majestic use of the*
*words "prudence," "careful consideration," "restraint," etc., I cannot understand*

why, under this well-intentioned vocabulary, a father has been so cruelly deprived of any family joy for four years. How do you see it that they want me to believe that I cannot have a single photo of my children? That they could not even write a word on the front of it, or to any member of my family...? Who stopped them from writing, if but once a month, to my unfortunate parents or sisters? Warned about the progressing deterioration of my mother's health, they let her die without being able to receive even a single line of kindness from the little ones, to whom she was so sweet. Was this because of prudence? No, no, my dear Louis, this is not prudence, for, if it were, prudence would be a very ugly thing. Since when has children's love for their grandparents been considered a political crime?

Poor Marie-Paule teaches me, with her courage and saintliness, the virtue of patience and gives me hope for future times.

I would like to believe, however, that all this will eventually end, that the barbaric and inhuman revenge under which an unfortunate woman is being crushed will end.

What a shame for a regime and for an era!

Belgium should not be known for the atrocity of its current hatred.

I repeat to you my desire to recover my wife and children as soon as possible after Marie-Paule's release. Besides, limited by our dear Bolshevik victors, our countries are now at the mercy of a catastrophe. As a soldier, I did everything possible to avoid the Bolshevik victory. I do not want my wife and children to have to suffer the catastrophic aftermath....

In your letters, my dear Louis, you have made clear that some conditions need to be included. You speak of "expressing sincere repentance," of "wise resolutions for the future." What do these mean? Do you think I risked my life for four years on the Eastern Front, where I suffered so much, without having carried inside me a great ideal? Should I disavow all this right at the moment when, everywhere, the fight against communism is the first rule of the day? One thing that we have understood for years and have shown, is that we offered our own youth to protect the world and Christianity from the communist tidal wave that millions of crazy people, attacking us from behind, have managed to use to take over half of Europe.

In this struggle, cooperation with Germany was the only reasonable course because it represented the only serious force on the continent. Now that it is knocked down, who is left to protect us? This will not be achieved until Europe again becomes stronger than ever, and then she will be able to breathe again. Besides, this is what the Americans are doing resolutely.

*In the same way, at the other end of the world, they are putting back together all the pieces of the other great anti-communist barrier: Japan. China is sunk by its communist allies of yesterday. They are realistic, they recognize their error.*

*You do not know, my dear Louis, how far the negotiations reach, what incredible offers have been made. I am perfectly aware of the most secret international agreements. There is every proof that our opponents of yesterday, the most lucid of them, see that the health of the world is only possible to the extent that they resume our work, of which we are the forerunners, and I must disavow it? Yes, I am sorry for myself since my great dream has been temporarily shattered. Sorry for the hundreds of millions of people, truly brave people, kept on the eve of an apocalyptic flood. Painful sorrow, yes, but sorrow only for having been beaten because the happiness and peace of the world depended only on our victory and not on our defeat.*

*Even if you take it from a religious point of view, for yourself, my dear Louis, you will find it amusing that half of Europe, and especially Catholic Poland and Catholic Hungary, has been ripped from Catholicism, while victorious communism, thanks to bourgeois schizophrenia, is now bringing down the missions of hundreds of millions of Asian Christians.*

*There were enemies of the Church near Hitler! They are all over the world, but there were also devout Catholics with Hitler, ardent ones, like Monsignor Tiso and me.*

*I had endless talks about this with Hitler and Himmler. One day I will make extraordinary revelations on this issue, especially on Himmler's religious crisis when it came to an end, partly thanks to me, on the threshold of his conversion.*

*He was absolutely sure that the new Europe would bring complete peace and firm collaboration with the Church. This was my job every second. Hitler knew very well that I would devote my life to it. I did not want to occupy a position as a political leader after the war, but to be the man who created harmony between spiritual and temporal powers, on the one hand, and between Germanism and Latinity[34] on the other. I know very well that for countless fanatics, we have been nothing but gross silhouettes, but I know personally what fervor and purity rested in our dream. I also know that one day Europe will rise again.*

*So, my dear Louis, do you understand the monstrosity of asking me to piously put on the slippers of repentance and sterility? In short, as a priest, you well know what it means to have a vocation. I also have one that embraces my whole being. It*

---

[34] [*Latinity* is how the translator has translated the Spanish *la latinidad*; this can refer broadly to the Latin or Greco-Roman influences in culture, language, and religion.]

is God who has given it to me. For me, to reject it would be to betray the gift of God and betray my own life.

This is not to say, my dear Louis, that tomorrow I cannot make a haven of peace away from all these human trifles with Marie-Paule and my children. I have been disgusted by the villainy and foolishness of men. They must, first of all, be smarter and more decent again before those who have sacrificed and suffered so much for them decide to put forth any new effort. For my part, you can believe me, I am carrying out a huge amount of preparatory work, but I am completely determined to let our old beasts first wither in their foolishness and fear before resuming any new action. So, Marie-Paule and the children, at this point, will find a husband and a father who lives with them in an intimacy and peace as we have never known before. This could last perhaps two years, maybe all our life, but when the cry of action and the ideal call out, I will jump right back on my steed that very day.

As for my children, I want them to always hold their heads high when they think of my work, instead of looking at a father who would have morally ended himself by preferring conformity and the cowardice of easy renunciations rather than a hard life…

As far as the children are concerned, see to their religious education above all, that is what is most important for me. Make sure they keep good company and attend to their moral life. Also see to their joy. Let them be natural, simple, content in everything, that they find that everything is going well in the best of worlds. In life, one must look at those who are less happy, whatever may be the case, and not those who are more fortunate and blessed.

In the past, I taught my little ones to sing joyfully and in chorus each morning: life is joy, and when one does not rise with a broad enough outlook, life quickly becomes sadness. There is a large part of self-suggestion in happiness….

Now look at this, my dear Louis, as soon as I send you a letter, as you can appreciate, it becomes an endless book. Given that we generally do not write to one another more than once every twenty years, the case will not be entirely too tragic.

Pray for me, I need it. I no longer know if my prayers are worth anything, for I am only a miserable sinner. Like all of you, I offer myself to you with great esteem and affection.

Sincerely from the depths of my heart.

## Back to Torremolinos

The Diplomatic Information Office echoed the dispatch of press agency *Internews* in Madrid, dated November 17th, 1948, in Madrid:

*It has been much discussed in the cafés whether the supposed hiding place of Léon Degrelle in Spain will be revealed. In monarchist circles, it is believed that the Duchess of Valencia knows the whole story behind Degrelle's mysterious disappearance from a Spanish hospital two years ago. The Duchess was preparing to implicate Franco's senior officials unless the charges against her were withdrawn.*

*The Duchess is now in the prison of Yeserías for violating her house arrest to attend the funeral of Carlos Méndez.*

*The Duchess, it is said, is furious at finding herself in the men's prison and not in the women's prison in Ventas, where she has been several other times.*

*Although the information concerning Degrelle cannot be confirmed and many are inclined to disregard it completely, one of the Duchess's closest friends assured the correspondent of its authenticity.*

As Christmas approached, Léon sent the following letter to his sisters:

*I want to take the initiative, first of all, to wish you all a Merry Christmas and a Happy New Year. On Christmas Eve I will be tenderly united with all of you, forgetting no one, as in the happier times of Christmases past at home. Mother, Father, and Edouard, will be spiritually united with us, healing our hearts with love. Also, our beloved and heroic Charles, our recent martyr, who marched to join the painful and glorious legion of the righteous, who died for a pure and noble cause!*

*Our dead are our strength! On Christmas night, they, you all, and I, from the confines of my exile, will form one soul, one familial tenderness, something painful but also strong in soul and blood! My best wishes to all for the New Year as well. This next year will not bring us, here, the great tragedy that plagues Europe.*

*It may be that one day we can all get together here. My heart's desire would be to soften the storm for you. I prefer to see you in more peaceful circumstances!*

*Be careful, as I know more about this than you do, and the dangers of a general outbreak are great, with the rapid shortening of the distance between the Pyrenees and the Rhine. They did not want to listen to us when we were striving to save*

*Europe in time! It will be very difficult for them to return to the work of the precursors, who are poorly appreciated and persecuted![35]*

*My health? The operation was very serious and, unfortunately, without great results. The hemorrhages have reemerged. I need a little happiness for my wounds to heal, and that is not my daily meal right now...*

*The horrible way I have been deprived of any news of my young children has put my health at low levels. Here lie the root causes of my illness: my ideal plundered by barbarians; my children uprooted from my heart; Marie-Paule (my wife) victim of the most ruinous and fierce hatred.*

*In spite of everything, courage! God will help us and save us!*

*I send you all my infinite affection*

Degrelle spent the Christmas of 1948 in Madrid. In the first days of January 1949, he traveled to Torremolinos, where he was a welcomed guest in the home of the du Welz family. His faithful Robert, the former field assistant who accompanied him, in May 1945, on the airplane adventure from Norway to their landing on La Concha beach in San Sebastián, and his beautiful wife, Marie Antoine, received him with affection. He spent several weeks recovering in Villa Santiago, Torremolinos. The beautiful weather and continual sunshine provided the new energy necessary to revitalize his exhausted body. During his extended stay, Robert and Marie Antoine had two children, Peter and Cristina. Léon loved them as his very own, having been deprived of his offspring and progeny by the cruel fate of history.

On June 15th, 1949, when he was forty-three years old, and still recovering in Torremolinos, Degrelle finished writing an autobiographical text which he named *La Soledad* (*Solitude*). It remained unpublished until 1999, five years after his death. When it was finally published, it was under the title *Mon Combat.*[36] Even though it had no reference to the publishing house, its seal, its address, or the place where the edition had been made, with the exception that it alluded to being "Printed in the European Community," it was not difficult to recognize its author.

---

[35] While this paragraph is not as clear as one would like, Degrelle appears to be concerned about the Soviet Union's further encroachment into Western Europe, thus "shortening the distance" between Soviet-controlled Europe and non-communist Europe; an encroachment that Nazi Germany's victory, the "work of the precursors," would have decisively made impossible.

[36] [French for *My Fight.*] This may have been a deliberate association with *Mein Kampf.*

## An "Incredible" Testimony

In March 1949, while Degrelle was convalescing among his compatriots in Torremolinos, the newspaper, *Vers L'Avenir*, in Namur, published some delusional statements by a random Belgian citizen. Without revealing his identity, the newspaper stated that during a recent trip he had just made to Uruguay, he came across Léon Degrelle. The newspaper explained to its readers that the name of the informant of such a sensational revelation, was kept secret "at the request of upper echelons." He pointed out exact and unlikely details, almost photographic, with a realism that neither the Spanish painter Segura,[37] nor Mother Isabel Guerra would have been able to capture in their canvases. The meeting, according to the anonymous informant, had taken place in a hotel in Santa Bellana, near the seaport of Punta del Este. He found Degrelle, according to his imaginative testimony, having a quiet drink; there was no doubt it was him. Everything was there to create a sensationalist montage to keep the flame of persecution lit.

Speculation about Degrelle's identity and whereabouts was still the order of the day. When the news of the location of Léon in Uruguay was known, the Spanish press took it with reservation and skepticism, questioning the news, which had more overtones of falsehood than of likelihood. Rumors were running around the streets of the old city of San Sebastián that Degrelle, while at General Mola Military Hospital, had undergone plastic surgery to alter his physiognomy and that the news published in the Belgian newspaper was therefore questioned. In the hypothetical event that he had undergone a face lift, it would be very difficult to recognize him. Even the name of the Basque surgeon who provided the cosmetic surgery was given. It was all false.

## His Relationship with His Comrades of the Women's Section of the Falange, Clarita Stauffer and Carmen Werner

Some in the hierarchy of the Women's Section had also watched over the fate of their heroic comrade in exile, giving him assistance of all sorts. This was the case with Clarita Stauffer and Carmen Werner.

Klara (Clarita) Stauffer was the daughter of the wealthy industrialist, Conrad Stauffer. He was married to Miss Loewe and was the general manager of the Mahou

---

[37] Likely a reference to Enrique Segura Iglesias (1906 – 1994), a portrait artist who painted portraits of King Juan Carlos I of Spain and Francisco Franco, among others.

Brewery and owner of the transport company Gil Stauffer. Clarita was born in Madrid, so she had both German and Spanish nationality. Her studies were carried out in Germany, and she excelled in swimming and skiing. Together with Pilar Primo de Rivera, José Antonio's sister, she was one of the founding members of the Women's Section of the Spanish Falange. She was in charge of the Press and Propaganda Secretariat. During the National Liberation Crusade, she and Onésimo Redondo's widow Mercedes Sanz Bachiller, and the writer Carmen de Icaza, were the architects of the aid organization Auxilio Social. Clarita is credited with the idea for the emblem that the organization adopted, inspired by an icon of a German National Socialist Association. A woman of great ideals, she was imbued with a doctrinal symbiosis of Falangist national-syndicalism and German National Socialism, to which she devoted herself with sincere enthusiasm.

Her work at the forefront of welfare and aid activities for Axis veterans and refugees was very outstanding and meritorious. Her linguistic skills made her essential for these tasks. Her home, located on calle Galileo fourteen, third, in Madrid, was the largest center of operations and networking for veterans in need of aid and relief in those critical post-war years.

In addition to providing supplies to the needy, she was also involved in activities to provide veterans with documentation for safe passage, both for refugees and those looking to settle long-term. Her efforts were worthy of high praise.

This exceptional woman was introduced to León Degrelle by their stalwart and common friend Otto Skorzeny, and from the first moments a sincere, intimate, and close friendship developed.

Clarita Stauffer died at the age of eighty in her hometown of Madrid in 1983.

Carmen Werner, León's other good friend, was, since the beginning of the Women's Section of the Falange in 1935, the Provincial Delegate of Malaga. Together with her father and brother, she played a very prominent role in the preparation and mobilization of the National Uprising in her province. In the early days of the uprising, she traveled to Seville to meet Pilar Primo de Rivera, who entrusted her with responsibility for the war hospital in Algeciras. Her entire family ended up being shot, but she managed to survive thanks to the intervention of the Mexican Consul in Malaga. Amidst the turbulence of the uprising, they managed to put her on a ship to Tangiers, thereby saving her life.

Carmen had an intimate and affectionate friendship with José Antonio who, in the prison of Alicante, was aware of his unappealable death sentence handed down by the People's Court. On November 19th, 1936, the eve of his assassination in the courtyard of the eastern prison, among the few farewell letters that he could write to his family and his most beloved comrades, there was the following letter to Carmen:

> *Dear Carmen,*
>
> *I have on the table, as my final companion, the Bible that you had the good sense to send me in the prison in Madrid. From it, I read parts of the gospels in these, perhaps the last hours of my life.*
>
> *Our friendship is too serious and strong for me to write a "death sentence" letter. I just want to reiterate my thanks for the book and tell you that your friendship is one of the good things in my life.*
>
> *If I see you again (whatever God does) I will tell you everything. If not, then for the last time receive my most true affection.*
>
> *José Antonio*
>
> *P.S. Yesterday, I made a good confession.*

Due to her effectiveness and dynamism, she was appointed Central Regent of Youth Organizations for the Women's Section.

In the summer of 1937, Carmen Werner, leading a group of comrades of the Women's Section, was invited to visit the preparatory command schools of the Hitler Youth in Darmstadt and the School Home of Training for Future German Families in Düsseldorf. She concluded her stay at the Congress of the National Socialist Party in Nuremberg, which was held that year under the slogan, "The Triumph of Will." When she returned to Spain, she wrote in her report:

> *We were at the big stop in Nuremberg. Dazzling! This detail matters a lot. Those who have not lived through those years will never understand the impact that those compact ranks of men moving in unison by the "impulse of will," made on those who watched them. It seemed to awaken an energy capable of moving the world.*

Starting in 1938, at the initiative of Carmen Werner, the first command school of the Women's Section began to operate in Malaga. Management was appointed to Justina Rodríguez de Viguri, future wife of Dr. Narciso Perales, who would later help Degrelle in his escape from General Mola Hospital in San Sebastián. In October 1938, Carmen accompanied Pilar Primo de Rivera when she had an audience with Benito Mussolini.

Carmen Werner got along well with Léon Degrelle from the very start. A good, solid, friendship between them lasted for many years.

## Change of Destination: Majalimar, Lora del Río

While Degrelle was still in Torremolinas, José Antonio Girón and some industrialists from Fuentes de Béjar, the García y Gascón brothers, agreed that Degrelle should be moved. The brothers owned a farm in Sierra Morena, which was 20 kilometers (12.5 miles) from Constantina and 17 kilometers (10.5 miles) away from Lora del Rio. In that Majalimar farmhouse, Degrelle stayed for five and a half years, recovering definitively in the healthy mountain air.

The surgery had been a success. Subsequently, no fatal injury was discovered that could not be healed. Convalescence was slow, but hope was something he never lost. His health improved day by day. Degrelle felt the taste for life again in the Majalimar countryside, surrounded by forests and hills, near the Andalusian village of Lora del Río. He felt his soul and his freshness of yesteryear being reborn, little by little, in the midst of nature.

It was as if the spring of a new dawn was coming back to life within him, giving color to gray, ancient shadows. He was passionate about works of art, about the beauty that human genius is capable of creating. He wrote:

> *Often in life, only beauty frees the soul from human misery. There are so many mediocre, low, or ugly things on earth, that one day you end up being drowned in them if you do not carry in yourself the fire of that which is beautiful, burning away the ugly, consuming it, and purifying yourself. There are thirty-six ways to bring art to life. It is necessary to cultivate them with passion and love. It is our inner health, our secret garden that, without ceasing, refreshes us and fortifies us. Poetry, painting, sculpture, music…no matter what it is, it is necessary to avoid the banal, to rise above the dust, to create the great rather than conform to the small, to make this extraordinary flame, which each of us possesses in ourselves, come to life and turn it into a great fire!*

During his quiet convalescence, he deeply studied the work of the brilliant painter, Domenikos Theotocopoulos, "El Greco":

> *In exile also, thrown from the violet sea that rang around Cyprus to these bare and tragic rocks, grandiose and ruthless, of Toledo's curved line! As genius is universal, it adapts to everything, is reborn from everything and is everywhere. El Greco has launched into eternity the most prodigious transposition of the mystical life into a sheaf of colors that the world has ever known: spiritually frozen bodies in spite of*

*their realism, elongated, almost discarded, stripped of their weight and their form,*
*aspirated by the divine among powerful radiance. Wagnerian three centuries in*
*advance! Graceless skies trapped by the calls of the invisible!*

*Giant victory of the spiritual, integrating, burning the natural! Extreme limit*
*of the human and the superhuman!*

A thick, revealing book, entitled *La Cohue de 1940* (*The Mob of 1940*), signed by
Degrelle, came to press in Lausanne, Switzerland on December 31st, 1949. It was
a chronicle describing what happened in Belgium from May 1940 to June 1941,
when the most prominent "collaborationists" appeared. Among them were
important, committed figures who cynically and shamefully held positions of
responsibility in various political posts in different leftist parties. Many of them
were dedicated to repressive assignments, even against those who had been their
former comrades. The book was a stark depiction of events, and unsurprisingly was
banned in Belgium.

It was the first volume of a series of four books, which he was preparing to
continue. He would collect in that broad, monumental work, all the ins and outs of
the small, but great, history of Belgium during those tumultuous years. The titles
of the following tetralogy would be: *Avec Hitler l'Européen* (*With Hitler the European*)
and *La Grande Noyada* (*The Great Noyada*), finishing it with what would be *Chef de Rex*
(*Head of Rex*).

On the first blank page of his 1950 schedule, he wrote the following slogan:
"*Ne pas gémir, agir!*" ("Do not cry, act!")

Meanwhile, from Brussels, Morales, Chargé d'Affaires of Spain, sent a
"confidential" cable to the Spanish Minister of Foreign Affairs on December 21st,
1951, in which he shared:

> *Last night at a dinner given by the President of Council Ministers, I had occasion*
> *to talk to him about the denial published concerning Degrelle's supposed stay in*
> *Spain. Foreign Minister of Trade also attended and told me that socialist pressure*
> *had not influenced this government and proof of this was that he had a plan to*
> *appoint an Ambassador to Spain this same year.*
>
> *Morales*

In that year of 1951, the large Paris publishing house, Flammarion, published the
novel *La Grande Bagarre* (*The Big Brawl*), which had resounding success. It was
authored by a Jean Doutreligne, a pseudonym used for the occasion by Léon

Degrelle. It took exactly one week to write it, with Degrelle working on it every day, all day, at the rate of forty pages a day.

That same year, twelve poems, until then unpublished, would also come to light with the title *La Chanson Ardennaise* (*The Song of the Ardennes*), in a careful collector's edition. He dedicated some of his copies to his friends, among them "to Roberto Reyes, one of the best comrades of the 'Falange,' with an Arriba España, from your friend. Léon Degrelle. 1951." These poems had been written during his stay at the General Mola Military Hospital in San Sebastián.

Léon published his poems again in Paris in the publication *La Feuille de Chêne* (*The Oak Leaf*). These were titled *L'Ombre des Soirs* (*The Shadow of Evening*) and they were punctuated with emotion in every verse.

In January 1951, Léon Degrelle broke his silence, giving the magazine *Europe-America* in Brussels an extensive interview, which was conducted by journalist Guy M. Frère and published in edition number 295, dated February 8th, 1951. In it he made clear, in an irrefutable way, his clean record at all times in action, both political and military, and the sly and devious attitude of the Belgian government, with its tortuous and unsubstantiated behavior, in relation to his thought and work. The publication, in which he spoke to his people for the first time since his arrival in Spain, sold tens of thousands of copies without anyone being able to refute the unquestionable authenticity of the interviewee. He then spoke to a correspondent for the United Press, an interview in which he further unmasked his detractors and slanderers.

## He Writes of His Feats on the Eastern Front

Léon wrote of his experiences and memories on the Eastern Front while on the Majalimar farm. He vigorously recalled fighting hand-to-hand, the sieges, and the battles that made him worthy of the highest distinctions and decorations of valor and loyalty. He knew every moment, every argument in his book; he lived as the interpreter of that action, together with his volunteers, on the front lines under fire on the Eastern Front. He thanked God for giving him encouragement and life to describe some of the most heroic and passionate deeds of war, loaded with courage and heroism, in defense of eternal ideals. The three volumes were designed to be a chronological epic narrative: *Au Caucase à Pied*, *Cerclés en Ukraine*, and *L'Agonie à la Baltique*.[38] All three works were completed by Christmas 1948. This detailed trilogy

---

[38] [French for *To the Caucuses on Foot*, *Surrounded in Ukraine*, and *Agony in the Baltics*, respectively.]

was too voluminous for publishing houses. They suggested that he merge all three books into a more compact summary, a single book of the exploits of his men on the icy fields of the Russian steppe.

These three books were the precursors to the single volume *The Russia Campaign*,[39] whose first edition in Spanish was published in February 1951. It was edited by his old friend and jonsista comrade Luis de Caralt, of Barcelona, and the translator was Eugenio Tejada. His book had previously appeared in Paris two years earlier as *La Campagne de Russie 1941–1945* (*The Campaign in Russia 1941–1945*), published by La Dissemination du Livre (Le Cheval Ailé), and was dedicated "to the memory and glory of the two thousand five hundred Belgian volunteers of the Walloon Legion, killed as heroes on the Eastern Front, from 1941 to 1945, in the struggle against Bolshevism, for Europe, and for their patria." The book would be republished ten years later in France, under the title *Front de l'Est 1941–1945* (*The Eastern Front 1941–1945*). Editions in Dutch (1971), German (1972), Italian (1978) and English (1985) would appear in succession, with new editions and reprints continuing periodically.

Commenting on *The Russia Campaign* in a full-page report in the daily *Arriba*, the distinguished journalist, José Luis Gómez Tello, wrote, "Ultimately, it is a book about soldiers," in which he advocated that a time would come "…in which at the head of each of our young people we will find this beautiful and cheerful book, like a banner, calling soldiers and men who want to remain free."

Degrelle and his men had fought in a clean and dignified way for a pure and superior ideal, as genuine soldiers of a Europe united by blood and soil, culture and tradition. A defeated Germany was an open door to Soviet communism and the plutocratic capitalism of the greedy, hook-nosed merchants of mankind. Degrelle wrote that the fighters on the Eastern Front, particularly those of the Walloon Legion, were already and forever soldiers of Europe:

> [They had left] *their beloved homes in Jutland, La Beauce, the Ardennes, Putza, Limburg, or Andalusia; not to serve the particular interests of Germany, but to defend two thousand years of the highest civilization, thinking of the Florence Baptistery, the Cathedral of Reims, the Alcázar of Toledo, or the Belfry of Bruges. They died by the thousands far away, not for Berlin's "Dienstellen," [40] but for their old homelands, gilded for centuries, and for their common patria, Europe*

---

[39] This volume's first English edition appeared as *Campaign in Russia: The Waffen SS on the Eastern Front*, published by Institute for Historical Review, 1985.

[40] [German for service units or service departments.]

*...scattered, we were persecuted all over Europe, but we could look to the future with our heads held high. History weighs the merit of men. Above the wretchedness of the earth, we offered our youth. We reached the extremes of sincerity and sacrifice; sooner or later, Europe and the world will have to recognize the justness of our cause and the purity of our sacrifice.*

The book flap reads:

*Léon Degrelle has been one of the youngest political leaders in Europe at crucial times for the life of our continent. His personality has gained him both the greatest hatred and the most fervent supporters, but no one has ever doubted that right or wrong, he has acted at all times with great aspiration and thoughtfulness exclusively for the greatness of his people.*

It should not be forgotten that Degrelle, during the four years of the conflict, was promoted all the way up to general. He was wounded on seven occasions, three of which were serious, and received various distinctions and decorations on twenty-three occasions. The writer José Viver, wrote a glowing and eloquent critique of Degrelle's work, praising him for his literary beauty and dedication to promoting great human values.

### Along the Path of the Stars: Pilgrim to Santiago

On the evening of Wednesday, June 20th, 1951, Léon Degrelle arrived in the Navarre Pyrenees, at the "coll" of Ibañeta. This was next to the field where the legendary battle of Roland took place, a feat that gave birth to the great *Chanson de Roland (Roland's Song)*, after sounding the ivory horn to try to save the twelve Peers of France who accompanied him. From that steep port that divides the valleys of the French and Spanish slopes, a short distance from the monastery of Roncesvalles, Degrelle was preparing to set out on the Camino de Santiago. He would go alone, packing light (hardly more than leather boots and a backpack), on the centuries-old path of pilgrims who sought in Santiago the tomb of the faith of Christianity. The tomb had been discovered in 813 during the reign of King Alfonso II El Casto, in the kingdom of Asturias, when Charlemagne ruled in the West.

It was the starting point of a very unique itinerary, the place from where pilgrims, arriving from all over Europe, knelt before a wrought-iron cross. It was placed at the point where, according to tradition, Charlemagne knelt and said a prayer, with his face turned towards Compostela. This simple action has been repeated since then by many pilgrims searching for strength to continue on the long and winding road that heads in the direction of Santiago de Compostela. The road towards St. James is one that pilgrims have traveled and continue to travel regularly, seeking mysticism and spirituality.

From the top of a hill, surrounded by dense forests of oak, beech, and giant fir trees, he contemplated the sunset and its purple hues, setting his view in the direction by which the Star King[41] was hidden, which would be the compass of his steps until he reached the destination on the pilgrim's walk.

The starting point inspired him to hum songs on his descent to the nearby monastery of Roncesvalles, which marks the first stage of the path.

It was an obligatory journey for Degrelle, who was persuaded that "Europe made a pilgrimage to Compostela," as Goethe had said, for the cause of devotion and an encounter with itself and its majesty. Opening the road through incessant journeys over the centuries since the Middle Ages, legions of men traveled that same path, leaving their ephemeral imprint: nobles and peasants, archbishops and princes, muleteers and devotees, kings and subjects. It was the path for those seeking forgiveness of their sins and inner purification until they find absolution and redemption.

Art emerged everywhere along that path, with Romanesque monuments lined up at the edge of the road; pure, simple lines, nothing gaudy. The Gothic followed the primitive art of those varied places, crossing that imaginary line, from east to west, like a compass. The monastic orders and the popes had cleared the difficulties with the topography and eased the path forward and westward. The Flamboyant Gothic style was followed in form by the Plateresque, and culminated in the Baroque, which can be admired in the areas surrounding the road.

Léon visited the monastery of Roncesvalles, where he received the blessing of a priest; the boon would help him to face the difficulties of the remaining journey.

At the end of each day, Degrelle wrote of his impressions, his experiences, his emotions, and the feelings he harbored in the depths of his mind. He wrote in the form of epistles. He stopped for the night in Burguete, the ancient town of Roncesvalles, that stretches in line with the length of the road. There the houses have red painted windows and the family crests, carved in stone, appear in the most visible and distinguished parts of the façades. From the shelter where he stayed that night, he could hear the noise of a nearby stream running with a gentle, muted rhythm.

---

[41] [In Spanish, *el Astro Rey*. A poetic reference to the sun.]

Waking up at dawn in Burguete on June 21st, he began his walk again, heading to Zubiri. As he walked, he noticed the squat houses with large doors and tiny windows compared to the dimensions of their stone wall perimeters, which seemed to him fortresses against the sullen winds and the heavy snowfall in the harsh winters. He had not been able to see them in the dark. The roof boards reminded him of the roofs he had seen in Estonia. He noticed over and over again the blazoned crests on the façades of the ancestral houses, carved and seated with pride of lineage and blood. He crossed both fragile and sturdy stone bridges of medieval design. He could periodically see massive church bell towers as he walked the path toward Zubiri.

He traced the heights of Erro, lined with oak, birch, yew, holly, and pine in abundance, forming a forest of all the hues of green imaginable, until he reached Zubiri in the evening, anchored at the bottom of the valley across the gothic bridge of Rabia.

On June 22nd, after five hours of walking in a torrential downpour, and, after having passed the Arga River, he arrived in Pamplona, which occupies the lower part of that hollow.

Arriving in the Irunian city, he crossed the bridge of La Magdalena and made his way to the cathedral to visit the Pantheon of the Kings of Navarre, Tournai's masterpiece. He noted the scenes on the capitals, as well as the moss-covered stone houses. He scrutinized the neoclassical façade of Ventura Rodríguez, gothic in its origins, that was saved from a fire in the eighteenth century. There he was recognized and entertained by the Secretary of the Provincial Council. Degrelle asked him to keep the pilgrimage secret, hoping to be able to enjoy the mystical silence, the sacrifices, and the trials of the road undertaken without interruption or interference. He toured the Navarrese and then planted himself in a knoll, from which he could see the Arga River, to sleep.

In the very early morning of Saturday, June 23rd, in the midst of chill and fog, he crossed calle de la Curia, the San José square, and calle de los Mercaderes, to go to the Town Hall square. He then took calle Mayor and went around the citadel built by King Philip II, the king whom he admired so much, and continued along the road towards St. James. This was the fourth stage of his journey towards his destination, Puente la Reina, "the small town that serves as a link, and in which groups of pilgrims coming from Roncesvalles meet up with those pilgrims arriving on the road from Arlés, the majority of whom are Germans. They then split through Catalonia and Aragon."

In his diary he wrote:

*At the entrance of the city, I once again admired (I have been familiar with it for a long time) the most magnificent carving of Christ that I have ever seen in my life. It is Rhenish, with a height of 3 meters (9' 10"), carved in wood in the year 1400; an expression of suffering without being dramatic; done with a realism without being frightening and very moving. The truest exponent of the most famous sculptures of Christ due to the virtuous hands of the primitive German, Grünewald. It was precisely the German pilgrims of those times who, despite the mass and weight of the sculpture, loaded it painfully on their shoulders, and brought it to this people to watch over it and protect it. Since then, it has been a guide to travelers and devotees. Those poor German pilgrims who suffered the derision of rascals and whom everyone walked over, threw in jail, and ridiculed. In the little hospital of the chapel, in spite of its semi-ruinous state, two German monks have come to settle.*

He heard the legend that Charlemagne stayed there. He left Puente la Reina on Sunday, June 24th, after attending Mass and receiving communion.

## Staying in Estella and Logroño

The fifth stage of the Camino de Santiago led him to Estella. He slowly crossed, ecstatic, the huge bridge of the Six Arcades. It had been commissioned in the eleventh century under the auspices of Queen Munia, wife of Sancho III of Navarre, to facilitate the passage of pilgrims over the mighty Arga River. He passed through the village of Cirauqui, with its houses on the hill intertwined as if they were a ring. The name of the village means "nest of vipers" in the Basque language. He reached the end of his travels at 2:30 p.m. Estella was the hometown of Julio Ruiz de Alda, the aviator who, together with José Antonio Primo de Rivera, founded the Falange Española. He was also head of its sister movement, the Falange Exterior, since 1934. From Estella he wrote that it was one of his favorite places on a political level.

Aymeric Picaud, in the *Codex Calixtinus*,[42] wrote about Estella: "The bread is good, the wine is excellent, the meat and the fish are plentiful, and they fill all the delights."

In the Royal Palace, Degrelle stood staring at a ducal capital on which the celebrated battle of Roland with the giant Saragut is carved. He remained for an hour, with solitude as his only companion, in the cloister of the Church of St. Peter

---

[42] Aymeric Picaud was a twelfth-century French monk and scholar; he is believed to be the author of *Codex Calixtinus*, sometimes referred to as *Liber Sancti Jacobi*, which is an illuminated manuscript containing information and advice for pilgrims following the Way of St. James.

"...under the white feather grass, with green pines, in front of such noble arches, the cypresses and the shiny box trees, while from the invisible villa, the whisper of the green river was heard..."

In the afternoon, he was lost in the maze of that trail of antiquities that is the old city. There he acquired some chests, a cupboard, tables, a copper kettle chiseled with hearts, and a sublime figure of Christ. When he wrote in his diary at night, he confirmed: "Life is beauty. To find the beautiful, to take hold of beauty, is of such high voluptuousness!"

On June 25th, he started out on the sixth stage of his journey from Estella. After a three-hour walk between Villamayor and Los Arcos, solitude began. He always walked at an even pace, without "asking my feet for any unusual effort." He stopped at the monastery of Irache, at the foot of Montejurra. The place was venerated by the Carlists, crusaders of the tradition who carry on their flag the cross of Burgundy, also a distinctive symbol of the Belgian Rexist Movement. He moved ever forward, meditating, pondering, and reflecting on what he was seeing ahead and what he was leaving behind.

The seventh stage ended in Logroño, on Tuesday, June 26th after Degrelle traveled 35 kilometers (22 miles) without stopping. The first village he encountered on the route was Sansol. The weather had calmed, and the sun shone, in a clear sky, as he went through La Rioja. He excitedly toured the charming streets of Viana, the city of César Borgia.

Upon arriving in Logroño, he stopped at the church of Santa Maria to study the Brussels altarpiece installed there.

For the eighth stretch of his journey, he prepared himself to crown the 35 kilometers (22 miles) that separate Logroño from Nájera. Fatigue, however, was making a dent in his weary body by this time. Instead of stopping to rest, which would have let his body and muscles cool down, he accelerated his pace and continued the march. Exhausted, he finally reached Nájera. It had formerly been the capital of La Rioja, and then a bishopric, and later an abbey dependent on Cluny. It was an obligatory stop for all the pilgrims heading towards Santiago.

That day he wrote:

*Ecstatic, I first spent half an hour on the bridge, with the backpack still on my shoulder, while admiring that spectacle: thousands of poplars, swaying in the wind, aerating the valley, thick white clouds, clear and transparent water, with all the windows of houses reflecting on it (the entire shore is nothing more than a glass window, facing northeast, all along the water). In the end, my thick shoes thudded up the staircase of a very old inn as if made of iron. It was a place where they still shod their horses.*

For two hours he toured the monastery of Santa Maria la Real, attached to the mountain like a fort, sheltered by huge rocky outcrops, and he recognized that he had never before found such majesty and grace, such a wonderful filigree of curves and nerves, carved in reddish-pink stone "…chiseled like a beautiful choir, with an oriental voluptuousness." He discovered, in the carved choir of the church, a young man and a girl holding the coat of arms of Burgundy. Alone, he enjoyed everything, without burden or fatigue.

The ninth stage passed between Nájera and Santo Domingo de la Calzada. He reached it on June 28th. Such was his enthusiasm that he recognized that every day that went by, despite the long walks he took, rather than feeling more exhausted and burdened, he was less so, as if it were simply youthful enthusiasm that kept him going. In the evening, in the twilight, he dreamed of his childhood.

It was the city of Domingo—the city of Santo Benefactor del Camino—where ninety years had been spent clearing the road and building a bridge over the river Oja, building churches and hospitals and attending to injured pilgrims who wandered toward Compostela. Degrelle drenched himself in the history of the city, even contemplating a hen house installed in a niche inside the cathedral. The place pleased him. He remembered Emperor Charles I, who, many years before, stopped at that same altar where he was now raising his supplications and prayers.

## He Makes His Way, Walking Through the Highlands of Castilla

The next day, he left for Belorado, and during the day on July 1st he reached Burgos. On the way between Belorado and Burgos, he observed what was a fortuitous discovery for him. He saw what looked like an oil deposit under the brambles, large puddles with blue and gold hues floating in the stagnant waters, a phenomenon that was repeated in all the puddles he came across during his journey of more than 1 kilometer (about 0.6 miles). He visited the village of San Juan de Ortega, then he directed his steps towards the old city of Castilla.

He stayed at the Hotel Condestable in a small room on the fourth floor. When he arrived, he visited the cathedral that same afternoon and also the following morning. He recognized that, by studying numerous photographs of the walls of the cathedral in flamboyant Gothic style, emotion overwhelmed him. He wrote:

*In art, as in all matters concerning the spirit, it is never necessary to treat oneself like a wharf. It is essential to receive, to let the numerous waves springing from the stone and the colors of the air penetrate the subconscious, and then retell, analyze. This cathedral is a splendid poem, its flamboyant Gothic—work of a German from Cologne—is not heavily entangled and overflowing, but an orderly, portentous song. The sunlight from here allows all the wonders of the materials to come forth, as the inspiration retains its stroke.*

He toured the churches of the Arrabales, stopping to enjoy the Flemish altarpieces. They were so endearing to him, he felt unspeakable emotion as he entered through the door of Santa Maria, which had been ordered to be built by the Emperor King. In Burgos he felt enchanted, fascinated. He walked through the monastery of Las Huelgas, where he again noted the Cross of Burgundy. He ascended to the Miraflores Charterhouse (Carthusian monastery), which moved him in much the same way as the impressive Hospital del Rey.

On July 2nd, he reached Hornillos del Camino. As he travelled, he stopped at a tavern along the way to eat and rest. On one of the walls in the tavern, a photograph of a "bizarre young man" was displayed in a field-gray uniform. It was the son of the tavern owner, a volunteer of the "Blue Division," a comrade-in-arms from the Eastern Front!

The following day he travelled to Hurlones and Castrogeriz. He always walked in the morning until noon, with the sun at his back. He stopped in front of a hospital where they treated those who suffered from fever from the "Fire of San Antonio." The July sun fatigued him, but still he walked, singing as if he were a reaper gathering up the harvest in the field.

In Castrogeriz, in the shop of an antique dealer, he bought some antique carvings of polychrome wood. In his reflections in his diary that evening, he confessed: "This great aridity; I like it, its effect of stripping away is amazingly spiritual. I also like the sun. Behold, five thousand years old, I ask God, strength, beauty, continuity."

On July 4th he slept in Frómista. It had been a very hard day, both because of the distance and because of the sun's merciless heat. In the evening the heat caused a burst of storms, dry in the beginning, with great tension and electrical energy, and then with strong gusts of wind. It finally let loose the contents of its black clouds, the rain cooling down the parched earth.

Due to the prevailing heat, he only made it to Carrión de los Condes. Six kilometers (4 miles) before arriving, he made a stop to admire the huge church dedicated to the Virgin of Villalcazar. He wrote: "This whole mystical route that I am traveling is nothing more than a cascade of amazing saints, fascinating miracles, and admirable heroes."

When he arrived in Sahagún, he had already made it through seventeen uninterrupted stages of walking without much rest. In spite of this, he wrote in his diary:

> *Nothing has worn me out, nothing has broken, everything in general is fine. I have gulped down the 50 kilometers (31 miles), although I would not say it was easy. Everything has gone as well as possible and this afternoon I find myself with a fresh body and in a good mood.*

He had already entered the province of León. From the Pyrenees, the provinces of Navarra, Logroño, Burgos, and Palencia were behind him. Lugo and the province of La Coruña were still ahead. He had traveled a total of 535 kilometers (332 miles) in little over two weeks. It seemed perfectly feasible for him, as it was a matter of faith. He reflected:

> *A mystical spirit overlooks everything, and the old holy saints, Saint James, Domingo, Juan de Ortega, and Mauro help me. We have become old friends. For almost three weeks, we have been walking the way together, without manners, with a punch or perhaps with a kick. When this does not work, I ask them for their help. It is also a matter of will. It is not worth wavering when the objective is there, already so close.*

Step by step the distance was shortened. On the horizon, Santiago, like a mirage, could be seen, getting closer and closer each time. On the feast day of San Fermin, he arrived at Mansilla de las Mulas, having advanced 100 long kilometers (62 miles) in two days. He continued to cross bridges, spotting convents, and old grain villages. The ash trees along the road seemed to reflect the silhouettes of the spears of Charlemagne's warriors, clearing the path of infidels. The landscape in this neck of the woods made him remember Ukraine. Storks gliding over the wheat fields flew over small village steeples, with adobe houses scattered about the plateau. The smell of chamomile wafting off the fields was distinct. His legs were lean and strong, barely resembling the limbs he had when he began the walk.

When he arrived in León, he was fascinated by the cathedral. He stopped to contemplate it. He did not want to leave, absorbed by its fantastic stained-glass window, the ancient polychrome stained glass causing him to fall into a deep meditation. He wrote: "I did not know when to leave. I came back ten times. Half of the time I stayed in León I spent it in the cathedral, attracted and fascinated by so much beauty."

As he traveled to San Marcos, he understood why the hospital there had become, in the sixteenth century, the most lavish of the rest houses along the pilgrimage, with its thousands of shells scattered everywhere. In San Isidoro, he was impressed by the masterpiece of the Pantheon, bringing to memory that wonder-working saint who accompanied travelers for three days until they obtained their repentance.

In Puente de Orbigo, on July 10th, he stood on that noble bridge, and, in his reverie, he dreamed of the virtues of medieval knighthood, remembering the famous joust held there in 1434. It was at that tournament where the knight of León broke three hundred spears. Settling at a bakery in the town, he wrote excitedly:

> *The pilgrimage to St. James truly satisfied everything: the mystical thirst, with all its proliferation of miracles, churches, works of art, transforming the spiritual into the real; the epic, with the immense legend of Charlemagne connecting with the wonderful divine being, planting in him his mighty deeds all along the way; and the spirit of chivalry, not only for this fact, but for all those carried out by European knights on their way to Compostela, who, preceded by a herald, would hold tournaments along the entire route.*

On July 11th he was already in Astorga, where he arrived with a fever and a sore heel, perhaps from having walked all day long with sweat soaking his clothes and the wind's gale in his face.

When he saw Ponferrada, he had already put 744 kilometers (462 miles) behind him in twenty-one consecutive stages. For a moment, seeing the mountains silhouetted behind the village, brought him the memory of Mount Auclin in Bouillon, his hometown. He went to the town hall to request a visit to the Templar Castle. He was accompanied by a municipal guard, who had also, unbelievably, fought with the glorious Blue Division on the Eastern Front!

When he arrived in Villafranca del Bierzo, he understood why many pilgrims, upon reaching this town, already felt they were at their strength's end and declared themselves unable to continue the road to Santiago. This is why a "Door of Forgiveness" had been set up in the Romanesque portico of the church in that area, invoking the supplications of St. James.

## Ultreya!

He made it to Piedrafita on July 15th. There, he prostrated himself and prayed before the Holy Chalice of the Catholic Monarchs in the small church surrounded by *pallozas*.[43] He passed through Triacastela on July 16th. Through this land he was already starting to feel close to Santiago. The next stage ended in Sarriá, but not before making a stop at the monastery of Samos and contemplating the Fountain of the Nereids in its courtyard.

On July 18th, the day of the National Festival of Spain, he arrived in Puertomarín, military stronghold of the Knights of St. James, protectors of the pilgrim's way, where he had the opportunity to tour the village in the company of its mayor. The next night, before the last stage of his pilgrimage, he stayed in Palas del Rey. On the night of July 20th, he stayed in Arzúa, keeping vigil over his spiritual weapons and feeding the fervent yearning that always accompanied him on his journey: to be able to successfully complete the determined path and finally reach that heavenly homeland he dreamed of.

On July 21st, as was planned, he reached the end of his adventure, having traveled 1,030 kilometers (644 miles) from his starting point in the Pyrenees. He arrived comforted and in good form. By noon, he was already approaching Monte Gozo, feeling his heart beating with force. Upon arrival, he knelt, gazing ecstatically at the profile of the city of Compostela. He sang the *Te Deum*. He prayed. He took off his leather boots and with bruised, cracked, and tired bare feet, he walked the last leagues that separated him from the Compostela Cathedral.

That day, he still had enough time to reach the city of Santiago and bow before the apostle's tomb in the crypt of the cathedral. He joyfully wrote: "All my being sings the joy of having overcome, of having been able to arrive, of having lived a few weeks of spiritual elevation, of having collected beautiful things."

Santiago thrilled him to the extreme. On Sunday, July 22nd, he attended the Pilgrim's Mass at the cathedral. He entered through the Obradoiro gate and stopped, lost in thought, before the *Pórtico de la Gloria*,[44] by Master Mateo. He was accompanied by new friends, a writer and a picturesque local anarchist poet who recited his literary creations in the Gallego language as a troubadour. They showed

---

[43] *Pallozas* are unique, traditional homes in north-western Spain, whose stone walls are low to medium height and are built as a circle, roofed with a kind of thatch; their style and technique dates to pre-Roman times.

[44] The *Pórtico de la Gloria*, mostly finished by 1188 by Master Mateo and his studio, features as the main gate to the Cathedral of Santiago de Compostela.

him the surroundings and then moved on to Iría Flavia. On July 24th, a canon from the cathedral spent four hours with him, showing and explaining the ancient palace of the archbishops, which dates to the twelfth century, and educating him on the Codex Calixtinus, jealously kept among the cathedral's most sought-after treasures.

On the Feast of Saint James, he attended the lavish ceremonies for the commemoration in the cathedral. One hundred thousand Galicians, together with countless pilgrims from all over, converged on the city. They participated in all the events in the surrounding area and inside the cathedral before the Blessed Sacrament. Bagpipes[45] left the air impregnated with the musical notes and cadences of *saudade*,[46] the dances of the giants with big heads, and the fireworks of the previous night. He attended the religious ceremonies that lasted three hours. With great pageantry he took a place in the sacred precinct, where the *botafumeiro*, that giant censor of the Santiago Cathedral, swinging like an enormous pendulum, filled the naves with incense. At the time of his departure he wrote, "My heart clenches in my chest, for this city is formidable, these festivals have captivated my soul, and my senses are full of a great melancholy because I have to leave."

On the morning of July 26th, before his departure, he again received communion in the crypt, before the small altar at the foot of the tomb. His soul was imprisoned. Emotion washed over him.

He left for Santa Cristina, on an invitation by the Rof family. He dined with them and at their urging, he shared his recent experiences, which for him would be unforgettable.

He began heading back to his place of residence in Lora del Rio, where he arrived on August 6th, to a joyous reception.

The stubborn and tireless pursuit of his enemies, while still unsuccessful, had yet to cease. The murderous and preying instincts that characterized them had not borne any fruit. Where was Degrelle? From Wednesday, June 20th, when he left Roncesvalles, until July 25th, he fulfilled the goal that he determined to accomplish, go on foot as a medieval pilgrim, or like a knight errant, upon the Camino de Santiago—the Way of Saint James—that Jacobean route that fills and infects the heart and mind with the spiritual. With a clean soul and sore feet, he was able to arrive in Santiago on the eve of the Feast of the Holy Patron of Spain and of Knighthood and bow before the tomb of the venerable apostle. Along the dusty road of his journey, he meditated on and wrote down his deep and serious

---

[45] [*Gaitas*, or bagpipes]. A traditional instrument in Galicia, as well as northern Portugal.
[46] [Gallego/Portuguese, *saudade*; refers to a deep nostalgia that can be represented a feeling or a song that speaks to that feeling.]

impressions, emptying his soul with verses from the heart and prayers upon his lips. It has been an honor to be able to rescue these pages from oblivion, and to translate them into Spanish; those pages written with a stately melody that, as a whole, form that beautiful literary narrative and description of that mystical path, so singular and without equal, his pilgrimage to reach an ever-renewing faith.

In total, during his walk along the road of Saint James, he wrote thirty-six letters. He kept them secret, for memory's sake, to remember intimately those vibrant emotions gathered with the spontaneity and immediacy of lived experience. He kept them among his private papers in a trunk full of his personal effects. He never spoke to anyone about them. He attached a cover to his writings with a drawing he made depicting an old pilgrim with his staff and cape, classic attributes on that spiritual path of faith.

Sometime after his death, his second wife and widow, Doña Juana "Jeanne" Brevet, showed me the letters. I read them, totally absorbed. They were like a precious literary document to me. I immediately translated them into Spanish, and in 1996, they would be published in a book titled *Mi Camino de Santiago*.[47] I tried to scrupulously respect the chronology of each of the stages of Degrelle's pilgrimage.

It was the first posthumous work to be edited after his death and was an indispensable artifact in understanding the arduous soul of Léon Degrelle.

Years later, Pedro Varela made me aware of his intention to republish that work, while requesting the plates from the first edition. I handed them over gladly. A very well-presented second edition was published, allowing readers to relive the adventures of Léon Degrelle's journey on the Camino de Santiago.

On July 9th, the journalist Ramiro Santamaría, wrote a cleverly misleading report from Tangier for the newspaper *Diario de Barcelona*. In it, he said that Léon Degrelle was "…one of the people that the intelligence services have been searching for most eagerly in recent years." Secret agents from Belgium, Britain, the Netherlands, France, and the United States sought him throughout Europe. They accused him of being a collaborationist, for the great sin of having organized the Flemish Legion[48] that fought against communism. This was why Spaak's masonic socialists had condemned him to death. At this time, he had supposedly appeared in Tangier, but since 1946, according to the correspondent's chronicle, if we look at reports from the British espionage network under Major Thompson, he had also been seen in San Sebastián. Another agent of the Gibraltar Secret Service claimed

---

[47] [Spanish for *My Way of Saint James*.]
[48] The author almost certainly means the Walloon Legion, not the Flemish Legion, although towards the end of the war, Degrelle commanded both legions in the SS.

to have seen him in Algeciras. There were also those who swore that he lived for some time in Portugal and even traveled around French territory. The journalist also reported that "...for four days he was in Tangier, in plain view, walking along the boulevards. He arrived on a ship from Europe and boarded another one in the direction of South America." The journalist, in a humorous tone, wondered:

> How could a "war criminal," who was bold enough to live a public life in a city, escape the international police? In Tangier, the police are overseen by a delegation of Belgian officers! Of course, Colonel Legrand never learns of anything. At best, he crossed Degrelle in the street and thought, "I know that face from somewhere..."

The year 1951 gave us another unprecedented surprise. The historian Xavier Casals, in his book *Neonazis en España*,[49] wrote:

> Sometime around 1951, the Belgian government organized an operation to kidnap him (Degrelle resided in a town near Seville at that time) and to drive him to Belgium, where he would be tried. Willy Verstrynge, who, during the Second World War, had been an agent of the Allied and German information services simultaneously, was responsible for executing the plan. Forty-eight hours before the planned abduction was to take place, however, a call was received from high-ranking Belgian authorities canceling the mission. This was due to the fear that eventual revelations from Degrelle would lead to political destabilization in Belgium since the latter had confidential information of which we are unaware. Degrelle likely did not know about this frustrated kidnapping attempt.

This amazing and criminal revelation was shared with Casals by the communist agent's own son, the chameleon Jorge Verstrynge,[50] in a conversation on October 28th, 1994.

Once again, the protection of the Holy Patron of Spain, Saint James, watched over and protected Léon from the treacherous plots being dangerously planned against his valiant life.

---

[49] Pg. 89. Xavier Casals Meseguer's book *Neonazis en España: de las Audiciones Wagnerianas a los Skinheads (1966-1995)* (*Neo-Nazis in Spain: from Wagnerian Auditions to Skinheads (1966-1995)*), was published in 1995, has not yet been translated into English.
[50] Jorge Verstrynge Rojas, born 1948, is a former politician and activist who, in earlier days, had been close to fascist parties, but who switched to leftist politics later in life.

*Léon Degrelle, commander of the Walloon Legion who fought on the Eastern Front against communism*

# III

## *The Burning Souls*

## *(1952)*

### A Mystical Book Written in Poetic Prose

Léon Degrelle's mystical and magical masterpiece, written in poetic prose and with captivating strength, as if it were a text of spiritual exercises, bears the scorching and incandescent title *Les Âmes qui Brûlent* (*The Burning Souls*).[51] It is made up of notes and reflections of peace, war, and exile.

The work is a call to spirituality and militancy, of commitment and faith, of idealism and of vanguardism. He writes: "without love and faith, the world is killing itself," and "the body is sick because the soul is. It is the soul that has to be healed and purified." Degrelle fleshes this out when he states:

*There is no choice: either spiritual development or failure of the century. The salvation of the world is in the will of the souls who have faith...no other country has been blessed with more love for the Virgin, your thousand-year-old Virgin of the Pillar, your Virgin of the Warriors of Covadonga, your Virgin of the Camino for those who grope their way, looking for their path.[52] Your Virgin of the Forsaken, for the drifting souls. Your Virgin of Sorrows, for hearts torn apart by pain...Spaniard! Child of God, keep your path straight. The century awaits you! Burning souls can do absolutely everything!*

---

[51] The English edition of *The Burning Souls* is published by Antelope Hill Publishing, 2020.

[52] The various "Virgins" here are references to the Blessed Virgin Mary, who is venerated and often recognized for specific acts of protection, taking the locale as part of the name for the Virgin.

*The Burning Souls* is a sublime book that was translated from French into Spanish, with a foreword by the distinguished physician, Dr. Gregorio Marañón. He had no difficulty in recognizing that it was a book "flickering like a flame," noting in his foreword that the book contains "pages of unsurpassed beauty and human pathos, full of hope for a common, better world, for which, to the best of our strength, we have polished, like the gold in which an emerald is to be set, with our loftiest and noblest Spanish."

Léon Degrelle met Dr. Marañón personally through his good friend and comrade, journalist Víctor de la Serna. Marañón was an outstanding man. Serrano Suñer said of him: "Apart from his many other values, scientific or intellectual, he was a kind man." When Léon took the book to Dr. Marañón, he was very impressed by its human and spiritual content, and committed himself to writing a foreword, a decision that was criticized by his liberal friends. In response to the reaction to Dr. Marañón's decision to translate the text and write the foreword to the work, Serrano Suñer wrote an article in the newspaper, *ABC,* entitled "Liberal Intransigence." In it, among other assessments, he said that it should be considered that, by profession and vocation, Marañón was an outstanding explorer of the humanities, and of painful humanities at that.

A previous work within the extensive Degrellian bibliography that could be considered a kind of preliminary and remote point of view is his book *Etat d'Âme* (*State of Mind*), published on March 19th, 1938 (the Feast Day of Saint Joseph), by Editions Rex in Brussels. It contains a series of varied writings and meditations, which dealt with an emphasis of faith in the most sublime ideal in political, historical, and poetic themes. In this earlier work he wove the emotions experienced in his native land, the sky above it, the customary patterns of his people, the shape of their dwellings, the faith of his people, and all those elements brought together by the invisible threads of homeland as a land of origin and destination. That same year, this earlier book was published in France under the very suggestive title, *Révolution des Âmes.*[53]

*The Burning Souls*, which Degrelle dedicated to his four children, "Chantal, Anne, Godelieve, and Léon-Marie," was published in 1952.[54] It is chiseled out in the best, glittering prose, deep in its sentiment and endearing like a sincere friendship. Numerous editions have been published in different languages. For the first edition, in its original version, the text was in *Weiss* font, size twelve. The print run was made under the direction of master printer Juan Pons at the Don Ildefonso

---

[53] [French for *Revolution of Souls.*]
[54] His youngest, Marie-Christine, was not included in this dedication.

Becerra workshop, in Lora del Río. It was limited to a hundred copies on large pure alpha paper, numbered in Roman numerals from I to C, plus another print of two hundred seventy-five copies on large veiled alpha paper, numbered one to two hundred seventy-five. The publisher was The Oak Leaf, Degrelle's own publishing company. The iconic emblem used in the design for the publishing seal was the oak leaf, similar to that on German war decorations. The cover was printed in two colors, red and black, which, with the white paper of the dust jacket, formed the three primordial hues. The only illustration inserted was a luminous bonfire, like the ones that were lit in the campfires of the Youth Front, or like those that usually illuminate the dark during traditional and festive fireworks, by M.A. Dans.

## The Oak Leaf Publishing House

The publishing house, The Oak Leaf, was listed as being on Calle Irati, number 6, a small, closed, and quiet street of family-friendly residents, located in the El Viso district in Madrid, almost at the end of calle Serrano, near the church whose patron saint is Santa Gema Galgani of the Redemptorist Fathers. There was not actually a publishing house there. The neighborhood was, and still is, residential. The cottage was the place where, during that period of ruthless persecution, Léon was a refugee for a long time. The room at the top of the property was a kind of loft. The owners of the house were Doña María Paz Díez Tortosa Mocoroa and her husband, Don Luis de Lorenzo Salgado. Don Luis was a volunteer in the Blue Division and a Falangist, who, in the War Council for the events of Begoña in 1942, had been sentenced to death. Given his status as a wounded gentleman, the death penalty was commuted to imprisonment by the Head of State. Luis kept a precious relic in his living room, a blue shirt with the yoke and arrows insignia on it that had been worn by his good friend and comrade Juan José Domínguez Muñoz at the time of his summary execution on September 1st, 1942. Dominguez was also involved in the bombing of the Basilica of the Virgin of Begoña in Vizcaya. [55]

In an interview I had with Luis de Lorenzo on December 10th, 2000, we recalled together an episode of Léon's stay in that cozy house, and he described him

---

[55] The bombing in the Begoña Basilica grew out of tension between two right-wing factions; the Carlists and Falange. During a funeral service for carlists killed in the civil war, carlists were allegedly heard denouncing Falangists. Eight Falangists, including Juan José Domínguez and Hernando Calleja, responded at a subsequent carlist commemoration by throwing bombs into the church. Domínguez and his accomplices were caught and held. Franco reportedly downplayed the event but delivered some justice. While Calleja's death sentence was commuted, Domínguez was shot.

as someone who was "exceptional, bombastic, quite cultured in the 'Mediterranean sense,' a man with an overflowing imagination and poet's soul, who, every time they met with the sun's rising, drew his attention to show him the dawn, as he repeated, 'Look, Luis, what a beauty it is to see the dawn.'"

In that home, The Oak Leaf's "bookstore" was housed. This was basically packages containing copies of *The Burning Souls*.

Luis de Lorenzo joined the Spanish University Syndicate (SEU) in 1934, a young student from Madrid, brave, fierce, and passionate about sports. He was one of the first to enlist in the Blue Division, where he held the post of SEU National Deputy Chief of Sports in the General Secretariat of the Movement. The comrades who joined him, also students associated with sports, were Jesús Luque, Virgilio Hernández Rivadulla, Mariano Sánchez Covisa, and even the National Sports Chief of the SEU himself, Jorge. They joined to go fight the communists in their own burrows. Luis de Lorenzo was seriously injured in Russia, in the battle of Lake Ilmen, and made it out alive thanks only to the quick intervention of Mariano Sánchez Covisa. Covisa saw Lorenzo fall in the snow and placed him on his coat, using it like a sled to gently pull him to the evacuation point at the field hospital. Due to the severity of his wounds, Lorenzo returned to Spain in April 1942. In this condition, and despite having to use crutches in order to walk, Lorenzo was designated to take Jorge's place as the SEU National Sports Chief

Luis de Lorenzo was a great skier, and it was while practicing that he met María Paz Díez Tortosa, who was affiliated with the Falange Women's Section in San Sebastián. Curiously, she was the daughter of Dr. Díez Tortosa, head of the medical team at General Mola Hospital in San Sebastián at the time that León Degrelle stayed there after his crash landing in Spain in May 1945. María and Luis soon married.

During his stay with the Lorenzos, Degrelle witnessed the birth of their daughter, María José de Lorenzo y Díez Tortosa. They asked their guest, "Don Juan Sanchiz"—the name he used during those times of secrecy—to be their baby girl's godfather at baptism. Degrelle took this very seriously, and in a very affectionate and endearing letter to Lorenzo, dated December 22nd, 1961, Degrelle mentions María Jose in one of his first paragraphs.

The second edition of *The Burning Souls* was smaller in size and was published in 1954. It was sold for forty pesetas a copy. Its dust jacket showed a photograph of Léon Degrelle's face and, to the right of it, vertically, a yellow border highlighting the name of the author, the title of the work, and the names of the translator and writer of the foreword. A brief description of "Degrelle the Political Man" and "Degrelle the Soldier" appeared on the front and rear flaps. Thousands of copies of this edition were printed and soon sold out.

The publisher "Tip. Cat. Casals," which had its offices at calle Caspe one hundred eight, in Barcelona, launched a new edition of its C.L.I.C. collection in 1962. The first title of this collection was a work by Jesuit Adro Xavier entitled *Los Concilios Ecuménicos*.[56] The second issue was the book *La Madre Educadora del Ideal*,[57] by Ch. Grimaud. The third issue of this collection was the new edition of *The Burning Souls*, whose cover was designed with the drawing of a field encircled by a ring of thorns, cut and open only at one end. The fourth title of the collection was the work *La Iglesia y el Estado*[58] by Fr. Francisco Segarra SJ. The publishing house where *The Burning Souls* was republished was a Catholic company under the patronage of the Jesuit Society.

## A Curious Interview in the Weekly *El Español*

In the December 19th, 1954, edition of the weekly *El Español*, published in Madrid, journalist Jiménez Sutil took up four full pages with a broad and frank "Dialog with León Degrelle." He was aware of the current news and related that "his book *The Burning Souls* just appeared in Madrid," describing the beginning of the interview this way:

> *I arrived, I saw him, and I knew him. I had never spoken with him, but there are physiognomies that time, however cruel it might be, does not age. The face of León Degrelle, leader of the Belgian Rexist Movement is one of them.*
>
> *JS: "If you are León Degrelle, please allow me a few minutes to chat. I am Spanish."*
>
> *To this he responded with an open, frank smile and very expressive gestures, so we chatted.*
>
> *LD: Oh, Spanish, Spanish!*
>
> *JS: I reaffirmed that yes, Spanish it was, and Andalusian at that, so we sat down. No more was needed. I felt, as a Spaniard, a great satisfaction.*
>
> *LD: I was a very close friend of José Antonio.*
>
> *JS: Do you know Spain well?*
>
> *LD: Quite a bit. As a youngster, I used to come here with my parents. During your Liberation Crusade, I toured several cities and even the front lines. Then...after the last European war, when the defensive organization of the fighters*

---

[56] [Spanish for *The Ecumenical Councils*.]
[57] [Spanish for *The Mother Educator of the Ideal*.]
[58] [Spanish for *The Church and the State*.]

*against Russia fell apart, I, a Belgian soldier in the icy fields of Russia, grabbed this firm rock of your peninsula, as one shipwrecked in a great tragedy. A man healed in the fight.*

JS: *Léon Degrelle, with his aquiline eyes wandering along the horizon, far from me, continued in a lower tone. He spoke to himself, for the sake of memory. He synthesized a deep and always living past in himself.*

LD: *I will not forget it. The memory of Spain will always be with me.*

JS: *I could not observe, however, the slightest hint of softness. He had a gratitude towards blood and life. The gratitude of a man who has been cured in the midst of struggle; hard, dynamic, vital, enterprising, mentally built to encourage. A man of thought for immediate action, of operative thought…At the age of twenty-nine he had behind him a large number of the Belgian people. He was the captain of a movement, a rexist, socially minded, based on the principles of Catholicism. Restless, easy and fiery of word, much of the youth was with him. He personally got more votes than any other delegate of his country…What can a man do, so separated from his homeland, a man condemned to death in his country? Does he live alone with the sun, with the air, with the clouds that pass overhead? Far from men, does he live alone with his memories and hopes? What does such a dynamic man think, in these circumstances outside his native land, outside his own continent, unknown, silent by force, with everything strange and sometimes suspicious?*

*There you have it. He will probably find what he is looking for. He gave me his book* The Burning Souls, *translated into Spanish and published in Madrid, with a foreword by Dr. Marañón. I read the subtitle: "Notes on Peace, War, and Exile." It was divided into five parts with a series of titles—all vital—of movement, of birth, of falling, where there is nothing but life, in its sunrise or its sunset. In a more intimate tone, I asked: Do you have a family?*

LD: *Yes. My parents have died after two horrendous years spent in prison. My wife and children were in Switzerland in 1946. The Swiss handed them over to the Allies. They sentenced my wife to 10 years forced labor. My children have changed their first and last names. After ten years, I do not know any of them. Neither my wife nor my children are at fault. Politics is a vocation. The politician alone is responsible. My wife is on probation after several years in prison.*

JS: *Why did you write this book, Mr. Degrelle?*

LD: *The politician must not only make laws. He must also give soul to the people. We have to write. The book is intended to ignite the youth.*

Sutil and Degrelle discussed several other important experiences in Léon's life. Sutil fluctuated between curiosity and amazement at those events that had made Degrelle a living legend, an incarnate myth. Again, he read aloud some paragraphs from *The Burning Souls*, concluding with the question:

*JS: So, the true revolution is...?*

*LD: The one that sets up not the state machine, but the secret life of souls.*

*JS: In the end, his feelings toward Spain again surfaced, when he referred to Spaniards as "the only ones with a universal mission in the world."*

*JS: What did you see in Spain?*

*LD: In the different and well-spaced stages of my visits to Spain, I could see many things, many good things.*

*JS: Léon showed an authentic and genuine love for our country. He has known our population, closely observing and learning from them.*

*LD: What healthy people of body and soul! What simplicity and what faith, free of the skepticism of our time! They constitute the reserve of our century. I have seen and heard them—with great satisfaction, on my part—react and enjoy in the cinemas when the good guys win. They seem to be anachronistic people, but what sincerity, what nobility! Their family life, their customs...everything!*

*JS: Spanish generosity, an open hand and heart, a total dedication to things, has also attracted his attention. We are, according to him, people of much inner life. Few victims are overwhelmed by the machinery of today's life. Good connoisseurs of time, without being slaves to it, as well as being gentlemen.*

*LD: On one of my trips a man came up, in Andalusia, and asked me for a peseta. "Why do you want a peseta?" I asked. He told me, "So I can buy a hat to be able to greet you."*

*JS: Degrelle laughed heartily with this anecdote. He later recalled that wherever the Spaniards have gone, they have left positive and flourishing traces of culture and civilization: they have tied perennial bonds of fraternity. Do the other peoples have such a testimony?*

*"Friend," he said, standing up and putting his hand on my shoulder. "What a pity that there are only twenty-eight million Spaniards in the world!"*

*Mr. Degrelle, do you want to write anything in this book?*

*He wrote and signed his name.*

*JS: It looks like a minister's signature.*

*LD: And what is a minister's signature?*

*JS: Degrelle responded with a good laugh.*

## His Friend Pierre Daye

In 1954, former Rexist Deputy Pierre Daye, a good friend of Léon, published a book that should be required reading: *El Suicidio de la Burguesía Europea,*[59] released by Claridad Editorial in 1952, Buenos Aires. Daye had moved to Argentina and was teaching classes at a university.

Pierre Daye was born in Brussels, in 1892, to an upper-class Belgian family. A tireless traveler, he was familiar with most of the countries of the five continents and had traveled them, depending on the occasion, as a soldier, journalist, or diplomat. He was a Catholic and a romantic. He participated as a volunteer combatant in the West Africa campaign in 1916 and in 1918 was appointed Belgian Military Attaché in Washington. In 1925, he was a correspondent for *Le Soir* in Argentina, a period that gave him an opportunity to build a friendship with the nationalist writer Leopoldo Lugones. In the 1930s, he was stationed in Tehran on a diplomatic mission at the Belgian embassy. He would soon become one of the most representative figures of the Rex Movement and work closely with Léon Degrelle. He fostered personal friendships with Hitler, Rudolf Hess, and Von Ribbentrop, with whom he met on several occasions. Degrelle offered him parliamentary leadership of the party after their election victory. In 1939, he joined the Belgian Catholic Party. During the Second World War, he resided in Paris, where, in 1943, he was appointed Belgian Minister of Sports. At the beginning of that same year, he received a private audience at the Vatican with Pope Pius XII.

He settled in Madrid in 1944. In the capital of Spain, he associated with like-minded journalists Víctor de la Serna, Mariano Daranas, José Ignacio Escobar, Manuel Aznar, and Eugenio D'Ors.

The masonic and communist revanchists, who rose to power in Belgium after the fall of the Third Reich, condemned him to death *in absentia*. With Brussels' request for his extradition for the sole purpose of executing him, he fled to Argentina, arriving in Buenos Aires on May 21st, 1947, on Iberia flight EC-DAQ.

Daye was a brilliant intellectual and a prolific traveler, who associated with notable characters such as Robert Brasillach and Lucien Rebatet, also strengthening ties with the Spanish Ambassador, José Félix de Lequerica. He was also a flowery and entertaining lecturer and author of more than thirty works on a variety of subjects. In his new book, he now included an enigmatic phrase: "The technique threatens to stifle man," and put his dreams and his fantasy of a "United States of

---

[59] [Spanish for *Suicide of the European Bourgeoisie.*]

Europe" as a future solution for the old continent. He recalled that an old Brussels tapestry of Toison d'Or that bore the heading: "Justice is the constant will to do right even by the defeated."

From his hiding place in Spain, Degrelle wrote to Daye, encouraging him to continue the struggle in Argentina without fail. In his letter he said:

> *In two, three, or five years, great hours will come. You will see, my friend Pierre, how we will do formidable tasks. All that has been done so far has been nothing more than patrol, reconnaissance, stealthy inspection. Real life has yet to begin. I firmly believe it.*

In his reply, in loyal agreement, Daye told Degrelle, "The future is ours. Experience and disgrace have shaped us. The martyrs, necessary for any higher cause, will see their names triumphantly rehabilitated."

### Finally, *The Burning Souls* Is Published in France

In 1964, the first French version of *Les Âmes qui Brûlent* (*The Burning Souls*), was published under the publishing label A la Feuille de Chêne, with the address fourteen, rue Weber, Paris XVI, although its printing was done in Spain under the technical direction of E.G. Coll, on calle San Francisco de Sales eighteen, in Madrid. It presented a small, handwritten dedication with Degrelle's signature: "A little fire in any corner of the world, and all great miracles will be possible." In the French edition, the foreword by Dr. Gregorio Marañón was inserted as an appendix at the end of the text. A brief introduction entitled, "The Immutable Man," was included in the front of the work, which read:

> *This work,* The Burning Souls, *comprises a series of spiritual notes that the author wrote during the various adventures of his life, before and during the Second World War.*
>
> *Each era has its style, naked or bombastic, classic or romantic. Through its style and apart from the writer himself, certain forms, certain ways of thinking typical of an era, come into play.*
>
> *A part of these notes are war-time reflections, written while the author— wrongly or rightly—fought as a European volunteer on the Eastern Front, from 1941 to 1945, against the Soviet Army.*
>
> *This manuscript, very likely, was doomed to never appear.*

It was discovered by the greatest Spanish writer of our time, the recently deceased Dr. Gregorio Marañón, a member of five academies in his country.

Politically, Dr. Marañón had nothing in common with the totalitarian movements of the twentieth century. He belonged to a gentle liberalism, far from violence. Then, like a meteor, the author of these pages appeared. Gregorio Marañón read the manuscript by chance and decided to dedicate the spare time of the last two years of his life to translating the book into the Spanish language, in a style of admirable purity. He presented it to the general public of his country with a foreword, which can be read here in the appendix. "These pages," wrote Gregorio Marañón, "are of an unsurpassed beauty, vibrant with human pathos."

The work, known in Spain under the title Almas Ardiendo (The Burning Souls), has had more than fifty editions published and continues to be republished.

The author, however, did not print this work in its original language. The French-speaking reader, after 1945, seemed more easily bored than the Spanish public and almost impervious to meditations of this kind. The curvatures of a female character in a movie are much more interesting to a modern audience than the anguished vibration of a soul. On the other hand, what does the soul even mean? Moral and spiritual problems today are a bother to the men and women who are said to be "with the times." They prefer to dilute these problems with a small dose of superiority, condescension, or mockery. At best, it does not affect them in the same way, nor do religious problems.

The ideas contained in these notes, the feelings that vibrate here, have resonated with considerable numbers of people. They can, therefore, still present a certain interest, though only as testimony.

In a preliminary confession, the author has made the point, has expressed his doubts, his disquiet; he has given himself, with few illusions, with a slight ray of hope. In general, across generations and differences of lifestyle and taste, there always exists, from man to man, spiritual connections. A boy of twenty years, or perhaps a few years older than the author of this book, may experience the same vibrations. They will remain with us until the end of the world. What does it matter then, at the end of the day, how they were expressed or the identity of the person who expressed them? [ . . . ]

Naive in spite of everything, it either remains pure by dint of struggle or is destroyed and stumbles by its faults and its stains. The heart of man is immutable, whatever is said and whatever is done.

These notes would have been addressed to him in the past, and they still address him today. Anyone who throws these pages into the stormy winds of his time cannot *know whether they will contribute to emotion or simply put a smile on the face of those who, in their inner death, have taken on the colors of irony.*

## The Latest Editions

On July 18th, 1978, the national Spanish holiday commemorating the Glorious National Uprising, the *Fuerza Nueva* (New Force) publishing house launched the printing of the fifth edition of *The Burning Souls* with the short subtitle "Notes on Peace, War, and Exile." On the front cover, Léon Degrelle appears in a famous historical photograph, a smiling face, in his military uniform, surrounded by his three daughters when they were young. On the back cover is another photograph of Degrelle.

The book carried the following dedication:

*To my ten grandchildren in Madrid and, through them, to "Fuerza Joven,"[60] faithful and proud, that keeps the red and yellow flag of Spain "united, great, and free," invincible to the extent that a fiery ideal infuses faith and hope in every heart.*

In March 1993, a new edition, the second in French, was published a year before Degrelle's death. It was odd in that it was the first one bound and printed in France among the publications of the National Association Pétain-Verdun and on the initiative of its president, Robert de Périer. A thousand numbered copies were printed. It was illustrated with various photographs of Léon Degrelle, the first taken in Spain on November 23rd, 1992, among others, and several taken in November in the years 1988, 1990 and 1992, the last of which was in the company of Didier Lestavel. The cover photograph was an excellent portrait by his photographer, Deschutter.

This short, but expressive, dedication was also included in this edition: "To all my French friends and all the others, spread throughout the vast world."

## Anthology of Texts, Maxims, and Thoughts

As Alonso Quijano wrote in his day, *The Burning Souls* is a poetic vision of ethics, a way of life, a song to every virtue that a man has to have like goodness, patience,

---

[60] *Fuerza Joven* (Young Force) was the youth wing of Fuerza Nueva, started by Blas Piñar in 1976.

obedience, renunciation, leading a straight life, being kind and merciful, but also knowing when it is time to be hard and firm. A beautiful portrait of the value of faith, the encouragement given to us Spaniards to be men of God and a meditation on the crucifixion of Christ, which is a moving experience to just read. We again, even today, abandon Jesus alone at the cross. In short, it is a work of shocking beauty, with that form of expression as accurate and as stunning as the one he always has in his essential texts.

To give an idea of the content of Degrelle's work, of the powerful inspiration, let us take a selection of aphorisms and phrases. This book is essential to understanding Léon Degrelle and his way of being and acting:

### Part One: Empty Hearts

**The Agony of the Century:** *Human beings have barricaded themselves behind their selfishness and pleasure. Virtue has abandoned its natural song. Happiness has become, for man and for woman, a heap of fruit which they devour in a hurry…Happiness only exists in the gift, the complete gift; his selflessness gives him the flavor of eternity.*

*The air is charged with all moral and spiritual denials. The lungs draw in vain for a breath of fresh air, the freshness of a spray thrown close to the sands.*

*Man's interior gardens have lost their colors and their birdsong.*

*The century does not fail for lack of material support. Never before has the universe been so rich, filled with so much comfort, helped by such productive industrialization. Never have there been so many resources or goods offered. It is the heart of man, and this alone, which is bankrupt.*

*From his conquests, or more precisely, from his mistakes and then from his falls, man acquired pleasures that seemed supremely exciting at first, and which were in fact only poison, filth, and falsehood.*

*What remains is only the passion for taking, for seizing, angrily setting themselves against all obstacles and against the stale odors of decay clinging to their ransacked and rotten lives.*

*Vain, emptied, their hands dangling, they do not even see the moment approaching when the artificial work of their time will collapse.*

*The disease of the century is not in the body.*

*The body is sick because the soul is sick.*

*This is what is essential, whatever it may take to cure.*

*The real, the great revolution to be made is there.*

*Spiritual revolution.*

*Or the ruin of the century.*

*The salvation of the world is in the will of souls who believe.*

*For this reason, mystical Spain, Spain of Santa Teresa and of San Juan de la Cruz, of San Francisco Javier, of San Ignacio, for this, I believe in your mission, in a mission together with which your passing misfortunes are nothing; a privileged mission among all, the one of shedding souls in agony the blood of your burning soul.*

*No country today has your faith.*

**The Right Path:** *Those who hesitate in the face of struggle are those whose souls are numb. A grand ideal always gives you the strength to overcome the body, to suffer from fatigue, from hunger, from cold.*

*Ease sedates the ideal. Nothing rights it better than the whip of a hard life; it makes us understand the depth of the duties to be assumed, the mission of which we must be worthy.*

*We are not on earth to eat on time, to sleep on time, to live a hundred years or more. All this is vain and foolish.*

*Only one thing matters: having a useful life, sharpening your soul, improving it at all times, monitoring your weaknesses and exalting your impulses, serving others, throwing happiness and tenderness around you, giving your arm to your neighbor, raising all by helping each other. Once these duties are accomplished, what does it mean to die at the age or thirty or a hundred years, to feel the fever throbbing at the hour when the human beast cries out at the end of its power?*

*Short or long, life is only redeemed if we have no cause for shame at the moment; we have to give it back.*

*It lives only to the extent that we die to ourselves.*

### Part Two: Wellsprings of Life

**The Land of Our Birth:** *As men, we belong always to a people, a land, a history.... They bring us back first to the men of our blood. Shameful or bright, family binds us together, ever tighter and firmer with time.*

*The country's past is embedded in the depth of our consciousness and our sensibilities.*

**Hearth and Stone:** *It is the home that forms us into who we are.*

*Life is fixed on hearth and stone; the rest flows away like broken wood floating on a winter stream.*

### Part Three: The Misery of Mankind

**The Blind Men:** *The money, the honors, the mess of bodies, the eagerness to seize an earthly happiness which leaks between the fingers and always escapes, has made of the human herd a pitiful horde, ruining itself, tearing itself apart to find a liberation which does not exist.*

*This baseness has poured out from the limited circles of the "elites" into the extended circles of the masses, tossing them about on waves of infinite desire, ambition and pseudo-pleasures which are just caricatures of joy.*

*There is great hatred between men, between classes, between peoples. Everyone is bent on the pursuit of material goods which ultimately avail nothing.*

*All abandon the goods, proffered to all, of the moral universe and the eternity of the soul.*

**The Lines of Sorrow:** *Happy again, those who are purified by invisible suffering!*

**The Saints:** *The saints show us that perfection is open to all. They too were simple men, simple women, charged with passions, weaknesses, and often faults.*

*They too sometimes tired, gave in, and told themselves that they would never be able to get rid of that smell of muck and sin that accompanies us all.*

*Still, they did not renounce themselves.*

**Nobody:** *Lord, You brought us the essential and the eternal, the bread and the wine, the breath and the sun.*

*We are overwhelmed at the threshold of Your tomb.*

*Lord, make the spark of the resurrection bloom in our defeated souls!*

**To Have Loved:** *To love is to give.*

**The Price of Life:** *We must reiterate the price of life. Life is the admirable instrument put in our hands, with which we forge our wills, raise our consciences, and build a monument of reason and of heart.*

*Life is not a form of sadness, but joy made flesh.*

*Joy of being useful.*

*Joy of mastering what could demean or weaken us.*

*Joy of acting and giving.*

*Joy of loving all that trembles, spirit and matter; everything under the impetus of a righteous life rises, lightens instead of weighing down.*

*You have to love life.*

**Despoliation:** *Happy is he who is not a slave to circumstances, who knows how to enjoy pleasure as well as privation.*

*To remain in good spirits, even to live with one's soul apart from the world when the exterior universe holds nothing but a yawning void, to live intensely in this "material absence," to live without regret, master of your desires, having bent them to the complete domination of the spirit marks the victory of man. It is the true, the only victory, next to which the greatest conquests and dominions are merely caricatures of power.*

*Happiness can be born everywhere. It comes, not from without, but from within us, holding within it infinite possibility.*

**The Power of Joy:** *Even when, through our strength, we are free of our desires, we are happy.*

**To Dream, To Think:** *Whoever does not know how to enjoy the possibilities of dreaming and thinking, offered to man every second, ignores the nobility of life.*

*To be bored is to give up the dream and the spirit.*

*Boredom is the disease of empty souls and brains.*

*Life quickly becomes a horribly dull chore.*

**Patience:** *Patience is the first of victories: victory over oneself, over one's nerves, over one's weaknesses. Patience delivers the joy of not having given in.*

**Obedience:** *No great work is accomplished in selfishness and pride.*

*Obeying is a joy because it is a form of gift, of clairvoyant gift.*

*Obeying is a duty, because the common good depends on the disciplined coming together of many energies.*

*Obedience is the highest form of the use of freedom.*

*It is a constant manifestation of authority, authority over oneself, the most difficult of all.*

*No one is really capable of commanding others who is not first able to command himself, to tame in him the proud wanderer who would have liked to throw himself madly into the winds of adventure.*

**Kindness:** *By affection and by example we can do anything.*

*Shouting and storming about rarely solves problems.*

**Happy Isolation:** *The company of others is, most of the time, nothing but restlessness, noise, troubles revolving around mutual loneliness.*

*To constantly search for what is called stimulation is to be afraid of being in the presence of yourself.*

*Loneliness is a wonderful opportunity for the soul to get to know itself, to keep watch, to learn.*

*Only empty heads or fickle hearts are afraid of remaining silent in front of themselves.*

**Grandeur:** *It is often by doing, with maximum nobility, a thousand bothersome little things that you are great.*

*It is infinitely more difficult to stretch your soul a thousand times every day, without relief, than to give a single grand impulse at the moment of a visionary event.*

*Greatness is the nobility of the soul wearing down, dripping with the desire to give, each according to our duties, especially when they are stripped of those things that give rise to vanity.*

### Part Four: The Joy of Mankind

**Stong and Hard:** *The sun is gone. In half an hour it will be shade.*

*The birds, who sing madly in the gardens, perceive it.*

*There are roses everywhere, so gorged with light that they will soon perish.*

*The wood is already sleeping around a few tiled roots.*

*As always, the birds now begin to utter their sharp cries and their pleas, no doubt for the two lovers sitting there, dreamy, with a huge white hat lying across their knees.*

*All of life seems condensed here. Nothing lives apart from these birds, this dog which barks at the end of the world and these two hearts which steadily beat in the evening calm, heavy with the vibration of June.*

*How can one believe in hatred? Has one never seen the last roses go dim in the light evening silence?*

*We will have to tear ourselves away from this great country oasis soon.*

*It will be necessary to take, again, at the end of the path, the road where the cars tear up the ground through a sputtering, relentless rain.*

*There will be brutal lights, empty faces, soulless eyes.*

*This evening landscape is so clear. It is given with such a complete generosity! These dying roses, these bouquets of trees, these oat fields shimmering and gray,* these grave fir trees, all so pure and so simple. A childlike wonder rises in our being near the eternal youth of grasses, trees, and flowers.

We cannot hear anything anymore.

The night slicks down the roses.

The woods cut their jagged silhouette in the dying gleams. The last singing bird stops as if he too, from time to time, must simply listen to the silence. The two lovers have disappeared, hands trembling, a light wind in their hair.

I should move on.

I will go slowly, without disturbing the branches and the variety of the life which slides through the shadows. I will guess the outline of things. I will feel the dew blooming at the end of the grass, which will refresh the sun tomorrow when it climbs over the top of the wood.

Where is the night of hearts, from which the tender morning would spring?

We will have to renew our sorrows, resume our journeys through the fields and lost woods, among cold hearts.

Who will understand later, in the savage glimmers, before our trembling eyes, that we have just left the forests and the wheat fields, the shade and the silence?

Why falter? At the end of the path, we watch as cruel life snatches everything up in wolves' teeth.

We no longer look at anything, we no longer think, we no longer breathe this air charged with the scent of passing death.

Put out the lights. Let the night weigh upon our hearts.

Tomorrow, when daybreak reaches the crest of the trees, we will have before us only the closed horizon of man.

We will have to be strong and hard, joyful through nothing but the radiance of our souls.

Dying evening, silent and sure of dawn, gives us the peace of awaiting the light that is reborn, renewed, from the immense and auspicious night.

### Part Five: A Man's Duty

**The Great Retreat:** *To die twenty years too early or twenty years too late is of no consequence.*

*All that matters is to find a good death.*

*Only with this goal in mind can we truly begin to live.*

*As a simple soldier, I would gladly die tomorrow. The humility of my lot in life at the front reconciled me to such an outcome. Not having lived as a saint, to die as a soldier would be the most suitable thing.*

*Are my weeks numbered? Then it is best to make the most of these chances to purify my soul. I once dreamed of dying after a long illness, to better prepare myself for the inevitable. Such a death necessarily takes place in an atmosphere of pollution.*

*On the front, our preparation takes place with a feeling of power, in the unfolding of the will. I realize how lucky I am.*

*Perhaps I will return alive, more alive than ever before?*

*Either way, this great retreat, which life or death will close, will have been a blessing. I enjoy it freely, fully, like a nourishing and beautiful sun.*

*The soldier learns to be great among the most mundane or the most painful things. Heroism is to stand, to struggle, to be always alert, happy and strong, in nameless, unrecognized misery of the front, in the mud, the excrement, the corpses, the mist of water and snow, the endless and colorless fields, the total absence of outer joy.*

*Every day we move further away from the blissful world of yesteryear. Are we not already half-dead, we who advance, gritting our teeth, through the mists?*

*Always look at those who have less than you and rejoice in what you have, never lusting after ephemeral desires.*

*Life is always beautiful when you look at it with peaceful eyes, the light of a soul at peace.*

*We soldiers, we have nothing, and we are happy.*

*The joy of an unencumbered soul can only flourish when one has cast off this jumble of mental slavery.*

*If the soul did not rise, straight as the barrel of a gun, straight as the crosses over the graves, we would quickly sink into moral decay.*

**The Taming of Horses:** *But poetry is everywhere.*

**Intransigence:** *We listen to cynics more readily than to the message of righteous hearts.*

*I would rather see ten years of cold and abandonment, than one day feeling my soul emptied, voided of its living dreams.*

**The Cross:** *There are so many mediocre things on earth, low or ugly, that one day we would be overwhelmed by them if we did not carry within ourselves the fire which burns away ugliness, which consumes it and purifies us.*

*Art is our inner salvation, our secret garden that constantly refreshes and soothes us. Poetry, painting, sculpture, music, anything to escape from the mundane, to rise above the drying dust, to create something grand, instead of submitting to the small, to let out that spark of the extraordinary that each of us possesses, and convert it into a grandiose, devouring, inextinguishable fire.*

*Everything in life is a matter of faith and tenacity. Trust cannot be begged for; it has to be won. The best way to conquer is to first give of yourself.*

*We all carry our cross. We must carry it with a proud smile, so that we know that we are stronger than suffering, and also so that those who seek to harm us understand that their arrows reach us in vain.*

### Part Six: To Give Completely

**The Reconquest:** *The world is more and more preoccupied with banal, material, or simply animal joys. It maintains itself only by the principle of maximizing material wealth. Each man lives only for himself and allows the domination of life both within his own home and within the country, through a constant egoism which has converted men into hateful, embittered, greedy wolves, or corrupt and soulless half-men.*

*We will come out of this downfall only through an immense moral recovery, by re-teaching men to love, to sacrifice themselves, to live, to struggle and to die for a higher ideal.*

*The time is coming when saving the world will require this handful of heroes and saints to make the great reconquest.*

These noble and altruistic thoughts, these spiritual exercises, this renewed mysticism, could not be read by the Belgian people because of the merciless censorship put in place by their new authorities. Article 123 of the Belgian Parliament prohibits any publication, sale, or distribution of any intellectual property condemned by the vengeful courts of the post-Second World War era. Therefore, even today, Léon Degrelle's books cannot be sold in Belgian bookstores. This is how the false and misnamed "democracy" of today's Judeo-masonic empire understands freedom.

*Léon Degrelle with Rex's flag during exile*

*IV*

*Life in Constantina*

*(1952–1963)*

### Constantina, an Encaladas City[61]

Constantina is a city built according to the traditions of popular Andalusian architecture, white and whitewashed like perpetual snow, albino-white like the dove's nest. Located in the foothills of Sierra Morena and nestled in Guadalquivir Valley, much of its district falls within the Natural Park of Sierra Norte. Mixed together in this park, in a varied mass of forests, are stands of chestnuts, holm oaks, cork oaks, oaks, alders, elms, ash trees, and willows. It is a place where one may silently contemplate; where one can see, soaring through the sky, the silhouette of imperial eagles. It began as a remote Beturian Celtic settlement for the families who sought, in the depths of those steep mounds, the copper and silver that abounded in these wild places. Soon the earth was pierced, the surface was dug, and they extracted the metals that later shaped the history of man. From antiquity, even the Phoenicians and Punics came to the call of the mining trade. Later, the Romans arrived, giving the emperor's name to the place and carving out the road that would link Artigi (Ecija) with Emerita Augusta (Mérida). During Muslim rule, Constantina was the capital of the Firrish district. Reconquered by Ferdinand III, the Holy One, in 1247, the Muslims handed over their proud Almoravid castle of seven erect towers. Constantina was later fully retaken and finally tamed by the warlike nobles of the Seville region under Isabel la Católica, in the 1478 campaign. In 1916, His Majesty King Alfonso XIII granted the town the title of a city.

---

[61] [Spanish for whitewashed; refers to the white color of the town's buildings, which are painted white or whitewashed. The term has no reference to hypocrisy, as is often understood in American English.]

Constantina counts among its local history a very prominent event. When the French forces of Napoleon invaded, the town tried to avoid being looted, which was a common tactic used by the French Army. On April 9th, 1810, it did not waver at confronting the French Army with odd tactics. In hand-to-hand fighting, man to man, street to street, from the Mesones to the Alameda, the locals, in their onslaught against the invader, used old blunderbusses, hunting shotguns, farmhouse tools, and cooking utensils to repel the invaders. The town, after such an unequal confrontation and in such singular combat, was littered with three hundred dead defenders. Its struggle was not in vain, however, despite the hardships that followed. Constantina was freed from that stubborn occupation army in 1812.

This page of Constantina's bloody and tragic history was retold and masterfully described by "Juan de Majalimar" (a pseudonym of Léon Degrelle) in an article published in 1952 in the municipal magazine of the local fair. Referring to the unequal battle between the people of Constantina and the Napoleonic Army, he stated:

*There are moments when one must dispense with all prudence and must sacrifice for national honor. Spanish honor could not allow an old free land to be occupied without a fight. It was necessary that patriots everywhere, selflessly, even at the price of their own blood, raise their banner with pride in every place before the invaders. The day would come where the example and the memory of these heroes and martyrs of the first hours would lead the liberators to victory. Constantina thought in this way in 1810. It did not want to let its ground be sullied with foreign boots. If the French arrived, they were ready to receive them! [...]*

*To be reasonable was to renounce national pride and prefer living conquered to dying free. In the face of this terrible choice, Constantina did not hesitate: three hundred of its inhabitants fell during that hard and unequal battle before giving way. Three hundred! The exact same number as the historical and forever remembered "May 2nd" in Madrid. The small Andalusian mountain town made, for the common homeland, a sacrifice as great as the one that Madrid had made two years prior; that powerful capital, standing upright in its heroic impulse against the invader.*

The most fervent in dragging the people to the fight against the invader had been the Franciscan friar, Juan de Oviedo. With his cassock rolled up, crucifix in one hand and rifle in the other, he led the fight, together with Mayor Don Cipriano Antonio Santa Maria, who died without resignation on that bloody day.

Léon reiterated these heroic deeds because:

*It is necessary for the descendants of heroes to know what their ancestors did, so that they can find in these glorious memories additional reasons to be proud of their homeland and people, always ready for everything, for the sake of their freedom and greatness.*

Degrelle's detailed article captured the spirit of those three days of struggle and courage, valor and sacrifice, of a whole people who wrote its history in letters of blood, showing that national pride could not be tamed.

In those days, Léon Degrelle, using various pseudonyms, collaborated with several local publications for which he developed and exhibited the results of his research into the historical past of Constantina.

According to its census, Constantina numbered some fifteen thousand inhabitants. The residences and shops were crowded around the stylized shadow of the old castle, in the sloping streets of the hillside that formed the area of Las Cuestas, in the neighborhood of La Morería, and in the parishes of Santa Constanza and Santiago.

According to the records kept in the Municipal Archive of Constantina, Léon Degrelle officially resided in the village between 1957 and 1962, the date on which he requested a cancellation of the municipal water supply for his farm at La Carlina. His arrival to Constantina was actually much earlier, since his article, "The Looting of Constantina by the French on April 9th, 1810," had already appeared in the fair magazine, sponsored by the City Council, in 1952. In 1955, the notary public notarized the adoption court order, with the new name of León Ramirez Reina. He remained in Constantina definitively for ten years, from 1952 to 1962.

As a simple curiosity and historical premonition, on Monday, June 15th, 1936, just over a month before the National Uprising began, the Madrid newspaper *Informaciones* published on its front page a literary portrait on *"What is the Leader of the 'Rex' Movement Like?"* The article was written by Pierre Bonardi and described the personality of Léon Degrelle. In the description box, the journalist wrote:

*Although in the village cemetery of his native Bouillon, in the Ardennes, twenty generations of ancestors' sleep, those sunken eyes—round, vivid, and black—reveal the fact that the Spanish left traces three hundred years ago in the confines of Flanders and Brabant. The manly cut of his face, the firm arch of his eyebrows, are frequent traits in Andalusia. There is something Spanish in Léon Degrelle, surely from this comes his heat, his magnetism, and his contempt for danger.*

The description was illustrated with a charcoal drawing. It seemed to point out and highlight in Léon a return to the remote origins of his lineage.

## New Credentials as a Journalist

In 1949, Léon Degrelle spent a season as a refugee in Extremadura, which he always called, with a good sense of humor, "extremely hard"[62] in the town of Fuentes de Bejar, in the area of Béjar. Before moving to Constantina, he resided near Lora del Rio, where he was involved in the construction and planning of the "El Molino Azul" development.

This was issued by the National Delegation of Former Combatants in Seville, dated December 4th, 1951, with provincial number 13.758. He was also provided with an identity card in the name of "Juan Sanchís Duprés," a native of Algiers, with a residence at calle Los Molinos, in the town of Lora del Río.

On January 19th, 1950, the director of the social outreach weekly *Afán*, the Falangist, Víctor de la Serna, provided Léon Degrelle with journalist credentials, number 24, issued in the name of "Juan Sanchís Dupré," a Spanish citizen, who was a native of Algiers. These credentials were awarded to him by the Press Section of the Ministry of Labor. Degrelle became the newest editor/ correspondent for Serna's *Afán*.

Víctor de la Serna y Espina was the son of the famous Cantabrian writer Concha Espina. He had been the director and founder of the newspaper *El Faro* in Santander during the dictatorship of Primo de Rivera before moving to Madrid, where he worked with the newspapers *El Sol*, *El Imparcial*, and *La Libertad*. He was also the director of the daily *Informaciones*. He defended the position of the new European order represented by the Axis powers with articles written under his own name or using the pseudonym "Unus." He remained in charge of the newspaper until 1948, when he replaced his comrade, José María Alfaro, as President of the Press Association of Madrid. Serna served in that role until 1951.

---

[62] The word play here is that the region's name *Extremadura*, although etymologically unrelated, sounds like a shortened form of *extremadamente dura*, or extremely hard.

## His Long Stay at the Majalimar Estate

In the province of Seville, Degrelle stayed at the Majalimar estate. It was owned by Empresa Majalca S.A., of which the García Gascón brothers, from the Bejar area in the province of Salamanca, were shareholders.

The Majalimar estate—Valles del Paraíos—was the place where Degrelle laid low from 1949 to 1954. There, he conceived the idea of writing a colossal work, that is, telling the story of the last few years through great portraits: "I knew Hitler," "I knew Mussolini," "I knew Franco," "I knew Churchill" "I knew Pétain," "I knew Laval," etc.

Degrelle lived there for several years, isolated from almost everyone, lost in that wilderness of Sierra Morena. He was 20 kilometers (over 12 miles) from the nearest village, where he only had access to an old crank-up telephone to communicate with the outside world. It was in Seville that he carried out his first dealings and commercial transactions that offered him a livelihood. He then helped to set up a metallurgical industry near Guadalquivir. He also executed some excellent deals in Australia related to cotton. Later, in 1952, he became a builder to help provide shelter for fifty families on an American base.

Léon lived his life in exile with maximum dignity, thanks to the work he was doing. He was not concerned about money. The only thing he was interested in having were some works of art that reminded him that, since the beginning of time, men have always been dominated by the passion for beauty.

José Antonio Girón had sought him out and provided that quiet place, that huge estate, not far from the Sevillian village of Constantina. Léon fondly remembered, "I went frequently to the village and always passed by a shop run by an old woman, Matilde Ramírez Reina, whom I came to know very well over time. Soon she adopted me."

After he arrived in those serene surroundings and got settled in, it was not unusual to see him riding alone, or taking walks, strolling along like the Cid Campeador,[63] or as if he were "Don Quixote"himself. Sometimes he was seen with his great friend José Antonio Girón de Velasco, the Minister of Labor. It was while Léon resided at the Majalimar estate, that his first pseudonym, "Don Juan de Majalimar," was born. He used it in his writings at the time. His identity, however, was already well known and he did not go unnoticed by the local countrymen.

---

[63] *El Cid Campeador* refers to medieval Spain's eleventh century warlord and knight, Rodrigo Díaz de Vivar, whose exploits and battles figure prominently in Spanish history.

Degrelle soon made friends with them. They professed great admiration and respect for his joviality, interpersonal skills, vitality, and exceptional personality.

Since his arrival in Spain, Degrelle was finally beginning to reintroduce himself into a more normal life.

There is no lack of anecdotes from that time. Now fully integrated into Andalusian life, he made the processional tour as a penitent during Seville's Holy Week. He wore the hood of the Brotherhood of the Great Power to which he belonged and would usually walk the streets on Holy Thursdays. One year, participating as usual in the procession of the Brotherhood during Seville's Holy Week, Degrelle walked carrying a heavy, wooden penitent's cross. He stopped a meter from the Belgian Minister of Justice who was on a stand, contemplating the parsimonious march of the Andalusians and listening to the *saetas* that intoned the eternal grieving of the Passion. The scene moved Degrelle intensely.

He earned his first financial resources by importing machines and equipment into Spain for growth and development in the country. He initially planned to build a large steel company that manufactured special steels, working on metal rolling, but this idea fell through. He did not make enough money, so his earnings went to works of art, and useful and beautiful objects to surround himself with. They inspired him with the emotion of the supreme creative action of the human being.

## The Fantasy and the Charm of Andalusia
## Made His House "La Carlina" a Reality

In the early 1950s, he acquired a small vineyard called "*La Carlina*" from a friend, near the urban center of Constantina. It was located on a hill overlooking the town in a northwest direction. He bought the vineyard for twenty-eight thousand six hundred pesetas. It was an estate with decent acreage that had only one building, a small farmhouse. It was the first property that Léon bought and fixed up. The farmhouse would later become the caretakers' house, a family with three sons.

The name *Carlina* is related to a plant of fusiform root, with sharp, thorny leaves, and yellowish flowers, better known as *ajonjera*, although its botanical name is *Carlina angelica*.

Degrelle worked also as the director of an urban development company called Inmuebles Andaluces S.A. He was involved in the construction of a set of buildings in the vicinity of his vineyard. The development was organized on both sides of a central axis designed to be the main artery. These were smaller constructions, respecting the surroundings and the environment. They were built according to the guidelines of the popular architecture of the area, beautifying the landscape and respecting nature. The complex culminated in a villa of larger dimensions on the highest part of the property, with a circular tower that served as a lookout post for the various nearby houses. Next to the villa, a deep cistern was built for the collection and storage of rainwater, which would also be the guarantor of the water supply for all thirty houses erected on the slopes of the hill. Those were built as terraces to take advantage of the nooks and crannies of the irregular terrain. The estate was protected and fenced in by a perimeter wall.

Once the construction was completed, the houses were rented to the workers and military personnel of the United States Army stationed at the nearby Air Surveillance Base, built as a result of the 1953 agreement between Spain and the United States. The base was in a place called Cerro Negrillo and had a tracking radar to control aerial navigation in the Strait of Gibraltar and the southern aerial overhead of the Iberian Peninsula. Degrelle's idea was to set up, in an artistic way, the rural environment as a forerunner to inland tourism, intended for future visitors or vacationers seeking alternatives to the more common, crowded distractions of the beaches. At the same time, this would revitalize the villages that could not benefit from tourist plans centering on sun and beach, but who were, nonetheless, guardians of countryside treasures and natural environments of unparalleled beauty. He thought that perhaps the North American marines of the amphibious base of Rota, in the province of Cadiz, might be interested in those "bungalow" facilities located in the southern foothills of Sierra Morena, only 80 kilometers (50 miles) from Seville.

In the archive of the Municipal Council of Constantina are kept a total of thirteen records filed by León J. Ramirez Reina, as representative of the company Inmuebles Andaluces S.A., concerning the construction of the tourist villas in the vicinity of Castillo Blanco and Castillo Rojo. Three are from 1958, eight from 1959, one from 1960, and another from 1962, the last year of Degrelle's permanent residence in the city.

Years later, when the journalist Win Dannau asked him, "Were you a pampered child of the Americans, stationed on their military base?"

Degrelle replied:

*That is not true. I was not stationed at all; it was they who were stationed in my house. It was I who built all their houses for them. Moreover, they were delighted to reside in them and came to visit me from time to time, although they broke a Roman statue of mine. The best friend of the Americans here is [Otto] Skorzeny; otherwise, the biggest American magazine. [ . . . ]*

*Time? Life?*

*No, it was 'Look' Magazine. Well, I gave a great interview to 'Look' and it was Skorzeny who put me in contact with the editor of the magazine.*

Indeed, in January 1951, news was widely publicized that former members of the SS, such as E. Dollmann, Otto Skorzeny, and Léon Degrelle had founded what they called the Foreign Organization. It was headquartered in Madrid with branches in Egypt, Sweden, Morocco, Italy, and Argentina.

Photographs from 1955 have been preserved in which Léon Degrelle is seen directing the construction work on the houses he later leased to the Americans.

He turned out to be an extraordinary and improvising architect, with a true and authentic artistic genius for creation. He explained:

*In life, often only beauty frees the soul from great human misery. There are so many mediocre, low, or ugly things on earth that one day you could end up being buried by them if you do not carry in yourself the fire of beauty that burns away ugliness, consumes it, and purifies us. There are thirty-six ways to make art come alive: it is necessary to cultivate them with passion and love. They are our inner health, our secret garden that constantly refreshes us and hoists us up. Poetry, painting, sculpture, music, no matter what it is, the goal is to avoid the banal! Rise above the dust! Create the big instead of elevating the little! Highlight the extraordinary star that each of us possesses within himself and turn it into a great fire! Deathly and black are the times in which souls flee in the face of struggle. Luminous times are those that have seen these great fires of the soul mark out and dominate spiritual mountains.*

On this great plantation of La Carlina, it seemed as if his rural ancestry had been awakened inside him. As always, he lived in the present moment intensely. He was passionately interested in the lives of the laborers who were working their lands, their herds, their trees, the harvest. He sent letters to his friends that reflected his intense mood:

*Poetry is never lacking. I discover beautiful things every day: The sweetness of dawns full of chants and chimes, fog, powerful foliage, brilliant with a thousand gleams of golden yellow; noon where everything shines, where everything sleeps, except this or that, highlighting a blue smoke that rises from the enclosed forest; green and*

*orange twilights over the violet mountains, while all the animals return, small*
*donkeys in rows, two by two, dreamy and melancholy…*

## The Lord of the "White Castle"

On the upper part of the estate was built the house that would be Degrelle's
dwelling, personally designed and laid out, with certain reminiscences and
architectural influences from the Arab style of castles. This was later baptized by
popular imagery as "White Castle," the name with which it is still known today in
Constantina.

The interior of the house-fortress was designed and decorated with exquisite
taste and refinement. In the hall's decor, one can see the remains of the altarpiece
of the high altar from the Church of the Conception, located in Plaza de España in
Constantina. Degrelle had recovered and restored what he could save from the ruins
of that church. The Church of the Conception had been designed in the Baroque
style, with a belfry that crowned the exterior façade of the temple, formed by a
nave on two sides.

The "Tower of Homage" of the White Castle, visible from a distance, had a
height of six floors, and was decorated in the purest Sevilla Mudéjar style with tile
work from the traditional pottery of Triana. Beauty and harmony mixed with an air
of modernity, perfectly combining classic colors with Mudéjar and Andalusian
architectural features, and the white chalk typical of the Serrano villages.

The house was surrounded by beautiful gardens and a pond excavated in natural
rock. A Romanesque theater had also been designed, taking advantage of the slope
of the land. Several tiers had been marked, ending in a freestanding colonnade
where the proscenium was located. It had at least fourteen fountains of different
and capricious shapes, all of them adorned with arabesque tiles and ceramic spouts.
These were surrounded by flower beds adorned with plants and benches finished in
plinths also made of tile.

Degrelle even situated some old bronze-cast cannon that he brought from
Cadiz and incorporated them into the landscaping.

As one entered the house, there was a mosaic, in the purest Roman style,
representing the Leonine map of his old Belgium. It was the *Leo Belgicus* by Petrus
Kaerius, the famous emblematic map that contains the meeting of the seventeen
provinces that form Belgium. Of this territorial composition, in the shape and figure
of a lion, there are a half dozen cartographic versions. The heraldic lion, as the
emblem of the Netherlands, was first used in 1583 by Michel Eytzinger and, as a

concession to nostalgia and a feeling of belonging, the following inscription[64] could be read on the back:

> *Je goustaray le bien que je vería present.*
> *Je prendrey les douceurs à quoy je suis sensible,*
> *Le plus abondamment qu'il me sera posible.*

> *I will enjoy the good that I see present.*
> *I will take the pleasures that I am fond of,*
> *as abundantly as possible.*

On the porch in the back of the garden, on both sides of a niche that housed a stone sculpture, there was another inscription with text by García Lorca: "*Aire de Roma Andaluza le doraba la cabeza,*"[65] that is, "The air of Roman Andalusia gilded his head."

Before committing himself to building La Carlina, Degrelle never had any experience in construction of any sort. He personally had to put his own two hands to work creating complementary industries, making lime, installing a woodworking shop, and opening quarries. He had to extract eighty thousand tons of stone under the unforgiving sun of Andalusia, cut paths and make roads, bring electricity, and find water for that sparsely populated area.

Léon Degrelle employed many people from the village and contributed knowledge and culture, along with all his initiatives. His collaborators were his secretaries, Lolita and Aurora. Under his adopted name, an emotional Léon Degrelle always received many gifts from the humble, simple, and grateful people of Constantina on the day of St. John: chickens, hens, bacon, cheese, wine, paprika...

The original name with which Léon Degrelle was known when he received these gifts had a paradoxical evolution and metamorphosis. Upon his arrival, the people in Constantina knew him first as "Don Juan de Majalimar." Later, his friends called him "Juan Sanchís," the name on his second set of identification documents, and by the end of his stay among the locals, everyone referred to him as "Don Juan de la Carlina." The national documentation that was initially provided was under

---

[64] The inscription that follows is in early modern French; the translation that follows is my own.

[65] This couplet—*Aire de Roma andaluza / le doraba la cabeza*—is from the *La Sangre Derramada* (Spilled Blood) section in Federico García Lorca's long poem *Llanto por Ignacio Sánchez Mejías* (*Crying for Ignacio Sánchez Mejías*).

the name "Juan Sanchís," but after his adoption,[66] the National Identity Document then contained the name "León José Ramírez Reina."

Interestingly, at the time Degrelle was building La Carlina, his photograph was published in a French newspaper with an article reporting that he was in Brazil in the company of his new wife and his recent son, a wonderful mulatto child. The press did not even know what to invent anymore!

## The Visit of His Countryman Jean Thiriart and Maurice Bardèche

In 1954, Degrelle received a visit in Constantina from Jean Thiriart. Thiriart championed the conception of Europe as a great, single nation, an empire of four hundred million people.[67] Jean Thiriart was born in Brussels in 1922 and during his youth he had liberal and communist leanings, even joining the Unified Socialist Youth Guard, which was a mix of communists and socialists. His ideological turn was motivated by a family event: the divorce of his parents and his mother's remarriage to a Jew from Germany. This circumstance changed his way of thinking and put him in contact with nationalist circles. When the war began, he enlisted in the SS, integrating himself into an anti-terrorist section aimed at neutralizing the clandestine activities of communists operating in conjunction with Allied forces (communism allied with capitalism!) against Europe. He was part of the AGRA association, *Les Amis du Grand Reich Allemand* (Friends of the Great German Reich). When the war ended, he was sentenced to three years in prison and the loss of his political rights. His name was included in a list of men to be killed that was broadcasted by the BBC in London in the spring of 1943. He was not politically active again until the 1960s, when he founded, the *Jeune Europe* (Young Europe) movement in Brussels in 1963.

During Jean Thiriart's visit to Léon Degrelle, he was accompanied by the French writer, Maurice Bardèche, one of the founders of the European Social Movement in 1949, and later, was the leader of the European People's Movement in 1953.

---

[66] Degrelle's adoption is discussed in more detail later on.
[67] This important work by Jean-François Thiriart has been recently translated in a new edition by Dr. Alexander Jacob, published as *Europe: An Empire of Four Hundred Million* in 2021 by Arktos Media Ltd.

## Family Reunion

Degrelle's wife Marie-Paule was released from a Belgian prison on September 1st, 1950, after serving five out of the original ten years of her unjust sentence. She was released thanks to the government's softened policy of reducing the convictions of "minor" collaborators. "Democratic" justice was proving to be more akin to "tribal justice" where law is applied in the use of force, not in justice or equity. It had been imposed on her in a shameful and inhuman manner as a way to punish Degrelle after the Second World War. When the humiliation and suffering, which she overcame with fortitude, came to an end, she chose to reside in her native France with her family. Her health was very delicate at this time, and she suffered from acute depression. In 1951, she appears to have spent a few days with her exiled and clandestine husband in Andalusia. Marie-Paule had paid for the cost of defeat in excess. The situation she encountered in 1951 was not at all flattering.

Léon and Marie-Paule had married on March 29th, 1932. The union was celebrated and blessed by Monsignor Picard in Tournai. There was some tragedy when they lost their son Françoise, born January 28th, 1933, prematurely. Overall, they formed a true Christian home, giving life to a large family.

On May 6th, 1950, she was able to regain custody of their five remaining children after her release from prison: Chantal, the eldest daughter, nicknamed "Brigitte"; Anne, born July 26th, 1936; Godelieve, born April 14th, 1938; Léon-Marie, born May 4th, 1939 (he later died in a traffic accident on February 22nd, 1958); and Marie-Christine, born July 31st, 1944.

Meanwhile, Degrelle, always with the threat of capture and death by Belgian authorities, was fighting for his very existence in Spain under fake names and false documentation. He did not have a job that could provide stability for a family. His was an uncertain and stormy future, and he could not be certain of any possible hopeful and permanent solution. For all these reasons, and for the good of their children, they agreed to lead separate lives.

In the autumn of 1954, Marie-Paule again went to Spain to spend a short stay in La Carlina with Léon. It was their second encounter after ten years of forced separation and absence. There remains evidence of her last visit to La Carlina in several photographs taken in October 1954 in Degrelle's garden, where they enjoyed the sunset over the profiles of that wild mountain range that could be seen from the terrace of the estate.

To avoid the grave dangers and problems that were continually surrounding him, Léon and his wife, extinguished their joint partnership and opted for free, voluntary, and spontaneous separation. The legal proceedings and matrimonial agreements that would henceforth govern their segregated lives and their private property were taken over by his wife's attorney, Mr. Thèvenet, who, after the appropriate procedural steps, finally succeeded in having the Court of First Instance in Brussels, on November 12th, 1954, rule on the granting of concessions and separation of property between the spouses Degrelle-Lemay.

## Léon Degrelle Speaks for "Youth"

On December 9th, 1954, an extensive interview with Léon Degrelle was published in number 578 of the Falange's weekly *Juventud*. The interview was conducted by his dear friend and comrade, the illustrious journalist José Luis Gómez Tello. Tello was a Falangist from its first days and also a veteran of the Blue Division on the Eastern Front, who had, reciprocally, a great admiration and a special affection for Degrelle.

The interview addressed topics such as Europe, spiritual politics, Spanish youth, and a book of meditations at this time of the world, whose text was published and contained three photographs. One photograph, taken in the aftermath of the war, is of Léon in campaign uniform surrounded by young enthusiasts. In the other two photographs, which were taken during a conversation, León appears dressed in a light-colored trench coat sitting on a sofa; in one of them he is alone, portrayed in the foreground, and in the other he is in the company of José Luis Gómez Tello.

Tello began his article by saying, "The man of Cherkassy's odyssey is before me," and then gave a short summary of what the epic was, with Degrelle at the head of his Walloon Legion volunteers, who, under his command, knew so well how to keep the flag of Belgium in the fight against communism on its own turf. The journalist gave the reader a tour of the combat zones, the fighting, and the heroic feats (Cherkassy, Donetz, Gromovaja-Balka, Jablenskaya, Elbruz, Tjerjakov, Túpass, Dorpat, Lake Peipus, Pomerania, Lindenberg, the Stettin Bridge, etc.), where his comrade-in-arms Léon stood out prominently, with "…seventy-two close combat engagements and five wounds," who "in 1941 came to the front as a simple machine gunner and by the end of the conflict had become a general on his war merits."

When asked about his work as a poet, writer, and speaker, Degrelle replied:

*My work as a journalist amounted to twenty articles per year. These were distributed throughout our publications Rex, Le Pays Réel, and L'Avenir. I have written since I was fourteen, whereas my work as a public speaker began in Mexico, when I fought beside the Cristeros who were suffering religious persecution.*

José Luis Gómez Tello observed that "deep inside this man there is a great fire, a faith, the desire to make a revolution of souls." He listened carefully to him say:

*The greatness of the virtues tempered in pain and sacrifice was never in vain, which is worth more than hatred or death; sooner or later they will shine, just as the sun that arises from the depths of night. In the future, rehabilitation will not suffice. Men will only bow to the heroism of the soldiers of the Eastern Front of the Second World War. They will also say that they were in the right, they were really in the right: negatively, since Bolshevism represents the end of any value; positively, because the united Europe for which they fought was the only—perhaps the last— chance of survival for a wonderful old continent.*

Since they had a copy of *The Burning Souls* in front of them, Léon indicated to Tello the paragraph that says, "The salvation of the world is in the will of souls who have faith," which led the journalist to formulate for himself, the following reflection:

*When I said a poet and a man of action—so I had defined Degrelle at the beginning of the talk—I think of ourselves, the Falangists, summoned by José Antonio for the wonderful synthesis of our doctrine. There are times that have a similar beat. Only a few years later, men of Degrelle's legion and men of the Blue Division would die together on the same Eastern Front defending a threatened civilization. Only a few years later, and in the memory of those dead, wherever their desecrated tombs may be today, I spoke with Degrelle about this Europe that must be born of the faith of those who fought and died or else she cannot survive. This is also my faith in the unity of Europe, which began in the unity of her fighters.*

The interview moved easily along the naturally emerging range of topics:

The Burning Souls

*JT:* The Burning Souls *is an intimate, spiritual book. Written in prose, it reminds us of the poetry of Gille and Gauchez; of Gilkin's "Cherry Blossom"; of Kinon's serene and fiery thoughts. These were daily meditations Degrelle was writing on pieces of paper he kept in his pocket. Later, he selected the ones that would make up the book.*

*Is politics over for you? Are you returning to the world of spirituality after these years of action?*

On hearing this question, he thinks for a moment, as if he were recalling his youthful years.

LD: *No because I do not conceive this separation of worlds. The book is spiritual, but at the same time political. Poetry is in the blood of politics; it is its foundation. It could be described as a lyrical book of political meditations. When it comes to the political, the social, the important thing is that there be something noble inside. Politics is both realism and idealism. Realistically we must know that man is dust, in the biblical sense. The mission of the politician is to make man an immortal being. Without the ideal, he becomes spiritually bankrupt. Great revolutions and great experiences fall apart when they lose this inner light, this fluidity.*

JT: *What are the differences between this book and your previous works?*

LD: *All constitute a continuity of thought. The seed of these pages lies in my time as an activist for religious action. When I used to explain Christ's life to the workers in communist neighborhoods, do you know what I intended? Only to live for the ministry. I did not feel the slightest enthusiasm for throwing myself into the political mudhole. It was then that I understood that redemption had to begin with the clearing of the land. I have always felt the melancholy of that past. I wanted to bring people to heaven, not to a political party. I wanted to free my country from what was vile. For me, politics is a work of faith in the living and real contact between the masses and power, in the fruitful union between citizens divided by artificial struggles. It is this faith that I have wanted to gather, my thoughts matured by pain; faith, as in the days when a breath of idealism spread out exalting spiritual forces and the excellent memories of a past of glory and struggle.*

JT: *I remember Willy Koninckx's message: "Our Lord, have mercy on our anguish. Let us be satisfied with bread and salt. Keep in us hope and a smile. Give us encouragement and strength." Without faith there is nothing solid. Our time suffers from a lack of faith. It is its most serious moral disease, which must be fought by all means. There is a singular and unique exception: Spain. He points out to me a paragraph in the book:*

*The salvation of the world is in the will of souls who have faith. For this reason, mystical Spain, the Spain of Santa Teresa and San Juan de la Cruz, San Francisco Javier and San Ignacio, for this I believe in your mission, a privileged mission among all: to pour into souls in agony the blood of your burning soul.*

LD: *Do you know what explanation I give to failures that seemed impossible, with their boast of material means, in the face of communism? To the fact that I had not been able to bring about a state of faith, of the crusader. Cold reigns in all souls. Struggling souls are equally materialistic: some have snow, others have refrigerators.*

Good Faith and Bad Faith

*JT: But communism is fanaticism; fanaticism comes from faith.*

*LD: That can be admitted, but there is good faith, which is authentic, and bad faith, which is false. This is also an absence of faith. Our mission was precisely to guide those people towards us with faith, even if it was bad, to purify it in our struggle. Even today, I believe that the world can be saved when people who are always wholesome are given an ideal.*

The Unity of Europe

*JT: Today it seems that this collective ideal is Europe.*

*LD: Yes, let us add Christian Europe. The time of nationalism has passed, as in the Renaissance, it passed from the province to the nation. The love of the homeland will be preserved, increased even, by joining it to a great common spiritual mission, but the normal and human union of Europe will be achieved. If we want to survive, we need to do so without hindrance. The current mistake lies in wanting to build that unity on economic material and materialistic interests. Even so, Europe's role will be diminished, in relation to the young people with immense resources, who are going to change the world's physiognomy. I am not just referring to North America, but to Asia and the Hispanic-American peoples. This is another reason to believe in the spiritual mission of Spain.*

*JT: So, what will Europe be?*

*LD: An immense bulwark of faith.*

Peaceful coexistence

*JT: There is now much talk of "peaceful coexistence" with communism...*

*LD: It cannot exist. Either communism is crushed or the civilized world sinks. There is no possible coexistence between angels and demons. It is necessary to have something better to offer people attacked by Marxist materialism than simply a materialistic anti-Marxism. It is time to offer, not time to ask. By this time, we must build up men and generous idealistic people...*

Spain

*JT: How Spain is perceived in the world is strongly influenced by Keyserling[68] and by those who consider us too idealistic...*

*LD: "Burning souls can do absolutely everything." It is the last paragraph of the first chapter of my book, devoted precisely to Spain. Your country has the ardor*

---

[68] Hermann von Keyserling (1880—1946) was a German philosopher and popular essayist.

*to give. Spain is the only people in Europe who know how to give. The Spaniard is detached from everything material. He is independent from it. This is his great moral reserve, the most necessary in Europe. Money...there is always too much money in the world. Force...there is always too much force in the world. The only thing lacking is this spiritual energy, which lives in the deepest layers of the Spanish people. Even in the peoples we admire today for their recovery, it is observed that they have been infected with materialism. This work by Francisco Franco and La Falange—making Spain a spiritual reserve—will not be appreciated much by the world.*

*The European Revolution*

*LD: There is no choice, either spiritual revolution or failure of the century. It is necessary for the souls of the people to make a heroic effort. National revolution, yes. Social revolution, yes. European revolution, yes. Above all, a spiritual revolution. This is a thousand times more necessary than external order, than external justice, than a brotherhood merely mouthed.*

*Spanish Youth*

*JT: We have closed a circuit of ideas. We return, of course, to our starting point.*

*LD: What I like most about Spanish youth is that they have faith. They have, like Spain, a healthy heart and the new and strong body like earlier times in the world. They are in a wonderful position to radiate their truth and faith.*

*Decisive Hours*

*The conversation has ended. Still, outside our talk, there are unfinished themes about the world's landscape, which parade with their anguish and restlessness. Just before I draw it to a close, I ask Degrelle, almost suddenly:*

*JT: Where is the world headed?*

*LD: (who has a powerful voice, responds in a low tone): Towards its redemption.*

On December 30th, 1954, in issue five hundred eighty-one of the weekly *Juventud*, a two-page article appeared, signed by Léon Degrelle and entitled "The Heart and the Stones." It was, in fact, a chapter from *The Burning Souls*, and was reproduced, as stated at the end of the text, "with special permission by the author."

## The Great Scandal

On December 15th, 1954, Spanish press agencies reported that Léon Degrelle attended a ceremony in Madrid, in honor of the Spanish veterans of the Russia campaign who were members of the glorious Blue Division. He was there, along with many others, including the Minister General Secretary of the Movement, Raimundo Fernández Cuesta.

The event was organized by the Madrid Municipal Council and was held in the Patio de Cristales at the town hall. The ceremony included awarding the city's silver medal to eight veteran citizens of the capital: Gerardo González García, Carlos Junco Díaz, Desiderio Morlán Novillo, Pedro Pérez Gallego, Regino Hernández Benito, Leonardo de la Peña Hernández, Mariano Remón López, and Timoteo Domínguez Quintana. They were all former prisoners of the Soviet Union who had just returned to Spain after their release from painful captivity, having finally been repatriated on April 2nd, 1954.

The event was presided over by the Mayor of Madrid, José Finat y Escrivá de Romaní, Count of Mayalde, who had previously been the Ambassador in Berlin and Director General of Security. He was a close, personal friend of Degrelle and also the mastermind, as will be remembered, of his adventuresome departure from the hospital in San Sebastián in August 1946.

The award ceremony for the Blue Division veterans was attended by many high-level personalities, among them the Minister of Air, Lieutenant General González Gallarza; the National Delegate of Health, Agustín Aznar Gener; the National Delegate of Veterans, General García Rebull; the President of the National Institute of Forecasting, Carlos Pinilla; the Duchess of Pastrana, wife of the City Mayor and Mayor of Court; the former Civil Governor of Logroño and a Blue Division veteran himself, Alberto Martín Gamero; and the Count of Montarco, who entered a room full of old comrades and friends.

The event began with the reading of the municipal agreement to award the medal to such heroic soldiers by the Secretary of the Town Hall, Mr. Fernández Villa. He then expressed gratitude to the mayor and duty to justice held by the city council, who were seeking to recognize those men of Madrid. They had all been through a terrible ordeal and still knew how to honor the name of their homeland so highly. A letter from the Minister of the Army, Lieutenant General Agustín Muñoz Grandes, was then read, celebrating the event "with a hug for those magnificent combatants who deserve everything." Minister of Air Lieutenant General González Gallarza dedicated an emotional speech to the fallen, those who died on the Russian steppe. Minister General Secretary of the Movement Fernández Cuesta emphasized the significance of the ceremony.

After the awards were presented to the Blue Division veterans, Gerardo González García, on behalf of his colleagues, read a few pages expressing the sentiments of all the honorees present, testifying to their gratitude to the nobility and generosity of the people of Madrid for their gesture.

Degrelle attended that emotional commemoration for his comrades of the Eastern Front who had fought with faith and courage in the glorious Blue Division. They suffered the hardness and martyrdom of the concentration camps and Soviet prisons as prisoners of war for eleven long years. Degrelle's presence in the municipal hall was highly celebrated by his Spanish comrades. This was his first public appearance since he left General Mola Hospital in 1946 and occurred only a few days after the Court of First Instance of Cazalla de la Sierra issued his legal adoption record by Mrs. Matilde Ramírez Reina. He was granted Spanish nationality by the adoption because he was legally stateless when Belgium condemned and deprived him of his Belgian nationality. Degrelle elected Spanish citizenship through this legal procedure.

The official news agency, EFE, disseminated news of the event to the media, including in its press release the name of Léon Degrelle among the other high-level functionaries. Degrelle's presence among such distinguished officials of the Spanish State did not go unnoticed. The publication of his name in the media triggered great scandal, fury, and controversy among the sectarian and irreconcilable Belgian authorities.

The Belgian press picked up the news of the discovery of Degrelle's whereabouts and put out great headlines on the front pages of its papers. Borrowing from the EFE news agency, the newspaper *Le Soir* published, on December 17th, the headline: "Degrelle in Madrid." The diplomatic uproar was stirred up again.

On December 19th, 1954, Degrelle gave an interview to the well-known weekly magazine *El Español*, which was headed by the former secretary of the Jonsista, Juan Aparicio. The "Dialogue with Léon Degrelle," which we already spoke of when referring to his work *The Burning Souls*, contained six well-selected, recent photographs, which had been taken a few days prior to the publication. The one that was featured towards the top of the conversation with reporter Jiménez Sutil was a close-up portrait of Léon proudly wearing the Iron Cross with Oak Leaves about his neck. In the second photograph, Degrelle is reading the English newspaper, *Manchester Guardian*, dated December 2nd, 1954, with the following caption: "This is the most recent photograph of Léon Degrelle." Among Degrelle's first statements during the interview, this one resounded: "And I was a very close friend of José Antonio."

> *JA: And why do you not return to your country?*
>
> *LD: Oh! I wanted to go back. I am not a war criminal. I was a soldier. There is no just cause for which I should be afraid.*
>
> *JA: So, what is going on?*
>
> *LD: I offered to return to be tried under conditions that they did not accept. I requested to be dressed in my uniform, to allow for wide publicity of my allegations and of my defense, and that they authorize full broadcasting of the trial.*

Concerning the other four photographs, in one, Léon is next to his daughter, two others are snapshots showing him with expressive, concentrated gestures during conversation, and the last is a photo taken some time during the war, with Degrelle dressed in a German military uniform.

A summary of this interview appeared in the Belgian press on Christmas Day.

On December 22nd, the Spanish Ambassador to Brussels sent the following note to the Belgian Minister for Foreign Affairs:

> *As a follow-up to the news published in the press regarding the alleged presence of Léon Degrelle at the ceremony that took place at the Madrid Municipal Council on the fifteenth of this month, I am authorized to inform Your Excellence of the following:*
>
> 1) *That he had not been invited; and*
> 2) *That, from a supplementary inquiry carried out after the ceremony, it turns out that he was not among the many individuals who attended.*

During a parliamentary session on December 21st, 1954, Belgian Senator Cornez, hurled a battery of questions to the Minister of Foreign Affairs, Spaak, interested in the discovery of Léon Degrelle in the capital of Spain, demanding he proceed immediately to renew the latent extradition request.

Interestingly, Degrelle's public appearance coincided with a ceremony in Belgium commemorating the tenth anniversary of the deadly battle of von Rundstedt's[69] Ardennes offensive, in which the then Colonel Degrelle had participated and distinguished himself as a combatant.

---

[69] Reference to Field Marshal Karl Rudolf Gerd von Rundstedt.

On the return of Minister Spaak from the NATO meeting taking place in Paris, Oscar Behogne of the Christian Social Party, the former Belgian Minister of Public Works, and a Member of Parliament in 1954, presented an interpellation in Parliament on December 22nd. He requested, as a matter of urgency, that measures be taken and the extradition of Degrelle be requested again now that he had emerged from hiding and his whereabouts were known. For his part, the President of Belgian Veterans and Resisters' Commission asked Spaak to make a strong written protest to Francisco Franco, for the "odious public exhibition of Degrelle accompanied by the ministers of his government."

Spaak addressed Parliament from the speaker's gallery, stating:

> *Since my return to Belgium yesterday morning, I have been concerned about the revelations made in the press regarding the presence of Degrelle at an official reception in Madrid.*
>
> *The Spanish government states that Degrelle was not invited to the Madrid venue and that, according to the inquiries it later conducted, it can be said that he was not present. Any debate on this point seems to me to be impossible, although it does not sway my conviction that Degrelle is currently in Spain. He has recently written a book that has been published there* [The Burning Souls*] and he also gave an interview to a magazine. I have asked the Spanish government to keep its promise to hand Degrelle over to Belgian authorities. I have also asked the Ambassador to emphasize that all Belgians would react with indignation against any protection, whatever it might be, by the Spanish government for someone who is not only a traitor to Belgium, but also an odious criminal of common crimes...*

Brussels once again mobilized its foreign ministries to order the extradition of Léon Degrelle ten years after the conclusion of the Second World War.

Faced with the new dust up, the Belgian government, on December 23rd, 1954, once again called for the surrender and repatriation of the former rexist leader with renewed intransigence and harsh terms. It may be recalled that the first request for extradition from the Belgian government had been made to the Spanish government on October 28th, 1946.

On December 23rd, 1954, the EFE news agency published a redaction, noting that, despite the news broadcast at the time, the presence of the "Belgian politician" at the event on December 15th in Madrid could not be confirmed. It was an attempt to quiet the diplomatic controversy that had arisen.

On December 24th, in the middle of Christmas Eve, the socialist leaning magazine *Pourqoi Pas?* released an issue with the same familiar hatred and viciousness with a caricature of Degrelle with a rope around his neck, hanging from a tree on the cover. The text below said "trapped."

The Spanish government continued to insist that it had no record of Léon Degrelle's attendance at the event of the Blue Division veterans.

For its part, the Flemish daily *Nieuwe Gazet* provided information that was more accurate and closer to reality. It reported that, since his arrival in Spain, Degrelle had never left the territory, living between Seville and Madrid, and using documentation under the name of "Juan Sánchez."

Journalistic disinformation did not cease. All kinds of stories were invented without any foundation, published only to stir up a big fuss through sensationalism. They were writing fiction nonstop, as if it were a mystery novel. Hack journalists would find an opening and pour in their insidious lies. It was written that he was "War Criminal Number One." At other times, it was brazenly asserted that he lived comfortably thanks to the hidden funds he had deposited in Swiss banks and then transferred to Spain. In other articles they pointed to Degrelle as the head of a great secret neo-Nazi political movement that was operational throughout the European continent. Everything was fair game. There were no limits to the shameless media deception.

Since it had been published that Degrelle might be using the pseudonym, "Juan Sánchez," the Spanish Minister, faced with contradictory versions, opened an investigation to clarify the facts. He concluded that Léon Degrelle was not on the guest list of the event and that perhaps, since the official EFE news agency's initial report had been revised, it could have been a mistake by the journalist who wrote the article on the event. Moreover, there was no news to confirm that Léon Degrelle was in Spain. His name, either as Degrelle or as the pseudonym, was not included in any document officially issued by the Spanish administration.

The response provided by Spain was by no means satisfactory to Belgium. Belgian Ambassador to Spain Prince Eugène de Ligne met with Spanish Foreign Minister Martín Artajo on December 27th, to remind him of the promise he had made in 1946 to hand over Degrelle in the event that he was in Spain. Artajo assured him that before deciding on the matter, an investigation would be carried out. De Ligne was called back for consultations in Brussels on January 5th, 1955. The next day, de Ligne met with his Foreign Minister, along with Secretary General Scheyven, and the Director General of Politics of his department, Baron Delvaux de Fenffe. At the end of this diplomatic summit, the Belgian Minister himself, at a press conference, provided an official note stating: "The Belgian Ambassador to Spain has been asked not to rejoin his post, but to remain at his disposal until the moment a response from the Spanish government is received in Brussels."

The intention of the Belgian government in not reinstating the Ambassador to his post was to continue tightening the rope until the Spanish government responded positively to their request for Léon Degrelle's extradition. The Belgian government was prepared to reject any claim by the government of Spain that Degrelle was a political refugee or any other type of excuse.

Meanwhile in Belgium, in activist campaigns and propaganda, left-wing organizations, socialists, communists, partisans, resisters, and *lumpen*[70] mobilized to spur their government on. Among other groups of rioters, revelers, and politicians of all Marxist stripes, they organized vengeful protests and demands through the Union of the Brotherhoods of the Secret Army, the Liege Committee of Action and Surveillance, the National Committee for the Friendship of Political Prisoners and Prisoners of Spain, and the Belgian Union of Political Prisoners.

The issue led to an institutional crisis. It was the most highlighted news of the last half of 1954 and the first weeks of 1955. The controversy played out in the streets and in Parliament. There was talk of little else. The Belgian government, nervous about the turn that events had taken, was impatient. The press, with large headlines on their front pages, ramped up their spin significantly. All the newspapers began a dizzying, long-distance race to print the most extravagant and sensationalist news using threatening and excessive language. *Le Peuple*, *Le Soir*, *La Cité*, *Nieuwe Gazet*, *De Standaart*, and *Het Handelsblad* printed their editions in a monothematic and concordant way, wanting to add some new piece of information with each subsequent article. They did not give up fanning the flames, hoping to set the story ablaze.

On January 4th, 1955, in the midst of this high tension, Degrelle wrote a letter, which he sent to the newspaper *La Libre Belgique*. It was published in the January 11th edition. Degrelle wrote:

> *I offer to stand before an ordinary court of justice, free, without traps or cheating, so that from the stand I can face, alone, the enormous machinery of a hostile regime. If this is accepted, I would present myself the next day, with my humble possessions, to the nearest Belgian Embassy. If it is not accepted? In that case, I will wait, assuming that, no one should be surprised if, from the outside, I speak from time to time...*

---

[70] [German; in Marxist thought, this is a lower-class stratum that has little class consciousness and is easily manipulated. The *Lumpenproletariat* thus had little revolutionary potential, contrasted with the *Proletariat*. The author's use of it here likely denotes simply "easily manipulated."]

When he demanded to appear in a regular court, he did so because a public hearing would be guaranteed in those courts, as opposed to being tried, as was the intention of Belgium's masonic government, by a war council, where, behind closed doors, a new political state-crime would be secretly carried out.

The notes presented by the Spanish Ambassador on the non-official invitation to the December 15th veteran's event were of no use, regardless of the investigation carried out to determine, at least from an official capacity, that Degrelle had not attended. In the *notes verbales* (verbal notes) and communiqués, in fact, it was doubted that he had attended under his real identity, although it was suspected that if he had come, he might have done so surreptitiously under the name of "Juan Sánchez."

In order to try to resolve the crisis, the Spanish government informed the Belgian government that Léon Degrelle had left Spain, so it was not possible to fulfill the extradition request. The rumor was put out at the same time that Léon Degrelle was in Tangier, thus outside Spanish jurisdiction. This diplomatic response was intended to put an end to this issue, which was keeping relations between the two countries strained and practically broken. As the Spanish response was considered satisfactory at the present moment, with respect to the Spanish government's promise to hand Degrelle over in the hypothetical assumption that he returned to Spanish territory, it was announced that the Belgian Ambassador would return to his post in the "very near future."

On January 11th, three weeks after the first note was made, the Spanish Ambassador formally delivered the Spanish government's reply, stating that, after a thorough investigation:

> *Degrelle, in effect, entered Spain clandestinely, but the search for his location has proved unsuccessful. This seems to show that he has once again left Spanish territory. In any case, the Spanish government wishes to emphasize that at no time has it allowed foreign refugees into its national territory to carry out political activities of any kind.*

The letter omitted any reference to the way in which Degrelle may have entered Spain and his location after December 15th of the previous year, an interval in which it appeared that he had been in Spain's capital using a pseudonym.

This response did seem to take care of the concerns expressed by the Belgian government and they seemed satisfied. An official record of Léon Degrelle's stay in Spain had now been registered, and from now on he could not remain on Spanish soil. So, the Belgian government sent the following communiqué to Spain on January 13th:

> The Belgian government deduces, from the note that was submitted to it, that the expulsion order concerning Léon Degrelle remains in force, and that the Spanish government will ensure that any contravention of this decision be prevented in the future. In the event that the person concerned violates it, the Spanish government will hand him over to the Belgian authorities in accordance with its own declaration of October 28th, 1946.

In order to calm public opinion, the content of the official documents between Madrid and Brussels on December 15th was provided to the media at that time. While they were accepted, most did not really believe it.

This exchange of notes put an end to the diplomatic crisis. On January 18th, 1955, Prince Eugène de Ligne, finally returned to Madrid again to take his post.

The British Embassy in Spain was not convinced. It drafted a comprehensive report to corroborate Belgium's suspicions concerning the uninterrupted stay of Degrelle in Spain since his arrival in May 1945, and the activities that he had participated in. The report described Degrelle's property in Seville and even mentioned the existence of a suspected business operation or small office in Madrid. The British memorandum also referred to the good relations that Léon Degrelle had with his Falangist comrades and with relevant and influential Spanish authorities.

Certain international media outlets did not believe the Spanish report, so they continued to question and cast doubt on the assertion that Degrelle had left Spain; however, some media confirmed his whereabouts in Tangier, as was the case with the American newspaper *The New York Times*. Perhaps through certain leaks in Spanish diplomacy, the *New York Times* reported in its January 27th issue that Degrelle had settled in that city in northern Morocco.

## A Forbidden Interview with the United Press Agency

On February 2nd, 1955, Degrelle gave an interview, which he sent in writing to the United Press's correspondent. It was immediately censored, mutilated, and misrepresented in the media governed by plutocratic elements. In a tacit pact of silence, Belgian newspapers did not reproduce the interview's contents or any of its explanatory statements, assuming that this would serve as political propaganda for the persecuted.

This attitude of concealing the truth and censorship forced his Belgian comrades of the Social Movement, led by Jean Robert Debbaudt and headquartered on rue de Serbie in Brussels, to distribute, on June 15th, 1956, the full text of the interview on the streets of the Belgian capital. They did so at great risk to themselves. This distribution took place a year after demonstrations were held regarding the interview's censorship and were also intended as a birthday present to Degrelle. A sepia-colored folio was compiled and dispersed. The front was a sharp photograph of Léon dressed in military uniform as a combatant officer on the Eastern Front, his war decorations shining, among them his Iron Cross with Oak Leaves and the saw-toothed cross of Saint Andrew, the emblem of Burgundy as well as a rexist symbol.

The text of the interview was as follows:

*UP: Are you aware, Mr. Degrelle, of the controversy surrounding you and of the demands of the Belgian government for extradition?*

*Degrelle: Yes, and I hate it so much. Ten years after the Second World War, I am astonished.*

*UP: The accusations against you are serious. How do you respond? Were you linked to Hitler's Germany before the war?*

*LD: In no way. In 1939, the Rexist Movement wanted to keep Belgium strictly neutral: neither with the Germans, nor with the anti-Germans. We wanted peace. This new European civil war seemed to me to be senseless, I wanted to avoid it for my homeland and, at the same time, preserve Belgium as a land of possible reconciliation between the two warring sides, which was still the expectation in the West at that time. This attitude was politically and humanely very defensible.*

*UP: And after the invasion of Belgium?*

*LD: In the summer of 1940, after the French defeat, almost everyone in Europe believed in Germany's ultimate victory, that they would be victorious for a thousand years, as the current Belgian Foreign Minister, Mr. Spaak, said. We, who had not wanted this war, tried, once it was lost, to limit the ravages. That is why we "collaborated," as it is said, not to serve Hitler's Reich, but to try to straighten out our country, which was in decline. How could we lift it up without working with Germany, which then had the fate of Belgium in its hands and that of almost all of Europe? What did Chancellor Adenauer do, on the other hand, with the Allies in 1945? Were we wrong? That is debatable. What is indisputable is our good faith and our love only toward our country, which is what led us into this difficult matter.*

*UP: And your activity on the Eastern Front?*

*LD: It was motivated exactly for the same reasons. Thousands of Belgians, two divisions, actually, were with me in Russia to fight Bolshevism, but also to win the glory and privileges that would enable us to deal more effectively with the Germans in the event of their victory. The Reich was defeated, yes, but it could have triumphed, and, in this case, the merits acquired on the anti-Soviet front would have served our homeland enormously. So, as you can see, it was for Belgium that we fought and for which so many of our volunteers died heroically.*

UP: *What about the war crimes?*

LD: *I have not committed any war crimes. Never, nowhere. To keep saying that I have committed them, as is still being done, is a horrible slander. Never has a court condemned me, nor tried me, for a war crime, whatever it may have been. I was sentenced to death in absentia on December 27th, 1944, as a political leader and as a volunteer on the anti-Soviet front, and for nothing else. They need to be logical here. A few years ago, Spanish General Muñoz Grandes was received in Washington and at the Pentagon with great honors. He was my colleague on the Eastern Front and commanded a division exactly like mine. He has now been awarded by the United States. So how can they claim that, for the exact same action, I should continue to be persecuted savagely? Volunteers from the Eastern Front were precursors. Without the millions of young Europeans who died in the snow on the steppes, the Soviets would have arrived at the Atlantic by 1943 or 1944. We did our best to cut them off. I see no criminal action in that.*

UP: *Do you forget that common law crimes have been laid against you?*

LD: *Yes, they have been alleged, even proclaimed in diplomatic notes, in the United Nations, and, with great alarm, in the press and on the radio. The trials held in Belgium against the real culprits, and the investigations by the commission for war crimes have shown, one after another, that not one of the accusations was justified. So, when they repeat this, they are lying. Even with the best evidence, not one court has tried or convicted me for even one of those allegations. It would have been easy for them because in my current circumstances I could not even defend myself.*

UP: *So why not return to Belgium to explain it clearly?*

LD: *Because I would not be allowed to explain anything, either clearly or in any other way. I do not understand how international opinion is still not aware of the unbelievable judicial situation created in Belgium after the war. If I were to present myself in Brussels, I would be shot, not tried. A new law, in effect, prohibits the opening of proceedings for a person convicted in absentia after six months from the time of conviction. This means that none of us, often condemned without knowing it, can demand justice. The sentence is executed without hesitation. We only have the right to silence ourselves and, in my case, to die against a wall in a barracks courtyard. Moreover, the courts that were created to try Belgian "collaborators" are nothing more than caricatures of justice relying on emergency decrees, made in London during the Second World War, by an exiled and highly questionable Belgian government. They were created without the interested parties knowing anything about them. These decrees, and the laws that followed them, however, are used retroactively, which has given all this repression a truly monstrous extra-judicial character. On this basis, "dossiers" have been opened against more than half a million Belgians (20 percent of the electoral body), condemning tens of thousands, some sentenced to face firing squads; for hundreds, a prison sentence amounting to more than a million years. This is madness.*

*UP: What if you could be tried normally?*

*LD: Then I would present myself to the Belgian courts immediately, for sure. I authorize you to say it publicly. I have already done so in writing to Brussels last January 5th. I simply want to be guaranteed an ordinary criminal court hearing; to have only Belgian legislation prior to the alleged acts applied; and to have the possibility of defending myself freely, broadly disseminating the trial for the Belgian public's consideration. With these considerations accepted, I would immediately turn myself in. I authorize you to repeat this loud and clear.*

*UP: Is that all?*

*LD: What misery, these hateful times that continue in Europe; this crime, poisoned by its own bile. What is the purpose of this whole community of coal, steel, or armament, if divided hearts hate one another, thinking no further than for vengeance? When will the United States of America, with its natural generosity of soul, vigorously recognize the need for forgiveness in Europe? When will they prepare amnesty and reconciliation for her? What a great mission for great hearts, and so necessary too. If Europeans do not all unite, laying aside their past grievances, tomorrow the Soviets will be in charge of unification, but for extermination. That is why this man hunt, of which I am the object, discourages me so much. Not for me. I have suffered a lot, and I am not afraid to die, but because of the miserable spiritual state that the incident reveals. Moscow is at the gates of civilization, yet they forget this danger and instead slander and ruthlessly hunt down a defeated soldier and outlaw. I am sorry for Europe!"*

Degrelle, faced with this delicate and conflicted situation, continued to live in Spain, but took many precautions and safeguards. He stayed in contact with Jean-Robert Debbaudt, his liaison in Belgium, to whom he wrote a letter in March encouraging him to continue the fight, and to not lose heart. Debbaudt, under strict secrecy imposed by the circumstances, sent him a letter of reply on July 9th, giving Degrelle a detailed account of the difficult situation created by his participation and desire to be useful, in addition to responding to incessant attacks from the press. In his note he said:

> *The most significant thing about your absence is that it is the main source of most of the divisions hindering a renewal of our ideas. It would be very useful if your voice could be heard from time to time among our scattered ranks, to achieve, once again, unity in our views and an uncorrupted doctrinal basis. Even if other means cannot be put into action, I believe that the reception of your texts could easily be distributed with the means that I currently already have control over.*

In mid-1955, Degrelle was still suspected of having taken refuge in Tangier. The news that appeared in the press from time to time pointed in that direction. Therefore, on May 5th, the Auditor General of the Military Court in Brussels requested that the Foreign Ministry should issue an extradition request to the authorities of that international city in northern Morocco. Belgian Foreign Minister Jean Gol made efforts to this effect through the French authorities who could produce positive results in the Tangier area, where the "fugitive" was presumed to be hidden.

Meanwhile, Degrelle worked tirelessly on civil projects, continuing to complete the construction of his residence, the "White Castle," in the Constantina area, and in building the small, cozy one-family apartments designed to be rented to American military personnel of the Rota naval base. He tried, as far as possible, to go unnoticed, waiting for the storm to calm, while eagerly endeavoring to move his real estate projects forward.

## A Historical Tapestry

Léon donated a tapestry of the Trojan War to the Madrid City Council when the town hall was overseen by the Count of Mayalde. It was hung at the head of the Staircase of Honor at the House of the Villa. It was a seventeenth to eighteenth century tapestry, woven in Brussels by Van der Borght. Its design was reminiscent of Boucher's work. It was quite large, 8 meters by 3.4 meters (26 feet by 11 feet) and was a grandiose representation of two almost consecutive scenes (lines 273-393 and 438-449) from Canto XX of Homer's *Iliad*. The first, according to the account, reproduced the end of the struggle between the pious Aeneas and Achilles when, unarmed by Achilles, Aeneas takes a colossal stone as a weapon and he is preparing to take away from his enemy a song worthy, in fact, of the sublime Homer's singing.

The second episode deals with Achilles' penultimate struggle against Hector. The Trojan has been shot down by the son of Peleus who is preparing to kill him. Apollo helps him by hiding him in a cloud.

An avid art lover, Léon Degrelle collaborated actively with the "Antonio Maura" Municipal Studies Center of the Madrid Municipal Council, in which he had been introduced and presented by his good friend and comrade Clarita Stauffer.

## His Faithful Dog "Dogo"

One fine day, some of Constantina's citizens came to La Carlina to make a courtesy call with their little son, Pierre, whom they all called "Pitchou." Pierre gave Léon a magnificent gift, a superb dog named "Dogo," who was trained to be a good companion and a vigilant watchdog. Degrelle was very appreciative and loved Dogo immensely. Unfortunately, the extraordinary guard dog was hit and killed by a vehicle. As Léon said, "in this world the most beautiful things know the worst fate." Degrelle, thinking of the grief of his little "comrade" Pitchou, wrote a poem full of freshness and happy philosophy, in which, under the title "Crushed Dogs," he explained to the child—certainly with his own children in mind—the feelings that weighed upon him. The poem was full of natural and exciting verse and was, at the same time, a kind of indirect justification for its author.

Léon Degrelle first described his dog in his "territory," that domain where tens of thousands of shrubs and thousands of funny and fabulous animals existed:

> *Watching him walk and run was an artist's joy. That time I stopped to admire this black creature that followed, like a living sculpture, to the rhythm of absolute perfection, the green and golden background of the grass under the trees. Then, suddenly, Dogo stood up, sensed something, some other life nearby, or simply adventure, the desire to create a myth. His long legs uprooted the earth at an unusual speed where he had sniffed, digging a pinkish brown hole in the pretty, undisturbed soil. What was it? Nothing! Yet, Dogo was like the poets and dreamers who want there to be something, even when there is nothing, and who delve madly in search of the chimera. I, and my little Pitchou, also pursued chimeras in the soil where there was no doubt anything left. Like Dogo, I dug with enthusiasm, throwing the dirt behind me with all my strength to reach that pretty prey!*
>
> *Dogo, like us, has followed a great dream, and was exceptional.*
>
> *Sometimes, our Dogo, hunter of chimeras, found something more! That is how it is. Dreamers pursue, with eyes illuminated by their inner faith, objectives that*

*others believe impossible. The great thing for Dogo was to see a small rabbit moving among wild plants, among the violet flowers, its small white tail, as if an arrow had been shot at him, a pretty feather in passing. Don José, who knew everything about this area, said, "There are no rabbits." That seemed to be the case to me too, as I kept repeating, I had never seen any. I would continue just the same, and then I found them! Dogo would chase behind the rabbits, in spite of everything, and he always found them! Every time! That is right, Pitchou! Faith creates. Those who seek the impossible find the impossible. For Dogo, the impossible was his rabbits. Every time rabbits would jump up, Dogo would be fast on their heels, flying at breakneck speed! The rabbit would throw itself into its burrow, and Dogo would put his snout down to wait for it, besiege it, and finish the feat. One could say that joy is not in the taking or the killing, but to feel the master close at hand. In the great forests, under the centuries-old trees, Dogo felt the master.*

*A master must keep his dog handsome. Warriors do something similar when they place a horse tail, or plume of feathers, brimming with color, atop their helmets. Dogo always wore a collar of wild forest flowers: fiery flowers of a light violet, or white flowers with a gold heart, or a bunch of margaritas. This was rather ridiculous, as dogs should not be given flower ornaments, but Pitchou, it was necessary to challenge ridicule. For those who mock are generally more ridiculous than those who are not afraid to defend what is beautiful! Dogo was beautiful, with the flowers about his neck, like a conqueror or a poet. He came back later frolicking, passing in front of the other dogs, and his flowers stood out against his black hair. The other dogs, who donned no flowers, looked envious of our Dogo, a poet who donned the flowers of great forests, where he, the seeker of chimeras, had found his chimeras, the pretty rabbits with tails of white pomp!*

*There were more animals than just bunnies. Dogo was interested in everything he saw because everything he saw was a mystery and a source of energy for him. He was interested in the plump, heavy partridges, which is to say lazy, that do not like to take flight or run. Dogo, who loved beauty and knew that the beauty of a bird is in the air, would run behind them as if yelling to them, "Get up! To the sky! Let there be beautiful colors and motley movements in the light!" In this way, animals—and people, Pitchou—must sometimes be pushed to do beautiful things. They do not like this because it takes effort. The duty of dog-kings and of man-kings is to force them to go beyond their clumsiness. The partridges would throw themselves into the air, their flight touching the horizon with the reflections of a warm brown, almost red, ending atop the brushwood. It was very pretty. Without Dogo, these partridges would have remained no more than thick, bourgeois lumps, only going on foot. Always remember this lesson from Dogo, Pierre! Later, like him, like me,*

*force people, even if they do not want it, to rise above their laziness and mediocre
situations. Make them fly, even if you have to bark very loud behind the partridges,
so that they can be birds upon the earth or beings with a soul in the undergrowth of
men!*

## Archaeological Works

During his long stay in Constantina, Degrelle carried out, on his own initiative
and at his own expense, an archaeological excavation of Cueva de la Sima, located
in a place adjacent to the Plaza del Naranjuelo, the ancient dwelling of the primitive
inhabitants of that agricultural and perforated mining area. The arduous
archaeological works, led by Degrelle, bore fruit when they discovered a site.
Immediately, he reported this to the provincial authorities of Seville, who, given
the importance of Léon's discovery of prehistoric remains, instructed the
archaeologists Don Juan de Mata Carriazo and Don Juan Collantes to continue the
excavations. Thanks to his work on the remains and to the continued excavations,
the pieces that they had found are currently on exhibit in the First Room of the
Provincial Archaeological Museum of Seville. The location of the site was cataloged
as *Cueva de Don Juan* (Cave of Don Juan). It was named after Léon Degrelle, who
was known by the locals as "Don Juan de la Carlina." During these exciting
archaeological excavations, on some of those tough workdays, he was accompanied
by his friend and comrade, Otto Skorzeny (there is written testimony of his stay in
La Sima).

## Degrelle is Nationalized a Spanish Citizen by Adoption

On September 17th, 1955, a significant event took place for Degrelle. Before
the local notary Don Luis Ávila Álvarez, Doña Matilde Ramírez Reina, who was
seventy-two years old, appeared to file a deed of adoption under protocol number
427, in favor of a Don Léon Joseph Marie Ignace Degrelle Boever."[71] This brought
to public record, from December of the previous year, the court order of the Court
of First Instance of Cazalla de la Sierra, approving the adoption and the granting of
the surname of the adopter to the adopted.

Degrelle, who at that time was forty-nine years old, was once again historically
under the command of Emperor Charles I and King Philip II. They had once

---

[71] The inclusion of Degrelle's mother's maiden name, never seen outside this context, is likely done
here in compliance with Spanish custom, which gives a child his father's last name as well as his
mother's maiden name.

extended their royal and imperial jurisdiction through the fields of Flanders, where the Degrelle's manor was located in his native land, and through the lands of Hispania, his land of adoption and refuge.

That kind old woman, Matilde Ramirez Reina, who ran a shop in the town of Constantina, simply adopted him. She lived on Pozuelo Street, number 13, in that municipality. She was a relative of the former mayor of the village, Juan Ramírez Felosia, a local doctor and a close friend of Degrelle.

The adoption was a completely legal act. Everything was prepared with absolute stealth. Blas Piñar, who was a court procurator in his role as National Councilor, advised him on the adoption procedure in accordance with legal procedures in force. Blas Piñar says of Degrelle in his memoirs:

> *I had a friendship with him. Some friends helped him, as his life among us was not easy. He was adopted in order to change his name, and as notary I authorized the adoption papers. He was renamed León Ramirez Reina. The economic hardship was difficult enough for him, but coupled with the assurance that his enemies, lurking, wanted to kill him and that his status as a political exile was not so sufficient as to enjoy generous protection from the Spanish government made life even harder. By being frugal, he could get out from under economic hardship. From persecution, however, he could not escape.*

In Spain, adoption only grants and carries with it the acquisition of the nationality of the adopter by the adoptee in the case of minors. Given that Léon Degrelle was a special case due to his death sentence in Belgium, which entailed the absolute loss of all civil rights, as well as the loss of his nationality, his case was legally comparable to that of a minor. The Court of Cazalla de la Sierra considered and kept these mediating circumstances in mind, and officially approved the adoption and consequent change of surname. Shortly after that date, his daughters born of his marriage to Marie-Paule Lemay, began to marry and give him the first of twelve Spanish grandchildren. In the Spanish legal system and for all purposes, Degrelle became León José Ramírez Reina, a Spanish citizen, with his corresponding national identity card, domiciled in Constantina. He even had a street named after him in recognition of his aid and contribution to development in Constantina.

## Cultural Activities

Léon Degrelle was immersed and fully integrated into the local life of Constantina, where the neighborhood looked up to, admired, and respected him. On December 3rd, 7th, and 10th of 1955, he summoned the locals to the Cervantes Theater, where he gave a series of scholarly cultural conferences. He lectured masterfully on the "Roman, Moorish, and Christian" past of the town of Constantina, in an effort to disseminate the historical roots of the place that he so thoroughly studied and researched.

The lectures at the Cervantes Theater were organized by the *Instituto Laboral San Fernando* (San Fernando Labor Institute). When the sponsors of the cultural event, in a tone of collective complicity, introduced the speaker to a crowded theater and a diverse audience, they referred to Degrelle as the well-known personality "Don Juan de la Carlina."

People still remember León Degrelle's speaking engagements at the Cervantes Theater. No one wanted to miss those lectures. Attendance was massive, usually with standing room only. The doors of the venue were opened hours in advance so that early comers could choose a seat. The audience sometimes waited several hours inside the venue until the lectures began.

The testimony of one of the theater assistants, is most eloquent:

> He appeared on the stage; he placed himself in the center, spread his legs a bit and put his hands on his hips. The silence was absolute. With that pose, before he even opened his mouth, the entire audience was already won. He was a real conductor of the masses, fascinating and disturbing at the same time. When he finally broke the silence to speak, he did it with a slow and penetrating voice, increasing the attention of the public. The lecture dealt with the entry of the French into Constantina on April 9th, 1810, and his words were almost literally those of the account of Louis Caro y Salamanca, published in a memorandum at the College of Nuestra Señora del Robledo on December 21st, 1988. Despite this, the epic tone he knew how to use was so fantastic that the audience was fascinated. Planted in the middle of the stage, he looked like a new Hitler.

His erudition captivated the natives.

Sometime later, the newspaper, *El Socialista,* lashed out at Léon with a bitter, tendentious article. It was full of hatred, lies and falsehoods, absolutely poisonous and vitriolic. It stated:

*A Shame. Degrelle, Master and Lord of Constantina.*

*Despite the repeated denials of Foreign Minister Martín Artajo, denials in which the whereabouts of Léon Degrelle were ignored, he was quietly living in the city of Constantina, in the province of Sevilla. Not only does he live in Constantina, but he acts as the master and lord of the people.*

*A few months ago, we received a pamphlet announcing three lectures that took place on Saturday, December 3rd, 7th, and 10th of 1955, at 7.30 p.m., at the Cervantes Cinema in that locality. The conferences, according to the announcement leaflet, constituted "an extraordinary event," organized by the San Fernando Labor Institute, under the Ministry of National Education, and were to deal with Roman Constantina, Moorish Constantina, and Christian Constantina.*

*The name Degrelle is not on the program. In order for Martín Artajo to continue denying the presence of Degrelle in Spain, when convenient, the announcement says that the lectures will be delivered by "the celebrated personality we all know by the name of 'Don Juan de la Carlina.'*

*Realizing the situation of his death sentence by the Belgian courts, it could be said that Degrelle has engaged only in the harmless work of historical research, but none of that. In Seville there is a true army, a special army, an authentic foreign legion, formed by Nazis from several countries who are there as refugees. These criminals at birth, even have among them a Spaniard with an English surname who responds to McLean. In Morón he became infamous for having murdered two hundred Spanish Republicans. This foreign legion trains under military instruction and does shooting exercises on the estate owned by Degrelle in Constantina. It has its headquarters in Bar Zahara and its militants behave like true sheikhs, frightening the population that does not feel protected by the authorities.*

*We knew that Franco ceded a piece of national territory to the Americans in exchange for a handful of dollars under an agreement that ended up published in the newspapers at the time, but what we do not know is under what secret agreement Franco has been able to cede to Degrelle and his crew the city of Constantina, to act there as master and lord with his related Foreign Legion.*

## Belgium Votes against Spain's Admission to the UN

Despite all the Belgian and Jewish counteractions, their devastating campaigns of harassment and disrepute against Spain, Spain entered the United Nations as a full member state on December 14th, 1955. The result of the vote for admission came to the following count: fifty-five votes in favor and two abstentions.

The only countries that did not vote in favor of Spain's membership were Mexico and Belgium. Mexico was against it because it was a den of exiled Republicans who looted the coffers of the public purse and the Bank of Spain in one of the most notorious acts of destruction and political theft; as for Belgium, one can speculate that it was because of the disagreement with Spain concerning the whereabouts of Léon Degrelle.

## Lights and Shadows

The burial of Rafael Finat y Bustos, the son of Degrelle's close friend and comrade, the Count of Mayalde, took place before the end of 1955. The body of the young man was finally found on December 19th on the banks of the Tagus River as it passes through the city of Toledo, next to the Safont dam. This was about 25 kilometers (15.5 miles) from where the tragic accident occurred that killed him and his cousin Luis, on February 25th of that same year. The unfortunate young man was buried in the cemetery of San Isidro. Attending the funeral was an enormous crowd grieving for such a sensitive loss. Léon shared his deep sorrow with that family. Little did he know that three years later he would also go through a tragedy of his own.

José Utrera Molina, who on separate occasions served as Minister of Housing and Minister Secretary General of the Movement, shared some recollections of Degrelle:

> I met Léon Degrelle in Ciudad Real at Christmas 1956. I had just recently taken charge of the civil government in that province and, coincidentally, I had finished reading with increasing interest, the book The Burning Souls. It has a foreword by Dr. Gregorio Marañón, who, incidentally, faithful to his liberal and human spirit, emphasized in his text, with sharpness and brilliance, the relativity of political circumstances, which must never create unfathomable chasms that hatefully divide the hearts of men.
>
> I can still recall that first conversation I had with him [Degrelle], which went on for several hours. I was then vividly impressed with his strong personality, undoubtedly valued for a truly fascinating life adventure. When I heard it, I felt like I was in the presence of a very significant part of Europe's living history. I found that his image corresponded faithfully to the figure of a fierce warrior endowed with incredible tenacity, of an undeniable hearty warmth and of a spirit whose emotional

*consistency was guessed at first sight. It resounded through his expressive, serene, and direct gaze.*

*I must admit that throughout my human, personal, and political trajectory, I have met very few men endowed with the intellectual and moral energy of Léon Degrelle. The whip of sorrow tempered his nature and strengthened his character. The more adverse circumstances were not able to rob him of his courage to renounce his combative will because his soul is peculiar, sustained by faith itself. His capacity for illusion is marvelous and continues, uneasy, in a kind of miraculous state of grace. It is that, above all, that Degrelle retains almost intact; the youth that, despite his age, remains an amazing organic reality, living and obvious. Degrelle is an idealist who never lost that characteristic, despite living surrounded by realism, and those who believe that man's life does not end in defeat. For him, living vitally is a complex of real hopes, desires, dreams, and yearnings. I sincerely believe that all this gives him an exalted lucidity, an undeniable mental freshness to maintain and advance the risky defense of his ideals.*

Meanwhile, the Belgian newspaper *Le Peuple*, published an article on August 2nd, 1956, insisting that Degrelle lived in Constantina. The Spanish Ambassador to Belgium, Count de Casa Miranda, drafted a cable to his minister the same day, sending him the article urgently by air. In his statement he said:

*Still do not know implications that this will have. This morning went to Foreign Affairs for other matters, and nothing has been told to me of all this. Still pending is signing of trade agreement next Tuesday and initial result tomorrow of working talks that have been quite fruitful.*

## Intense, but Quiet, Political Activity

Degrelle maintained discreet contacts with people he trusted, like his countryman Gilsoul, to whom he wrote on August 8th, 1956, to explain the delicate nature of his situation and to tell him not to receive anyone important at his home.

On August 23rd, 1956, the French nationalist weekly *Rivarol* published an interview with him. It was a real firestarter. Again, they brought back to life the speculations and fantasies of the French-speaking press concerning his person and his legend. He was assumed to be the supreme leader of a well-structured network of anti-communist commandos who trained in clandestine camps in the province of

Sevilla. He was charged with being the mastermind of secret machinations and plots. His figure always remained in the unknown, in myth, in mystery, in the twilight, but always at the top of things.

Even Belgian Socialist Deputy Arthur Gailly in the same month, wrote for the Belgian newspaper *Le Peuple*, that in Seville there was "an authentic foreign legion, made up of 'Nazis' of various nationalities, who had found refuge in these places," and also "that this legion was under military instruction and did shooting and training exercises on an estate in Constantina, owned by Léon Degrelle…"

He was identified as the shadowy commander-in-chief of the National Socialist international which had spread into all the corners of the world, with close connections to Nasser's Egypt.

In other media, Degrelle was thought to be the mentor, and brains behind the former "European National Congress," under the auspices of Per Endhal, which had been held in Malmo, Sweden, on May 12th, 1951; this group brought together sixty representatives from the Scandinavian, French, German, Austrian, Swiss, Italian, Spanish, English, and Belgian countries, and even Hungarian representatives in exile. Among the attendees was the writer Maurice Bardèche, brother-in-law of the ill-fated and distinguished poet Robert Brasillach, murdered in France during the "democratic" cleansing. At the end of the sessions, the representatives drafted a final document, the so-called "Manifesto for a European People's Movement in the Service of National and European Independence." This was the basis for the birth of the European Social Movement, which, according to the most speculative and visionary analysts, was inspired by Degrelle, who would have attended the meeting under the false identity of "Martinez." This was stated at the Hebraic freemasonry meeting of the B'nai B'rith (The Children of the Covenant) held in Luxembourg in April 1957.

## Before Spain's Entrance into the Organization for European Economic Cooperation (OEEC)[72]

On October 8th, 1956, Spanish Ambassador to Belgium, Count de Casa Miranda, sent an encrypted communiqué to the Spanish Minister of Foreign Affairs, in which he referred to his previous telegram of August 2nd, and informed him:

---

[72] The OEEC, created in 1948, was reformed into the Organization for Economic Cooperation and Development, or OECD, in 1961 and opened to non-European countries.

*In recent days, the newspapers Le Peuple, Le Drapeau Rouge, and La Libre Belgique have taken up the subject again. They coincide with certain statements made by Belgium's representative in the OEEC, when Spain's entrance to the organization was discussed last Friday. My wish was not to return to the Degrelle affair until the former issue had been resolved, but our acceptance in the OEEC and the activities of our enemies, who do not cease raising the Degrelle issue if they believe it will harm us, obliges us to reconsider the matter in light of the following premises:*

1) *It is not possible to continue eternally in the misinformation that Degrelle entered and left Spain and that we do not know any more about him, mainly because of the lack of discretion of the interested party, who makes it public knowledge that he is still in Spain;*

2) *He cannot be handed over; and*

3) *We do not plan to expel him.*

*If Your Excellency agrees with me on the certainty of the three previous premises, I see no other solution but to grant him political refugee status. This obviously brings with it a great deal of unrest in this country that will trigger a violent press campaign, etc. Appointing a new ambassador to Madrid may be delayed, when, as it is necessary, the current one is withdrawn for health reasons. Eventually, things will calm down and we will be able to remove this eternal sword of Damocles from above us. Please tell me whether we are prepared to arrive at this solution and if so, whether I will be authorized before putting it into practice, to use it as a threat if they speak to me about Degrelle. In a few days' time, I will visit these authorities to see what Belgium's attitude will ultimately be at the next OEEC meeting.*

*Casa Miranda*

## The Meeting with Jean-Robert Debbaudt and Its Consequences

Jean-Robert Debbaudt was born in 1926. He was ten years old when, in Saint-Gilles-lez-Bruxelles (also the place of his death), he stopped at 37 Lombardie Street, the local address of the Rex movement. That was where he first saw Léon Degrelle, when Debbaudt, as a youngster, was active in a Catholic youth scout group. He heard the then twenty-year-old Degrelle speak at a rally and was impressed by his eloquence. When the first volunteers, Léon among them, set out for the front on August 8th, 1941, Rex's youth section was mobilized for the farewell and to participate in the parade. It was necessary to be at least seventeen years of age, with mandatory parental consent, in order to enlist. Given that Debbaudt was only fifteen and a half years old in 1942, he had to falsify his identity card in order to volunteer for the engagement. After a period of training, he was assigned to the Fourth Company operating in Ukraine, who fought until the end of the war on the Eastern Front. Debbaudt earned First-Class and Second-Class Iron Crosses. After the war, with the repression that broke out in Europe against defeated veterans, euphemistically called "cleansing," he entered the Saint Gilles prison, and was then transferred to the Petit Chateau headquarters in Brussels, also outfitted as a prison. In January 1946, he was tried at a war council, and sentenced to some time in prison, the same morning on which Degrelle's secretary, Félix Franck, had been tried and sentenced to death. When he got out of prison, he became an activist, linking himself with the various patriotic parties and movements of post-war Europe. He founded and launched different political groups, among great difficulties and persecution, around the ideas that remained latent in his heart. He often had to change the name of his political formation, but never his ideas. He always said, "I consider it as the honor of my life to have been led in combat by a real leader, by a man of Léon Degrelle's mettle," even writing it in a letter to the weekly newspaper, *Spetial,* in 1967.

Since 1950, Debbaudt had participated in the formation of the European Social Movement (ESM); he founded *Nouvel Ordre Européen* (New European Order), with Maurice Bardèche, in that same year. In 1953, he organized the Belgian Social Movement. In 1955, he traveled to Spain to meet Léon Degrelle, in Constantina for the first time since the end of war. In 1957, he founded the monthly magazine *Le Peuple Réel*, which the following year changed its title to *L'Europe Réelle*, becoming the official publication of the New European Order.

In 1966, he formed the Federal Fascist Front. In January 1970, Debbaudt founded the International Rexist Movement in Belgium, which, from the beginning, established contacts with the Spanish group *Guerrilleros de Cristo Rey*. It was linked to Mariano Sánchez Covisa, who affirmed that the name of the group had been adopted in tribute to Léon Degrelle. In 1972, Debbaudt founded *Faisceau Belge* (Belgian Beam).

In the 1974 elections, he ran as a candidate for the National Popular Front, obtaining two thousand seven hundred sixty-four votes. In 1982, he launched the Social Nationalist Movement.

Following the publication in Belgium of the famous *Letter to the Pope*, written by Léon Degrelle on Pope John Paul II's visit to Auschwitz, Debbaudt was sentenced to two years in prison for publishing political writings of former death row inmates. In the face of such a legal monstrosity, he sought exile, meeting with Degrelle in Spain, both in Madrid and in Andalusia.

The enthusiastic Debbaudt arrived in Spain in July 1957 to privately meet with his undisputed political leader. He spent a few days in Constantina with Degrelle, which for him were unforgettable. From the conversations he had, he wrote an article entitled, "*Léon Degrelle M'a Dit*," which he published in the monthly *Le Peuple Réel* in Brussels.

During the meeting, Degrelle confessed to him:

*It is not exile that makes me suffer. It is the inactivity, it is feeling immense dreams deep inside that cannot be fulfilled, and also the idea that they have made noble, righteous, generous, human beings, who imagine monstrous things about me, who have been able, for ten years, to listen to all the infamies they have poured on me. It is easy to insult someone defeated, someone who is prohibited from responding, someone who cannot talk or explain himself. I have offered it ten times; obviously, what they want is for me to return there, but not to let me speak so they can kill me. I do not care if they kill me, but I first want to explain myself, I want to say everything about those fat liars who are so sure of their impunity. What are they so afraid of? I am alone, defeated, I do not have a newspaper, I have nothing at my disposal, not even money. I speak of returning with the only good civil right left to me because I do not even have the means to pay a good lawyer. I know well what this breed is. I have offered to come back and am answered with silence and lies. I gave an extensive interview to United Press, where I laid out all the details. I asked for simple things: a large trial with all the necessary publicity and that it be broadcast. In short, I could be wrong or right. If I was found wrong, I would have been a bandit, a traitor, a murderer, it was very simple: that would have been made evident in the trial. If it was broadcast by radio, that would be better for my enemies, my confusion would be complete. It would be stupid if I were wrong to ask for these things. You would think my own adversaries would answer immediately, rushing to say, 'Okay, we are going to place Degrelle before all of Belgium...' They know that my name has never appeared on any list of war criminals, neither in those of the Allied countries, nor in the one drawn up by the Belgian government. They know that there is not a single word of truth in anything they argue about this matter. Not only is this known, but it is also proven. They have no argument to give me because they know they are lying. They systematically lie, it is proof that they have a bad conscience. They can lie, but sooner or later the truth gets out. Exile and suffering will pass, but the truth, sooner or later, will be imposed. It will win and with it, us too. We are sure we will win."*

Jean-Robert Debbaudt, on whom the weight of Degrelle's representation and political defense in Belgium had fallen, and with whom he maintained regular contact through letters, spent the week with Léon in his house writing out, in solitude, all his affairs with reserved anonymity and quiet. Léon took advantage of the meeting with his faithful comrade to record a message intended for his children, whom he had not seen since 1945, which he entrusted to Debbaudt to send to them. Degrelle also wrote a manifesto for his compatriots, to give them a political proclamation, so that Debbaudt could try to give it as wide a dissemination as possible in Belgium. The proclamation was published in the bulletin of the Belgian Social Movement, *Le Peuple Réel*, which Debbaudt had it printed with the subtitle, "*National Combat Newspaper*," in Brussels, as a modest, revolutionary bulletin in March of the same year. The document manifesto in the December 1957 issue with the title "*Mes Chers Camarades*" ("My Dear Comrades"). In the style of Fray Luis de León in his "We decided yesterday…," León began his broad appeal to his war comrades with these words: "It has been more than twelve years since the misfortune of the last battles dispersed us from the Eastern Front. I remember with deep emotion those last days. Those titanic battles were on stage from Stettin to Lübeck…" He told them of all the vicissitudes and adventures that occurred during his exile. He encouraged them to continue in the struggle for the future, telling them that "History evolves. Political life has great turns and, above all, has new projects and developments. It was up to us to live in a stormy period where a new world was being built…" and he exhorted them, saying, "It is necessary now to see much further and say that we are not only men of Europe, but men of the universe. For the men of our generation there is no longer a European problem, but a global problem." He outlined for them, appealing to his sense of authority and unity of command, the way to follow, the path to be traveled, the role to play, as only spiritual guides, leaders of people, and warlords trace it. He ended the broad manifesto like this:

> *What we need is to be in a state of grace, to be prepared, to preserve faith and the will to fight and to overcome. I could have fallen into despondency, but I assure you that I have not. I keep all firmness and I am determined to throw myself back into combat without a second thought, to open a path and build the great work on behalf of all the comrades who have died, and also on your behalf. You do not want your dreams to die, and so you still remain faithful to our ideal. My dear comrades, let us have faith in a great future that surely awaits us. God will provide us with it, and our indomitable will can accomplish it.*

The modest bulletin *Le Peuple Réel* was the trench fence, the newspaper barricade for Léon Degrelle in Belgium. The small four-page newsletter changed its heading in 1958 to "*L'Europe Réelle*," perhaps at the suggestion of Léon, the great defender of the idea of *Magna Europa*. It expanded its number of pages and its radius of influence, increasing its circulation to reach fifteen thousand copies over time, a "David" resistant in the face of all odds against an insatiable, spiteful, faithless "Goliath," with an increasingly hooked nose.

During his stay at La Carlina, Debbaudt also made a photographic report of Léon, both as a souvenir of the visit and for dissemination in print media. In some of the shots, Léon appeared wearing his uniform and all his decorations.

In October, through a press agency, some of those snapshots, surprisingly, made it into Belgian newspapers. When they were published, they caused a rash of hot rage among the socialist-communist extremist organizations of the former guerillas and resistance terrorists. They held a protest on November 17th, 1957, in Brussels, against the government's failure, for years on end, to capture General Degrelle dead or alive.

Debbaudt's surge of activity and his interview with Degrelle alerted Belgian police and intelligence services. They easily discovered Léon's abode in the Seville highlands and brought this to the attention of their Spanish colleagues at the direction of their own Foreign Minister, Victor Larock, in that same month. Larock expected his Spanish counterpart, Fernando María Castiella, to respond in favor of Belgium's old aspirations to hunt down the great hero of the past world war. Instructions were again sent to the Belgian Ambassador to closely follow up inquiries in this regard and to insist on a prompt response. Spanish Minister Fernando María Castiella, a devout Catholic and former volunteer in the ranks of the Blue Division, did not reply until March 1958, saying that there would be an investigation into the matter, and if the person requested were found, he would be handed over. The conditional and subjunctive tenses in the language of the Minister's note highlighted the disinterest and lack of will he showed in the capture of Degrelle,[73] a capture which undoubtedly would only get him killed. Spain would later confirm that the investigation had produced no results and, therefore, the matter was closed.

---

[73] The author is referring to grammatical tenses in Spanish—including the past subjunctive, which is often translated as a conditional—that signify an action as hypothetical, virtual, not-yet-real, etc. While used rarely in English, a feel for what the author is referring to would be something like this: "Were he to be found, one might be able to initiate some process, etc." The entire tone is non-committal.

When Léon Degrelle died, in the midst of the sorrow that befell him, Castiella said:

*Léon Degrelle defended his convictions with extraordinary lucidity until his last breath. He has left us something: the example of uncompromising fidelity. He has become a moral guide because of the mysticism that he has bequeathed to us, particularly in his precious book* The Burning Souls.

Debbaudt died at the age of seventy-six, on June 28th, 2003, in Waterloo. In his obituary, published to make known this sad news, it said, "More than ever and like no one else, his slogan was up until the last day: "My Honor is called Loyalty."[74]

## A Visit by the Writer François Brigneau and the Cartoonist Paul Jamin

In the winter of 1957, the French writer François Brigneau traveled to Constantina to interview Degrelle and write up a large piece, intending it be published as a serial in *Paris-Presse*. After holding meetings and conversations with several major figures of the Second World War, their responses and impressions were later compiled and published by the Gallimard Publishing House in a volume entitled *The Adventure is Over for Them*. It was later republished in 1991, by the author himself, as *When the Weapons are Silent...*, in which interviews with Léon Degrelle, Otto Skorzeny, Colonel Remy, "El Campesino," Leni Riefenstahl, Turco Westerling, and Arthur Koesler were included.

The French writer had found Degrelle and arranged the interview with him thanks to the journalists and writers Henry Charbonneau, François Gaucher, and Claude Martin, from the nationalist outlet *Rivarol*.

Brigneau titled his in-depth interview with Léon Degrelle, "Degrelle, the Magnificent." In the introduction, he pointed out:

*This man can present himself today as an architect or teacher. He can display three passports, one in the name of Enrique Durán, a Polish citizen, and a second in the name of Juan Sanchiz, a Spanish national. Nothing can make him forget that he has been one of the most extraordinary political agitators known to the West: the head of rexism; the last great man in fascist Europe; the one to whom Hitler once*

---

[74] Obvious reference to the German *Meine Ehre heißt Treue*.

said, *"I would have liked to have a son like you"; he who will always be called Léon Degrelle. I have mentioned three passports, but I have identified only two. The third is one that Degrelle asked me to keep secret.*

The "White Castle" of Constantina peaked Brigneau's interest, especially its Arab styled tower of 27 meters (88.5 feet) in height "where the muezzin would make the call to prayer or to combat in that valley." He continued:

*I see hanging gardens, arches, statues, a monumental porch, pylons, giant amphoras, terraces. It was a mansion for an oriental count, full of magnificence and mystery. A large mall, drawn on the slope of the hill, led one there through orchards, but before that, one had to cross a porch where he could read "La Carlina," and then pass in front of the caretakers' house, from where two black eyes observed me.*

He fixed on a peculiar detail:

*Surrounded by golden dahlias, an arc de triomphe held on top a Lion of Flanders which stood over England and had his legs on Lorraine. A verse by Joaquín du Bellay, written by hand on artistic tiles, could be read with melancholy.*

A Belgian lady, Ivonne Ransy-Leroy, was serving as secretary to Léon Degrelle. She had two sons who were young militant rexists, of whom she was very proud. One of them had died fighting in the battle of Korsun-Cherkassy. The other was in prison in Belgium, convicted of being a faithful follower of Degrelle. She had white hair, a thin, sweet, porcelain-like face, and that resigned and distant air that mothers often have when living under the weight of war and its aftermath.

She was the one who told François Brigneau, when he approached the house, "You are going to have the opportunity to see Degrelle. Stay in Seville tonight, behind the Reales Alcázares, next to the Guadalquivir River, you will see a garage, on a walkway."

The last talk between Brigneau and Degrelle took place in front of a large fireplace in the hall. A large fire was blaring, which consumed the wood logs tossed in by Léon. He finished his account beside the roaring fire, under a phrase engraved on one of the beams of the chimney: "A small fire in any corner of the world and all miracles of splendor will be possible." This concluding scene could not have been more fitting.

Degrell's hospitality extended to many friends and comrades, including the Belgian cartoonist Paul Jamin, who signed his works as "Jam." He later on became better known as "Alidor."

Jamin had met both Hergé[75] and Degrelle while writing for the magazine *Le Vingtième Siecle*, in the late 1920s and for the Catholic magazine of Father Wallez, his promoter and mentor. He was considered the best Belgian cartoonist and overall cartoonist of the twentieth century. With his brilliant strokes, he illustrated for Degrelle's political campaigns, including promotional posters, and publishing his brilliant drawings and cartoons in the magazines of the Rexist Movement. The designs and illustrations of "Jam" contributed powerfully to the success of Degrelle's campaign runs. His visits with his old comrade were regular and brotherly. On one occasion at La Carlina, his visit overlapped with Germaine Kieckens, the first wife of his friend Hergé. She had married the creator of "Tintin" on July 21st, 1932.

## The Painful Longing for His Family since Exile and the Great Tragedy

Degrelle thought of his children in his moments of solitude and prayer. A melancholy weighed on him because he could not have them at his side, or watch them grow, or share their smiles. He stated this in his letter to his sister Suzanne in May 1957, when he confessed, "Twelve years like this, waiting, without having read a single line from my children, is truly barbaric."

Léon Degrelle, during the almost thirteen years of adventure and survival of his long exile, had not seen his children; to his greater desolation and torment, he had no news of them at all. The tape that he recorded for his children, in July of 1957, was approximately fifteen minutes long, and he entrusted it to his loyal comrade, Jean-Robert Debbaudt, to deliver. It was finally received by his firstborn daughter Chantal.

His only son, Léon-Marie, who was then eighteen years old (born on May 4th, 1939), after hearing the recording, insisted on coming to Spain to meet with his father, despite the advice of his mother. She discouraged it precisely because of the instability and uncertainty of his father's position as a political and persecuted exile, with a risky and uncertain future. With natural, youthful rebelliousness, and

---

[75] Georges Prosper Remi, whose pen name was Hergé and who created the beloved Tintin character, will be discussed in more detail later in the book.

resolutely attracted by the call of blood, Léon-Marie dismissed his mother's advice. He showed up at La Carlina in October 1957, to his father's delight and joy.

Those were happy days for both father and son. They exchanged much conversation, trying to make up for lost time. So as not to delay his school studies and to correctly learn the Spanish language, Léon-Marie took private classes and moved to Seville. The weekends at La Carlina were reserved for father and son alone.

Degrelle's new-found happiness in the company of his only son, was about to be ripped apart by a horrific tragedy.

On Saturday, February 22nd, 1958, Léon-Marie died at the age of eighteen, a victim of a fatal traffic accident. He was riding a Vespa motorcycle (registration SE-51.867), which had been given to him by his father, when he was hit by a taxi on Avenida de la Palmera in Seville.

At around 4:00 p.m., he left the house of his private tutor and headed off to spend the weekend with his father at La Carlina. A few meters from his tutor's house, Léon-Marie swerved to avoid a trolley. The wheel of his motorcycle got wedged in the trolley rail for a moment. As he got the wheel unstuck and started moving, a taxi suddenly appeared. Although Léon-Marie stopped abruptly, he was not able to avoid the spectacular collision. It threw him violently, head-first onto the sidewalk, breaking his neck and cervical vertebrae. He instantly went into a deep, irreversible coma. He had no time to realize his impending death. His face retained his serene, tender, youthful smile, which would now accompany him forever to eternity. At the time of the accident, he was not carrying any documentation. A bystander, a young man of his age, immediately recognized him and indicated the place where he was staying, the house of Cernuda, the head of the local Falange.

A priest in the vicinity gave him extreme unction. He was immediately taken to the hospital, where they could only certify his death due to the deadly impact of the crash. Degrelle was then notified of the loss of his son.

At 10:30 p.m., the body of the ill-fated Léon-Marie arrived in Constantina, and the funeral chapel was set up in the mayor's house. Degrelle was filled with misery, bitterness, and sorrow. In those desolate, insufferable moments, when despair emerges with such a sensitive loss of a life, Léon was surrounded by his friends, all those good rustic people, both rich and poor, from around that wild countryside. Women dressed in full black kept vigil over the coffin throughout the night; they spent those hours of mourning in permanent prayer with an uninterrupted chain of rosaries.

The burial took place the following day, Sunday, February 23rd, at 1:00 p.m. The transport of the coffin to the cemetery was on the shoulders of Léon-Marie's friends from the village. The entire village went to the funeral in silent procession.

Ivonne Ransy-Leroy, Degrelle's secretary, notified his sister, Suzanne, of the death of Léon-Marie in a letter dated the same day, sending it by express mail after the burial.

The press agencies also got word of what had happened on the day of the funeral and reported the death through their corresponding dispatches. The partial similarity of the father's name and the son's name created some initial confusion. The newspapers mistakenly reported the death as if Léon Degrelle had died in a traffic accident in the city of Seville. The mistake was unanimous. On February 24th, the major Belgian newspapers reported the incorrect news on their front pages. The Belgian Embassy and Ambassador Viscount Berryer, in the exercise of his duties, fell into the same error during the first hours, which helped to corroborate and confirm the fallacy. The Belgian radio broadcast the end of the Belgian leader's existence, reporting that the news had been confirmed by the embassy. Everyone in his homeland was convinced that he was dead. It took at least forty-eight hours to undo the mess and clarify the confusion.

Having to rectify the news, revenge came later. As Léon Degrelle's definitive whereabouts had now been verified, given where his son's funeral was, there could be no excuses or pretexts to delay his immediate handover. In the face of such an untimely claim, made on the basis of the news of that tragic event, the Spanish authorities denied Degrelle's presence at the official funeral. They held, as irrefutable proof, that he had not participated in the funeral and liturgical ceremonies for his son, arguing that had Degrelle been in Spanish territory, he definitely would have attended.

Belgian Foreign Minister Larock did not miss the opportunity from such a terrible event to renew his obsessive demand upon the Spanish government for Degrelle's extradition. Just one month after the event, the Degrelle case was once again the center of debate at the Belgian Senate session on March 27th, where Senator Moreau de Melen accused his own government of not applying enough pressure to apprehend Degrelle. This forced Minister Larock to defend the tireless and persistent harassment by the Belgian government to secure the handover, even turning to international bodies for support.

He considered calling back Ambassador Berryer for consultations, but this did not take place. On April 22nd, 1958, the Belgian Embassy in Madrid submitted a secret and confidential request for extradition. This led the Spanish Foreign Minister to reply, on May 27th, with an extensive memorandum concluding that the Spanish government's definitive position was that it would not hand over Degrelle. This document was not disclosed by Belgium to its public and thereafter remained secret.

On April 16th, 1958, the Mayor of Constantina himself published an edict, expressing the feeling of the entire municipality and conveying to Degrelle everyone's sympathy for the death of his son. After almost thirteen years of no contact, Degrelle only enjoyed the company of his son for barely four months before he was permanently taken from him.

A few days before the tragic accident, Léon-Marie wrote, perhaps his last letter, to a male cousin:

*Dear Cousin,*

*Father and I received a letter from mother a few days ago, as well as my old newsletters and report cards from school during my studies in France and from various schools I have been to. I am very discouraged once again by the poor results. I have decided to prove by my actions that I am not an idiot and to not give up on high school, which would be a shocking slight against father. I have been with father for almost four months. We are both very happy, but he is very concerned about my studies, and I am really afraid to disappoint him. Besides that, I have an inferiority complex, which is quite normal, but it annoys me a lot. I am studying for the high school exam, another door to open, but whose lock is rusty.*

*I live in the home of the Cernuda family, good people and good friends of my father. I have had to adapt to Spanish life and discover many things that I like, and I have learned Spanish. Father's situation, being more stable, makes us think that we will be able to live quiet for some time. Also, I visit with my father every weekend at his house. He has bought me a motorcycle, which I am really happy about, so I can make this weekly trip.*

*Father and I have had a good Christmas and New Year's holiday, the first time in twelve years that he has not spent them alone.*

*I hope you and the whole family have had a good time this holiday. Father takes care of a number of different issues; he is very efficient in everything. I have a lot of acquaintances here and enough friends; we go out together and they have helped me explore Seville and have taught me to love the city.*

*We have not had any news of Chantal and her husband for a long time. I know they will write, if they have time, but a month has passed since Christmas, and nothing has arrived. Now, if they want to come here for Easter, I think this would be the time to arrange things.*

*The house gets a little prettier every day. Father arranges it with much satisfaction and dedication. He always finds beautiful pictures, beautiful furniture; in short, the house is wonderful.*

*I have received the box of chocolates from Aunt Louise. I thank her very much and I send her a hug with all my heart; I have written a letter to thank her for it. I would be grateful if you could send me two or three birth certificates as soon as possible, as I need them to enroll in high school. I have received one, but it is over a year old. Specifically, two certificates, with a date of issue not exceeding three months, must be submitted in March to Madrid for registration. If you would be so kind as send them to me, I would be very grateful to you.*

*Now I must leave you, dear cousin, because I have to get back to work.*

*Sending you a hug with all my heart, as well as to my whole family in Belgium.*

*Léon-Marie*

In Belgium, Jean-Robert Debbaudt's magazine *Le Peuple Réel*, published an emotional article by Debbaudt himself in its March 1958 edition. The piece, expressing sympathy and condolences, began as follows:

*There is no one among us, whether former members of Rex or the legion, activists for the Belgian Social Movement or supporters of Le Peuple Réel, who make up the great family of the censored, who are not deeply dismayed by the announcement of the tragic news released by the press agencies on the afternoon of February 23rd, 1958. Such a blow had not struck us with such strength and intensity since the capitulation of May 8th, 1945…*

The article, communicating heartfelt pain and sadness, ended with these words:

*Léon-Marie is already at peace in the noble land of Spain, where another significant young man also sleeps. As a Spanish comrade told us, he was a victim immolated by the same repression, the noble son of General Moscardó,[76] the heroic defender of El Alcázar de Toledo. He ended his letter with a few words rich with meaning: "Léon-Marie, present!"*

---

[76] General José Moscardó Ituarte defended El Alcázar, holding out seventy days against Republican forces. During the siege, the Republicans caught his son and called the general's office inside, offering his son to the general in exchange for El Alcázar, (Thomas, 2001). General Moscardó asked to speak to his son and reportedly told him to commend his soul to God and cry "Long live Christ the King!" His son responded, "That, I can do." The Republicans shot him.

*Yes, Léon-Marie is present with our young heroes of the Eastern Front, the Abrassarts, the Tevernes, and also our martyrs, fallen on the interior front.*

*May Léon Degrelle, our chief, our friend, if by chance these lines get to him— in whichever part of the world—let him know that we share his grief and affliction. In the painful ordeal that he has suffered again today, if it will lessen his sorrow, let him also know that, as always, we are all unconditionally at his side.*

## Parallel Lives

When Marie-Paule Lemay received the news of the tragic accident and death of her son, she fell into shock and despair. With her nerves shot, under anguish and discomfort, dazed by the tragedy of her son's demise, she wrote a letter to Sister Anne-Marie Degrelle, a nun and the sister of her husband, containing this line: "I blame him for having taken away my son and I hold him responsible for his death." Having already given instructions to her lawyer Thèvenet, this tragic accident was the pretext for applying for divorce.

On February 25th, seventy-two hours after the painful event, Léon wrote and sent a letter to Attorney Thèvenet, expressing the following:

*Despite the pain in which my son's death has plunged me, I am responding to the typewritten note you have sent me, on behalf of your client Marie-Paule Lemay.*

*Declaring in the same that she has nothing in common with me, that carrying my surname produces constant trouble for her, and that she wants a divorce, I do not see how I can oppose bringing into effect her desire. So let her do what seems best to her. I do not want to participate in this initiative, even if I accept it, since it is unavoidable.*

*I hope she has the moral elegance to keep the matter discreet. I, for my part, ask only one thing: to be able to see my children. Depriving me of them, as has been done deliberately for so many years, is monstrous. It is not I who have broken up the home, let no one forget.*

*I do not wish for controversy or resentment. Why go against the impossible and try to revive what is dead? I just ask that justice be done and that a father be able to see and love his children again.*

*Apart from this, I can only wish for peace and sweetness to the one who is leaving. I feel pity for her.*

*If it were possible, I would prefer to be left out of all these procedures, which, as a Christian, are reprehensible to me.*

The intervention and mediation of friendly priests, such as the Reverend Fathers Geuser and Moereels, ultimately prevented the divorce from being recognized in its strict canonical-legal sense, but they maintained their marital separation. Marie-Paule Lemay continued to live in Nice.

In Holy Week of 1958, one of extreme sadness for Degrelle, the perennial emptiness left by the death of Léon-Marie, his daughter Anne decided to move from France to Constantina to comfort her father and to keep him company in La Carlina. Being quite taken with that land and its inhabitants, she stayed to live with him until she married the young Falangist attorney Servando Balaguer Parreño. The following year, his daughters Marie-Christine and Godelieve also arrived at La Carlina, with the intention of staying to live with him. They eventually changed their residency to Spain. Finally, his eldest daughter Chantal began traveling quite frequently to Constantina to visit him.

## The Attempted Kidnapping Perpetrated by Belgian Judge Albert Mélot

In August 1958, the judge of the city of Namur, Albert Mélot, attempted to kidnap Léon Degrelle. Mélot had distinguished himself during the war with the cruelty of his terrorist acts as a partisan with the resistance, in which he had served as a captain of the guerrillas. He later joined the British RAF.

Since Albert Mélot, had been a résistant, this was apparently the greatest "merit" that earned him the "title" and promotion to Magistrate-Judge of a regional court after the "liberation." It was Mélot who, in 1945, approved the persecution of the whole Degrelle family. He was a small, mustachioed man, physically quite disadvantaged, with one of his eyelids falling like a dry fig.

He began to conceive of the criminal kidnapping project in 1956, being encouraged all the time by his communist colleagues. It is impossible to believe that a man whose country had entrusted him to uphold justice was, in fact, able to prepare to carry out criminal acts in violation of all international laws in order to achieve the kidnapping of a political refugee, motivated only by his irrepressible desire for some sort of revenge. For two years, he and his cohorts worked on preparing the operation's logistics and studied all the details to carry it out with the least risk to themselves. During this interval between 1957 and 1958, Mélot made three trips to Seville and Madrid to study the terrain and to contact some local criminal elements, who would provide support and cover.

Mélot chartered a private plane, which was able to land discreetly at the military airfield in Seville. Taking advantage of the fact that Degrelle then lived alone at La Carlina, Mélot was relying on the collaboration of a commando group composed of ten men, all former communist members or similar members of the Belgian resistance, to execute his plan.

In July 1958, Mélot even traveled to La Carlina, knowing that Degrelle was absent from his home in those days. He posed as a comrade who was very faithful to the rexist cause when the gardener, who also guarded the property, met him upon his arrival. During the days in which Léon was, by chance, momentarily absent, the "Judge" convincingly persuaded the gardener to believe that he had arrived, as it were, on pilgrimage and to keep a promise to Degrelle. His lies succeeded, and he was given access to the estate. He thus had the opportunity to closely study all points of access to the property. Surreptitiously and with great stealth, he visited every one of the rooms and outbuildings of the house, photographing even the smallest corner as well as all the access doors. He developed a rigorous plan that he believed could be executed with a strong guarantee of success and with little risk. He also studied, in a calculating and meticulous way, the surroundings and landscape of the estate.

During Mélot's surveillance, in order to study Léon's movements and to be familiar with his itineraries and habits, he even attended mass in the village on one occasion, sitting a few pews behind Degrelle.

The kidnapping would be carried out, according to the plan, in the purest mafia style. At the time of apprehension, Degrelle would be forcefully knocked out with chloroform. Once neutralized, he would be sedated and placed in a car that would take him to Seville's San Pablo Airport. An airplane would be ready and waiting to take off immediately for Belgium, staying on the periphery of French airspace.

When he had everything prepared and calculated down to the smallest detail, Mélot went to meet with Count Jean d'Ursel, the secretary of the Belgian Embassy in Madrid, to inform him of the plan, and of the imminence of its execution.

He assured d'Ursel that Degrelle would be on his way to Belgium very soon, and he would be plucked as "a bunch of grapes from the vine." The Belgian Ambassador immediately transmitted the information entrusted to him by Mélot.

If Degrelle had indeed been kidnapped by Mélot at that time, as was intended and expected, and brought to Brussels, it would have caused a major scandal that was both inappropriate and ill-timed. The event would have tarnished the figure of then Belgian Prime Minister Spaak and even cost him political privileges, due to the sensitive information that Degrelle could bring to light about him. Therefore, in response to the information Spaak received from d'Ursel, he sent an urgent order to the embassy in Madrid to call off and cancel the operation.

Unlike Colonel Lovinfosse, Judge Mélot would recount his disappointment and defeat in not carrying out his terrorist plan years later. This was published in the November 1977 issue, number 61, of the magazine *Confluent*. His version of the "facts" has been recounted many times and by different media outlets, such as in the magazine *Vers l'Avenir* in 1984, and in *Le Soir Illustré*, in 1988.

In order to get Mélot to abandon his initiative and stand down, the Minister of Justice promised him that Léon would be officially handed over and, therefore, legally extradited to the country. Mélot now had no reason to carry out his completely illegal kidnapping plot. In his story, Mélot commented, "I was quite surprised to be told that the Belgian government did not wish to see Degrelle returned."

It was absurd that a Belgian magistrate would even consider perpetrating an act of international terrorism, counting on absolute impunity on the part of his government.

At the insistence of his government, Albert Mélot wrote to Attorney General of Liège R. Tahon on August 11th, 1958, sharing the cancellation of his fateful kidnapping plot.

The Degrelle affair, therefore, remained unresolved in Belgium. Senator Moulin, in his speech to Parliament on March 5th, 1959, acknowledged with resignation and impotence that Degrelle "was an untouchable man."

### Conversations with the Writer Henry Charbonneau

Degrelle, meanwhile, continued his tireless work. He now had almost two hundred residences constructed on the outskirts of Constantina. He took care of everything. He was constantly traveling to Seville and Madrid to resolve any matters related to his business activities. He seemed tireless. He himself used to say he would have time to rest when death came, and that life was given in order for one to take the opportunity to live out a sense of service and mission, where the greatest satisfaction was a job well done.

In January 1959, he received a visit from the French journalist Henry Charbonneau, who spent several days with him. Charbonneau wrote a serial, entitled "Intransigence," which was published in the daily *Paris-Presse* on February 3rd, 4th, 5th, and 6th.

Degrelle and Charbonneau agreed to place their meeting point at an imaginary meeting place, thus giving false clues to potentially malicious people. They pretended to have their conversation in the vicinity of Tangier, presenting Léon as a tireless traveler who was traveling across five continents, under several different identities, using three different passports for different nationalities. The hope was that the deception would allow him to be left in peace and for his persecuting enemies to stop their eternal harassment.

There was an assertion, in this long serial interview, that did not go unnoticed by the Belgian government. Degrelle said that he might play an active role in politics again at some point in the future, leaving the Belgian authorities, once again, on the brink of a nervous breakdown. The possibility of Degrelle reemerging into political life, with his overwhelming personality, influence, and gravitas, whipped them into a frenzy. Foreign Minister Wigny wasted no time in calling the Moroccan Chargé d'Affaires to his office in Brussels in order to urge him to expel Degrelle from Moroccan territory. The Belgian Minister had taken the bait, and consequently, was then subjected to the most dreadful ridicule. The minister himself informed Parliament during their March 5th session of the measures taken with the Moroccan government to resolve the matter. Since there was no signed extradition treaty between Belgium and Morocco, they hastily signed one on February 27th, 1959. Extreme paranoia was the order of the day. At the behest of Brussels, the Rabat government scoured the Casablanca and Tangier area, trying to locate Degrelle, but coming up empty-handed.

### The Alarm Goes Off in Belgium:
### An Article Published in Turin's *La Stampa*

On Sunday, October 11th, 1959, a fresh news scandal broke out in Europe. The newspaper *La Stampa* in Turin, managed by Giulio de Benedetti, published an article by Sandro Volta with the following, well-known headline: "A Fascist Center is Discovered in Belgium." It was a scandalous claim. The headline, according to the reporter, emerged from "the inquiries about the activity of the 'Red Hand.'" The subtitle of the long article was "It is led by the Nazi Degrelle, who is condemned to death. He is located in Spain and has contacts with French and Italian fascists and former SS officers, including Skorzeny." The article spoke of "terrorist activities by a far-right group that was agitating Belgium under the name "neo-rexism," composed of former followers of Degrelle. It also referred to the fact that:

*If the information published by the newspapers in Brussels is accurate, he not only directs the "neo-rexist" organization while in exile but has also established contacts with Skorzeny and other former representatives of international Nazi-fascism to coordinate common actions in their various countries. Participating in this organization are former German SS officers, other elements from Pétain's France, and elements from the Repubblica di Salò.[77]*

The piece continued:

*The Belgian authorities are now trying to discover the hiding place of a certain Debbaudt, who appears to be the head of the Nazi-fascist organization in Belgium. Debbaudt was sentenced to death in his country because during the war he had worn an SS uniform and participated in atrocious actions. He managed to disappear from Belgium and for several years no one knew anything about him. It is true that he was present on November 20th last year in a violent street demonstration that took place in Antwerp to demand amnesty for all the former collaborators.*

There was also talk of "international danger, about which the authorities of all European countries should be concerned." The article was not ignored, nor did it go unnoticed in Spain. It was translated by the Office of Diplomatic Information of the Ministry of Foreign Affairs, and on the cover of the official document it read: "According to *La Stampa*, there is an international nazi-fascist organization led by Degrelle and Skorzeny." The case file included a photocopy of the article as it appeared in the Italian press and the Spanish translation.

### The German Weekly *Der Spiegel* Echoes the Drunken Campaign

Following *La Stampa*, journalistic sensationalism mounted rapidly. On October 21st, 1959, the German weekly *Der Spiegel,* from Hamburg, published an extensive report on these same activities with the title: "Degrelle, Uncertain Footprints in Spain Since 1945," which the Spanish Ministry of Foreign Affairs ordered to be translated. They did not hesitate to describe it as "romantic."

In the extensive news article, *Der Spiegel* pointed out that:

---

[77] The Italian Social Republic, often referred to as *la Repubblica di Salò* because of the town where it was headquartered, was based in northern Italy where Germany set up Mussolini after his rescue.

*The fact that Degrelle's shadow occasionally emerged in other countries, like in Argentina or Morocco, was only due to a skillful ruse that deceived not only Belgian diplomats, but also the authors of German encyclopedias. We read this in an edition of the Bockhaus: "Degrelle…went to Argentina in 1946." It is alleged that the Spanish government did not take the slightest trouble in finding out anything about him. The regime made up for this ignorance by saying that Degrelle had never bothered to hide from the Belgian police who visited Spain in their search for him. Degrelle had realized, rather, from the beginning, that he could only remain in Spain as long as his presence did not prove to be a compromising burden to the regime.*

In the extensive and detailed article, reference was made to the fact that Degrelle, after leaving the hospital in San Sebastián in the summer of 1946, subsequently found safety and shelter through the mediation of the Falangist Eduardo Ezquer. Ezquer had been linked, in the spring of 1943, to an operation in concert with the Third Reich to facilitate the entry of Spain into the Second World War on the side of the Axis. The story continued that Degrelle knew how to win the friendship of Eduardo Ezquer:

> *[B]y very convincing means: a discreet reference to a certain microfilm held by the Supreme Command of State Security, which included the correspondence between Ezquer and Berlin and a list of the men in his trust in various Spanish provinces. This was enough to achieve the most effective hospitality of Don Eduardo to Léon Degrelle.*

In another section, reference was made to the Duchess of Valencia's proposed initiative to the Americans, which they welcomed with enthusiasm: "Degrelle would organize, to the south of the Pyrenees, a whole series of anti-communist nests to oppose the feared invasion from the East."

For this reason:

> *Léon Degrelle went to the provinces seeking among the refugees of the Third Reich and other Axis countries active persons who could be useful to him, and finally found two separate places where he instructed his legionaries in guerrilla warfare. One of these places was located in the Guadalquivir Valley, near Seville, and the other on an estate in southern Spain, in Constantina. The necessary weapons were provided by the Americans.*

Among more half-truths, Degrelle was referred to as "opening a way through his friendship with the conservative Marquis de Valdeiglesias for Otto of Habsburg's European Documentation Center." It claimed that Chancellor Adenauer accused the Belgian government of not having been alert about tracking the fugitive Degrelle "who had been in correspondence from Spain with the Nau-Nau Circle." The article reported that he left for Tangier, although it also speculated that this might have been a ploy by the journalist François Brigneau of *Paris-Presse* to sow false clues.

## The Puzzle in Plato's Cave

Even with the enormous allocation of men and resources having been deployed to Morocco, the search had been unsuccessful. Suspicions focused once again on Andalusia. On January 17th, 1960, the Belgian Foreign Minister Wigny paid an official visit to the capital of Spain. Among the items on the agenda to be discussed with the Spanish government was "the Degrelle Case," and the imponderable legal complexities for its final resolution.

A game similar to that of "hide-and-seek" or "blind man's bluff" was thus begun. In June 1960, a rumor popped up that Degrelle was in Ireland, specifically in Dublin, along with his good friend Otto Skorzeny. The one who started this rumor was the Hungarian Jew Joel Brand in statements published on June 1st by the daily newspaper *Le Soi*. The situation was further complicated by false information leaked by interested circuits, which necessitated the Irish government to make an official denial by confirming that, "He [Degrelle] has never set foot in Ireland."

Later that summer, the mysterious Degrelle was in Cairo, next to the pyramids. This was revealed by a "generally well-informed" source, no less than Hubert Halin, editor-in-chief of the Belgian sectarian newspaper *La Voix Internationale de la Résistance*. The news did not go unnoticed by *Le Soir*, who reproduced it on October 9th and 13th, 1960. The imaginations of compulsive liars know no bounds. It was also reported that Degrelle had had a conversation with Gamal Abdel Nasser, at a special hearing that was granted to him, and that in Egypt he had connected with Dr. Johann von Leers, who worked closely with Dr. Goebbels, Minister of Propaganda of the Third Reich.

On January 9th, 1960, Degrelle's daughter Godelieve was married in Constantina in the strictest privacy. Amidst the joy of this happy event, Degrelle faced some financial trouble.

In relation to his business as a real estate promoter, he was hit with an unexpected setback, complicating his economic situation. The builder who had been carrying out the construction of the houses and bungalows had an economic crisis. The rental of the houses was not as profitable as had been expected. This threatened suspension of payments and uncertainty loomed over the project. The builder's bankruptcy seemed inevitable, which in turn would pull down Léon, since he owned the land on which the buildings were being erected.

On January 13th, 1961, General Perón, former president of the Republic of Argentina, living in exile in Madrid in the so-called *Quinta 17 de Octubre*, a villa located in the residential area of the Puerta de Hierro development, received for the first time an emissary of Léon Degrelle: his friend Gil, the great traveler. He would later meet General Perón again over the years, on the following occasions: May 7th, 1965; May 24th and November 2nd, 1966; June 17th, 1967; July 1st, 1974; and October 7th, 1985.

The year 1961 began with a new rumor. This time, it was a plot urged by Mossad, the Jewish intelligence services, who understood Degrelle to be in the capital of Lebanon, Beirut, where it was reported that he had attended an ultra-secret meeting with Alois Brunner and General Otto Remer. These three outstanding characters were brought together in the Middle East in order to plan the liberation of Adolf Eichmann, who had been kidnapped in May 1960 in Argentina, under the mandate of President Arturo Frondizi. Eichmann was forcibly removed from Argentina by his undesirable captors and brought to Israel. Obviously, the intention of this new lie was to divert attention towards Degrelle and his companions and away from Eichmann, already clenched within Israel's claws, so they could convict Eichmann in a pantomime of justice. He had already been prejudged and condemned in advance. Eichmann was found guilty and executed, his victimizers having perpetrated a new Zionist state crime that wrapped up in December 1961. An entire operation had been carried out without any kind of protest by the Argentine government for a citizen resident in their country, and for whom it provided no defense or protection. It was a crime that continues to enjoy the most absolute impunity.

The only real truth about Degrelle's eventful life is that, during his forty-nine years of exile in Spain, he never left Spanish territory.

## The Dangerous Jewish Plot

Degrelle suffered at least six attempted abductions or kidnappings during his long exile, but the most dangerous and sinister plan was the one devised by the

Zionist secret service, the Jewish Mossad, who was prepared to undertake an attempt in July 1961.

On a Sunday afternoon in April, Director General of Security Carlos Arias Navarro warned Degrelle that they had discovered a sinister plot against him. Navarro could not give many specifics on the date or place of the criminal intentions of the Jews. Navarro was a friend and knew Léon well. He had even given him shelter once at his home in Logroño. Almost at the same time, Degrelle was warned of the plot through another channel, from a source of the highest confidence and credibility: his good friend the Count of Mayalde, who had been updated by the German government. Their BND services had detected that a terrorist attack or action was underway against Degrelle. The German government sent three high-ranking officials from Bonn to alert Spanish security services, who took the threat very seriously because of the reliable source of the information and because of the danger of those who planned it. It was learned that Israel's security and espionage services wanted to abduct him with such conviction that they thought they could carry it out at any time, with no obstacles whatsoever.

Degrelle received a third confirmation of the plot from his good friend Horia Sima, commander of the Romanian Iron Guard. Sima was exiled in Spain, along with a handful of faithful and associated old legionaries, and he had access to sensitive information because of the leaks within the Gehlen network, which collaborated with the CIA during the Cold War period against Soviet communism.

Since the plot was known, it was agreed that Degrelle, for his security, would move to Madrid. For several months, he lived there in a small apartment on the Paseo de los Jesuitas, number 1, guarded by five police inspectors who never left him so as prevent and thwart the action of organized Zionist crime. The officers slept across the floor of the small apartment, so they would not lose sight of him at all! At all hours, day and night, his bodyguards kept their superiors informed by relaying the results of their surveillance through continuous telephone calls. This unending, almost suffocating, close-quarters cohabitation became a horrible situation for him that was almost unbearable. Degrelle even made the remark to Carlos Navarro, his protector, that, "I prefer to be killed by my enemies than guarded by my friends."

There was no doubt that the Jews, in mafia style, intended to kidnap Léon, and their plan was already set in motion. It would be the most serious attempt, prepared with great care and attention to detail. During their thorough preparations, Jewish agents had even planned to take him to Tel Aviv, although they later abandoned this option. The Jews had mounted the operation with treacherous, rigorous fanaticism and with that millennial rancor that typically characterizes their behavior.

The state security forces were on alert, but they decided to postpone the action until surveillance and escorts died down or until Degrelle's protection service was canceled.

In that uncertainty, Degrelle spent three months waiting and worrying. When three months passed and it was believed that the kidnappers had given up on carrying out the plan, the Director General of Spanish Security himself explained to Léon that the measures they took had succeeded in dissuading and disrupting the operation and that, therefore, their plan from every point of view was unachievable. This was good news; he could return quietly to his home, since the intentions of the perverse plan were discovered and derailed.

After his confinement in Madrid, in what seemed more like house arrest than protection, Degrelle returned to his home at La Carlina on June 30th. As soon as he arrived, however, he found that the electric lighting around the house had been disconnected and that the dogs of all the neighboring estates had been poisoned. It was evident that before the operation was set in motion, at least two well-paid communist accomplices in the area had proceeded to cut the lights at the estate and kill all the dogs. In a letter dated July 24th, Degrelle recounted this to Paul Jamin.

While still in Madrid, Degrelle received a letter from his Swiss friend François Genoud on June 18th. Genoud warned Degrelle:

*My dear Juan,*

*I am writing today to advise you to exercise caution. Chance has allowed me to discover that an attempt similar to the one that was carried out a year ago in Argentina has been planned against you. It is easy to imagine all the benefits that the country in question would enjoy internationally...*

*Be suspicious of all those whom you do not know perfectly well...be wary of your own shadow..."*

On June 22nd, 1961, Degrelle replied to Genoud:

*The plot in question? It is not safe. If these individuals truly want to achieve their goal, they will achieve it. They have powerful means, and I cannot keep ceaselessly annoying the government here. Furthermore, you know this country: strict measures are quickly relaxed, and my abduction is just a kid's game. Simply put, all I can tell you is that if the operation is carried out one day, they will not find me alive.*

*On the other hand, am I still alive? Everything has died around me, great ideas and great dreams. The years pass, and with them the golden years of strength and faith; everything is frayed and is breaking down. I am like the dead man who has been left with his eyes open in his coffin. From time to time, a hopeful breeze blows in, refreshes the atmosphere and puts me into action, but our time now is no more than jumping from miscarriage to miscarriage, like a woman who can give no more of herself. The great masses are brutalized by the enormous forces of the beasts and the corruption that dominates everything. How do you blow all this up? I would certainly jump for joy if there were but still a possibility of rebuilding a great Europe, but my hamstrings would go numb before the chance to jump ever came, if this possibility can still be given to a world that does not deserve it. In short, Michelangelo used mud, not to honor clay, but to create beauty and the eternal! Man is made of mud that can serve the worst (today) or the best (if the time of destiny comes again)...*

François Genoud was born in 1915 in Switzerland, although his father was French and his mother of British descent (Colingwood). Some of his studies were carried out in Germany and at the age of seventeen he personally met Hitler in Bonn. He would always remember Hitler's words to him at their greeting: "It is with your generation that we will build a brotherly Europe." He soon identified himself as a National Socialist and fascist, having been an activist in Switzerland, since 1933, in the National Front. In 1936 he visited the Grand Mufti, Hadj Amin al-Husseini, in Jerusalem, and a good friendship was born between them. During the Second World War, he worked with the Abwehr. After 1945, in his native homeland, he dedicated himself to helping Axis veterans and became a defender of the memory of the Third Reich. In 1947, he gained notoriety as the publisher of *A l'Enseigne du Cheval Ailé* publishing house, managing the copyrights of Léon Degrelle and Joseph Goebbels. He ensured that the reprints of works written by their authors were not used, manipulated, or misrepresented to vilify their ideals. He took care that the income generated by the publications that he sponsored would go to the legitimate heirs of the deceased authors. He was also a great defender of the Palestinian cause in the face of criminal Zionism.

Genoud wrote back to Degrelle on July 2nd, informing him that the last details of the operation had been carefully studied in the Swiss city of Lausanne and that its execution seemed immediate.

This revelation was providential and was due only to a happy stroke of luck. While Genoud was a writer and publisher, he was also a banker. As administrator of the Arab Commercial Bank of Geneva—depository of the copyrights of the works of Hitler, Martin Bormann, and Goebbels—he was having dinner one night at an upscale restaurant in Lausanne when he overheard five suspicious men. Their hushed discussion piqued his curiosity, so he strained his ear to try to catch some of their secret conversation.

The one whose voice sounded "in charge" and was coordinating the details and final preparations during the dinner was Zvi Helbert Aldouby Cidevans (originally "Dubensky"), the then Deputy Director-General for Security in Israel. This malefactor was a Jewish journalist, who held a high position in the Zionist intelligence services and who had collaborated in the writing of the book *Eichmann, Minister of Death,* published by Cassel in London that same year. In the past, he had been a dangerous activist in Israel for the terrorist group Shin Bet and was later arrested for Jewish espionage. After the kidnapping of Eichmann, all his efforts were focused on the persecution of Martin Bormann, which first led him to Degrelle, whose extensive range of high-level correspondence, would, so they thought, provide the necessary clues to lead them to the former Minister of the Third Reich.

Jewish hatred towards Degrelle was brought about because he was regarded as "Hitler's successor." That is why he had to be kidnapped and tortured to the limit of his physical endurance in an attempt to obtain information on Bormann's whereabouts, and then they would toss him like leftovers to the Belgian authorities to finish him off. Their Tel Aviv sponsors were aware of what was planned and agreed to it. They also counted on the sympathies of the International Union of Belgian Resistance and Deportation, whose Secretary General Hubert Halin was also aware of the preparations and even gave them some background on where they could find Degrelle in Spain.

Ten Jewish personnel were involved with Aldouby in the operation, some of them drawn from the lowest ranks of Irgun,[78] including a son of Yigal by the name of Avital Mossinsohn; a former bodyguard of General Degaulle; a retired police officer; a consanguineous Algerian official; the twenty-seven-year-old Jewish journalist Jacques Simon Feinsohn, often based in Paris; and even two female agents.

Genoud was quite stunned with the parts of the conversation he was able to overhear and miraculously managed to understand the gist of it, despite the low, hissing voices of the conspirators. After dinner, Genoud, with growing nervousness, quickly went to the airport to take the first plane departing for Madrid.

---

[78] *Irgun* (Hebrew אָרְגּוּן ) was an offshoot of the paramilitary organization Haganah in British Mandate Palestine. Taking a hard line in Zionist goals, many of Irgun's operations have been considered acts of terrorism.

According to their plan, agents would overpower and drag Degrelle to a ship anchored in a Mediterranean port.

The team of Jewish criminals arrived in Spain, armed with sophisticated and deadly weapons, and with abundant financing.

The American magazine *Look*, supported by Jewish capital and where Aldouby contributed regularly, had financed part of the Jewish criminal operation with the guarantee of an international exclusive on the kidnapping. They had been advanced the significant sum of one hundred thousand dollars for the exclusive, stating that:

> *It would be very good to have an informative report explained by the agents who carried it out it themselves, how they violently took possession of a political adversary and led him to death. As you can see, there are people in America, and certainly elsewhere, who pay for that sort of thing. Even so, virtue prevails!*[79]

A publishing house, a few film studios, and a German newspaper, all contaminated with Jewish capital, had also subsidized the cost of the kidnapping. The proceeds amounted to tens of millions of dollars, an amount more than sufficient to cover the planned abduction and to ensure that it did not fail due to lack of resources. They were convinced that they had everything under control.

The first one that Aldouby recruited and disclosed his evil intentions to was the former lieutenant of the shock and punishment battalions of the Palmach,[80] and former police captain and torturer Avital Mossinsohn. Mossinsohn resided in New York, from where he worked with the Mossad under the cover of carrying out media services. This scoundrel gave his consent immediately. In a few hours, through a bank in Manhattan, Aldouby transferred ten thousand dollars in traveler's checks to Mossinsohn.

As the kidnappers were heading into Spain, it was at this time that Director General of Security Carlos Arias Navarro received word about the impending plot. Genoud was also enroute to Spain to warn Degrelle. A high-alert police unit was mobilized at the border to thwart the action and cut it off at the root.

Some of the agents entered Spain and then Madrid via different routes, each one on his own so as not to raise suspicion. In Madrid they waited for Zvi Aldouby and Jacques Simon Feinsohn, who traveled together, carrying the discreetly hidden weapons and equipment in their car.

---

[79] It is unclear where the author has taken this quote from; it is almost certainly not from *Look* magazine.

[80] *Palmach* (Hebrew פלמ״ח) was an elite fighting force drawn from the Haganah.

Once the last details were cleared up, Feinsohn crossed into Spain on July 6th, through the Junquera border post in the Catalan Pyrenees. The car in which they were traveling was possibly a red Renault Dauphine model—although I think I remember that on one occasion, speaking with Degrelle on the matter, he referred to the car in question as a "Simca"—with a Parisian license plate. The car stopped next to the customs booth, where the civil guard routinely controlled the passage of light vehicles. Aldouby showed his documentation; a forged U.S. passport, issued on behalf of Alduide Idelon, containing a residence in the city of Tel Aviv, Israel. The passport quickly alerted the guard and he asked Aldouby to pull the car over. During the registered search, between the roof and the upholstery, they found an arsenal of pistols, three submachine guns, very strong nylon strings, steel shackles, bottles of chloroform and narcotics, a map of Andalusia with a target on the town of Constantina, and even a detailed plan of Degrelle's house. The cache was uncovered by the operational brilliance of the Political Social Research Brigade of Barcelona, which was then commanded by Commissioner Antonio Vicente Creix. When members of the Political Social Research Brigade interrogated the Jew Feinsohn, he confessed like a coward. He revealed almost all the details of the operation, including the existence of the ship, the name of the accomplices, and the local cronies involved in the kidnapping. Feinsohn did omit the meeting point of the operatives scheduled for that same day.

Meanwhile, Mossinsohn waited impatiently on the yacht docked in Malaga for news about the kidnapping operation. As the hours passed and there was still no contact, he started to get nervous. Like the rogue that he was, he waited as long as he could, but started to suspect that the plan might have gone awry or possibly been postponed for a better time. He traveled to Barcelona, but when he arrived there, ignorant of what had happened, he was arrested and interrogated. Unfortunately, the police were unable to tie anything to him, and he was released after being questioned at the police station.

The inventory of items that Zvi Aldouby carried in his luggage, two suitcases, at the time of his entry on July 12th, 1961 into the Barcelona prison, was as follows: eleven shirts, a towel, two full suits, a pair of slippers, a pair of black shoes, eight pairs of underwear, two rubber pads, a corduroy jacket, pajamas, a pack of razor blades, a bottle of Diademunde, three pairs of cufflinks, seven t-shirts, four handkerchiefs, five pairs of socks, a pocket handkerchief, a swimsuit, seven neckties, three ladies' undergarments,[81] a shaving razor, a plastic case, three tie

---

[81] There is no indication, from the author or otherwise, as to why Aldouby was carrying ladies' undergarments.

pins, two belts, a bottle of soap powder, a bottle of intesticarbine, a handkerchief holder, a bottle of Williams and an Adrecte ointment tube .

At the time of their arrest, six million pesetas were also seized, intended to fund the operation and to pay off communist accomplices in Seville and around Constantina.

The police also seized a large-capacity vehicle, a Lincoln Continental model with French registration,  in which they found narcotics which were intended to subdue Léon and a coffin in which to transport his unconscious body to the port of Malaga. There the operation's boat was docked, waiting to set sail for France. Degrelle would later be handed over to Belgium.

In the custody of the General Captaincy of the Military Region IV, case number 67-IV-61 was filed against Israeli citizen and Mossad leader Zvi Aldouby (a native of Romania), and against the French Jew Jacques Simon Feinsohn. Based on the statements given by Feinsohn and Aldouby during their interrogations, two Spanish collaborators were also arrested and prosecuted by the Seville police.

In seizing the weapons, various letters of introduction for individuals identified as anarchists from Seville, handcuffs, chemical/pharmaceutical products, and maps, the charges that were filed against them were illicit possession of weapons, currency trafficking, and subversion. The offense of attempted kidnapping was excluded, but only because it had been planned and originated abroad.

On July 12th, 1961, the Chief Commander and Judge Examiner of the case, Don Bernabé Abalos, of the Special Military Court of E. and O.A., appointed Artillery Lieutenant Don Rafael Díaz de San Pedro (Armed Regiment Seventy-Two in Barcelona) as legal counsel for the accused. The defense attorney was advised not to mention the attempted abduction at all and that the wisest course of action was to limit the proceedings to the "weapons cache," which the accused were found in possession of.

Since Feinsohn had a French passport, defense attorney Díaz de San Pedro contacted the French consulate in Barcelona to bring the criminal act to their attention. The news was not well received, and the presence of French activists and terrorists was embarrassing for the consulate.

On July 28th, these wrongdoers were tried by a War Council, in the Council Chamber of the Military Government, at la Puerta de la Paz, in front of the shipyards in Barcelona.

At the War Council held on August 2nd, 1961, in Ciudad Condal, the defense secured the acquittal of the two Spanish citizens, but the military court found Aldouby and Feinsohn guilty for the offense of "weapons possession," and sentenced them to six and nine years, respectively. This was less than the nine and ten-year imprisonment requested by the prosecution, since the major crime in question, kidnapping, had not been planned on Spanish soil, nor had it succeeded.

Nothing happened to the anarchists in Seville who were implicated, except for the additional information being reported on their police records. The sentence was firm, but attorney Lauderto Franco, who was a Jew with ties to Zionist intelligence services, and who worked at the French Consulate, was allowed to give his opinion against the military defense. He found that the judgment was legally sounds in all its terms but criticized the defense for not having appealed it.

The Captain General of Catalonia was Don Pablo Martín Alonso, who, in order to avoid problems related to this case at the Modelo prison, sent the convicts to other prisons in the interior of Spain. Aldouby was transferred to Burgos. Feinsohn was eventually transferred, and they both served time in the Burgos prison. In December 1963, Feinsohn returned to France. On February 10th, 1964, Aldouby, left the Burgos prison; he had been granted house arrest, until his provisional release in March 1965.

Nicolas Franco Bahamonde, the brother of Franscisco Franco, was involved in the early release of the two Jewish terrorists. He had interceded for prison benefits to be applied and that Aldouby and Feinsohn be released as soon as possible. At that time, Nicholas had held the position of General Manager at the Renault Car Company in Spain. Pierre Dreyfus, a Jew, was the director of the Renault headquarters in France. Between them they had managed to get Aldouby and Feinsohns released with the promise that they would not speak to each other ever again. They broke this promise several years later, when they collaborated on the book *Les Vengeurs* (*The Avengers*), published in Paris in 1968 by the Fayard Publishing House. In the book, they hypocritically narrated that they had intended to kidnap Martin Bormann because they believed that he was hiding out on Degrelle's estate. The book also said that Degrelle was the only person who could have known the whereabouts of Martin Bormann's place of refuge. According to Jewish lies, Bormann had been saved in Italy, hidden in Madrid, and then sent, together with friends, to South America. The fact was that Degrelle had no idea what happened to Bormann after Hitler's death on April 30th, 1945, even though Bormann's fellow escapee, Artur Axmann, was a good friend of Léon. Artur Axmann, head of the Hitler Youth, explained that Bormann died the day after the Führer's suicide when he tried to leave Berlin surrounded by the Soviet Red Army.

Léon Degrelle, in a series of letters sent to the brilliant cartoonist Paul "Alidor" Jamin on July 24th and 27th and August 10th, 11th, and 17th of 1961, gave him an account of everything that happened.

During the proceedings and after the sentencing passed at the War Council, the Civil Guard put guards around La Carlina. This surveillance was even extended two more months after the sentencing of Aldouby and Feinsohn.

Blas Piñar relates in his memoirs:

*From persecution he could not escape. Someone would come from abroad, periodically, for the purpose of taking his life. On one occasion, in order to avoid an attempt, he sought refuge in a monastery; on another was admitted to a hospital; and on another he was hidden in a village in the province of Ciudad Real.*

Léon, even after everything that had happened, commented humorously, "Outsmarting the Jews…I like it!"

This was not the only occasion the Jews tried to kidnap him. On another occasion, a Jewish expedition came out from Anvers with the same criminal intentions. Surprisingly, a Jewish woman showed up one morning at the home of Léon's sister Suzanne, who was married and living in Flanders. Suzanne was completely removed from any political involvement, although she had also been imprisoned twice in 1944 and 1945 in Belgium. Suzanne worked hard for the survival of her large family of six children. When Suzanne let the woman inside, she said to her:

*Madam, I have finally been able to find your address. Your brother Léon saved my life during the war. I would like to thank you for that. He is going to be kidnapped in Spain and I have come to warn you. The team will disembark in Bilbao.*

She then recounted all the details of this new operation. It was possible to thwart it in time. When the ship on which the kidnappers were traveling arrived in Bilbao, the Spanish police were already waiting for them. They were arrested and interrogated on landing.

A similar plan had been hatched in Morocco, even with a helicopter ready to take off from Larache and land on Degrelle's estate. Degrelle had installed a Roman-style theater on the terrace of his house. It had to be completely remodeled in such a way as to make it impossible to land a helicopter on it to avoid kidnapping attempts by air. He also reinforced the security measures at La Carlina by installing a machine gun on the tower, just above his bedroom.

The operation out of Morocco was mounted with great financial means and orchestrated by more Jewish operatives. Just as Adolf Eichmann had been the black beast of the Jews during the war, Léon Degrelle was their black beast of the post-war period, and an objective to be taken out. Yet again, this attempt was unsuccessful.

There was one last attempted abduction during the Easter holiday of 1962. A French friend offered Degrelle refuge on a fenced-in property in good condition not far from the capital. His French friend, short of cash, had been renting this property to an American colonel for the then considerable sum of forty thousand pesetas a month under a six-month lease. Since the colonel would be away from the house, Degrelle's friend said it would be a perfect place to stay. Degrelle quickly accepted and moved in.

When the house was once again inhabited by the colonel three days after Léon left, he awoke at 1:30 a.m. to the frantic barking of his huge guard dog. He looked through the large windows overlooking the garden, trying to see what was happening. He saw one individual hidden right next to the bedroom window that Degrelle had occupied during the three months he stayed in the house, and another individual climbing the fence near the tennis court, appearing to have the intention of jumping over to join the person near the window.

The colonel, because of his military background, had an arsenal of weapons at his disposal. He began shooting in all directions to intimidate the criminals but failed to hit anyone. The kidnappers, with a new failure to their credit, managed to escape. This American colonel, one of the chief officers in his country's intelligence services, had no idea why there were trespassers on the property, and if not for the alertness of his dog, he might have been harmed in the kidnapping attempt. Once again, Degrelle escaped certain death.

## The Eternal Return

On August 12th, 1961, Léon Degrelle sent a letter to the director of the newspaper *Soir*, who refused to publish it. He finally had it reproduced in *L'Europe Réelle* in Brussels. It was a response to a defamatory article that had been published on August 1st in *Soir* with the title "The Degrelle Case Begins Again." The letter opened by saying:

> *I just learned about the article you published on August 1st, 1961. In it you republished, with evident venom, the slander, a hundred times thrown, and a hundred times refuted, of "Degrelle, a war criminal." Criminal of what? You know perfectly well that the lamentable accusations of "war crimes" leveled against me in 1945 and 1946 have totally collapsed and have been so for a long time.*

In his extensive letter, he once again dismantled, point by point, the unceasing slander. In one of the paragraphs, he said openly:

> *You manage to stay in your position as a patented slanderer by condemning your adversaries to silence! Banned from publishing our version of the facts! Banned from disseminating our works, labeled as "uncivic" in bookstores! Banned from appealing a trial held in default, that is, where the accused has no possibility of explaining himself! Prohibitions! Bans! Why so much prohibition against everything if you are right? No, Degrelle cannot speak! Degrelle cannot write! Degrelle cannot be judged fairly! Gags everywhere!*
>
> *You call yourself Democrats! You are really nothing but freedom-farces!*

Once again in his response to *Soir*, he insisted on the chief argument of his firm position:

> *For fifteen years, I have been proposing a real judicial debate, without subterfuge…an exiled man alone, without anyone's support, offers to return to Brussels and stand before the court where he knows that he risks his head, showing his face…I offer my head, but not in silence.*

## A Letter to the Belgian Monarch

A few days later, on August 20th, 1961, Léon Degrelle sent an extensive letter to King Baudouin of Belgium to inform him of many things that occurred while he was a youth and Degrelle was in exile,[82] and things that those around the King did not allow him to know with exactitude, issues around which violent controversies continued to erupt from time to time. Degrelle enlightened the king on such essential issues as: "What had been the motives of the political action of rexism from 1940 to 1945? Why did two divisions of Walloon and Flemish volunteers fight

---

[82] Young Prince Baudouin was evacuated to France during the German invasion in May 1940, and then to Spain, while his father King Leopold III personally commanded the Belgian defense. After Leopold III unconditionally surrendered to the Germans, the children eventually returned to Laeken, Brussels in August. After the Allied landing at Normandy in June 1944, the royal family was taken to Hirschstein, Germany and then to Strobl, Austria until the U.S. Army took over the area in May 1945. The royal family was unable to return to Belgium, however, because the self-declared "Belgian government in exile" in London, who were never joined by the king, accused King Leopold III of collaboration with the Nazis. By referendum in 1950, the public voted to have the king return, although government dissent and protests eventually caused King Leopold III to abdicate in favor of Baudouin, who then became King Baudouin in 1951.

during that period on the Eastern Front against Communism?" and "What 'war crimes' have I been convicted of?" He did so "by appealing to a Christian sense of truth and justice" when answering these questions.

In the letter he referred to his sixteen years of relentless persecution following the Second World War, carried out against all rexist patriots, by rabidly partisan improvised magistrates. They enforced illegal arrests, death sentences in abundance, were carried away by hatred, muzzled any opposition, did not allow them to make their voices heard and criminally prohibited the dissemination of their writings, nullifying any freedom of expression and thought in a ruthless manner, and discriminating against citizens before the law. He informed His Majesty of how the publication in France of *The Russia Campaign*, in which he describes the four years of struggle endured by Belgian combatants on the Eastern Front, in addition to being banned in Belgium, provoked the ire of Prime Minister Spaak. Spaak also succeeded in getting the book banned and requisitioned in France thanks to the pressure he leveraged. He also made him aware of the publication of his work *La Cohue de 1940* (*The Mob of 1940*), which dealt with the political explanation of Belgian collaboration in an extensive document of more than five hundred pages. The tyrant Spaak, under the orders of the former king, obtained cooperation from the Swiss government to not only have the book confiscated from the second day of its publication, but that even, in order to avoid any vestige of it, to have the lead plates for its manufacture be melted down right there in the presence of the police. This clearly demonstrated the stark fear of the revelations contained in the work.

He also informed King Baudouin that:

> *It is true that, in 1940, we merely fulfilled the instructions of King Leopold that he sent to us through his secretary, Count Capelle, and also because our country was down and dying, and we wanted, with all the fervor of our patriotism, to stand her up, come to her aid, and save her. We acted as we did because the King, your father, wanted it and because our patriotic duty required it of us.*

He told him of the ignoble Spaak's maneuvering in those days, and how, in the month of May, in Limoges, he rudely insulted his father, King Leopold. Soon afterwards, Spaak actually offered himself to Hitler, and talked like the socialist Henry De Man. He said that "Hitler's victory was, for Belgium, a liberation." He described to King Baudouin a great deal of paradoxes about the contradictory behavior and cowardly attitude of this miserable politician who was never a man who stood for anything and appeared without conviction or principle.

He reminded King Baudouin that:

*Our good faith was total. One does not die for what he does not believe in. Thousands of my comrades died for an ideal. That is why we must have, at least, the decency to listen to the defense of the survivors, to let them honestly say what their dreams were, their struggle, and, in defeat, their hopelessness!*

He made him aware of the unprecedented degree of intolerance in Belgium, where slander against the defeated was common practice. Degrelle reiterated to him that he had never been charged with anything, nor convicted of "war crimes," despite the political propaganda campaigns unleashed by his adversaries to massacre the vanquished. Spaak, with his nauseating slander to try to secure Degrelle's extradition, was repeatedly rejected by the Spanish government for the request being politically motivated. He then tried to get the extradition through by altering the request with the allegation that "he [Degrelle] is an odious common criminal," but without being able to present the least evidence or testimony of such a terrible assertion. Degrelle also expressed to the king his pride in having fought against communism.

He continued:

*The Belgian constitution that he [Spaak] had sworn to respect proclaimed that "all Belgians are equal before the law." Then, Sire, it is time for Your Majesty to set this out little by little…We the defeated, the insulted, the outraged people demand the right to defend ourselves, the right to speak, the right to write, the fundamental rights of every citizen in any civilized country. We call on the courts before which we are asked to appear that we be able to explain to our people our reasons and truths freely and fully, rather than be rejected from every courtroom through illegal detentions that prohibit any remedy through a conviction in absentia. This is what happened in my case. I found out about my conviction eight months after the fact!*

*This entire horrible repression is unique in Europe. No other country exists where this manhunt, since 1945, is currently practiced!*

Degrelle addressed Baudouin because he was king "of all Belgians, both the persecuted and the persecutors," and he hoped the king could intercede on his behalf.

In its September 2nd, 1961, edition, the newspaper *Métropole* published, "If Degrelle entered Belgium tomorrow, he would be immediately imprisoned. He would have the opportunity to defend himself during his trial. He has also been very lucky not to have voluntarily shown the tip of his nose." Léon wrote a courageous and forceful response on September 22nd. They did not dare publish it, so it was printed, like all his previous responses, in *L'Europe Réelle* by his unconditional friend Debbaudt.

## A Letter to a Young Comrade

In reply to a letter sent to him by a comrade, dated November 11th, 1961, Degrelle sent the following letter:

*I have received your letter with joy and with emotion. Nothing is as hard for me as having been cut off from the youth, and nothing comforts me so much as receiving a letter from a young and idealistic person like you, who understands the ideal that encouraged us and for which we have let ourselves be devoured rather than yield. What weighs upon one in exile is neither loneliness (this is often, to the contrary, a wonderful blessing) nor the bitterness of defeat, but rather it is that feeling of impotence, being unable to project all the forces that roar inside of one and to convince others born to transmit these forces as I was born to carry them. This is the torture of every day, every hour; that nothing happens. At least, in the shadows of this drama, a sincere and beautiful letter like yours is a little light, a bit of a rainbow...*

*Rise up with valor! Everything can change abruptly! Our generation, too, had to climb out of the abyss. Living, this means fighting, believing, struggling up until our very last breath! We have what is essential: willingness and faith!*

## Letter to the Belgian Parliament

On September 10th, 1962, Léon Degrelle wrote to the Belgian Parliament a long epistle that began by saying:

*Mr. President, gentlemen, and dear old companions:*

*I am the former representative of Brussels, Léon Degrelle, who writes to you today.*

*A debate is being announced in Parliament, during which my specter will be evoked. Fearing that what is essential will not be said, I shall take the lead in the discussion.*

*By reading the preliminary statements of the recorded interpellants, it is easy to imagine that, once again, the subject of my extradition will come back to the fore.*

*For your part, the desire to see me again in Belgium is very kind of you! I would gratify said desire solicitously if your intention were not covered with the appearance of an old cheat! In short, on numerous occasions, I have offered to return among you, without the need to make so much clamor in foreign embassies, and even in New York, at the UN.*

*Try to get a country, whichever one, to extradite me today? You know very well that this will not happen! Even though I am among wild Indians, or with the Grand Turk, or among General Franco and his government, you will not get them to hand me over, to hand over to you, twenty years later, a politician for the sole cause of being the object of the hatred you profess!*

*This cannibalism, with retroactive effect, is perceived as very strange abroad. They doubt the Belgians, their humanitarian feelings, and, more seriously, their sense of humor.*

*If your vehement wish were to have some chance of being fulfilled, then it would be necessary that you do not disqualify yourself by continuing to support your old extradition demands based on long-unmasked lies.*

*Be that as it may, "honorable" parliamentarians, as you proclaim yourselves, you have lied, you have long lied…*

He continued to irrefutably dismantle the unsustainable arguments alleged for his extradition, which, to his mind, had provoked international discredit of its politicians and its form of justice to the world.

It was foolish nonsense to continue insisting on lies, especially since it had already been shown that they were unfounded, such as those held, for example, by the socialist government and Parliamentarian Georges Bohy. The missive, with brave and challenging pluck, continued:

*If you sincerely wish that I return to Belgium, you do not need to continue lying. It would be enough, as I ask you, to simply accept fair play, a fair justice on the day of trial. You would have seen me show up in Brussels immediately. Twenty times I have offered my return. Each time, you, and the press devoted to you, have squandered my offer. You have hidden behind laws of exception, prohibiting an accused man from explaining himself, from publishing something even in the most insignificant newspaper, from writing a book or an article where he might explain, through direct testimony, why he took the position he did, in a different way from yours, to serve their homeland from 1940 to 1945!*

He later remarked that, "you are the legislators! You could repeal unjust laws and create correct laws tomorrow!"

After plausible legal and logical arguments, he ended by exhorting them:

*Under no illusions (for I know your hidden ways!) I challenge you: adopt legal provisions so that a real trial is possible regarding the collaboration and combat of Belgian volunteers on the Eastern Front; guarantee, under the control of an international body (the UN, for example), the publication and radio broadcast of the hearings in their entirety, where the defense can express itself freely, with full latitude; and vote on and organize these guarantees for the big trial. In this way, you will not need to scream yourselves hoarse or chafe against this apoplectic crisis by demanding my extradition from Franco, or Nasser, or Hassan II. I would present myself in Brussels without further ado, very calmly, to your satisfaction and to mine. This depends on you, the Belgian Parliament and the government that has come out of it! This depends on your fear (in which I believe), or your courage (in which I do not believe).*

*Which do you choose? The drowning man of the past? Or, finally, the light? I know well what is going to happen. You are going to writhe and shout, finding a virtuous great escape!*

*Do you think the public will be content with these wild gesticulations? To you, there, at the foot of the white wall? Black? What do you respond? Me, me?*

*I send you my greeting.*

## Letter to the Belgian Catholics

On September 22nd, 1961, he wrote the "Letter to Belgian Catholics," which he addressed to the important Catholic newspaper *La Cité*, and which was also published in *L'Europe Réelle* and the conservative weekly *Métropole*. The Catholic newspaper had spoken out in the debate in Belgium's left-wing press about Degrelle's once again having offered to stand before Belgian justice if a number of minimum guarantees were given in order for him to attend a fair and serious trial and to be able to explain himself to the public.

In this extensive letter, he reviewed the key issues of his personal and political situation. He once again reiterated the shame of Belgium's six hundred eighty-two thousand eight hundred fourteen post-war judicial dossiers and the thousands of people sentenced to death in the heinous "democratic" repression unleashed by the government. He provided further evidence of the vile behavior of current Belgian policy makers in relation to Hitler during the war and their shameless betrayal after, as was the case with Prime Minister Spaak and several of his ministers, including Hendryk (Henri) de Man, Chairman of the Belgian Socialist Party. These cowards converted into political cannibals against their own countrymen who were loyal to a higher ideal. He discussed the true enemies of the monarchy, camouflaged within power networks, and the attempted kidnappings by Israeli secret services, which were thwarted by the Spanish police, as well as the position of the Belgian press in its wild slander campaign, etc. He ended the writing with a postscript:

> *Considering that no judicial explanation is possible at the present time, and if you are willing to open in your newspaper a loyal debate on what rexism, collaboration, and our struggle on the Eastern Front were, I am at your disposal to answer all the questions that you want to ask me, either in writing for your columns or verbally. I am willing to receive an envoy (or several) from your newspaper, accompanied, if you wish, by one or another genuine résistant. They can ask me, point by point, without time limit (hours, days, weeks), whatever pleases them. We would jointly establish the answers in writing, in an honest way, in order to avoid any future objections.*
>
> *I would ask, in order to avoid complications of a diplomatic nature, not to reveal, under any circumstances, in which country the interview, or interviews, would be held if we do them. These are all my conditions.*
>
> *The decision is in your hands. Fifteen days after you have made it discreetly known in your newspaper that this proposition is accepted, the address of the meeting place will be communicated to you.*
>
> *Surely you will consider my offer. I hope that you will, without the showiness of an annoying parrot. Finally, as far as I am concerned, what should be done will be done.*

### The Force of Reason, Not the Reason of Force

The presence of Degrelle in Spain slowly began to be officially recognized and accepted by Belgium as of May 22nd, 1962, as evidenced by a letter from the Belgian Foreign Minister to Member of Parliament Glinne in response to his parliamentary question. Time would show Degrelle to be consistently in the right.

In the newspaper *Le Monde*, on June 1st, 1962, statements by Léon Degrelle were published, highlighting the phrase "This is going to have consequences." This led a collaborator of the Information Services of the Spanish General Directorate of Security to draft a note on June 5th to the Minister of the Interior:

*Brussels, May 31. Again, Léon Degrelle, head of "Rex" and the SS Walloon Legion, who managed to take refuge in Spain in May 1945, is being discussed. Answering a question in Parliament, Spaak has stated that the Belgian authorities have, for years, been in possession of information indicating that he is indeed in Spain. Unfortunately, the minister explained, of the many interventions to obtain his extradition, none has ever succeeded. Indeed, the Spanish government has excused itself with various pretexts, and for several years Madrid has maintained that, due to the time that has elapsed since the end of hostilities, there is a real "moral principle" at stake.*

*The Belgian government has rejected the Spanish thesis and the Degrelle affair is a permanent dispute between the two countries, Spaak concluded.*

*Meanwhile, Degrelle continues to have contacts with Belgian "collaborators" and, principally, with former SS member Debbaudt, who runs the neo-Nazi newspaper 'L'Europe Réelle' in Belgium. In its last edition, Degrelle attacked several Belgian personalities, calling them "political cannibals, bloodsuckers, public criminals, hyper-capitalistic sharks, etc."*

*He also claims that the Israelis have tried to kidnap him in Spain, just as they did with Eichmann in Argentina.*

*Degrelle is threatening Belgian Senate President Mr. Paul Struye.*

*Referring to the O.A.S., whose procedures he clearly approves, Degrelle concludes: "With correct people, correction. With others, chastisement, and chastisement can take on less peaceful aspects than just epistolary responses. Much has evolved in this regard in recent times. You must stop insulting us and gagging us at the same time. Either you allow us to defend ourselves before real justice or you stop slandering us. If not, one day or another this will have consequences. Many consequences. It will then be too late to complain..."*

## The Last Days in Constantina: His Daughter Anne's wedding

On July 21st, 1962, the National Holiday of Belgium, Degrelle's daughter Anne Degrelle Lemay married a young Falangist lawyer named Juan Servando Balaguer Parreño in Constantina. He was the son of the local dentist, and the brother of three good Spaniards, also all Falangists: Conrado, a police officer based in Seville; Francisco, who studied political science; and Alfonso, a practicing attorney.

Léon Degrelle was the godfather of the religious ceremony, entering the church with Anne on his arm. He wore the Falangist summertime gala uniform, in ivory white, and all his war decorations: the Iron Cross, Second Class; the War Merit Cross, with swords; the Insignia of the Wounded; the Iron Cross, First Class; the Silver Badge of Infantry Assault; the Order of the Cross of Burgundy; the Golden Close Combat Clasp; the German Cross in Gold; the Knight's Cross with Oak Leaves; and the Medal of the Spanish Falange Old Guard.

The fruit of this marriage would be four Spanish sons.

When I met Léon Degrelle, he was kind enough to sign a studio photograph for me in which he is standing between the young spouses.

In number 695 of the French magazine, *Paris Match*, dated August 4th, 1962—widely distributed in Belgium—they published on page thirty-two a photo of Léon Degrelle taken during the wedding ceremony. It was featured next to a long article entitled "Return of the Swastika: Degrelle, the Rexist, Appears at His Daughter's Wedding in a Göring-Style Uniform." In the article, it read:

> *The head of the Belgian Rexist Party, who fought on the Eastern Front with the Walloon Division, has retired in Spain. On July 21st, he married his daughter Anne-Marie, 26, to Juan Servando Balaguer, 24, a Spanish lawyer. After the ceremony, Degrelle offered a reception at his property in Constantina (near Seville) to his one hundred fifty guests.*

Among the guests who attended the wedding were Jaime de Mora y Aragón, the brother of Fabiola, the Queen of Belgium; the former minister and brother-in-law of Franco, Ramón Serrano Suñer; and Colonel Otto Skorzeny. The "Nazi uniform" was actually the dress uniform of the Spanish Falange. Degrelle was authorized to wear it because of his status as a member of the Falange Old Guard since 1934.

## The Magazine *Triunfo*

The writer César Alonso de los Ríos, in his recent work entitled *Yo Tenía un Camarada (I Had a Friend)*, published by Áltera, Barcelona in 2007, reveals a curious side anecdote in relation to the then popular weekly *Triunfo*, which was dedicated to shows and especially to the cinema. In the section, "Francoist Past of the Left-Wing Masters," de los Ríos states the magazine was owned and managed by Luis Angel Escurra and his family. It had come to have significant clout because of the services it provided to the previous regime. In 1962, the weekly became a regular publication of general information, turning its editorial line to left-wing positions after being sold to multimedia company Movierecord, led by the Belgian journalist

Jo Linten. Linten was of the same political bent as Léon Degrelle. The weekly served as a springboard to progressively take over the Moro Film Studios with Movieplay. In addition to *Triunfo,* this old rexist would later edit the magazines *Mundo Joven* and *Teleprograma.* As Alonso de los Ríos points out in his book, "he was a former Nazi, in the good times still to be had under Franco and was the one who made possible the creation of the cultural magazine of the left. Manuel Fraga ended up shutting this down."

## The Departure

León Degrelle's departure to Fuengirola, his new destination on Costa del Sol, took place in 1963. There were more than just memories and experiences left behind in Constantina. In Holy Week of the following year, Anne Degrelle and her family inhabited that beautiful "White Castle" La Carlina.

At this same time, his beloved neighbor of the La Carlina estate, Mrs. Ivonne, a great friend of the Degrelle family, donated an important part of her personal library to the Constantina Public Library. Today, the bibliographic legacy is preserved in its Ancient Books Section.

Years later, Degrelle unexpectedly showed up in the village. The locals greeted him with heartfelt affection and tenderness when they saw him walking along calle Mesones once more.

In Costa del Sol, Degrelle settled in a single house known as *La Cabaña,* [83] surrounded by a beautiful Mediterranean garden, in the sunny town of Torreblanca del Sol. The home was situated on top of a hill belonging to the municipality of Fuengirola, from where you could gaze upon, as far as the eye could see, the mythological *Mare Nostrum.* [84]

---

[83] [Spanish for cabin, cottage.]
[84] A Roman name for the Mediterranean Sea.

*Léon Degrelle in the uniform of the Spanish Falange*

# V

# Settling in the Watchtower of La Cabaña (Fuengirola)

# (1963–1985)

## The New Dwelling on the Costa del Sol

Coming from Constantina (near Seville), Léon Degrelle arrived in the municipality of Fuengirola (Malaga) in 1963, to live on top of a hill from which one could see the whole coast. The hill was crowned by an exclusive house, surrounded by a subtropical garden called La Cabaña. This would be his new dwelling for almost a quarter of a century.

Fuengirola is sheltered by Mount Calamorro and is situated on a coastal strip of 8 kilometers (5 miles) of Mediterranean shoreline. It stretches approximately 30 kilometers (18.6 miles) west of the city of Malaga. The city center today used to be, in early antiquity, a tiny Iberian town, before being expanded by the Phoenicians. It may have been the site of the fortified town of the Punic colony of Syalis, later to become the Roman settlement of Suel. Suel was a federated city of which there are still remarkable ruins, such as the remains of a temple, baths, mosaics of a patrician village, and fish salting workshops. At the foot of the hill where the castle was erected, a funeral urn and a statue of the goddess Venus are located.

If, during the Roman period, the maritime strip enjoyed some importance, in the low Middle Ages it was transformed into a wasteland due to depopulation in the area. Various disparate reasons are given for this, ranging from harassment and looting to the effects of an earthquake or the devastating passage of some Gothic tribe en route to the south of the peninsula.

The Arabs, after crossing the Strait of Gibraltar in 711, repopulated those solitary lands, calling the town Sohail, and erected a castle, which was enlarged in the time of Abd al-Rahman III. They put in a watchtower which they named after the star Suhail, for that is the promontory from which the guiding star of the desert Bedouins could be seen. The Moorish town ended up being burned in August 1485, and its castle taken during the Christian Reconquista in the time of the Catholic Monarchs. It was taken on the day of Saint Cayetano, under the command of Garcelán Requesens and Rodrigo Ponce de León, who established it as a defensive fortress.

The town of Fuengirola became, over time, a district of Mijas, with its meager population centered on the shops of muleteers and fishermen passing through, forming a village of a few shacks.

The castle was occupied by the French for two years (1810–1812) during the French invasion. Beginning in 1841, the district was separated into an independent municipality with the name Fuengirola, reminiscent of the Genovese seafaring vessels, or "girolas," which gave their name to the river that crosses that area. The municipality's highest population was thought to be a thousand inhabitants, although in reality it was no more than half that.

La Cabaña was located in the upper area of the town, in Torreblanca del Sol, a residential neighborhood of Fuengirola. It was a place which until recently had been a small, secluded fishing port situated midway on the road between Malaga (24 kilometers or 15 miles) and Marbella (23 kilometers or 14 miles). Fuengirola, with its enormous beach, has along its shoreline a promenade of 7 kilometers (4 miles) that borders the sea. In from the coast, towards the west, is the Mijas mountain chain and its town some 8 kilometers (5 miles) in.

Léon began to remake his life there. In that house, dominating the slopes that go down to the sandy beaches of a warm and soothing sea, Léon received German Admiral Karl Dönitz, who traveled to Torreblanca del Sol to pay his compliments. He was also visited by Professor Juan Rof Carballo, whose ideology differed profoundly with Degrelle's, but who nonetheless was a friend. Carballo stayed there on one occasion for fifteen days to write. Otto Skorzeny was another visitor who frequented Degrelle's La Cabaña. Degrelle also periodically hosted Abel Bonnard, Jaime de Mora y Aragón, Clarita Stauffer, Prince Junio Valerio Borghese, and many others.

Léon's friendship with the well-known French actor Alain Delon was quite talked about in the area. During the filming in Spain of the movie *El Zorro*, which was a huge box office success, Degrelle and Delon could be seen together in friendly company. One photograph in particular, taken in 1973, was seen around the world. During their visits while Delon was filming, Degrelle stated, "Alain Delon comes to visit me; sometimes I receive him at home and other times he invites me to the set to watch the scenes that he is playing in. Does this mean that he is a rexist?

Certainly not, but he is one of the characters who arouses the passions of those who have nothing to do with the battles of the Forum…"

The Walloon Legion Corporal Henri Moreau, a volunteer in the first contingent of volunteers that left Brussels on August 8th, 1941, for the Eastern Front, was a war veteran who lost both arms. He was the author of the book *La Neige et le Sang* (*Snow and Blood*), which was published in France in the 1960s under the pseudonym "Paul Terlin." He was a social thinker of renown and the author of various works on political economics. In the June-July 1963 edition of the monthly magazine *Dossier du Mois*, a special edition dedicated to Léon Degrelle, he published an article titled "*Léon Degrelle, tel que je l'ai connu…*" ("Léon Degrelle, as I Knew Him…"), in which he says, "Degrelle was, in my view, the most attractive Belgian political person of the sad 1929 to 1945 period, and the most discussed too…. Degrelle was a good soldier and a brave soldier."

*Léon Degrelle with the famous French actor Alain Delon,*
*during the shooting of a film in Malaga, Spain*

## Under the Shadow of the Cross in the Valley of the Fallen

In August 1963, Léon Degrelle stayed in the Monastery of Santa Cruz del Valle de los Caídos (Holy Cross of the Valley of the Fallen). He stayed in the community of the Benedictine monks, caretakers of the holy places, in the shadow of the great granite cross. He spent several days in meditation and prayer, leading a contemplative life, serene, austere, monastic, occupying a cell and attending all the religious services and prayers dictated by the monastic rule. He took part in the Eucharist. He wrote pages in meditation on his faith. He kept a private diary, where he reflected upon the singing and psalmody in voice, without musical accompaniment, which formed solemn Gregorian chant. He found relief from his fatigue and struggle in the oasis of his deep and sincere religiosity, living next to the tomb that houses the mortal remains of his admired comrade José Antonio, the founding initiator of the Spanish Falange.

*Léon Degrelle in the Basilica of the Valley of the Fallen*
*in front of the tomb of José Antonio Primo de Rivera*

During his stay in the monastery, he wrote down all that he contemplated in his diary. On August 8th, in an atmosphere of silence and incense, he attended the divine offices, from where the monks go out intoning their chants to the refectory to break bread. At the entrance of the refectory, two lay brothers waited for the procession and would offer to those who came, in processional silence, water in a basin to wash their hands and a towel. During the light meal, a monk from the monastery recited prayers in monotone, which seemed to Degrelle to "ruin one's appetite rather than encouraging it." All fathers and brothers wore the brown habit of the order. On the heads of the younger ones, the tonsure could be clearly seen, while the heads of the older ones were bald or graying. He noted that the atmosphere that he took in during the meal was sad and dull. In his diary he wrote that if he was "the abbot, during the meal I would play moving music to give some joy, the joy of God!"

When the *melopea* (music) was finished, everyone remained silent with their eyes fixed on the emptiness behind their glasses. He noticed that almost everyone wore glasses, probably from reading in the dark or from tiring their eyes so close to the missals, or so far from the chanter stands, or from trying to read the minuscules in the song books. After the meal, a passage from the recent *History of Spain* was read; specifically, on that day, the atrocities of the Asturias Revolution in October 1934 were recounted. It was finished by singing the *Miserere*.[85] When the abbot rose and left the dining room, Léon returned to his austere cell. He reflected on the frugal and spartan-like food that he had just eaten, not so much for its austerity, with that white bread and the somewhat sweetened wine that accompanied the potato stew, but because of the gloomy atmosphere in which all the experiences in the refectory unfolded. In his cell he wrote, "My God, yes, you are the house of misery, but You are also life, You who have created it, and You are joy itself."

On Sunday, August 9th, the sky at dawn appeared clear. He looked up at the huge cross pointing toward infinity, like a divine finger, like an immense menhir,[86] placed like a space rocket high on the peak of Cuelgamuros Mountain. When he fixed his gaze on the stone monument, firmly seated on the steep rock, it seemed to sway slightly.

He attended the community breakfast. The bells rang for matins at 5:30 a.m. The first lights of the day, after a serene night, began to lighten in a range of blues that flooded everything with indigo. He began to adapt his life to this cadence of

---

[85] Latin for "Have mercy on me, O God."
[86] A standing stone.

stillness and reflection. In addition, the only noticeable noise was the ringing of the bell.

The monks had changed their brown habits from the previous day to white robes. He discovered the choir that precedes the procession of priests, through the arches, toward the depths of the carved rock. He attended the divine office. The Mass was concelebrated and sung.

The days passed in the greatest of tranquility. From time to time—as he noted in his diary—his thoughts would go back to Andalusia, to his tiles of polychrome colors. He thought of the devout silence of the flowers in his garden, of the fragrance of its nights, and he meditated "I am still a little there, a piece of my soul continues there." Sometimes, in his barren cell, he felt alone and shipwrecked. He thought about his loved ones.

On Tuesday, August 11th, the Father Prior invited him, after the mortifying *miserere* at lunch, to have a cup of coffee, accompanied by a Benedictine liqueur, in the intimacy of his "command staff." The abbot of the monastery was Fray Justo Pérez de Urbel, a native of the village of Pedrosa del Río Urbel, in the province of Burgos. He had been born there in 1895. At the age of twelve he entered the monastery of Santo Domingo de Silos in Burgos and was ordained in 1918. He was a wise and cultured man and who, from very early on, wrote about theological and liturgical themes. Pérez de Urbel wrote seventy-one books during his fruitful life and more than seven hundred of his articles have been recorded to date. He was also very passionate about history and art. He received his doctorate in Philosophy and History in 1948, obtaining the chair of Medieval History of Spain in 1950. When the Valley of the Fallen was inaugurated in 1958, he was named its first mitered abbot, a position he held until 1966. Pilar Primo de Rivera, José Antonio's sister, appointed him as religious advisor to the Women's Section of the Falange, for which she was its national delegate. It was Fray Justo Pérez de Urbel who gave shelter and refuge to Léon Degrelle, to protect him from his eternal enemies who persisted in their endeavors to kidnap him.

Inside the religious community, Degrelle was pleased to see community hierarchy, choir stalls, reverence, and respect. "The fathers were very gentle to me," he said. He shared with them his eloquence and wisdom.

When Wednesday came, Léon Degrelle realized that it was the day of Santa Juana Francisca de Chantal. He remembered that during his childhood, he and his young companions all marched to a small sanctuary of the patron saint of the blind. He recollected and enjoyed those old moments, reflecting on the color white, the color of light. All these thoughts persisted as he accompanied the monks toward the immense grotto built in the cloister of that holy mountain.

On Thursday, four members of the police visited. He detected their presence while attending Mass. From the place he occupied, he could see his four "guardian angels." Among them he recognized the "Chief" who had organized his stay at the monastery of the Holy Cross of the Valley of the Fallen. He began to ask, with some anxiety, what their unexpected visit meant. Was there anything amiss? Any new circumstance? Would he be sent elsewhere?

When the service ended, the "four horsemen of the apocalypse" kindly addressed Léon. His escorts were quiet and peaceful. The conversation was cordial. It was 5:00 p.m., and the Chief took him to a room where there was a television set. The bullfight of Semana Grande de San Sebastián was being broadcast. They watched it together. The bulls were bad, and the bullfighters were limited to performing dressing tasks. He thought attending a good bullfight was a luck of the draw. Of those he had attended, only one in twenty seemed to be a great bull-fighting show. The bullfighters gave their capes to Franco, who was in attendance.

That day, some of the church hierarchy arrived at the monastery.

On Saturday, August 15th, as soon as he woke up, his first thoughts and memories went to his mother. That was always a very special day for him. He remembered those days in her company in that cool house of large stone walls on the banks of the Semois River, from where he could see, through the haze of dawn, the enormous mass of the rock castle of Geoffrey de Bouillon. The day used to be for their family reunion. In that house, all the cousins, uncles, and aunts enthusiastically came together to eat and celebrate the feast day of the Assumption of the Virgin. It was a great gathering, like a kind of family convention. Sometimes forty or fifty family members gathered to celebrate that great day of Christianity. His heart and his thoughts moved across those unforgettable memories.

At 1:00 p.m., he attended High Mass, officiated by two mitered abbots with all the pomp and solemnity of the Benedictine liturgy that the day required. Resonating in the basilica were the clear and sharp voices of the choir of Escolanía del Valle, in their red and white robes. It was exciting for Degrelle to see the fluid beauty of Christ in the Eucharist, illuminated in the middle of the great nave of that immense crypt, as darkness flooded the temple. Under the Christ figure was a grail held aloft in the hands of Abbott Pérez de Urbel, imbuing a profound solemnity for the parishioners.

The place was breathtaking. The calm atmosphere was a sedative for him. Days were repeating themselves. Unchanging schedules, the same bronze clang of the bell that unfailingly sounded at the appropriate times, the songs and litanies, meditation, prayers, the holy sacrifice of the Mass, the sacred readings, the *Miserere*, the atrocious silence during mealtime in the refectory, the inner purification, the white color of the four walls of the cell, the hard bed of the Castilian style furniture; above all, the uninterrupted presence of his escorts who, although discreet and affable, always had that look that followed his footsteps through the solitude of the Sierra del Guadarrama. The next day, Léon decided to sneak out to seek refuge in the southern lands.

From his stay at the monastery, from that guarded refuge, Léon has left us twenty-nine written pages, composed during his meditations in his cell. They contain many of his emotional and intimate secrets, whose disclosure here would be indiscreet.

The Falangist writer Adriano Gómez Molina relates an anecdote that happened to him during Léon Degrelle's stay under the tutelary protection of the Holy Mother Church in the Valley of the Fallen. Gómez Molina was born in Abarán (Murcia) in 1935. He was an active and enthusiastic young man of the Youth Front who, after the field courses of Covaleda (Soria), founded a Centuria. He belonged to the Spanish University Union (SEU) of Murcia and the Faculty of Law of the Complutense University of Madrid, where he received his doctorate in Law. He was Chief of Studies for the "José Antonio" Upper College and Editing Secretary of the magazine *Cuadernos de Orientación*. He specialized in the history and life of José Antonio y Ramiro Ledesma Ramos. In the second week of August 1963, Adriano and seven comrades went to the Valley of the Fallen monastery with the intention of preparing, in the peace and quiet of that place, some monograph editions of the publication that he directed.

When these eight young people ate in the monks' refectory, there were three other people there in civilian clothes that they did not identify. As soon as the light meal was finished, one of those people went to the group of students and asked them who the head of their party was. Adriano replied that he was responsible for the group of writers. He was asked by the man to accompany him. They left the dining room and settled in an adjoining office. The man identified himself as a police officer of the Social Political Brigade and asked Adriano if he knew who Léon Degrelle was. When Adriano answered yes, the police officer told him that Degrelle was currently in the Valley of the Fallen monastery, incommunicado, and with permanent police surveillance, for fear of an attack or attempted kidnapping. He warned him that if Léon tried to contact them, to give them a letter, a communication or anything else, that he had an obligation—and the warning was serious—to turn it over to the police, and that it was very important that he comply very strictly with this guidance. Nor should they comment to anyone outside, and he emphatically emphasized this, about Degrelle's presence there for reasons of security. Adriano gave these instructions to his seven companions, who were captivated by this news. Léon did not entrust any message to them, nor did he ever come into contact with the group. Adriano and his seven comrades had partaken of that frugal meal, oblivious to the fact that they were in the presence of a historical figure of such an important historical figure, so appreciated by the Falangist youths for his fidelity and nobility.

Sometime later, through a comrade from Jerez called Santos, who worked at the Osborne shops—Osborne was a friend of Léon Degrelle—Adriano Gómez Molina got a copy of the book *The Burning Souls*, with a personal dedication by Léon. Adriano would go on to become the Director of the "José Antonio" Command Academy, become a prominent member of the Institute of Political Studies, hold various positions of responsibility in Radio Televisión Española and also became a member of the Board of Directors of the EFE News Agency. He would forever hold the memory of having been, although unknowingly, in the presence of a great hero at the monastery who was very dear to his heart.

Léon Degrelle, during his long exile on Spanish territory, as evidenced by the abundant photographs that have been preserved thanks to the selfless work of his photographer Schutter, returned on multiple occasions, to the Valley of the Fallen whenever he traveled to Madrid. He would pray and bow before the tombs of Franco and José Antonio, whose mortal remains rest there in the tomb of faith, in the shadow of the Great Cross and in the company of the fallen on both sides during the National Liberation Crusade.[87]

## Reunion with His Great Friend Raymond Van Leuw

One of his closest friends, Raymond Van Leuw, having just regained his freedom in 1961, traveled to Spain to join Léon in exile. He considered him to be of his inner circle and one of the most faithful and beloved coworkers of the same creed and political ideal. At last, fate had led to a new meeting with his compatriot.

Raymond Van Leuw was born in Brussels on August 3rd, 1924. He was active in the youth of the Légion Nationale in 1939. At that time, he was a member of the League for the People's Defense, moving in 1941, after the dissolution of the League, to become part of the Rexist Youth Movement, *Jeunesse Nationale Solidariste*, along with John Hagemans. He enlisted in the Walloon Legion and left for the front on March 10th, 1942, with the youth contingent. He was distinguished in the

---

[87] In 2019, General Francisco Franco's remains were exhumed from *El Valle de los Caídos* (Valley of the Fallen) and reburied in a family cemetery near Madrid, next to his wife.

fighting in Cherjakow, where he was wounded and evacuated to a hospital in Germany. He stayed in Germany for the two months of his convalescence and then returned to the front lines in January 1943 as an instructor of the Wildfecken camp. He found himself again on the Eastern Front on November 11th in the Cherkassy sector, in the great encirclement. On February 17th, 1944, he was again wounded in combat and was evacuated to field hospitals in Poland and Germany. Finally, in May 1944, he was operated on at the Bruggman Hospital in Belgium. Upon discharge, Van Leuw began serving in the General Staff of Youth Legionnaires. Once he had fully recovered, he returned to the front, where in 1945, he joined the Twenty-Eighth SS Division Wallonie. After Germany's surrender, he was taken prisoner by British forces. Although they wanted him executed, he was ultimately sentenced to fifteen years in prison. At twenty-one, he was sent to a British concentration camp in Neuenham, and then transferred to Nivelles, where the so-called "collaborationists" were interned. Five years later, in 1950, he was released on parole, and then fully released on June 29th, 1961, but deprived of his civil and military rights. Among his military awards were the Iron Cross Second Class, the Infantry Assault Medal, the Special Weapons Medal, the Bronze Close Combat Badge, and the Medal for Wounded in War.

When he was able to obtain full freedom, Van Leuw and his wife, the Dutch citizen Maria Antonia, transferred their residence to Spain, living in Madrid and working for French companies based in the capital. It was here that he met with Léon Degrelle again, who remained a great friend of the family until his death. For decades he assisted Léon, becoming something like a political secretary. In the last years of his life, Van Leuw, now retired, moved to live in Malaga, to be closer to Degrelle. Van Leuw would be with Degrelle until his death, a sad and inevitable event, which affected Van Leuw deeply. Raymond Van Leuw, one of Degrelle's most faithful comrades and friends, also died in Malaga, with a clean service record and his duty fulfilled, on May 5th, 1998.

## The Shameful Lex Degrelliana

It was 1964. Twenty years ago, Léon Degrelle still had his act of National Deputy in force and therefore still enjoyed parliamentary immunity, a position for which he was democratically elected by voters in the pre-Second World War elections. The War Council trial at which he was sentenced to death *in absentia* was held shamefully; the council provided no guarantees and no legal or procedural formalities, and at a time when there was not yet a legal, or legitimate, government chosen by the people in any election, nor duly seated and established in that country. Belgium had been in a state of war and invaded by the military forces of allied foreign powers, with capitalism and communism simultaneously in tandem.

The period of twenty years that had now elapsed between 1944 and 1964, since the passing of Degrelle's absurd death sentence, without any legal basis or grounds, implied the automatic prescription and expiration of the sentence; that is, these sentences handed down by the Belgian war councils against those whom they called "collaborationists" with Germany were limited by law. Therefore, according to their own legislation, this meant the possibility of Léon Degrelle's return to his homeland, free and clear of any and all charges. He had expressed an intention along these lines the previous summer when he was asked about his future and stated to the press that, after the time of the prescribed fulfillment and expiration of the conviction, in accordance with the Belgian legal system itself, he was prepared to return to his country and immediately resume political activities in Belgium. He would clear and defend his honor and reputation against all the frauds and lies that had been poured onto him from the revanchist government over the last two decades.

In order to prevent Degrelle from carrying out that intention and to prevent him from benefiting from the conviction expiration, a reprehensible and hate-filled act was committed. A new and undefinable legal monstrosity was cobbled together in the Belgian Parliament as a matter of urgency. The new law stipulated a mandatory extension, by another ten years, for the exclusive conviction, with the death penalty, for the case of Léon Degrelle. This would be to approve, "democratically," a "nominating law," in spite of violating the general rule of law to which this applied and being contrary to the most elementary legal principles.

On November 19th, 1964, the Belgian Lower House passed the law and approved the extension of the statute of limitations for accusations of "collaborationism" during the Second World War, known as *Lex Degrelliana*. During the phony pantomime of a debate that took place in Parliament, three brave women who were near the gallery spoke up in favor of Degrelle. One of them, Adrienne Tart, shouted loudly, "It is time for Degrelle to return!" This caused a big stir and all three were forcibly and quickly removed on the order of chairman Achille Van Acker.

After the war, Adrienne Tart had suffered the harsh effects of "cleansing," and became ill in the sinister camp of Casteau, where she was held under the "uncivic" laws by her country's new authorities. After the purge, she regained her freedom. Although she was in weak health, she sought her former, scattered comrades. This brought confrontations and political and government persecutions. She joined the

Belgian Social Movement, assuming leadership responsibilities in the organization's press and propaganda activities, which reported on countless arrests and judicial proceedings. Severe fines and deprivation of liberty were imposed on these activities. The bravery and courage shown by Adrienne Tart at that parliamentary session in 1964 got her fifteen days of solitary confinement and a heavy fine.

The law extending the expiration by another ten years was passed by one hundred forty-eight to five votes. With this vile and cowardly resolution, they indignantly supported the rancorous words of that partisan "Judge" Mélot—the one who had tried to kidnap Degrelle in Spain in 1958 but failed—who had declared to the journalist Jean Michel Charlier, "The law can be changed for an individual."

The *Lex Degrelliana*, in addition to being a legal travesty, was a markedly illegal act, even more so as it was being applied retroactively by twenty years. Moreover, enacted laws must be applicable to all equally and not according to the cut and measure of whoever is defining the law. They cannot be applicable only to one person at the exclusion of all others. This atypical proceeding constituted a flagrant violation of the most elementary principles of law recognized by any civilized people.

It was not even considered that in 1944, when Degrelle was convicted, he was a popular leader and a democratically elected deputy in the Belgian Parliament. His sentence was imposed on him without his having the slightest opportunity to defend himself, as he was fighting on the Eastern Front to contain, and to protect Europe from the communist avalanche.

The aberration had been consummated and Belgium's revenge was complete.

### Repeated Visits by His Compatriot George Gilsoul

Another regular visitor at the time was his compatriot George Gilsoul, whom everyone knew as "Gil." Upon his return from Argentina, Gil visited Degrelle in May 1960, in January 1961, in May and September of 1965, again on the same dates in the following year, and in June of 1967 and 1968.

Gil, a great amateur photographer, travelled to Constantina on May 9th, 1965, and May 26th, 1966, to photograph the tombs of Degrelle's son, Léon-Marie Degrelle and Mayor Georges Jacobs, whose remains also rested in the cemetery of that Andalusian locality.

George "Gil" Gilsoul had been called by the Mandatory Labor Service (STO) to work in a factory in Germany in 1944. He met Léon Degrelle when, in the summer of that year, the latter was visiting prison camps and factories to recruit soldiers who might want to enlist to fight communism on the Eastern Front. Gil, who was then twenty years old, listened attentively to that call for the "crusade against Bolshevism," which needed combatants. He enlisted immediately, seduced by the ideal of whose torch was carried by the commander of that legion of volunteers. He was assigned to the Twenty-Eighth SS Division Wallonie. His campaign lasted three hundred days, the hardest and bloodiest of the Second World War. After the conflict he was taken prisoner, serving a three-year prison sentence for having fought for his homeland against Bolshevism. When he was released, he proudly stated, "When I was born, I received the baptismal waters within the Catholic Church. When I was of age, as a man, I put my faith in the Führer. This is all my life."

He immigrated to Argentina in search of a better future and hoped to meet some of his old comrades in Latin America. He eventually returned to Belgium. He worked in the most diverse trades, as a bricklayer, a sweeper, and a janitor. With his small savings he bought a Lambretta motorcycle, on which he traveled more than 300,000 kilometers (186,411 miles) on his vacation throughout Europe, and he used it to travel to Spain to meet his esteemed commander, Léon Degrelle, and spend a few days with him and Colonel Otto Skorzeny. Gil died in the fall of 1997.

A string of handwritten correspondence between the two survived. Gil became a kind of correspondent and clandestine agent for the distribution of Léon's books in Belgium, where his works were strictly prohibited and relentlessly targeted by the authorities. With his motorcycle, Gil would amble throughout the villages and visit comrades and sympathizers, gathering and passing information around. Everything was done with the strictest stealth, as the penalties involved in reading certain books in Belgium were severe.

In a letter that Léon sent to Gil, dated June 9th, 1969, he announced the publication of the work *Front de l'Est* (*The Eastern Front*), which was published with La Table Ronde, sharing that "as of a few days, it is now a reality; it is a thick volume of four hundred fifty pages, very well presented and priced at twenty-six French francs." In the same letter, Léon shared with him his sorrow in hearing about the sudden death of an old acquaintance and mutual friend by the name of Blanc, to whom he had written only a few days ago. In another personal letter, Degrelle asked Gil to send him some magazines—*Rivarol* and *Europe Magazine*—by post, and he commented on the distribution strategy and a method for sending some copies of his works in a camouflaged way. On another occasion, he provided some copies for one of his drops at the request of letters sent through intermediaries. In one, Degrelle asked, "Would you be kind enough to send to our friend Gilsoul the copies of *The Russia Campaign*, in Flemish, that are in your house? I would like to sell them because I need the small support."

On one occasion, Degrelle had to send a small reprimand to Gilsoul for exceeding his authority. In a letter dated October 18th, 1975, he was spurred to say:

> *My dear old Georges:*
>
> *Well! Here is the photo.*
>
> *In truth, you often drive me mad. No one has charged you, nor have you been conferred with the right, to interfere in the private life of those who receive you and to devote yourself to informing the universe of things that are not your responsibility and which are not of interest to anyone.*
>
> *Also, your hobby of using personal dedications urbi et orbi[88] is inadmissible. If I write to you a personal dedication, it is not to be thrown around to the four winds.*
>
> *Having said this—and without acrimony—I repeat to you once again that I deeply admire your activity, your zeal, your constancy in serving the cause. I can see your ease and your boldness, although it sometimes goes too far! That is why I reprimand you for your excesses, sometimes I even have to send you to the devil!*
>
> *You will therefore fulfill the following penance:*
>
> *First of all, you will distribute Saint Loup's book, which I am sure you will do wonderfully.*
>
> *You will also be responsible for the distribution of "Letter to My Cardinal" and, in this case, you will need to really put yourself into it. If Saint Loup's book succeeds and can be freely sold everywhere, then "Letter to My Cardinal" should also have normal access in the usual dissemination circuits.*
>
> *Once again, give me the proof of your sacred courage by taking back this "lion," roaring and rampant!*
>
> *Conclusion: you must give your eagerness to this enterprise and, with or without motorbike, we have to get everyone to read them.*

After commenting on some other more personal issues he ended the letter saying "… I am sure you are going to beat records!"

On another occasion, on June 19th, 1977, Gil received the following letter at his home, sent to him by a former Flemish rexist comrade, who he had supplied with a book by Degrelle:

---

[88] [Latin for "to the City (of Rome) and to the World."]

*My dear Gil,*

*I was pleasantly surprised to find in the last book a photo signed by the Chief. I warmly thank you for this pleasant surprise. This is the first time that this lucky honor has come my way, which may seem strange because occasions for it have not been lacking, being an old man like me…but, look, I never approached the Chief to the point of being able to obtain a dedication in a book or on a photograph.*

*I would often hear Degrelle speak during some rally…but really, I just heard the applause, considering that for most of the time I was placed near an exit, or even outside the room, which I considered to be an act of service, for I was already absolutely convinced and so I let other people enter the interior to have an opportunity to listen to him and be convinced.*

*This printed page, the paper already a little yellowed, shows you that I am a "veteran." This paper with the letterhead is what I used in Antwerp, as early as 1934. I am Flemish…but I was seduced by Léon Degrelle when I read (by pure chance) a small book of his called "Meditations on Louis Boumal" (published in 1931); a strictly literary work, certainly, but in which the author shares his ideas, between pages fifty-nine and sixty-five, about how to get Flemish and Walloons to understand each other. To tell the truth, I do not know if he captivated me simply for having made Louis Boumal's thought his own. One could even say that I became a rexist through Louis Boumal, who had died in October 1918…I wonder if you can inform me whether some rexist who is older than me still lives!*

*Seventy years…I congratulate myself on it…having already surpassed my sixties, and on the threshold of an announced physical decline, like everyone. A useless life? We have not been able to achieve our objectives, nor do we see a ray of hope, but the fire is still embers and will one day be able to fire up the whole world. From the beginning, we knew that we could not work for ourselves, but for one or two generations to come later. If it takes until the third or fourth generation, what does it matter? It is not at all necessary to wait in order to undertake something, or to succeed in order to persevere.*

*Very cordially,*
*Braeschaat*

In 1979, Degrelle sent Gil another letter with the following text:

*In exile, May 2nd, 1979*

*My dear Georges,*

*I read with joy the letter you sent to our friend Raymond, who thanks you, for having made him aware of the press reaction, as well as of the publicity and presentation in the bookstores of the new book. Are you waiting? Will the bookstores receive it well? Are they under pressure? Right now, on Swiss radio, there is an interview which is discussing the articles that have appeared in the press, but you must know that the interview they allude to is completely pure invention. For years now I have not received any journalist, either Belgian or from any other place! I have had no connection whatsoever with the radio station that they are referring to! So, from what I have read, this is about some poor man who has taken some sentences and paragraphs that are found in my book* Hitler for a Thousand Years *and with it he has produced a kind of interview, in which I have not taken part at all! I did not even know that it has spread!*

*In short, rumors in the press continue! They have even invented for me a black family in Brazil, without ever having set foot there in my life!*

*From what I read in the book, I have been able to detect some errors because I did not have the possibility, in the end, of reviewing it, since I wrote it in twelve three-hour working sessions, from 4:30 a.m. to 7:30 a.m., for twelve consecutive days. The most prominent of the errors is that which says, "the VI Army Corps," rather than "Paulus' VI Army," but the public does not know these details. Either way, it will be corrected, as well as some other details that have slipped by.*

*The book* The Russia Campaign *will be published again under the title* Eastern Front. *The issue here is the photos. I am missing a lot. It will make a great deluxe edition with the photographs. Try as hard as possible to get me some good photographic documents.*

*I have some things prepared along the lines of* Hitler for a Thousand Years, *which are to be published next: in total, about twenty books. This will be a great surprise in the coming years.*

*Regarding my health, I have spent a few days with back pain as a result of a herniated disc.*

*Receive my affectionate greetings.*
*As always, L.D.*

*P.S. - In the coming days I should receive copies of the book,* Hitler for a Thousand Years. *I will send you a signed copy immediately.*

On June 24th, 1983, Degrelle sent Gil the following acknowledgment:

*To readers afar off: thanks to our friend Gil, a veteran of the Eastern Front, who has had the courage to stay in the trenches, as on the front! Here you will find the admirable poems of Brasillach and, very importantly, some poems of mine, written*

*from the bondage and hope of exile, always in contact so that the faith never dies*
*and is maintained with the same strength as in our youth.*

*Affectionately, L.D.*

## General Charles de Gaulle Tries to Kidnap Degrelle

Independent of the thwarted attempts by Jewish organizations, the French police also put together a kidnap plan in which you could clearly see General de Gaulle working behind the scenes. He commissioned Colonel Argoud to capture Degrelle in a new attempt. To this end, he conceived an astute, Machiavellian plan, which would not only lead to Degrelle's capture, but would also hinder the European policy of Belgian Foreign Minister Paul Henri Spaak, with whom de Gaulle differed as to his approach to structuring the European continent.

De Gaulle knew very well that Léon Degrelle could reveal terrible things about his adversary, Minister Spaak, who slavishly humiliated himself in 1940 trying to work with the Germans and who failed in that only because Hitler did not want him by his side. General de Gaulle hoped to set off a big media scandal against Spaak with this information, and to humiliate his visceral political opponent among European leaders.

De Gaulle's plan was to offer Léon the guarantee of a suitable defense before a neutral court, where he could openly reveal all of Spaak's political and moral chicanery, which would definitively put an end to Spaak's political career. De Gaulle was convinced that by kidnapping Degrelle, although somewhat paradoxical, he would say everything he had to say against the despicable Belgian minister. Without Spaak's malicious intent to eliminate Degrelle, the constant harassment and persecution suffered over many long years would end. De Gaulle believed Degrelle would accept this offer.

This new operation, carried out by a group of kidnapping specialists, took place in the last days of July 1965. When he was staying in Madrid, Léon lived in a discreet apartment, on Pasco de los Jesuitas, number 1, third floor. His residence was not known to anyone, and he exercised extreme prudence and reserve. The information that revealed Degrelle's whereabouts was provided by a real scoundrel, a failure of a man who weighed more than 280 pounds. He earned the miserable amount of two thousand pesetas as a reward, much like the "thirty pieces of silver" that Judas Iscariot received for his betrayal of Jesus. The information was provided in the first days of July, and the kidnappers showed up towards the end of that same month.

Léon was completely oblivious to the trap that was forming around him. He had been planning to go on vacation on August 2nd to Costa Brava, invited by one of the candidates for the French presidential elections. He was meeting there with a good friend of his, Jean-Louis Tixier-Vignancour.

On Saturday, three days before his departure to the Catalan coast, he felt affected by a real physical anguish. He had the sense that something was going to happen to him. He perceived a danger that seemed to loom about him for no apparent reason. It was a warning, a premonition and disquiet that caused him some uneasiness, without any explanation.

Léon had to board his plane to Barcelona on Monday morning, but because of that mysterious inner voice that insistently warned him, as if he felt death was hovering over him, he decided to start the trip in advance, without further delay, on Saturday, two days ahead of schedule. When he arrived at the Madrid-Barajas airport and arranged to change the ticket, he was informed by Iberia airlines that this was not possible because the requested flight was already completely booked and only two first-class seats were available. Although Léon really could not afford a first-class ticket on his tight budget, without thinking twice and making an unusual exception, he exchanged his economy class ticket for one of the two first-class vacancies.

He telephoned Tixier-Vignancourt to apologize and announce that he would arrive three days ahead of schedule. Meanwhile, the malicious French police, called at Léon's apartment not long after he had left.

De Gaulle had sent three of his "*barbouses*" ("beards")—the police officers used by France's first president to carry out political crimes and shady operations—to kidnap Léon. They had been instructed to beat him into submission if he resisted.

It was not even half an hour after Léon had left his apartment that the three barbouses appeared at his door. When they did not find him at home, they went down the street to the nearest bar to make inquiries about him. While having a few coffees, they said they were old friends of Léon and had come because they wanted to pleasantly surprise him with their unexpected visit. Not knowing the neighborhood, they were in, this was the same bar in which years ago, when the dangerous circumstances of Degrelle's life necessitated Spanish police escorts from the Ministry of the Interior to protect him in the event of a possible incident, Degrelle's police protection would spend their off-hours. Therefore, when insistently asked about Degrelle by people with a marked foreign accent and who had never been seen in the area before, the owners of the bar and the patrons became suspicious.

The French police drew the attention of two former officers who had fought with the Red Army, with whom Léon maintained good, cordial relations. They called and warned Spanish security forces that three men were inquiring into Degrelle's life, anxiously and desperately, trying to find out where they might find him. The Spanish police came immediately, stopping the three barbouses when they returned to the apartment to make another attempt to take Degrelle.

The three French policemen were arrested and interrogated by the Spanish police, who, after having held them and ascertained that their stay in Spain was political in nature, released them. This was due to the fact that, since the officers were from France, a government decision was made to return them, with a serious warning, to the French border.

While all the commotion of the failed kidnapping attempt was happening in Madrid, Degrelle was embracing his distinguished French friend, who was already eagerly awaiting him upon his arrival in Catalonia. Jean-Louis Tixier-Vignancour was a personal and political adversary of General de Gaulle and a candidate running against him in the presidential elections in the French Republic. He and Degrelle were going to spend a few days in his villa near Bagur.

When Degrelle left his apartment ahead of schedule, he did so without saying anything to anyone, not even to his daughters. When the Spanish police detected his absence, it was immediately communicated to the Count of Mayalde, who began looking everywhere. He was so dismayed, he exclaimed, "They have taken him, he has disappeared." Everything was cleared up when the Governor of Gerona was able to communicate to his superiors that Degrelle was safe and sound in a coastal locality within his provincial borders.

When Léon Degrelle was asked on one occasion about why all the kidnapping attempts against him failed, despite having been so thoroughly prepared and sophisticated, his answer was frank:

> For very simple reasons. Firstly, because I am very lucky, always protected by a special "baraka."[89] Secondly, to kidnap me, they have to resolutely risk their necks. I was not an easy man to catch. I got my training during my seventy-five close combat engagements on the Eastern Front. The kidnappers, even knowing that, always acted within the shelter of protective operations that were too complicated. It was evident that they did not want to die in their attempt. In the end, those "gangsters" in the service of certain low-level politicians, and even the naive Lovinfosse, wanted nothing more than my blood. Lacking a great ideal, they did not

---

[89] *Baraka* (Arabic بركة) means blessing. Its use here by Degrelle is curious.

*know how or want to risk anything of themselves, and so they failed outright. I could always face them because I have what they do not have: faith in a cause. I sympathize with those whose lives were only shadows without light. I prefer to be on the top and not on swampy ground.*

## Business Initiatives

On December 7th, 1965, Degrelle acquired an attic apartment in Madrid with unbeatable views from its terraces on calle Joaquín García Morato, number 37, eighth floor, letter C. It was his usual place to stay when he was away from La Cabaña in Fuengirola. He had the deed notarized by Enrique Jiménez Arnau y Gran in the name of his commercial company, Comercio y Decoración S.A., which had been constituted, in the month of November 1964, by his good friend and comrade, Blas Piñar López.

He worked with the French European newspaper *Le Dossier du Mois* and in issue seventeen, December 1965 of that publication, Degrelle used the pseudonym "Philippe Dastier" to publish a wide thirty-nine-page report entitled "Franco et Son Régime" ("Franco and His Regime"), which was subtitled "Spain, an Impossible Topic."

In 1966, León had the opportunity to acquire some plots adjacent to his La Cabaña property, an area of more than 6,000 square meters (1.5 acres) on land known as *Colina de la Cabaña*. They completely surrounded his picturesque and strategic dwelling and were suitable to try to carry out a construction project. León managed two companies at that time. One of them called Madrid Europa S.A. (MADESA), with an address in Madrid at the apartment of León José de Ramírez Reina, in Paseo de los Jesuitas, number 1, fourth left, with telephone number 247-0130. The other company, as we have already mentioned, was Comercio y Decoración S.A. (CODESA). Documents and agreements related to these real estate and commercial transactions were signed and notarized by Blas Piñar in 1972.

In 1968, Degrelle launched a business initiative by setting up a chain of dry cleaners in Madrid. He shared this start-up with his acquaintances by means of a handwritten letter, which he reproduced and printed with the following text:

*In exile, 1968.*

*Dear friend and colleague,*
   *I am General Léon Degrelle, former head of Belgian Rexism and of the two Walloon and Flemish volunteer divisions on the Eastern Front.*

*Some of my officers, heroes of the Eastern Front who are exiled in Spain, have assembled in Madrid, with much effort, a network of dry cleaners and laundries called TINTEBEL. The German material is second to none, as you can read in the supplement just published in the newspaper Pueblo, which we gladly attach.*

*I would be very much obliged if you and your family could encourage and support these fellow exiles by entrusting TINTABEL with your clothes, curtains, lace curtains, carpets, etc.*

*The work, carried out in 24 hours, is perfect. Prices are current. The collection and delivery service are done <u>at home</u> at the client's request, without additional charge.*

*Materially, it cannot be done better. <u>Morally</u>, you have the opportunity to allow these colleagues, who have suffered so much, to earn a living and to rekindle some hope.*

*I can ask for no more, dear friend and colleague. You will have understood me. I entrust this case to your honor, to your own heart, reiterating my affection.*

*Léon Degrelle*

*Léon Degrelle, 1968*

## A Tragic Event

A tragic and sad event took place in April 1969 at the house of Léon Degrelle in Madrid. One of Degrelle's countryman, Raphael Roorick-Aura, aged forty-seven, was found dead in his office. He had recently returned from Madagascar and had been settled in Madrid for only a few months. The first person to discover the body was Carolina Charbonneau, who was then twelve years old. She was the daughter of Juana "Jeanne" Brevet, Léon's faithful and inseparable companion. Roorick-Aura had shot himself.

Raphael Roorick-Aura had committed suicide at a time of psychological unrest, in those unfathomable moments of darkness that sometimes disrupt the enigma of the human mind and lead a man into the abyss. Léon was very affected by the tragedy and mourned the sudden death of his close friend.

## His Daughter Marie-Christine's Marriage

On October 9th, 1969, the youngest daughter of Léon Degrelle, Marie-Christine, married Antonio de la Rosa in the aristocratic church of San Jerónimo El Real in Madrid. The godfather of the matrimonial bond was Léon, who on this occasion wore a jacket on whose flap a silver oak leaf was clearly visible.

Among those who attended was SS-Obersturmbanführer Otto Skorzeny, who signed as one of the witnesses. Skorzeny was going to write the foreword to Léon's book of political memoirs. His signature was also stamped, as witness of the ceremony, by the National Movement Councilor, a notary of Madrid, and the President of Fuente Nueva, Blas Piñar López, in whose political movement Léon's son-in-law, attorney Servando Balaguer Parreño, was an active leader.

Other notable guests at the wedding were Jaime de Mora y Aragón, brother of Queen Fabiola of Belgium, whom Léon familiarly called "Fabiolo." De Mora y Aragón considered Degrelle an old comrade, having first met him during his long convalescence at the General Mola Hospital in San Sebastián in 1945. The former Minister Serrano Suñer, brother-in-law of the Generalissimo Franco and the Count of Mayalde were also there, and there was no lack of deputies, magistrates, senators, and generals in uniform.

Several Belgian journalists covered the joyous occasion, including the special correspondent of *La Libre Belgique*, the director for the *France Press,* and the Belgian journalist Theo Knol, from the weekly *De Post*.

The Belgian Ambassador to Spain, Mr. Poswick was outraged by the openness and acceptance of the event and hurried to send a note of protest to the Spanish government.

## An Interview with Journalist Marino Gómez Santos
## Is Published in the Daily *ABC*

The journalist Marino Gómez Santos published a long interview in the Madrid daily *ABC* on October 11th, 1969, which filled three pages under the title "*Peripecia Humana de León Degrelle.*"[90] It highlighted the phrase "We enter politics, really, as apostles." The interview took place in Madrid, while he was there to help in the preparations for the marriage of his daughter Marie Christine. Santos opened the article with, "Only a few months ago we learned that you lived in Brazil, through extensive reports published in a São Paulo magazine." The truth was that Degrelle had not set foot in that country outside the imagination of certain media outlets. Santos continued, "…when the war ended and with it the associated military and political activity, León Degrelle had turned thirty-eight years old. Since then, he has published some thirty books."

Some questions asked were as follows:

*MGS: What has Spain meant in your career?*

*LD: Spain is my whole life. Even when I was a child I came to Spain. I have known the Spain of the monarchy; the Spain of the Republic. The latter impressed me by how the Republic had failed before the Civil War. Despite all its promises, it did absolutely nothing for the working class. The worker continued with six pesetas in wages and lived without any social security. This is one of the things that convinced me most of the impossibility of achieving the welfare of a country with methods that were already called democratic at that time.*

*MGS: When the Spanish war broke out, the Rexist Movement, which you commanded, was at that time victorious, and stood beside Spain. What was that like?*

*LD: It was our young rexist boys who were the first in Europe to expel the staff of the Red Embassy in Brussels to bring in the few Spanish nationals who were there at the time. We had a lot of young men, volunteers in Spain. Thus, in the winter of 1938 or 1939, I came to spend three weeks as a guest of honor in Spain. This allowed me to see the wonderful Spain of patriotism, of faith, and of youth. Twenty-*

---

[90] [Spanish for the *Human Journey of León Degrelle.*]

*five-year-old governors were seen; thirty-year-olds, thirty-five-year-old ministers. I think this was what saved Spain. In addition to the genius and the military effort, Spaniards made a great moral effort at all times. During the war on the Eastern Front, the memory of Spain accompanied me.*

*MGS: You had a friendship and a political relationship with José Antonio Primo de Rivera since 1934. Can you tell me about that?*

*LD: I can say that we had a great spiritual communion. The Falangist Movement and the Rexist Movement were united by a great Christian base. We were both more concerned about spiritual values because, for us, to gain power was not just to take political command or the possible material interests of men. Above all, our spiritual responsibility was not to turn our movement into a new religion, but rather to allow the free expansion of moral and religious values.*

*MGS: In 1934, José Antonio Primo de Rivera named you number one among the Falange Exterior, correct?*

*LD: I am the only foreigner in the world authorized to wear the Old Guard medal. As a curious detail, I will say that my connection with José Antonio was through a rich gentleman, whose surname is known to all Spaniards because of his industries, among which his most popular is beer. I am referring to Alfredo Mahou. He sent me the letters of José Antonio and carried mine to him.*

The interview was conducted in an affable tone. The history of the Rexist Movement, its beginnings and triumphs, its economic hardships, youthful enthusiasm and ardor were discussed. The last question raised was in regard to Degrelle's super-human activity, of which he commented:

*When one is in activity, sleeping is a surrender. I had to sleep little in order to work a lot and I remained that way for several years. The doctors told me that I could not keep doing this for much longer. I am now sixty-three years old, with four of those spent in war. I am completely maimed and not too long ago, I went on foot to Santiago de Compostela—1,030 kilometers (640 miles)—from the French border. The more you work and fight, the more the body gets stronger. The same is true for wounds: each broken bone is later made harder; each leg that has been cut by a bullet walks better. We must not believe in diseases; we must have faith. It is faith that gives health.*

## The Opinion of Mexican Writer Antonio Ríus Facius

On October 14th, 1969, Léon Degrelle enjoyed a cordial meeting with the Mexican poet, writer, and historian Antonio Ríus Facius, a member of *Acción Católica de la Juventud Mexicana* (Catholic Action of Mexican Youth), whose publications were prolific. Among the most noted were *La Juventud Católica y la Revolución* and *México Cristero*, et al.[91] At the meeting, Léon recalled for Facius that, in 1929, the Mexican Andrés Barquín y Ruiz lived in the Catholic Action of Belgian Youth house in Louvain, in a room next to his when he was studying law. Andrés, his neighbor, belonged to the National League, an advocate of religious freedom. He also told Facius that during his time on the Mexican war front, during *La Cristiada*,[92] he was invited to the house of the engineer Jorge Núñez, the vice president of the National League, who welcomed Degrelle into his home.

Antonio Ríus Facius recalled his unforgettable interview with Degrelle in this way:

> *He lived in a small apartment and used an assumed name. In his first words he praised and lauded Mexico and his former companions of the Cristero ideal. The dialog became monologue and in the span of a few moments, I relived the experiences of a life rich in adventure and thought. Meeting Léon Degrelle was for me a satisfaction that is difficult to explain. In saying our farewells, he gave me a copy of* The Burning Souls *and on a whole page, without hesitation, he wrote this expressive dedication: "To my dear Mexican friend Antonio Ríus Facius, in heartfelt memory of your beloved Patria, a guide and example for all Catholics, a country in which, in my most formative days, I lived the most beautiful months of my youth. With brotherly affection, Léon Degrelle."*

---

[91] These books, whose titles translate respectively as *Catholic Youth and the Revolution* and *Cristero Mexico*, pertain to the Cristero War, or the Cristero Rebellion, in Mexico starting in 1917. This was a reaction against the introduction into the Mexican constitution of secularizing and anti-clerical articles. These were interpreted by many as anti-Catholic. The Cristeros were the Catholics who fought against the government and its imposition of these new articles.

[92] *La Cristiada* is another term for the Cristero uprising.

## An Interview by Journalist Pedro Rodríguez
## Is Published in the Daily *Arriba*

On December 6th, 1969, the Director General of Popular Culture and Entertainment drafted and sent a document from the Ministry of Information and Tourism to Léon Degrelle, with registration number 11995-69, in which he communicated:

> *In response to your inquiry dated November 18th, 1969, concerning the work, Memoirs of a Fascist, we inform you that its publication is not an inconvenience, of which the prior deposit required by the current Press and Printing Law must be constituted in due course. God grant you many years.*

Two months after the interview for *ABC* with renowned journalist Marino Gómez Santos, another extensive in-depth conversation with journalist Pedro Rodríguez was published on December 10th, 1969, in the official Falangist Party newspaper, *Arriba*, founded by José Antonio. The article was titled "León Degrelle, el Último Fascista," ("Léon Degrelle, the Last Fascist").

One day when Léon was preparing to buy the Parisian newspaper *Le Monde* at the newsstand near his house, Rodriguez approached him in the street. At that time, during his visits to Madrid, Degrelle was living in his attic apartment on calle García Morato in the central, traditional neighborhood of Chamberí. The talk, which began in the middle of the street, continued in his home. The journalist described the room where the dialog took place as follows:

> *PR: The Iron Cross is immaculately laid out on a silver platter, as if the Führer had been here yesterday. There is a bust of Queen Isabel the Catholic, a check book, a hammock with lambskin, two stone lions "in honor of my name," a mirror, a wrap-around chasuble crossed with a foil, and the terrace. The terrace has hawthorn bushes and surrounds the home, and you can see Madrid from four directions: the Sierra, the Francia highway, the ABC, and the Palacio de Santa Cruz.*
>
> *LD: Oh, a beautiful terrace from which I can pray the breviary!*
>
> *PR: When will your book come out, Mr. Degrelle?*
>
> *LD: Well…my book. I hope that it will come out soon in Spain. There is still some work to do, some obstacles, but I hope soon. This is a historical book. It is the explanation of the fascist phenomenon in the world, although we do not necessarily accept that label. It is the explanation of a phenomenon that arose at the same time,*

*in the same way, in various countries, with the same tendencies, and the same reactions. As in every country, it was championed by a particular man, but the explanation of the differences the movement had in each country are varied. Fascism was not the same as rexism, just as National Socialism was not exactly equal to the Falange. Yet, they all agreed on the need for strong, enduring power for their countries. They all agreed on replacing the bourgeois order with social justice because every country had its national spirit, much more so than now. For example, in Belgium, I was not trying to be socialist per se, but rather to give life to social ideas, which is different. Hitler was a tyrant, they say. A tyrant, when six million communist workers, plus Marxists, plus Christian Democrats, threw themselves into his arms. Now, that is something. Furthermore, we all agreed that we were poor and young. I was the eldest of eight children...Mussolini had only one mandolin and in his wedding car, he carried only an umbrella...None of these fascist leaders had external support, social connections, or advanced age. I won my election campaign at twenty-nine years old.*

The book they were referencing was *Memoirs of a Fascist*. It had already been on the market in several European countries.

Rodriguez was aware of the attempted kidnappings and abductions perpetrated against Léon Degrelle and asked him about this openly:

> *PR: How do you go about on the street? How is it that I can run into you on the corner, buying Le Monde?*
>
> *LD: I cannot live with a poisoned life. I could not live without going out on the street. I want to continue living my life. I do not want to cut life short because of fear.*
>
> *PR: What would Europe have been if fascism had won?*
>
> *LD: That is the big question, the smart question...I am convinced—I cannot deny it—that if Hitler had won, Europe would have been made. Yes, I know; it would have been done through force, but nothing has ever been done without force. Spanish unity was not made by clicking castanets, but on horseback for centuries. France was made through bombardment. Garibaldi came out with cannons and not with blessings from the Pope. The United States itself had its Civil War. When I was his [Hitler] age, I had finished my political career and was serving on the Eastern Front. Then there was the great idea of socialism, and the great method of strength. Think about what happens now when Europe is just a little slice. Think of this selfishness, where because of French butter, European integration is denied to England. Then put yourself in that situation. Against this selfishness, some man*

*needed to say, "This is how it is going to be done." Do you understand? For sure, force is not enough. Force can either impose a great ideal or crush it. That idea of unity, that idea was on the Eastern Front where we were, where we met boys from twenty-eight European countries. Two hundred thousand non-German boys died there, for a common ideal, which after four years of war came to be known. That youth could have secured the moral side of the post-war era, and what would have happened, in the end, in Europe? This youth would have had the most fantastic possibilities that any youth could ever dream of. Millions of boys would have had a homeland stretching from Vladivostok to Cherbourg, passing through Vigo.*

### A Second Interview with *ABC*

In the first days of January 1970, another interview with Léon was included in the Sunday edition of the Madrid newspaper *ABC*, titled "*León Degrelle, Abuelo de Seis Niños Españoles*" ("Léon Degrelle, Grandfather of Six Spanish Children"), in which he stated up front:

*I am living a third stage of life in exile. The first stage was a bitter time of physical and familial suffering and, of course, economic hardship. In the second stage, not too long ago, I financially remade my life, thanks to a series of businesses that earned me my first significant income. Now, more recently, I have begun my third stage enthusiastically as a writer and I am going to write a collection of more than thirty works, with titles that include "Hitler and..." (the Jews, the concentration camps, the Yankees, Mussolini...). In addition, I am finishing up several volumes of my memoirs. I write a book in less than a fortnight, sometimes less than a week. I always write by hand because I have noticed that I manage to impart a more personal thrust in my writing than if I typed them out.*

In the interview, he says that he has made a living in Spain, first by setting up an iron sales business, with which he earned his first significant income, then a network of dry cleaners, construction projects, and his published book sales.

*Interviewer: Mr. Degrelle, how do you divide your day?*

*LD: I get up very early, at about 6:00 a.m., and I immediately write. Then I attend to my business and soon I am back to reading (I read at least one book a day) and publishing my work. From time to time, I talk with friends. I like to be open to the opinions of others. In the evening, I read until quite late. I despise the need to sleep, it is a humiliation, and I do not usually grant this requirement any more than three hours a day.*

The only physical exercise he did was walking about 10 kilometers (6.2 miles) a day. He had no car, so he moved about on foot. He also took refuge in music, which he considered the purest art of all, being a determined enthusiast of Wagner and, to a lesser extent, of Beethoven. He rarely went to the movie cinema or theater.

He liked to read Spanish maxims frequently and, in those days, he was preparing a French edition featuring the best of them, which he thought to title *Sagesse Espagnole* (*Spanish Wisdom*). The saying he liked most of all was the one that goes *"a lo hecho, pecho!" (What is done, is done!),* which he made one of the slogans of his prodigious life.

### Journalist Win Dannau Publishes a Thirteen-Volume Work of Degrelle's Recordings Entitled *Ainsi Parla Léon Degrelle*[93]

On December 10th, 1965, the writer and journalist Win Dannau interviewed León Degrelle for the first time at the Hotel Luz Palacio in Madrid. This was the first of a series of lengthy interviews conducted over several years. The manager of the hotel happened to be the son of Léon's Field Adjutant, Robert du Welz. As du Welz certainly recanted to his son, he had arrived in Spain in 1945 with Degrelle, and they endured that violent crash landing on the beach of La Concha in San Sebastián together. The interview was very cordial. On that occasion. Degrelle signed a copy of his book *Les Âmes qui Brûlent (The Burning Souls)* for Dannau, with the following words: "To my dear friend Win Dannau, in memory of the interview I have not given him and also of the Prince Borghese, and the delicate sun of December 1965, which floated upon my silences."[94]

Degrelle met with Dannau again in January 1970, although this time at his apartment in Madrid. When Dannau entered, he saw, just beyond the threshold behind the door, a mean-looking club Degrelle kept as a defensive measure. The small floor was the setting for endless hours of recording conversations, anecdotes, and the most minute details of Degrelle's life.

The following year, through the De Schorpioen publisher in Belgium, Dannau would publish a book in which he collected a small part of his recorded

---

[93] [French for *Thus Spake Léon Degrelle.*]
[94] This dedication appears somewhat strange to us as readers, but "the interview I have not given" is likely tongue-in-cheek; the rest probably refers to details that only Degrelle and Dannau knew.

conversations with Degrelle, entitled *Face à Face avec le Rexisme (Face to Face with Rexism)*.

Dannau described, in detail, the ambiance and environment in which his meeting took place:

> *Going up the small spiral staircase of cold stone at number one, Paseo de los Jesuitas in Madrid, on the third floor on the left, there was a door protected with iron bars and multiple locks, with a discolored label: Mr. Juan Sánchez. Under this pseudonym, Léon Degrelle has lived here. In 1935, he was the young leader of the Rexist Movement, with thirty-five deputies in the Belgian Parliament, and commander of the Walloon Legion on the Eastern Front. He was personally decorated by Hitler, who told him "If I had a son, I would want him to be like you." Degrelle was named Volksführer of Belgium during the offensive of the Ardennes, and was the youngest general of the Waffen SS.*

Dannau was struck by the fact that Don Juan "*de Tonnerre*,"[95] had never hidden his admiration for Hitler.

On a wall in Degrelle's home, ten historical flags were displayed. Two flags were of the SS Walloon Legion; one, between the blades of Burgundy, bore the motto "*Dur et Pur. Rex Vaincra*"[96] the other: "*Qui s'y frotte s'y pique*"[97] the remaining eight flags carried the numbers of their respective combat units.

Another thing Dannau noticed was that there was no security in front of the closed door, but he could see four uniformed guards, in pairs of two, walking a hundred feet to the right and left, discreetly, in the street. The porter, with a tip, also warned him that two security teams were in the bar on the corner. He also noticed a black SEAT model 1500[98] parked in the vicinity, which he suspected was a police vehicle.

Degrelle, who had been protected by General Franco and General Agustín Muñoz Grandes, Commander-in-Chief of the Blue Division, complained to Dannau at that time about the new technocrats, members of Opus Dei,[99] who had come to power.

---

[95] [French for "of thunder."]

[96] [French for "Hard and pure. Rex will conquer."]

[97] [French for "Whoever rubs it, gets stung," implying if you go looking for trouble, you will find it.]

[98] The SEAT 1500 was a Spanish-built six-seat sedan.

[99] Opus Dei (Latin for "Work of God") is a peculiar order that was founded in Spain in 1928. The majority of its members are laymen, while the rest are secular priests; it has no monastics. The order, which focuses on uniting the spiritual life with every day, professional and social life, has been criticized by some as "dangerous" and "secretive," although its founder Josemaría Escrivá de Balaguer

The third time Dannau and Degrelle met was in a small restaurant where they ate together, recalling their yet undisclosed adventures from 1945, what they witnessed in history, and recounting a kind of "political testament" of their experiences.

In January 1972, Degrelle and Dannau were together again holding another interview. Degrelle handed him a copy of the book *Degrelle, Face à Face avec le Rexisme*, published the previous year by De Schorpioen in Belgium. In the book, Dannau had compiled and commented on some of their interviews, whose dissemination had been prohibited in Belgium.

When Dannau met him again in Malaga, in March 1973, he stopped to comment on the club he had first seen in Madrid now hanging behind the entry door. "To settle accounts," Degrelle replied.

Dannau compiled more numerous recorded conversations and published, in 1975, a thirteen-volume set with copious photographs, entitled *Ainsi Parla Léon Degrelle (Thus Spake Léon Degrelle)*.

## Those Who Do Not Forgive: Belgium Issues an Order for Extradition

On January 28th, 1970, at the age of one hundred and two, Mrs. Jeanne Caton, the widow of Marcel Lemay, mother to Marie-Paule, and mother-in-law of Léon Degrelle, died in Nice. She was buried in the family grave in the Auberchicourt cemetery.[100]

At this time, Spain was determined to enter the European Economic Community, the economic-financial club that acted as the common market of the six countries that were signatories to the Treaty of Rome since the 1950s. Once again, the Belgian government, seeing Spain's excessive interest in gaining free access to the international economy, used this as another opportunity to force the Degrelle case back on the negotiating table in exchange for their support.

Since December 12th, 1969, Gonzalo Fernández de la Mora, Secretary of State for Foreign Affairs, had given assurances to the Belgian government regarding Léon Degrelle: "Do not worry, we will take as many measures as are useful so that we do not hear about him again." Spain's own Foreign Minister, Gregorio López Bravo, a prominent member of Opus Dei, had confirmed and ratified these "good intentions"

---

argued that these were misunderstandings (see https://www.escrivaworks.org/). Controversies include misleading members about canon law, alleged cover-ups of sexual abuse, recruiting teenagers, et al.

[100] Auberchicourt cemetery is near the town of Douai, in northern France, close to the Belgian border.

to his Belgian colleague, Harmel. During his visit to Brussels in mid-January, López Bravo assumed the obligation of handing over a stateless passport to Léon Degrelle in order for him to be expelled from Spanish territory. Degrelle's statements in *ABC* in early January 1970 had triggered another political storm.

When Minister López Bravo offered this commitment, he had been too hasty and had not considered the legal aspects of the matter. Léon Degrelle was legally a Spanish citizen, with the full legal name of "León José Ramírez Reina" since his adoption in 1955. This remedy offered by the Spanish minister was absolutely unworkable and illegal because a Spaniard could not be denied Spanish nationality and even less be expelled from the country.

José Finat y Escrivá de Romani, Count of Mayalde, along with the father of his recent son-in-law (the husband of Degrelle's daughter Marie-Christine), who was a judge, made Spain's chief diplomat understand that his promise to reduce a Spanish citizen to statelessness in order to authorize his expulsion constituted a legal offense.

The Belgian authorities continued to insist that the Spanish government extradite Degrelle and demanded his immediate delivery. This was still an issue of insatiable desire, a pathological obsession for the Belgian government. On October 29th, 1969, General Franco had appointed a new government in Spain, with a great influx of technocrat ministers and members of the controversial and secretive Opus Dei.

The Belgian government presented a petition to the Spanish Minister for Foreign Affairs, Mr. López Bravo, during his visit to Brussels on January 12th, 1970. López Bravo was a member of Opus Dei, as was the Belgian Foreign Minister, Mr. Spaack. Since they were both members of this sectarian group, they quickly agreed to cut a deal to get Spanish authorities to hand over Degrelle in the hope that this would facilitate Spain's entry into the European common market.

Minister of Foreign Affairs López Bravo proposed the appointment of the career diplomat Gonzalo Fernández de la Mora y Mon, also a member of Opus Dei, as secretariat for his portfolio. The López Bravo-Fernández de la Mora partnership signed a preferential treaty in 1970 with the European Economic Community.

In the memoirs of Gonzalo Fernández de la Mora, published under the title *Rio Arriba* (*Upstream*), there is the following testimony in relation to this issue:

> *One morning I received the Ambassador of Belgium, I think he was a baron. He was extremely nervous and could not control a facial tic. In choppy French, he expressed his protest at some statements made by Léon Degrelle. The diplomat was quite right, since the Spanish government had granted asylum to the banned Belgian leader on*

*the usual condition that he would refrain from political activities in the country that hosted him. I announced to the Ambassador that I would intervene, and I did so personally, at the request of my friend the Marquis of Valdeiglesias, who was also a friend of Degrelle. I met Degrelle soon after. He was of medium stature, athletic, with scars on his face and a high and sustained look. From his extensive work, I had only read one lyrical book whose foreword was written by Marañón. The interview was very brief. Essentially, I told him that if he continued with his political activity he would be expelled and put on the border.*

*He stated "I promise I will not. I am a soldier and a man of honor."*

*Indeed, he had commanded the Belgian volunteer brigade in Russia fighting the Red Army. I believed what he said.*

*Two weeks later, the Ambassador visited me again. Courteous, but pale and in a state of extreme agitation, he gave me a clipping from a Madrid evening newspaper that included statements from Degrelle, which I only glanced at.*

*"He has broken his word and must be expelled," the Ambassador stutteringly and solemnly exclaimed.*

*"That seems to be the case. I will inform you of my government's decision."*

*I referred the matter to the Minister, who gave me carte blanche, and immediately summoned Degrelle. He presented himself as stiff as a robot. I did not invite him to sit and, standing up, I said:*

*"You have deceived me."*

*"In no way. I made those recently published statements last month, weeks before our meeting, and I thought they had already been dismissed and would not be published," Degrelle explained.*

*Although I was impressed by the argument, I tried to intimidate him:*

*"That should have been foreseen. I am sorry, but I am afraid that I will have to propose to the minister that he issue an expulsion order to the government."*

*The truth is that, with such a warning, I hoped to dissuade him definitively from similar actions. I hoped that it would not be necessary to hand him over, as was done with Laval, to the vengeful anger of his socialist countrymen who, in an unusual case, periodically renewed his death sentence so that its statute of limitations would not expire and would even prohibit the repatriation of his mortal remains.*

*"Since this Foreign Ministry sends me to death, I will shoot myself right now in the yard," he said undeterred.*

*He promptly exited my office. To the usher at the door, I ordered:*

*"I hold you responsible for seeing that this gentleman immediately leaves the Santa Cruz Palace."*

> For a couple of minutes, I was afraid I might hear a shot, but that was not the
> case. The rexist leader, away from the main square, continued to publish books in
> French that were generally historical and poetic. Being a naturalized citizen, he
> died in Spain without giving rise to another incident. He could never visit his
> homeland, being threatened with immediate execution. Like him, my French
> teacher, Paul Werrie, was also never amnestied, and died in exile. The vengeful
> Belgian rulers, in the name of democracy, did not give the rexists any better
> treatment than the cruel legionaries of Scipio did to the Carthaginians and the
> Numantines.

In Belgium, there was an absolute prohibition on printing, selling, distributing, or
even transporting and possessing books of Degrelle's authorship and ingenuity. The
publication of a simple booklet was punishable by years of imprisonment or an
exorbitant fine.

A complicated dilemma arose. Belgium was once again requesting extradition,
but Spain could not legally hand him over under their bilateral agreement from
1870, which was still in force. It expressly stipulated that they would neither claim
nor hand over political exiles. Léon Degrelle's lawyer, José Luis del Valle Iturriaga,
dean of the illustrious Bar Association of Madrid, had demonstrated this. In
addition, as of 1957, Léon Degrelle held a Spanish National Identity Document
under the legal name of León José de Ramírez Reina.

Léon Degrelle was sixty-three years old, his three daughters were married to
Spanish citizens, and he had six grandchildren born in Spain, all of them of Spanish
nationality.

Unlike in previous years, the current Spanish government, which was then
largely composed of ministers who were numeraries and supernumeraries of Opus
Dei,[101] summoned Léon Degrelle to request that he leave Spanish soil within forty-
eight hours, and that he would be provided with a stateless passport. Léon did not
appear at the summons at the stipulated time, so the police were ordered to locate
him to notify him of the precarious and imminent period of expulsion from Spain
and to give him the passport, without which the government's formal requirements
would be impossible to fulfill. An arrest and detention order were issued for his
search and capture. Degrelle, harassed by these Opus Dei-affiliated ministers, once

---

[101] Opus Dei has several classes or ranks of members: *Supernumeraries* are the largest category whose
members are married men and women who devote a part of their day to prayer; *Numeraries* are celibate
members who make themselves fully available to the organization. Other categories include the
*Numerary Assistants* and the *Associates*, as well as the *Clergy of the Opus Dei Prelature.*

again saw the need to seek refuge by going underground. He sought security and protection from harassment in eleven different hideouts during February 1970.

The pretext for proceeding with his arrest and subsequent expulsion from Spain was the publication of a number of statements, otherwise innocuous, that he had made to the Madrid daily *ABC* at the beginning of the year, in which he explained how his life was getting along in Spain, pointing out that on six occasions, he had almost been kidnapped.

The arrest warrant was also justified because of the appearance of a series of twenty-nine chapters under the title *Memoirs of a Fascist*, that had been published from October 7th to November 13th, 1969, in the Madrid daily *Pueblo*. The series met with great success and received an extraordinary welcome from readers of the newspaper. The *Pueblo* was managed by Emilio Romero, a journalist from Avila and a native of Arévalo. The series was later compiled into a book of which fifty thousand copies were printed in its first run. The books were seized and destroyed but would be reissued in Barcelona several years later in 1975. This edition had a prologue written by Otto Skorzeny for the Bau Publishing House. Later, more editions of these political memoirs followed, although some of them appeared with the title *Hitler for a Thousand Years*.

The place where he remained hidden the longest that year belonged to journalist Bernardo Gil Mugarza. It was a tower located at the end of Arturo Soria Street. The apartment was newly built; the owner had just acquired it, so it was not yet inhabited. The only furniture inside the property was a single three-seater sofa in the center of the living room. Words echoed off the walls because of the hollow emptiness of the place. In this refuge, with absolute secrecy, he spent almost six months, visited only by the closest members of his family. The flat was high and sunny. Léon read voraciously sitting on that lonely couch. In his lonely silence, the thought occurred to him, just in his imagination, that should the police discover his hiding place, he might throw himself out the window into the open air and fly, dream-like, like a winged being, toward the constellations.

His daughter and her husband Servando Balaguer lived in Madrid where their home was located on calle Enrique Sotomayor. In those days, the residence was being discreetly monitored by the State Security Services, since they were convinced that, at some point, Léon might show up there. Soon Anne would move from that house to a flat on calle María de Guzmán, next to Glorieta de Cuatro Caminos.

From the Pinar de Chamartín apartment, on calle Arturo Soria, number 330, Degrelle moved to a villa offered to him by his friend, Colonel D. Fernando Sanz Esteban, who had been the Chief of the Almansa Armored Regiment and who lived in Madrid on calle General Ampudia. He was linked to the Spanish Youth Organization (OJE). In that villa, Léon found himself in a discreet and secluded place, in the middle of the countryside, close to what is now the Monte Príncipe development. From the window of his bedroom, Léon could see a small grove and the pine forest of the estate owned by the Oriol family.

Another safe haven where Léon lived was in the Moratalaz neighborhood, in the house of Victor Barrado Alonso, who had just married his young wife, Coca. There he spent time tirelessly devoted to reading and writing. Reaching that place was not without mystery and happenstance.

Víctor Barrado Alonso was the son of José Barrado Ruiz, a prominent member of the Spanish Confederation of Autonomous Rights (C.E.D.A.) of Salamanca, well known because he wrote regularly in *La Gaceta Regional*, a local paper linked to Catholicism and civil rights. There he met and developed a friendship with Onésimo Redondo, founder first of the Juntas Castellanas de Actuación Hispánica and later of the Juntas de Ofensiva Nacional Sindicalista (J.O.N.S.). José Barrado considered Redondo an excellent person and a great idealist.

José Barrado Ruiz was one of the first managers of the French cosmetics company L'Oréal in Spain, where Henry Deloncle, Jean Filliol, Jacques Corrèze, and Roger Bretcher worked. The prestigious company was founded on July 30th, 1909, by the chemist Eugène Schueller (1881–1957). Schueller was an intimate friend of the engineer and Knight of the Legion of Honor, Eugène Deloncle (1890–1944), who together with Joseph Darnand, began the armed, clandestine organization *Comité Secret d'Action Révolutionnaire* (Secret Committee for Revolutionary Action or CSAR) in 1935 in France. [102] It was also known as *La Cagoule* (The Hood). Deloncle was also the founder, during the Vichy Government, of the party called Social Revolutionary Movement, a political movement in which Schueller and Deloncle were active and held high responsibilities. L'Oréal financially supported La Cagoule, and even some of La Cagoule's meetings, in preparation for their expeditious actions of sabotage, were held under the greatest secrecy in the French offices of L'Oréal. Deloncle had visited Salamanca during the Spanish Civil War, when he traveled there to meet Franco at his headquarters. It was there that he met José Barrado.

Jacques Corrèze (1912–1991) was the adopted son of Eugène Deloncle and one of the officers in charge, together with Jean Filliol, of La Cagoule. He was known by the pseudonym *La Bûche* (Lump or Log) and was also a member of the

---

[102] The organization was a highly secret, right-wing organization responsible for several violent operations.

Social Revolutionary Movement. After the death of Deloncle, on January 17th, 1944, he married his widow. He was a veteran of the French Legion (LVF) in the Charlemagne Division, which was integrated into the Waffen SS on the Eastern Front. At the end of the conflict, he was arrested and spent several years in prison until he was released in 1949. That same year, Eugène Schueller set him up as a director at L'Oréal-Monavon, overseeing the company's cosmetics in Spain and Latin America, and he collaborated with José Barrado. Henry Deloncle, Eugène's brother, also began to work there.

Roger Bretscher, a great friend of Léon Degrelle, who was of Swiss origin and a member of the SS, along with Henry Deloncle and Jacques Corrèze, asked their friend and colleague José Barrado Ruiz, another leader of the French subsidiary, to help Léon Degrelle in that period of ruthless persecution and potential deportation to Belgium. Barrado Ruiz immediately agreed and asked his son Víctor Barrado Alonso, who also worked for L'Oréal, and who had just settled in a flat in the Moratalaz neighborhood, to hide Degrelle in his house and to say nothing to anyone about the whereabouts or identity of his illustrious guest. There Degrelle was visited by Juana "Jeanne" Brevet, who was his only link to the outside world. The time spent in that house in Moratalaz gave rise to a long-lasting friendship between Degrelle and his hosts Víctor and Coca.

During that series of displacements and constant transfers from house to house, Degrelle also spent a few days at the home of Dr. Mur, on calle Claudio Coello, in the heart of the Salamanca neighborhood of Madrid. In his incessant flight from death, which was always right on his heels and narrowing in on him, sometimes his stays were no more than an overnight, leaving the very next day to head to another safe place.

A great deal of confusion and misinformation on this situation occurred both in the Madrid and Belgian newspapers. In Madrid, the newspapers *Arriba* and *Ya* gave ample coverage of the news. For its part, the Belgian newspaper *Le Soir* published a note by Jean Robert Debbaut, interim head of the Rexist Movement, who, in order to spread disinformation, confidently placed Léon Degrelle in Cairo. Belgian television pointed in another direction, Portugal, although the authorities considered that news to be "unfounded rumors." A Belgian radio correspondent in Madrid, Edouard de Blaye, referring to a statement by a so-called "Degrelle spokesman" in Madrid, said that he "intended to return to Belgium." For its part, *La Dernière Heure* in its last edition, concluded "that the best thing for Belgium and Spain is that Degrelle not be found."

That time was life at a standstill. Degrelle had to learn how to rest again. Up until then, he had been accustomed to eighteen-hour workdays. For several years, he had never taken time to rest or relax. Even if just temporarily, he discovered the *dolce far niente*[103] imposed upon him. In the midst of the political storm, his mood remained serene. He saw things calmly. Perhaps his gaze was set on the horizon of 1974, the year in which he hoped to see the final expiration of his judicial sentence, and thus to be able to return to his homeland. He had the intention, the intimate need and desire, to return to his homeland as soon as possible. He was kept vigilant by the hope of being in Brussels for Christmas in 1974, in the company of his whole family.

The magazine of *Círculo Español de Amigos de Europa* (Spanish Circle of Friends of Europe, or CEDADE) published in issue twenty-one, corresponding to January and February of 1970, an editorial in defense of Léon Degrelle, taking a strong position against his extradition:

> *Léon Degrelle is the living symbol of all that the anti-communist crusade has meant here since 1936. He is the leader of a nonconformist youth movement who sacrificed himself on the battlefields for an ideal: Europe. Yes, we already know. They will say that he has not respected his status as a political refugee, but since when has a comrade of the Falangist Old Guard been considered a political refugee in Spain?*

In his memoirs, Blas Piñar has written:

> *The resolution issued by Minister of Foreign Affairs Gregorio López Bravo is scandalous proof of the lack of interest in providing him [Degrelle] with governmental protection. Ordering his search and capture in order to hand him over to the Belgian authorities is a murderous decision because in Belgium, under the law on the non-expiration of the sentences of certain crimes, Léon Degrelle would have been shot. I published an article in edition number 163 of "Fuerza Nueva," dated February 21st, 1970, criticizing such a brutal decision. I titled the article, "Those who do not forgive." This article brought me some criticism—like the confiscation of that issue of the magazine, although the article later appeared in one hundred sixty-four—and some satisfaction, including a visit of recognition and friendship by Juan Servando Balaguer Parreño, son-in-law of Léon.*

In that article, among many other sensible reflections, Blas Piñar said, "The Belgian government asks us to hand over Degrelle and the Spanish government is looking

---

[103] [Italian for sweet nothingness, or idleness.]

to capture and deliver him. Reading this news is offensive. A sense of disgust, servility, and foolishness assaults our dignity."

During Degrelle's exile, Blas Piñar shared friendship and camaraderie with him. In 1964 Degrelle dedicated a copy of *The Burning Souls* to him in which, on the dedication page, he wrote, "To my esteemed friend Blas Piñar, champion of the ideal. With the most affectionate sympathy, Léon Degrelle, Easter 1964." Degrelle reiterated years later his appreciation and friendship in the dedication he wrote for the fifth edition of the book, published by Fueza Nueva Editorial S.A.: "To the greatest and most noble of friends and comrades, Blas Piñar, knight of the faith and of the fatherland, without fear, always in the front line of the fight. With admiration and brotherly affection, Léon Degrelle, February 22nd, 1979." It should not be forgotten that Blas Piñar, in the mid-1950s, had worked to bring about Léon Degrelle's adoption by Mrs. Matilde Ramírez Reina of Constantina, which paved the way for his new Spanish nationality. He also signed as a witness at the marriage of one of Léon's daughters.

The following year, speculation and rumors started up again, so on March 25th, 1971, the socialist newspaper in Brussels, *Le Peuple,* published an article asking whether Degrelle, in the absence of news about him for a little more than a year, was still in Spain or a refugee in South America. The article stated that for many years he had lived in Constantina (Seville) under the name "Juan Martínez." The article concluded by quoting the testimony of a Spanish journalist, who said he was a friend of Léon, reporting that he was very likely to be in Brazil or Uruguay.

## Correspondence with Blas Piñar

Blas Piñar and Léon Degrelle had an extensive exchange of correspondence. In his memoirs, Blas Piñar, transcribed some of these letters:

*I cannot resist the temptation——I think noble in this case——to reproduce, albeit partially, the text of some of the letters I received from Léon Degrelle:*

*On May 16th, 1970, he begged me to provide my services to Juana "Jeanne" Brevet, the woman who would later become his wife: "I am Léon Degrelle, your friend now more than ever. In the sadness and tragedy of my life, your brotherly support has given me much strength to resist despair." This letter concludes as follows: "I congratulate you on FN, as interesting as it is dynamic, and above all courageous (in a time of cowards). A thousand thanks, again, for your solidarity."*

*On April 19th, 1971:*

"Dear Don Blas, this is your friend Léon. My situation remains difficult. With diabolical rage they continue to pursue me, despite my absolute silence. We know, from an indisputable source, that only in the course of last week, the Belgian Embassy in Madrid sent three encrypted telexes about me, proof that they are preparing something again. See you soon, dear Don Blas. With brotherly embrace."

On April 25th, 1971:

"Dear Don Blas, I am sorry to bother you. You have a lot to do. I would be sorry to leave Madrid without seeing you for a little while, at any time at your convenience, it does not matter to me. I would also like to recover the sole copy of my poor Memoirs of a Fascist. Of this book (ten thousand copies stacked in the printing press), I would also like to speak with you. Embracing you as a friend and comrade"

In repeated congratulations, on the occasion of Christmas, he said to me in 1977:

"Dear Blas, To you and your family, a very Merry Christmas!

1978 is not looking good. You will have to fight heroically to save Spain! May God bless you, Blas, giving you enlightenment of the soul, courage, and physical strength. You will always have me by your side, fraternally.

Cheers! You will win!

Very affectionately yours."

In 1986:

"Dear Blas,

Happy Easter! May God bless you once again in 1987! May we, your friends, have the honor of seeing you elected as member of the European Parliament! I do not doubt, not for a minute, your victory, so precious to Spain.

Congratulations also to your dear family.

With a brotherly embrace, your old friend."

In 1987:

"Dear Blas,

The happy days of Christmas are coming. I do not forget you. I know your faith and I want to tell you with what affection I share in your spiritual joy.

I wish for you, for your family, and for your beloved Patria, the blessings of God! You have earned them a thousand times!

With a brotherly embrace."

The newspaper *El País*, on December 15th, 1982, manipulated and distorted statements attributed to Léon Degrelle, in which he allegedly said:

*I was a friend of Fraga and also a good friend of Blas Piñar. I always told Blas that he was wrong, that he could not be a notary and a politician. He set up a party around a very rich social class. That is why it failed.*

In the fourth volume of his memoirs, Blas Piñar refuted these fallacies, "I never heard that from Degrelle, to whom I was a close friend.

### An Interview Is Published in the Magazine of the *Círculo de Amigos de la Historia*

*Historame* was a highly regarded and widely disseminated French magazine on historical issues. In issue two hundred twenty-eight of the publication, dated November 1970, eleven full pages, from fifty-three to sixty-three, were dedicated to an in-depth interview with Degrelle. This "explosive" interview with the chief rexist was conducted by the journalist Claude Bourgeois, who considered the transcribed text to be a true document, calling it:

> *A fiery encounter with Léon Degrelle, former head of the Belgian Rexist Movement whom Hitler would have wished for a son…passionate admirer of National Socialism and fascism, condemned to death in his country, exiled for twenty-five years, he does not hold his tongue; Degrelle unconsciously—or maybe consciously—lets it all out about what he thinks of yesterday's Germany and today's Europe.*

Bourgeois opens with a wise and timely statement that Degrelle's way of thinking is that of "a man who can say whatever he wants, as long as he is not sincere."

The interview begins with a series of quick questions to get Degrelle's opinion of particular people and countries:

> *CB: De Gaulle?*
> *LD: A false fascist and a false democrat who capitulated at the decisive moment of action.*
> *CB: Spaak?*
> *LD: A politician who has been playing demagogue for thirty years.*
> *CB: Hitler?*
> *LD: Genius in its pure form.*
> *CB: Mao Tse-tung?*

*LD: A man with a higher sense of life.*

*CB: China?*

*LD: A billion men who in twenty years oriented the world in one way or another.*

*CB: The Soviet Union?*

*LD: A kind of South America, a dream of small bourgeois people.*

*CB: Europe?*

*LD: An impossibility that for a long time will busy itself with butter, milk, and meat.*

*CB: France?*

*LD: The country that refused De Gaulle.*

*CB: Life?*

*LD: Heroism.*

Bourgeois reflects how, for twenty-five years, Degrelle has lived under different assumed names. With a desire to start his life again, Degrelle responds, "Look, at the age of thirty-eight, my life as a political leader was smashed to smithereens and my military life left truncated." The interviewer acknowledges that Degrelle, during his exile, continued to be "an amazing character, a kind of mercenary swordsman and friend of the arts, both passionate and tormented. When he speaks, he finds those words that made him, in his youth, a most ardent and reputed hero and great orator." In order not to disclose the location of the meeting, Bourgeois dropped a false hint: "When I proposed to meet him, he suggested that the appointment be in a village on Italia Road, where he had some friends."

Bourgeois observed that:

*Degrelle does not deny anything. Until death, he will not disown anything. Up until now, death, unconcerned, does not appear to want him. The only thing Degrelle wants, truthfully, is to return to his country because exile is too heavy a burden.*

*LD: I want to be able to return, to defend the ideas for which I have fought.*

*I do not want to be judged by an emergency court because it is the Belgian people who should judge me. I have been repeating this for twenty years. I was sentenced to death for having fought on the anti-Soviet front. I consider that condemnation unfair because it is based on retroactive decrees and effects. The essential thing for me is to be able to explain to my people that I have lived for them and that on the Eastern Front, for years, we fought and suffered in order to achieve, for the people we represented, their rights in the event Hitler's Germany had triumphed.*

*Well, for twenty years I have made the same offer and during this time I have repeated, "I will return" only asking for a normal trial. I have even gone further by saying, "I am ready to return unconditionally. They can lock me in prison as long as they want, but just allow me one thing: to stand in the elections in Brussels so the people themselves can judge me."*

*Are the people democrats? True democracy allows people to express what they think, and this would be the most beautiful of justices.*

*Five years ago, I offered to return an hour before the expiration of my sentence, asking only that it be the people who judge me. What was the Belgian government's response? The Minister of Justice himself said, "If Degrelle returns, he will be expelled that same day as a foreign citizen..." A foreigner! I was elected a Member of Parliament in Brussels with the highest number of votes that a parliamentarian had ever achieved until then!*

Commenting on the long journey of exile, Degrelle stated:

*The life of an exile for me is, first and foremost, not being able to realize my vocation. If a sculptor's arms are cut off, or a painter's eyes are gouged out, it is the end of his vocation. For a politician, the case is the same. The politician lives to lead the masses, to excite them. For him, from the moment he gets cornered in exile, action becomes impossible, and his existence is over.*

*For me, this quarter century of exile has been a quarter century of death.*

*The material question has no importance in life. The politician does not live to make money, nor to have it. He does not live in order to eat, to drink...He lives in order to create; he lives to realize a work. The material question has never occupied a moment, a second of my existence. When we were on the Eastern Front, we had nothing to eat, nothing to drink, and we were completely happy. I prefer to live with a piece of bread and direct a people than to have a palace and not to be able to carry out the mission that is essential to my life.*

He still considered Hitler "a genius in its integral state, and that is what for many small-minded people is incomprehensible."

When asked about the Jews, he does not shy away from the question: "These people are unable to be assimilated. This is the fifth column. They never belong to a country."

At the end of the long line of questions, when asked about Europe, Degrelle replies:

*Frankly, it is no longer imaginable, as we find nothing but mediocre people. Europe will not be built through a congress, let alone by thirty-six commissions or by miserable disputes over milk, butter, or meat, which get delayed for days and days with clocks that seem to have stopped. No, Europe can only be forged by the will of one man. Napoleon, Hitler, De Gaulle have failed. In the future, maybe we will see a Europe of merchants, but there will never be a Greater Europe.*

The last question is about China. Degrelle posits:

*From my point of view, the Soviets and the United States will end up reaching a big settlement. Communism has gone beyond Siberia; it has been set up in Central Asia. Seven or eight million human beings live there who will be a billion in twenty or twenty-five years. A billion Chinese, to whom Mao Tse-tung himself, who has a superior sense of life, this is obvious, has given a reason for hope and another reason to live. Mao Tse-tung, this great poet, despite all the foolishness in today's Chinese system, is otherwise orienting another world. So, it is possible, and I am convinced of this, that one day they will oppose the enormous materialistic civilization of the United States, overflowing onto Soviet Russia and an immense Asia adapted to another form of civilization. Amidst all this is our little Europe and its little bourgeoisie.*

As an aside, when the interview was over, Degrelle's daughter Marie-Christine was present

In Spain, the *Círculo de Amigos de la Historia* magazine, published in full, in the May-June 1971 edition, on pages twenty-six to thirty-six, Claude Bourgeois's interview.

## Léon Degrelle's Offense in Europe

On Monday, March 12th, 1973, Léon Degrelle made some bold statements which were broadcast to a fairly large audience by the Netherlands television station AVRO. The interview took place in Spain with a film crew led by Marcel de Groot from AVRO. De Groot, as Degrelle had demanded, was a reporter under the age of thirty. After the interview, they returned to the studio with an hour and a half of recorded tape, of which only twenty minutes was actually broadcast.

Since people could also tune in to AVRO from Belgium, when the exclusive interview was announced, the number of viewers was enormous, but the political scandal it generated was even more dramatic. In short, Degrelle told viewers that fascism was good and that, if possible, he would begin the struggle to achieve that ideal again, as he defended the ideal of greater Europe. He did not regret having founded Rexism, nor commanding the Walloon Legion that fought in Russia, side by side, with the Waffen SS. He did not regret being a personal friend of Adolf Hitler, quite the contrary.

The Belgian government immediately asked the Spanish authorities, once again, with serious warnings, to prohibit the rexist founder from speaking about politics. When the Belgian Foreign Ministry spokesman appeared at the weekly press conference, he talked about Degrelle's interview, and said that orders had been sent to the Belgian Embassy in Madrid to silence Degrelle. This prompted a journalist to ask him intentionally: "So, have we asked Spain to censor Degrelle's objections?"

On April 4th, 1973, the magazine *Knack* published the news that the RTB and the BRT[104] outlets had censored the AVRO documentary. They made it known to their readers that *Knack* was preparing to publish the interview in its entirety. This news was keenly and bitterly felt in Brussels.

## A Letter from Germany to Léon Degrelle: "Das ist Kamaradschaft"

In April 1973, Degrelle received a letter from Germany, translated into French by comrades Abel Delannoy and Georges "Gil" Gilsoul which was subsequently published in *L'Europe Réelle*. It read:

*Dear comrade Degrelle,*

*It is a curious thing that leads me to write this letter to you. Three weeks ago, I gave a lecture in Munich before an audience with very diverse political opinions, which dealt with camaraderie and my memories of the war. I spoke, among other things, about the experiences we shared together during the siege of Tcherkassy. I was then the Viking Division surgeon, and the hospital was installed in the Korsum School. That is why I have kept a very vivid and accurate memory of the visits you made to the wounded, always accompanied by your driver. These boys were sometimes so seriously injured that they could not even bear being talked to, but when you arrived, those heavily wounded, sleepy, and feverish soldiers would*

---

[104] *Radio-Télévision Belge* (RTB) and *Belgische Radio- en Televisieomroep* (BRT, now the VRT) were both state-run public broadcast stations in Belgium. They were basically the French and Flemish language stations of the same outlet. Today, they are separate entities.

*suddenly wake up and sit up in their beds, yelling jubilantly and full of joy, "My commander! My chief!"*

*At that time, we had dinner together on several occasions. On one occasion, I asked you, considering the impact of our desperate situation, why you did not exert political activity in your country and why you remained at our side, despite the desperate situation we were already in at that time? You answered me: "We are now at war, and I will not return to politics again until this crusade ends." I remember it like it was yesterday. Shortly before the siege broke, the Führer's order had been received in which he expressed his desire to get you out of the infernal siege by putting a plane at your disposal, as he needed you for other political tasks. You refused the tempting proposal, saying, "I will stay with my men through the good and the bad." Indeed, you led your men heroically, breaking through the enemy siege after the death of the commander-in-chief of the besieged forces.*

*This is camaraderie! That was the general theme of the lecture I gave.*

*I have just read in the weekly Der Spiegel a detailed article on what happened to you afterward, plus it includes your Madrid address. For my part, it only remains for me to tell you that I am a surgeon and I have a very comfortable economic situation. I would very much like to hear from you and I affirm my absolute fidelity, just as before.*

*Very sincerely,*

*J.K.*

## New Business Projects on Costa del Sol

On May 28th, 1974, before notary Javier Cabañas Rodríguez, the act of constitution was signed for a company called Torre del Sol S.A. It was established with one million two hundred thousand pesetas in capital, in which the Spanish citizen Léon José Ramírez Reina was the majority shareholder and functioned as its president. The headquarters of the new entity was located in his own home in Fuengirola, in Torreblanca del Sol, in the Villa La Cabaña located on Cerro Alto.

Later, the company Torre del Sol, S.A. would acquire a plot of land in Fuengirola, located next to the old coast road, on National 340. The goal was to build on this land, but the construction project could not move forward, when in 1981, archaeological remains of Roman thermal baths were discovered. The plot was declared an archaeological zone in the municipal planning of the Fuengirola Town Council that same year. It was described as "a monumental archaeological site of the first degree and is declared a historical artistic monument of national character by legal decree."

The ruins that were found were part of a Roman villa of some noble patrician from the first century, of which only part of its thermal baths plus two chambers to heat the pools of the luxury villa were preserved. They were in a deplorable state, and the primitive building had suffered great deterioration in the fourth century when a salting factory was being installed on the site. Later, the land was used as a Visigoth[105] necropolis.

## The Belgian Government Prohibits
## Léon's Return to Belgium Indefinitely

December 27th, 1974 should have been the definitive end date of the illicit ten-year extension of Degrelle's sentence, per the controversial *Lex Degrelliana,* which had been handed down thirty years prior. Thirty long years of relentless persecution had already passed.

The Belgian authorities morally, politically, and legally, feared that Léon Degrelle would return to Belgium victorious and triumphant, when the illegal extension on his sentence was over. On October 24th, 1974, two months before the expiration of his sentence's extension, the government decided to prohibit him from entering the country "on grounds of public order." For this reason, Leo Tindemans' center-right executive promulgated a Ministerial Order to apply a Royal Decree from 1965 to Léon Degrelle, stipulating that entry into Belgium "may be denied by order of the Minister of Justice when the presence of a foreigner in Belgium is considered to be liable to compromise public tranquility, public order, or the security of the country." The order was signed by Justice Minister Vanderpoorten, a Flemish civil-rights liberal, and was applied to Degrelle by treating him as legally "foreign," having been stripped of Belgian nationality in 1945. The government, before signing the order, had studied the possibility of a further extension of the sentence, but a legal commission ruled that the procedure was absolutely illegal, as well as a denial of human rights. For this reason, the Order of the Minister of Justice, which appeared in the *Official Gazette of the Kingdom*, resorted to the public order. Degrelle was nearly seventy years old at this time and continued to challenge an entire government made up of cowardly, timid, irresponsible, and mendacious political puppets.

---

[105] The western tribe of the Goths (a Germanic people) who settled west of the Black Sea sometime in the third century.

Léon, however, was still in the saddle, as they say. In issue one hundred forty-two of the French magazine *Défense de l'Occident*, some of his statements to Jacques Vanden Bemden were published about his motivations and feelings in April 1941, when he:

> *...was not thinking about calling up volunteers. The war against Russia had not yet begun. I did not even seek the extenuating circumstances of the struggle against communism, but because I did not want to entangle my country in an absurd military adventure, I went on my own.*

## An Extensive Letter to His Daughter Chantal

In December 1974, Léon Degrelle wrote to his daughter Chantal the following letter:

> *You already know that I have collected complications like postage stamps in the past! I am unable to stay in any one place for six months without playing hide-and-seek with my enemies. When a statement comes out in a large newspaper that explodes in their hands like a bomb; when a terrific hour-long interview is broadcast on Dutch Television, which all of Belgium listens to, loving a good joke, but which causes half a dozen strokes (a highly appreciated result) among the big idiots who want my head. Then their survivors, obviously unhappy, muster together some outrage before the Spanish government, demanding that they muzzle my snout. This amuses me a lot every time it happens, but it does not prevent me from having to lie low for a few months, towing huge suitcases of books, living on cans of sardines and cooked potatoes! I will never capitulate! I am in the right, and I will repeat it with a bellowing voice until the end, and the end is not near. I already have in mind an interview I will give at a press conference on the first day of January 2000. You are going to see that I will be gallant and waiting by then! Those who are rabid, completely burning themselves up inside to see me dead, can see it and weep with their jaws dropped, one after the other. Van Zeeland, the former Belgian Prime Minister, whom I once turned upside down? Buried! Pierlot, our enemy of London? A bag of bones, as bare now as his bald head once was, varnished like a shiny saucepan! And that fat Spaak! Paunchy flab planted on two small legs like bowling pins? Rushed back to Brussels in a United States Army plane, sweaty, snorting, leaking like a sieve everywhere, trapped by the devil by the bottom of his underpants*

*after two days of agony! Everyone has died!*[106] *Yet I, well healed by the sun, happy to be alive, full of good humor, standing next to the tombs of my gravediggers! Will I pass by one day on my way back? That is possible. It would be fine, but I am not sure. Why will it be really necessary to die? I have no envy for them. I am full of dynamism. Life is a magical charm. To be alive! To see the sky bursting with the gold of dawn! Alive! To take in big, deep breaths of air! To live! To feel the brain turning everything on, creating original, beautiful, great things! To live! To feel like one is a piece of the plot of immense universe, nourishing, shimmering power, whirling like a picture of Van Gogh! To live! To be one of the human stars that God has cast on the most diverse soils through space! It is a spell to live! It is a conquest, a joy every second! Like missing a minute of this party, letting it stop a minute too soon!*

*Then, the sorrows, the exhausting work, the catastrophes can bring my faith to an end; sovereign is the life that always stirs in me!*

*Have I aged? Certainly, but I deny it. I have had no lack of obstacles, for sure. First of all, I have thrown myself from the top of an old oak, 10 meters (33 feet) high! Listen to this! Two years ago, I had to hide out in a house, not far from large mountains, that a senior official had put at my disposal (I was being harassed again). Fine. I lived there completely alone with my books (that is, I had the company of hundreds of passionate interlocutors). Three times a week, a van passed 100 meters (328 feet) from my shelter, along a narrow forest road, carrying tomatoes, potatoes, vegetables, soaps and other stuff for the few inhabitants of the region. I boiled the potatoes in water and made a huge salad, which I served myself from when I was hungry. Complications? None. I listened to the bees hum, the sparrows singing, and my great inner voices. Perfect, well, but behold! In the afternoon, I watched the sunset, hiding behind the trees of the oak grove. I said to myself, from the top of these trees, one should be able to contemplate the formidable display of the golds, the violets, the light greens of the twilight between the slopes of the mountains, whose lush vegetation hides me. To help me get a better look, there was no choice but to climb to the top ("à la copette," as it is said in Walloon) of the largest of the green oaks. So, I went up. I got to the very top. It was enormous. The entire range of the great Guadarrama mountains was like a fire, but a fire much more sumptuous than the ordinary fire that is nothing more than red and gold. This was a fire that was like a thousand giant orchids, gladiolas, and lilacs, springing among the immense sunsets. I was completely captivated. So fascinated was I by these wonders, that my feet, vulgar material hooks, escaped my subconscious and,*

---

[106] Paul-Henri Spaak died in 1972; Hubert Pierlot in 1963; and Paul van Zeeland in 1973.

with the speed of a sea lion bursting the surface of the water, I plunged myself into the midst of the abundant foliage below! Bam! I hit the ground like a sack of potatoes. My left foot was broken, and my right knee was dislocated! I could not even walk two feet away! Apart from the playful squirrels shelling their acorns and the voles rubbing their little snouts in the weeds, there was not a human being within 10 kilometers (6 miles)! I spent the night at the foot of that tree, very sensitive to the charm of darkness, to its furtive noises, to its perfumes, but also to the throbbing pain in both of my legs!

The next day, around 12:00 p.m., a forest warden, after having taken me for a poacher, came to my help and put me on an old couch. Go to the doctor's office? Unthinkable! I should not be located by anyone. I wrapped my foot up as best I could with a bandage, and despite having a dislocated knee, with the aid of a chair I was able to move around 2 or 3 meters (7 to 10 feet) every day, which allowed me to eat from my pot of unvarying salad, potatoes, tomatoes, and lettuce, tossed in mayonnaise that I scooped out of a large, increasingly yellowish jar (the mayonnaise!) as time passed. The bone was mending, and autumn was coming. They were still looking for me. My knee still smarted when I turned around on the pad. Unimportant misery. The incident was over.

Last winter, a new alert! One of my officers quickly picked me up and rushed me over to the same deserted shelter. There was nothing more than an old wood burning fireplace. Very poetic, the fire's love of logs! It did not work, and thick, teary, gray smoke spread all over, which made me cough. My guide had now returned, and the fire also realized that the time to disappear had come. It went out, leaving me in the company of a numbing cold. It was in the dead of winter. The temperature dropped to 5° or 10°F. My teeth were chattering. My whole body was shivering. I had gathered up all the rags of this summer shelter to cover myself. Nothing could be done. I felt invaded by a devilish fever, and then was bitten by a sharp pain in the back. When my friend came back, two days later, I told him to take me to a clinic urgently. He asked me where I would want to check in? I would risk everything now: to Franco's clinic! I had bronchopneumonia and was running a 104° fever. My dear daughters, I thought, would cheer me up with their visits...

So, I had to appear, for the second time, in this clinic. Moving from a shelter in Madrid one night at 1:00 a.m., dragging two huge suitcases of books that weighed as much as a tank, I suddenly felt a great pain, and like an apple falling off in my belly, I had a hernia burst!

This time they had to operate on me. I was taken to Franco's clinic again, as if I were a Spanish colonel. The lieutenant drove me on a stretcher to the operating room. When they were about to operate, the doctor asked me, "What is your name?"

*Good grief! I had forgotten my colonel's name! The one they were going to operate on did not even know his name! Neat story? I pretended as if the sleeping pill had transported me to an apple vendor. The doctor shook his head, and started getting the scalpel ready, click, scrape! That was the noise I heard!*

*That is life: comedies and tragedies! That is why it is necessary to maintain balance, until the end, on the rope of fate!*

*I have seen everything, the whole spectrum of colors during my life: strenuous political work, a terrible war, relentless persecution in exile, but the truth is that all the people of my age are "hardened," and I walk straight like a pine full of sap. Now I am working on a large, historical work. I have never had a headache. Every day I walk my usual six miles on foot. I am happy (and God knows that I have not lacked reasons to be sad). Above all, I am possessed with the passion for that which is beautiful: finding it, possessing it, creating it, produces in me untold joys, nourishing sources of my existence...*

*Ordinary life is often drunkenness, monotony, brutish, but it can also be beautiful, and happiness is at your door if you recreate it without ceasing, if you put your mind to it. It is like fireworks; they can be nothing more than stupid firecrackers in a box, or they can also flood the sky with dazzling-colored lights. Even by closing your eyes, bright colors are discovered. Beauty and happiness, in everything, are within our reach, in the contemplation of a blade of grass, or in the mysterious impulse of a gaze. Everything is inside us. We can do everything, but look, it is not necessary to be just a small ant walking to and fro stupidly and uselessly. There are ants, millions of ants, there are also lions, some are lions, and eagles, some are eagles. You need to be a lion or an eagle...*

*Above all, it is essential to get out of mediocrity, avoid it at all costs, and escape that which will otherwise invade us everywhere and oppress us just like the metastasis of a cancer. In the background, the noblest evasion, that which, in any case, comforts everything, is God. You know, truly, that this was my true great ideal. I wanted to be nothing more than this. This interested me much more than politics. I do not know if you have my little book,* The Burning Souls, *where I evoke all this, but this is not simple these days. The Church, like everything else, is all mixed up, but the heart of men is always the same, it will always be the same, and conflicts, temptations, endless aberrations will never choke the great inner calling of every being, their thirst for truth, justice, their need for surrender, and above all their hope for eternity. If not, what is living? If it is nothing more than walking in circles for fifty to eighty years inside a pot—or inside a mink coat— what does it serve, if we accumulate a lot of grudges, disappointments, sadness, which, sooner or later, eat away our chest, as if an infestation of rats were gnawing at us under our clothes?*

*Happiness is the peace of the soul, it is nothing else, it is to have a soul that believes and gives, that is nourished by great inner light that illuminates and comforts by the joy that it brings to those who strive not only in material complications, but in the long, interior shadows of spiritual sterility. In fact, the vast majority of men are very unfortunate, even if they do not appear that way, even if they say they are not, even though they bustle and cover themselves with an outer cover of a joy that almost always is nothing more than a show, an escape...*

*If you have crossed the artificial barrier of false, creative joy of a world that is nothing more than pretty dust, you will understand that sooner or later it will decompose; you have to be attentive to the essentials. The only thing that does not lie, that never disappoints, is the great inner peace, that secret vocation that transcends everything. To have discovered this vocation, to have allowed it to gush forth (there are so many wonderful springs that never gushed forth), to have made of life, poor in itself (even when the brightest tinsels camouflage it), a wealth always renewed. Normal life is rain. True rain is the sea, always in place, always powerful, eternal. Both are water. One, a flowing banal water, the other a water that will live, powerful, with its immense rhythm, always so beautiful, until the end of times.*

*This is the story of both the happiness and misfortune of humanity, which otherwise adapts, and winds up diluted in mediocrity, this is the fate of accommodation of the vast majority of people. So, how many mediocre people surround one! They end up being satisfied with, or unconscious of, their semi-mediocrity, becoming accustomed to it, thinking nothing more beyond this vague comfort that pleases everyone equally, like a car (like everyone else!), a television (like everyone else!) a vacation (like everyone else!), and a certain cavalier agreement that makes one become too engulfed in family or in the midst of being crushed by the weight of life....*

*Holding all of you to my chest and embracing you tenderly.*

## A Restaurant That He Frequents in Marbella

On the beach of Marbella, is a large, luxurious restaurant, with terraces on the fine, blond sand of the coast. It is a place is frequented by Léon, where he is always received with a hearty welcome and respect. The owner of the establishment is Alex Stroïnovski, a friendly, extroverted man with a last name that betrays his Russian origin. His young son Dimitri is in charge of keeping things fresh and vibrant in the famous and busy restaurant, whose clientele are mostly foreigners or passers-by on the Costa del Sol.

The premises are decorated simply but tastefully. Wooden beams and tiles on the walls in a curious mixture of rustic and Andalusian styles combine perfectly. The roof is thatched, a feature characteristic of the area, and one can see the sun setting outside.

Alex's restaurant was relatively close to La Cabaña where Degrelle lived. He celebrated special events there and invited guests to lunch when they visited him.

Alex and Léon were old friends. He was a descendant of a family of Russian emigrants. After the communist revolution, at the age of sixteen, he volunteered for the National Socialist Motor Corps, or NSKK,[107] in Germany. During the Second World War, he volunteered on the front serving in a mortar platoon. He then served with the Walloon Division, where he developed a friendship and camaraderie with his commander Léon Degrelle. Fate would bring them back together in Spain.

There were several birthdays that Léon celebrated in Alex's restaurant, and countless meals enjoyed in the company and fellowship of comrades. On June 15th, 1976, while dining, he wrote on a photograph the following dedication to a friend: "To Dira, who shares our passion for greatness, with all the affection of his faithful friend." Several years later, celebrating his birthday again in that place, on June 15th, 1989, he dedicated another photographed card, with several smaller pictures of himself, to Alex's son: "For you, dear Dimitri, this memory of youth, with all my affection." Two years later, on June 15th, 1991, while serving the birthday desserts, he signed a picture in which four images were captured while reading the adventures of Tintin. At the foot of the portraits, he wrote: "For you, dear Dimitri, on this day of my birthday, with all affection, L.D."

On April 20th, 1987, on the anniversary of Hitler's birth, Léon also met for lunch with a group of his close comrades. Some of the diners were old friends of his for more than twenty years. The feast took place in Alex's restaurant and from that celebration some written testimonies of Léon are preserved.

Léon also went there frequently with his loyal comrade Mariano Bolaño Lozano, a man of refined fidelity and absolute confidence. Lozano was a former chief of the Second Centuria of the Guard of Franco, the "*Ramiro Ledesma Ramos*"[108]

---

[107] The Nationalsozialistisches Kraftfahrkorps (National Socialist Motor Corps, or NSKK) was a paramilitary organization of the NSDAP and served the training and transport needs of various German military units.

[108] Ramiro Ledesma Ramos (1905—1936) was a Spanish politician, writer, journalist, and philosopher. He was a pioneer in introducing fascism in Spain.

of the district of Tetuán in Madrid. He lived and worked in Torremolinos. They both felt a special predilection for this restaurant.

Léon Degrelle reading *The Adventures of Tintin*

## Teodulfo Lagunero, Political Adversary and Yet a Friend

Léon had friends of all persuasions, of all classes, and of all ideologies. One of them was the wealthy economist Teodulfo Lagunero, whom Degrelle had met on the Costa del Sol. For a long time, Lagunero was one of the most solid pillars of the Communist Party of Spain. It was Teodulfo Lagunero who, in 1976, secretly snuck into Spain, in his large white Mercedes. He brought with him the infamous individual responsible for the Paracuellos del Jarama Massacre (Madrid, 1936), Santiago Carrillo Solares. Carrillo was disguised in his famous wig and feigned cluelessness to achieve entry into the country.

The two men exchanged pleasantries and stimulating conversation and dinner at each other's homes. They talked about everything, from politics, to art, and even business. Lagunero had a dozen tiles by Picasso and over two hundred gouache paintings by the communist poet Rafael Alberti. They had a mutual respect and friendship for each other on a personal level, but in the realm of politics, they vehemently disagreed.

It would have been a curious happenstance if Léon happened to have crossed paths with the abominable, genocidal mastermind of the massacre of Paracuellos del Jarama, Santiago Carrillo, when he was hiding in a luxurious villa in the exclusive, aristocratic El Viso neighborhood in Madrid, wearing his false wig. This almost happened when Degrelle wanted to have his war medals polished. He consulted a Jeweler, who advised him to take them to a woman who turned out to be a niece of Carrillo. He became friends with her and one day she told him that her uncle Santiago wanted to meet him and proposed that they meet in his luxurious hideout. Léon did not accept because he himself was under surveillance, and also because he thought that if the authorities had trapped Carrillo in that house while he was in disguise, they might think that some sort of trap had been set, or maybe there was a tip-off.

On another occasion, when Tierno Galván, whom he considered a prolific intellectual, was convicted and his typewriter confiscated, Degrelle tried, by all means, to lend him his own. In an interview he even said that he was an interesting leader, and he considered him a man of great culture. One should keep in mind that Tierno Galván was a fanatic of the political regime of General Franco. For political opportunism and pure, calculated convenience, and as he was a professor at the University of Salamanca, he joined the Spanish Socialist Workers Party (PSOE), despite being rather advanced in age. His admission was endorsed by a "friend of Felipe González, Antonio Villar Massó, who would eventually become Most Worshipful Grand Master within freemasonry."

## An Evening with José Luis Jerez Riesco

A very special evening took place on October 10th, 1975, when, in the company of my wife, I was invited to dine with Léon Degrelle by his daughter Anne and Servando Balaguer in their home in Madrid on calle María de Guzmán.

Balaguer was a personal friend of mine and had been on attendance at the act of my registration as a practicing attorney with the Bar Association of Madrid. He was one of my sponsors and signed the admission file.

It was a memorable dinner, and it lasted into the wee hours of the morning. We were wrapped up in a conversation of revealing, intimate, familiar, and endearing complicity. In the end, as a reminder of that unforgettable encounter, when it was already dawn and the first light of day was making its way over a waking Madrid, Degrelle offered me a copy of the French edition of the book *Les Âmes qui Brulent (The Burning Souls)*. He autographed it and inscribed the following dedication:

"For my dear friends and comrades, Flory and José Luis Jerez Riesco, the 1,000 percent idealists, with the admiration and fraternal affection of Léon Degrelle."

The anecdotes that Léon Degrelle told of his heroic life on that relaxed and familiar evening are notes that remain reserved for the future publication of another book about his intimate memories and encounters.

On October 11th, 1975, I took a trip to Italy, where I gave a speech in front of a large crowd of people gathered in the Piazza della Repubblica in the city of Reggio Calabria. They were there to demonstrate support for the Franco regime and in support of Spanish justice, that, in a sentence handed down by the War Council, known as *Proceso de Burgos* (Burgos Process), prosecuted dangerous terrorists and criminals who had been sentenced to death for serious and horrendous crimes.

*Léon Degrelle, with his daughter Anne and his son-in-law Servando Balaguer,*
*in a photograph dedicated to José Luis Jerez Riesco*

### A New Edition of *Memoirs of a Fascist*:
### Otto Skorzeny Writes the Foreword

A new edition of the book *Memoirs of a Fascist* was published on January 9th, 1976. Léon Degrelle and I met once again to celebrate the recent publication of the autobiographical work. Léon gave me a copy, writing a heartfelt, autographed dedication: "To my dear friend and comrade…" It was the second copy I obtained from him. The first, published under the title *Hitler pour 1000 Ans* (*Hitler for a Thousand* Years) in its French version, he dedicated and gave to me on December 6th, 1972, four years prior. During that day we commented, as was customary between us, upon the experiences and adventures that he liked recall, remembering his close and intimate comrades who had fallen on the Eastern Front. Saying our farewells, Léon had prepared a more than pleasant surprise; he gave me a copy of the first French edition of his book *La Campagne de Russie* (*The Russia Campaign*), which he had reserved for me with his usual generosity and unlimited affection, and with a very special dedication. It was a difficult book to find in Spain and, like all of his works, was confiscated and banned both in France and in his native homeland of Belgium.

With the first French edition of *Hitler pour 1000 Ans* (*Hitler for a Thousand Years*), he used to give a copy to friends who came by La Cabaña, as was the case with Fermín Echeverría. In September 1968, Degrelle gave the book with the following dedication: "To my dear friend and comrade Fermin Echeverría, so idealistic and so noble, with affection, L.D."

Skorzeny had also written the forward to Degrelle's *Hitler for a Thousand Years*, the first edition. For the foreword of Degrelle's *Memoirs of a Fascist*, his friend, the legendary Otto Skorzeny, wrote:

> *The author, Léon Degrelle, is an old comrade of mine. This camaraderie of the Second World War front is a very special thing. Today, when I meet, almost thirty years later, a sergeant or a colonel among those who, like me, knew what the battle of Russia was, we immediately begin to exchange impressions and memories, even though they are almost always linked to our dead friends, to hunger, to hardships, or the dreadful cold past.*
>
> *Everyone who fought in Russia feels very close to other comrades. We know, every one of us, why we fought.*
>
> *… The volunteers of those times who fought with us were treated, after losing the war, as traitors in their respective countries; they were sentenced to death or*

*have spent long years in prison. They had only one fault: they believed in a united Europe at that time and hoped that they could realize, with the help of Germany and together with Germany, that vision of a better future. Their will and aspirations, their hopes, were justified and were valid also for these times; their vision only blurred by being young.*

*My comrade Léon Degrelle was already, in those years, a man of politics. He had his admirers, especially in the southern part of Belgium, among the French-speaking Belgians. He was convinced that, as a volunteer in the German uniform, he was fulfilling his duty to his homeland. No one can deny or question this conviction in Léon Degrelle. I am convinced that Léon Degrelle, with his Walloon Legion, wanted to fight until he achieved a right of self-determination for his homeland in a future Europe.*

*There were very few volunteer units in the German Army that fought or fought as bravely as the Belgian volunteers under the command of Léon Degrelle. This brave soldier at the head of his units, was wounded many times, and received, by rights, the highest German military distinctions.*

*Between February and March 1945, when I was commanding a division in Schwedt, east of the Oder River, Léon Degrelle was fighting with his division near Stagart, a few kilometers north of Schwedt. Our two divisions on this front were the units that fought in the most advanced positions to the east.*

*I, and all the old comrades of the Eastern Front, wish great success for this new book of Léon Degrelle, but especially we hope that now, twenty-five years after the end of the war, there will very soon be a possibility for him to return as a free and respected man to his homeland. A brave soldier who has fought and risked his life according to his honest conviction deserves, in my opinion, at least respect in today's world.*

*Otto Skorzeny*
*March 1969*

Léon Degrelle and Otto Skorzeny often had lunch at the Horcher restaurant on Alfonso XII Street in Madrid. It was owned by Otto Horcher, who had ties to some German political personalities during the Third Reich. Horcher later opened a new restaurant with the name La Fonda in Marbella.

Otto Skorzeny, his legendary friend, a commando of the Waffen SS who was personally commissioned by Hitler for the risky mission of the liberation of Benito Mussolini, the Duce of Italy, also lived out his exile in Madrid. A Knight of the Iron Cross, Skorzeny was also a man of legendary exploits, who never renounced his ideology or disavowed Hitler. Born in Vienna on July 12th, 1908, he was the son of a very famous engineer. In May 1932, he joined the National Socialist Party of Austria, and then the SS in 1934. He completed his university studies as an engineer. The annexation of Austria by the Third Reich gave him immense satisfaction and joy in seeing the German people reunified. When the Second World War broke out, he first entered the Luftwaffe barracks for pilot training, although he was immediately transferred to a Waffen SS combat unit, joining the *Germania* battalion and participating in the Western Front campaign. He was then made a lieutenant in the *Das Reich* Division, which was involved in the Yugoslavia campaign. He later went on to fight on the Eastern Front. In 1943, he was appointed head of the Hunters Battalion in the SS *Oranienburg*, also known as the *Jagdverband* (Hunting Band), a group of SS commandos that was set up near Berlin in what had been, in former times, a hunting pavilion for Frederick the Great. On July 26th, 1943, then Captain Skorzeny went to Hitler's headquarters in Prussia. He had been summoned by Hitler to be entrusted with the location and rescue of the Duce of Italy, who had been kidnapped the previous day and hidden in an unknown place. Immediately the search began, and they finally located Mussolini in the high mountain hotel Campo Imperatore on the Gran Sasso massif. It was an impregnable place, at an altitude above 2,000 meters (6,562 feet) in the Apennine Mountain range. The dangerous and near impossible rescue mission was carried out with twelve gliders on Sunday, September 12th, 1943. This difficult and risky operation earned him a promotion to commander, and he was awarded the Iron Cross.

In the July 20th, 1944, assassination attempt against the Führer, Skorzeny again proved his loyalty by working with Commander Otto Ernst Remer in controlling the situation. In the winter of 1944, he participated in the great German counter-offensive to stop the advance of the Allied forces. At the head of the unit he commanded, the One Hundred Fiftieth Armored Brigade, he launched Operation Griffin, a cover and infiltration operation of commandos behind enemy lines. On May 8th, 1945, at the limit of their forces and with the last three hundred of their commandos, they were captured by the Americans in a hellish encirclement. Skorzeny was interned for three years as a prisoner until, on July 27th, 1948, he managed to escape from Darmstadt.

After a journey through various countries, he settled in Spain with his wife, Ilse Lüthje, niece of the former National Socialist Finance Minister, Hjalmar Schacht, on January 12th, 1951. In 1952, Skorzeny gave an interview to the daily *ABC*, and on April 7th he also made statements to Charles Foley, the foreign editor for the British newspaper *The Daily Express* in Spain. They had lunch at the Horcher restaurant in Madrid. Skorzeny was linked to the General Gelhen Network, and to the Odessa Organization, a clandestine organization to assist in the evasion of comrades-in-arms. He was even associated with the creation and leadership of an organization of former SS known as *Die Spinne* (The Spider). He traveled frequently to Cairo, Buenos Aires, Cape Town, and Montevideo.

Upon his arrival in Spain, Skorzeny started an engineering company on Avenida de José Antonio, number 14, under the name of *Rolf O.S. Steinbauer*. He later moved the company to de la Montera street, number 25, in Madrid.

He had connections with Spanish Minister of Foreign Affairs Alberto Martín Artajo and with Deputy Secretary of the Presidency Admiral Luis Carrero Blanco whom he met through his friend, the diplomat Pedro Prat y Soutzo. Through German engineering and construction companies, he contacted American forces and collaborated on their projects to build military bases and housing for their personnel in Spain. He also cultivated activities in the area of foreign trade. On one of his initiatives, he had the collaboration and advice of his great friend and comrade Léon Degrelle. Their friendship was one of high esteem, respect, and genuine affection. Otto Skorzeny died on July 4th, 1975, at the age of seventy-seven at his home on calle Castellón de la Plana in Madrid.

Degrelle wept bitterly at his death. He had lost one of his best friends and comrades in Spain, with whom he had shared many memorable moments. They were unconditional friends, and on some occasions, they were business partners. On May 23rd, 1993, eighteen years after the death of his friend Skorzeny, the American journalist Martin A. Lee asked him about his relationship with Otto. Léon replied:

> We ate together every week. He was a great friend of mine...the Americans were convinced that there would be war with the Soviet Union, and they wanted his assistance...He was a soldier, not a philosopher, who had a fairly simple view of the world: Europe should be a unified and anti-communist continent.

The appearance of the second Spanish edition of *Memoirs of a Fascist*, with the foreword written by Otto Skorzeny, sold extremely well.

For the future edition and dissemination of *Memoirs of a Fascist* in Argentina, which took place in 1976, he conferred and ceded the rights of his publication to Editorial Milicia, a brave publishing house in Buenos Aires that was headed, against all odds, by the intrepid intellectual Federico Rivanera Carlés, a bastion of Spanish culture in the lands of the Southern Cross. On June 7th, 1976, Léon Degrelle sent him the following note:

*June 7th, 1976*

*To Editorial Milicia,*

*I fully agree for the Argentine publication of my book Memoirs of a Fascist (or Hitler for a Thousand Years, a title I like more) to be done by Editorial Milicia.*

*Léon Degrelle*

Two months after the publishing agreement, in August 1976, he directed his overseas comrades to deliver to Federico Rivanera Carlés the following message: "To my valiant Argentine friends, who defend our civilization and our ideal in their great homeland, with brotherly greetings, Léon Degrelle."

### Tribute to Francisco Franco

After the death of Francisco Franco on November 20th, 1975, Degrelle published a long, sixty-four-page essay entitled "*Hommage a un Grand d'Espagne Franco*" ("Homage to a Great Man of Spain: Franco") in the French magazine *La Pensée Nationale* in Paris in February 1976. In July of that same year, it was published by Éditions du Baucens as an independent book.

On April 9th, he received a young friend, Joaquín, at his La Cabaña house in Fuengirola. Degrelle gave him the book *Franco Chef d'État (Franco, Head of State)*, with this dedication: "To my dear Joaquín, a splendid example of Spanish youth, sure of himself, open to the future, telling him of the pleasure that his first visit has given me, to which many others will follow, with the most affectionate sympathy, L.D." Léon opened the doors of his home and his soul to everyone who approached with noble intention.

### The Incessant Visits

In order to meet the legendary rexist chief, when the summer period came in the month of June, countless Belgian compatriots decided to spend part of their holiday in Spain: former and endearing activists, with the longing and memory of those courageous older days; his Burgundian comrades, who had fought under his orders on the Eastern Front and with whom he shared blood and suffering, glory and dignity. They all came, accompanied by their wives and children. Everyone wanted to take a picture with him; he represented the very the image of fidelity; unscathed and standing tall. They wanted to embrace him, to talk to him, to feel the emotion of a reunion after many years.

Young Europeans, who were inspired by his life and convictions, also wanted to meet him. Each year, the groups of young people surrounding Degrelle grew larger.

On one occasion, Degrelle asked one of those young people, "What moves you to visit me?"

The response was spontaneous and sincere: "All the lies that they told us about you."

It was clear that they wanted to see which side the truth was on. Everyone left cheerful, enlightened, convinced, and enthusiastic.

Another frequent visitor Degrelle entertained at his home in Madrid on calle Joaquín García Morato, was the leader of *Avanguarda Nazzionale* (National Avant-Garde), Stéfano delle Chiaie. Chiaie also lived in exile in Spain, along with a group of Italian comrades from various national-revolutionary and patriotic organizations such as *Ordine Nuovo* (New Order), *Fronte Nazionale* (National Front), *Nuova Fenice* (New Phoenix), *Fronte Nazionale Rivoluzionario* (National Revolutionary Front), *Movimiento d'Azione Rivoluzionaria* (Revolutionary Action Movement), and *La Rose des Vents* (The Rose of the Winds). Chiaie had been introduced to Degrelle by Luis Antonio García Rodríguez, and there are several photographs of these encounters. Stéfano delle Chiaie had attended the CEDADE Congress in Barcelona in 1969 at Ciudad Condal. After the failed coup attempt in Italy, supported by Prince Junio Valerio Borghese,[109] delle Chiaie went into exile in Spain, where he remained until after the death of Francisco Franco. He then embarked on a journey through various Spanish-American countries until his final return to Italy several years later.

Degrelle also had visits from several well-intentioned members of the wartime resistance, with whom he carried on profound dialog and conversations. These people were mainly Allied military, especially paratroopers and pilots. Sometimes he could even be seen at 8:00 a.m., having breakfast in his home with some senior Belgian Army officer or another. Some of those high-ranking military men had been in London while Léon fought on the Eastern Front.

Some days visitors arrived from Brussels on private chartered flights, but it was not only Belgians who visited him. There were appointments with foreign people from many different countries, historians and researchers from various universities and, from the Americas, as was the case of the Leaño family, governing rectors from the famous and magnificent University of Guadalajara, Mexico. Léon had a special

---

[109] Junio Valerio Borghese was nicknamed the "Black Prince," and he was an Italian aristocrat of House Borghese and a naval commander during Mussolini's regime. He remained a fascist politician in post-war Italy. In 1970, he helped plan a coup, often referred to as the Golpe Borghese, which was called off after the media got wind of it.

affection for the young Mexican Juanito Leaño. He held him in great esteem, as he reminded Degrelle of his own deceased son. The Leaños had been introduced by the American editor Henry Fisher from the Institute for Historical Review (IHR). Degrelle maintained editorial relations for his works with this revisionist organization.

Degrelle had become a paradigm of myth and legend. His epic past, his immortal deeds, and his role as a writer had created an aura of intrigue and sensationalism around him.

The most insistent and tenacious visitors were the journalists, who were keen to get his statements on tape and his image on film. There was no shortage of television crews, who filmed hours of interviews. One such case was for French television, that broadcast an extraordinary program of more than three hours. Another was for Belgian television, recording footage intended to be broadcast over a span of five days. When it was finished, however, Belgian politicians, always fearful and on the defensive, with their cowardice and dishonesty obvious to all, prevented its dissemination.

In Degrelle was a unique blend of eloquence, vibrant faith, an inextinguishable sense of humor, and a love for God and natural life, the wonderful and perfect work of creation.

## An Interview Given to the Argentine Weekly *Siete Días*

On July 19th, 1976, the Buenos Aires magazine *Siete Días* published an extensive interview conducted in Malaga by their correspondent in Spain, the prestigious and learned journalist Armando Puente. These were the first statements Degrelle made for a Buenos Aires media outlet.

The interview touched on a timely and highly controversial event at that time: the request for extradition by the Argentine government of the former secretary of the Ministry of Social Welfare, López Rega, who was an intimate colleague of Juan Domingo Perón during his exile in Madrid. Armando Puente, titled the article, "What Will Spain do with López Rega?" Puente stated:

> *The case of León Degrelle, a Nazi refugee on the Spanish peninsula since 1945, allows us to deduce what fate the Argentine fugitive José López Rega might have, who ended up in the Spanish capital almost a year ago. Degrelle fled and has since eluded the pursuit of his enemies, which is what the former Argentine minister did in turn.*

Puente details the testimony of Léon and the circumstances and the events surrounding the arrival and settlement in Madrid of López Rega, who, when harassed in Spain, moved to Switzerland and from there to the United States, the country in which years later he was finally arrested. He died in jail in Buenos Aires, without ever having been tried.

The interview began with Puente recounting a unique and unknown fact, which occurred on November 20th of the previous year, the day on which Generalissimo Franco died. Puente writes:

> With a steady step, a man with graying hair entered the Palacio de Oriente, approached the coffin of Francisco Franco, came to attention and gave the fascist salute. The man donned the Iron Cross with Oak Leaves, which Hitler had personally awarded him thirty years earlier. It was on that occasion that the Führer said to him, "If I had a son, I would like him to be like you."
>
> In front of his friend Franco's body, the man remained for two hours in a thoughtful mood, in a mood of recollection. When he left, it was dawn on the great square. Soldiers were completing preparations to raise the altar and stands where the funeral would be held hours later. Then the artillery caisson would be set in motion, on the way to the Valley of the Fallen, the final resting place of Franco.
>
> That tall and strong man, Léon Degrelle, founder and head of the Belgian Rexist Party, hesitated and fell against the door of the Palace, knocked down by chest pains.

Degrelle recalls:

> I was once again on the verge of death, as in May 1940, in Abbeville, when I was placed before a firing squad with twenty-one other comrades. All were shot except me. They left me alive, believing that I could reveal Hitler's war plans to them. The only things they took from me were ten teeth. They would not have been able to get anything else out of me because I knew nothing.

Smiling mischievously, he continues:

> I have more lives than a cat. In Ukraine and in the Caucasus, when I fought at the head of the Twenty-Eighth SS Division Walloon Panzergrenadier (mechanized infantry), I survived seven wounds and eleven fractures. I also escaped death when I crashed in a plane in the Cantabrian, and then in Sevilla, although with all those broken bones, they still wanted to kidnap me.

He resoundingly affirms: "I am the last of the great fascist leaders and that is why I have to survive."

The interview also recounted the last days of May 1945, after Hitler's death, when Himmler told him on the evening of May 2nd, "*Mein freund* (my friend), Degrelle, you must survive...." Himmler had called Degrelle to announce that he had been promoted to General of the Waffen SS. Degrelle told Puente everything that happened from that point up to his arrival in Spain, "the only friendly country."

At this point, in contradistinction, the events of José López Rega's arrival at the Madrid-Barajas airport, suffering from an illness and "on diplomatic mission" with thirty-one pieces of luggage and six bodyguards, are inserted into the article. López Rega was the strong man in the government of Isabel Perón and a big fan of esoteric astrology. He arrived in Spain on the morning of June 21st, 1975, albeit less dramatically than Degrelle. He ended up in a villa located in the residential neighborhood of Puerta de Hierro in Madrid.

Puente shifts back to Degrelle and his stay at the General Mola Hospital in San Sebastián, for sixteen months (from May 1945 to August 1946). Degrelle even reveals to him a well-kept secret that he never confided to anyone before. Following the request of the Belgian government for his extradition, "some young people, among whom were Torcuato Fernández Miranda, now President of the Spanish Courts, and the Argentine Juan Carlos Goyeneche, planned to take him from the hospital to prevent him from the same fate as Pierre Laval."

Upon López Rega's arrival in Spain, Perón's head physician Dr. Francisco Flores Tascón gave him a general and routine check-up at the "Incosol" clinic. Meanwhile, events in Argentina were unfolding and the courts were beginning to act against him. There was the possibility of Isabel Perón's imminent arrival in Madrid, and Rega was already planning his route to Switzerland.

Returning to Degrelle's exile experiences and the ridiculous news in the international press concerning his whereabouts, he explains:

*I have a "dossier" of news articles that say I am supposedly living in a score of different countries. A journalist discovered me in Lima, another in Panama, a third in the Argentine Pampas, naturally protected by Perón, or in a villa owned by Nasser on the banks of the Nile. There is someone who interviewed me in Brazil, where I was married to a black woman, and he even published the photo of my alleged mulatto son. The most sagacious of them followed my trail to the Vatican. Some called me "E. Duran" and reported that I was traveling on a Polish passport; for others, "Lucien Demeure" and I was passing as French; for many, I was called "Juan Sanchiz."*

Puente adds that while he was being sought around the world, the truth was that he had been adopted by Doña Matilde de Ramírez Reina right there in Spain.

Returning to López Rega, his case had less publicity and involved no diplomatic notes or parliamentary actions. A simple note put out by the EFE News Agency—in which he was considered a fugitive of justice, saying that the former Minister of Social Welfare "had left Spanish territory to avoid an extradition request by the Argentine government"—was sufficient to make speculations as to his whereabouts in news outlets inevitable. From Libya to Brazil, disguised with a new face after cosmetic surgery, etc., they latched on to every rumor and piece of scuttlebutt.

Puente recognized that:

> *López Rega does not have the intellectual and political personality of Léon Degrelle, he who held activist card number one from the Falangist Foreign Section, signed by its founder and chief José Antonio Primo de Rivera. He always had important political connections, but also had friendships with such prestigious and liberal men as the philosopher José Ortega y Gasset and Dr. Gregorio Marañón. In contrast, López Rega, apart from being a union leader and a partner in several businesses in the Canary Islands, had as protectors only Dr. Flores Tascón (sponsor of the Perón marriage, whose wedding was held at his home) and the lawyer José Antonio Hernández Navarro, a deputy and union bureaucrat, who came to his defense when his extradition was demanded by Argentine authorities.*

After a review of the great difficulties and upheavals during Degrelle's exile in Spain, Puente asked if he met some illustrious exiled colleagues, such as Perón.

Degrelle replied:

> *I was introduced by my comrade Otto Skorzeny. With Perón, we talk a lot about the Eastern campaign. He was a specialist on the battles in Pomerania and Silesia during the First World War, especially in Tannenberg, and he was sympathetic to Mussolini. He said that like the Italians, the Argentineans are a people with little discipline, which showed up in criticism. He admitted that much like the Duce, he had no more vocation as a man of war than a rural guard.*
>
> *On the other hand, he had a helpful and clever secretary beside him who worshipped Hitler, but not the Hitler I knew; rather, one forged from an unworthy slop of newspapers and pamphlets written by illiterate people. I remember that at one time the secretary interrupted our conversation to say that Hitler had a mysterious liquid and when he put out his hand, he discharged through it powerful spiritual forces. I do not quite recall what he said about the Führer's gaze and the*

*twenty-first century seeing the triumph of Nazi ideals…I never understood how Perón could have that man at his side…his name was López, was it not?*

## A Visit by Joaquín Ruiz Jiménez

On November 6th, 1976, Léon held a meeting with his comrade Joaquín Ruiz Jiménez, to whom he offered a copy of his work *Lettres á Mon Cardinal* (*Letters to My Cardinal*), a book that had been published the previous year. They were united by a long-standing friendship and their connection with Catholic Action, where Léon Degrelle started out long ago in Belgium. The dedication he put on the acknowledgments page read: "To my great and dear friend Joaquín Ruiz Jiménez, as Christian as he is Spanish, with the old affection of L.D."

These visits with Jiménez were maintained with some regularity, but always with a certain reservation and total discretion, owing to the timidity of his Spanish comrade.

## Degrelle, Correspondent in Madrid for the Magazine *Valeurs Actuelles*

At the end of the 1970s, Jean-Claude Valla, a committed and brilliant French writer, worked indefatigably as editor for the weekly *Valeurs Actuelles*. Valla secretly hired Léon Degrelle to be his correspondent in Spain. He signed his articles under the pseudonym "Luis de Velasco." On one of the two or three occasions when Jean-Claude Valla had to travel to Madrid, he met Degrelle and the two became instant friends.

A curious anecdote surfaced regarding Degrelle's work with the magazine:

*This was towards the end of the 1970s, in the offices of Spéctacle du Monde, located on rue d'Uzès in Paris. I was, as usual, in the office of Jean Lousteau-Chartez, who was the editor-in-chief of the monthly magazine.*

*Michel Gurfinkel arrived, a manager in the international politics section of the weekly Valeurs Actuelles. Generally, Lousteau received him with a feigned hostility, saying "What brings you around here?" On this occasion, however, he received him normally and began to talk with him about the last issue that had just been published. They spoke about Gurfinkel's work; he was at the time the "official" representative of the pro-Jewish and pro-Zionist trend of the Likud group of Rue d'Uzès (money compels!).*

*Lousteau said to him, "Yes, I read the article from Spain. There would be a lot to comment on this…"*

*Gurfinkel, whom everyone knew as "Gurf" replied, "Yes, in fact, I hesitated to publish it, but at the last minute, I decided to do it. After all, the article was signed by 'Luis de Velasco,' the official correspondent of Valeurs Actuelles in Madrid."*

*Lousteau, again took the floor to say, "Good man! You know well that with Velasco you do not have to be amazed at anything…sure enough! You know who it is…"*

*Gurf gets petrified, and he crouches behind his glasses, "No, who is it?"*

*"Come on, it is Degrelle…"*

*"Do not tell me that! It cannot be true! I did not know anything!"*

*Lousteau sunk in his deep black leather armchair, looked at Gurf.*

*"Shit! What have I done! I did not know anything, you realize! What a blunder!" Gurf is pale as he continues to defend his ignorance and innocence.*

*After twenty minutes and a couple glasses of Poitou wine, Gurf regained his composure, stating, "Bah! After all, I had to know…"*

## An Interview Is Published in the Magazine *Cambio 16*

On August 14th, 1977, the tendentious tabloid magazine *Cambio 16* published an extensive interview with Léon Degrelle. Journalist Jeannine Camps interviewed him at his home. A photograph of Léon toasting with Jaime de Mora y Aragon at a social event in Costa del Sol, was included.

When Camps arrived at Degrelle's house, perched on the top of the hill from where one could scan the horizon and the entire coast, Camps commented to Degrelle about how it was a privileged place to live and how great the panoramic view was that dominated. Léon greeted Camps in a hospitable way, as was his custom. Here follows part of the aforementioned interview:

*"First of all, I like beauty and art. Politics is also art." These were Degrelle's first words of welcome, with a deep satisfaction, while we were admiring the garden full of flowers. There was an Iberian lion that he rescued from the bottom of a warehouse, a Roman amphora, a Visigothic well…*

*Inside the house are two huge paintings flanked by golden Solomonic columns. "They are from a student of Murillo, El Soriano," he says proudly. "Rather than a checking account, I prefer to have artwork."*

During the interview, Degrelle politically defined himself as a National Socialist, "but more socialist than nationalist since nations are losing importance. I am a Euro-socialist."

When asked by Camps whether the Rex Movement he founded in Belgium had some points in common with the Spanish Falange, he acknowledged:

> *They seemed as though they were spiritual movements. José Antonio was a spiritualist, an inspired person, a poet. While we were a movement of the masses, the Falange got no more than a few thousand people before the war. Yes, we had contacts, and I am member number one of the Foreign Falange."*
>
> *With pride, the Belgian "lion" pulls out of his pocket an old membership card signed by José Antonio in 1934. "My liaison with José Antonio was Alfredo Mahou, the beer producer, who was then a Falangist."*

Of Otto Skorzeny, who was one of his comrades in arms and a great friend, he said:

> *He was a beautiful person and had a heart of gold, and he was very lucky. He published his memoirs in Le Figaro, which provoked a strong communist reaction. He came here in '48, where, in collaboration with the High Staff and fearing that Spain would enter a war, he prepared for the arrival of all German youth.*

In 1977, Rodolfo Martín Villa, who held the interior portfolio, made a commitment to provide Degrelle with a passport so that he could travel abroad. The Count of Mayalde promised Léon that he would remember him, and, in case the delivery of the document was delayed by the unreliable and chameleon defector Martín Villa, he would ask for it directly from King Juan Carlos himself.

### A Foreword by Degrelle Is Published in an Edition of *Mein Kampf* in Italy

In 1977, Léon attended the great political rally held by the Fuerza Nueva (New Force) Movement at Plaza de Toros de las Ventas, in Madrid. He could be seen with his arm held high, singing the *"Cara al Sol"* ("Facing the Sun") at the end of the political event. Blas Piñar also participated with his singular and masterful oratory.

In November 1977, the Italian publishing house *Sentinella D'Italia* (Sentinel of Italy) published the full text of Adolf Hitler's famous *Mein Kampf* in two volumes in

Trieste. The novelty of this edition was that it appeared with a foreword written by Léon Degrelle, in which, among other assertions, he wrote:

> *I knew Hitler and interacted with him for more than sixteen years. I was at his side at his moment of glory, right next to him, in the universe of his achievements and dreams. I know, I know very well who he was: the political chief, the great leader, the man, the man in flesh and blood, simply the man...What matters is the truth, and that is what I know.*

In the foreword, Degrelle highlighted the curses that had been cast upon the Führer and the slander and historical falsehoods attributed to him. After sharing a number of thoughts on the magnetism and identity of the German Chancellor, he emphasized:

> *Hitler was simple, very careful. His ears always amazed me, gleaming like shells...His suits were neatly pressed, what more can I say. His military jackets were all the same, without any grace. He wore a size forty-three. One night, when I was putting on my worn-out Russian felt boots in front of him, he went to his closet and took out another pair of boots and offered them to me. He placed a folded piece of newspaper in the toes of each boot as a filler so that they would not pinch, since I wore size forty-two.[110] This anecdote highlights what this uncomplicated man was like.*
>
> *He had no need for anything except beauty. With the royalties from his book Mein Kampf, he bought a wonderful Boticelli, which he placed at the head of his bed. Additionally, it never had a frame on it. When he died, he did not have a penny. For him, the question of personal property, of money in particular, was irrelevant. I am sure that during the last years of his life he did not think about it once.*
>
> *He used to finish eating in ten minutes. Even his food was a surprising spectacle. For that man, who went to bed at five or six in the morning each day, and who was already up at eleven with his glasses in his hand, in front of his documents, barely ate. Moreover, his food was, for the most part, food that "did not stick to your ribs." He managed all that terrible effort for the war without tasting, not once, an ounce of meat. He did not eat eggs. He did not eat fish. Normally a*

---

[110] European shoe size forty-three is equivalent to U.S. size ten; Euro size forty-two, to U.S. size nine or nine-and-a-half.

*pasta dish, or a vegetable dish. Something sweet. Water. Always water. Hitler's culinary feasts were made up of these quite spartan meals!*

*He felt a passion for music. To a surprising extent, he possessed an auditory memory worthy of the oral memory of de Gaulle. A musical motif, heard by him once, was internalized by him forever. He registered it without difficulty, however long it might have been. Wagner was his god. Not a single nuance of Wagner escaped him. He could have confused, from Spanish history, Isabel la Católica (fifteenth century) with Isabel II (nineteenth century), but he would never have confused two notes of Wagner's entire musical repertoire.*

*He loved his dog. One was stolen from him during the First World War. It was one of the biggest disappointments of his youth; yes, that was the case. I met Blondie, his dog during his last years. The brave animal measured its steps along the desk, pacing, as if it were weighing the risks of the Eastern Front. Hitler himself prepared the dog's food, even excusing himself from visitors who were present to go and feed his faithful companion.*

### An Emotional Letter

Degrelle's great friend and comrade from Milan, Giancarlo Rognoni, leader of the Italian group Nuova Fenice (New Phoenix), whom he had known and visited in Madrid during his exile as a *latitante*,[111] was in Italy serving a politically motivated sentence. Sandra, Giancarlo's wife, continued to live in Madrid with their son, working as a cashier in a small café near Puerta del Angel, next to Paseo de Extremadura. Léon, always endearing and sensitive to the pain of his friends and neighbors, wrote a letter to her on Tuesday, December 8th, 1977:

*Dear friend,*

*We often think about you. With great sadness we have followed the painful trek of Giancarlo. We too carry your grief, with great affection.*

*We are very sorry to never see you. Be encouraged! Come to our house, and you will be received, always, with great affection. We know nothing about your plans. Are you going to stay in Madrid? Or will you travel to live closer to Giancarlo?*

*For him, when you see him or write him, and for you and your child, we send a hearty embrace from his great friend.*

*Léon Degrelle*

---

[111] [Italian for fugitive.]

## President Adolfo Suárez Attempts,
## Without Success, to Hand over Degrelle

In 1979, on the occasion of the visit of Spanish President Adolfo Suárez to Strasbourg, a Belgian deputy, Dejardin, once again personally requested, before the European Council, the extradition of Degrelle. The defector, turn-coat Spanish president promised him an investigation and a review of the case.

The overseeing government office considered that there were no grounds to grant such an investigation. The renegade "Falangist" Adolfo Suárez, former Secretary General of the Movement, was the designated successor of one of Léon Degrelle's great friends, Herrero Tejedor. Tejedor had been Attorney General of the State, and later, Minister Secretary General of the Movement. Tejedor was a prominent member of Opus Dei, and died in a tragic and controversial, car accident in the village of Villacastín on National Highway 6, the road that links Madrid with La Coruña.

On February 3rd, 1979, in the Madrid newspaper *Ya*, journalist Luis Carlos Buraya published statements by an indignant Léon Degrelle, in which he categorically affirmed, "I never killed anyone in my country, not even a bug." Léon had sent a letter to the newspaper refuting the accusations made against him before the European Council by a Belgian socialist parliamentarian, which had been published in the paper. Degrelle explained his current situation, his actions during the Second World War, and the dogged motivation driving him in the letter that follows:

*I have read with surprise in Ya on February 2nd, 1979, on page nine, under the title "A Belgian Member Raises the 'Degrelle Affaire' to Suárez," such strange statements that I have no choice but to impose on your kindness to correct them. I have no doubt about the good faith of your correspondent, Mr. Colchero, but I have to say that he is completely wrong. It says of me: "Léon Degrelle, leader of rexism, collaborated in the Nazi repression of his people and in plans for the extermination of the Jews." This is a complete error. I did not ever participate in any Nazi repression against my people, nor in any "plan for the extermination of the Jews." I fought, like many distinguished Spaniards (including an illustrious candidate for the next election on March 1st), on the Eastern Front against communism. Due to these strictly military actions, a special court sentenced me to death on December 24th, 1944, without summons, without a defense, in absentia, in a "trial" that lasted a quarter of an hour. A hundred times I have offered to stand before a normal tribunal, broadcasting the hearings. My offer was in vain, for in my case all human rights were trampled upon, and they are still doing it.*

*I was never convicted of a "war crime," nor prosecuted for that reason. The War Crimes Commission published the results of a long investigation against me, and the report found that I was absolutely innocent.*

*French Television, in its famous "Dossier Noirs" (RT3), has just finished a long two-and-a-half-hour film about my life. The full text will be published in one volume, of which I have here attached proof of three hundred fifty pages. The same director of "Dossier Noirs," Mr. Jean-Michel Charlier, explains in the prologue how French TV contacted me and decided to make this film.*

*As you can see, indeed, we can find out in that book, there is no conviction against me for a war crime, no accusation.*

*How can a man be frivolously accused of a "genocide in which thousands of Belgian patriots died" when not a single patriot died because of me?*

On February 10th, 1979, a letter sent by Degrelle to the director, of the Madrid daily *Informaciones* was also published:

*By means of this letter, taking advantage of your chivalry and the existing provisions, I would like to reply to the content of an article published without signature in this newspaper today. It is entitled "Leka of Albania Finds Refuge in Rhodesia," and in it my person is alluded to in an insulting and slanderous manner, and which could cause me very serious harm.*

*This article states, verbatim, "Degrelle, guilty of the death of thousands of Belgian patriots during the Second World War," which is absolutely incorrect, and I hope you will realize the magnitude of this malicious accusation.*

*I fought as a volunteer on the Eastern Front against Soviet troops, having been in Russia throughout the whole war, resigning, prior to my departure from Belgium, from my position as head of the Rexist Party. For having participated in that war, and for never having been guilty of any death of my compatriots, I was sentenced to death by special tribunal on December 24th, 1944, in absentia. This penalty, according to Belgian law, was to expire after twenty years, which was subsequently extended retroactively to ten additional years. This is a legal monstrosity, and this period ended quite a long time ago. I could produce innumerable pieces of evidence of what I affirm, but I believe that this would be more appropriate for the courts and not convenient for a simple letter of reply. I will not refrain, however, from transcribing a phrase contained in the text of the film about my life shot for French Television (RT3) as part of the famous "Dossier Noirs" series, directed by Jean-*

*Michel Charlier. It reads as follows: "The Minister of Justice of the Belgian government in London, Antoine Delfosse, would later confirm to me, before the cameras, that Degrelle had never been a war criminal. The list of reasons for his conviction contains no accusations relating to war crimes, or ever even participating in retaliatory acts."*

*It has been almost thirty-five years since I forcibly abandoned politics and devoted myself to a modest subsistence through writing and books. I have three of my daughters in Spain, married to Spaniards, who have given me ten grandchildren in Madrid, among whom I hope to spend the last of my days peacefully. I do not believe, therefore, that anyone in good faith can approve of the incomprehensible attitude of the person who edited the article or report appearing in your newspaper, which only seeks to draw attention to me and potentially cause me irreparable harm.*

*History will judge whether or not I acted rightly in my past, but I must exercise my legitimate rights to prevent malicious people from impeding upon the peaceful survival of the few years I have left. It is monstrously unjust that in my own country, while the whole press kept absolutely silent about the involvement of President Suárez here in Spain, there was interest in throwing about garbage concerning my past.*

*Léon Degrelle*

The following day, February 11th, the journalist Ernesto L. Feito interviewed him for the Madrid newspaper *El Imparcial*, with the headline: "Léon Degrelle, to Men…" In reference to the extradition that was demanded of Adolfo Suárez, during his participation at the European Council, by the Belgian leftist representative Dejardin, Degrelle said:

*It is a well-defined plan. They want to provoke my expulsion or murder. One day, if someone reads that I killed thousands of Belgian compatriots, thousands of Jews, he might say, "Well, you will pay for that." Bang, bang, and that is the end of Degrelle. It is clear that this left-wing mess has this idea in mind. I, on the other hand, in Spain, have not kept very quiet because I know what could happen. That is why these provocations are not good for me, and it is a provocation. I have not provoked anyone. I, in Spain, live very quietly while writing, dedicated to purely intellectual work. I do not get involved in Spanish or European politics, and never, in thirty-four years of exile, have I gotten mixed up in any Belgian political operation. I have never been reproached for anything. This is so obvious that it seems that even Mr. Suárez did not know my identity. That is proof that I have quietly minded my own business here. [ … ]*

*Let us get to the facts. This Belgian representative is a man who makes a laugh, who is worth nothing, as I have been told…but what is monstrous and unworthy of a journalist is to throw this slander around without any evidence. Neither the French press nor the Belgian press have said a word. So then, he was something of a provocateur, a man who has tremendous hatred and is allowed to throw about any accusation, even if it is totally unfounded because there are documents that prove the opposite.*

Referring to the extradition request, which took advantage of Suárez's visit to Strasbourg, Degrelle stated:

*Extradition? Mr. Suárez said, and he said very well, that he would investigate. The investigation had already been done and the Council of State had this in its hands and declared that there were no grounds for extradition. If I offered to go back…and do not forget that I was, in 1944, an elected Belgian representative with the highest number of votes in preference… but I have been named "an undesirable alien"…they do not want me to return because I can explain a few things. Afraid of going back? I will go back tomorrow if they want. All I ask is that I be allowed to stand as a representative. I will present myself to the public in Brussels any time they want, but I have been named "an undesirable alien" to prevent my reelection by the same ones who have demanded amnesty for Carrillo, and do not forget that Belgium is the only country that has offered the least amount of amnesty to anyone. They present me as a murderer in the press, and when millions of people have read that, anything could happen. For me it is all the same. I have lived quite a bit, but it is inelegant…in an industry like the press, it is necessary to have a sense of honor.*

The final comment of the interview was this:

*Thus, Léon Degrelle spoke; this old fighter, his body tattooed with scars that tell the tale of a hundred battles, this man accused of collaborationism, of murder, and of so many other things that, apparently, no one can prove. Thus, the last fascist has spoken.*

## The Interview Published in *Playboy* Magazine

The magazine *Playboy*, in the April 1979 issue of its Spanish edition, published a long interview by Michel Bibin, about Degrelle:

*"Lucien Demeure," alias "Juan Sánchez," alias "José Ramírez," alias "Pepe," whose real name is Léon Degrelle. His story is fascinating. As a trade union leader, he led more than six hundred thousand workers in the most important strike Belgium has ever known, entered the Second World War as a private and left with the rank of general. He is proud to have been elected as a Member of Parliament in Brussels in a free election and with an overwhelming majority of votes. Léon Degrelle admires Adolf Hitler, whom he knew very well. He thinks Franco was a great man, but that he should have stepped down in the 1960s.*

When Bibin interviewed Degrelle, he could not help thinking that Degrelle was a living piece of modern history, a seventy-two-year-old man who looked fifty and appeared to fully believe in his ideals.

He described him as "enterprising, business savvy, and fearless." He also told him how he had spent a season in Fuengirola carrying out some work in one of the Girón de Velasco developments and how his relations with Herrero Tejedor and Carlos Arias Navarro were always very good, so much so that Navarro once hid him in his house in Logroño.

The in-depth interview was a review of Degrelle's life from his early days. Among the anecdotes that he shared was the following:

*I have had so many surnames that I do not remember all of them anymore. I remember a meal at Serrano Suñer's house, in which various acquaintances of mine happened to have gotten together, and they all came to greet me, saying, "Hello Pepe!" "Hello Juan!" The director of a major bank smiled at me and asked me what they actually called me, and I answered him, "Benito Mussolini."*

Bibin asked him, "How do you see the future of Spain?"

Degrelle answered, "I do not see a future for Spain without Europe; no country can stand alone today." .

The American journalist Ted O'Keefe also visited Léon at the beginning of 1979, writing a report entitled: "Léon Degrelle and the Crusade for Europe," which was published in the magazine *National Vanguard* in March of that year. The text of the interview was then inserted into a book published in 1983 by the Institute for Historical Review (pages fifty-nine thru sixty-eight), along with a history of the Waffen SS.

## Letter to Pope John Paul II

On May 20th, 1979, Degrelle sent a letter to Pope John Paul II concerning the "millions" of Jews "gassed" by Hitler at Auschwitz. He called into question the lies that had been blasted, like an insidious buzz, into the ears of humanity stunned by the monothematic persistence of a historical scam and war propaganda turned into undisputed dogma. What was even sadder, was that questioning this dogma was stigmatized and penalized by various criminal codes. Degrelle would later say, "There is no historical truth if it rests on lies and hatred!"

The official stamp of receipt of this letter was assured by His Holiness John Paul II; it carried, after the order number 951, the reference "Cittá del Vaticano," P2-26.5.79, and was followed by the signature of His Holiness.

The booklet did not go unnoticed. Both Degrelle and the Belgian publishers of *Letter to the Pope*—the book would also later be published in a Spanish version by CEDADE—could be sentenced to more than three years in prison. The Belgian police confiscated from the home of the publishers Adrienne Tart and Jena-Robert Debbaudt about three hundred copies that had not yet been sold. The legal justification for this was the famous Article 123 of the Belgian criminal code, an example of "democracy," which, since 1948, prohibited those convicted of "collaboration" with the National Socialists from writing in magazines, newspapers, or authoring books. By 1961, this generic prohibition had been reduced to the publication of their writings in political journals, newspapers, or books.

The publishing house responsible for its publication in Belgium—*Les Éditions de l'Europe Réelle*—was viciously prosecuted and after having exhausted all the remedies in a Court of First Instance, the case was brought before a Tribunal in Strasbourg. Adrienne Tart was responsible for the publication of *Letter to the Pope on His Visit to Auschwitz* and was sentenced to fifteen months of solitary confinement and fined a penalty of four hundred thousand Belgian francs.

Several editions of *Letter to the Pope* were published. The third technically appeared in June 1988 as the second monograph, inserted with the number 161, chronologically, in the *Boletín del Círculo Español de Amigos de Europa* (CEDADE).

As an introduction to the topic, let us look at some excerpts:

*Most Holy Father:*

    *I am Léon Degrelle, the Chief of Belgian Rexism before the Second World War, and during the war, Commander of the Belgian Volunteers on the Eastern Front, fighting in the Twenty-Eighth SS Division Wallonie. Certainly, this is no recommendation in the eyes of people, but I am a Catholic like you and I believe, by this fact, that I am authorized to write to you as a brother in the faith. [ ... ]*

*The Church is always much better informed than anyone else. Through two thousand years of circumspection, she has always avoided hasty positions, and has always preferred to judge on proven facts, with calm, after time has separated the wheat from the tares, fury, and passions. The Church always distinguished herself by extreme restraint throughout the Second World War. She always carefully kept herself from spreading crazy speculations that ran rampant then. [ ... ]*

*Countless lies, with increasingly stubborn anger, have been repeated in thousands of books. They have been republished in color, in apocalyptic movies that furiously flog not only the truth and likelihood, but even common sense, the most elementary arithmetic and even the facts themselves. [ ... ]*

*You, most Holy Father, were said to have been part of the resistance throughout the Second World War, taking physical risks involved in a fight contrary to international law. Certain people report that you were hospitalized in Auschwitz. Like so many others, you left there, for you are currently the Pope, a Pope who, with all evidence, does not at all smell like the famous Zyklon B gas. Your Holiness, who has lived in these places, should know better than anyone that this massive gassing of millions of people was never a reality. As an exceptional witness, has Your Holiness personally seen a single one of these large collective massacres take place, which are constantly repeated over and over again by sectarian propagandists?*

*People certainly suffered in Auschwitz, as in other places too. All wars are cruel. The hundreds of thousands of women and children who were atrociously burned alive—by direct order of the Allied Heads of State—in Dresden, Hamburg, Hiroshima, and Nagasaki, experienced far more horrible suffering than those who were interned as political deportees, resistance (these two categories were 25 percent of the total population of the camps), conscientious objectors, sexual deviants, or common criminals (75 percent of the camp population), and sometimes died, in the concentration camps of the Third Reich. [ ... ]*

*The personal suffering of most of the exiles would have happily ended on the long-awaited day of the beginning of peace, had they not been hit, largely during the final weeks, by the catastrophe of exterminating epidemics. These were made even worse by the Allies' fabulous bombardments that shattered railway lines and roads and sank boats loaded with prisoners, as happened in Lübeck. Those massive air strikes destroyed electricity grids, pipelines, and water reservoirs, cut off all supplies, imposed hunger everywhere, and made any evacuation transport impossible. Two-thirds of the deportees killed during the Second World War perished* at that time; victims of typhus, dysentery, hunger, and of the endless delays on the shredded communication routes. Official figures state this. [ . . . ]

It is shown that Allied air terrorism no longer had any military utility because by the beginning of 1945, Allied victory was already fully assured. Therefore, such Allied air terrorism was no longer necessary in any way. Without this crazy, brutal, blind obliteration, thousands of internees would have survived, rather than becoming, between April and May 1945, macabre exhibition objects, around which herds of necrophiles from the media pushed and shoved, greedy for photos and movies with stunning angles and shots, and guaranteed business performance; visual documentation that is carefully doctored beforehand, overloaded, deformed and serves as generators of growing hatred.

These information brokers could also have taken miles of similar photographs of corpses of German women and children, a hundred times more numerous, killed in exactly the same way, from starvation, cold, or machine-gunned on the same frozen, uncovered wagons and on the bloody roads. Those pictures, like those of the immense extermination of German cities, which eventually documented six hundred thousand corpses, they now hide under the table! They could have generated some sympathy and tempered the hatred. The truth is that in 1945, typhus, dysentery, hunger, and continuous machine-gunning by air, struck both the foreign deportees and the civilian population of the Reich indiscriminately, all trapped by these abominations typical of end times.

Furthermore, Most Holy Father, as far as a formal policy of genocide is concerned, no document has been able to provide the least official proof of this for more than thirty years, especially as regards the alleged cremation at Auschwitz of millions of Jews. The claims launched and constantly repeated for so many years, in a fabulous campaign, cannot stand up to serious scientific examination.

It is crazy to imagine, and above all to maintain, that twenty-four thousand people could have been gassed in Auschwitz every day, in groups of three thousand, in a four hundred cubic meter room or less, with seven to eight hundred persons in a 25 square meter (269 square feet) floor, at 1.90 meters (6.2 feet) high, as has been said about the Belzec camp. Twenty-five square meters is roughly the size of a bedroom. Could you, Holy Father, manage to put seven hundred or eight hundred people in your bedroom?

Seven to eight hundred people on twenty-five square meters is about thirty people per square meter. A square meter, 1.90 meters high is a telephone booth! Would His Holiness be able to stack thirty people in a telephone booth at St. Peter's Square or at the Great Warsaw Seminary? Or in a simple shower?

*If the miracle of the thirty bodies planted like asparagus in a telephone booth or that of the eight hundred people crowded around your bed could have happened, a second miracle had to have occurred immediately; the three thousand people— the equivalent of two regiments!—were so fantastically crowded in Auschwitz's chamber, or the seven hundred to eight hundred people apprehended in Belzec at thirty occupants per square meter, would have perished almost instantly, suffocating for lack of oxygen! Gas chambers would not have been needed! Everyone would have stopped breathing, even before the last ones had been shoved in, before the doors were closed with the gas spreading throughout the room. How did this last thing happen? By a few cracks? By a few holes? By a fireplace? In the form of hot air? With steam? By pouring it onto the floor? Each one contradicts the other! Zyklon B only being used on corpses would have served no purpose!*

*What about the United States? Have they not risen to power thanks to the enslavement of millions of negroes branded like cattle and thanks to the almost total extermination of the Redskins who owned the land they desired? Was it not they who dropped the atomic bomb in 1945? Just yesterday, did their troops in Vietnam not include unquestionable executions?*

*Not to mention the tens of thousands of victims of the USSR's tyranny and the present-day gulags, of which I fear nothing will be said or that you will ever visit there as you have done at the Auschwitz camp, which has been empty for decades. [...]*

*The holocaust, regardless of how widespread it is or its impact among fools, has been nothing more than a gigantic Hollywood uproar of a rare vulgarity, whose primary aim is to empty the hundreds of millions of pockets of unsuspecting viewers. [...]*

*"Homo homini lupus," the sectarians say. "Homo homini frater,"[112] says every Christian who is not a hypocrite. We are all brothers, the deportee who suffers behind barbed wire, the fearless soldier tense at his machine gun, all of us who have survived 1945, you, the persecuted man who became Pope, me, the warrior who became a persecuted man, and millions of human beings who have experienced in one way or another the immense tragedy of the Second World War with our ideal, our desires, our weaknesses, and our faults. We must forgive, we must love. Life makes no sense otherwise. God has no other meaning.*

In November 1979, in a copy of the French edition by the *L'Europe Réelle* publisher, Degrelle wrote the following dedication: "To Jeanine and Roger Bretcher, my

---

[112] [Latin for "man is a wolf to man" and "man is a brother to man," respectively.]

admirable friends, in evidence of my greatest affection. Léon Degrelle." Roger Bretcher was a French officer of the SS unit from France. After the war he spent some time in Argentina and later returned to Europe, settling in Spain. He settled down definitively in Madrid, where he worked in a position of responsibility for a major French cosmetics company. He was very close and faithful to Léon.

Degrelle, in the absence of a response to his letter to the Holy Father, wrote an *Answer of His Holiness John Paul II at Auschwitz*, which in the manuscript is signed with the pseudonym "Jesús Palacios." When it was published in 1979, along with the *Letter to the Pope* by Ediciones Bausp in Barcelona, it was signed by "José Martínez."

When the text of *Letter to the Pope* was republished in 1979 by CEDADE in Barcelona, based on the previous Bausp publication, Léon wanted to expand it with the annex entitled *Reply by His Holiness John Paul II at Auschwitz*. He preferred that this text be signed by another person even though he had written it; initially he signed it as "Jesús Palacios." This was a name that, without having been proposed by the author, coincidentally was the same name as that of an old Madrid comrade of CEDADE about whom, at that time, there were well-founded doubts and suspicions of alleged political infidelities in exchange for favors and money. When they finally published it, they decided to change the pseudonym to "José Martínez," which was absolutely anodyne, generic, and impersonal. The text was a clear revisionist plea:

> The American university professor of Evanston, Illinois, Arthur R. Butz, has radically shattered that myth (the "holocaust") in his book The Hoax of the Twentieth Century. This great yankee sage is nothing of a Nazi, nor is the French scientist[113] Robert Faurisson, professor at the University of Lyon, who has scientifically proven, in the newspaper "Le Monde" and other publications, the material impossibility of the massacres in "gas chambers" using Zyklon B. He has established that the total of all Jews having died in Auschwitz—dying, of course, of physical fatigue, of demoralization, of diseases, of tremendous epidemics, and not from any "extermination"—did not exceed fifty thousand over four years, that is, an average of twelve thousand five hundred per year, which is quite far from the figure of four million in four years, invented by communist, or Hebrew propaganda.
>
> When Soviet troops approached Auschwitz in January 1945, the Germans quietly left the six thousand deportees who were in poor health with seventeen doctors

---

[113] Robert Faurisson was a professor of French literature, not a scientist, although his work was indispensable to honest discussion of whether gas chambers existed or were used.

*to care for them. There is obvious proof that the Nazis did not put these sick internees in "gas chambers," as six thousand were thus perfectly attended to, waiting for the Soviet invaders. It is also evident proof that the Third Reich was not particularly worried about leaving these six thousand eyewitnesses of life at Auschwitz in enemy hands. If the Germans had committed mass exterminations of Jews, as holocaust merchants have so loudly stated, they would never have so easily put the SS in jeopardy by quietly handing over six thousand future accusers. If they allowed these prisoners to be available to the Soviets, then they were not afraid of accusations. This is very clear. [...]*

*Moreover, why would the German railways have carried millions of deportees so far, uselessly, when they unfortunately lacked train cars, engineers, coal, etc.? They did not even have enough to transport soldiers and ammunition to the Eastern Front. Above all, why would the Third Reich have dedicated itself to "exterminating" millions of Jews who were indispensable in Europe's factories and workshops? Due to its labor shortage, Germany had no choice but to commandeer innumerable foreign workers from across Europe, thus provoking opposition, hostility, and very violent resistance. Hitler, under duress, needed workers not corpses! [...]*

*It was also difficult for the Pope to remind the communists of other exterminations, for example the massacre in Katyn, with its thousands of Polish officers, first-class patriots, killed in that forest with atrocious cruelty. [...]*

*What is significant about the Holy Father's speech at Auschwitz was not what he said, which was more or less forced, but what he did NOT say.*

*He did not say a single word about the most obvious thing, that is, about the "exterminations" in the "gas chambers," even though he spoke only a few feet away from the huge "gas chamber" that can be seen at the camp. This is a fake gas chamber (there never was a gas chamber, just a shower room and a tank), totally new, built from the first brick to the last by communist propaganda services AFTER the Second World War.*

The Pope made a second reference to Léon Degrelle's letter, when, leaving his official text, he improvised some words that, first of all, clearly pointed to the crimes of the Soviets and, secondly, cited almost verbatim the rexist chief's quote 'Homo homini frater' (man is a brother to man).

The newspaper *Ya* in its June 8th, 1979 issue (page ten, column five) mentioned with great curiosity the reaction of the nine hundred journalists after hearing, very strangely, these words suddenly improvised by the Pope, absent from the official text already distributed to the press.

The letter continues:

*They want to make us swallow another candy myth—Nazis, this time—with millions of poor little, humble, soft, holy Jews, gassed and burned all on Hitler's orders, these Jews who now walk around all over the world, more flamboyant and more exhibitionist than ever, overflowing with health and fanaticism, bloated with phenomenal compensation, swindled pensions, and stolen territories.*

*The navel, the flesh, the brains of the universe are created, although the artificial state of Israel does not represent one thousandth of the world's population. The dramatic oil crisis stems from Israel's insatiable ambition and bloodthirsty intolerance. The pyromaniacs of this intruder State have used up the Arabs' patience and have provoked the collapse of the world economy. Its territorial voracity, its blackmail, its revenge, and its military crimes, repeated and condemned a hundred times, compel humanity to live under the relentless threat of a new international war. An international war for a handful of Jewish imperialists who always want more and more and more, accumulating, to achieve its end, legends and lies of the "gas chamber" and "holocaust" type.*

## Goodbye, "Holocaust"

The screening of the film *Holocaust* on Spanish Television in June 1979 raised a lively controversy. Many personalities spoke out with arguments for and against the event, laying out their respective points of view.

On July 1st, 1979, the newspaper *El Imparcial*, published the opinion of Léon Degrelle, a person competent to speak on the subject. Statements, comments, and articles, including those of the president of the Jewish community, had been reproduced in their pages in a public forum style layout. Léon Degrelle gave his opinion in an extensive letter:

> As chief of one of the large military units of the Waffen SS during the Second World War, I would like to reply to El Imparcial's article dedicated to Holocaust on its front page, published June 27th, 1979. It is not my intention to get involved in a political controversy, but in a problem of history.
>
> "Holocaust" is a novel, nothing more than a novel, in which characters are invented to the author's liking: all Jews are very good, cultured, generous, and Hebrew women are blond goddesses, irresistible. The Germans, on the other hand, are unclean and degenerate, gross. The movie deforms and invents facts, pretends that millions of Jews died in "gas chambers" that never existed, who are now more alive, more numerous, and more powerful than ever: one million in France, rather

*than the three hundred fifty thousand that existed during the Second World War. In Madrid, fifteen times more than a quarter of a century ago; two million five hundred thousand Jews arrived in Israel, coming mainly from Poland.*

*A version of Jewish events in Hitler's time, however, as it appears in "Holocaust," would have had been more convincing had it been accompanied, or preceded, by a free, complete, and above all, public examination of "the truthfulness of the figures, the data, and the circumstances of the series that is doing so well on Spanish Television," as El Imparcial called for.*

*What examination was done? In advance, the one who was over-graciously referred to as a "moderator" of the previous debate intervened with a few sharp statements: six million Jews died, which quickly passed to seven and eight million! Two million or so, what did it matter? Where did this man get these varied numbers from? Even the Jerusalem Tribunal, during the Eichmann trial, did not dare to specify the figure, but the "moderator" on television did!*

*Deliberately, from the first minute, he offered millions of viewers a false debate. The only people who had been invited were those whose thinking agreed with the film, and who knew absolutely nothing about the real facts. In fact, they did not even need to know anything because they simply had to bless Holocaust with holy water.*

*To have a documented judgment on the capital problem of whether or not millions of Jews were exterminated in Europe, it is enough to read the works of a first-hand witness, like French historian Paul Rassinier. Rassinier was an important leader of the French Resistance. He spent a few years in concentration camps, such as Mittelbau-Dora and Buchenwald. His behavior was so exemplary that, after the war, he was elected as a socialist representative. Not "fascist," but socialist. What happened? Surprised by the story of the six million Jews killed, he investigated and quickly became scandalized. He published decisive books explaining that in no way could six million Jews have died, that this claim was totally inaccurate. He, a victim of the Nazis, had never seen a single gas chamber and, by way of studying the case, of questioning witnesses and visiting the camps one by one, had no other choice but to conclude that, in the entirety of German territory, not a single gas chamber had ever been used throughout the course of the Second World War.*

*The historian Rassinier has had successors of the highest intellectual quality, whom TVE could have invited to its colloquium. One is American, and he is not a Nazi. Professor Butz is a great scientist at the University of Evanston, Illinois. Surprised by the very implausibility of these stories of gas and Jews, he decided to study American archives of the war in depth. He then visited and thoroughly examined each camp. He finally published his findings in a now famous book called,*

*The Hoax of the Twentieth Century. In it, Butz states emphatically that we are facing the "biggest scam of the century," and that this "mass extermination" of Jews only comes from a lie. His study of Auschwitz is scientifically overwhelming. No gas chambers, no genocide. Is that true? Is it not? If his claim is false, why did Spanish Television not invite Professor Butz to the debate, rather than presenting to us a clumsy German who bored everyone? It was the perfect occasion, if the historical report by Butz is to be criticized, to demonstrate that his conclusions were false. This would have given Holocaust greater credibility. What was TVE afraid of? To see, as they certainly would have seen, Professor Butz convincing the viewers?*

*Without going as far as Illinois, Spanish Television could have invited at least another great specialist, also a professor, Professor Robert Faurisson, from the French University of Lyon. This gentleman is also not a Nazi. He is an anti-nazi who personally shocked me by welcoming the assassination of Marshal Pétain's minister Philippe Henriot in June 1944. That is to say, he is nothing of a Hitlerite.*

*Professor Faurisson was, in his position, dedicated to the study and analysis of texts and documents. This is how, as an exclusively intellectual project, he and his students happened to study documents on a well-defined problem: gas chambers and Zyklon B gas. Over time, Professor Faurisson had his doubts and checked the "dossier," made numerous visits to the German archives, consulted all the specialists, made two visits to the Auschwitz camp, etc. Fourteen years of intense, strictly intellectual work on this sole problem!*

*His scientific conclusions finally appeared in the form of letters to the well-known daily Le Monde, as well as in studies collected in other publications. Faurisson points out that the use of Zyklon B gas, in order to carry out extermination, contrary to the claim in a thousand books and in Holocaust, is a technical impossibility. This extremely dangerous and flammable gas would not have allowed the corpses to be handled for twenty-one hours. Professor Faurisson has studied every detail of the gas chamber that is shown to visitors to Auschwitz: it is fake, built after the war. The French sage finishes his study categorically: this whole story of gas chambers is insane; it is only a myth.*

*The thesis of Professor Faurisson has had such a profound impact that Switzerland's Italian-language television invited him to participate in a debate that preceded the Swiss broadcast of "Holocaust." Why, with Lyon only two hours by plane from Madrid, did TVE not invite Professor Faurisson like the Swiss did? Possibly because his participation, strictly scientific in nature, had a considerable impact in Switzerland.*

*TVE did not accept my testimony either. I have known Hitler and Himmler up close. I could explain many things. I have publicly offered to participate in TVE's discussions and have kindly reiterated my offer in writing.*

*They should have allowed historians, learned men, witnesses from both sides, to appear in a gentlemanly way before a public capable of judging for themselves and not have deceived them with a prefabricated, unilateral debate.*

*Léon Degrelle*
*ID: 27.761.932*

## An Interview Requested by the Weekly *Poble Andorra* That Was Not Published

On October 25th, 1979, Léon gave an interview to the weekly *Poble Andorra*, which the publication had requested, but was rejected by the editor just before publication. The questions were about the position of rexism in relation to regionalism on the day that the Statute of Catalonia was being voted on.[114] Degrelle had stated:

*Thinking more of the unity of Europeans, of a great National Socialist unity, in which the nation would play a less prominent role, with the socialist part having a larger aspect, we saw that all states had a complex of unity. Unity is not opposed to diversity; one can have a unified state, on the basis of two important points, but one that enriches itself from the variety of different regions.*

### *La Nostra Europa*

In 1980, the Italian publishing house Edizioni di Ar de Padua in Italy published the book *La Nostra Europa* (Our Europe), which had been translated from the original French into Italian by Franco Giorgio Freda. This publication saw the light of day in the month of September. In a brief note to the publisher, Giorgio Freda wrote:

---

[114] Catalonia is a unique region in northwestern Spain, including its distinct Romance language of Catalan. Many in the region have agitated for political independence from the Spanish State, although the status as Autonomous Region today, with its own parliament-like *Generalitat*, has been in place for hundreds of years. During the civil war, the *Generalitat* was loyal to the Republic, although much of the territory was effectively controlled by other socialist and anarchist groups; support for republican and socialist elements was strong in the region. Relations with Spanish nationalists and patriots, who tend to emphasize Spain's non-negotiable unity, have often been strained.

*Léon Degrelle has honored us by sending us this writing from exile.*

*Léon Degrelle has not come to be a "literato,"[115] he remains a warrior.*

*The last great warrior of the European imperial space.*

*In September 1944, Adolf Hitler told him, "If I had a son, I would want him to be like you."*

*We think that Waffen SS General Léon Degrelle will regret not being able to count, among his own decorations, the most glorious distinction that is set in his gentlemanly heart by this recognition of the Führer.*

The book is an essay on the nature and being of Europe, her culture and traditions, her civilization and her soul.

## An Interview Published in the Weekly *Interviú*

In November 1980, the journalist Ernesto L. Feito, who already did an interview with Degrelle the previous year for *El Imparcial*, spoke again with Léon, giving the tone of his work a sensationalist character. This new interview was published in the magazine *Interviú*, which described it as a "World Exclusive" and in whose double-page heading, in a large, alarming font, reported "Léon Degrelle, 'Hitler's Son,' We Find in Spain the Most Sought-After Nazi in Europe."

The first part of the interview responded to a number of historical questions about his relationship with the Axis and his active, enthusiastic, and heroic participation on the Eastern Front.

When the issue of racism was addressed, he responded with ease:

*Nazi racism? Our racism is not what people imagine. It is clear what we wanted and what we still want because nothing has changed from that perspective: a strong race, with good physical and moral health. I do not see what is wrong with that. I prefer to see strong boys, singing along the road and working, as were seen in Hitler's time, rather than those miserable guys who get high and have no ideals…and it is the victors who are to blame.*

---

[115] [Spanish for "man of letters."]

## Eviction from His Apartment at Number 1,
## Paseo de los Jesuitas, Madrid

Degrelle continued to receive all kinds of different people at his home. There were plenty of young people who wanted to know the living myth personally, the very definition of a hero, the paradigm of the tireless struggle for the redemption of Europe, the position from which he had always embarked on the path of social justice as the goal of his political aspirations. On February 27th, 1980, he welcomed four young people to his home in Chamberí: Amador Sanz de Galdeano, his girlfriend Immaculada Varela, his brother, and the young painter Víctor Zarza. He spoke with them, pointed out the horizon to them, excited them, and they left there comforted, fortified, and convinced that another vision was possible.

On May 23rd, 1980, the news agency *Colpisa*, where Léon Degrelle's goddaughter, Pilar Cernuda worked as a journalist, published information that she had passed to them, reporting that Léon Degrelle had been evicted from his house on Ribera del Manzanares and that the Madrid City Council had seized the apartment as if it were a military operation.

They knocked the door down, throwing the bolt 3 meters (over 9 feet) from the entrance, and took away his art objects, which were transferred to the municipal warehouse. The agency added:

> *Léon Degrelle is to Belgium what Hitler was to Germany or what Mussolini was to Italy, with the difference that, while the German Nazis were engaged in sending Jews to the gas chambers, Degrelle was fighting on the Eastern Front and suffered dozens of wounds from the war, all of them in close combat.*

Degrelle remarked on what happened with the eviction:

> *I saw everything because I happened to be there that day and it looked like a military occupation. Two police trucks, several private cars, a moving truck, men from the City Council… The least they could have done was to let me know earlier. Not a letter, not a phone call, nothing. They did not even ask for the key from the neighbors who had one. They knocked the door down. You would have thought they were storming El Alcázar again.*

The confiscated apartment was never returned to him.

## *Folie de la Répression Belge*

For three days, from June 23rd to June 25th, 1980, Léon Degrelle wrote page after page, his pen flying. It would later be reproduced with the title *Folie de la Répression Belge.*[116] Even forty years after the end of the Second World War, Belgium still continued to butcher freedom of political expression.

In these nearly eighty-four handwritten pages, he referred to the "Process of September 1980 and the Central Israelite Council," which gathered on September 5th against Jean-Robert Debbaudt and Adrienne Tart for political thought crime, having tried to spread among their compatriots Léon Degrelle's literature.

In view of the impossibility of being able to publish, in print form, the contents of these exculpatory and justifying pages, the hand-written text was copied, bound, and then made public.

On April 24th, 1981, a copy of this book was also dedicated to his faithful friend Roger Bretcher, with the following dedication: "To my most cherished friend and comrade, Roger Bretcher, and his wife, of admirable intelligence and dynamism, in witness to the deep affection I have felt for them for so many years." I recorded the visits Bretcher made on December 3rd, 1981, and June 12th, 1984. On the second occasion, Léon gave him a copy of *La Nostra Europa* (Our Europe), writing in the dedication: "For my dear Roger, heroic companion during the honorable and glorious hours of European struggle, with the most affectionate testimony of your friend, L.D." They were also together on August 24th, 1986. Léon appreciated him very much and, in the conversations I had with him, he referred to Bretcher as "magnificently faithful."

### An Enthusiastic Follower

There is eloquent testimony from a follower from Asturias, a resident in Gijón, who said of Degrelle:

*Back in the 80s, as my only letter of recommendation was being the son of an ex-combatant of the Spanish Civil War, he received me on a stunning day in November in his flat in Madrid. From the very first moment, I realized that his figure radiated a great enthusiasm and contagious joy, coupled with an unwavering faith in his ideals, not without a fine irony. His face lined with wrinkles denoted a tenacious*

---

[116] [French for *The Madness of Belgian Repression.*]

*and indomitable spirit, his thin and delicate hands, prepared both to handle a machine gun on the Eastern Front and to put on paper songs of love, fidelity, and hope. His house is a small museum: figures, porcelains, Renaissance paintings, objects of Roman and Iberian art, books and notes everywhere filled showcases and corners, and in a prominent place, his cherished Iron Cross.*

*At the many meetings I had at his home, I was told and reminded with passion of the faith of so many young people from all over Europe who, under a common ideal, were part of the Waffen SS; most of whom, some four hundred thousand, would give their lives in pursuit of a European ideal, as distant from communism as from capitalism. He remembered the days he had spent in Asturias, invited by Franco, and above all his experiences and dealings with Hitler and Mussolini. I was told how the great cartoonist and humorist Hergé had been inspired by him to create the character of Tintin, saying that in his youth he quite resembled Tintin.*

## Léon Degrelle Takes Part in a Barcelona Rally on January 30th, 1980, the Anniversary of Hitler's Rise to Power

The famous European historian Jacques de Launay, a long-time résistant and not one to typically make kind concessions to Léon Degrelle, wrote in the October 1979 issue, number 113 of *Europa Magazine*, the following: "It is necessary to speak with those from Hitler's entourage who are still alive, to understand that Degrelle had great possibilities of becoming, perhaps, the Führer's successor."

Léon Degrelle's first involvement in the commemorations of January 30th, the anniversary of Hitler's rise to power, took place in 1980. In front of a young and disciplined crowd in the auditorium on the premises of CEDADE (the Spanish Circle of Friends of Europe) on calle Seneca, number 12, in Barcelona, he showed that at his seventy-four years of age he had not lost a single iota of his energy and oratorical skills.

Ramón Bau, at that time Secretary General of the Spanish Circle of Friends of Europe, recalled his first meeting:

*I met Degrelle when I was secretary general of CEDADE. When we went to see him, I went holding this respect for "a great figure, a historical personage," but I met a man, a person who was affable, funny, simple to his credit, far from any "self-importance," yet at the same time he was wholly National Socialist, solid as a stone. He did not hesitate a moment when asked to speak at our venue, to explain and share National Socialist ideas. Despite being exiled, persecuted, and with a sure death penalty if he were expelled, he did not even mention those problems and accepted with that simplicity of "everyday normal," the "hero of normality."*

At the scheduled event, CEDADE President Pedro Varela spoke first, with a few preliminary words, referring to the significance of January 30th in National Socialist organizations and in the group he presided over.

In his presentation, after remarking upon the glorious meaning of the commemorative anniversary, he spoke the following words:

*The Jews are going to make an impressive holocaust campaign, while our revisionist campaign, which, with great effort, was able to launch a thousand copies of the book by comrade Joaquín Bochaca or to spend many nights making a documentary. All this great sacrifice is intended to be canceled in a single minute. Hollywood simply has to give the order that a particular film be shoved in the face of the European nation and every night some film like Holocaust, or some series like "QB VII," or "Roots," is shown. Or something like "Rich Man, Poor Man," so that the campaign of truth might be torn apart that same night, in a single minute.*[117]

*By broadcasting their great TV series and films, the people, who watch them unsuspectingly and passively, learn to spit on us in the street because they have been told to do so in movies, that we are killing blacks, burning Jews, that we have got knives in our mouths like pirates, and we are walking around with chains to hit people on the street. Judaism is the cause of all of this, as it was already proclaimed back in 1925, in the famous twenty-four points of the NSDAP in Munich, which brought Adolf Hitler to power. Hitler warned us, until the war was lost, that Judaism was the culprit and pointed it out directly—and precisely because they cannot allow it—but in spite of everything we continue to selflessly maintain in an unprecedented chapter what is asked of us from above and what helps us, and it is the hand of God that protects us. In the United States, as in Germany, and everywhere, National Socialist parties, groups, organizations, and formations, like us, keep poking them in the eye, as Hitler did in his time. That is why they want to eradicate these groups and mercilessly put an end to them much more quickly than what happened to Hitler. He came about because at the beginning they did*

---

[117] In all of the TV series or movies mentioned above, the White man, the traditional man, or sometimes the specifically German man, is depicted as bigoted, bumbling, or cruel; while in some of the series, the progressive, multicultural character is depicted as the good protagonist, or in the case of *Roots*, the anti-slavery White and oppressed Blacks are obviously the "good guys." The screen writers and directors for these series—Dean Riesner, Edward Anhalt, Boris Sagal, Marvin Chomsky, and others—were largely Jewish.

*not take him seriously, but when they realized this, it was too late. For he had brought together a very healthy force that made it easier for him to move forward with an impressive coalition of resources and political might. Meanwhile, they can bring us to an end with a simple signature on a form from any ministry, or by putting three or four of our best comrades in prison, or simply by shutting down our premises, which for the moment have not closed. There is something we always say, destiny, faith, blind faith, that guides us on this path and protects us, we do not know why.*

*Just as I said before, like many young people, without experience and without any personal wisdom, but being whole, they come to our ranks simply because they believe in the truth and because they have a deep faith in idealism and in our way of being.*

*From here I want to thank comrade Hans-Ulrich Rudel, a Stuka pilot that many of you know well, who promised to come today with comrade Léon Degrelle, to participate in the event. Unfortunately, he was not able to fulfill this desire due to his being very ill and paralyzed mid-body. He is under intensive medical care, so we will not have him with us on April 30th, like we had planned, although he is convinced that by January 30th of next year, he will be here with us.*

*Of course, I would also like to thank comrade Léon Degrelle who has traveled so far to be with us on this special occasion, despite the great amount of work he always has in Madrid, setting aside all his projects, and despite the inconvenience of the trip.*

*Now, to conclude, I will read the speech that Adolf Hitler delivered on January 30th, 1945.*

After his speech, Pedro Varela read Hitler's speech with the masterful and almost supernatural music of Richard Wagner's *Rienzi* in the background.

After the Führer's speech was read, and with a welcome ovation, Léon Degrelle took the stand and gave an energized address.

There is a small anecdote that occurred at the beginning of his speech. When he began to speak, he addressed the audience in French, his mother tongue; perhaps because of nostalgia, he was transported unintentionally in his mind to forty years prior, when he appeared at the Palais des Sports in Brussels before his dedicated, enthusiastic, and fervent audience. When he realized that he was speaking in a language that many attendees did not know, Degrelle continued his masterful discourse with a smooth shift to Spanish. He spoke about Hitler's personality, which he knew from his own experiences. The raucous applause was the crowning moment of his brilliantly delivered piece of oratory.

Degrelle's speech is here transcribed:

*Spain is my second homeland and although I do not speak the Spanish language as well as I would like, I will speak to you with my heart, to explain how behind death, behind all the hard trials, at a time like this, if we believe in the immortality of a man like Adolf Hitler, he is together with us now, overjoyed to see that there are always young people who live and fight for an ideal, just like he lived and sacrificed himself for a great ideal.*

*We have heard so many atrocious things about Hitler that one is almost afraid to talk about who the greatest genius of our century was. For where is there another like him?*

*To think that there are thousands of fools, cretins, filthy people, who are allowed to make fun of this man, but what do they really know about him? What have they analyzed from his enormous work? What effective study have they done?*

*Hitler lived through the most dramatic circumstances of Europe. His struggle was a superhuman struggle in all respects. His life was a constant revolution: In his way of seizing power, no one seized power like him; in political and social revolution once he came to power, completely changing the social structure of his country, which had been in ruins, to remake it and convert it into the most important country in Europe; and in military revolution, winning many battles, with resources in a precarious state, but completely renewing, in an extraordinary way, faith in strategy.*

*I had known Hitler closely for many years, as a human being, in his simple life, how he worked, how he loved, how he sacrificed himself, and how he was preparing for Europe an immense future, which from the East has been destroyed in the wildest way. Instead of Hitler's project, something else has been provided, but what has it brought? Forty years have passed, and we have countries destroyed materially and morally, always talking about crisis, not to mention incapacity, and this when one imagines that Hitler took over a ruined country when he came to power, with six million unemployed, and in two years no one was left unemployed, while now in all the countries of Europe, full of professors, full of great technicians, unemployment continues to rise more and more, without prospects.* (Applause)

*When I started my political struggle, I bought a fifteen-day rail credit because I had no other resources, which cost one hundred ten francs. Every day I learned where some socialist or communist rally was held, taking place in the "houses of the people," in those "palaces of the people," as they said, where the big meetings took place. They ended with contradictory lectures in the places where I went because no one wants to get a beating. I would show up just as you have done, and when they ended by asking if anyone wanted to speak, I took the stand. It was not easy to start when there were three or four thousand absolute Marxists, complete communists, then a right-wing fighter shows up; imagine the show they got!*

*My first participation was on a Sunday. It was a great tumult. The next day, the big socialist newspaper, called Le Peuple explained what happened and how I had done. That was what I expected and therefore I was going to go again the next day. Without planning it, they had turned me into formidable propaganda, and everyone began to wonder, does anyone know anything about that boy? Let us see who that young man is.*

*They went to find out who that guy Léon was, and every time Léon went to the podium, he got hundreds of supporters and followers. Those idiots furnished a huge audience for me in their events for free.* (Applause)

*I remember when Hitler laid upon me the medal of the Ritterkreutz. Then we were up until 3:00 a.m. with Geitel and the other marshals eating something. When we returned, he opened the door and offered us two bottles of champagne. He was a man of great simplicity. I can tell you that he loved his dog very much. I never trust people who do not love animals or who are cruel to them. You had to have seen Hitler, with all the work he had, pause at midnight and say, "I am sorry, gentlemen, I am going to prepare some food for my dog." A dog knows that his master is the one who feeds him, and he truly realizes it. Animals are often superior to men; God was already tired when he created man.* (Laughter and loud applause)

*I met boys who went to the Eastern Front who never understood a single word of what people spoke to them in German because their language was French, but there was an energy that passed through, which doctors cannot perceive, as happens in love; such a banal thing that lasts an entire lifetime because, at that moment, the energy passed through. The energy that moved through was produced by the force that Hitler transmitted in his radio broadcast speeches, which became an invincible weapon. Every day he spoke three, four, five times. It was what had to be done. One day I happened to speak fourteen times. The first rally I started at 7:00 a.m. There were already people there at that early hour. The last speech took place in the town square of some village at 3:00 a.m. with its square completely crowded.*

*You have to make people come because they want to, so they can attend a great show. I have never given a meeting without charging for entry. I noticed that you sold tickets at the entrance of the event, although I do not claim anything. People have to pay. I used to tell the audience that if they had to pay for entrance to see an idiot, then to see me, one who does not consider himself an idiot, they also had to pay* (laughter and great applause).

*People no longer want to fight because they do not know what to die for. A young man nowadays does not know what happens in the homeland or what happens in his life. All noble values have been shattered for him, while the Russians have an immense army that faces demoralized peoples who have lost their soul. The enemy has millions of communists who are capable of any national betrayal. If we are where we are, it is because we must have what we have to have, that is, a strong head, walking united. In this way, everything can change in a day. In 1940, democracies used to say, "We will win because we are the strongest." A month later, they were all on the ground. Everything can change.*

*It should not be forgotten that Lenin made the USSR with twenty thousand people. What happened was that he was a leader who martyred the population.*

*There are thousands of young people who can make things change, but you have to be prepared. You have the strength to be numerous. It is said that in Spain there are not many people with good ideas. There are more here than in any country. I know that here among you there are French comrades, and in every country, there are thousands of guys waiting to do what needs to be done. One day a young Russian could come along to end slavery. Russians are Europeans like us. When the French were living through the Reign of Terror,[118] who thought of Napoleon?*

*It may be that six months later a young Russian might save Europe, and stand up against its tyrants, and mobilize this people, who are a wonderful and generous people and who maintain their great virtues. Everything is possible when you have faith, faith, faith, the faith that Hitler had.*

*Heil Hitler!* (Loud applause)

When the event ended, comrade D. Julia played the hymn of the National Socialist Party, "*Horst Wessel Lied*" the sharp notes of his trumpet echoing in the midst of an impressive ceremonial silence with everyone standing at attention.

## The *Express* Interview, Conducted by Eva Muns

After the event at the CEDADE premises in Barcelona, on January 30th, 1980, comrade Eva Muns asked Degrelle a series of off the cuff questions for CEDADE's journal, *Express*:

*EM: What is the main feature in your character?*

*LD: The spirit of conquest.*

---

[118] Reference to the French Revolution.

*EM: What is the quality you want in a man?*

*LD: Courage.*

*EM: What is the quality you want in a woman?*

*LD: Sweetness.*

*EM: What do you appreciate most about your friends?*

*LD: Loyalty.*

*EM: Your main flaw?*

*LD: I think others should speak to that.*

*EM: Your preferred occupation?*

*LD: Writing.*

*EM: What is your dream?*

*LD: To rise to power.*

*EM: What would be your biggest misfortune?*

*LD: To die.*

*EM: What would you like to be?*

*LD: The one who rebuilt Europe.*

*EM: Where would you like to live?*

*LD: In Andalusia.*

*EM: What is your favorite color?*

*LD: Blue.*

*EM: What is your favorite flower?*

*LD: The rose.*

*EM: Your favorite bird?*

*LD: The eagle.*

*EM: Who are your favorite prose authors?*

*LD: Napoleon.*

*EM: Who are your favorite poets?*

*LD: Rilke.*

*EM: Who are your fictional heroes?*

*LD: Charles the Bold, Duke of Burgundy.*[119]

*EM: Who are your fictional heroines?*

*LD: Agustina of Aragon.*[120]

---

[119] Charles the Bold, Duke of Burgundy, is obviously a real duke of history, whose lands and expansion of Burgundy are situated roughly in what is now Belgium, so identifying him as a fictional hero may appear odd. Degrelle may have had a novel or film in mind based on the life of Charles the Bold.

[120] Agustina de Aragón, or Agustina of Aragon in English, is a patriotic historical figure who was a heroine in the Spanish War of Independence against Napoleon, most famous for her brave participation at the Siege of Zargoza, 1808. She is listed as a "fictional heroine" likely because of two films about

*EM: Who are your favorite composers?*

*LD: Wagner and Beethoven.*

*EM: Who are your favorite painters?*

*LD: Goya.*

*EM: Who are your real-life heroes?*

*LD: Hitler.*

*EM: Who are your historical heroines?*

*LD: Eva Braun.*

*EM: What are your favorite names?*

*LD: Those of my parents: Édouard and Marie.*

*EM: What do you hate most in life?*

*LD: Vulgarity.*

*EM: Which historical characters do you despise most?*

*LD: The murder of Europe by Churchill.*

*EM: What military act do you admire most?*

*LD: The breakthrough in the Ardennes in Sedan in May 1940.*

*EM: Which reform do you admire most?*

*LD: The National Socialist reforms.*

*EM: What natural gifts would you like to have?*

*LD: Loving others (spiritual) and the strength to never get tired (physical).*

*EM: How would you like to die?*

*LD: Fighting for my ideal.*

*EM: What is the present state of your spirit?*

*LD: Optimistic, with faith in life.*

*EM: What facts inspire greater indulgence in you?*

*LD: Those which derive from loving.*

*EM: What is your motto?*

*LD: He who does not expose himself, does not impose himself.*

The interview appeared in issue ninety of CEDADE's *Express*, which was published in June 1980.

---

Agustina of Aragon: a silent film made in 1929, and the historical drama *Agustina de Aragón* filmed in 1950, staring Aurora Bautista as Agustina, produced by Cifesa.

## Letter Addressed to His Bourguignon Comrades

On November 15th, 1980, Degrelle sent the following letter to his Bourguignon (Burgundian) comrades, his former comrades in arms:

*In exile, November 15th, 1980.*

*My dear comrades,*

*In spite of the distance, to which this unending exile has condemned me, my thoughts unite me every day with all of you, my glorious comrades of the Eastern Front, so courageous over the course of those four years of terrible fighting, so dignified even in prison, when it was meant to annihilate your ideal. You have always behaved well, in spite of everything. After that, you have suffered from misunderstanding and hatred, leading a life often with hardship that is difficult for you, difficult for your families. You have always held your heads high, and you have continued to be true companions, affectionate and faithful, among yourselves.*

*Likewise, you have remained unchangingly united with our hundreds of thousands of comrades, volunteers from some twenty different countries, who heroically stepped up to counter the Soviets, to achieve among all a united Europe after the armistice, based on tradition and blood.*

*It is this friendship and camaraderie on the Front that brings us together, especially in the month of November every year, to honor our dukes of Burgundy, the great patricians of the most famous times in the history of our ancient people. Today, more than ever, I am fraternally united with you.*

*Not being able to meet with you, let us put on our best attire! I send you my encouragement, more than ever, far from our homeland, with my most enthusiastic support! As a comrade, nothing more, as the simple soldier I was when we left together for the Eastern Front, on August 8th, 1941, I ask you to enlist me among the members of your association "Les Bourguignons." I do not aspire to be anything more than a simple bugler among others, who does not even have the comfort of seeing you in person, but who is with you, from the depths of my exile, with all my heart as an old comrade.*

*To your health, all of you, Bourguignons, yesterday and forever!*

*To your health too, the women, sons, and daughters of our soldiers and brave supporters of their deeds and epics.*

*Embracing you all,*
*Léon Degrelle*

## "Europe Will Live!" Speech Delivered on January 30th, 1981

On January 30th, 1981, in another event also organized by CEDADE in Barcelona in celebration of the forty-eighth anniversary of National Socialism's rise in Germany and Hitler's taking over the Reich Chancellery, Léon participated for a second time by giving another important speech. This was later published in a booklet, reproduced by the publishing label Huguin, entitled "Europe Will Live!" Léon Degrelle was the main guest of the event and in his address, reiterated his message of resistance to the destruction of European values.

In his speech, he raised fundamental questions, such as: What is Europe? What kind of Europe do we want? Where does she come from? How can she be rebuilt? What role does she play? Who are we? What hope can she bring to the world? He methodically answered these questions throughout his speech.

The energetic discourse began with:

*Comrades,*

*I have heard our comrade talk about the importance of the Eastern Front. I was reminded of the thousands of young men his age who died in the snows of Russia to save Europe. If now, when that immense conflict has been lost; now that Europe is torn apart—one half Soviet, the other half the West—you can see nothing but decadence. Many of us say, "Europe, Europe is wealth; we are going with Europe." This word is not miraculous in and of itself. It is not a miraculous solution that can fix everything that way, without effort.*

*What is Europe? What kind of Europe do we want? Where does she come from? How can she be rebuilt? In the new world, what role can she play? Those who speak of Europe usually do so in an empty way. We know what our homeland is, but who can explain well what Europe is?*

*Last night I was in the hotel with folks watching Mr. Suárez on television. One incident came up: in the Europe of today and tomorrow, what is a government that destroys itself? I was surprised to see that people watched Mr. Suárez without enthusiasm. They were just looking at him, and then what? He finished and everyone got up and left, leaving me by myself to watch the international news. I said to myself, "Are these people interested in Europe? Are they interested in the world?" So, let us not fool ourselves. This Europe, of which you know so much, how do we see her? What hope can she bring to the world?*

*First: where does she come from? What is a European?*

Many think of today's Europe, but Europe is two thousand five hundred years old, at least! Europe is an immense civilization; she is a way of living.

We almost know Europe before we know our own homelands. Where did Europe emerge from? She emerged from those first peoples of the Mediterranean who have created the culture of Europe, the political order of Europe, their civilization.

One day, I said to Hitler, I asked him, "What is your country? Who are you? He answered me, "I am Greek," and he was right. It is Greece who has given us all our spiritual life.

If the European world exists, if it makes sense, it is because two thousand five hundred years ago, this small country, Greece, with few inhabitants and little wealth, was able to forge the supreme wealth that is civilization. When has a civilization like the Greek one ever been seen? Art, temples, sculptures, philosophy, science, and this wonderful balance of life. A life that lived almost amicably with its gods; that lived in the joy of the spirit, because it had these strengths that are worth more than any material strength. They projected in a few centuries their civilization to all the known world of their time.

We live here near Ampurias.[121] Who built Ampurias? When one walks around these ruins, when one goes to the Archaeological Museum of Barcelona, when all these extraordinary works of immense beauty are seen, it must be said that Greece existed here twenty centuries ago. But it existed in the same way in Naples, nea polis (the new city). There was Sicily; there was Egypt. Who built Alexandria? Alexander! With a library of four hundred thousand papyri. Four hundred thousand papyri! What culture! What knowledge!

It was Greek ships that surrounded the entire Mediterranean: Marseille, Ampurias; who went in the same way to Cadiz; who had come through the Gates of Hercules, the Strait of Gibraltar; two thousand five hundred years before the English, the Greeks were in Gibraltar, just as they were in India. With Alexander, this king of a small land, who goes with his warriors (and with his culture!) throughout the whole of Asia in the East and he arrives with everything at the Indus River.

Small European people (of Germanic blood!) which is always forgotten.

Every time civilization is sought anywhere in Europe, the blood of the North is seen. The Germanic peoples, the Celts. All these famous barbarians of antiquity who can be seen with a dagger clenched between the teeth. Barbarian means

---

[121] *Ampurias*, in Spanish, or *Empúries* in Catalan (from the Greek Ἐμπόριον; trade place, marketplace) is the site of an ancient Greek colony located on Costa Brava in Catalonia. The ruins of the colony, which date from the sixth century B.C., are still a popular tourist attraction.

*"foreigner," and nothing else!*

This Indo-European blood that came from Russia, which reached the Baltic Sea, then Greece, Italy, Spain, is the blood of the first journey. We racialists,[122] we know that it is pure blood that makes people strong. These White, strong, intelligent races, with few people, are setting up this world of Greece. When Greece had given the world its civilization for all time, then came the second wave of European strength: Rome. Another extraordinary example.

In our time we have giant nations, like the United States, with fabulous wealth, but powerless in the face of civilization; unable to win a war, even unable to disembark seven helicopters! (Laughter and applause) You see, in this time, when you had to do everything on foot or on horseback or in very small boats, with little force, without motors, only with sails, you see: the first inhabitants of Rome again cover the whole known world with their order.

So, we have two great assets: Greek Culture, the clear, lucid brain; and Roman Order.

*Léon Degrelle's speech in Barcelona, 1981*

---

[122] I have translated the Spanish word *racistas*, which literally means "racists," as "racialists" in order to remove the derogatory tone that the word carries in modern English. Much like the men of his time, Degrelle's use of "racist" does not imply a uniquely derogatory or stigmatized meaning, but implies rather one who thinks in racial terms.

Degrelle then categorically states that "Europe is, above all, a civilization."

To emphasize the strength of the patrician peoples' spiritual power and the threats they faced, he gave the following explanation:

*Why was the spiritual power, which the Roman empire had, which was an immense wealth for all, everything, in half a century leveled to the ground?*

*The fall of Rome has several origins. First, a phenomenon we know now: decadence. To play a great role, to spread a great civilization, you have to have a strong center and a pure center. You see, when the center is broken down in a country—you don't have to look far—*(laughter)*, you see how in a few years everything crumbles, and it happens at the sound of "Oh, my! I cannot take it any longer. I am leaving."* (Laughter and applause)

*The Roman Empire had reached a point of enormous wealth, and money always corrupts. The religious orders that have been saved are those that lived poor, and the political leaders who seek money, who want money, are no longer politicians. I remember of Hitler that he never had a "pfennig." He died, and he had nothing. No material wealth was left. The same with Mussolini. His poor wife, twenty years after the war, with great sorrow, has only now gotten a pension. For power is supreme joy. What is money next to power? To take human clay[123] and mold it...I think humanity is like that, it is clay. Mud can smear your pants, but if Michelangelo gets a hold of it...he makes an immortal work. The great politician gets a hold of the human clay and makes a great people, a great civilization, like what Napoleon did, like what Hitler did. We are waiting for what will be done, in the same way with everything as it is now, with the mud on the ground.*

*The great Romans had this sinful love of money.*

*Second, we have to remember it well, another sin: race. The race was corrupted, as in today's Europe, where there are four million Moors or half-Moors in France* (laughter), *four hundred thousand Turks in Berlin, and, in Madrid, twenty times more Jews than twenty years ago.*

*Once the blood is rotten, everything is lost. We were lucky in Europe to have the same race at last. The truth must be said: those in the Baltic states, those of the Apennines in Italy, the Spanish, the Russians, we are the same. The Russians are our brothers. We are all Europeans. We are the same. The decline of Rome came when, like in Athens, human forces from the East had come en masse. It was a*

---

[123] [The Spanish word *barro*, which I translate as *clay*, means clay in a secondary sense, but normally means *mud*. In English, of course, *mud* and *clay* are not interchangeable or synonymous. Either way, Degrelle's use here is not the image of a professional molder's clean, washed clay, but rather the image of something dirty that can be made beautiful.]

*temptation for a wild African; it was a great adventure to come and live in Rome, even as a slave in Greece. The Athens of decadence had only—or what was left—seven thousand Athenians. The others were slaves, or semi-slaves, who came from outside.*

*Similarly, the Roman race, which dominated through strength, through its spirit, through its will, was disintegrated...*

*By breaking Roman unity, they allowed, or obliged, each people to use their own resources and to seek a small form of political existence. This is how one notes the breaking apart, of that great European unity into twenty different pieces. From that moment, separated politically from Rome, and with little union with ecclesiastical Rome, every people, abandoned, developed their own language, followed their immediate customs, and lost contact with the rest of the world.*

*It was like that up until fifty years ago. Since the fall of Rome, we have lived one thousand five hundred years separated, not only by the political form of state, but by languages.*

With regard to the plurality of languages he made the following reflection:

*Languages can be given an exaggerated importance. Regional and provincial languages are beautiful and perfectly respectable, but if we want to have a European spirit, we have to look a little farther, too especially if we want to belong to a universal culture. Truly!*

In referring to communism, he did not hesitate to call it what it was: "Communism is a typically Jewish phenomenon!"

Degrelle spoke of the great forgers of European unity: the spirit of Greece; the Roman Empire; Charlemagne's endeavor as Emperor of Europe; the Hohenstauffen, with Holy Roman Emperor Frederick II and his quest for cultural unity; Charles V; Philip II; Napoleon, and the latest example featuring Adolf Hitler, who, had he achieved final victory, would have reunited Europe from the North Sea to Vladivostok:

*Hitler played a role: to prevent the Soviets from conquering Europe. At once, in every country, hundreds of thousands of boys, just like you, understood the meaning of this struggle and came to the Eastern Front. At that moment, that dream which seemed so impossible, that dream of Charles V and of the Hohenstauffen, of Napoleon, could finally be brought to life. On the Russian front, in the ranks of the SS, weapons, shock troops—we were 60 percent of the non-German troops—the million SS soldiers had six hundred thousand non-Germans. This is obvious proof that Hitler did not want Germany to swallow up Europe, but that he wanted a fraternal union of Europeans, just as he had done with social classes and their reconciliation, once Europe had been protected from the Soviet danger, finally uniting Europeans.*

Degrelle concluded his magnificent speech by saying:

*These democratic forces have sunk the family, the idea of homeland, the idea of religion; they have taken away all ideals. There is no longer a spiritual life, and spiritual life is the main thing. Without the life of the soul, there is nothing!* (Applause)

*In other words, the only salvation for Europeans who remain lucid is to have strong souls! To have a great social ideal, a great patriotic ideal, a great religious ideal, to maintain all the strength that can be maintained for when the day of salvation comes. All great things that have been done in the world have always been done by a few people. There is no need to have millions of lazy people. We must have strong hearts, ready to sacrifice until death, if necessary. You need to know what you want; you need to know where the future is. Thus, will Europe be saved.*

*If in Europe, everywhere, there are guys and girls like you; if everyone tries to convince others, the day of the great reckoning will come! These thousands of young people will appear throughout Europe, and they can save what remains.*

*These young people exist. They exist here. They exist in all the countries of Europe. It is they who one day, in God's Day, when God will help us, and inspire us, will achieve our salvation.*

*Huge risks, but a huge potential. This depends on us.*

*Long live Europe!* (Great applause)

## An Unpublished Book

On February 23rd, 1981, two monarchist generals, defenders of the Spanish crown, two centurions of great weight in the Spanish Army, the generals Alfonso Armada Comín and Jaime Milans del Bosch, with the top ranks pulling the strings in the shadows, staged an attempted coup. This was ultimately thwarted by Lieutenant Colonel Antonio Tejero Molina of the Guardia Civil, who knew how to put his patriotism and his military honor first when he was warned about the machinations that had surfaced among the political parties (the right wing UCD, the socialists, and the communists), together with the monarchist military. This happened under the anxious gaze of the great would-be beneficiary of the operation in order to push forward an integrated "concentration government," as would be seen months later, by elements of questionable reputation. These included socialists such as Felipe González, who the following year led Spain in its state terrorism with the use of the GAL[124] and its greatest period of corruption; the Jewish-Zionist Enrique Múgica Herzog; the American agent and socialist Javier Solana; and the communist Jordi Solé Tura.

The attempt was unsuccessful and was postponed for another year, until Felipe González, who appeared as vice president on the government's list of His Majesty's coup plotters, took power, starting a period in the government marked by state terrorism, financial scandals, and unprecedented corruption.

Léon (I reveal here a well-kept secret) as if it were a chess game, wrote a "blind book," not to be published, in relation to these events. Rivers of ink have flowed about it, but the whole truth of what "really" happened has not yet been revealed.

Its author left a handwritten note on the first page of that unpublished and secret book that says the following: "Confidential writing. Photocopying this text is absolutely prohibited. It is strictly personal and not for commerce, including any passage from it." Respectful of his desire and will, after having studied it carefully, I must omit its content.

The title of his analysis was "El Putsch Tejero" ("The Tejero Putsch") (Madrid, February 23rd–24th, 1981) and he signed it as "General X." The work, "*ex ungue leonem*,"[125] runs through two hundred and five typed pages, with a documentary appendix as an annex. The index is made up of twenty chapters, which correspond to the characters involved: all the characters, without beheading the "invisible head," the political parties involved, the press, and the background.

In the lines of the text are innumerable annotations, comments, handwritten footnotes and notes in the margins, so as not to miss nuances and to correct the text that would be definitive. The sole copy is kept hidden on an island called "Dignity."

---

[124] The *Grupos Antiterroristas de Liberación*, or GAL, were illegal units financed by officials under Spanish Socialist Workers Party (PSOE) administration in the 1980s to assassinate Basque separatists, most notably those in Euskadi Ta Askatasuna, or ETA. The GAL's long list of assassinations came to an end in 1987; many PSOE officials were convicted for these.

[125] [Latin for "from the claw, a lion"; meaning, one can judge from looking at the claw whether it is a lion, or one can deduce the whole, from looking at a part.]

## Letter to Jef François

On July 29th, 1981, Léon Degrelle sent a heartfelt letter to his comrade in arms and a hero also decorated on the Eastern Front, Jef François:

*My dear friend and comrade François,*

*I often think of you with great affection and also with admiration. Above all, for over sixty years, you have always been the perfect idealist, unwavering in faith in our doctrine and in the unforgettable lesson of your Chief Joris Van Severen.*

*Like him, first and foremost, you have been a lucid man, always trying to behave in a way befitting the great and worthy past of our western lands, making it endure in the real and in the possible, enriching it by the exaltation of the highest spiritual virtues.*

*With our great and dear Van Severen with whom I shared, as you know, the terrible suffering on Abbeville's fatal road, and with our heroes of the Eastern Front, the epic was continued. You, dear comrade François, were, in truth, in all the territory of Flanders, one of the most noble symbols of our faith.*

*You have also endured the harshest trials; the purity of your convictions had to collide with the most blind hatred, but you have always been the same, unavailable to discouragement, always calm, courageous.*

*You are our pride. I wanted to tell you again, with all my affection, as an old comrade in arms, in this gallant year in which you will be turning eighty years old.*

*Forward! We must outlive and bury all those vile people who, provisionally and materially, have defeated us. They have been unable to create anything; they have defiled everything; they have desecrated everything. Sooner or later, the time will come when the youth again fly our unstained banners and live their lives in service of the great ideal for which so many of our comrades have died.*

*We, at least, can be proud of our lives and with clear consciences look, not only back to the glorious past, but ahead to the future, which will see the day that our dream is realized.*

*Alive or dead, we will overcome. We were right. Our plans had an objective, to save the West and all of Europe. We gave back to men the honor of living; we gave meaning to our peoples.*

*There is no one who can stop faith. Sooner or later, they will understand us. So then, what does it matter to have suffered so much!*

*Dear comrade François, I send you my faithful greeting.*

*Accept my brotherly embrace, Léon Degrelle*

## Why Did I Believe in Hitler?

The publication *Histoire Magazine* published an interview with Léon Degrelle, done by Jean Kapel, in issue nineteen, September 1981, which was entitled "Why I Believed in Hitler." The interview began with Kapel's question to Degrelle about his first meeting with Hitler, which took place in the summer of 1936 during a trip Léon and his wife took to Germany with some rexist friends. Hitler invited them to tea. From the very first moment the Führer and Léon met, there was a mutual empathy, an eternal alchemy.

Throughout the interview, Degrelle went on about his favorable views toward the National Socialist movement and its social achievements, ardently defending his convictions. He reminded Kapel that Hitler came to power democratically, backed by the votes of millions of Germans.

Kapel then asked, "You are the leader of a Belgian nationalist movement that claimed to be Catholic. Is there no contradiction with your alignment on the side of Hitler's armies?"

Degrelle responded:

*People have lied about Hitler in this regard. He was intensely devout and frequently invoked the name of God. His beliefs were Christian, and even in his childhood he was part of the choir in his parish church. It is true that some National Socialist leaders were hostile to the Church, like Borman and Himmler, not to mention Rosenberg, but their influence on Hitler in this regard was rather negligeable. He did not take Himmler's interest in ancient Germanic religions very seriously, and his policy was very favorable to the Catholic Church, even when opponents of the regime emerged from the Church. On one occasion, I met him one morning when I was on my way to receive communion, and when I told him my intention he was not surprised, telling me that his mother, had she been alive, would have joined me. He was very discreet in this regard, but had a true devotion to his mother's memory, and what Kubizek has stated in his memoirs is very revealing. To me, my religion did not seem to be at all in contradiction to my siding with the principles and ideas promoted by Hitler; he understood that very well, to the extent that one day he told me, "If I had a son, I would have liked him to be like you." [ . . . ]*

### Political Event at the Barcelona Conference and Exhibition Center

In the December 1981 bulletin *CEDADE*, one of CEDADE's publications, a political event was announced that was to take place the following month, on January 29th, 1982, at 7:30 p.m., at the Conference and Exhibition Center, room three, located on María Cristina Avenue, in Montjuich, in Barcelona. It was the forty-nineth anniversary commemoration of Hitler's rise to power and his arrival to the Reich Chancellery. Léon Degrelle would once again speak, this time on the theme "The Epic of the Eastern Front and its Validity Today."

This was the third time that he appeared in the CEDADE gallery before an increasingly large, dedicated, and enthusiastic audience.

Eva Muns introduced Degrelle as a brilliant speaker and political head of one of the most important fascist movements of the 1930s, who, at only thirty years old, had become a consummate *Volksführer* (*people's leader*). He had won this recognition from his years of political struggle, and it was apparent on the Eastern Front with his magnificent young men of the Waffen SS.

Later, CEDADE President Pedro Varela made a sincere appeal to the audience about the all-out fight against the destroyers of all that is beautiful and noble:

> *Europe has no guarantee of living forever. If there are no young people willing to fight for her, Europe will disappear.*
>
> *Those who have heard the "Belgian Lion" in some speech know how he speaks, with heart, with soul, with the truth, and with complete logic; with demolishing argumentation; with his characteristic accentuation and enthusiasm. Even today, at seventy-six years old, with numerous scars from combat, he is "still a kid," as everyone confirms.*

The room was packed with an enthusiastic audience, including Ms. Juana "Jeanne" Brevet.

When the memorial event ended, a banquet dinner took place, after which Degrelle shared an emotional anecdote about Rudolf Hess, the martyr of peace sacrificed in the sinister prison of Spandau. León spent hours signing autographs and dedications to all the comrades who requested it during the dinner. Young admirers formed a never-ending line before the one who gave the best years of his life for the National Socialist idea and who was still on the front line fighting tirelessly to keep alive the flame of that ideal.

Among those who heard him was the untiring Ramón Bau. Recalling those days sometime later, Bau wrote:

> *Perhaps the most relevant personality of the Third Reich that we were able to work with, and get to know in person and in truth, those of us who lived in the 60s, was undoubtedly Léon Degrelle. His penetrating and lively personality impressed those of us who formed the leadership at CEDADE in those years in a way that certainly marked us forever. He made it clear to us that those men of the SS, those European National Socialists, had nothing to do with what the press said about National Socialism.*
>
> *Degrelle represented to us that ideal of a different man, a man of action, a fighter, but at the same time mystical, spiritual, clean, and heroic, sensitive and dynamic. Both Catholic and National Socialist, he spoke to us of Hitler and Himmler, and at the same time he continued his fight through books and events despite his exile, despite being under a death penalty by Belgian democracy, despite kidnapping attempts by the Mossad, despite being the target of a special law, the Degrellian law, that thwarted the legal expiration of his persecution or the possibility of being buried in his homeland.*
>
> *With a brilliant humor, a spontaneous and direct discourse, Degrelle, together with Hess, were our heroes. We could not see Hess because of the brutal democratic tyranny* [that imprisoned him], *but they could not take away the living example of Léon Degrelle.*

## "Léon Degrelle, A Hero's Life"

With the title "*León Degrelle, una Vida de Héroe*" ("Léon Degrelle, A Hero's Life"), journalist Alexis Maulnier published, in the January 1982 edition of *CEDADE* magazine, an interview whose introduction ran as follows:

> *Léon Degrelle… a man, a legend; but a legend that is quite alive. In fact, Léon Degrelle, of whose life you could write a dozen novels and fifteen movies, remains a solid rock. Brown hair, the energetic face of a man of action who has suffered quite a bit, athletic build, in whose eyes shines a flame able to revive the dying, a man who seems to be barely sixty years old, let alone seventy-six. Friendly and cordial, with a frank, warm smile. No one could tell from his appearance that since the 1920s, this man has fought to defend his ideals and those of his homeland despite all the adversities that have been put before him. He was the Director of Rex Publishing in the 1930s, founder and head of the Rexist Party of Belgium, and*

*during his political campaign of 1935—1936, he held from ten to fourteen rallies*
*a day, with great electoral success. He was locked in the concentration camp of*
*Vernet, in the Pyrenees, until his release by order of Marshal Pétain, enlisted in the*
*Wehrmacht in 1941, fought on the Eastern Front, and was promoted to general*
*shortly before the end of the war. He fought in seventy-five close combat battles, was*
*wounded five times, was awarded a gold medal for his wounds and received the*
*highest military awards during the war. On February 23rd, 1944, he became the*
*only non-German to be a Knight of the Iron Cross with Oak Leaves. Hitler*
*personally gave him this highest distinction. After Germany's defeat, he fled on*
*Speer's plane and arrived in San Sebastián. He is accused of war crimes, but his*
*innocence is proven. In vain, Degrelle continues to offer to stand before a court if he*
*is simply guaranteed full publication of the hearings and their broadcasting. His*
*offers fall on deaf ears.*

*Léon Degrelle welcomes us very kindly into his home. Léon Degrelle does not*
*give us an interview, per se, he simply speaks to us as if he were speaking to old*
*friends whom he had not seen in a long time.*

The interview proceeds with an extensive round of questions that touch on issues
such as the current political situation, the oil crisis, unemployment in Europe,
democratic censorship, the economic crisis, and the fallacies of the "holocaust."

Degrelle answers these questions resolutely:

*We return to the same story of the Jews and the holocaust. No one can speak his*
*mind on this issue. If one does not completely agree, it is a crime. Not even a learned*
*man can ask the question, "Are you sure that it really happened like that? Are you*
*sure you can place seven hundred to eight hundred people on a surface of 25 square*
*meters (269 square feet)?" There is the Gerstein document, which was presented at*
*the Jerusalem Tribunal, and Eichmann was convicted first and foremost on the basis*
*of documents like that one. Seven hundred to eight hundred people on 25 square*
*meters is about thirty people per 1 square meter (10.8 square feet); a square meter*
*is the size of a telephone booth. In Paris all of them died, yet there were three*
*hundred fifty thousand after the war; now there is a million. They are everywhere.*
*They have populated Israel and there are three million in Russia.*

*AM: You have just mentioned Israel, so what do you think of this state?*

*LD: It is a totally artificial state that lacks meaning. Above all, if the Germans*
*had committed an atrocious crime against them, they should have granted Bavaria*
*to the Jews. Why take land from the Arabs? They had nothing to do with this whole*
*story. They say it is because that was the country they had been in, but by this way*

*of thinking, the Arabs should be given Córdoba, Toledo, Zaragoza, and Poitiers, and the United States to the American Indians, and so on. People also seem to forget that the oil crisis came about because of this people. All the money that has been given to them could have been used to turn the Sahara into bottles of mineral water, and all this to take the Jews to a country they do not want to go to. A seventh of their entire population does not live there, and never even goes. However, the Americans created Israel more as a province of their own. Israel was created by force, following a series of horrible crimes ordered, organized, and carried out by Menachem Begin, the current head of the State of Israel, and who was also said to have disappeared in a crematorium. Israel was a preconceived plan of the hyper-capitalist world. They have planted some tomatoes there, with the sweat of a few thousand people, but that is worth nothing. What they wanted was the oil around them. Today oil is the blood of the universe, and what do they want? To eliminate the Arabs. There is clearly a risk of triggering a new global conflict.*

When broaching the subject of Russia, his opinion was optimistic:

*A figure may appear in Russia and the youth would follow him. I spent four years in Russia. It is a sensational country, a powerful, noble, and intelligent race, a race with a sense of philosophy, art, and music, and that has also received great currents from our civilization. Obviously, it has its policy, and communism governs it, but opportunities arrive. We have been carrying on this way for sixty years now, and it is going to explode. Just as we tempted our fate in our day, Eastern Europe can tempt its own. The Europe that we want might one day be created by a Russian, and it makes no difference to me. If Hitler had been French or Portuguese or Italian, it would all have been exactly the same for me.*

The interview ended with Degrelle recognizing and praising Hitler's genius.

## A Great Documentary on the Epic History of the Waffen SS

In the winter of 1982, a recording team from the American publication *Journal of Historical Review*[126] traveled to Spain to film a video about the Waffen SS. From his home, Léon Degrelle spoke about the epic meaning of unity among the SS in a

---

[126] *Journal of Historical Review* was the publication of the California-headquartered Institute for Historical Review (IHR). Their publication ceased in 2002, although IHR still markets their flagship books and valuable translations.

lecture-type format with a broader message to illustrate this to the American public. The content was largely unknown at that time, but it was widely publicized. The following year, the publishers also released a book with the text from this speech, entitled *Epic: The Story of the Waffen SS*. The first edition sold out in 1983, the first year of its publication, so in October 1984, the book was republished in California. Copies of this publication are located in the U.S. Library of Congress, where it is included in its bibliographic file.

During the filming, Degrelle began his monologue by saying, "In a certain sense, it is surprising that this organization, which was both political and military, and which during the Second World War brought together more than a million volunteer combatants, continues to be officially ignored."

He continued: "A very likely answer is the fact that the most salient feature of the Waffen SS was its composition, made up of volunteers from about thirty different countries."

A tight synthesis of his overall view would lead us to highlight, in light of his documented and lived experience, the following paragraphs:

> *Young people were shown why they were fighting, what kind of Germany was resurfacing before their own eyes. They were shown how Germany was being morally unified through class reconciliation and physically rebuilt by recovering lost German territories. They were made to clearly see their relationship with other Germans living in foreign countries, in Poland, in Russia, in the Sudetenland, and elsewhere in Europe. They were taught that all Germans represented an ethnic unity.*

He drew attention to "the self-styled Western democracies [who] allied with the Soviet Union to surround and destroy Germany's democratic government," emphasizing that:

> *National Socialism was a people's movement in the strictest sense of the term. The vast majority of National Socialists were working class. Seventy percent of the Hitler Youth were made up of children of manual laborers. Hitler won the election because so much of the working class had stood solidly behind him. One often wonders why six million communists, who had voted against Hitler, turned their backs on communism after Hitler was elected in 1933. There is only one reason: they witnessed and experienced the benefits of class cooperation. Some say they were forced to change parties. It is a lie. Like the other loyal Germans, they fought for years on the Eastern Front with great distinction.*

*The workers never abandoned Hitler, but the upper classes did. Hitler carried out his formula of cooperation between the classes, as a response to communism, with these words: "Cooperation between classes means that capitalists will never again treat workers as mere economic factors. Money is only part of our economic life; workers are more than just machines that they can throw a paycheck at every week. Germany's true wealth is its workers."*

*Hitler supplanted gold in favor of labor as the foundation of his economy. National Socialism was the exact reverse of communism. Extraordinary achievements followed Hitler's election.*

*We always hear about Hitler and the concentration camps, Hitler and the Jews, but we never hear anything about his immense social work. Much hatred has been generated against Hitler by the international bankers and by the servile press, and it is precisely because of his social work. It is obvious that a genuinely popular movement, such as National Socialism, had to collide with the selfish interests of big finance. Hitler made it clear that the control of money did not confer the right to a rapacious exploitation of an entire country because there are also people living in that country, millions of them, and these people have a right to live with dignity and without suffering want. What Hitler did and said gained him the enthusiasm of the German youth. It was this social revolution that the SS felt compelled to spread throughout Germany and to defend with their lives, if necessary. Thus, the war turned the SS from an internal political force into a national army fighting outside German borders and, later, into a supranational army.*

*It is difficult to wrap our minds around the idea that, out of a total of one million SS members, three hundred fifty-two thousand died in action and fifty thousand were missing in action. These are cruel figures! Four hundred thousand of the best of European youth sacrificed their lives, without hesitation, for the ideal they believed in! They knew they had to set the example. They were the first in the line of fire, as a way of defending their homelands and their ideals.*

*In both victory and defeat, the Waffen SS always sought to be the most prominent representative of every people. The SS was a democratic expression of power; people gathered together by their own free will.*

*The consensus at the ballot box is not the only possibility; there is also the consensus of the minds and hearts of the people. In action, the Waffen SS were a plebiscite in that the German people felt proud of them, that they should be given their respect and their affection. Motivation like this made the Waffen SS volunteers the best warriors in the world.*

*The SS had proved themselves in action. They were not politicians of hollow words, rather they gave their lives; they were the first to go and fight in an extraordinary burst of camaraderie. This camaraderie was one of the most distinctive characteristics of the SS: one SS leader was the comrade of all the others.*

*It was in the line of fire that the results of the physical training could actually be observed. An SS officer had the same rigorous training as his soldiers. Officers and enlisted men competed in the same sports tournaments, and the best won, regardless of hierarchy or rank. This created a true brotherhood that literally filled all the Waffen SS with energy. Only teamwork, embodied by a superior ideal, would be able to unify Europe. [...]*

*The relationship of equality and mutual respect between soldiers and officers was always present. Half of all division commanders were killed in combat. Half of them![127] There is no other army in the world where this has happened. The SS officer always personally led his troops into combat. I myself participated in seventy-five close combat engagements because as an SS officer, I had to be the first to make contact with the enemy. The soldiers of the SS were not sent to the slaughterhouse by officers behind the lines; they followed their officers with passionate loyalty. Every SS commander knew and taught all his men; and he often received unexpected and valiant results.*

Degrelle included a very significant, but little-known, anecdote of personal character:

*One time, two of my soldiers took out their identification cards for the Belgian Resistance Movement. They had been sent to kill me. In the line of fire, it would be very easy to kill someone from behind. It happened that the extraordinary esprit de corps of the SS had won them over. SS officers could expect loyalty from their men, by virtue of their example.*

Degrelle continued:

*The life expectancy of an SS officer on the front was three months. In Estonia, on a Monday, I received ten new officers from the Bad Toelz Academy. By Thursday, only one remained and he was wounded.*

---

[127] In typical Western military doctrine, divisional commanders (and even lower-ranking brigade commanders) are rarely placed in the direct line of fire for obvious command-and-control reasons; losing this many divisional commanders would be very rare. Degrelle's point is to highlight the personal sacrifice of even high-ranking SS officers.

*In conventional armies, officers speak to the troops as superiors to inferiors and rarely as brothers in combat and brothers in ideology. That is why, by 1939, the Waffen SS had won the public's admiration and respect.*

*The name "Waffen SS" was more than just a change of name. The Waffen SS became Germanic while volunteers were accepted from all Germanic countries. The SS had discovered for themselves that the people of Western Europe were closely related to them. The Norwegians, the Danes, the Dutch, the Flemish...all belonged to the same Germanic family. These Germanic peoples were very impressed by the SS and so were, incidentally, the French.*

*People in Western Europe marveled at this extraordinary German force, which possessed an incomparable place in history. If two SS scouts arrived in a village before the rest of the unit since they were on motorcycles, before presenting themselves to the authorities, they first put themselves in order and cleaned up to make their appearance spotless. People could not help but be impressed.*

*The admiration that young Europeans of German descent felt for the SS was very natural. Thousands of young men from Norway, Denmark, Flanders, and Holland had been stunned with both surprise and admiration. They were irresistibly attracted to the SS. It was not Europe but their own Germanic race that so deeply drove their emotions. They identified themselves with the victorious Germans. For them, Hitler was the most exceptional man ever seen, and Hitler understood them and conceived the remarkable idea of opening the doors of the SS to them. The bargain was quite risky. No one had thought of that before. Before Hitler, German imperialism had merely consisted of swapping some goods with other countries with no idea of creating an ideology called "communitarianism," an ideal common to all their neighbors.*

*Suddenly, instead of swapping and haggling, here was a man who offered a glorious ideal: a broad social justice, which all of them had yearned for, in vain, for years. A generous new order, instead of the shapeless cosmopolitanism of the so-called pre-war "democracies." The response to Hitler's offer was overwhelming. Legions from Norway, Denmark, Holland, and Flanders were created. Thousands of young people were now wearing the SS uniform. Hitler created for them, specifically, the famous "Viking Division."*

*How do you find officers who could speak all these languages, and how to coordinate such a crazy situation? To overcome these problems was the miracle of the assimilation program of the Waffen SS. This return of the various "tribes" was seen in the Waffen SS as the foundation of true European unity. The three hundred thousand Germanic volunteers were welcomed into the SS as brothers and their reciprocity was demonstrated when they were seen to be as dedicated, loyal, and heroic as the German SS.*

*In the course of a year, everything changed for the Waffen SS. The barracks were full; the academies were saturated. The admission criteria and the strictest requirements applied equally to Germanic volunteers. They had to be the best in every sense, both physically and mentally. They had to be the best of the Germanic race.*

*German racialism[128] has been deliberately distorted. It was never a racism that was "anti" any other race. It was pro-Germanic racialism. Its concern was to make the Germanic race strong and healthy in every sense. Hitler was not interested in having millions of degenerates if it were in his power not to have them. Today one finds alcoholism and a flourishing drug addiction anywhere. Hitler was concerned that Germanic families should be healthy, and that they should raise healthy children for a healthy nation. German racialism meant the discovery of creative values in its own race, a discovery of its own culture. It was a search for the excellent, a remarkable idea. National Socialism was not against other races; it was, rather, in favor of its own race. It aimed at defending and improving its own race and wanted all others to do the same for their respective races.*

*This was demonstrated when the Waffen SS expanded their ranks to include sixty thousand Islamic SS members. The Waffen SS respected their lifestyle, customs, and religious beliefs. Each Islamic SS battalion had its imam, each company had its mullah. It was our common desire that their qualities would find their highest expression. That was our racialism. I was present when each of my Islamic comrades received a gift from Hitler, personally, on the occasion of the New Year. It was a pendant with a small Quran. Hitler honored them with this little gift. He was honoring them with what constituted the most important aspect of their lives and history. National Socialist racialism was loyal to the Germanic race while fully respecting all other races.*

Degrelle later pointed out that:

*Personally, I have always vigorously defended the Russians and, finally, succeeded in convincing Hitler that the Germans should live with the Russians as partners and*

---

[128] Similar to a footnote above, I translate the Spanish word *racismo*, literally *racism*, as *racialism* to avoid the immediate stigma in the English word racism. Degrelle partially explains its meaning in the following lines; were he speaking to contemporaries of the early twentieth century, this would not necessarily have to be explained.

*not as conquerors, but before achieving any such collaboration, the issue of eliminating communism was a priority.*

He then highlighted a memorable fact:

*Throughout the war, the Waffen SS never pulled back by ceding ground. They would rather die before retreating. You cannot ignore the numbers. During the winter of 1941, the Waffen SS lost forty-three thousand men on the Eastern Front. The "Der Führer" regiment fought almost literally until the last man.*

*Only thirty-five men survived from the entire regiment. The men of the "Der Führer" nailed themselves to their posts and there were no Soviet troops who could pass through. They had to try to surround the SS in the snow. This was how the famous Russian General Vlasov was captured by SS Division Totenkopf. Without its heroism, Germany would have been annihilated in December 1941.*

*Hitler would never forget. He appreciated the willpower that the Waffen SS had shown in front of Moscow. They had shown character and courage, and that was what Hitler admired most of all: courage.*

*From all over Europe, volunteers ran to help their German brothers. It was then that the third great Waffen SS was born. First there had been the strictly German Waffen SS, then the broader Germanic component, and now there was the "European Waffen SS." Some one hundred twenty-five thousand men would volunteer to save the civilization and culture of the West. The volunteers joined fully aware that the SS had the highest number of casualties. More than two hundred fifty thousand men out of a million would die in combat. For these volunteers, the Waffen SS was—despite the death toll—the birth of Europe. Napoleon had said in Saint Helena, "There will be no Europe until a leader emerges."*

*The young European volunteers had observed two things: first, that Hitler was the only leader able to build Europe, and second, that Hitler and only Hitler could overcome the global threat of communism.*

*For the European SS, the Europe of little envies, politics, border disputes, and economic rivalries, was uninteresting; that Europe was too false and petty; that Europe was no longer valid for them. At the same time, the European SS, however much they admired Hitler and the German people, did not want to become German. They were men of their own people and Europe was the gathering together of all the peoples of Europe. European unity was to be achieved through harmony and not through the domination of one over another.*

*I discussed these issues at length with both Hitler and Himmler. Hitler, like all men of genius, had risen above the merely national stage. Napoleon was first a*

Corsican, then a Frenchman, and finally a European; he ended up being, singularly, a universal man. Similarly, Hitler had been an Austrian, then a German, then a greater German, then more broadly Germanic, and then he finally had understood the magnitude of the task of building Europe.

After defeating communism, the Waffen SS would have the solemn duty of gathering all its strength and all its power to build a unified Europe, and with no inclination that non-German Europe should be dominated by Germany.

Before joining the Waffen SS, we had been through very difficult conflicts. We had gone to the Eastern Front, first as units attached to the German Army, but during the battle of Stalingrad, we had realized that Europe was under serious threat. A great common effort was becoming imperative. One night I had a debate with Hitler and Himmler that lasted eight hours about the "status" of non-German Europeans within the new Europe.

For now, we expected to be treated like equals, fighting for a common cause. Hitler fully understood this and from then on, we had our own flag, our own officers, our own language, our own religion. We had a totally equal "status."

I was the first to have Catholic priests within the Waffen SS. Later, priests from all denominations were made available to all who needed them. The Islamic SS Division had its own mullah, and the French even had a bishop! We were pleased that, with Hitler, we Europeans would be federated as equals, and we felt that the best way to merit this place, as peers among peers, was to defend Europe, at this critical hour, just as well as our German comrades did.

For Hitler, what mattered above all was courage. He created a new chivalry. Those who deserved the Ritterkreuz (Knight's Cross) were really knights again in a new sense. They deserved this nobility of courage. Each of our units, once they returned home after the war, would be the force that would protect the rights of the people in each of our respective countries. All the SS understood that European unity meant the unity of all Europe, including Russia.

The European SS saw the new Europe in the form of three major components: Central Europe was like the factory of Europe; Western Europe, as the cultural heart of Europe; and Eastern Europe, as the potential of Europe. Thus, the Europe that the SS imagined was alive and real. Its six hundred million inhabitants would live from the North Sea to Vladivostok. It was in this area of 13,000 kilometers (8,078 miles) that Europe would realize its destiny. A space available for young people to start a new life. This Europe would be a beacon of the world, a unique ethnic group, an ancient civilization, a spiritual force, and the most advanced technological and scientific complex. The SS was preparing for Europe's higher destiny.

*It was this faith in higher ideals that inspired four hundred thousand German SS, three hundred thousand "Volksdeutsche," or broader Germanic SS, and three hundred thousand European SS from different countries. All volunteers. One million builders of Europe.*

*The paradox was that the closer Germany was to defeat, the more volunteers came to the forefront. It was something phenomenal. Eight days before the final defeat I was able to see hundreds of young people join the SS on the front. Until the very end, they knew they should do the impossible to stop the enemy...the Waffen SS had as many as fifty divisions in 1945.*

Léon Degrelle concluded his filmed lecture with these words:

*If the Waffen SS had not existed, Europe would have been completely swept through by the Soviets in 1944. They would have gotten to Paris long before the Americans. The heroism of the Waffen SS stopped the Soviet steamroller in Moscow, Chercov, Cherkassy, and Tarnopol. The Soviets were more than twelve months behind. Without SS resistance, the Soviets would have been in Normandy before Eisenhower. People showed great gratitude to the young people who sacrificed their lives. Since the great medieval religious orders, such an altruistic heroism and idealism had not been seen. In this century of materialism, the SS rose up as a bright light of spirituality.*

*I have no doubt whatsoever that the sacrifices and incredible achievements of the Waffen SS will have their own epic poets like Schiller. Greatness in adversity is the hallmark of the SS.*

*A curtain of silence was drawn over the Waffen SS after the war, but more and more young men are somehow aware of their existence and achievements. Fame is growing, and young people demand to know more. In a hundred years, almost everything will be forgotten, but the greatness and heroism of the Waffen SS will be remembered. It will be the reward for an epic history.*

## Interview in the Newspaper *El País*

Degrelle's public life came to a close that year with an interview for the newspaper *El País*, given on Tuesday December 14th, 1982, in his home at calle Santa Engracia, number 37, in Madrid. This was conducted by its editor Ismael Fuente. To open the interview and to describe the environment and ambiance of Degrelle's residence, Fuente began:

*IF: His house is an entire museum, with display cabinets with artifacts from the Roman period exquisitely cared for, religious carvings of the sixteenth and seventeenth centuries, priceless paintings, unique coins, antiques of all kinds, period furniture, and Persian rugs. It is adorned everywhere with Nazi symbols.*

*LD: Back in the day, these things cost next to nothing. When I had recovered from the last of my war wounds, already in Spain, I made my way to Santiago from Roncesvalles, and I would buy things in the villages. In Andalusia, too, many things were given to me by the rural folk in those poor villages, because as you know, I am actually Andalusian...*

*IF: On the walls of his impressive office hang the flags of the companies of the Waffen SS Division he commanded as a general, and the two flags of the Belgian Rexist Movement (fascist) that he founded before the Second World War. On a small copper plate, placed on top of a small chest also made of hardwood, the great Ritterkreutz medal can be seen.*

*He apparently does not enjoy police protection. The passage is open until the eighth floor of the estate. He himself opened the door to me, although the appointment was agreed upon. During the three-and-a-half-hour talk, the house remains silent and apparently uninhabited. Léon Degrelle walks around his office throughout the conversation. He speaks with compelling power and speed and carries the weight of the conversation because he hardly stops talking.*

*LD: [...] To us, the survivors of the European crusade against Soviet communism, the veterans of the Eastern Front, torn by wounds, overwhelmed by mourning, consumed by sorrows, what rights are still left to us.*

On fascism Degrelle specified, "I do not believe in that word. I repudiate it. I speak of National Socialism because it is a global concept. Fascism is a strictly Italian concept."

Fuente commented that Degrelle had hired a major American multinational publishing house to publish his memoirs. They would be fourteen volumes, fourteen videocassettes, and fourteen films. He had to deliver a book every four months.

He also commented, "He writes by hand with a black felt-tip pen, in large ring notebooks, which he deposits one on top of the other until they are full. He tells me, 'The pulse of the hand is what best reflects inspiration.'"

Degrelle remarked, "I admired Serrano Suñer. Then, in the subsequent forty-five years, I had relationships of all kinds, with people like Girón, Dr. Marañón, Ridruejo, Laín Entralgo, Rof Carballo, Cossío, Sopeña, de la Serna, Mayalde,

Carrero Blanco, etc." To the last two, he gave a valuable picture to each. He was a friend of Fraga and even more so of Blas Piñar.

At that time, in relation to his death, he said, "It does not matter whether it has already been decided where I will be buried (at his Fuengirola estate called La Cabaña) or what they will put on my tomb (a gigantic stone lion I found many years ago at the door of a bar on a provincial road in Seville)…"

## Pilar Cernuda Interviews Him for *Interviú*

On January 30th, 1983, the fiftieth anniversary of Adolf Hitler's rise to power was celebrated. Coinciding with this anniversary, the Madrid newspaper *Diario 16* published a lengthy report by Mark Williams, full of resentment and spewing hatred in every adjective and epithet he could use. It included, in addition to the usual defamations, historical inaccuracies.

The half-century that had passed since that historic event made Léon Degrelle even more relevant because once again a Belgian left-wing MP insisted on his extradition. Belgian Minister of Justice Jean Gol, who happened to be Jewish, was obligated to explain, once again, to the country that extradition was legally unfeasible due to Degrelle's acquisition of Spanish nationality.

A spokesman for the Belgian Ministry of Justice on that occasion stated:

> *Léon Degrelle was sentenced to death in Belgium. He had taken refuge in Spain and his extradition was requested on several occasions. These petitions led to some conflicts before the Spanish Minister for Foreign Affairs, a friend of Degrelle.*
>
> *After one of these conflicts, the Belgian Ambassador to Spain was recalled home for consultations. The Spanish government rejected the extradition every time. When he was sentenced to death, for collaboration with the enemy, Degrelle was deprived of his Belgian nationality. Upon becoming stateless, he applied for Spanish nationality, which was granted to him immediately. At present, the prescription of his sentencing makes it impossible to continue pursuing Degrelle.*
>
> *In Belgium, the dissemination and sale of his books, like others who have committed "uncivic" behavior, continues to be prohibited. It is clear that in our country he is still regarded as persona non grata.*

An exclusive new interview titled "León Degrelle Speaks, the Belgian Nazi Refugee in Spain," was conducted on February 16th, 1983. It was published, with great fanfare, in issue three hundred fifty-four of the weekly sensationalist *Interviú*, on

February 23rd. The interview was conducted by journalist Pilar Cernuda, who, as we pointed out, was Degrelle's very own goddaughter.

The interview took place at his home in Madrid "with a Spanish table and with the flags of the Eastern Front as the only decorations on the walls," which gave Degrelle an opportunity to add, "A journalist has come here saying that I live surrounded by Nazi symbols, but I do not have any. They do not know what the Cross of St. Andrew is."[129]

When Cernuda asked him, "Are you a normal Spanish citizen?" Degrelle replied:

> *Yes, a Spanish citizen. I even went to the Congress of Socialists, the twenty-eighth Congress, when Felipe González resigned. I went there accompanied by one of my sons-in-law, who is a socialist and was a delegate, who walked there wearing a huge red carnation. I have been to many meetings with Felipe González, Fraga and Carrillo, and Piñar…I have been everywhere.*

After a review of the main historical issues, and some international current events, Cernuda closed the interview by saying:

> *Degrelle lives quietly in Madrid, surrounded by his books, his papers, his documents. A lot of journalists of all nationalities pass through his home. An American channel has just made a series about his life. French television has just broadcast a program about his life. TVE produced a program for the "In Depth" segment, although it was never broadcast. It was made in two parts, highlighting the special characteristics of Degrelle's personality, who speaks on and on, telling fascinating stories about the protagonists of history. He constantly writes articles, books, collects data, researches and studies…*

## La Clave

On March 4th, 1983, on the Spanish television program *La Clave* (The Key), hosted by the well-known journalist José Luis Balbín, one of the guest commentators was Léon Degrelle.

The program was about "war crimes." In addition to Léon Degrelle, the following participants made an appearance: the journalist and lawyer Miguel Ángel

---

[129] Degrelle is probably referring to Ismael Fuente who had interviewed him for *El País* in December 1982.

García Brera; Michel Cojot Goldberg, from the Association of Children of Deported Jews of France; Mark Raginsky, assistant to the Attorney General of the USSR and Soviet prosecutor in the Nuremberg Trial; Francisco Muñoz Conde, professor of criminal law, and the rowdy, leftist troublemaker José María Mohedano, President of the Association for Human Rights in Spain, who was married to a Jew.

On March 15th, journalist Javier M. González interviewed Degrelle. The interview was conducted as a result of the publication of Mark Raginsky's earlier interview during the debate on the La Clave television program several days before.

Degrelle refuted the falsehoods of the communist prosecutor and emphasized, while vehemently gesticulating, that the Russians committed great atrocities and continued to do so, "so if there are trials, let them be for everyone," and he added, "the least the Russians can do is keep quiet."

## A Letter of Reply

On March 7th, 1983, Degrelle had to address a new slander against him. He sent a "Letter to the Director" of the newspaper *El País*, which read:

*Despite my desire not to waste time in controversies, I have to protest against an article that your newspaper published on Saturday, March 4th, 1983, with the title "Degrelle, More Criminal than Barbie, According to Victor Alexandrov."*

*Quoting this man, whom I do not know, El País reproduces the following statement:*

*"In Estonia, he [Léon Degrelle] managed to hang underage minors who were favorable to Allied forces, hanging them light posts."*

*How can a newspaper as serious as El País reproduce such grave and gruesome statements without checking anything?*

*According to your newspaper, this Alexandrov added, "There are witnesses of all this." Has El País seen this testimony?*

*It clearly has not, and for a very simple reason: it does not exist, and it cannot exist. I have not hanged anyone, neither minors nor adults, in any country, nor did I see anyone hanged in Estonia. I did not even see a light post!*

*The day his book comes out, I will sue this Alexandrov in court to make him answer for his speculations.*

*How has El País, the best made newspaper in Spain, been able to carelessly reproduce such senseless extravagances?*

*You, Mr. Director, speak frequently and with emphasis on human rights. That is well enough, but what are you doing about a man's right to honor, the most important of human rights?*

*Do you think that one can, in good conscience, trample the honor of a man without having the slightest proof of the veracity of these wild accusations?*

*I have the right to see my life as a soldier and my opinions respected. I have daughters. I have ten grandchildren in Madrid. Does it seem right to you that they should read that their grandfather is a criminal? Is this not a total lack of justice, correctness, and prudence?*

*I am one of the few military leaders that the Soviets did not include in their list of war criminals. In Estonia, as in any corner of Russia, I always protected the civilian population, who suffered and were defenseless.*

*Neither did the smallest incident ever occur in my military sector in four years. That is right. This Alexandrov, for whom the newspaper El País has become a spokesman, seeks nothing more than sensationalism. How did El País not ask this gentleman to provide some evidence?*

*Why not organize a debate in Madrid between Mr. Victor Alexandrov and me, about his dossier of supposed hangings which El País has just spoken about? Henceforth, I agree to such a public debate.*

*Léon Degrelle*

## Hitler's Fake Secret Diaries

Two months after the interview with Pilar Cernuda for the weekly *Interviú*, the Parisian weekly *Présent* published some statements by Degrelle collected by journalist Hugues Kéraly on Wednesday, April 27th, 1983. Kéraly spent nine hours in pleasant conversation with Degrelle, from which he extracted many of his views and insights on the issues discussed.

In 1983, a piece of sensational news was published in all the media, marking an unprecedented finding over the last forty years. Sixty handwritten booklets, bound in black, quietly resided inside an armored steel chest, left haphazardly in a haystack in East Germany. In the chaos of the end of the war, according to this unusual story, the plane carrying Hitler's secret diaries crashed along the road to Brtsne.[130] The sole survivor dragged the chest with Hitler's papers—dated from 1932 to 1945—into a nearby country house. The German weekly *Stern* published the arcane secrets of those manuscripts. A media storm exploded. Historians and scientists were

---

[130] Most retellings of this story place the event at Heidenholz forest, not Brstne.

divided. Was it a fraud or would they have to revise history? With only a partial reproduction of Hitler's supposed handwritten diaries, an English weekly offered an amount equivalent to eighty million pesetas, a fortune at that time, to acquire the rights to publication. An American editor was willing to pay half a million dollars if experts certified that they were genuine. There was a wave of opinions from graphologists and laser analysts. Wild speculation was fully unleashed in every form.

On Monday, May 2nd, 1983, León Degrelle stated his position on the sensational news with a full page in the Malaga daily *Sur*, saying, "I think Hitler's secret diaries are fake. There is too much of it for a man who tended to communicate through dictation instead of writing."

On the porch of La Cabaña at 5:00 p.m., reporter Luis Torres held an interview with Léon, from which we have the following paragraphs:

> LT: *A chalet without exterior showiness, manicured lawns, bougainvilleas, red geraniums, cat claws, and spring rose bushes. Léon is accompanied by Heliodoro Pomar, an Italian nuclear engineer. His first statements are:*
>
> LD: *I believe that the authenticity of Hitler's diaries, published by the German magazine* Stern, *is unlikely, although not impossible. These writings are too extensive for a single man whose time was fully occupied; he hardly had any time. Now, to falsify six thousand pages, a total of sixty volumes, you need a team of people who are experts on the time period, on the atmosphere then, in detail, and, by the way, who command the same level of Hitler's good German. Also, the punctuated changes over the course of time, now that is an incredible, phenomenal job. Who could be interested in all that? Jews? No. Although they have always dominated the media and have fabricated many other books, they appear in the diaries under a new light that in no way benefits them. Hitler is moderate with them in his judgments, and the Jew has profited from these famous six million dead. His hatred never calms down. It comes from the Bible.*

Torres then asked Degrelle, "What profession appears on your identity card?" Degrelle answered, "Writer. Like the Führer."

Time proved Degrelle right. The *Hitler Diary* was a gross forgery. He had already qualified it in one of his answers during the two-hour long interview:

> *If we are talking about counterfeits, let us start with the famous memoirs of Eva Braun, Hitler's companion, who suddenly writes: "This morning we took a long trip. I was very afraid because Adolf was driving one hundred miles per hour." That is a*

*fat lie. Hitler never drove a car. Never in his life. Here is another: the famous diary of the Dutch girl Anne Frank; fifty million copies sold. With such a tear-jerker, in Spain there would not be a drought. Well, after some years, an examination of the ink with which the manuscript was written shows us that it is false. A good part was written in French Bic ink, which did not exist during the war since it was not invented until 1950.*[131]

## The Law of Silence

In 1984, the Belgian authorities were still determined that Léon Degrelle should end his days without ever seeing Belgium again. Convinced at last by their failed repatriation plans and frustrated thirst for revenge, they renewed the prohibition against his possible return to Belgium, which expired that year. A decade after the Ministerial Order was signed, approving the first ban to his returning to his country, the *Official Gazette* reiterated the Order of the Belgian Ministry of Justice renewing his status as *persona non grata*. Another of the laws in Belgium levied against Léon was the "law of silence," stipulating neither his books, articles, messages, nor his images could be disseminated in his homeland.

The Ministerial Order even reproduced a list of some of the names used in Spain by Degrelle since 1945: Juan García Álvarez, José Sánchez, Juan de la Carlina, Juan Sanchís, León José de Ramírez Reina, Juan Martínez, Leo Negrelli, Jesus Palacios, Enrique Durán, Luciano Demeuré, Pepe, etc.

## Remarriage

In June 1984, Léon Degrelle gave an interview to his good friend Theodor V. Soucek for the German monthly magazine *Nation Europa,* published in Coburg, which appeared under the title "*Sozialisten, Kommunisten und Europa.*"[132]

---

[131] Degrelle is referring to the report that parts of the "original diary" appear to have been written in Bic ball-point ink, which had not been invented until after the war. The Anne Frank House, a museum and organization devoted to the book and the Frank story, claims that the ball-point "myth" is based on loose leaves written by a researcher whose notes were placed among the pages of the diary. In 2015, the Anne Frank House/The Anne Frank Foundation added Anne's father, Otto Frank, who died in 1980, to the work as co-author to avoid the copyright's expiration (the diary would have been 70 years old at that point and would have entered public domain; by adding Otto Frank, it would extend the copyright enjoyed by The Anne Frank Foundation to 2050). Controversy and questions of authenticity still surround the diary.

[132] [German for socialists, communists and Europe.]

On June 15th, 1984, Léon Degrelle was seventy-eight years old, and he was celebrating his new marriage to the second great love of his life, Doña Juana "Jeanne" Brevet, widow of the French writer Henry Charboneau, member of the French Royal Academy. Juana Brevet was sixty-one years old. She was a refined and intelligent lady, of a traditional and fervently Catholic background. She had worked closely with Léon in editing his literary and historical writings for many years. Both were perfectly attuned to one another and imbued with an everlasting love.

The ceremony was simple, discreet, and took place in the strictest intimacy. León José Ramírez Reina and Juana Brevet exchanged their vows of love and fidelity until death. Two close friends were present as witnesses to the ceremony. One was Mariano Sánchez Covisa, a volunteer of the glorious Blue Division, a fellow combatant on the Eastern Front, a beloved friend and an exemplary Falangista. He later died on a pilgrimage to Santiago when he saw Monte del Gozo, and in the remoteness of the Galician countryside he could make out the pinnacles of the Compostelan Cathedral. Degrelle considered him a "great friend and comrade, the sincerest of Spaniards," and felt a "sincere and profound affection" for him. The other witness on that great day was Miguel Baillo, a good and noble comrade from the province of Ciudad Real, an inseparable friend of Sánchez Covisa.

## The Visit of Chilean Ambassador Miguel Serrano

Another of Léon's great friends who visited him in 1984 was Chilean diplomat Miguel Serrano, a distinguished writer of esoteric Hitlerism. Miguel Serrano was a native of Santiago in Chile, where he was born in 1917. In 1947, he made a trip to Antarctica in search of secrets under the ice, the oases of temperate waters, and the southern entrance of the hollow earth. The Chilean Army named a mountain after him. He was appointed Chilean Ambassador to India in 1953, establishing a personal friendship with Nehru, Indira Gandhi, and the Dalai Lama, and he remained in that post at the head of the diplomatic mission until 1962. He was then appointed Ambassador to Yugoslavia, with accreditation to Romania and Bulgaria. In 1964, he presented his credentials to Austria as Ambassador of Chile, where he remained until 1970, having also occupied the post of Ambassador to the International Atomic Energy Agency and to the United Nations Industrial Development Agency while in Vienna. He was a member of the "Hermetic Circle," which Carl G. Jung and Hermann Hesse were a part of as well, and with whom he lived for ten years at Casa

Camuzzi in Motagnola, Switzerland.[133] He shared a friendship with Ezra Pound, in whose honor he raised a monument in Medinacelli in the Soria province of Spain.

## Interview with the Magazine *L'Histoire Insolite*

In January 1985, Léon Degrelle gave an interview to the magazine *L'Histoire Insolite*[134] in which it was reported:

> *Léon Degrelle, the last great military and political chief of the Third Reich, has agreed to answer L'Histoire Insolite's questions about his role in the course of the Ardennes offensive in December 1944. This is an impressive historical document that must be appreciated considering the personality of the interviewee, who, although his statements may be surprising, is already an integral part of the history of our century.*
>
> *L'Histoire Insolite: Léon Degrelle, what was your participation in the Ardennes offensive?*
>
> *LD: I was in the Ardennes as the future head of the West. For me, the big issue was this, the West. I had moved from the Belgian theater to the Bourguignon theater, as it was the only one available for me to be near Hitler. Not a single Frenchman had been able to achieve this. For the unfortunate Laval, Pétain was a second Hindenburg disaster, not to mention Doriot.[135]*
>
> *Hitler had recognized me as "Volksführer" (people's leader) with full political, civil, and military rights, in all the regions liberated from the Allied presence, and not only in Belgium, but also in France! In short, I was chief and commander of all the armies that were on the ground there. By no means did Hitler want these people dominated by Germans. He had thus rejected that by giving me a mandate.*
>
> *L'Histoire Insolite: Where were you during the offensive?*
>
> *LD: I arrived on Christmas Eve in a small German village near the Belgian border, in Sepp Dietrich's sector. He was one of the great leaders of the operation, and he accommodated me at his headquarters. The next day I went to Mass. For the first time the sky was clear. What would have helped the Germans a lot, however, would have been an overcast sky so that American and English aviation could not*

---

[133] The exact dates of Miguel Serrano's time here are unclear.

[134] [French for *Unusual History*.]

[135] Jaques Doriot was a French politician and eventually a strong supporter of German fascism prior to the Second World War. During the war, he spent some time in Vichy, France, and later served in a French unit on the Eastern Front for Germany.

*have operated while the Luftwaffe did its job. The Wehrmacht troops marched along the roads, crossing almost undefended land, with nothing in the clear sky above. Well, that morning, while I was attending Mass, I saw planes flying over civilian positions; it was a hideous carnage. I had guessed what would happen.*

*Later, I entered Belgium and saw the city of Stavelot blow up.*

*Fortunately, if I had not run out of gas, I would have found myself under those bombs. We stayed there for a week in the midst of an extraordinarily friendly population. Along all roads you could still see a large "REX" painted on the walls, dating back to my 1936 campaign. At the new year, I organized a party with all the people of the region. We celebrated with absolute fraternity, and there were no brawls. At the Front, the Germans were increasingly cornered by the American counteroffensive.*

*L'Histoire Insolite: What, in your opinion, was Hitler's role in the conception of the offensive?*

*LD: In September 1944, I was summoned by Hitler to be awarded the Oak Leaves; he sent me his plane on the Estonian front, where the battle had just ended. I spent a week with him. It was there that I first heard the news of an offensive in the West in September 1944.*

*The defeat of the West was hardly accomplished, English troops were beginning to enter Brussels, and Hitler told me, "Léon, do not despair, in three months, you will recover your homeland." I found this to be so extraordinary that I could not believe it. It seemed unthinkable. Only a military genius could rebuild a significant army, and he did so with divisions that had been annihilated in France, namely the "Hitlerjugend" (Hitler Youth).*

*The history of the Ardennes, like all the great German victories during the war, was only due to Hitler; it was in the military field where his genius was most clearly seen. Take any successful operation; he was always a part of its concept and planning.*

*L'Histoire Insolite: What was the reaction of the Belgians, according to how you see it?*

*LD: When the Belgian government found out about my presence on the front, it quickly sentenced me to death and then chartered two planes to prepare for the eventual flight to London. In prison, the guards rushed over to our people, especially my sisters, to ask them to sign a paper to attest that they had been well treated.*

*L'Histoire Insolite: What is your overall judgment of the operation?*

*LD: This offensive, which lasted for a week, was achievable, not only because Hitler had assembled a formidable shock force, but also because the Americans we were facing had been a nonentity. I can still see the train cars with open doors, enemy troops fleeing; no one had resisted, except for a handful of people who appeared dead in the snow. The Americans evacuated so precipitously and with so much haste that when the first troops arrived in Laroche, a small town next to the Ourthe River (a place that is dear to me, as my mother was born there) within twenty-four hours, the G.I.s had fled leaving the bridge intact. The U.S. Air Force then killed two hundred people in town who had not been able to reach the bridge!*

*Everywhere, German troops swooped in and managed to reach the Meuse River. They were only stopped a few kilometers from Dinant in Celles for lack of fuel. Without this stroke of luck for the Allies, the battle could have been won and the fate of Europe would certainly have changed.*

## Signature and Rubric

In Paris, in 1985, publisher Jean Picollec published the text of various interviews compiled for French Television by Jean-Michel Charlier, with the title *Léon Degrelle: Persiste et Signe* (the following year the Spanish version was released as *León Degrelle, Firma y Rubrica*, translated by José Ignacio San Martín)[136]. It was a book that illustrated the exemplary and edifying life of this legendary hero of the twentieth century in great detail. In a captivating way, it gave fine granularity to his thoughts, experiences, emotions, and dreams.

Back in 1977, French Television filmed a movie over two hours long on the life of Léon entitled *Autoportrait d'un Fasciste* (*Self-Portrait of a Fascist*) for one of the most famous programs in France, "Les Dossiers Noirs," where, among others, the Kennedys had also appeared. The program director J.M. Charlier came to Spain to interview Léon. He spoke with him at his home for ten days and returned to Paris with a plethora of information from Degrelle.

In Belgium, the broadcast of the documentary on Gala television produced a shocking effect among the corrupt political class. They planned a special, restricted viewing session in one of the halls of Commercial Center forty-four in Brussels, attended by high magistrates and representatives of the Ministries of Justice and the Interior. The cartoonist, Paul Jamin caricatured this political gathering in a parody cartoon sketch.

From his statements in the film, a full explanation was published about how they asked all the "Allied" countries, including even Israel and the Soviets, for their

---

[136] [French for *Léon Degrelle: Persists and Signs*. The Spanish version translated it as *Léon Degrelle: Signs and Initials*.]

lists of war criminals, and had concluded that the name Degrelle did not appear on any of the lists. No one brought allegations, not even the Belgians. Thus, the directors at French Television found that Léon had no direct or indirect participation in anything related to the so-called "war crimes." He was a soldier, a warrior from Europe and nothing else.

In the prologue to the book, Charlier pointed out that he asked for the lists of war criminals from various countries to verify what Degrelle had sworn to him: that he had never been wanted as a war criminal. Charlier stated literally, "Your name is not on any of the lists." Even the former Minister of Justice of the Belgian Government in London during the war, Antoine Delfosse, would later confirm to Charlier in front of the cameras on French Television: "Degrelle was never a war criminal."

The Parisian weekly *Rivarol* commented on the book, saying, "It is explosive, a tremendous historical document, the history of a life, the history of a man, and also of a loyalty; an authentic, complete, and living document," and, "What most impresses the reader about Degrelle is the incredible vitality of this man who gambled with death a hundred times."

For its part, the Parisian magazine *Panorama* referred to the book as showing "a tumultuous existence, which emanates a vital faith and tension that inspire respect," where:

> *Degrelle appears as one of the last "condottieri"*[137] *in Europe. A general at age thirty-eight and holding the highest number of German war decorations...he was not just an exceptional soldier. He was also a politician of those who stood their ground until the death.*

The Parisian *Le Quotidien*, also referring to the book, made the following witty comment: "A man too big for that small country...their allegations deserve to be heard."

In Spain, on July 31st, 1986, in the literary section of the newspaper *El Alcázar*, Cratés de Madrid wrote an extensive article entitled "*Futuribles y Premociones*"[138] in which he analyzed the book:

> *It is not literary, but historical, and I point out the possibility that, above all, it may be political. This kind of spoken autobiography is, historically, a*

---

[137] [Italian for leaders, warlords, or commanders.]
[138] [Spanish for "Prospects and Forecasts."]

*transcendental book, precisely because it accurately collects a story, that of the "Rexist" Movement, which was not, however, carefully forgotten or intentionally forgotten, any less interesting.*

De Madrid analyzed the trajectory of the Rexist Movement and concluded his commentary and critique by saying: "The possibility that Rex, now, and not only in Belgium, could be a movement of unity and respect around a new political formula, is the best lesson in this book, with all its historical and human interest. Precautions about possible premonitions should be understood."

On October 24th, 1986, Léon dedicated a copy of the book to me, saying, "To my great friend and comrade…"

He signed a publishing contract with Art et Histoire d'Europe in Paris, to narrate twenty volumes under the general heading of *The Century of Hitler, the European History of the Twentieth Century*, in which he so prominently acted as a protagonist. The first of the series that was published was *Le Traquenard de Sarajevo* (*The Sarajevo Trap*), followed by *Le Pseudo-Guerre du Groit 1914-1918* (*The False Legal War 1914-1918*), *Les Tricheurs de Versailles* (*The Cheats of Versailles*), and *Hitler Démocrate* (*Hitler Democrat*).

## Degrelle Testifies: An Interview in the Parisian Magazine *Rivarol*

The French weekly *Rivarol* published, in 1985, an extensive and in-depth interview with the title "*Degrelle Témoigne*,"[139] which addressed historical issues and various commentaries on current politics which were being debated in Europe at that time. The interview was also reproduced in the seventh issue of the magazine *Contact* in July of that year.

The interview went as follows:

> *Rivarol: April 30th, 1985, marks the fortieth anniversary of Hitler's death. What reflections does this date inspire in you?*
>
> *LD: I knew Hitler well. The image of him that I hold, understand this well, is very different from the grotesque caricature that is painted of him since his death. It is very easy to insult the mortal remains of a defeated man. What interests me is the truth.*

---

[139] [French for "Degrelle Bears Witness."]

A statesman who was backed by a hundred million enthusiastic men and women is not a monster; millions of young people died for the ideal he embodied. Apparently inflexible, Hitler was generous. Also, however incredible it may seem to those who hate him, to those who actually met him, he seemed to have a great heart and a good sense of humor. He was endowed with an iron will, he was the catalyst for a prodigious array of energy.

National Socialism is, with Marxism, one of the two great revolutions of the twentieth century. A real revolution took place in Germany, with the establishment of institutions in the service of the nation. Hitler, from 1933, sought to unify his people and to root out the aberration of class struggle. He provided work again to the six million unemployed. Under Hitler, German workers enjoyed a standard of living hitherto unknown. Each could acquire a house, thanks to a system of very original credits, some to promote the birth policy, amortizations were according to the number of children, etc. Workers benefited from paid vacations, long before the measures of the Front Populaire[140] …Hitler's political revolution was adapted to a social revolution, and this was what capitalists and Marxists could not admit! The doctrine of National Socialism preached class reconciliation, ending with the oppression of both capital and communist trade unions.

Rivarol: Is that what prompted you to align with the Third Reich?

LD: The revolution that was realized in Germany announced another one: the revolution in Europe. Hitler's vision was long term and far-sighted. He was a Europeanist, as of 1941. He confided to me that after the war he would change the name of Berlin so that there would be no misconceptions about it. This formidable transformation was due to the brotherhood of European combatants. This giant enterprise, with which we were associated, was tragically interrupted by the decapitation of Europe. Yes, April 30th, 1945, was for us, the Waffen SS, a day of pain, the death of a great hope. Our victory would have meant the end of communism and the independence of Europe regarding the United States. Forty years later, the countries of Europe are torn apart into small quarrels, petty things, operations caused by ridiculous politicians.

Rivarol: This April 30th, did not it not mark the end of a Europe of concentration camps as well?

---

[140] The *Front Populaire* was a coalition of communist and republican parties in France during the inter-war period. They won legislative elections in 1936 and formed a government made up entirely of republican and communist ministers, led by Jew Léon Blum. Conservatives still held a majority in the French senate. The *Front Populaire* introduced generous increases in wages and workers' rights and benefits, although they petered out under a stagnant economy and wild price increases.

LD: *We would be made to believe that the Third Reich was an inhuman machine destined to make farm animals of deportees just to suit its sadistic instincts. This would be comical if it had not led to an abominable revenge, cynically baptized as the "Nuremberg Trial." There, the victors assumed the right to treat the defeated as "war criminals," and to kill them without mercy, appointing themselves as judges. The trial made it possible to camouflage the terrible massacres committed by the Allies which could not be justified militarily! All those cities destroyed, summary executions, torture...those atrocities went unpunished! The thousands of Polish officers liquidated by the Soviets in Katyn, an ignoble act that they originally tried to attribute to Germany. The hundreds of thousands of defenseless women and children massacred in Dresden and Hiroshima![141] These cruel Allied abominations strangely escaped the categories of war crimes and crimes against humanity.*

Rivarol: *You do recognize that this was a relentless war...*

LD: *The forces of the Third Reich certainly contained among its ranks some criminals, but no more than the others! If we want to be objective, we must be against any violence of this kind. My soldiers and I never committed any war crime whatsoever. Not even the Soviets listed anyone from our unit on a single list of "war criminals." Despite this, for forty years now they have been pounding our ears with the inexhaustible theme of "Nazi barbarism"...*

*It will do, at last, to recognize that the victors of 1945 have hanged, tortured, and imprisoned people simply for their opinions. The blindness or calculations of these "holocaust" sectarians fortunately have not prevented the former camp internee Paul Rassinier, Professor Faurisson, the American historian Butz, and so many others from denouncing the fraud. The living conditions in the concentration camps were certainly very difficult, especially at the end of the war, mainly because of Allied bombing, typhus, and restrictions. We do well to remember, coincidently, that today in 1985, Soviet concentration camps are still in operation. Which head of state is bothered enough by this to throw it in Gorbachev's face? How many "democrats," in the name of human rights, would surely scoff at the law if retroactive laws were enacted, which is a sinister farce at minimum? These abject comedies, this hypocrisy cannot last long. In 1983, I participated in a four-hour long Spanish television program, where I debated with the Soviet deputy prosecutor from Nuremberg. My participation stunned the prosecutor. The result? Within a month,*

---

[141] The firebombing of Dresden and other civilian targets in German cities was very poorly known or discussed in English language sources until David Irving's breakthrough publication *Apocalypse 1945: The Destruction of Dresden*, 1963, published by William Kimber & Co. Ltd. Current copyright is held by Parforce UK Ltd., 1995 and 2007. Many argue that it is one of the least discussed Allied war crimes to date.

*two hundred interviews with me were requested and the New York Times published a six-column article!*

*Rivarol: The image that people have of you, in general, is that of a brilliant speaker. Is oratory talent indispensable to a political man?*

*LD: The true political man is a man of action, who lives according to his ideal. It is not about being able to make a career and settle into whatever circumstances, or to be able to obtain some ministerial post or another. One cannot at the same time be attached to material matters and lead the destiny of a country. Politics must be devoted to the realization of a great work.*

*A political man must be a real leader; there can be no question of yielding. Working class men, those who perform rough tasks, are able to perceive courage and sincerity. That is why it is necessary to always be present. It was the communists who gave me my launch; when the communists gathered an assembly to discuss issues at the beginning of our struggle in Belgium, it was very important to attend these assemblies to affirm everywhere the presence of our movement. In this way I won over numerous supporters. It is necessary, without interruption, to dare to face danger if one wants to be victorious. In Searing, for example, on September 15th, 1936, I tried to speak at a workers' commune, but the socialist-communist municipal government wanted to ban me from speaking; all the roads were cut off by guard barriers. They forgot about the river! So it was from a boat that was equipped with powerful megaphone equipment that I was able to address ten thousand workers. The Marxist bosses rushed us and three of my comrades were killed, but we did not give in to their terror: we won! We had won the hearts of the workers.*

*Rivarol: How do you perceive the beginning of the third millennium?*

*LD: With pessimism. Europe, if she wants to get out of her decadence, needs true statesmen and not political hacks who betray our people. Europe will likewise remain disabled for a long time so long as her politicians only worry about butter, meat, or wine. Now more than ever, strong men, that is, men who have Europe's best interests at heart, will be needed, given that the peoples of Europe are going to be invaded by immigrant peoples who are foreign to her civilization and genius. In this regard, Jean Raspail's book, The Camp of Saints, seems to me prophetic. It is urgent for people who are tragically sleeping to wake up. History has shown, countless times, that rejection of combat in a just cause leads to disappearance.*

*Rivarol: The books you have published are sold out. Do you have any new projects?*

*LD: Well, certainly, young people show a lot of interest in the activities we carry out. This indicates, on the other hand, with sufficient evidence, that they do* not always take seriously the slander that pours out every day on the radio, on television, or in the press.

At the moment, I am working on a series of at least twelve volumes whose central theme will be "The Century of Hitler." The century I am writing about begins with the First World War, called "Born at Versailles." The first three volumes are dedicated to the advent of Hitler and his rise to power. Here I am interested in his political life: "Democratic Hitler"—Hitler, do not forget it, came to power democratically through his resounding victory at the polls—"Hitler the German Unifier"; "Hitler the Great Reich's Architect"; "Hitler and Danzig." Hitler was also a military genius, which I will deal with carefully. I will also examine, in detail, the relations between Hitler and the French, Churchill, Stalin, Mussolini, Roosevelt...A study of this magnitude would be incomplete if it did not address the "dust storm" of "Hitler and the Concentration Camps." It is for that reason that this large work will handle themes such as "Hitler, the Jews, the gassing, the ovens" and "Hitler and His SS." Finally, I will examine the religious question about Hitler in one volume entitled "Hitler and God."

The publication's English language edition is already assured in the United States. I would very much like a French publisher to publish these books as well. The time has come to restore the truth too long disguised. Readers will judge. I have been a politician and a soldier, that is why the work is a synthesis of my personality.

*Rivarol:* You have continued your struggle in adversity; why this constant effort?

*LD:* Because it is necessary. When you have an ideal, the risks of combat cannot extinguish the inner flame. Abandoning the struggle is out of the question, even if one has the right to be pessimistic at certain times. A little forgotten journalist, eager for sensationalism, asked me in 1983 if I regretted anything. How can you regret having fought for an idea when it seems just and great to you? I believe in this example: the heroic battles that we waged forty years ago have been recorded in the memory of eternity. For it was not just a struggle of arms; it was, above all, for us, a struggle for civilization and the rise of man against subversion and decadence, the great integral duel of youth and greatness against old models and old chimeras.

## Was Bitterness and Hatred Their Currency? Simon Wiesenthal

The presence of Léon Degrelle on the lists of persons being persecuted by the Simon Wiesenthal Center in Los Angeles caused commotion among Belgian public opinion. The Belgian daily *Le Soir*, on July 10th, 1985, described the project announced by the president of the center, Rabbi Abraham Cooper, to allot a million dollars to the search for Léon Degrelle, who "lives in Madrid, where he apparently carries out regular neo-fascist activities." Belgian politicians were skeptical that Degrelle, now seventy-nine years old, would ever appear before the courts of his country after the expiration of his death sentence.

News of this was also echoed in Spanish media on July 13th, 1985. The newspaper *Diario 16* published on the cover of its Andalusia edition the terrible and threatening news, accompanied by a big photograph of Degrelle's face in the foreground, with the following title: "A Jewish Foundation Offers a Million Dollars for His Head."

Questioned by journalists about Jewish plans, Degrelle replied calmly that he was "not afraid of any Nazi-hunting. Why be afraid? During the war I was wounded a thousand times, I am 100 percent maimed, I have been through seventy-five close combat engagements and here I am very happy."

The campaign was unleashed with great intensity. Given free rein to execute sickly obsession, Rabbi Cooper took to the charge and made some statements that were reproduced on July 29th, 1985, in the Spanish magazine *Tiempo*. In a report entitled "Nazi Hunters Will Come to Spain to Capture Degrelle," he pointed his accusing finger, saying, "Léon Degrelle is guilty of promoting Nazi ideas among young people around the world. We are going to follow him closely and we will make him pay for this." The rabbi's sense of treachery was such that, in trying to "hunt" Degrelle, he was blinded to some facts. The special envoy of the magazine *Tiempo*, Juan Girón Roger, wrote an extensive piece on the matter. When Roger got in touch with Simon Wiesenthal, the killer of Axis survivors of the Second World War, who had his sinister downtown office in Vienna named after himself, the editor was cynically told by Wiesenthal that:

> *Belgium will not ask for the extradition of Degrelle and there is no reward for getting him. This is a rather theoretical question. For years, the Belgian government asked Franco to extradite him, and Franco refused. Then enough time passed, and the criminal sentence expired. There is no reward offered by Belgium or by us. Léon Degrelle is a war criminal, but in the end, he will get away with it and will not pay for his crimes.*

Roger wrote that Cooper did not seem to be of the same opinion, as he had already initiated actions to bring about the capture of Degrelle.

Rabbi Cooper stated bluntly:

*We are in contact with the Belgian government to see what legal means we can activate against Degrelle, and we are going to do the same with Spain. We know that there are Nazis in Spain and that this is a problem inherited from fascist Spain, not from the new democratic Spain. Degrelle lives peacefully in Spain in luxury and without having changed his Nazi positions. We will ask the Spanish government to annul Degrelle's asylum and make him leave the country. Several Jewish businessmen in the United States have earmarked a million dollars to capture Nazi war criminals, and a part will go towards the Degrelle case. If they bring him in dead, there will be no reward. That is why this is not so much a price on his head, as it is a stimulus for a fair trial and for justice to be done. He would be tried in Belgium, Federal Germany, or Israel, depending on the nature of the crimes committed. We are not seeking murder, but a criminal conviction. Degrelle corrupts young people with piety, racism, and fascism, and the curious thing is that he is not on the run, but free.*

Specifying his malevolent intentions, he added:

*In Federal Germany, there is no capital punishment, and the legal process is very democratic. For the capture of Degrelle, we have earmarked a sum of one hundred thousand dollars, which will be paid to whoever delivers him to one of the countries mentioned above. We are counting on the participation of Spanish authorities, of Spanish democracy.*

The threats and merciless words were tantamount to an official complaint against Léon Degrelle in the United States. The procedural machinery was started and, as Léon wrote, "They spent more than a million dollars for their lawyers' time, who had as many members as a soccer team to catch me. Better this way."

The contradictions and lies between Simon Wiesenthal and Rabbi Cooper were obvious, so much so that their extortions fooled no one.

Although no charges of war crimes were formally brought against Léon Degrelle, Cooper nonetheless made the following points:

*Degrelle claims that he is innocent of these charges, but if he belonged to the Waffen SS, I would not be surprised if a Belgian expert could provide evidence that he has committed violent crimes. The first goal is to ensure that he does not feel safe, in 1985, in a comfortable retirement. We need the help of democratic regimes to prevent the torch of fascism from continuing to spread to the youth.*

Despite all the time that had passed without a single piece of evidence against the absolute innocence of Léon Degrelle, this rabbi still harbored, in his limitless rancor and unjustified yearning for revenge, the hope that some "Belgian expert" would fabricate some kind of evidence to indict an innocent man forty years later. This was simply miserable, ignominious, and inhumane. Rabbi Abraham Cooper had put a price on Degrelle's head worth "sixteen million," and this was published as a piece of sensationalist news by *Tiempo.*

Roger recognized that Degrelle was not afraid of the possible "bounty hunters" that might get close to him at Costa del Sol and kidnap him. With serenity and balance, he said, "It is not worth taking any precautions. My brother, who was very cautious, was killed by someone with a gun in his pocket."

When asked about issues of a political nature, he replied:

*The National Socialist ideology is not dead. Its social policy is usable today because if they voted for Hitler once, it was because they lived a better life under him. Believe me, it hurts me not to be fifty years old, to know that I cannot initiate the conquest; instead, I find myself in exile.*

Regarding the question of genocide, which the cursed Jews so cunningly contrived and manipulated against him, his answer was categorical:

*No court in the world has ever condemned me on such an issue. No government has ever charged me for violent crime. Do you think that in 1941, with Belgium being an occupied country, we went to Russia to be able to talk face to face with the Germans about the Jews? Look, the Germans did not take Belgian Jews. I had nothing to do with that. Of course, since there are so many of them now, it is difficult to believe that they came out so alive from the crematorium furnaces. The problem with the Jews is that they always want to be the victims, eternally persecuted, so much so that, if they have no enemies, they invent them. Their persecution was not only in Germany, but also in Poland, where they were almost exterminated. As always, they wanted to form a state within another state.*

Roger found that Degrelle spent no less than fifteen hours a day writing at La Cabaña, producing a multitude of historical works commissioned by American publishers. In the mornings, Degrelle would place a rose on the lips of a bust of Aphrodite in the middle of his splendid garden. He used to walk around the city and receive visits.

Referring to the maneuvers that the Jews were making against him at that time, he replied:

> It is a game of Wiesenthal's madmen, and he is a very murky individual, of whom it is said that he was a Gestapo spy in the camps. They have taken the bones and even the teeth of Mengele... Where does their hate end! In my opinion, Dr. Mengele was a normal doctor and I doubt very much that gas chambers ever existed because two years ago there was a reward in the United States for whoever could provide proof of the gas chambers. It was fifty million dollars, and no one has collected it yet.

The latter reference referred to the amount offered by The Institute for Historical Review, founded in the United States in 1979.

In Degrelle's view, the recent campaign against him by international Jewry had but one cause:

> It is a money problem because, in order to pursue Dr. Mengele, Wiesenthal's adventurers took at least a million dollars out of the pockets of rich Jews in the U.S. They did not have to look for long, since it is now known that Mengele had been dead for three years. Surprised, those rich Jews want to know where the money went. Now they explain that the reward is to capture Degrelle.

Degrelle continued:

> If they return me to Belgium, they will achieve nothing. If they kill me, that will be proof that they cannot refute my ideas. No one in the world is demanding my handover. I live defenseless and I will continue doing so. They can get me kidnapped or killed, and it is clear that there is no shortage of candidates who would do this. Protecting myself serves no purpose because what counts is not simply survival, but rather living with faith and honor. Genio y figura hasta la sepultura,[142] as they say in Spain. Here I have no other activity except for writing.

The interview ended with these words:

---

[142] [Spanish that literally translates to "character and form up to the grave." Its meaning is more akin to "a leopard cannot change its spots."]

*I am neither a former Nazi, nor a neo-Nazi. I have only clear ideas as to how to implement a true democracy with authority and responsibility. This case with Wiesenthal is as if Julio Iglesias or Jaime de Mora were awarded the right to seek and capture conscientious objectors in Argentina, Bolivia, or Spain and then claim a humble grant of eight hundred twenty-five million from the Central Bank or from the Extremadura regional government to cover their expenses.*

### The Jewish Plot: Violeta Friedman versus Léon Degrelle

In mid-1985, the body of German physician Dr. Mengele was exhumed at Embu Cemetery in Brazil. At the request of Jewry, confirmation of Mengele's death was sought through DNA testing so that they might cease hunting him down. It was an odious and perfidious persecution that they had been carrying out and which the doctor had been subjected to for forty years.

Televisión Española, in an evening news program, interviewed Léon Degrelle who commented with surprise about, among other issues, the desecration of that tomb. He was critical of the sinister para-police activities of the paranoid Simon Wiesenthal Center. He once again reaffirmed, with honor and pride, the ideals for which he had fought and for which he was willing to continue to defend until death.

On July 17th, 1985, the newspaper *El País*, in its "Letters to the Editor" section, published a letter from the Jewess Violeta Friedman. In it she protested, with the arrogance of one who assumes the power to muzzle their neighbor, against the fact that Léon Degrelle used his legitimate freedom of expression and opinion on Spanish television.

Violeta Friedman was an agent of the Jewish Anti-Defamation League (ADL). She had been another wanderer, born in 1930 in Marghita, in the Transylvania region between Hungary and Romania, who was able to study and live quietly in Hungary throughout the war. Since the Jewish element in the rear were saboteurs of soldiers who bravely fought on the Front, in May 1944, when the fate of the war was practically sealed, and as a preventative measure, that element was detained in order to prevent the German Army from being stabbed in the back while they were fighting in retreat. Her family was regrouped and housed near the market of her hometown. Sometime later, with several others of her ethnic group, they were housed in the city of Oradea Mare. Later, they were gathered into a concentration camp, analogous to those in the United States or in France which set up camps to house citizens of enemy countries. It is clear that Violeta was obviously not gassed, although she did go through preventative disinfectant showers, like all prisoners did, for reasons of hygiene and public health. Her sister Eva, who resided with her, was placed in an aviation factory for labor. In the month of November, she was housed in the Hochwald area in better conditions. On January 20th, the communists took over the town, leaving her, safe and sound, in the enclosure.

In 1946 she went with her sister to live in Cluj, Romania; the following year she decided to move to Canada. She falsified personal records to do so, even changing her name to Alice Goldman, married to a certain A. Neufeld. Having become Alice Neufeld, although she also fraudulently used the name of Ibolya, she got married again in 1951 to a Hungarian Jew whom she met in Caracas, named Jancsi, although to camouflage himself, he appeared as Protestant in his documentation. They had two children, Riki (1954) and Patricia (1956). She divorced in 1963 and came to Madrid with her children, who at the first opportunity, left their mother to go to Canada to live with their father. Her life was irregular. She lived in Budapest, Hungary, and in other European cities. She was in psychiatric treatment as of 1973. She later began working for the nefarious ADL. She collaborated with the Jewish mafia, the infamous *B'nai B'rith* in Spain.

In her letter to *El País*, among other considerations of her own, Friedman said:

> *I find it outrageous that Televisión Española has granted time and prominence to Léon Degrelle, a former SS general, and the opportunity for him to declare his total loyalty to Hitler until death, his pride in his participation in Nazi activities and his sorrow for Hitler's defeat.*

Later, with a supine ignorance of history and manifest lack of knowledge and recklessness, manipulating facts and lying naturally, she dared to say:

> *I do not know the specific accusations against Léon Degrelle, but I do know what the functions of the Waffen SS were on the Eastern Front, where Degrelle said he had fought "with great pride." In the rear, the Waffen SS committed gigantic massacres, and I assume that he, in his capacity as a general, must have unceasingly given orders. Degrelle did not lie when he said he had not killed anyone; he just gave the orders.*
>
> *Despite everything, he has managed to live peacefully in Spain, with official protection and influential friends. I still remember his participation in a colloquium on television and his statements to a Madrid newspaper, where he said that the Jewish holocaust and the concentration camps and extermination camps were lies. You should ask the victims, not the executioners.*
>
> *Violeta Friedman, Madrid*

Friedman forgot, or completely missed the truth, that it was Léon Degrelle who was the victim of Jewish persecution.

## A Resounding Reply

On July 23rd, 1985, Léon published a rebuttal letter in *El País*:

*I am Léon Degrelle. It pains me to contradict a woman, whether or not she is Jewish. Mrs. Violeta Friedman (Violeta! What a beautiful name!) described me in her letter to El País on July 17th, 1985, as an executioner, ordering "gigantic massacres. In the rear, the Waffen SS committed gigantic massacres, and I assume that he, in his capacity as a general, must have unceasingly given orders. Degrelle did not lie when he said he had not killed anyone; he just gave the orders." I must answer that I never gave orders like those imagined by this lady's enthusiasm. I did not give them, nor did I ever have an occasion to give them. Firstly, I never fought in the rear; I did not miss any of my soldiers' fighting on the front lines. Secondly, I doubt very much that any Waffen SS unit has ever engaged in such "massacres." We, that is, a million volunteers in the Waffen SS, of whom six hundred thousand were non-German, had to assume the sole and very dangerous role of shock troops, always the first ones to open a breach in the offensive, or to contain Soviet breakouts. Thus, four hundred two thousand boys of the Waffen SS died: Belgian, French, Dutch, Norwegians, Danes, Hungarians, Croats, Romanians, and so on, and even Spaniards!*

*They did not have the same convictions as Mrs. Friedman, but they offered their lives in faith and courage for their ideal. I find it inelegant to treat them and their commanders as "criminals," when their only act was not to kill anyone in the rear, but to die, wrongly or rightly, to save their respective homelands and Europe from communism.*

*Nor can I let Mrs. Friedman claim that I said that "concentration camps were lies." That is false. I challenge her to reproduce a text of mine with such a statement. There were concentration camps in Germany, obviously, as there were under British control in France between 1939 and 1945. In the latter, some fifteen thousand Spanish "Reds" died, as El País has reported. Twice as many as in the German camps! Anyway, neither I nor any of my Belgian soldiers in the Waffen SS ever knew anything about such camps. Our only camp was the battlefield, where Jews were not often found. I saw one, just one in four years, in a valley of the Caucasus. I did not touch a hair on his head.*

*I do not fully understand why we have to feed endless hatred with ramblings. Are we going to poison the world for centuries? The Spaniards knew the horrors of Napoleon's troops. Do they constantly throw this in the face of the French? Among Spaniards themselves, are you going to forever label yourselves "criminals," left or right, depending on your location in the trenches between 1936 and 1939? What is worse is that the "crimes," such as those this kind lady Friedman has laid against me, are totally false.*

*I have no doubt of her sincerity. Forty years of blind controversy has wreaked havoc. Whenever you want, come and see me, I will gladly welcome you and convince you.*

*Léon Degrelle*
*Fuengirola, Malaga*

Friedman's rejoinder was reproduced in *El País* on July 26th. It was once again the same stereotyping and the same gibberish cooked up by the Jews after the Second World War in relation to Hitler. Thankfully, history's revisionist school is taking care to correct these false accusations with irrefutable arguments and evidence. What she was blaming him for was that he said, "I will feel united with Hitler until my death." This incomprehensible loyalty cannot be understood by those who have made a lucrative living in the history of betrayal, hypocrisy, or self-righteousness.

On July 29th, 1985, the magazine *Tiempo*, in its issue one hundred sixty-eight, published some statements from Léon Degrelle, which contained a free and truthful review of history on the question of the "holocaust." In these statements he questioned the exaggerations and manipulations by the Jews concerning this issue. The journalist asked whether there was anything that Degrelle regretted. His answer was clear and straightforward: "I regret only that Hitler lost the war."

## The Judicial Process

Violeta Friedman, as stated earlier, came from the small town of Marghita, located in Transylvania, which belonged to Hungary until 1920 and later was under Romanian control as a result of the Treaty of Trianon, although she always considered herself a Magyar Zionist. She was fourteen years old when the German Army took up positions in Hungary in March 1944. Her family was part of the fifth column that stabbed the regular army in the back during the campaign, which now was in outright retreat, and despite her fantasy of being in an "extermination camp," she lived freely dedicated to being an agent of international Zionism. In Spain, according to the experts, she worked closely with the Israeli secret services and had a friendship with the Israeli Ambassador, Shlomo Ben-Ami, and with the Jew Max Mazin, President of the Jewish-masonic B'nai B'rith in Spain, as well as with Alberto Benazuly Azulay.

In her memoirs, that she did not really write (the journalist Angeles Caso played the role of "black servant" and was paid to write and embellish the book), Friedman wrote the following:

> *Given that my financial straits did not allow me to embark on a long and costly legal battle, I thought I would turn to B'nai B'rith, which has about half a million members spread around the world. I spoke to the President of the Madrid area (now all of Spain), Max Mazin, about the resolution he had taken. I asked for his help. He considered it [the Degrelle case] very difficult in view of the legal vacuum in Spanish jurisprudence, but as I insisted so much, he took care of me and spoke to his lawyer, Jorge Trias Sagnier, who agreed to take charge of the matter. Since then, I could count on the valuable, total, and unconditional support of Max Mazin, and at all times I fully supported the entire B'nai B'rith.*

In order to initiate legal proceedings against Léon Degrelle, the pretext used was the revisionist statements made by Degrelle in 1985 on Televisión Española. Friedman also hoped to curtail freedom of expression without considering that this is enshrined in the Spanish Constitution. Moreover, she was trying to condemn, in her unbridled pride and limitless arrogance, someone who had differing opinions than those imposed by Zionism on debatable, historical events of the Second World War. She did this after expressly recognizing that Léon Degrelle had not committed any punishable act against the Jewish people in general or against any particular Jew, neither in Belgium nor during combat on the Eastern Front.

### The Media Duel

On September 16th, 1985, Léon Degrelle again wrote a letter to *El País* in response to the insults of those "unrepentant maniacs who love filthy rumors":

> *The open controversy in El País about my case has resulted in something positive.*
> 1) *No impostor dares to repeat this slander of "Degrelle, the war criminal." The reader Mrs. Friedman (letter from July 17th, 1985) entrenched herself in your newspaper in a distinctly withdrawn position when she acknowledges that she*

*knows nothing of my "crimes," but claims, without having the smallest reason for suspicion, that "as head of a division of the Waffen SS," I had to "give unceasing orders" for "gigantic massacres." Which ones? Where? On the moon, surely.*

Her second spontaneous collaborator (letter from July 31st, 1985), being more prudent, does not risk relapsing into such fantasies. This man "does not want to judge right and wrong." He does well, understanding that there is no trace of my responsibility of this sort. As he cannot wield anything against me, he has preferred to entertain himself with some digressions about the Waffen SS.

2) *This gentleman denies that the Waffen SS had brought together a million men, apart from some thirty-eight divisions, which would be wrong. Never in world military history has an army with thirty-eight divisions of volunteers been known, representing twice the number of Napoleon's Grand Armée. Thirty-eight divisions (they were mobilizing as many as fifty) corresponds roughly to seven hundred thousand men, but what her collaborator carefully ignores in his calculations are the four hundred two thousand combat casualties, which were replaced without delay by other volunteers. The famous Viking Division that was decimated in the course of the Battle of Cherkassy had to be replenished almost entirely in the spring of 1944. The same was true of the Hitlerjugend Division, almost wiped out during the Battle of Normandy (summer 1944), which did not prevent it from reappearing four months later, in December 1944, in the Ardennes offensive, with almost twenty thousand new volunteers.*

We too, the Walloons, lost three quarters of our troops, counting both the dead and wounded, during those months of heavy fighting in the Caucasus mountains in 1942. In 1944, two thirds of our troops were eliminated when we, along with the Viking Division, had to break out of the Soviet encirclement at Cherkassy. Not only were our units renewed to full strength immediately, but we reorganized from a battalion (1941) to a regiment (1942), then to a brigade (1943) and finally to a division (1944). Is this, curiously, in your esteemed reader's letter, a "regiment"? Frankly, if I only had an insignificant number of troops under my command on the Eastern Front, it is unclear why, after forty years, such an uproar is mounted against me internationally, repeated so consistently and with so much rage.

3) *To downplay the historically important fact of the presence of hundreds of thousands of volunteers who were anti-Soviet and non-German in the ranks of the Waffen SS, Mr. Valdés claims that "the divisions that most successfully and expertly fought in the Waffen SS were German." These divisions, did, in fact, prove a thousand times their extraordinary effectiveness and heroism, but many*

*of them were not entirely German either. The Viking Division, for example, had thousands of volunteers from countries outside the Reich, and one regiment in particular, the Nordland, was entirely made up of Dutchmen, Norwegians, and others. After all, establishing these distinctions is neither here nor there. On the Eastern Front, there was not six hundred thousand non-Germans and four hundred thousand Germans. There were one million Europeans.*

4) *The "gigantic massacres" of which Mrs. Friedman epically spoke are reduced in Mr. Valdés' letter to some local persecutions in Normandy (the same Normandy in which, on May 21st, 1940, French troops killed twenty-one of my Belgian political comrades, all civilians (including some women), in Oradour (France) and in Malmedy (Belgium).*

The case of the small town of Oradour, its property and inhabitants destroyed in the summer of 1944, remains highly debated. It was caused by the murder of a senior staff officer from the Das Reich Division of the Waffen SS in the town. What is most astonishing, is that during the French War Council's session, it was discussed that many of the accused were Alsatian volunteers, that is, that they were French. The French Chamber of Deputies had no choice but to grant them amnesty the following night.

The case of the American soldiers shot in Malmedy (Christmas 1944) is no less confusing. It is now considered almost certain that they died in combat. At the request of a scandalized American colonel, a Senate Commission traveled from Washington to Germany and officially established that the confessions of the young Waffen SS who were indicted were only extracted by heinous torture. There is something more. In his letters to his wife, published two years ago, General Patton, the famous commander of the Third United States Army, explained that his troops murdered groups of German prisoners in the same region and on the same dates. Who knows if the graves that President Reagan honored in Bitburg in the spring of 1985 are not covering the remains of some of those victims!

I would add that in such cases (Normandy, Oradour, Ardennes), the total number of human lives lost, fortunately, did not exceed a few hundred. In Dresden, Germany, however, British and American aircraft exterminated at least one hundred thirty thousand civilians, totally defenseless elderly people, women, and children, in one night in February 1945.[143]

The Soviets were even more barbaric. As the great historian Jacques de Launay has shown in La Grande Débâcle (The Great Debacle) in 1985, Stalin's hitmen, entering Germany, killed a whopping two million two hundred eighty thousand

---

[143] See David Irving's *Apocalypse 1945: The Destruction of Dresden*

*civilians during the first months of 1945, not to mention the eight hundred thousand missing, including French and Belgian prisoners also murdered as "vulgar Nazis." Fifty thousand Belgians of the army of 1940, interned in eastern Germany, barely liberated by Soviet troops, disappeared forever. At the same time, an American terrorist bomb blew apart more than one hundred thousand Japanese civilians in Hiroshima. These "gigantic massacres" perpetrated by the Anglo-American-Soviet side do not seem to have excessively moved your delicate reader.*

*The only thing that the vigilant Valdés can finally throw in the face of the Waffen SS is the Nuremberg Trial, a pretty awkward reference! This verdict against the Waffen SS is so extravagant and unjust today that it was not long ago that we saw how the former Austrian head of government, the socialist Kreisky—who happens to be Jewish!—defended the head of the liberal faction Friedrich Peter, who was an officer specifically in the Das Reich Division at Oradour, and he harshly attacked Simon Wiesenthal. In the democratic Germany in Bonn, former Waffen SS officers, up to the rank of colonel, have been allowed to serve with absolute equality in the Bundeswehr Army. In other words, tomorrow, some of these "criminals," according to Mr. Valdés's expression, could participate in NATO maneuvers alongside, and as allies of, the military of democratic Spain. Only a fanatic, burdened by irrepressible hatred, could even rumble out these stories of German war massacres forty years later, wildly exaggerated and easily dwarfed by Allied war crimes and genocides. There are unrepentant maniacs who love "black legends." I insist no more.*

*Léon Degrelle*

*Fuengirola, Malaga*

On February 4th, 1986, the German magazine *Diagnosen*, On February 4th, 1986, published an article entitled "*Degrelle Nimmt Stellung*" ("Degrelle Takes a Position"). In the same issue, journalist Alan Marlowe wrote another piece called "*Die Erinnerungen Degrelle*" ("Degrelle's Memories").

## Filing the Lawsuit

The filing of the legal action against León Degrelle was undertaken by the Jewish quarter based on a piece entitled "*Cazadores de Nazis Vendrán a España para Capturar a Degrelle*" ("Nazi Hunters are Coming to Spain to Capture Degrelle"), published in issue one hundred sixty-eight of the magazine *Tiempo*, dated July 29th to August 4th, 1985. In this article, as we have already written, León Degrelle made several statements concerning the perverted intention of Rabbi Cooper of the Simon Wiesenthal Center to kidnap him in Spain, offering a large reward for the job. This criminal act was disclosed and disseminated by the media.

Degrelle laid out a series of factual truths in his reply: 1) The Germans did not deport Belgian Jews from Belgium, but rather foreigners; 2) He, Degrelle, had had nothing to do with that affair; 3) If there are now so many Jews, then it is difficult to believe that they died in the crematorium ovens; 4) The Jewish problem is that they always want to be the victims, the eternally persecuted, and that if they have no enemies, they invent them; and 5) He doubted very much that gas chambers had ever existed, given that, for two years, a substantial reward had been offered in the United States for anyone who could provide reliable evidence for their existence and, despite offering the impressive figure of fifty million for this, no one had gone either to facilitate the tests or to collect the prize for their work in clarifying the truth of what has ended up becoming a widespread and very profitable lie for its exploiters.

The first court hearing of the legal action was held in Madrid's Sixth Court of First Instance.

On November 7th, 1985, Violeta Friedman, who was not mentioned at all in the statements published in *Tiempo*, filed a lawsuit for civil protection of the right to honor, under Law 62/78 of December 26th, 1978, against Léon Degrelle for his statements, against journalist Juan Girón Roger as the author of the article, and against Julián Lago as director of *Tiempo*.

Violeta Friedman was called to testify in April 1986. Friedman's lawyer Jorge Trias Sagnier had to be warned by the judge to maintain correct procedural behavior during the hearing, otherwise he would be forced to find Sagnier in contempt of court. The writer J. Cuyas Rigau recalls Trias Sagnier was a frequent collaborator with *ABC*, who proclaimed his status as "tacit," a defender of parliamentary democracy and monarchy with its micro-nationalism, its taifas,[144] and its coalition of parties, effective destroyers (by deed and omission) of Spain. Rigau observed how the attorney's surnames (Trias and Sagnier) were two of the components of the first municipal government of Barcelona liberated by nationalist forces, being as they are very expressive of the noblest traditional Catalan dynasties. The name of his father, first a traditionalist and later a Falangist, still appears as the name of a

---

[144] [The word *taifa*, from Arabic إطيفة refers to the little Muslim principalities of Al-Andalus in Spain and Portugal.]

street in Madrid. His brother's name is connected to persons murdered by the "*Rojos*"[145] in August 1938, who are among the graves of Montjuich.

## Open Letter to Violeta Friedman

At the beginning of the judicial proceedings, the irreproachable Mariano Sánchez-Covisa, wrote a letter to Violeta Friedman. Backing Léon's thesis, he said:

*While raising the issue, in court, of gas chambers in the German concentration camps, it should be remembered that no one, not even the efficient Allied Intelligence Services, was able to discover the spectacular disappearance of millions of Jews. This was despite the fact that, on a regular basis, the camps were visited by members of the Red Cross, consular representatives, and clergy of various religions who, in their reports, never remarked on anything abnormal, or on the existence of gas chambers. No government was aware of a "holocaust," nor were well-informed leaders like Roosevelt, Churchill, or Pope Pius XII. Even the Jews who supposedly witnessed the purported extermination only discussed this after the war had ended, and thus it could not be verified.*

*A school of historians has emerged after a reasonable period of time, to weigh the facts objectively, and are demonstrating how the Jews lie. They have reached the following conclusion: "There was no extermination program in the National Socialist regime, nor did the gas chambers exist."*

*No serious historian today holds to the existence of gas chambers. The gassing is a falsehood invented by the Jews. The British historian David Irving offered ten thousand dollars to anyone who proved that Hitler gave an order to gas anyone. Bertrand Russell acknowledged that there was no gas chamber in Belsen. Cardinal von Faulhaber stated: "There were never gas chambers in Dachau." Even the Austrian Hebrew Social Democrat, Bendikt Kautsky, declared in 1945 that, "I have never found an installation that was a gas chamber in any concentration camp."*

*Of the thirty concentration camps, the Jews have classified seven as extermination camps, and these were found in communist territory. They are impossible to verify.*

*International Jewish pressure demanded economic reparations from a defeated Germany for millions of alleged gassed victims, forcing it to pay the State of Israel,*

---

[145] In this context, the Spanish *Rojos*, the Reds, refers to republican and communist forces in the civil war.

*which did not exist prior to 1947, compensation as spoils of war. This was the greatest scam in history, given that among the victims is the brand-new former President of the European Parliament, Simone Veil.*

*Many authors who have studied the subject agree with the points outlined: Henri Roques' doctoral thesis with outstanding qualifications at the University of Nantes; Wilhelm Stäglich's The Auschwitz Myth; Serge Thion's Historical Truth or Political Truth?; Heinz Roth's Why Do They Lie to Us?; Michael A. Hoffman's The Great Holocaust Trial; Joaquín Bochaca's El Mito de los Six Milliones;[146] Leo Ferraro's El Último Protocol;[147] Richard E. Harwood's Did Six Million Really Die?; Arthur R. Buzt's The Hoax of the Twentieth Century; Robert Faurrison's "The Myth of Gas Chambers in Agony"[148]; Thies Christophersen's The Auschwitz Lie; Léon Degrelle's Letter to the Pope; Paul Rassinier's The Lie of Ulysses; Uri Walendy; Manfred Roeder; Harry Elmes Barnes; Carlo Mattogno; Ernst Zündel; Enrique Aynat, etc.*

*To sustain the existence of extermination policies and gas chambers is an offense to the German people and is detrimental to the International Declaration against the Incitement of Hatred among Peoples.*

*Yet, the smoke from the supposed gas chambers cannot quite hide world opinion from the actual genocide of the Palestinian people by the Zionist leaders, whose aim is: "To destroy Christianity and enslave humanity."*

*Mariano Sánchez-Covisa*

## The Hearing is Held

The hearing was held on June 11th, 1986. Degrelle testified about the controversial facts that were attributed to him, which outraged the plaintiff. His son-in-law Servando Balaguer Parreño was his attorney. In his testimony, referring to the much-vaunted "gas chambers," he exposed the doubt about their existence, taking into account two arguments: "He has not seen them, and many historians refute their existence."

The ruling was handed down on June 16th, with the judge ruling in favor of Léon Degrelle. The ruling expressly stated that at no time had Degrelle attacked

---

[146] The book by Bochaca, *El Mito de los Six Milliones,* which translates as *The Myth of the Six Million,* is different from the book of the same title in English written by David Hoggan.

[147] This book, *El Último Protocol (The Last Protocol),* by "Leo Ferraro" is actually the work of Jorge Luis Jerez Riesco.

[148] The translator is unaware of a book by this title in French (Robert Faurrison's native language) or in English. This title, however, may refer to the transcript of Faurrisson's trial in French. This transcript has also been translated in full into English and Spanish.

the honor of Violeta Friedman, also because he, like any other citizen under the law, enjoyed basic rights, including the right to freedom of expression as set out in Article 20.1 of the Spanish Constitution. It was clear that the plaintiff had taken legal action that not only lacked standing, but also purported to violate a constitutional right. The sentence fully considered the objection to the plaintiff's lack of standing raised by León Degrelle's attorney, arguing that, in this case, Violeta Friedman had no standing for the protection of her honor because she had not been attacked in the article. None of the statements specifically referred to her. Without these requirements of determination and specification of the person involved, the plaintiff could not argue that her honor was defamed, and thus in need of the protection granted by Organic Law 1/82, of May 5th, neither could the plaintiff sue on behalf of her ethnicity, race, or people.

On June 26th, 1986, the Madrid newspaper *ABC* published a letter sent to its director by Léon Degrelle's son-in-law Servando Balaguer Parreño:

*Mr. Director:*

*I would like to highlight some of the points contained in the information appearing in ABC on the acquittal of Léon Degrelle, whom I represent.*

*The complaint was filed on the basis of Organic Law 1/82, of May 5th, for Protection of Honor. The proceedings are of a civil nature, not a criminal nature, as one might deduce from the news that the media reported, such as Léon Degrelle not appearing at the hearing, or that Léon Degrelle was tried. In said hearing, only attorneys and prosecutors were required to participate and attend.*

*The ruling wholly upholds the thesis that I maintained on Mrs. Violeta Friedman's lack of standing because Degrelle's statements to the magazine Tiempo did not in any way threaten her honor, since these were opinions on historical persons and facts which the Spanish Constitution freely authorizes and which did not affect, specifically, the person of the plaintiff.*

*Finally, it is important to clarify that Léon Degrelle did not state that he "denied the Jewish holocaust," but that he doubted the existence of gas chambers, as many well-known historians have done. His doubt concerning this is based on the fact that he never saw them, despite having been fighting on the Eastern Front on the front lines with the Waffen SS, which should not be confused with the simple SS. Given this, he never committed any war crime, nor was he ever convicted of such a crime. The accusation by Mrs. Violeta Friedman that "as a general of the Waffen SS he must have committed gigantic massacres in the rear," published in ABC last year is injurious.*

*Balaguer Parreño, Madrid*

## Interview in the Newspaper *El Faro de Vigo*

In the Sunday supplement to the newspaper *El Faro de Vigo*, dated July 20th, 1986, under the title "*León Degrelle, el Eterno Guerrero*" ("León Degrelle, the Eternal Warrior"), journalist Marta Arroyo made the following statements: "Despite the constant accusations by the Jews that associate him with Hitler's extermination policy, his name does not appear on the lists of war criminals drawn up by the Allies, Soviets, or Israelis." She then highlighted his extensive intellectual work, stating "working fifteen hours a day, he [Degrelle] admits that he is dedicated to this task, which he considers necessary for the world to know what was great about the genius of this man [Hitler] who changed history."

Arroyo added:

> *Léon Degrelle strikes again. Having recently just turned eighty, the old general of the Waffen SS is ready to embark on what may be his last battle. After many years of threats, unproven accusations and a legal complaint filed against him by Violeta Friedman (dismissed by the judge), the one who was called the "last fascist" is prepared for a counterattack. The stage, far away now in time and space, that Eastern Front, will be the court of justice where the politician-soldier will fire his last cartridges "to end the lies and slander, for my honor." Even in the autumn of life, the "Old Lion" says that he does not give up.*
>
> *He is as healthy and strong as an oak, despite the years and the scars, and he is sure that his spirit is serene, and his mind is clear.*
>
> *LD: For the entire war, I was on the Eastern Front and did not see a single Jew. I never did anything to them. I never even killed a bug in my country. They believe that they are the only thing on earth. They did their best to get Europe into a war and now they want to take revenge on the Germans. They call me a murderer...but at the Front we did not have a clue about things like Auschwitz. I do not deny it is possible, but I have the right to doubt it."*

It was precisely his expressed doubt that motivated the complaint against him in court. The Wiesenthal Center put a price on his head, one hundred thousand dollars,[149] to take him alive, thus igniting the Jewish-Degrelle confrontation. His legal battle was about to begin.

---

[149] The author has given a couple different figures for this bounty; this may be due to thinking in pesetas and then thinking in U.S. dollars.

At the age of eighty, he continued to tell the press that "the only conceivable salvation for Europe would be for a 'Russian Napoleon Bonaparte' to appear." He was convinced that the following verse from the Psalms was written for him: "But my enemies live, and are stronger than I: and they that hate me wrongfully are multiplied" (Psalm 37:20).

In that same interview, the journalist reported:

> *In mid-July 1986, a trial was held in Madrid in which the Venezuelan Jew Violeta Friedman accused Léon Degrelle, a Spanish citizen, of having doubted the death of Jews in gas chambers. The judge handed down a ruling in favor of Léon Degrelle, in which he expressed the argument that, as a citizen, Degrelle enjoyed the right to freedom of expression and his own judgment.*

## Appeal to the Provincial Court of Madrid

Mrs. Friedman, supported by the Jewish community, with Max Mazin cheering her on, was not happy with the outcome of the trial in the Court of First Instance, so she appealed the judgment to the District Court of Madrid (appeal number 572/86). The appeal hearing was held on February 3rd, 1988.

A Jewish-led media campaign was orchestrated to try to intimidate and frighten the magistrates of the district court. The same morning of the hearing, the radio show host Iñaki Gabilondo, from the first hour of his broadcast, issued proclamations and slogans asking people to go to the court *en masse*, in the Palacio de Justicia de las Salesas, where the hearing was to be held, to support these "poor Jews" in their claims against Léon Degrelle. Gabilondo himself moved to a mobile unit to broadcast the development of the trial live, as if this were a circus. He wanted to manipulate public opinion, thinking that perhaps with this kind of theater and pressure, it might be possible to influence the judge's decision. He desperately tried to get in contact with Friedman so that her voice alone, partial and self-interested, would be heard. Everything was crazy, hasty, stifling for the media agitators whose scandalous action attempted to deliver a large crowd to the doors of the courthouse. So that the hearing would be widely disseminated, and at the same time to try to overturn the initial unfavorable judgment, at the suggestion of the Jewish secret service units, several media outlets sent reporters to the court room to cover the hearing.

What that nest of vipers did not count on was that supporting the cause of justice and historical truth was a large group of young law students and several members of the Spanish Circle of Friends of Europe. They were also in the halls of the district court with their Madrid representative Cristián Ruiz at the head.

The media propaganda orchestrated by the Jews fell apart. In all the photographs taken of Violeta Friedman, who presented herself as a diva, banners calling out the reason and justice that Léon Degrelle defended were also present. A few simple posters carried by young idealists ruined the Jewish attempt at manipulation. Even when a television camera went to get some footage inside the hall to try to politicize the trial, it was not tolerated and at the request of the judge in the court room, one of the civil guardsmen told them to respect the chamber and maintain order. He did the same with Violeta Friedman, who was given no chance to push her provocative plan by hysterically drawing attention to herself and provoking scandal by getting the cameras and photographers to capture her rehearsed scenes playing victim; it was a ridiculous theatrical display. The photograph that made the rounds in Spain was that of Violeta Friedman against a backdrop of posters with slogans supporting Léon Degrelle. Their trick had gone completely wrong.

The court again dismissed the charges brought by the Jewish community against Degrelle. This outcome triggered the Jewish-controlled press to launch a "victim of anti-Semitism" campaign in Spain, as well as around the world.

Friedman's attorney in the appeal was again pro-Zionist Jorge Trias Sagnier. Léon Degrelle's defense team was again led by his son-in-law Servando Balaguer. I had the great honor to accompany and assist Balaguer at the bench as his partner.

The Jews intended for Degrelle to be convicted on statements he had made in 1985 to Televisión Española and to the magazine *Tiempo* referring to Doctor Mengele, as well as gas chambers. According to Degrelle, Mengele was a normal doctor, and then he called into question the existence of gas chambers as a system for killing internees. His doubts were supported scientifically by a report from the American expert and engineer Fred Leuchter. In those statements, he had never once mentioned Violeta Friedman by name, nor alluded to her person at all. The truth hurts, especially when that truth is totally opposed to the falsehoods propagated by the Jews. Their aim was to obtain a judgment in favor of their mendacity.

Acting in court via Violeta Friedman, the Jews wanted to muzzle and silence Degrelle definitively, hoping to deny him his fundamental right to freedom of expression and thought, which every human being possesses in a system protected by the rule of law. In the lawsuit filed by Friedman and Trias Sagnier, they asked that Degrelle "be condemned to perpetual silence." They intended to outlaw historical revisionism that argued with the credibility and plausibility of the alleged killing of prisoners in gas chambers.

The district court acquitted Léon Degrelle because of the appeal's absolute lack of standing. On the way out, Friedman spoke to the press photographers covering the hearing, almost commanding them to "Photograph them [Degrelle's supporters] so they can all be registered."

The ruling of the First Chamber of the District Court, dated February 9th, 1988, upheld the judgment of the Court of Justice Number Six in Madrid (ruling number 1284/85), dated June 16th, 1986.

The First Chamber ruled that: "the statements denounced as illegitimate meddling in the personal sphere of the plaintiff cannot be regarded as such because they do not refer to personal expressions or events that defame or denigrate the plaintiff in the consideration of others."

## The Supreme Court Intervenes in Cassation

With an abundance of financial means at their disposal, the stubborn Jews returned to appeal this recent judgment of the District Court, bringing an appeal of cassation for violation of law before the First Chamber of the Supreme Court (Appeal No. 771/88). On December 5th, 1989, the High Court confirmed every point of the District Court's ruling, dismissing the appeal and finding Degrelle in the right, yet again. The court based its ruling on the fact that his statements were manifested under his fundamental right to free expression of thoughts, ideas, and opinions under the Spanish Constitution, and that they did not imply an offense to the honor of a particular physical person or the person's family. Therefore, the Right to Honor, which according to Organic Law 1/1982, is personal and non-transferable, pertaining to the subject and, in any case, to her family if she were affected by discredit or contempt. Since this was not violated, the appellant was not in a position of *legitimatio ad causam* and *ad procesum,*[150] which is required to appreciate injury or claim damages.

---

[150] [Latin for legitimacy of cause and of process. This is similar to the American legal notion of having "standing" in a case.]

## The "Politicized" Constitutional Court "Fails" and Years Later Amends its "Ruling"

An appeal for relief was then filed with the Constitutional Court, with entry into the register on January 12th, 1990. This initiative enjoyed strong support, both direct and indirect, from the Minister of Justice, the recalcitrant Zionist Enrique Múgica Herzog; the President of the Constitutional Court, Tomás y Valiente, who had such a controversial and dishonorable role in the Rumasa case; the President of B'nai B'rith of Spain, Max Mazin; and the President of the ADL (Anti-Defamation League), Alberto Benasuly.

The case was heard in the First Chamber of the Constitutional Court, which included Justices Francisco Tomás y Valiente as President, Fernando García Mon y González Regueral, Carlos de la Vega Benayas, Jesus Leguina Villa, Luis López Guerra, and Vicente Gimeno Sendra, who acted as rapporteur in appeal for relief no. 101/90, submitted by Violeta Friedman. Friedman was represented by attorney José Luis Ortiz Cañabate, assisted by Jorge Trias Sagnier. Her latest appeal was against the ruling of December 5th, 1989 of the First Chamber of the Supreme Court, rendered for cassation no. 771/88, arising from the civil protection trial of the right to honor, heard in the Court of First Instance Number Six, in Madrid. Léon Degrelle was represented by attorney Francisco de las Alas Pumariño y Miranda, assisted by Juan Servando Balaguer Parreño.

The Public Prosecutor's Office, in its statement of allegations, requested the inadmissibility of the appeal for relief in this case, given that the preliminary courts had stated the plaintiff's lack of standing to act under Organic Law 1/82. The Constitutional Court itself had stated that questions of standing in the underlying judicial process were mere legality and therefore not subject to review, unless they affect a fundamental right, which was not the case. Furthermore, because the right to such relief is not conferred on a party to the proceedings, but rather on the person actually affected, that is to say, the holder of the right infringed, it was patently obvious, one could say even tautological, that the appellant for relief was not a person directly affected. According to the Public Prosecutor's Office, it is one thing to feel affected and another to have been actually affected, a requirement that obviously was not satisfied in the previous proceedings.

Despite these legal fundamentals, it was still allowed to be heard.

Léon Degrelle's defense argued that "the defendant did not make the statements in question on his own initiative, but rather they were solicited from him by the magazine *Tiempo* following the statements made by a representative of the Wiesenthal Center that the money available to him to locate Dr. Mengele was now going to be used for hunting down and capturing Degrelle, and also "that it is not legal to analyze phrases, which the writ of appeal transcribes, isolated from the rest of the interview, taking them out of their general context." On the other hand, at no time did the plaintiff Violeta Friedman substantiate during the process that she was Jewish, that she was in Auschwitz, or that her relatives perished there, recognizing instead, in the opposite sense, that it was not easy to prove all this reliably and that this lack of substantiation is sufficient to conclude that she lacked standing to exercise the action that she presumed.

What was evident and of note, and legally more relevant, was that the statements of Léon Degrelle contain no insult, or slanderous or insulting phrase, or offense, or attack on the honor of a collective, an ethnicity, or a group, and therefore much less a personal attack on Violeta Friedman, whom he did not even cite and who was completely unknown to him. In the interview, Degrelle had not stated or denied anything categorically. He did not even state that the concentration camps did not exist or that no murder was committed in them. He merely expressed doubts about certain aspects, such as the existence of gas chambers. He said much less than many well-known historians from various countries who denied them outright, such as Roques, Stäglich, Thion, Roth, Hoffman, Bochaca, Ferraro, Mattogno, Faurisson, Rassinier, etc. In addition, it is absolutely legitimate to give an opinion, or a sense of doubt, about historical facts. One may or may not like it, it may provoke indignation in many, it may provoke in others irritation, it may be more or less politicized, but no one can deprive another of the right to comment on events that have occurred, in the distant or recent past. Furthermore, the plaintiff lacked standing to exercise the action derived from the Law on Civil Protection of the Right to Honor.

Judgment 214/91 of the "politicized" Constitutional Court for the selection of its co-components was dated November 11th, 1991. The Constitutional Court has been a body where the appointment of its magistrates becomes a struggle between political parties to place their attorney pawns under their jurisdiction. In the latter instance, Judge Vicente Gimeno Sendra was responsible for the proceedings as rapporteur, and it reflected the political doctrine maintained by the Jewish "lobby" in its claims to list and criminalize the ideas of those who defended, with honor, the positions of the Third Reich. It was the consecration of the criminalization of the right to freedom of opinion on certain historical facts. The judgment was brief and stated:

1) To declare null and void the judgments of December 5th, 1988 of the First Chamber of the Supreme Court; of February 9th, 1988 of the former Civil Chamber of the District Court of Madrid, and of June 16th, 1986 of the Court of First Instance Number Six of this capital city, all of them arising from the Incidental Case No. 1284/85 on Civil Protection of Honor;

2) Recognize the right of the plaintiff to honor.

Judge Fernando García Mon made a resounding private vote that differed from the arguments of the judgment rendered in the appeal for relief no. 101/1990 and showed in writing his legal discrepancy with the controversial judgment.

What was evident is that the judgment of the appeal and its content still annulled all the aspirations of the Jewess Violeta Friedman exercised in the preceding process and, therefore, without ruling or decision from the Courts of Justice on any of her basic claims, which gave rise to her judicial action in an attempt to get them recognized:

1) That the defendant committed an illegitimate aggression against the honor of the plaintiff and that such aggression generates serious damages that must be repaired by the defendant;

2) That he be ordered to refrain perpetually making similar statements hereafter;

3) That the literal text of the judgment rendered by the Court be inserted in the magazine Tiempo at the expense of the defendant;

4) That the text of the judgment likewise be reproduced on the first channel of the second edition of the newscast; and

5) That the defendant compensate the plaintiff by way of reparation for the non-pecuniary damage he has caused and that the amount of the compensation be allocated to the Association of Spanish Citizens who suffered persecution in Nazi concentration camps and extermination camps.

None of the claims requested by Friedman could be obtained, and therefore no Spanish Court of Justice sentenced Léon Degrelle to carry out any of Jewry's claims, for which, in this case, Friedman had been used.

Alberto Benasuly welcomed the forced decision, which was not even shared by all the judges who were members of the Chamber, and in a spirit of media propaganda rather than legal rigor, rushed to state the following: "It was given at a particularly delicate time by the resurgence of racism and xenophobia in Europe and Spain. The European Community and, of course, Spain, which occupies the complicated southern border, is inevitably going to assist with in the coming decades, the peaceful or impetuous invasion of Africans, Asians, South Americans, and Eastern Europeans." One must question this premonition from this ADL Jew and ask if they, the Jews, are the ones behind all the current human trafficking, the invasion of Europe by furtive immigrants, all of which is not accidental?

After the ruling by the Constitutional Court, the world's Jewish "lobby" threw all its weight behind it and launched a campaign to penalize disagreeing with the official version. Denying the assertion of it would be punishable. The Constitutional Court's judgment on November 11th, 1991, was ambiguous, but the Jews, encouraged by its precedent, managed to gag any contradictory version. With the help of conservative Member of Parliament Robles Fraga, so submissive to Jewish interests and so docile to the mandates of Israel, they managed to bring an amendment to the Spanish Criminal Code and introduce a crime of opinion on a historical event.

Seven days after the death of Léon Degrelle, on April 7th, 1994, Violeta Friedman went on Televisión Española to continue her farce. She was interviewed on the program "*Gente de Primera*," which was directed (just by chance!) by the journalist Iñaki Gabilondo, curiously the same journalist who was a left-leaning activist and a person of the most rancid brand of socialism. He had cackled over microphones of the SER channel in agreement with Mossad talking points, telling listeners to go to the Provincial Court, in order to obtain a favorable sentence for the Zionists. In a rare coincidence, he joined his voice in his program with that of the communist singer Milanés.

When the government, in the Council of Ministers held on July 27th, 1994, approved sending a new draft of the Organic Law on Criminal Code to the Courts, Jewish organizations in Spain were mobilized and created a Commission of Jewish Organizations of Spain, coordinated by Alberto Benasuly. This was composed of the Federation of Jewish Communities of Spain, the B'nai B'rith of Spain, and the Anti-Defamation League (ADL), plus other Zionist and Jewish organizations, in order to intervene and interfere in the proposals of Spanish parliamentary groups.

The plenary meeting of the Congress of Deputies, in its session on February 16th, 1995, approved the proposal for a law presented by the conservative representative, Robles Fraga, which "defined the defense of the crime of genocide" in order to suppress certain conduct.

Violeta Friedman, a heavy smoker, died in Madrid on October 4th, 2000. Five years later, the lawyer of the B'nai B'rith, Jorge Trias Sagnier, still remembered her and, as a personal tribute, he dedicated a column commending her in the monarchist daily *ABC*, where he continues to collaborate regularly.

## Léon Degrelle, Like El Cid Campeador,
## Wins a Legal Battle after His Death

On November 7th, 2007, the plenary of the Constitutional Court issued a ruling on the question of the unconstitutionality of Article 607.2 of the Criminal Code concerning denial of the "holocaust," in which it decided "to consider the question raised by its unconstitutionality" and, consequently, "declaring unconstitutional and nullifying the inclusion of the term 'deny' in the first subparagraph of article 607.2 of the Penal Code."

The legal basis on which this decision was made is logical and easy to understand. The second paragraph of article 607 of the Penal Code reads: "The dissemination by any means of ideas or doctrines that deny or justify the crimes set forth in the preceding paragraph of this article…." The crimes referred to in the above-mentioned precept are those of genocide.

The paragraph in question was contrary to the constitutional right to freely express and disseminate thoughts, ideas, and opinions through word, writing, or any other means of reproduction. It is clear that the behavior defined as criminal by Article 602.2 of the Criminal Code could not be framed within the concept of provocation to commit an actual crime, nor within the concept of defending a crime, since the literal content of the provision indicated did not require, as an element thereof, that it be aimed at inciting the commission of crimes of genocide, nor that it praise or extol genocide. The behavior in question was the mere dissemination of ideas or doctrines that denied or justified the existence of historical events that would have been described as genocide, therefore: "the Chamber considers the conflict of such a definition with the right enshrined in Article 20.1 of the Spanish Constitution obvious…in the sense that it protects subjective and interested opinions on certain historical events, however erroneous or unfounded they may be." Article 20 of the Spanish Constitution guaranteed the right to free expression and dissemination of thoughts, ideas, and opinions.

Both the State Attorney and the State General Prosecutor shared the view that the behavior penalized by Article 602.2, consisting of disseminating ideas or doctrines that deny or justify genocide, could not be interpreted as a defense of genocide.

The Constitutional Court repeatedly affirmed:

*Article 20 of the Constitution, in its various paragraphs, guarantees the maintenance of a free public communication, without which other rights enshrined in the Constitution would be emptied of real content, reducing the representative institutions to hollow forms and absolutely falsifying the principle of democratic legitimacy set forth in Article 1.2 of the Constitution, which is the basis of our entire legal-political order. The preservation of this free public communication, without which there is neither free society nor, therefore, popular sovereignty, requires the guarantee of certain fundamental rights common to all citizens, and the general interdiction of certain actions of power.*

Similarly, the European Court of Human Rights, since the ruling in Handyside vs. The United Kingdom of December 7th, 1976 reiterated that freedom of expression is one of the essential foundations of a democratic society and one of the primary conditions for its progress and development.

The Spanish Constitutional Court says:

*The rights guaranteed by Article 20.1, therefore, are not only an expression of basic individual freedom, but are also configured as forming elements of our democratic legal system. Thus, Article 20 as a fundamental rule, in addition to enshrining the right to freedom of expression and to communicate or receive freely truthful information, guarantees a constitutional interest: the formation and existence of a free public opinion, a guarantee of special importance, since, as a prerequisite and necessary for the exercise of other rights inherent in the functioning of a democratic system, it becomes, in turn, one of the pillars of a free and democratic society. In order for the citizen to be able to form his opinions freely and to participate responsibly in public affairs, he must be broadly informed so that he can ponder diverse and even conflicting opinions.*

*A direct consequence of the institutional content of free dissemination of ideas and opinions is that, as we have reiterated, freedom of expression encompasses freedom to criticize, even if it is tasteless and can annoy, disturb, or upset whomever it is directed at, as is required in pluralism, tolerance, and the spirit of openness, without which there is no democratic society. For this reason, we have firmly stated that it is clear that the protection of freedom of opinion covers everyone, however wrong or dangerous it may seem to the reader, even those who attack the democratic system itself. The Constitution also protects those who reject the Constitution. That is to say, freedom of expression is valid not only for information or ideas that are welcomed or considered harmless or indifferent, but also for those that are contrary, shock, or offend the State or any part of its population.*

The Constitutional Court continued to argue:

> *On previous occasions, we have concluded that the statements, doubts and opinions about Nazi activity with regard to Jews and concentration camps, however reprehensible or misrepresented they may be...are protected by the right to freedom of expression, (Article 20.1 of the Spanish Constitution), in relation to the right to ideological freedom (Article 16 of the Spanish Constitution). Therefore, irrespective of the assessment of these, which is not the responsibility of this Court, they can only be understood for what they are: subjective and interested opinions on historical events. This same perspective has led the European Court of Human Rights, on several occasions when collaboration with Nazi atrocities during the Second World War was put in doubt, to point out that "the search for historical truth is an integral part of the freedom of expression."*

In so ruling, the Constitutional Court, in order to be able to judge historical events that occurred during the Second World War, removed the gag imposed by Jewish demands with which they have subjected much of humanity, at least for now in Spain. History can be revised in a way that searches for truth. The strong Jewish monopoly on punishing dissenting thought—true or false—has ended.

Léon Degrelle won this legal battle because he was in the right, even after death.

*Léon Degrelle with José Luis Jerez Riesco*

# VI

## Residential Move to the Boardwalk City of Melilla, Number 23, Malaga Capital

## (1986–1994)

### Correspondence with His Former Driver on the Eastern Front

One day, towards the end of summer 1986, the postman gave Degrelle a letter that would fill him with joy. It was from his trusted driver during the last years of the Russia campaign, who had located his address and sent him the following letter:

> *To the Commander of the Walloon Legion Léon Degrelle*
>
> *Dear Commander,*
>
> *This is one of your veteran soldiers writing to you, your former driver Pierre who entered the Legion in 1943.*
>
> *I served with the Flemish NSKK in France and Russia.*
>
> *With Stürmbrigade Wallonie, as part of the Fifth Viking SS Panzer Division, I campaigned in Ukraine and joined the Fifth Pak Company in the Cherkassy encirclement, also in Novo Buda, where our Commander Lippert fell.*
>
> *I was wounded in the left leg by the explosion of a grenade; my feet were also frozen when we broke out of the encirclement and crossed the river Guilai Tikis.*
>
> *After a long evacuation, I arrived in Galiza at the military hospital 920 MOT.*
>
> *I then got to Berlin and Brussels, where I lived on Avenue Jean Volders, number 14, next to the door of the Saint-Gilles market hall.*
>
> *After a stay at the Brugmann hospital, I returned to service.*
>
> *I was then part of your guard at Drève de Lorraine where Mrs. Degrelle and your children were.*
>
> *During the evacuation from Brussels, together with my comrades, we took Mrs. Degrelle and your children to Germany.*

*Later I was your driver and accompanied you on various missions in Germany, together with the French and Belgian political refugees in Berlin, in Sieg-Maringen, with Mr. De Brinon, and where Marshal Pétain was also present. I met Mr. Otto Abetz, former German Ambassador to Paris, and I also accompanied you to Vienna, Prague, etc.*

*We left the Castle of Bokerode for the offensive of the Ardennes in December of '44.*

*At the end of the war, you instructed me to accompany your family, passing through Bavaria and Austria, in order to try to get them into Switzerland.*

*This was my last mission, sir.*

*Mrs. Degrelle was accompanied by other people, and this complicated the situation.*

*For me, personally, it was simpler: I had a Swiss passport, being a Swiss citizen (although during the war I also passed for Italian). The guard post was very suspicious because of my military trousers and boots, and I was held together with other German prisoners in a column of English, American, and French soldiers who had arrived from Germany and were to be handed over to the Allies.*

*Sir, even after so many years my conscience today is still not clear, and I think of those sad moments for your family.*

*I have tried to write to you many times, but I thought my letter would not get to you, so I waited.*

*Your former legionaries always think of you. For us, you continue to be Modesto First Duke of Burgundy. I kept my uniform, the suit, the belt, and the military kepi, sneaking them into Switzerland in a small suitcase. After the Cherkassy encirclement, you decorated me with the Iron Cross, Second Class. I had a photo of you with the dedication: "To Pierre, my brave brother in arms, most sincerely, Léon Degrelle," which was unfortunately lost.*

*I heard the news that little Marie-Christine got married. From the bottom of my heart, I wish you the greatest happiness possible.*

*I am now 80 years old, but I enjoy good health, and legionaires are hard to break.*

*Sir, please convey to all your loved ones, Mrs. Degrelle and your children, my most distinguished and sincere greetings.*

*Ever faithful,*
*Pierre*

The reply was not long in coming. On September 16th, 1986, Léon Degrelle sent him the following letter:

*My dear old Pierre,*

*It gave me great joy to receive your letter. How can we ever forget the courageous and faithful Pierre, companion on so many adventures, and also of our most meritorious ideal! Sometimes those thousands of kilometers come to mind, along which you transported me amidst great fumes of gas!*

*I wondered what happened to you after I had given you the chance to try your luck at reaching a safe haven in peaceful Switzerland once the catastrophe calmed down.*

*I appreciate hearing all your history. I do not blame you for failing in the last mission of saving my wife and children. At that time, everything was impossible.*

*Everyone suffered much. My wife spent seven years in a dungeon, then later died. My father and mother died too, in abominable prison cells. For my part, I spent fourteen years not knowing anything about my children. Finally, thanks to some friends, I found out where they were—under different names—and had them brought here to me. Another tragedy: as soon as he arrived in Seville, my son Léon-Marie (who had been four years old when I had last seen him and was eighteen when our reunion took place), was hit by a taxi and was killed. My four daughters are fine and happy and have a total of twelve children between them. Godelieve has also just become a grandmother as of last week! To think that you took her to Germany when she was just a little girl in September 1944!*

*I have heart and am determined to never die!*

*Did you read my book The Russia Campaign, which has been translated into several languages? I send you my latest book, as a little memory (Léon Degrelle, Persiste et Signe).*

*Apart from this, I lived quite hidden, as two Jewish commandos wanted to catch me!*

*I wish you much happiness, my dear old Pierre!*

*Sincerely...*

## Conversation with Portuguese National-Syndicate Leader Zarco Moniz Ferreira

On October 24th, 1986, the Portuguese nationalist leader and great polyglot from Lisbon, Zarco Moniz Ferreira, visited him at his home with his distinguished wife Pilar.

Zarco Moniz had already met him before in January 1980. At that first meeting Degrelle offered him a copy of his book, *Les Âmes qui Brûlent (The Burning Souls)* with the following dedication: "To our dear Dr. Zarco Moniz Ferreira, this book contains the essential of our mysticism, so that beyond the borders, souls might gather together, in homage of affection and friendship. Léon Degrelle. January 12th, 1980."

The Portuguese Julio Prata and José Carlos Lópes Craveiro also visited him on one occasion.

## Meetings with Olivier Mathieu

The first time Olivier Mathieu met Léon Degrelle was in Madrid in 1986. This young, courageous maverick and controversial journalist was in Madrid writing a biography of the French Minister of National Education (from 1942 to 1944), Abel Bonnard. Mathieu had the original manuscript of Bonnard's personal diary. His work was carried out at the house of the book merchant Alain Couartou (better known by his pseudonym "Arnaud Imatz"), an accommodating French civil servant based in Madrid, on calle Raimundo Fernández Villaverde, near the Glorieta de los Cuatro Caminos. When Olivier Mathieu was writing about Bonnard's life, little could he have imagined that when the book was published, it would be enriched with an epilogue by Léon Degrelle. Léon had the opportunity to meet and maintain a cordial friendship with Abel Bonnard in Madrid between 1945 and 1968, where Bonnard lived in humility and dignity until his death.

Olivier Mathieu, who had Belgian citizenship, was born on October 16th, 1960. He was the grandson of the Belgian writer Marie de Vivier, born in Belgium on October 14th, 1899, and died in Paris on January 17th, 1980; in 1922, she married Marcel Mathieu, one of the founders of the Belgian Communist Party. His grandmother was the first one who spoke to him of Léon Degrelle during his childhood. His mother, Margarita Mathieu, an eminent linguist, was a teaching assistant to Professor Henri Grégoire at the Free University of Brussels. She spoke extensively to Olivier about the aesthetic side of Rexism, often mentioning August 8th, 1941. It was a memorable date in the history of that movement, for it was the day that the Walloon volunteers set out to fight against Bolshevism in the Soviet Union.

Olivier Mathieu recalled that first encounter with Léon with the following touching words:

*One fine day in 1986, when I was twenty-five, I came into the presence of Léon Degrelle for the first time in Madrid. He had undertaken the task in Belgium before the Second World War of trying to establish a strong, Christian-inspired power, a social corporate system, and to end a Parliament that was tainted by countless abuses. In the attic of a building on a street still unnamed after Spanish democratization, but which the Madrid taxi drivers and the people still knew by the name it had during the Franco regime—that of an Ace pilot in the Francoist air force—a very upright man of noble stature appeared, opened the door to me, and shook my hand.*

Olivier found Degrelle in his home on calle Santa Engracia, number 37, eighth floor, letter C, which, during the Franco regime, was called Joaquín García Morato. The building where Léon resided was almost at the height of Plaza de Chamberí.

Not five minutes into the conversation in the living room of the house, Degrelle said: "The Left is really us." He immediately explained to Mathieu the nuances of that emphatic statement, and in his discourse, the rational and paradoxical arguments were as solid as a rock. Olivier's instant conclusion from this meeting was that "Léon Degrelle was, if you want, a nationalist of the left. Or, if you prefer, a right-wing socialist. A non-Marxist left! A non-capitalist right! He is above that. He is something else."

At this time, he recalled Benito Mussolini's famous phrase, which his mother repeated to him frequently during childhood: "It is better to live one day as a lion than a hundred years as a lamb."

Throughout his personal relationship with Léon, he found that he opened the door of his home generously to all visitors, even the most anonymous. He was always willing to sacrifice so that anyone who came, sometimes traveling very long distances to pay tribute to him, never left disappointed. His patience was inexhaustible, memorable, even his health would have been sacrificed if necessary.

In his apartment the objects of are illuminated and decorated by the light of stained glass, which demonstrated Degrelle's unalterable passion for Roman antiquities, European art, and the history of greater Burgundy. In the presence of such beauty, a sudden and pleasing feeling filled the visitor.

That meeting would be the first in a series of subsequent visits. Mathieu himself has written that Degrelle received him about a dozen times. He kept a recording he made of more than eight hours of conversation with Léon Degrelle by telephone, a genuine historical treasure.

Mathieu left us an interesting testimony. It was in 1987 that, once again, he visited Léon at his home in the company of journalist Angel Bayod Monterde, a magnificent Falangista and extraordinary person, the last director of the movement's newspaper *Amanecer* in Zaragoza. Angel Bayod was an old acquaintance of Léon Degrelle, who in a dedication to her in a copy of *The Burning Souls*, referred to Bayod as "the true Spanish knight." When they left his house they met Alain de Benoist, the flag bearer of the French *Nouvelle Droite* (*New Right*) and promoter of the "*Nouvelle Ecole*" ("New School") on the corner of the street. De Benoist was a recognized and prestigious European intellectual. He carried a bouquet of flowers in his hand, and he was also going to visit Degrelle. A few hours later, when Olivier Mathieu returned to Léon's house, Alain de Benoist had already left, but Mathieu found Degrelle surrounded by young Belgian activists, one of them being Yannick Stoefs, who died tragically in 1993. When the young Belgians left the house, they saluted him with arms extended, a triumphal arch in the Roman manner. In the late afternoon, they took a taxi to the Casa Botín restaurant in the Plaza Mayor area. In his hands Degrelle carried the bouquet of flowers that Alain de Benoist had given him, which he then placed on the table they sat at in the restaurant.

The *Antigua Casa Sobrino de Botín* restaurant, located on calle de Cuchilleros, number 17, was frequented by Léon regularly. He took many friends and visitors there. This old corner of Madrid was a silent witness to many of the events that took place in the village and court for almost three centuries. A former muleteer inn, it was known for savory meats and wines of memorable vintages. Many transactions were settled at its tables. In the place where the building was situated, in the sixteenth century there was a wine cellar which was converted into a dining room. The date of 1725 at the entrance marks precisely the age of its famous Castilian roasting oven, decorated with period tiles.

The last time Olivier Mathieu saw Degrelle was at the end of 1993, when Olivier was thirty-three years old. On this occasion, he went to his flat in the boardwalk city of Melilla, in Malaga, and found Degrelle with his usual vigor and strength. They spoke on the balcony overlooking the Mediterranean Sea. He recognized in Degrelle that same exuberance that was found in his books, with the utmost precision of feeling, with his characteristic generosity, and by the wisdom of expression that he showed in his dedications.

The impact of Léon's personality on Mathieu was immense. He cherished the masterful pieces of advice Léon gave him, based on long experience. Mathieu was affected by the letter of condolences that he received from Degrelle, sending his sympathy at the death of Mathieu's mother on August 12th. He wrote:

*In exile, September 13th, 1988*

*Dear Olivier,*

*I have received this morning and read with great sadness the admirable obituary—worthy of a great priest and a philosopher—announcing the death of your beloved mother. Her final happiness, of course, will have been to have a son like you.*

*You were able to give her, at her end, your presence and affection. Here, I had to face a very cruel shock, when the front page of a newspaper published the notification of the death of my mother, at the age of seventy-nine, having died in an abominable "democratic" dungeon. Forty years later, I continue to carry this raw wound . . .*

*Writing a great book can console you somewhat. You are of the strong race. You are lucky! We will meet in the measure of our luminous and divine pulse. The great powers of the sun, trees, and winds will keep us. May God protect you!*

*Sincerely,*
*Léon Degrelle*

Olivier acknowledged with joy, "I have been lucky to benefit from your wisdom, your help and, to put it briefly, from that feeling that is a rare and precious thing, your friendship."

It was in that same year of 1988 that Mathieu, accompanied by the Breton painter Yann-Ber Tillenon, traveled once more to Madrid to meet with Léon again, so Mathieu could introduce his companion. Together, as if they were all old friends, an excellent poet, a brilliant writer, and an avant-garde painter, they wandered about through the Austrias neighborhood in the older quarter of Madrid, savoring the atmosphere of the ever-traditional part of the city, finishing their tour when the light of twilight was seen on the horizon, in the distance of Casa de Campo. They watched the sunset with pleasure from the viewpoint of Las Vistillas.

### The Epilogue to Abel Bonnard's Biography, *An Unfinished Adventure*

It happened on a winter afternoon in Paris on November 20th, 1988. The writer Olivier Mathieu was at Rue des Pyramides, number 10, on the first floor of the Ogmios bookstore, in the offices of the publishing house where he worked as a literary advisor, when Léon telephoned him from Spain to read him the epilogue he had written for his book. Léon scrupulously, like a schoolteacher, read him every word. A few weeks later, the book *Abel Bonnard, une Aventure Inachevée* (*Abel Bonnard, an Unfinished Adventure*) appeared in early January 1989. On January 12th, 1989, Olivier Mathieu sent a copy of his book to me, and because of my friendship with Degrelle, included the following handwritten dedication: "To my dear friend José

Luis Jerez Riesco." We were both great friends, and, as proof of this unconditional friendship, Mathieu even sent me another of his earlier revolutionary works.

Léon Degrelle's epilogue to the book on Bonnard began as follows:

*Since the Second World War, almost half a century has passed. Therefore, the exile to whom the book we have just read is devoted seems to still be here, two steps away, with his ironic look, his malicious smile, drafting his writings on two miserable overlapping apple drawers of white wood, as could be seen every morning in front of the greengrocer's shop window. The small room was sad, almost gloomy. This is how one of the finest, most successful minds in Europe has survived in Madrid; a member of the Académie Française, the former Minister of National Education, Abel Bonnard, banished from his homeland, ruined, and helpless. His spirit was always so biting, and, at the same time, fiercely charitable, as in the happier times when he was in Paris. He was the author of epigrams whose fires illuminated the solemnity of the salons of old men with white beards and viscounts. Abel Bonnard had as much sense of observation as Proust. He also, at the beginning of his life, fluttered among the butterflies. The noise of his wings was that of a brilliant period, as are the sunsets, but expiring also like its last gleams, rejoicing in autumnal shades. The man was strangely racial. Through his veins ran blood worthy of a chief magistrate of the Italian Renaissance. The buzz of human wasps mixed in his writings with the harmony that flowed from the vowels. [...]*

*A bitter exile had certainly hit Abel Bonnard hard, but it could not damage his fineness, nor his dignity. The writer published an article from time to time, in a Madrid newspaper, for which he—a famous academic—was actually paid a one hundred peseta bill. This assured him access to a plate of food every day during his frugal week and did not at all prevent him from taking a little crumb from his crust of bread to give to the pike sparrows that came begging at the ledge of his window. They were his friends, simple as he was, and like him, willing at every moment to go back to the air, to that enchanted region of free beings. He also died as the birds die. What is the testimony of his return to nothing, of his disappearance among the shadows of the groves and forests, after a last song? [...] Abel Bonnard vanished like them. Around his tomb, today, other birds return to find him, hanging their fragile legs next to the water of the clear basin that is located nearby, dominating this last, very narrow, dwelling of the great disappeared.*

At the end of this literary piece, which reads like a polished work for its beauty, he recognized Mathieu as "a new Celine,[151] reappeared on the lava of a petrified world."

### The Voice of Experience: A Letter to Olivier Mathieu

In 1989, Degrelle was counting on Mathieu to write his biography, and for that reason he sent him to Mexico that year, in search of some of his earlier history. He put him in touch with some of his good friends in the states of Jalisco and Colima, what had been the battleground of the Cristero Rebellion.

In 1990, a few days before Mathieu was scheduled to give an advertised and awaited lecture in Brussels on "Léon Degrelle and Tintin," he met up with Degrelle in Madrid. In the presence of numerous witnesses, León complimented him beautifully, saying, "I wish him the best, as usual, but above all, do not 'discover' *me*!"[152] Never between 1986 and 1990 had they mentioned Tintin in their conversations, nor did they associate Hergé with Léon, but between 1990 and 1993 they frequently discussed it, such that Olivier was one of the first to read the manuscript written by Degrelle called *Tintin, Mon Copain* (*Tintin, My Buddy*).

On September 18th, 1991, Léon sent him an extensive letter from Malaga, with a supplementary annex, giving him some fundamental, friendly advice before an upcoming hearing for a judicial appeal, in October, of an earlier decision that had sentenced Mathieu to eighteen months in prison. The letter's tone was kind and paternal, full of advice and morality:

> *My dear Olivier,*
>
> *I frequently ask about you. I have also read, with great interest, your last message. I worry about you, and I want to show you my friendship.*
>
> *I would especially like to tell you not to torment yourself over this! Throughout all our fighting and, above all, at the beginning of the war (enduring twenty-one prisons, on the threshold of death every day), then, for four years on the Eastern Front, we also had to see death's face again many times! Then the years of imprisonment of one hundred thousand rexists! I certainly would not want to*

---

[151] Reference to French writer Louis-Ferdinand Céline, whose real name was Louis Ferdinand Auguste Destouches. Céline was both an award-winning novelist—arguably one of the greatest French novelists of the twentieth century—and a physician. Due to some of his criticism of Jews in 1937 and his support for a military alliance with Nazi Germany, Céline remains a controversial figure in French letters.

[152] This is likely a cute reference to the many adventures and discoveries of Tintin where something dangerous quickly ensues.

change; I prefer a thousand sufferings accepted with joy to the routine inertia of today's living! It is you who have to say that you are not entering the same hell! In any case, you must accept the misfortune with head held high and to be proud of not buckling!

You faced your trial last April. You have made them a nervous wreck, but there has been no talk of them being able to strike again. My humble advice: do not shy away from them! If I were in your shoes, I would stand before the court on October 10th, and I would say nothing, except, "Here, you can lock me in prison for a hundred years, if you want, but I want to remain, if not free of body (which you can confiscate), still free to direct my thought according to my conscience and my passion."

Jail? Then what? They will not "break your mouth"...they will not torture you! In the worst case, this still will not be as tragic as being told every day that you are going to be shot at dawn on the following day! I heard that lovely news every night, for several months, and I was always full of optimism! Besides, I will tell you, it will be a chance for you to finally be at peace and write that book! Complete solitude! Without the company of womanizers to bother you. Every day with fifteen hours of peace of mind to balance your thoughts. Then, you will be well employed, my dear Olivier Take advantage of everything, even being behind bars, if you have to go to jail! You are now thirty years old. Life is beautiful, whatever else it may be! Beautiful like the dawn! Beautiful like the woods! Beautiful as the splendid animal that nests in us! Be ready for everything! Do not let yourself be polluted by pessimism, that disease of the defeated!

A strong hug,
Léon Degrelle

At the end of the letter, as a supplementary note, he added five edifying pieces of advice:

1) Don't ask for financial help. It is humiliating! It is better to earn four bucks a day killing yourself at work; you can pick up trash, load packages! Work is an honor, whatever it may be. Hitler said this clearly!

2) Do not hang out with women! On the Front, for four years, they never got close to our guns! Woman is the warrior's rest, but after the war!

3) Great words must be pronounced in the realm of great events: heroism, holiness, are too great to describe them as events, or incidents, and trying to do so would just be a bunch of words.... Life will offer you a hundred opportunities to

*imitate Bayardo or St. Francis of Assisi, but it will be when having a soul as strong as iron is necessary.*

4) *Never run away! Not to South Africa or anywhere! You have to face danger with a serene countenance. Besides, where could you run? Why? You will make life more complicated. A little work will allow you not to starve. Out of this, the immense panorama of creation!*

5) *Solitude! Blessed solitude! Part of the antechamber of paradise!*

## Mathieu's Books on Degrelle

The first book that Olivier Mathieu published after Léon's death was *Léon Degrelle Tel Que Je l'Ai Connu* (*Léon Degrelle As I Knew Him*), published in Belgium by the publishing house Aux Bâtons de Bourgogne in April 1994. In it, Mathieu recounts his impressions, emotions, and personal memories of Léon, analyzing those aspects of his personality that most powerfully drew his attention.

*The first thing that struck me about Léon Degrelle was his eloquence. He spoke with a serious, powerful, and calm voice, in a very pure French where he mixed Belgian and Spanish accents. He had the art of fascinating his friends and guests...his memory was prodigious. He spoke of himself, but with such passion, and at the same time with such discretion, that one was not aware of it. When the interview, hours later, came to an end, it was as if the conversation had lasted only a few moments.*

Another detail Mathieu highlighted was Degrelle's hospitality and sacrifice of his time:

*He was infinitely generous in everything, he spared neither his fatigue, nor his time to demonstrate his hospitality to those who visited him from all over Europe and even from America. The topics of conversation he covered were quite varied, such that several days were not sufficient to take it all in. He was not chained to the past. He alternated the past with the present in a reciprocal way; moreover, what really hits you about Léon is his unprecedented youth.*

He emphasized another detail. He perceived that Léon not only had the intelligence to see evil, but also had the will to counter it. His conscience was active.

Léon spoke with natural excellence, just as he wrote. It was not lost on him that Degrelle was also someone who could bring about or provoke some of the funniest scenes.

After this first volume, *Aux Bâtons de Bourgogne* published another book on May 8th, 1994, entitled *En Réponse à la Presse lors de la Mort de Léon Degrelle* (*In Response to the Press after the Death of Léon Degrelle*), in which Mathieu opened a debate of ideas.

For Olivier Mathieu, Léon Degrelle was not a mythical figure but a living legend. They corresponded regularly and had frequent telephone conversations. Mathieu fondly remembers when, on April 20th, 1989, he was in a small village of the Jura, in the company of a friend from the pharmaceutical sector and a dozen other people. They were gathered to celebrate the one hundredth anniversary of the birth of Adolf Hitler. A surprise telephone call suddenly hushed those gathered together. It was Léon Degrelle sharing a few words with those gathered. Those long-distance calls had also been made several times between 1987 and 1990 at Solstice celebrations that were organized at the Château du Corvier in the Sologne region. In religious silence and in that magical environment, Léon's words resonated like strong beats in the pulsating hearts of those participating.

In his book, Mathieu confides that:

> *Each time I had to face some extraordinary situation during the period of 1988 to 1991, such as, for example, an evening attendance on some television broadcast or the summons to some legal proceedings brought against me, I always telephoned Léon Degrelle, not only to keep him informed of developments, but to ask for advice. Even when he wrote text—as he wrote to us—you seemed to hear his warm and courageous voice: "Good luck! Whatever it is, whatever happens, whatever follows, remember our sufferings on the Eastern Front. God bless you."*

## Be Strong!

Degrelle had good relations with the Madrid delegation of the Spanish Circle of Friends of Europe (CEDADE), whose representative in Madrid in the late 1980s was Javier Pascual. For the activists of this organization, Léon was an example of dedication and fidelity without fail, always upright in the face of the harshest adversities, a benchmark of bravery, coherence, and intelligence. He was the last of the great European leaders to survive the great storm of steel. To be received by Léon, to have a conversation with him, for those idealistic and unbroken young people was the greatest and most exciting political event of their lives.

On January 17th, 1987, a group of teenagers, members of CEDADE, visited Léon at his home on García Morato Street. Javier Pascual, as a local delegate, introduced these enthusiastic comrades. They were young, cheerful boys, among whom was a young man named Eduardo Núñez Barrado. He was the grandson of José Barrado Ruiz, from Salamanca, one of the executive staff of the multinational cosmetics company L'Oréal, who, in 1970, had asked his son Víctor Barrado, the uncle of Eduardo Núñez, to give shelter and refuge to Léon when a wave of persecution was again unleashed against him. Léon spoke with those young comrades in his office and, at the end of the meeting, gave a signed photograph with a personal dedication to each of them. He wrote to Eduardo: "For my dear friend Eduardo Núñez, with the most affectionate memory. L.D." The following year, on November 20th, 1988, the seventieth anniversary of the assassination of José Antonio Primo de Rivera and the thirteenth anniversary of the death of Francisco Franco, Degrelle delivered a lecture at CEDADE's local venue. Eduardo Núñez retained another photograph that Degrelle dedicated to him on the date of that anniversary: "To my great friend Eduardo Núñez with the affectionate memory of Degrelle. November 20th, 1988."

*Léon Degrelle with Pedro Varela and Eduardo Nuñez, 1987*

In March 1987, in CEDADE's magazine, a bold slogan was published in issue one hundred forty-eight: "Be Strong!" In that issue, Degrelle states in an article:

> *My dear comrades of CEDADE, I would have liked very much to be with you this afternoon, but you know my situation and the dangerous life that I have to endure, the displeasure that Jewish persecution provides me…but, in spite of everything, my spirit, my heart, go towards you.*

It was an extensive, dense article, with a clear and courageous message, no ambiguity, in which he recognized that:

> *The young people of CEDADE are the only ones who are truly Hitlerites. This word gives fear to many people; all the cowards of the bourgeoisie, and the semi-bourgeoisie are afraid to hear it, millions of people of good faith are surprised, and sometimes scandalized. Why? Because they do not know what the truth is, who Hitler was, what Hitler's work was. To have the courage to repeat what Hitler's social policy was, Hitler's great social revolution, the only social revolution of the century.*

In the article, he highlighted the impact and magnitude of the Führer's social policy, the universal aspect of National Socialism in his European policy and the anti-communist bulwark that he made Germany, becoming the engine to build up the continent.

He finished the writing with a few words of order: "Be strong! You have to be strong intellectually, strong morally, in the face of the assaults of corrupt people and idiots, strong looking toward the future, that is, toward victory! Heil Hitler!"

He added a postscript in his own handwriting, written in December 1979, which, on the occasion of the forty-seventh anniversary of the rise of National Socialism in Germany, had already been printed in CEDADE's special bulletin number 88 of January 1980, in which he said: "To my young comrades, so brave, of CEDADE, faithful to the great example of our heroes of the Eastern Front! Your friend. Léon Degrelle."

## An Unpublished Writing by Degrelle:
## A Commentary on Point XVI of the Falange Program Standard

On the feast of the Three Wise Men in 1987,[153] León Degrelle gave me a gift, a manuscript that has remained unpublished until now. Degrelle, having the honor of being the holder of the very first membership card of the Falange Exterior, granted by José Antonio Primo de Rivera in 1934, had been asked to comment on Point XVI (Sixteen) of the Falange Program Standard, which reads:

> XVI. *All Spaniards who are not disabled have a duty to work. The National Syndicalist State will not pay the least consideration to those who do not perform any function and who aspire to live as guests at the expense of others.*

Providing commentary on the twenty-seven points of the program standard with exegesis, footnotes, annotations, and glossaries was an exciting project that I was working on at the time as a contribution and update of the National-Syndicalist message on the fiftieth anniversary of the assassination of José Antonio in Alicante. I had already collected comments on some of the cardinal points of the program doctrine, written by my friends and comrades, Blas Piñar, Tomás Borrás, Felipe Ximénez de Sandoval, Manuel Ballesteros, Juan Moso Goizueta, the Count of Espoz y Mina, Ernesto Giménez Caballero, Francisco Alemany, Dionisio Martín Sanz, Patricio González de Canales, Fray Pacífico de Pobladura, Fernando Vizcaíno Casas, Jaime Alonso, Antonio Gibello, Raimundo Fernández Cuesta, Carlos de Meer, Ángel Alcázar de Velasco, Julio Pino, Jesús Suevos, etc. As I was the youngest of the writers who contributed to the project, I reserved the commentary on Point Twenty-Seven of the Falangist Program Standard for myself. It was the only one that was adjectival, exclusively strategic in content and, perhaps, the most compromised, for having been taken out of hand and out of context on the most disparate occasions to justify, depending on how it was interpreted, all the good or all the evil that later occurred to the Falangist Movement.

León Degrelle's article on Point Sixteen, in its entirety, reads as follows:

---

[153] *Los Reyes Magos*, or the Three Kings Day, celebrates what is better known in American English as the *Three Wise Men*—from the Gospel of Matthew, chapter 2—on January 6th and is a holiday in its own right in Spain, and to a lesser extent in France as well. This is the holiday that was traditionally the day for exchanging presents.

## THE DUTY TO WORK

I was a friend of José Antonio. We were both filled with the same faith. In 1934, two years before he was killed, he gave me member card number one of the Falange Exterior.

For the Falange, as for the Rex that I led, the basis of all social life was the obligation of honor to the work that every human being must respect.

Indeed, this "duty to work" is stumbling upon the material impossibility of working that has hit millions of young people head on. The so-called democratic Europe at the end of the twentieth century drags behind it, like a ball and chain, the tragic chain links of its unemployed.

The drama is not only economic, but also political. The real problem is no longer the duty to work, but the duty to be able to work. In order to give due consideration to work, it is first and foremost necessary to make it accessible. Even more so than in the time of José Antonio, a total political renewal is indispensable to restore order, longevity, competence, and strength to the State, essential bases of all wealth, both economic and social, for the one is linked to the other.

In a regime where any calamity can be a deputy or minister provided that he has captured enough votes and where it is never known whether, three months later, the government will still survive, no major plan is possible. The honor and the possibility of work are concerned most with political stability. [...]

Moreover, they are only conceivable to the extent that a strong state subjects a hyper-capitalist society to the law of the common good, and taming the pursuit of profit, the mediocrity of industrial elites, and the cruelty of competition at any price, which make man a manipulated object according to the very laws of economic materialism.

The Falange, inscribing in its principles the obligation to work, inserted in them the sacred duty to do so in a human and balanced society.

José Antonio, when he fixed the rules of his National-Syndicalist State, did not just think of the working class's obligation to work. At that time, back in 1936, the people worked very hard, and were miserably paid, under a front that was called Popular. This Popular Front, because of its fundamental anarchy, its political fanaticism, its constant calls for social hatred, led the Spanish working masses to stagnation. The miserable wages that workers received under the Popular Front are often forgotten today. Young José earned two pesetas a day as a typographer.

To camouflage its failures and its inability, the Popular Front resorted to escalating violence. It dragged Spain into its civil war. Before losing the war militarily in 1939, the Popular Front had already lost the war socially in 1936. [...]

These Popular Fronts, both in Paris and in Madrid, had failed. They were plunged into chaos from the very moment when the declared anti-Marxist Adolf Hitler had been democratically empowered in Germany, supported in every election and in every plebiscite—even in Saarland under Allied control[154]—by more than 90 percent of voters.

In three years, not only had the leader of the German people returned work and dignity of life to six million unemployed, but he had created two million more new jobs. He was able to renew the energy and creative spirit of the elites, fostering the encouragement of the best with super modern industries, and creating new sources of labor. He transformed the factories, humanized them, aerated them, provided them with sports facilities and swimming pools. He benefitted the working class with paid leave and vacations up to twenty-one days. He built two and a half million comfortable houses. He created the popular car, Volkswagen, payable at the rate of five marks per week. He inaugurated the layout of several thousand kilometers of highway for the general economy and for the leisure of workers. They were glad to be able to drive to the Norwegian fjords or to the sparkling waters of Madeira Island. The people had regained, at the same time, comfort and dignity.

In "democratic" Madrid, what had the freemason liberals and the ruling socialists done for the people, other than gaining power...? Where was Social Security in Spain? Who took care of the pensions of workers, peasants, and the disabled? What about paid holidays? Misery prevailed everywhere. Desperate day laborers had even been killed in Andalusia. [...]

José Antonio opposed the demagogy of the Popular Front. He certainly considered Spain's quest according to her own identity, within her own interior, and not through the models of foreign countries. What he wanted above all was to dignify work, to make it the true title of nobility of a regenerated national community.

When he spoke, in Point Sixteen, of those who aspire "to live as guests at the expense of others," it was not only the struggle of the working class that he had in mind. For him the class struggle was <u>multi-faceted.</u>

Contrary to what many obese bourgeoisie think, class warfare is not just a concern for the proletariat. It is also often a fact of the powerful class, committed to enjoying their privileges, the privilege of hogging sterile wealth, and living as such without collaborating for the common good.

---

[154] After the First World War, in 1920, the German territory of Saarland was occupied by France under a League of Nations mandate. In 1935, after a status referendum, the territory was returned to Germany.

*This class, because of its blindness and selfishness, has also been afraid for social peace, as Karl Marx's teaching points out.*

*José Antonio wanted to bring this wealthy class to heel, to force it to serve and not just to enjoy; to endow the nation with true elites who considered the manual laborer a respected collaborator and not a servant, whose only value is determined by profitability.*

*On the part of the Falangist chief, it was not a question of demagoguery but of giving meaning to the life of a so-called managerial class whose arms hung limp, useless, in the face of the reality of the masses that formed the country.*

*At the instigation of comrades who survived José Antonio, Franco sought to increase work opportunities and to depart from the economic backwardness of his country, introducing an exclusively agricultural Spain to the industrial reality of the century. The well-off classes had long been relegated to disregarding creative economic activity. Therefore, it is thanks to this industrial evolution undertaken against the tide, especially by constructing the seventy large industrial complexes of the INI as a decisive stimulant for the future, that Spain is not, economically and socially, backward at this time. Without this high-level industrialization, like that imposed by Franco, what would happen to the millions of surplus farmers in Spain? In 1975, Spain ranked eleventh among the industrialized countries of the world. The fact is there. History will take note of it. [ . . . ]*

*It was still necessary that this industrial activity that was offered to the "elites" propel them to get in contact with the innumerable industrial and agricultural discoveries, as well as the ambition to expand in certain industries.*

*To be locked up, and spiritually dead in the past, or to refuse this indispensable evolution for lack of curiosity or because of laziness, was to prevent the Spanish worker from an awakened nature and becoming equal to the best foreign technicians.*

*To be apathetic, to reject modernization, would have been like putting into practice another form of class struggle, that of capitalism closed to progress and the needs of the social community.*

*Only a conquering mentality, coupled with a team spirit among all classes, can save Spain's economic life from stagnation. To aspire to live no more than "as guests at the expense of others" is too simple. Modern society cannot live unless everyone, the industrialist, the landowner, the worker, and the peasant, progress technologically at the same cadence. The "duty to work" should aim at developing all new forms of production and the competitiveness of workers. To stagnate is to remain at the tail of modern life. [ . . . ]*

*Thus, José Antonio gave no consideration but to those who fulfilled a role in society, modest or eminent. Even more, he said that it was intelligence that led the physical effort.*

*To work, to honor work, is not only handling the pickax or giving orders in a workshop, but it necessarily includes the work of the mind, the brain of the responsible employer, as of the mental work of the laborer and the peasant, who must, both the one and the other, assimilate new knowledge and use it in full and fair collaboration.*

*Without work, un-adapted and scattered, it would be utterly vain. Moreover, in modern life, they would not be doing their function, but would be like manipulatable, part-time, expensive, and unproductive robots, who would be inexorably eliminated by competitors.*

*Such is the teaching that José Antonio has bequeathed to us, to bring together everyone's energy and effort.*

*Léon Degrelle*

## An Iberian "Nazi" Lion

Sensitivity to the world of arts and culture always had an impact on Degrelle. He often repeated a particular phrase of his, in which he insisted, "I love beauty. After God, it is what counts most in my life, even including politics, which I have always considered a work of art." He was convinced that the vulgar passes away, just as beauty is immortal.

One summer morning, back in 1973, while traveling with two friends from Andalusia, they stopped at a roadside inn on the highway linking Osuna to Sevilla. It was a quick stop on the road to quench their thirst from the summer heat. Among the stacked boxes of soft drinks, there was an old stone lion, left haphazardly, with two bulging eyes that seemed to fix their gaze on them. This was a granite lion that could be dated back to antiquity and was some two thousand four hundred years old. It weighed one ton. He asked the innkeeper if he was selling the lion. The innkeeper was relieved to get rid of it and agreed to sell it to Degrelle.

A few days later, that lion occupied a central and dignified place, with full honors, in the garden surrounding Degrelle's La Cabaña house. From then on, the stone Iberian lion was his faithful namesake and companion. There it remained until 1986, the year in which Degrelle moved his residence to a spacious flat, on the eighth floor of building number 23 on Paseo Marítimo Ciudad de Melilla, in Malaga. Due to its weight and size, and considering the move to an apartment, the piece was stored on the premises of the Nereo shipyard until it found a new location.

On April 12th, 1988, a great scandal, designed to be artistic in nature, but in reality, was political, erupted in the city of Malaga. The intent of the great uproar was to make it seem that an Iberian lion, "of priceless archaeological value," was about to be sold and illegally shipped to a foreign country. A large number of police were mobilized, and radio, press, and television media were called up. The next day it was revealed that this whole trick had been nothing more than an operation carried out by provocateurs. Using the lion as an excuse, they were trying to discredit Degrelle publicly.

A campaign of disrepute was orchestrated by the Jewish quarter against León Degrelle, in collusion with the socialist mayor of the city and the city council's cultural advisor, Francisco Flores. Malaga's municipal police agents prepared a spectacular deployment and a very special plan to carry out an operation that had been fed to the media at the national level, so they could broadcast the concocted plot. A whirl of photographers, hack journalists, reporters, and television cameras concentrated on the square at the Nereo shipyards in Malaga, happy to continually report that they were about to witness an exclusive event, a hidden, unusual discovery, propelled by a false accusation: the lion had been stolen by a "Nazi" and was about to be smuggled abroad.

Everything supposedly started from "an anonymous phone call."

The ruse worked. The large news agencies EFE and LOGOS unleashed their reporters, who carefully took note of the information leaked to them by the agents within the municipality.

In fact, the Iberian lion had been exposed to the public for over ten years at La Cabaña in Fuengirola, where it had been admired and contemplated by dozens of friends, politicians, and journalists who had photographed it on numerous occasions.

Televisión Española, in its first news broadcast for that day, put out the false news of the illicit origin of the archaeological piece, and that Degrelle planned to illegally transport the work of art to Italy. The news was mixed with images of a Jewish woman from Hungary who had just lost a case in court against Degrelle, obviously added to the story to push more Jewish propaganda.

While the police deployments were taking place, Léon was traveling elsewhere in a Citroen from Madrid on the way to Malaga, where he had an appointment with the dentist. He was completely unaware of the events unfolding. He had been away from Malaga for more than a month, staying in Madrid and Figueras, writing a book entitled *Hitler and Dalí* for a Paris publisher. Few people knew that, in 1938, the brilliant painter Salvador Dalí painted a portrait of Hitler in oil on canvas called *Hitler's Enigma*. In 1984, Dalí produced a work representing a moving truck, where a white-whiskered Hitler appeared on one of the vehicle's doors, inside a large number 21.

When Léon Degrelle entered his home in Malaga, the phone was ringing off the hook. The owner of the shipyards informed him that he urgently needed to go down to the Municipal Police Office, on Avenida de la Rosaleda nineteen. From there he was taken before Judge Don Fernando González Subieta, Court One, who was on duty. When Degrelle was asked about his ownership of the Iberian lion, he immediately and fully reported purchasing it fifteen years ago, where he obtained it from, the witnesses present, and the receipt of the check given to its former owner. In less than fifteen minutes, everything was cleared up and Léon Degrelle left the judge's chambers. The complaint was filed, and the mysterious case was closed in terms of its legal significance, but not in terms of the journalistic assembly that was supposed to herald the "alleged scandal."

Two newspapers in Malaga, *Sur* and *La Gaceta de Málaga*, on April 13th, 1988, devoted eight columns and seven columns, respectively, to the "big news" with great headlines and with an important and unusual typographical display. The news in *Sur* reported, "The police discover alleged illegal trafficking in art objects. The Nazi collaborator Léon Degrelle may be involved in this alleged trafficking of art objects." For its part, *La Gaceta de Málaga* reported, "an alleged illegal movement of archaeological pieces was detected by the municipal police. There were suspicions that the far-right Belgian Degrelle intended to smuggle them out of Spain."

Slander, without any foundation, multiplied like a domino effect.

The gutter tabloid *Diario 16* distinguished itself by stating: "The Nazi Degrelle is caught in Malaga smuggling three archaeological pieces. One of them dates from the third century BC." The Madrid newspaper *El País* published the news sent by its correspondent, Elena B. Castilla, with the following headline: "The municipal police of Malaga discover archaeological pieces of great value. According to the shipyard owner's account, the archaeological pieces could belong to Léon Degrelle, who resides in Torreblanca del Sol (Fuengirola)." This newspaper, in its edition the following day, referred back to this news, reporting that, "The judge investigating the alleged sale of archaeological pieces by the Nazi collaborationist recused himself from the case," and continued to report that the previous day Degrelle had declared to the correspondent of the Belgian newspaper *Le Soir* that "this was all a defamation campaign and a disgrace," since the pieces in question had been legally purchased and he had receipts for them.

Also on April 13th, with the perfidious maneuver now falling apart, the LOGOS News Agency released the following news:

*Malaga Thirteen. The head of the Court of Instruction One of Málaga, Fernando*
*González Subieta, has recused himself from the case of the archaeological pieces*
*located yesterday in the Nereo shipyard, next to the Baños del Carmen campsite. It*
*appears that the alleged attempt to export these pieces clandestinely could not be*
*demonstrated.*

*Léon Degrelle, the protagonist in this event, provided, at the request of the*
*judge, sufficient information to demonstrate ownership of the pieces found. They*
*were unable to demonstrate the possible sale of these pieces.*

The EFE News Agency expressed itself in similar terms: "The Judge has recused
himself in the case for not having shown that these pieces were being moved out of
the country," adding that "Degrelle, eighty-two, provided sufficient evidence to
ensure that these archaeological pieces are his property."

At 10:00 a.m. on April 13th, the judge, fed up with so many foolish articles,
closed the case and ordered it filed away, finding it senseless. The judge had torn
apart the ridiculous plot of Degrelle's enemies.

As is often the case in these defamatory, disinformation campaigns, on
Thursday, April 14th, the press, which had pumped up the fake news, got their
balloon popped and the malicious information completely vanished; they had no
choice but to retract it. *Sur* buried its retraction in the inside pages, hoping it would
pass unnoticed, reporting, "Degrelle demonstrates ownership of the archaeological
pieces." Some newspapers, such as *Málaga*, went so far as to recognize that they had
been deceived.

The leftist newspaper *El País*, however, continued its defamatory campaign
against Degrelle, despite the exculpatory court order, and continued to completely
distort the judicial decision, proclaiming with the huge title of a four-column
article: "Degrelle will have to show that the archaeological pieces identified by the
Malaga police are his own." They were stubborn about it and repeatedly insisted
and denigrated only because of their desire to sow suspicion and uphold the slander,
without even pausing to note that the case had already been resolved by the court.

Televisión Española kept the incriminating news in the spotlight until two days
after the judicial resolution. This was not the first time that Léon Degrelle had been
baselessly reviled in the media. Televisión Española's "Weekly Report" program
was labeled by viewers as "*Infamous Weekly*"[155] in August 1987, when it was directed
by the judaizing Ramón Colóm. This was because of a report entitled "Barbie in

---

[155] [Play on words here: "weekly report" and "infamous report" in Spanish are, respectively, *informe semanal* and *infamia semanal*.]

Madrid" that broadcast an intentional falsehood, inventing the story that a German Army lieutenant, whom Degrelle had never known before and whose name was even unknown to him, had set up a large arms and drug trafficking business in partnership with Otto Skorzeny, who had already died in the 1970s, along with Léon Degrelle. His detractors continued to stoop lower and lower with their malicious lies.

Léon Degrelle wrote, "I prefer being a Nazi to an architect or accomplice in the production of such garbage, like Televisión Española, champion of lies and cowardice."

*Diario 16*, evidently refusing to recognize reality, continued insisting on the false news all the way up to April 15th and 16th, stubbornly maintaining its defamation and confusing public opinion, which forced Léon Degrelle to file lawsuits against journalist Juan María Rodríguez, who authored the false news; the Andalusian director of *Diario 16*, Francisco Rosell; the Managing Director of *Diario 16* in Madrid, Pedro J. Ramírez; and the President responsible for the newspaper's publishing company Información y Prensa S.A., Juan Tomás de Salas. The incidental claim for jurisdictional protection of fundamental rights was filed with the Court of First Instance of Malaga on May 28th (decision 595/88). The judges would eventually rule in Degrelle's favor, condemning the defendants.

In one week, *Diario 16* had dedicated nineteen whole columns to this defamation campaign. The four defendants thought they would go unpunished forever. They gambled on the fact that Spanish justice was expensive and to litigate risked hundreds of thousands of pesetas over a slow process. In this case, the delay demonstrated that fact in Madrid as the dossier of warrants was lost, incidentally, for four months. They had the previous case file and the number of the case filed later, but the one containing the warrants for the *Diario 16* defendants in Madrid had vanished! General Léon Degrelle had to personally confront the Madrid court, protesting vehemently. He gave the court officials four days to find the case file before giving a press conference at the same Palace of Justice. On the fourth day, the case file miraculously reappeared!

On March 9th, 1989, the judge of Court One delivered a condemnation with the following judgment:

> *That on the part of the journalist Mr. Juan María Rodríguez Caparrós, editor of Diario 16, there has been illegitimate interference in the honor of the plaintiff, and in consequence I must condemn it and I require all the defendants to put an end to the unlawful interference or meddling that is here denounced; likewise in the future they shall refrain from defaming the plaintiff. All of them are ordered jointly to pay*

*the plaintiff the sum of eight million pesetas for damages and non-pecuniary harm*
*caused.*

On March 10th, 1989, *Diario 16* issued its opinion on the convictions of three of its managing staff, and was silent about its President, Juan Tomás de Salas. *Diario 16* appealed the sentence at the provincial court, which rejected the appeal and confirmed the sentence, although it lowered the amount of compensation.

When the matter of the Iberian "Nazi" Lion finally ended, on Saturday, April 16th, 1988, *Sur* published one of its "Letters to the Director," signed by Juan Jesús Gómez Rivera along with fifty-two young Malagueños, who said the following:

> *The ideal will live to the extent that we give ourselves to it until death. What a drama it is, truly, to live a righteous life!*
>
> *These phrases, written from the hardness of his own experience, define the human and political profile of its author, one of the most prominent characters in the recent history of Europe: Léon Degrelle.*
>
> *Léon Degrelle is, in his life, in his sacrifice, and in his unshakable fidelity, an exceptional example for all young Europeans committed to the defense and rebirth of our civilization. Therefore, in the face of this insidious and clumsy campaign waged against his person by the eternal pharisees, dogmatics of "freedom," and their professional liars, the young Malagueños here undersigned want to make public our unconditional support for this man, one of our most illustrious neighbors.*
>
> *At the same time, we express our rejection and our disgust toward the vile and crooked promoters of this campaign who have shown themselves to be so irreverent to the dignity and personal honor of a Spanish citizen.*
>
> *For Léon Degrelle, our respect and our recognition; for "the usual ones," our absolute contempt.*

The Iberian lion plot at least unmasked a whole lot of liars steeped in political hatred.

All these incidents were exposed in a work entitled *Un León Ibérico Nazi (An Iberian Nazi Lion)* dated and signed in Malaga on April 30th, 1988. It would be published in full by CEDADE in number 160, as a double copy, from its magazine dated April/May of that same year, unmasking the great political and journalistic scandal that fell apart. One recalls the commandment of the law of God which says, "Thou shalt not bear false witness against thy neighbour" (Exodus 20:16).

On Saturday, October 28th, at 8:00 p.m., the book *Un León Ibérico Nazi (An Iberian Nazi Lion)* was presented at Hotel Málaga Palacio, a public event organized by CEDADE, for which the corresponding invitations were made as follows: "Léon Degrelle is pleased to invite you and your family to the public presentation of *Un León Ibérico Nazi (An Iberian Nazi Lion)*," indicating the place and time as well as the organizing entity. The invitation cards for the book event were all personally signed by Léon Degrelle.


## He Celebrates His Birthday in 1988 with the Portuguese Poet Rodrigo Emilio and a Group of Portuguese Comrades

On June 15th, 1988, eighty-two years after his birth, Degrelle was visited by five Portuguese comrades at 5:00 p.m. at his home in Madrid: Rodrigo Emilio Ribeiro de Mello, Antonio Carlos Rangel, José Carlos Craveiro Lópes, José Manuel Ferreira, and Julio Prata Sequeira. They arrived from the sister country to wish him well, congratulate him, and celebrate his birthday with him. The time spent with this group of "*Viriatos*,"[156] who admired him as if they were his "Portuguese disciples," included book dedications, autographs, and souvenir photographs in memory of the historical visit. It also brought together those two great poets of the millennium, the Lusitanian Rodrigo Emilio and the Belgian Léon Degrelle.

During the meeting, Rodrigo Emilio read aloud, in French, a letter he had written:

*My General:*

*I have to tell you that it has been beautiful to meet you in person. With my knowledge of your person, I have fulfilled the first dream of my life. That is, I have already reached the highest peak of my life. To see you, to look at you, to speak to you, to listen to you, above all, being able to shake your hand—your warrior hands, your hands as an artist and a writer, so brave in everything, and so heroic in all things like those of the combatant—all of this has for me the myth itself and, what is more, the myth lived.*

*I cannot fail to feel a kind of historical shiver remembering that your hands, which I have had the honor of shaking, were also embraced by those of the Führer, just twenty-four hours before I was born. Your last meeting with Hitler took place on February 17th, 1944, is that not true?*

---

[156] The name *Viriatos* in both Spanish and Portuguese refers broadly to those Portuguese volunteers who fought for the Spanish nationalists in the Spanish Civil War. The name itself is borrowed from the second century BC leader Viriathus of the Lusitanians who resisted Roman conquest in the peninsula.

*Well, I was born on February 18th, 1944.*

*This leads me to say that I, then, entered life at just the right time, just at the best moment that I could have been born. It was already getting too late, no doubt, to reach this world…*

*In Spanish, now, I would like to thank you, in short, for the simple fact that you were born, my General.*

*Rodrigo Emilio*

In the evening, Degrelle dined with his Portuguese companions at the Casa Botín restaurant, where his magnetic conversation entertained everyone in an atmosphere of friendship and camaraderie. One of his comrades stated, "he celebrated with Portugal, transmitting to his young disciples his contagious vibration, his impetus, his energy, and his magnetism, which literally set us aside and made Degrelle the ideal image of youth, which Brasillach talked about so often."[157]

As a culmination to such a pleasant and enjoyable meeting, they went out to the terrace of his upper floor to admire the crests of the Sierra del Guadarrama against a beautiful backdrop, and to contemplate the old roofs of Madrid resembling a red tide in the labyrinth of the Castilian city.

From that encounter, Rodrigo Emilio has left us a superb chronicle, which he titled "Léon Degrelle or the Known Soldier":

*It was 5:00 p.m. It was 5:00 p.m. on all the watches of Madrid, when we were lucky enough to reach our goal, so long awaited and always desired.*

*As if by the work of a spell or an enchantment, there we were finally, knocking upon the most sacred of doors and seeing them open. They opened wide, allowing our passage into the temple of the last terrestrial god whom we worship, a constant, unconditional worship, at all hours.*

*In a stroke of magic, we had before us nothing more and nothing less than Léon Degrelle.*

*For us, it had been years, years and more years of longing and hopeful expectation and now, and for the first time, they were satisfied: To see Degrelle, and now we can die in peace!*

*We expected, an effusive lesson of liveliness, of life and adventure fully enjoyed and fully attested.*

*However incredible it was or seemed to be, there he was, at last, at his full height, in front of us, welcoming us like a gracious prince and comrade of all time,*

---

[157] It is unclear exactly which of the Portuguese friends the author is quoting here.

*introducing us with the finery of Athenian delicacy and with his affability into the most private chambers of his stronghold, reserving for us, exclusively, the right of admission. [...]*

*With deepest admiration for the host, to have the satisfaction of seeing him, enjoying the honor of being able to serve him on the day of his eighty-second birthday as his honor guard (For him! Can you imagine!), who is the only one, and continues to be, for all intents and purposes, the greatest colossus of that heroic and combatant Europe from the 1940s. He is the lord of war and of war's glory, fighting, without truce or quarter, for the petty littleness of peace at any price. He is the living and reviving myth of the irresistible crusade against the Soviet escarpment, the supreme portent of the Russia campaign, and of another thousand terrible "exploits," against that titan par excellence of world defeat and of the hours of despondency and debacle that followed. He is the depositary, legate, and privileged transmitter of the flame of Aryan faith and charm and fidelity to the Führer; the unwavering agent of the tradition of Europe from the day before yesterday to the day after tomorrow, there he was, suddenly, in person, within reach, at our complete disposal, think of it!*

*Degrelle immediately and without delay opened the book of history in his memory as a man of arms and called upon the man of letters to break forth, equally incomparable, that which dwells within himself, so he could recite it to us very well from beginning to end. Then Léon Degrelle began to tell the saga of an extreme and palpating existence, of a full and simply fabulous life; for his life, his existence, is all of it well worth a long, long film, sown with marvels and wonders. I mean to say, a film about brave men, full of action and suspense, imbued with magic and tests of combat. That is worth, for all and above all, and at the end of the day, a great and heartbreaking song of deeds.*

*The narrative arch of the exhibition transferred us and then moved us from rural and deep Wallonia of the beginning of the century to the advent and triumphal march of the political proposals inherent in the waves of the Rex Movement, and from there to the turning point and then the point of no return from the fury of the battlefields themselves.*

*Always making "grand état," and a superior and permanent boast of his extraordinary "rex-appeal," our passionate interlocutor then set out the underlying reasons, compelling reasons all of them, which pushed him to sacrifice his aura and prestige as a charismatic domestic leader (with benefits, moreover, and a future situation guaranteed within a rather small range of action and in a smaller sphere of influence) and obligingly leave off making a career, in a selfish sense, just to be*

oppressed by others in his native Belgium. He wound up living a destiny of epic and
widely European remembrance in Spain.

Adolf Hitler's clarion call had the effect of mobilizing, both inside and outside,
the greatest and best of its recipients: in the end, Degrelle was the only being on
earth whom the Führer considered as being molded, carved, and created in his own
image and likeness, and 100 percent worthy of him. There is still no one like
Degrelle, who has not ceased to emphasize it himself, who asserts his status as a true
Belgian, a genuine Belgian, alongside the German high-ranking leaders,
systematically refusing to accept or slavishly obey their "diktaten" (dictations) and
thus to play the passive role of either a gate guard or a bugle boy, if not a day officer
or an officer on the orders of pan-Germanism.

He evoked, in sequence, the circumstances, understanding that it was up to
him to meet with the one who would be the first and best of his panegyrists and
biographers, the great, the brilliant, and ill-fated Franco-Catalan writer and poet
Robert Brasillach, the martyr of Fresnes.[158] To talk to Degrelle, he would approach
him directly in the 1940s, by going up to the front lines as a war reporter sent to
the Eastern Front by the weekly "Je Suis Partout." He interviewed Degrelle at length
on the war front, drawing from him a moving and expressive physical,
temperamental, and psychological portrait. Degrelle suspended the superb debate to
take us to the more intimate corner of his office.

He sat in front of the creative furniture of his worktable and then exchanged
with us books and autographs, authenticating one by one the innumerable titles,
volumes, and pamphlets of his authorship, just the thing we had traveled to Madrid
for, that he might sign them with his own hand.

He then went, and we with him, to the roof of the building and he called us to
contemplate, from the top of a panoramic terrace, the four cardinal points of the
Castilian capital, until lost to sight, open and projected, against the western screen
of the horizon.

From there, in a few moments, we took up the conversation again, continuing
thereafter, sitting at the old warrior's table.

To celebrate fully, Degrelle had requested, or perhaps even demanded, the
friendly escort of his Portuguese apostles, after taking us to a well-known restaurant
in the city (a kind of oasis in the Thousand and One Nights, like a mirage in the
midst of the chaotic pulse of the city).

---

[158] Robert Brasillach, an important journalist and writer in French fascist and nationalist circles, was
imprisoned in 1945, tried for "collaborationism," and executed by firing squad. His death sentence,
opposed even by some of his enemies, remains controversial because he was executed for his words
and thoughts, not for any political or military action or crime.

*Degrelle described the Wagnerian chronicle of the Axis military campaigns, both on the continent and on the sea; the betrayal of von Paulus, the motive that dictated it and the catastrophic weight of consequences it had; the general apotheosis of the final hours that preceded the chaos, the hemorrhage, the catastrophe; the huge, Dantesque magnificence of the last skirmishes, clashes, and fighting, and the admirable example of the last devotions, self-sacrifice, and loyalty; the magnitude and grandeur, excessive even, of those who resisted and fought "jusq'au bout et au delà du bout";[159] the gratuitous and nefarious stench of all the selective and massive acts of vengeance that were then doled out from everywhere (large-scale butchery, such as Dresden, slaughterhouses like Dongo, and many more... which he witnessed; the gallows at Nuremberg; the crematorium furnaces of Hiroshima and Nagasaki... and so on...); the suffering, torture, and death of Degrelle's own parents and brother, as well his father-in-law, Joseph Darnand; the agony, passion, and crucifixion "d'il caro Ben,"[160] of Clara Petacci, and of thousands of faithful followers of the Duce; of a thousand other pathetic and eloquent episodes that fed the wild and unleashed fury and insanity that marked the so-called end of the war. An entire, detailed panel of all the anti-fascist reasoning that was then poured out upon the four corners of the world, were just an appetizer to this ceremonial dinner (perhaps our last and only dinner with the legendary fighter).*

*As time ran out and the night progressed, "Master" Degrelle kept getting younger, and when the time came to congratulate him for all the days of his life, he reverberated with youth, sharpness, animation, and brilliance.*

*He was by far the youngest and most jovial of us all, by word and by "verve."*

*His contagious animation, his impetus, his energy, his magnetism literally placed us in a song and made Degrelle the ideal image of youth, which Brasillach spoke of so much.*

*When the time came for farewells and the round table of friendship took leave of this knight, this primus et impar inter pares,[161] Degrelle remained the living, perfect, and divine image of time recovered.*

*With eighty-two years to his name, our old and fearless "Lion" could be said to have broken and transgressed all the laws of aging, and then some.*

---

[159] [French for "up to the very end and beyond the end."]

[160] [Italian for "of dear Ben," likely a reference to Benito Mussolini and specifically the manner of his mob execution.]

[161] [Latin for "first and unequal among equals," that is, he has no equal. This is a play on the historical Latin phrase *primus inter pares*, which defines the bishopric of the Pope of Rome as the "first among equals" among the ancient Christian patriarchates.]

> *On the way out, he sealed and united us in esprit de corps and unto ages of*
> *ages…the sacramental covenant of the brotherhood of arms (and souls). He*
> *ceremonially looked us in the face, kissed us respectfully on the cheek, gave us a*
> *brotherly embrace with all the strength that his years allowed him. Miraculously*
> *overflowing, he disappeared into the night, a spring in his step, extending his arm*
> *eternally in our direction.*
>
> *He left an imprinted, inextinguishable trace: the trace of a plethoric and*
> *winged being, Apollonian and fiery, Nibelungic and fantastic.*
>
> *Upon our foreheads, he engraved a magical and fascinating trace: the trace of*
> *a god, of an earthly god, a subsolar god.*
>
> *The only god in flesh and bone that one happy day I was allowed to know, to*
> *recognize, and to identify as such. The only one whom I encountered on the wayward*
> *roads of this world, after José de Almada Negreiros.[162] The only one also, until*
> *today, that it was possible for me to approach in person, to contemplate before, and*
> *to question face to face.*
>
> *Apart from Almada, the only god, in person, whom I saw up close and alive*
> *was Degrelle.*
>
> *Yes, the only one. The only one; and with certainty, the very last of his race…*

Rodrigo Emilio wrote this piece, next to a Manueline window at his home at Parada de Gonta in the Viseu neighborhood, in San José, Portugal, on Día de la Raza in 1991.

## Censorship of Editorial Planeta

In the year 1988, Léon had already finished the first three volumes of what was to be, unfortunately, the unfinished great European history of the twentieth century. He was looking for a publisher and thought of the possibility of publishing his magnum opus with the most universal publisher of Spanish letters, Editorial Planeta, owned by José Manuel Lara. Boldly and with resolve, on November 2nd, 1988, he sent the following letter to Mr. Gonzalo Fernández de la Mora, after a previous telephone conversation to which he refers in his writing:

> *As we agreed by telephone, I am sending to you, with this letter, the three volumes*
> *of my work, The Century of Hitler, that have already come out. For good or for ill,*
> *it must be admitted that Hitler was the man who most marked this century. The*

---

[162] Reference to Portuguese artist and writer José Sobral de Almada Negreiros (1893 – 1970).

*First World War was "pre-Hitler." Our age now has almost nothing to do with the past, ground up by Hitler.*

*It is the Americans who first encouraged me to write this great historical work: they pay well and in advance; thus, I was able to have the financial freedom to think and write.*

*These three volumes constitute only the first part of my work. The general title of the three volumes is "Hitler, Born in Versailles," for it was indeed the Treaty of Versailles that allowed Hitler's development and ascension. The first volume is entitled Le Traquenard de Sarajevo [Sarajevo's Trap], which provides many revelations about 1914, a year full of lies and ambitions. The second volume is entitled La Pseudo-Guerre du Droit, 1914-1918 (The Pseudo-War of Law, 1914-1918) a war very different from what has been explained to the public so far. The third volume, "Les Tricheurs de Versailles" (The Cheaters of Versailles), needs no further explanation as the wording is sufficient.*

*Each of these volumes could be published alone and independently, without having to frame them within the general title. Next is El Hitler de la Paz (The Hitler of Peace),[163] also a broad heading divided, likewise, into three volumes: Democratic Hitler; Hitler, Unificador de los Alemanes" (Hitler, Unifier of Germans) and Hitler, Constructor del Gran Reich (Hitler, Builder of the Great Reich).*

*Then will come in chronological order El Hitler de la Guerra" (The Hitler of War), developed in three different volumes: Hitler, Piège à Dantzig (Hitler, Trap at Danzig), Hitler y Sus Waffen S.S. (Hitler and His Waffen S.S.), and Hitler Genio Militar (Hitler, Military Genius).*

*Already in North America and France the books (the three I am sending) are enjoying great success. I would very much like its Spanish edition to be of interest to our esteemed friend, José Manuel Lara, an extraordinary man of entrepreneurial dynamism. Even better, if these books are of interest to Mr. José Manuel, would it be possible to meet and have a meal one day at my place?*

Gonzalo Fernández de la Mora responded to Degrelle in the following terms:

*I perfectly remember our meeting, through José Ignacio, (the Marquis of Valdeiglesias) many years ago. I suffered a very serious heart attack in February, so my physical condition is quite weak and, of course, in jeopardy.*

---

[163] At this point in Jerez Riesco's original Spanish text, the titles of Degrelle's works listed in this letter change from French to Spanish. The reason for this is unclear.

> *With your letter came the first three volumes of your initial work. I had not heard of them. In order not to waste time, instead of reading them, I will send them directly to José Manuel Lara, as is your desire. As soon as I have any news from the publisher, I will pass it along to you.*

In Gonzalo Fernández de la Mora's writings is found another letter, written on the same day as the one responding to Degrelle. It is dated November 3rd, and is addressed to the publisher Lara, the owner of Editorial Planeta:

> *Many years ago, my unforgettable friend José Ignacio, Marquis of Valdeiglesias, introduced me to the controversial Léon Degrelle. Today, on the basis of that encounter long ago, the very controversial character sends me three volumes of a history of Europe from the German point of view, which will cover events starting from the Great War. I have only skimmed through them, and the truth is that I know of nothing similar because almost all of the current writing on that period is made from the Anglo-Saxon angle. If you are not interested in the work, I would be grateful if you could have these three volumes returned to me.*

Two weeks later, on November 16th, the publisher Lara replied:

> *I have had the originals of Léon Degrelle's work that you kindly sent me read by a well-trusted person, and the report that you have given me is high praise enough for the work itself, highlighting the intelligence of the argumentation and an extraordinary narrative talent in presenting the topic. Along with all these accolades, which I do not doubt are well deserved, it indicates that this history of Europe is very difficult to fit in with a publishing house like Planeta; first of all, because of its sheer extent, given that twenty volumes are planned (and judging by the first three, likely to be very thick) and, of course, for the evident tendentiousness of the author, despite his indisputable talent. In the background, it seems, he is making an unreserved apologia for Hitler and the Nazis.*
>
> *As you can understand, for these reasons, while being fully aware of the quality of the work, it is impossible for me to take charge of its publication and, in fact, it should be noted that the French edition was published by an almost unknown publisher, evidently associated with Nazi ideology.*

On receiving the letter above, Mr. Gonzalo Fernández de la Mora wrote again to Léon Degrelle on November 21st, 1988, to update him on the result of his unsuccessful correspondence with the publisher:

*On the same day that I received the first three volumes of your historical work, I sent them to my publisher José Manuel Lara, as was your wish. He has returned them to me today, saying that he is not interested in the translation and subsequent publishing of the book. I am very sorry that my advocacy has not been effective.*

## The One Hundredth Anniversary of the Birth of Adolph Hitler

On April 20th, 1989, the first centennial of the birth of Adolf Hitler, the Führer, Reich Chancellor, and founding leader of the German National Socialist Party, was commemorated. To celebrate the anniversary, the Spanish Circle of Friends of Europe (CEDADE), launched a special one hundred sixty-fifth issue of its magazine as a tribute of historical recognition to the great German statesman.

For the occasion, Léon Degrelle contributed an article entitled "Hitler, One Hundred Years Later," which began as follows:

*It has become increasingly clear that the twentieth century will be marked by the work that Adolf Hitler carried out.*

*The greatest political events of our time, the most prodigious military confrontations in our history, bear his signature and have been stamped with his seal, not only for our time, but for eternity.*

*After the disappearance of the ideal of which he was a bearer, the world changed its skin and, above all, its soul...*

*The unconditional idealist was succeeded by simple and foolish materialism. Any fool can become a vibrating fanatic of motorization, a slave-disciple of "consumerist civilization."*

*The frayed pants of young Europeans or Americans, and even Japanese, are marked with the labels of the Levi-style Jewish "tailors."*

*They no longer appreciate the rebirth of spring in the tree leaves and in the fields 100 meters (328 feet) from their homes, but they travel the world, without understanding much, with high tech cameras!*

*The cities have been transformed into huge prisons, with tight housing like cigarette packs. Evenings are nothing more than endless sessions of television applause, featuring annoying jerks, or vicious, stupid vampires, showing their breasts like grapefruits, or scandalous epileptics gesticulating in the crossfire of dazzling, multicolored spotlights. Decline, decay, baseness.*

*All this because a tremendous genius, who had created a new man, secure and strong, was defeated, slandered, and thrown into the trash as if he were some old and repulsive thing.*

*Here, however, the human being from half a century ago is the same today. He had eyes and ears…but he had one thing that no longer exists today, and which is the only thing that counts: FAITH.*

*It was a time when millions of wonderful and determined young people, behind big drums and flags, symbols and badges, toured our great avenues and illuminated with their looks, as well as with their torches, the gray streets of our cities.*

*From the depths of nowhere, Hitler raised millions of waves of these young bearers of enthusiasm.*

*They believed.*

*Their songs proclaimed their faith in life…*

*Hitler, a firm and sure soul, made this miracle possible, the greatest of miracles: to make man, who is nothing more than clay to be molded, as on the first day of creation, a being vivified by spirit.*

To the question that Degrelle formulated in the text on *Who was Hitler?* he responded without hesitation: "First and foremost, he was an artist."

Léon continued:

*Hitler was different from the rest of the children. He had an inner strength, and he was guided by his spirit and instincts. He could draw skillfully when he was only eleven years old. His first drawings and watercolors, at the age of fifteen, were full of poetry and sensitivity. One of his most remarkable works from his early days, "Fortress Utopia," shows us that he was also an artist of rare imagination. His artistic orientation took on several forms. He wrote poetry ever since he was a boy. He dictated an entire work to his sister Paula, who was surprised by his pride. At the age of sixteen, in Vienna, he embarked on the creation of an opera. He even designed the stage, as well as the costumes; and, of course, the protagonists were Wagnerian heroes. More than an artist, Hitler was above all an architect.*

*Hundreds of his works are remarkable, both for his painting and for his architecture. He could describe from memory, and in detail, the dome of a church or the complex curves of wrought iron. It was undoubtedly his dream to become an architect, and this was what led him to Vienna at the beginning of the century. When you see the hundreds of drawings, sketches, and paintings he created at that time, as well as his mastery of three-dimensional figures, it seems surprising that the examiners at the Academy of Art suspended him on two separate occasions. German* historian Werner Maser, who was not exactly a friend of Hitler, criticized his examiners: "All his works revealed an extraordinary knowledge and mastery of architecture. The builder of the Third Reich gave reasons for the Academy of Arts to be ashamed."

Who was Hitler? First and foremost an artist. An unknown artist who would be depicted to us as a second-rate dauber of buildings, when, in reality, certain paintings of his, especially those he painted during the First World War on the Flanders front and on the French front, are works of art of balance, of ideas, of serenity, of transparency of color. There are no great men who are not, first and foremost, great artists. Any work, whether political or not, that does not enhance the splendor of beauty, is nothing more than a tree without roots, ready to be knocked down by the next gale.

As an artist, Hitler finds in the background of himself, for no one will help him, the great nutritional forces that beauty needs. When man is possessed by beauty, what power will not nourish his faith? Then nothing will resist him. In just ten years, an entire people handed themselves to Hitler in body and soul.

In a thousand years and until the end of time, Hitler the great, dominating the centuries, will continue to live.

Degrelle not only reflected on Hitler as an artist, but he also made an extensive analysis of the achievements on all fronts by National Socialism because "both in politics and on the battlefield, Hitler was, history will tell it, the great man of our century."

The extensive article, written for the unique occasion of the one hundredth anniversary of Hitler's birth, which Léon Degrelle closed out the extensive article with these words:

In this year of his centennial, hardly will one evoke his name, but, despite the bellowing and barking of a thousand gross deceptions, his genius is unable to be swept away. He will resurface one day from the very mud they wanted to stain him with. Greatness is immortal.

A small fire in any corner of the world and all miracles of greatness are possible.

Everywhere in the contemporary world, these fires, still weak, are now reborn. From them will resurface, on the day of truth and justice, the great brazier of genius that was the life of Adolf Hitler.

For great men, time is of no importance.

One hundred years is nothing but a brief lapse of history.

During the month of April 1989, the cultural organization CEDADE carried out an intensive propaganda campaign throughout Spain to commemorate, without complexity, without groveling to the powers that be, without disavowals, the centennial of the birth of the man who, despite the incessant discrediting by his detractors, defined the twentieth century, which could well be described in the future as the "Century of Hitler." The results of the campaign reverberated throughout all international press and media.

The Canadian revisionist historian Ernst Zündel designed the commemorative poster for the occasion, with great beauty and success, of which forty thousand copies were published in Spain. It was a poster full of symbolism, color, and hope, rather than old nostalgia. The poster presented the word "anniversary" in large typographical fonts in four widely known European languages: Spanish, German, French, and English. At dusk on April 19th, during the vigil of that stellar commemoration, the great cities of Spain were wallpapered with that joyful and colorful poster, and the façades of their buildings were illuminated by a note of color in keeping with spring. In total, more than thirty thousand copies were pasted and hung, with the remaining ten thousand copies sent to Switzerland, Germany, and Austria to achieve joint and coordinated action on the great anniversary. Also, in Argentina and Chile, many alluring posters were seen in the central streets of their respective capital cities of Buenos Aires and Santiago. There were also sixteen thousand smaller stickers made in support of the campaign.

In order to contribute enthusiastically to the centennial campaign, Degrelle offered to sign photographs, dedicated to so many friends and supporters who requested them as a keepsake on such a symbolic anniversary. The autographed photographs were sold at three thousand pesetas each, and the proceeds were donated to cover the considerable expenses borne by CEDADE. The photograph selected was of Degrelle, illuminated by the first light of dawn, leaning out of an open window to feel the first rays of sun and the fresh air of that spring morning. The photograph contained the following handwritten text: "To CEDADE's friends, Heil Hitler! Léon Degrelle. April 20th, 1989."

Léon Degrelle spent the evening of April 20th dining in celebratory fellowship and friendship with his comrades. They came from various countries to Madrid to participate in the numerous events. The meal was reserved almost exclusively for foreign visitors, by the express desire and deference of the national organizers, so that the guests could dine with Degrelle privately. The dinner was held at Casa Botín, one of Léon's favorite restaurants, in the heart of the Austrias neighborhood, in the vicinity of the arcades of Plaza Mayor and Arco de Cuchilleros. With its peculiar, old, and evocative atmosphere, this was the perfect place to host this ceremonial dinner with Degrelle. That evening, guests who dined with Degrelle were enchanted by the contagious and friendly enthusiasm of his strong personality.

The Casa Botín was filled with visitors and friends alike, there to celebrate with the last of the surviving warlords of the great European catastrophe, French comrades, even some former combatants of the SS Division Charlemagne, Germans, Canadians, Belgians, Portuguese and even Mexicans. To ensure that the foreign guests, having traveled so far, could enjoy the company of Léon Degrelle and his distinguished wife Juana Brevet de Degrelle on that special night, only two Spaniards attended that dinner, both of whom were knowledgeable in various languages and served as helpful interpreters.

The Mexican comrade who attended the dinner was the writer Juan Guerrero Zorrilla, member of the editorial committee of the magazine *Elbruz* and author, among others, of the works *La Muerte de un Pagano* (*Death of a Pagan*), *El Mago de Variantes* (*The Wizard of Variants*), etc. He had arrived in Barcelona and from there he traveled to Madrid to be present at the centennial celebration for Adolf Hitler. He arrived in the capital on the afternoon of April 20th. When remembering that dinner, he affirmed that it was the opportunity to interact with "the most important man I have known in my life. I greeted him at the Casa Botín restaurant and told him that I had come from Mexico. He was pleased and told me that he had been there in the past. I waited for him to speak. He spoke first in French and then in German."

The Portuguese delegation was made up of the unforgettable poet Rodrigo Emilio Ribeiro de Mello, hailing from the manor on Parada de Gonta, in the Viseu neighborhood. He was already then an immortal figure in the Parnassus of the Elect. From Oporto, capital of the north and the origin of the name of Portugal, came Antonio Carlos Rangel, who recited in French, with an Occitan accent, several stirring lyrics for the occasion. There was also Alberto de Araujo Lima, whom everyone affectionately called "Nonas," with his militant enthusiasm, always proclaiming to the four winds his deeply rooted convictions, and to whom Léon wrote this dedication: "*En souvenir d'une heureuse soirée au Botín* (Remembering a happy evening at the Botín)! April 20th, 1989." From Lisbon, the comrades José Manuel Ferreira, Julio Prata Sequeira, and José Carlos Craveiro López attended the gathering.

Among Degrelle's other friends was the writer and businessman Theodore Soucek; Mrs. Florentine Rost van Tonningen-Heubel, always faithful to the ideal; and the revisionist author Thies Christophersen, who gave a brief speech, addressing the attendees in German. The young German Hans Ewald Althans was also present. At important dinners, the figure of "Judas Iscariot" is always represented, who, despite having finished his brief four-minute speech with a loud "Heil Hitler!" seemed very likely to be there in service to shady interests.[164] Only two Spaniards attended: Bernardo Gil Mugarza, who declined the invitation to speak during dessert, limiting himself to a brief "good night to all," which motivated Léon to comment aloud, with a certain smile of complicity, "Bernardo, always the most discreet"; and Alberto Torresano, who acted the Harlequin[165] at the ceremony. When a photograph was taken during the dinner showing Hans Ewald Althans and Alberto Torresano sitting together, this was commented on by some of the diners with that Castilian saying "Dios los cría y ellos se juntan!"[166]

At dessert, the time of the toast, some of the attendees took the floor. The last to speak was Léon Degrelle, who addressed his comrades affectionately:

> *My dear comrades, mes chers camarades, meine lieben Kameraden,*
>
> *I will speak in Spanish for a moment to thank all our friends who speak my second language. Now I will continue to speak in French because it is a language that most of you know, and I want to tell you a little story of our comrades on the Eastern Front.*
>
> *Today we have gathered to celebrate the memory of Hitler, but also in memory of the million faithful young people—and this is a real miracle—who fifty years after his disappearance continue to fight for the ideal. These are young people from all over the world. Wherever we meet there are thousands of people who have this faith even though they have not met Hitler; we were so lucky, and I, in particular, to have had the fortune of meeting this genius of the century.*
>
> *For years now, for decades, they have presented Hitler to us as a kind of monster; in my opinion, all this is done very well because the point is to obscure the fact that the man they make out to be some sort of executioner was a genius. They do this to ignore the essential thing, that he was, I repeat, a genius and, in particular, a political, social, and military genius. I can tell you that forty years ago, when Hitler was advancing toward power, starting from the time he had fought*

---

[164] The name Hans Ewald Althans is uncertain here. The author may be referring to Bela Ewald Althans (born 1966), who was a former German neo-Nazi in his younger days. He would have been in his early twenties at the time of this dinner. Bela Althans was jailed in 1995 for holocaust denial, although he reportedly offered German intelligence services extensive files on the neo-Nazi movement in exchange for three hundred sixty thousand German marks. If this is accurate, then this may explain why the author characterizes Althans as a Judas figure.

[165] From the Italian *commedia dell'arte* (street play). Harlequin is a comical, witty, resourceful servant, often acting to thwart the plans of his master in the play. He pursues his love interest, Columbina, with perseverance and humor, often competing with the brooding and severe Pierrot. He later develops into a prototype of the romantic hero.

[166] [Spanish for "God makes them, and they gather together."]

*as a mere corporal and then in 1919, when he had only a hundred followers, this gentleman, in about twelve years, was able to bring together millions of followers, millions of patriots, because he was able to establish a faith and a doctrine, and not like those miserable people who no one will remember twenty-five or thirty years later. For the young people of that time, who were twenty-five or even twenty years old, what future did they have but a huge intellectual, sentimental, and spiritual desert ahead of them, but we, those of us who lived at that time, were very fortunate to have immense momentum across Europe. He conveyed his passion to all of us, and in the most democratic way we could imagine. All the politicians we see and hear are talking nonsense in our Parliaments, like François Mitterrand in France, who came to power with a meager margin without even having the confidence of half the electorate, since millions of French abstained or did not vote for him.*

*While Hitler had all his people behind him supporting him, he always had between 90-95 percent of the vote, always, and this was repeated every year, and this is recognized even by his most bitter adversaries. The Saarland plebiscite took place two years after his coming to power, and he was elected Chancellor there while the Saarland was still occupied by enemy troops in Germany. Hitler, Chancellor of this territory and of the whole of Germany, was not allowed to speak during the campaign for the plebiscite, nor to even set foot in the Saarland. Despite all this, he got 91 percent of the vote. No one could say that it was rigged because the plebiscite was done under Allied control. This man formed for himself and brought the Germans not only political peace but also social peace; as you all know there were six million unemployed people, which was an issue he resolved. Can you imagine that in a democracy? He eliminated workers' misery. When it comes to democracy, it is really a plutocracy; democracy and plutocracy are the same thing. Workers must be paid good wages and their factories must be modernized, and Hitler had a generous building policy, constructing some one million seven hundred fifty thousand homes for them when they had previously been living in popular prisons. He gained respect for faith and family, and he achieved one million eight hundred thousand births every year. When people start having children, that is when they feel happy. For the Germans it represented peace and family happiness. As for wage earners, they could rest assured for their future, as Hitler had guaranteed. Finally, he also provided them with comfort, making possible for them the first popular car, which they could acquire by paying five marks a week. It was not only the wealthy bourgeois who could enjoy their vehicles. He succeeded in unifying the country through a policy of racial unity, and then he reunited all the members of this race: the Austrian comrades, the comrades of Sudetenland, people who had lost their homeland years ago, and he managed to bring about a huge reunification of some eighty million Germans. This is why they cannot forgive him. He had succeeded in making Germany the first country in Europe. In these regions of Europe, he managed to sweep away Marxism; that could not be forgiven, that was his great crime. Marxism, in all the countries where it had been imposed, had failed, even in the Soviet Union, for then in Italy anti-Marxism had already countered it.[167] As for class struggle, he countered it with cooperation between the classes. With this enormous work he managed to save his country. He succeeded in bringing all his country's social classes together, united in the same faith. That is why they wanted to bring him down.*

*He was not the one who wanted war. He never wanted or was interested in war against the West; what he wanted was to fight the Soviet Union, annihilate communism in that immense country, and to bring a decent and human life to its people. There were hundreds of millions of individuals from Russia who were our brothers, Europeans like us. If we had won, we would have had the whole of Europe. Today's Europe is just half of Europe. We would not just have what had not been handed over to the Soviets; we would now have a Europe that stretched from the North Sea to Vladivostok. We would be a Europe of hundreds of millions of Europeans. Now, we do not know what the future holds for you. Millions of your comrades are condemned to unemployment. This is what you, young people, have understood, the great epic of war.*

*They have repeated to you for years and years that the generals who won the war did so because Hitler was not a good strategist. On the contrary, Hitler was right, despite the opinion of the old generals, like Badoglio in Italy, Von Paulus in Stalingrad.[168] The war was won by the young. We were twenty and thirty years old, like millions of other combatants. It was the young people who had the faith and imagination so necessary in combat. They had the sense of cunning needed to overcome. Unlike those old warlords of 1870 or 1914, Hitler understood this kind of war and had detected its faults, which he corrected in the new war, and which helped him win many victories. Hitler invented a completely revolutionary tactic. The combination of air power and armored vehicles. He counted on his elite forces and French soldiers on the Eastern Front, as well as the Dutch soldiers. The Germans managed to sweep the Western Front with one hundred thousand men. Due to Hitler's military genius, he invented a new phase of war. He did the same in the Balkans and Russia. Let us compare Napoleon's campaign to Hitler's: Napoleon's war was nothing more than a march along the large communication roads, and his*

---

[167] Degrelle's reference to anti-Marxism in Italy here is unclear.
[168] These names are associated with military failures that Hitler had warned against.

*return was along those same routes. Hitler remained in Russia despite the harsh winter, while Napoleon had left Moscow in October* [1812]. *The Berezina River crossing was in November. On December 6th, the last of Napoleon's French soldiers were in Poland, while Hitler's war in Russia was along a front of some 3,000 kilometers (1,864 miles). German troops, who were supposed to defend the west from Norway to the Pyrenees, had to fight in the sands of Africa with Rommel, as well as fight in the air and under the sea in the submarine war. It was an immense military epic deployed throughout the world. Hitler was impassive, calculating everything down to the last detail, and fought to the end. He managed to do that because of his extraordinary genius. Without ceasing, new tragedies occurred. When everything was thought to be lost, he launched the Ardennes offensive, which was poised to destroy the United States Army. All of that is what we, who have faith, cannot forget. We were soldiers and you, young people, have received the legacy of the great myth, of the great genius of the twentieth century, in contrast to the miserable little politicians. Who remembers them, like Badoglio in Italy? They are finished. They are no more. The proof that Hitler continues to exist is what panics all current politicians. It panics all of them throughout the world, and all the newspaper, radio and television outlets. At the same time of the survey, completely neglected by German public opinion, it is similar today, 44 percent of Germans recognize that Hitler was a great statesman and 66 percent recognize that Hitler did not want war.*

*My dear comrades, you need to be strong and have faith. We are in a unique position, when everyone has capitulated, immersed in a capitalist civilization, if you can call it that, where people only think of vulgar things, we are the bearers of a doctrine that brings happiness to people. We are the bearers of an immense historical memory, such as Europe has never seen and as the world has never contemplated. All of this was because of Hitler, and it is because of him that we are gathered together tonight thinking about him. In spite of everything he had to suffer and the outrages he had to endure, we cry out with all our strength, Heil Hitler!*

In the days prior to the official event, CEDADE had extended an invitation to activists and sympathizers with this announcement: "We cordially invite you to the great public rally that will take place to commemorate the centennial of Adolf Hitler's birth, in a serious and dignified manner that such an occasion deserves. Location: Palacio de la Música cinema, Gran Vía thirty-five." The date of the rally was set for Sunday, April 23rd, at 12:00 p.m. One had thought that among the orators of said event, Léon Degrelle might speak, given his life history, loyalty, and rank. Unbelievable pressure and trickery from the enemies of freedom prevented them, at the last minute, from leasing the central cinema auditorium on the old Avenida de José Antonio, in Madrid. The venue had to be relocated to the Cinema Benlliure, located on calle de Alcala in the Salamanca neighborhood of Madrid. The original theater did not object to the event being carried out, but the government in turn, very "democratically," saw to it that it was suppressed and closed with an arbitrary, unjust, and cowardly prohibition order.

At 12:00 p.m. on April 23rd, in defiance of the government's provocation to prohibit the event, more than 500 people, against all odds, surrounded by intimidating and coercive police cordons, concentrated at the doors of the Cinema Benlliure, which the police had closed and sealed. The atmosphere was seething with tension. On the beveled staircase that gave access to the large auditorium of the cinema, they managed to openly proclaim their loyalty to National Socialism and to Adolf Hitler. In the twentieth century in Germany and for the whole continent, he raised the banner of Europe's liberation over the two parasites that strangled it with pandemic dimensions: communism and capitalism, both by-products of the same perfidious mentors. In the access wings, at a height of four or five steps above the level of the sidewalk, under the warm spring sun, the rally attendants proclaimed the evangelical doctrine that only the truth makes men free. Pedro Varela delivered a harsh speech. The event was attended by various European personalities, including Thies Christophersen, who also shared some moving words, the Argentine-Croatian Marinko Bolcovic, Portuguese poet Rodrigo Emilio, writer Wilfred von Oven, Mrs. Rost van Tonningen-Heubel, and Léon Degrelle. The "Salute to Victory" was chanted by the attendees and the unanimous cry of "Freedom of Expression!" was shouted out forcefully by all the participants, as it was being denied to them by the halls of power, who were trying to muzzle their event.

The newspaper *El País* reported in its April 24th edition, "The Nazi gathering in Madrid was held in the street," and referred to the lecture Léon Degrelle gave in the afternoon at the premises of CEDADE.

Also on Sunday, April 23rd, at CEDADE's local chapter in Madrid, located on the third floor of calle Infantas, number 32, Degrelle was a keynote speaker, who raised euphoric enthusiasm in the auditorium with his fiery speech and his brilliant oratory. The energy was felt by all the attendees who filled to overflowing the assembly hall and all its side rooms. The space was clearly insufficient because people filled the large wooden staircase of the building's three floors, plus a large crowd was on the nearby sidewalks out in the street, as they were not able to enter. Pedro Varela introduced Degrelle. I personally occupied one of the seats a short distance from the podium. The auditorium, composed mostly of young people, fervently and attentively followed Degrelle's centennial speech. The words electrified them, captivated them, exalted them. The applause was thunderous. The Italian writer from Turin, Giuseppe Franco, took photographs of the eighty-three-year-old Degrelle, who, despite his age, had the vitality of a young dreamer and revolutionary.

Degrelle, stood next to a fireplace in the assembly hall, in front of a polymer lectern, beside which an extraordinary commemorative anniversary poster had been put up. The poster showed the world as a ball, encircled by a swastika whose arms were depicted as the blades of a windmill, wrapped in a crucible of bright and radiant colors forming a kind of rainbow that emerges when the sun shines behind the dark, black storm clouds.

It can now be revealed that in 1989, Léon gave some thought to running in the European elections to try to get a seat in Strasbourg. He talked about this with some of his close comrades. He analyzed the pros and cons and, indeed, how to achieve his return to his beloved Belgium that he had not seen since 1945. He brainstormed a powerful photograph of himself on the stairs of the Brussels Palace of Justice, with a *Soir* newspaper under his arm. His friend who was a photographer, Jacques Schutter, was going to help him. The project was left as food for thought for the future.

## The Reunion with His Veterans

On June 12th, 1989, an event took place that significantly marked the life of Léon Degrelle. After forty-four years of forced separation, with the natural joy of that exciting moment, a reunion with his comrades from the Eastern Front took place in the Balearic Islands, in Palma de Mallorca. He shared several hours with those veterans of the Walloon Division, who had hired a chartered flight to take them to the archipelago located in the middle of the Mediterranean Sea.

Among those attending the reunion, despite his advanced age, was Jef François (born in Ghent, 1901; died in Lochristi, 1996), along with Joris van Severen, founding member and board of directors member of the Verdinaso Movement, and a great friend of John Hagemans, the champion of the young rexists. In 1941, Jef François was naturally one of the first to enlist in the Flanders Legion on the Eastern Front, ending the war with the rank of Obersturmführer in the Waffen SS. After the conflict, he had the honor of being twice condemned to death by the Belgian government, spending endless years in the dungeons of "democracy." When he was finally released, he returned to his position in the struggle as a political soldier, immediately joining Flemish nationalist movements and the association of veterans of the Eastern Front known as "Hertog Jan van Brabant." The reunion with Degrelle in 1989, after so many years apart and so many hardships suffered, was emotional. They embraced one another and the two spoke excitedly together for a long while, making plans for the future.

*Léon Degrelle with Van Leeuw, 1989*

On that exciting and beloved occasion, Léon Degrelle, "Commander in Exile," awarded the Medal of Honor and the unit decoration of the Walloon Legion 1941/1945, "Gold and Blood," to his faithful and inseparable comrade Raymond van Leeuw. The medal was listed as number 116 by the Association of Mes Bourguignons.

As 1989 drew to a close, Léon took stock of the year, writing in secluded intimacy:

> *One more year gone by! Yet, a year that has been marked for me by an event of the most noble meaning. Indeed, on June 12th, 1989, after forty-four years of separation, I had the overwhelming joy on the Baleares of seeing, for a few hours, a charter plane filled with my comrades, my very dear veteran comrades of the Eastern Front! I will never be alone again, near my birthday, in my distant exile...*
>
> *In the bright moment of their prime, while these magnificent boys lined up at my side on the Eastern Front to participate in the crusade against murderous*

*communism, Anglo-Saxon hyper-capitalists would, from 1941 to 1945, become powerful and imbecilic allies of these same communists. They handed over half of Europe to slavery under the monstrous USSR, which we had tried at that time to defeat. The communists massacred, for more than seventy years, millions of victims and plunged the economies of twenty nations into total bankruptcy! Now, finally, they begin to realize that we were right, that we sacrificed our youth and offered our blood to save Europe from that plague! With Hitler, with Mussolini, with the six hundred thousand European volunteers of the Eastern Front, we had a gap, but it was fifty years before the dupes would open their eyes, remaining deceived by the Churchills and the Roosevelts!*

*Looking at each one of you, looking into your eyes, I find my old brothers. I see again, always shining in each of your eyes, the great ideal that has filled your lives with honor. It was worth it. History is proving you right. Be faithful to your heroic life. Faced with the blind of yesterday and today, be happy to have consistently accomplished your goal without failure. Hail, my faithful Bourguignons! I embrace you all!*

*Léon Degrelle*

## Statements Are Published in the Lisbon Magazine *Sabado*

On May 5th, 1990, issue ninety-eight of the Portuguese magazine *Sabado*, in Lisbon, published a color photograph of Léon Degrelle, dressed in a Waffen SS general's uniform, on its cover. It publicized an exclusive interview with "The Last Nazi," by Paulo Freitas, to which the weekly paper dedicated five full pages, profusely illustrated, with photographs done in Madrid by José Carlos Pratas.

In the article, Portugal was noted as the only country in Europe that Léon Degrelle did not know, although there were supposedly traces of his passage across the Lusitanian border in the late 1940s. One will recall that it was not the real Léon, but a double impersonating him who crossed the border when international pressure forced the Spanish government to plan out Degrelle's fictional trip to Portugal in August 1946. An official of the Spanish security services impersonated Degrelle and wound up in the presence of a solicitous Portuguese colonel who confirmed "Degrelle" had departed from Spain. In the interview, Léon Degrelle recognized that his going to Portugal, "…was another alternative, as [Salazar's] good friend the Count of Mayalde had a privileged relationship with Salazar and spoke to me several times about that possibility."

The interview with Freitas and Pratas was held in the presence of Mrs. Juana "Jeanne" Brevet de Degrelle, her daughter, her granddaughter Sabine, and a Belgian journalist who was a friend of the family.

When asked about the famous "gas chambers," Degrelle, with a naturalness and spontaneity that all truth emanates, stated:

*The gas was used to kill lice and only for that. I myself was in a gas chamber when I returned from the front and before entering Germany. We stopped the railway cars at a station, got off, and went into a gas chamber. It was nothing dangerous, on the contrary. You know that Jews and Russians often had fleas and those carried terrible diseases.*

*The holocaust is the world's biggest lie! No holocaust ever existed! This is a very important issue today. I hope that Gorbachev, in line with perestroika, will order the archives of Auschwitz to be made available to historians. Germans are very meticulous people, they note everything, there is no detail that has not been written. Of course, there were deaths in Auschwitz, it was no five-star hotel, but you know how many? Not the millions that they talk about, but seventy-four thousand. The French concentration camps were not much better. Why did Germany have concentration camps? Who was there? The reputed Professor Richet, dean of the Sorbonne Medical School, described very well those who were there in the German concentration camps. More than 85 percent were criminals, murderers, and homosexuals...the rest were political prisoners.*

*PF: And the Jews?*

*LD: They were there too. Do you know who encouraged the war? They did, the Jews, starting in 1933, when they realized that they had no chance of taking power in Germany. They moved and promoted in the international press a campaign calling for war. At the height of the Western campaign, and I have those written orders, German commanders had instructions to regard the Jews as any other soldier. When the West's campaign ended victoriously in June 1940, all Jewish soldiers who had been imprisoned were able to return to their countries. That other nonsense about the badge that, according to some, they were forced to wear on the chest...one day I asked Hitler what the reason was and why the color yellow. Do you know the real reason? He is the one who told me that in the Vatican, it was the Popes who decided that the Jews of Rome would use this badge, so that they could be recognized. It was not to humiliate them; it was only for the soldiers on the street to be able to recognize them and to know that they had a potential enemy in front of them.*

*When we entered Russia, all the Jews allied themselves with the communists. The only solution was to put them in concentration camps, out of the way, in the ghettos they had always liked to live in. They formed those ghettos to protect themselves, to protect their beliefs and customs. We made the ghettos whose aim was to prepare the Jews for the creation of a Jewish state. Do not forget that before the war, the Poles sent many of them to Madagascar.*

When asked if he was an admirer of Hitler, Degrelle's answer offered no doubt:

*I admired him because he achieved an extraordinary social reform. He brought work to six million unemployed, improved working conditions for another two million workers, doubled wages, built more than a million and a half homes, built a network of highways, regenerated the social fabric with abundance, well-being, and respect.*

When questioned if he was "a practicing Catholic," Degrelle replied, "Yes, of course, and I commune. Several times a day I pray 'My God, I love you!' I honestly do not see happiness in any other way."

On November 8th, 1990, he dedicated a photograph "To my dear Portuguese friends of 'Last Redoubt,' with the affection of Léon Degrelle."

On November 18th, 1990, Léon returned to give another lecture at CEDADE's premises in Madrid for a political event where the speakers included Italian activist Di Piaggio, having arrived expressly from Rome, and Swiss comrade Roger Wüthrich, all of whom were introduced by Pedro Varela.

### Half a Century after the March toward the Eastern Front

August 8th, 1991 marked the fiftieth anniversary of the march of the rexist volunteers from the railway station in Brussels to the Eastern Front. It was a day of deep emotion and affectionate farewells, tears, joy, applause and cheers for the brave who headed to the front to fight. Among that contingent was the chief of the rexists, then private Léon Degrelle. The volunteers paraded through the avenues on their way to the station, with heads held high, proud of the commitment made and ready to fulfill their noble duty in the face of that call to arms. They knew that hard times awaited them. They were heading out to fight against the communist hordes. From that point on, and until the end, they would wield the sword as the vanguard of European culture and civilization, to maintain the sacred principles. This was an unforgettable date that forged and cemented the European ideal of young Belgians with the youth of Europe, battling together and with the same hope.

Fifty years later, Léon wrote a letter to the survivors of that campaign:

*In exile, August 8th, 1991*

*My brave and dear comrades!*

*On a day like today, fifty years ago, we marched, our eyes narrowed, but with a proud soul, toward the immense and mysterious Eastern Front. From that point, death stalked us! How many wonderful comrades fell on those distant steppes, glorious heroes whom we will never forget…*

*Before facing that terrible destiny, we had to separate ourselves from everything we loved most, and yet we left with joy, with pride. First, we wanted to liquidate communism, and we were the forerunners, understanding that it meant the death and the ruin of peoples. Secondly, to give our homeland, back in 1940, the prestige that only a grandiose epic could restore at that decisive hour. Although at the cost of enormous difficulties, it was hoped that an indispensable Europe would finally emerge.*

*For this noble ideal, at the moment when so many of your cowardly and powerless compatriots were hiding in their mediocrity, you, while suffering, you would offer your blood and sacrifice your youth! You have wished to commemorate this deed today by recalling our Great March of August 8th, 1941. Separated from you by a harsh exile, yet my thoughts are devotedly with you! Hail, heroes!*

*Most sincerely,*
*Léon Degrelle*

## The Book *Dr. Leuchter and the Fascinating Hitler*

The book *El Dr. Leuchter y el Fascinante Hitler* (*Dr. Leuchter and the Fascinating Hitler*) was completed on November 9th, 1991. It was published and distributed by Librería Europa in Barcelona. This book comprised the first chapters of a larger and more ambitious work, which still remains unpublished today. In a serious and unapologetic way, it revealed the finer details of the controversial Jewish question.

In issue one hundred seventy-four of CEDADE's magazine, it comments on the recently published book, stating: "In these pages, with the sparkle and charm so characteristic of him, and supported by the most recent studies, Léon Degrelle analyzes and shreds the most infamous legends concocted by humanity's great enemy."

Leuchter is not a mythical character, nor is he one of Sir Arthur Conan Doyle's sleuths. He is a chief engineer who built gas chambers for several prisons in the United States.

In the last two chapters of this work, Degrelle noted how, in a similar way, the most defamed character in history, Adolf Hitler, was gradually recovering his true human profile in public opinion.

The drawing that illustrates the cover of the book is an original by Acacio L. Friera. It was a skull, the jawbone being elongated in laughter, with a clown nose placed over where the nose should be.

The work was divided into twelve short chapters touching upon controversial subjects such as: "Hitler? What Hitler?," "The Gassing of the Third Reich," "The Work of the Experts," "The Crematory Ovens," "How Many Died?," "Centuries of Exaggeration," "The Camps Without Gas," "The Communist Executioners in the Camps," "Fifty Years of Falsehoods," "The Screams of the Ungassed," and "The Jenniger's Hitlerite Text and Public Opinion." In the book, Degrelle refuted, point by point, with rigorous and scientific criteria, the greatest black stain invented by the true victors of the Second World War, who, of course, were not those who actually fought, but those who shifted about, and were always hidden among the murky interests of economic and political maneuverings.

When he claimed in the book that "the famous 'gas chambers' of Dachau, Buchenwald, and a whole series of camps in the Third Reich never existed," he corroborated it on the basis of fact, not on personal or subjective opinion or on a particular vision or interpretation. He founded his arguments on official confirmation that has been maintained throughout years of research by Dr. Martin Broszat, the famous director of the prestigious *Institut für Zeitgeschichte,*[169] which was dependent on the then German Federal Republic. Dr. Broszat was known for his antifascism, but he had no choice but to proclaim, consistent with his investigations, that after fifteen years of studies, analysis, and comparisons, he had come to the conclusion that no gas chamber ever operated in any camp and that "neither in Dachau, nor in Bergen-Belsen, nor in Buchenwald, were Jews or any other kind of prisoners gassed," a conclusion entirely in line with the testimony of socialist MP Paul Rasinier, a former camp inmate. He made this camp declaration on August 19th, 1960, in the newspaper *Die Zeit*. It was also in line with professor emeritus of the University of Lyon, Robert Faurrisson, whose mother was English and who was decidedly anti-Nazi during the war. He was also a scholar of recognized prestige, who, in front of the microphones in radio station Europe number one, did not hesitate to say, "Hitler's purported gas chambers and the supposed genocide of the Jews form a single and unique historical lie, which has allowed a gigantic political-

---

[169] [German for Institute for Contemporary History.]

financial scam of which the State of Israel and international Zionism are the main beneficiaries."

Léon Degrelle relied on these conclusions for his book along with those reached by other renowned scholars, such as Judge Wilhelm Stäglich, author of *The Myth of Auschwitz*, or American university professor Arthur R. Butz, who published *The Hoax of the Twentieth Century*. Additionally, there were the irrefutable theses of exhaustive scientific evidence on which his arguments were based. The great specialist in American gas chambers, the engineer Fred Leuchter, in 1988 wrote a one hundred- and ninety-two-page report as a result of his on-site work at the camps, assisted by the technicians Howard Miller, an industrial designer, and Jürgen Neumann, a filmmaker. They relied on verifiable facts, mathematical calculations, and samples subjected to the most rigorous examinations by all kinds of American experts, to dismantle the hoax, that has been repeated a million times, with paranoid delirium, in order to brainwash people. These are just some of the important references and bibliographic sources used by Léon Degrelle for the elaboration of his work.

Dismantling a lie of such proportions was not an easy task, especially when contradicting the official version is treated as a crime. Léon Degrelle did not hesitate to argue and base history on truth and not on what we have been told, which is typically based on bastardized interests.

Degrelle finished his book with:

*We have wanted, throughout these pages, to bring a little order to the mess of postwar exaggerations and lies.*

*We have done so without hatred. With humor when it was fun. With heart, thinking of the millions of honest people who seek truth.*

The book was due to be presented in Madrid on November 17th, 1991, at 5:00 p.m., to coincide with the 20-N events.[170] The event, however, was banned by the government deputy Segismundo Crespo because more than four hundred young people had confirmed their attendance at the presentation.

In November 1991, Pedro Varela, the owner of Librería Europa in Barcelona who was responsible for publishing the book, spent a week in Malaga as a guest in the home of Léon Degrelle.

---

[170] 20-N is a symbol/abbreviation that represents the anniversaries of both José Antonio Primo de Rivera, who was executed on November 20th, 1936, and General Francisco Franco, who died on November 20th, 1975.

## Letter to King Baudouin: "Your Majesty, You and I"

In 1991, a letter sent to the Belgian King Baudouin, who married Spanish aristocrat Fabiola de Mora y Aragón, was also published. The Spanish edition, published and distributed by Librería Europa, was entitled *Majestad, Vd. y yo*. This was an interesting political letter from Degrelle to the King of Belgium, where he recounted the most recent history and asked him to be consistent with it.

It was an extensive epistle asking for justice: not for himself, but for the "thousands of fearless boys who went…to offer their youth and blood to protect Europe from the spread of communism."

This was not the first time Degrelle had written to the Belgian king. He had sent another letter to him in 1961 to explain and clarify the situation in which many Belgian compatriots were being viciously persecuted by the socialist, masonic government under his reign, for having marched in their youth to fight joyfully and resolutely against communism together with young idealists from across Europe.

The letter was written on November 15th, 1991, addressed to King Baudouin in his palace in Brussels:

> Your Majesty,
>
> Finally, even the least savvy of your subjects has come to realize, during these months, the definitive collapse of what was the Soviet Union.
>
> So, do you not think it would be time (and God knows how late it is!) to do justice to the fearless boys of your people who fifty years ago, went thousands of kilometers from their native soil to offer their youth and blood to protect Europe from the spread of communism?
>
> Many people, because of their low mental lucidity, have not until recently understood the danger that ideology has posed to all humanity for three quarters of a century. [...]
>
> Everything that came from them was tolerated: so-called "democratic" governments endorsed their millions of crimes like so many other magical potions. [...]
>
> And as for us, the rexists, who since 1936 have been carrying our national battle with the cry of "Rex or Moscow!" we have since been registered in the archive of accusations that, in 1945, caused us to be crushed under the pylon hammer of "anti-fascism." [...]
>
> Europe had to wait fifty years (1991) to partially recover her sight, the very victims of Stalinism being those who were blind.

Yet, several hundred thousand European volunteers, coming from more than twenty countries, went to do their duty. Among them were two legions of young men, Flemish and Walloon, carried by the most ardent patriotism. They behaved on the Eastern Front with a heroism that no one would dare question...They eventually formed two divisions, the Langemark and the Wallonie. In the course of four years of combat, several thousand young, living, breathing souls were sacrificed to defend Europe and their country. [...]

Because of your father's sensible and realistic appeal, Your Majesty, the Belgians decided to "collaborate" (more than 90 percent in the summer of 1940). Some by sudden conviction, such as Socialist Party President Henri de Man, who called the 1940 disaster "the liberating defeat," others simply to survive; most so that their homeland, threatened with dismemberment or disappearance, could recover its life.

It was absolutely necessary, and without further waiting, to provide proof, despite the disaster in our country, that the bravery of Belgium's sons remained intact, and that, charged with history, culture, and glory, she was worthy to reappear with honor in the new Europe which, inevitably, would be created by the end of the conflict.

This was the spirit with which we departed, in early August 1941, toward the Eastern Front. Helping to save Europe from the invasion of an overwhelming communism, we thus embraced the providential opportunity to recover, through our sacrifice, the right of our people to decide their fate on the final day, in a dialog of equals, from victor to victor, through the respect that heroism imposes.

That, Your Majesty, was the reason we fought, and the reason several thousand comrades died.

Certainly, "collaborating," as your father asked, became more difficult from year to year. [...]

Since June 21st, 1941, communist terrorism, Stalin's international hub, has implanted its blackmail everywhere.

Our volunteers for the Eastern Front had barely left before the wave of Soviet attacks was unleashed in Belgium, as elsewhere. A thousand of ours—especially the grandparents, parents, or children of the soldiers—would be killed, with exemplary cowardice, in remote villages, where they had no protection. [...]

The arrival in Brussels of English and American troops took place in early September 1944. It was then, once any danger of retaliation had truly been eliminated, that the "super-valiant" heroically began their witch hunt.

One hundred thousand civilians were imprisoned and treated with unspeakable savagery, stacked like pigs in nauseating cells or put in zoo cages, men were beaten *abominably, mothers uprooted from their children by for thousands, countless young rexist women raped and sold for cigarettes to American negroes. Those who were executed by firing squad can be counted in the hundreds, especially the brightest intellectuals of Belgium, such as José Streel, Victor Meulenijser, and Paul Herten. Monseigneur Kerkhofs, Bishop of Liege, was a blessed priest, who, in 1949, defined the most exact form of this fierce "repression," saying, "it was of a hardness that had nothing of Christianity, much less anything human." [...]*

*It was the work of communists, launched against all those who participated in the European crusade against Bolshevism, as well as those who supported them with their votes.*

*The most unusual motives were invented to annihilate us. [...]*

*Unbelievable as it may seem today, the main crime that they attributed to our soldiers and their families in the courts to repress the events of 1941-1945 was their anti-Soviet behavior. The main reason for my death sentence in absentia, handed down within ten minutes without a subpoena and without a defense at trial, was most formal: "Having fought against an ally of Belgium." [...]*

*The modern world is threatened with death by two monsters: on the one hand, communism, invalidated from the very first moment by the economic aberration of Marxism; on the other hand, hyper-capitalism, moving man into social selfishness, unlimited speculation, immorality of money, and becoming the sole guide of human destiny.*

*Sweeping out one serves no purpose if the other is not swept out as well, instead of turning one of them into the only global arbiter, as it is at the moment.*

*It would be necessary to replace these two heresies against nature with a liberating system that would bring social justice to humanity, based mainly on a balanced collaboration of the classes, the dignity of work, and respect for the human being, owner of the material.*

*Switching out Moscow for New York does not solve anything, and who can guarantee us that New York, with its deified gold, its inhumanity, its domineering pride, and the economic bankruptcy that lurks behind it, will not jump up one day as well, like a galaxy seized with madness? [...]*

*Treating our Eastern Front heroes as outcasts, dishonoring them abominably despite all the cruelty of their defeat, incarcerating them for years, was especially shameful, but this disgrace toward the glorious defeated still endures in Belgium.*

*Do you realize, Your Majesty, that your Kingdom is currently the only country in the world not to have granted the slightest amnesty to the losers of the Second World War? [...]*

*Will you, Your Majesty, finally turn your gaze toward the best of your compatriots, who, as recent history proves, were the most lucid, and grant them, at least, amnesty, an almost indecent term in itself and hardly morally admissible? It has been done already everywhere for some time now; but has it been granted to veterans of the Eastern Front? After forty-six years of waiting, will you return their honor, their identity, and their property to them, reparations to which they have always been entitled for their admirable valor as soldiers? [ . . . ]*

*What are you waiting for, Your Majesty? Take into your hands a great sponge and a giant cauldron of water (and you would be the last to have to do it!) and wash away, throughout your country, the grudges, the bitterness, the hatreds fermented in the acid of a half-century old past? [ . . . ]*

*Your Majesty, you and I are Christians. Sooner or later death will gather us together. Perhaps in a sly way, gnawing at our life little by little, or maybe suddenly, with the thunder of its funeral drums.*

*For you, for me, death is God.*

*So, that will be the time to reckon accounts. Have we loved God enough, and, through Him, have we loved Man enough?*

*Before my heroic soldiers, before one hundred thousand "cursed" Flemish and Walloons, pilloried by unbridled persecution after the Second World War, what, Your Majesty, will have been your reaction during the forty years of your reign? Your concept of human fraternity? Your observance of Christian charity? [ . . . ]*

*Your Majesty, I salute you, just as I saluted your unfortunate father, man to man, when he received me in distant times.*

## An Interview Given to the Portuguese Weekly *O Diabo*

On May 15th, 1991, Degrelle gave an interview to the Portuguese weekly *O Diabo*, conducted by the Portuguese writer Antonio Marques de Bessa. It was entitled "*El Último de los Irreductibles*" ("The Last of the Unyielding"), where he used the motto: "*Chance Degrelle-Chance Eternelle*" ("Degrelle's Luck is Eternal Luck"). De Bessa wrote "living in Spain, at the age of eighty-four, Degrelle is today the last survivor of an era left behind, but his story is only half-told…it is clear that we find ourselves before someone who is out of the ordinary." The conversation lasted for more than two and a half hours. De Bessa perceived that "his [Degrelle's] speech is neither that of a dispassionate observer nor that of an unprincipled propagandist. In the way he describes the events he lived so intensely, there is a mixture of enthusiasm, deep conviction, and humor."

Among many anecdotes, he recalled referred to an incident that happened to him with Hitler on one of his trips back from the Eastern Front when he was received by the German Führer. When the Reich chancellor noticed the wear and tear on the boots that Léon was wearing, Hitler sent for one of his own pairs of boots to offer him, and after learning that Degrelle wore a smaller size, he handed him a few sheets of the *Volkischer Beobachter* newspaper to stuff into the toes of the boots to make them fit without hurting his feet.

The article concluded with the consideration that, for Degrelle, as for many of those who fought at his side, his perception was that of a life-and-death struggle for the survival of Western values, even though fifty years after all that tragedy, the victors still continue to inherit directly from their propaganda of 1939 to 1945. They promote Manichean mythologies of opposite meaning, without considering the courageous and heroic deeds of the European volunteer fighters, at the head of whom were men who marked the ages, like Léon Degrelle.

Marking the anniversary of the assassination of José Antonio in 1936 and the death of the former Spanish Head of State, Generalísimo Franco, on November 20th, 1975, Degrelle gave a masterful lecture of historic character at CEDADE in Madrid in front of hundreds of young people filling the hall. It was wonderfully decorated on this occasion for the speech from the immortal European.

## Statements to the Weekly *La Nación*

In the Madrid weekly *La Nación*, in the December 11th-17th, 1991 edition, an interview with Léon Degrelle was published. Journalist Alejandro Morcillo conducted the interview, wherein Degrelle expressed his opinions, thoughts, and concerns about, fundamentally, a Europe that, even then, could be blown to pieces.

The first question, asked point-blank, was about the dates of the 20-N calendar:

> *AM: What consideration does the violent controversy in Spain concerning the anniversary of Franco's death deserve?*
>
> *LD: This quarrel has revealed to me the extent to which the old political forces have been disturbed, which are otherwise in the process of decomposition. Remember, a thousand "skinheads" were going to invade Madrid, attack its population, and usher in a reign of terror. Bus columns would bring them from Barcelona and Valencia. The press published some terrifying drawings of those killers armed with clubs, and what did we see? Nothing, absolutely nothing! Some journalists with hawk eyes claimed to have spotted four or five of them. Is it true? In any case, during*

*those days, nothing significant happened in Madrid. The media tried to intimidate the population so that they would not go in large numbers to Plaza de Oriente. That was all, for the lie had no other purpose. What a clear-cut confession! This fake left's media has reached the point that it is only capable of replying with trickery.*

*AM: What can you tell us about CEDADE?*

*LD: The same observation. CEDADE is a serious movement of level-headed guys who no longer buy the lies that have been imposed on public opinion since 1945 and are given as official history. History is not so fixed that it should be treated like the final score of a football (soccer) match. It can only be the result of lengthy research. The basis of history and its essential duty is doubt; that is, to call into question every piece of data until its final verification. Is this what the newspapers do, running in search of simple details, judging them in a hurry? Or the magistrates who suddenly become historians, scholars, or engineers? The young people of CEDADE try to understand, and, after lengthy research, come to certain conclusions that they try to make known in a serious and non-violent way. When have their activists been seen to resort to any procedure other than intellectual analysis? For the Left, nowadays, reflecting, studying, and weighing means being "Nazi." The great fear of the old regimes is that a worthy elite might dismantle the legends on which they based their entire strategy. It is comforting to see this obtuse policy seems to be coming to an end; the old, devalued parties are increasingly discredited, which are in the doldrums everywhere.*

Degrelle answered all questions brilliantly. The interview ended with the question "How do you see the future?" In his reply, Degrelle made a series of digressions and considerations about the future of Europe and its threats "in extremis," and proffered this conclusion: "Greece, in former times, perished for not fighting. The same thing happened to the Roman Empire. Europe in the graveyard or Europe ready to rise again. We have to choose one or the other!"

## On the Television Network Antena 3

On Antena 3 Televisión, correspondent José Luis Balbín hosted a segment that was very well received, judging by the size of the audience who watched it. The format of the program La Clave was to show a film beforehand concerning a specific, determined theme whose argument served as a prologue or introduction to bring the topic into focus, which would later become the axis of a dialectical discussion among the guest speakers. Towards the end, the topic of the evening was addressed in depth, with a long discussion that lasted until the wee hours of the morning. The speakers invited to the program were typically popular, famous, prestigious, or had some relationship with the proposed topic, bringing their own version or testimony to the lively debate.

On February 8th, 1992, the program La Clave generated some additional excitement due to the presence of Léon Degrelle as one of guest speakers. The program had a large percentage of screen time and marketing. After the film, the debaters took the floor and laid out their opinions. Léon Degrelle was brilliant and forceful; he was definitely the winner, not in terms of points, but in an absolute sense, in terms of intelligence, candor, experience, presentation, and oratorial skills.

## Russia "Revisited"

In 1992, Léon Degrelle would visit Russia again, by way of an interview published in the Moscow weekly *Den*, in the twenty-first issue, March 24th–30th, 1992 edition. It had an important social impact and a considerable circulation of hundreds of thousands of copies. At the time, I was a correspondent for that paper in Spain and I was able to get the interview set up. The interview took place at Degrelle's home at Santa Engracia thirty-seven in Madrid, on February 28th. Léon and I were old friends, teacher and disciple sharing ideas and opinions. We both wanted to carry out a figurative incursion into the heart of Russia, to let the Russian people know from a source without misrepresentations, the thoughts of Léon Degrelle, the last survivor of the great leaders who tried to forge Europe's destiny in the 1940s, a prominent protagonist in political and military history of the old continent during the twentieth century.

It was a shared moral victory after the persecution and merciless harassment that Léon Degrelle had been subjected to. His statements had a surprising impact. The Russian people read with amazement in their own tongue, in Cyrillic, words coming from Madrid (that was the year of the Barcelona Olympics and Seville's Expo-92) that were addressed to them by former SS General Léon Degrelle. He was sincere with them and encouraged them not to give up their desire for freedom, while trusting in the traditional virtues of the Russian people, beginning to awaken from the long tyranny of communism. The interview was illustrated with a photograph of Léon, wearing the Iron Cross with Oak Leaves, and included the following handwritten dedication in French: "To my Russian friends of 'Den' with greetings from Degrelle."

In the introduction, I emphasized that it was his capacity, intelligence, courage, charisma, and overwhelming and convincing oratory that made him, even in his youth, the undisputed leader of the Rexist Movement in Belgium, which he had forged out of the European nationalist and fascist movements of the early part of the century. He raised a social idea in the heart of Europe out of Christian principles. We must again recall that Degrelle enlisted in the military confrontation against communism as a private, and he became a general through field promotions. Wounded seriously five times in combat, he rejoined the front lines every time with bloody scars, fighting until the very end of the conflict. There were already more than fifty books published that promoted his thoughts, his life adventures, and his ideal. Degrelle was introduced to new Russian generations as "a soldier and a warrior, a leader and a politician, an intellectual and a poet who cherishes the best of memories from the Russian people."

He had finally reconnected with the people he lived with for four years, whom he, at the head of his volunteers in the "crusade against Bolshevism," wished to free from the communist yoke.

The interview went as follows:

*JR: In several of your books you mentioned that you believe that someday, in Russia, a man, perhaps a military man, will appear whose mission is to save Europe from her liberal and capitalist decadence. What is your view of Russia?*

*LD: I have a great admiration for the Russian people. Russia, for me, is the great biological reserve of Europe. It is a strong and splendid race. It is a beautiful and honored race. I spent four years in Russia and never saw the people fight over things. I saw a great family unit with many virtues. There are three hundred million people in Russia who will always be able to change something in a semi-rotten Europe.*

*JR: What do you think of the war between the Russians and the Germans in 1941?*

*LD: That war had to come about sooner or later because Stalin, like Lenin, wanted to conquer the whole world and turn the planet into a world of slaves. It was not the Germans who provoked the war, but Stalin, who did it according to his plan. He had made an agreement with Hitler, which was a provisional and very hypocritical pact, to allow Europeans to destroy one another and then take to conquest. The plan failed because Hitler had conquered everything so quickly. The conflict in Yugoslavia was mounted in order to stage armies to the south, and Hitler wasted two months while Stalin was preparing five and a half million men on the border for the advance. Indeed, what Hitler did was a preventive defense. There was no other remedy. He could have freed Russia entirely had it not been for the massive support from America. It is they who allowed Stalin to win. It is they who handed over a hundred million more European slaves to Stalin.*

*JR: Do you think it could have been a geopolitical mistake?*

*LD: It was not a mistake on Stalin's part. He had maneuvered. He became the most important conqueror in the world, greater than Gengis Khan. It was not a mistake of his, neither was it a mistake on the part of the Germans because had they not gone in, others would have. There was no mistake.*

*JR: You are the only one of the leaders of historical European National Socialism who continues to defend his ideas. Do you believe this ideology can one day become important on the international level?*

*LD: I always believe that salvation can come if the Russians bring it. I believe that Europe no longer has sufficient strength to do it. It is a broken continent. In fifty years of democracy, since 1945, its results have been catastrophic. Nothing has changed for the better and everything has changed for the worse. These are countries that are all ruined. These are countries with tremendous racial corruption, countries that have lost all the old virtues that made up Europe. Europe is a hyper-capitalist territory without hyper-capitalism. They have no money, but they have the vices that American hyper-capitalism has given to Europe. The Russian people have been left as a fairly healthy people who can recover and, as I have said from the very beginning, it is always to be hoped that out of their three hundred million people someone will come who can raise up the Russian people and give decisive support to Europeans who still seek the resurrection of a great ideal.*

*JR: Who today is the main enemy of the Eurasian nations?*

*LD: The enemy right now is the enemy of all time: hyper-capitalism. For us, there were two great enemies in the world: Marxism, which throws classes against each other, inevitably ruining the entire economy and leading people to ruin; and hyper-capitalism, which turns every man into a machine, and makes him a pawn placed on the American board, instruments of the Americans. That is what we saw in the Gulf War. They went in like fools to participate in this stupid Gulf adventure that has led to three hundred thousand corpses. American capitalism is the great enemy, but an enemy as weak as communism. Just as communism fell once because it was a false doctrine, hyper-capitalism can sink. It is completely ruined. It has the highest deficit in the world. It has many races mixed together who hate each other and has a materialism that eliminates all spiritual life. That is how they will bring themselves down. This is necessary because, otherwise, the Pacific world will become the masters of the next century.*

*JR: Mr. Degrelle, what political forces, parties, or movements in Spain seem to you the most positive?*

*LD: Unfortunately, now I do not see a lot of important momentum defending our ideas. There are wonderful people in Spain who could raise up this country again, and yet there is also mediocrity, corruption, and a tremendous weakness of the democratic parties that represent nothing.*

*JR: What about in Europe?*

*LD: In Europe, yes. There is the Le Pen phenomenon, which is important,[171] very important, actually. They see that nothing can be done without him, but it is yet to be seen if he can achieve something by himself. The basic problem is that people in every country are upset about the democratic formula, which is an idiotic formula. The worst of fools is equal to the most elevated mind. They have done polls in France before the elections, and 54 percent of the people say they do not want to vote. Additionally, 14 percent of those who do not want to vote, tend toward the Greens.*

*Now we see the same phenomenon even in liberated countries such as Poland, where, in the last election, 60 percent did not vote. It was their first election and people no longer want those formulas, which are for fools. The people want a real leader. Popular democracy has you choose a man or a leader, like you might do in normal life, where you choose your wife, or your wife chooses you. We must choose a man who can think, who can lead, who can build, rather than abandoning countries to half-wits or uneducated folks who know nothing, who watch their interests going into the pockets of the political class; this is what sinks all countries. That is why Russia's great potential is that it has the people, three hundred million people, a healthy people to whom God will one day send someone to free them and to free us.*

These hopeful words marked the end to that relaxed and joyous conversation.

In the interview, Léon had alluded to the Le Pen phenomenon, which found itself in an emerging and growing phase in France. On May 21st, 1992, the undisputed head of the *Front National* in France, Jean-Marie Le Pen, declared on French television (channel TF-1) that he had had the opportunity to meet Léon Degrelle. The Front National as a political party was the heir of the *Ordre Nouveau* movement, whose sources of information and training materials for activists

---

[171] Reference to Jean-Marie Le Pen, long-time leader of France's far-right party *Le Front National* (The National Front). The party has been led by Le Pen's daughter Marine Le Pen since 2012; in 2018 the party changed its name to *Le Rassemblement National* (National Rally).

included, towards the end of the 1960s, the books *Hitler Pour 1,000 Ans* (*Hitler for One Thousand* Years) and *La Campagne de Russie* (*The Russia Campaign*), both by Léon Degrelle. The very name of the movement, *Ordre Nouveau* (New Order), was inspired, and later adopted, by the frequent repetition of this expression in the text of *Hitler Pour 1,000 Ans* (*Hitler for One Thousand* Years).

On July 11th, 1992, Degrelle received a visit at his home from his countryman Drea Diller, to whom he wrote the following dedication in one of his books: "To my dear friend Drea Diller, honor of the Flemish youth, to whom I express my full affection and also my admiration toward your beloved and great country, Flanders."

## A Tribute from the Verdun-Pétain Association

On the commemoration of 20-N, thousands of patriots and numerous foreigners were present at the memorials and the political events scheduled in the capital of Spain to commemorate Franco and Rivera. The government system in Spain sought, as usual, to organize campaigns to discredit and dismiss the occasion and minimize the large attendance at these events. The year 1992 was no different in the political strategy used by the government to poison public opinion with falsehoods about the former Head of State and the founder of Spanish Falange.

On November 23rd, 1992, his French comrades from the Verdun-Pétain Association, with its President Du Perrier at the head, paid Degrelle tribute at the El Faro restaurant, near Palacio de El Pardo, the official residence of the Caudillo of Spain. On the way out, all the diners formed a line in the large courtyard that gives access to the restaurant, and saluted him with arms raised high, making an arc of honor under which Léon passed, excited and satisfied.

## "Appeal to European Youth"

In the summer of 1992, precisely on August 8th, Léon finished writing "*Appel aux Jeunes Européens*" ("Appeal to European Youth"). It was a document as a status report and forecast of the world situation and offered a remedy to the anguish and rampant problems that would have to be faced by the generations born into history at the dawn of the twenty-first century. It was a proclamation and a political testament, where Degrelle once again stressed the need to maintain the ideals of youth.

The manifesto was published in Paris by the Avalon Publishing House that same year. It consisted of nine panels or large sections, from which we summarize the following:

1) *Against the Democratic Farce*

*[…] We were also twenty years old. Our days will no longer return, but our spirits, our hearts, are still vibrant with ideas and spiritual impulses that will certainly still be found in you, our young comrades of today.*

*Fervent nationalists, we stirred to the depths of their consciousness the soul of our homeland. We wanted to withdraw it from the political swamp in which it was immersed, restore faith in its mission, put order in its institutions, restore social justice with an indissoluble collaboration between the classes and, above all, to realize the revolution of souls that would liberate men from that sticky materialism. […]*

*Friendship in diversity. Europe breathed in us. After the storm, each of our homelands, proud of the honor of their troops and the sacrifice of their dead, had, in the bundle of our united civilizations, the deed of emphasizing and magnifying the personality of their people.*

*Defeated, our drums put away, we saw our nascent Europe of 1942 shrink after 1945 into banality, mediocrity, giving itself over to madness, without even guessing the ephemeral fragility, in a furious desire for pleasure.*

*This has tarnished the soul. It decomposed moral and spiritual characteristics.*

*Tomorrow, everything must be recreated.*

*This devotion to our homelands and to the Europe that brought them together, we your elders of the Second World War, have paid a terribly high price for it. […]*

*If it is still necessary, up to the present moment, to render aid from the bottom of an exile as endless as it is cruel, we are, dear European comrades, accompanying you until our last breath. […]*

*To stress that nine-tenths of the Members of Parliament, unknown and incompetent, serve no purpose at all, other than to enjoy fabulous benefits, you must become intolerable killjoys!*

*Opponents who denounce the sterility of these nonsense assemblies with three hundred, four hundred or five hundred heads (most often hollow!) are prohibited from access on television, as well as in the mass rallies, where they could clarify something for the people who are mocked. […]*

*Every country is burdened with insane taxes that kill any profitability from creating something new. […]*

*You, young people, boys and girls of real Europe, must replace this mess and this ruinous trap with a union of healthy States, under the authority of a true leader who is loved, respected, and freely chosen by the people.*

*He will be socially just and racially protected. [...]*

*To touch the omnipotence of the "democratic" pashas, plotting intrigues in their nurseries, is to play with dynamite. Often, you will have to watch your back; so many parasites and cancers. It does not matter; it must be faced with an unshakable consistency, and you must not betray yourself. The people must know that our doctrine—responsibility, hardness, cleanliness, the competence of a strong power, intelligent cooperation between classes, exaltation of the fundamental virtues of society—is necessary; life serves no purpose if it is not oriented toward perfection and greatness. We believe in the resplendence of stars. [...]*

*We will need pesticides to help clean out a corrupt, anarchic, and ruinous regime and replace it with a clean, strong, and popular State.*

2) *Terrorist Wars and U.S. Imperialism*

*[...] Since 1945, the revanchist tactic of terrorist warfare has been continually revived everywhere U.S. imperialism has wanted to impose itself. [...]*

*In Iraq, one hundred thousand or two hundred thousand civilians (we do not know how many exactly!) have been systematically killed, with impunity, by monstrous computer-guided terrorist blasts of American bombs!*

*Why?*

*To keep intact the medieval and racist machinery of a slum country, Kuwait, recently manufactured by the English, as well as the Emirates, foot-lickers and rapacious like vultures, flush with dollars, official oil well holders so coveted by the American gangsters of hyper-capitalism, eternal thieves and thugs!*

*Saddam Hussein, Iraq's unquestionably popular leader, wanted to recover that lost province of old Mesopotamia, and above all, he led the solid state in an oil-rich region. [...]*

*Lebanon, partly occupied by Israeli troops, without anyone making them crawl back to their own burrow; in Jordan, in Mecca, in Yemen, in Syria, too, where the Golan Heights were occupied, to mention the lands of the Hashemites! Washington had found an opportunity to assert its supremacy in the East. The strident crisis threatens the whole world.*

*They said it was about saving Freedom! Law! Civilization! while camouflaging the barrels of oil that were the real reason. Who would not have agreed, hearing such virtuous appeals? [...]*

*Saddam Hussein knows well that the fight will be unequal, that his troops and his people will be crushed. Silence. Wait. [...]*

*Americans possess a unique terrorist material in the world. [ . . . ]*

*Never in the history of the universe has such gesticulating hypocrisy been known…the whole bitter game of coldly self-interested rejections and the worst shamelessly religious compromises for oil!*

*That is where the rot of today's world lies.*

*First law: Base material profit. Then, disorder, powerlessness, and hypocrisy in the States, however immoral it may be! [ . . . ]*

*That is the case. This present world, hypocritical, powerless, phony in the midst of tragedy, is the one that beat us in 1945; this, because of its futility and harmfulness, is what you, oh European youth today, must bring down.*

3) *Europe in Misery*

*The democracy that we see decomposing before our eyes is anarchy, broken railroads, and bandits. [ . . . ]*

*The decline of principles is impressive. Man believes in nothing more than "greenbacks," "making some dough," the Buddha to which everything returns and on which everything depends. The ideal is a joke. "Quiero vivir!" as the Spanish say, "I want to live!" In fact, they are living with their feet in the air, on ground that is collapsing everywhere. This scandal is like a saxophone calling the tune of collapse, the collapse of nations, of customs, of the divine and the human, but in a euphoria that everyone believes is real. Life, you see, makes a boom! Makes a society! [ . . . ]*

*In this slum, an administrative Europe called the Common Market has succeeded, at the pace of a turtle, to unify the Europe that we fought for. She makes her camp in Brussels. She lacks a figure. This is, first and foremost, a conglomerate, an omnipotent potpourri of twenty thousand officials of motley "budget-holders," entrenched in limitless material privileges. No popular community has chosen them. It is a congress of the negotiation bosses. Democracy, in this whole issue, is nothing more than a colorless, inconsistent bubble, which, at the littlest gust of air, is blown away and disappears.*

*Deified yesterday, democracy at the end of the twentieth century is just a fool's farce. [ . . . ]*

*The various States massacre their populations—those who still work!—with exorbitant taxes. In this mess, they devour half, if not more, of the fruits of the labor of any bold creator.*

*The same so-called "democratic" parties, who had to provide an economic solution to the misery of the so-called third world, which they had tossed out like a trash bag in their "liberation" of 1945, are now powerless in the face of the massive, multiracial invasion of huge, ragged contingents of foreign populations, misguided by what these parties did, which are overwhelming social benefits at the present.*

*Above the market, these political liquidators are irredeemably corrupt, either by electoral necessity (at the national level, an election, with all its advertising and fanfare, costs a fortune!), or by personal or familial greed (wives, who often show up out of nowhere and are quickly accustomed to official cars and free trips to Los Angeles or Tokyo, do not want to go back to being janitors or cleaning ladies!).* [...]

*If a reformer of genius, with broom in hand, arises tomorrow in Europe, or in Russia's vastness, someone who brought the masses a true economic and social program of popular health, the pseudo-democratic mafias would quickly see their oily bustle of piglets swept away.*

4)   The Millions of Drugs and the Future of Russia

*[...] The international drug mafia has billions of dollars coming from a thousand massive frauds. It extends its tentacles everywhere. Sometimes some of these are cut off, but this is not very significant. [...]*

*The mafia has realized that this immense, almost untouchable shelter could, in addition to natural drugs, allow the manufacture of chemical drugs, which are by far the deadliest.*

5)   The Power of Asia and the Drama of Africa

*[...] There are important new forces that risk consolidating their power in the course of the next century. The twenty-first century will be, first and foremost, the century of the Pacific Ocean. Not only Japan, Korea, Taiwan, Hong Kong, Singapore, fertile in resources and already in full swing, but also, the one and a half billion Chinese workers who carry in their intellect the synthesis of many thousands of years of a high civilization. [...]*

*Restructured, the Chinese, in twenty-five years, will be able to gather a vast cohort of two billion tenacious Asians, who will possess the world's most advanced technology.*

*All together, they will lead their very strong alliance against a Europe of "democracies," poorly united, or disunited, a fifth of the size, with blood contaminated by AIDS and gangrenous by millions of new upstarts suddenly fleeing from Africa or infiltrating from the East.*

*She will also be devoid of moral sense, of social ideal, and of faith itself.*

*She will have no more weight.*

*In spite of everything, we cannot stupidly hunker down in our European anthill. We must draw lessons, observing closely from the technological discoveries and social methods so effective in the Asian world. All of this, at the threat of perishing...politically unbalanced?*

6)   The Past and Happiness

The agricultural world was, before the Second World War, the very essence of European peoples. They watched carefully for the beauty and quality of the products of their crops, masterpieces of patience. Now they feel immersed in the world of American-style business.

In anticipation of the ever-possible decline of the worker, thousands of households found it necessary to double their earning potential by placing the woman outside the home to work so her salary could make up the difference in case the one salary proved insufficient one day.

Hence the disorder of intimacy: fatigue of the couple, lassitude in the face of housework, clashes and misunderstandings, divorces, smaller families with fewer children who are entrusted to anonymous day cares. [ . . . ]

The state has become the financial monster of the modern world, every year increasing its taxes, plundering the economy by the handfuls, taking from a family's finances—already quite little, but nevertheless hard acquired and able to balance itself—not caring whether some economic shock might unexpectedly crush it.

Humanity believes itself free, but where is it? Hyper-capitalism dominates society. This is the new form of slavery, a slavery in which the gold barely camouflages the cruelty. The poor man, however poor he may have been in the past, could still get a morsel; when having next to nothing was still sufficient. Today, the relentless rigor of modern life, with its overconsumption and its unceasingly increased expenses, dominates or strangles the penniless; the man who started out honest ends up being considered a fool. It is the evilest, the most calculating, the least scrupulous that counts. If someone lacks money, he freely consents, beyond his means, with their sword at his throat, to being tyrannized by creditors. Living on credit has become, for the nine out of ten lured by it, a false passport to the trap of wealth, believing that once they get it, they can keep taking on limitless debt.

A young man does not understand that, before, one could live in another way.

Modern life, of course, is theoretically easier than yesterday, but only for some. It throws entire undeveloped countries into torment. The truth is that most men and women, even if they work hard, are only rich in terms of money that is eclipsed, that slips between their fingers and disappears like water in the sand.

Modern man bets on a million different cars that give him the illusion of escaping reality, but these roads are wrong. The asphalt stinks in the most overcrowded cities. The air pollutes the lungs, it taints the blood. In our noisy avenues, from those same trees, with faded leaves, the last birds are leaving.

The pollution from the factories is showing up everywhere, increasingly asphyxiating.

*In the next century, factories will be installed even in the farthest rice or cassava fields, in Laos, or Manchuria, or in Polynesia.*

*This immense human chaos is being devalued everywhere, like a river with a musty smell. Nature itself has become a swallow with her wings clipped.*

*Faced with the almost superhuman difficulties that beset Europe's entry into the twenty-first century, can these be overcome through new discoveries, even with the extraordinary benefits that they provide?*

*An excellent question!*

*Are modern inventions going to fix everything?*

*Scientific progress in the contemporary world is often dazzling, but does its brightness hide its shortcomings?*

*Thanks to the genetic and pharmaceutical developments of modern research and its worldwide spread, older people live longer; women who, as we know, never die, have now surpassed the average age of eighty years.*

*Who will pay the pensions for these millions of fearless octogenarians? [ . . . ]*

*The States, crushed under their current burdens, will have to face these additional burdens in the future. [ . . . ]*

*By dint of cunning, intelligence, and passion for the new, television has become a real wonder. The result: the masses are stuck in front of their television screen for three and a half hours a day. They end up being completely confused, at the mercy of whatever viper's tongue or whatever garbage happens to spew forth. . . . These passive viewers do not think any more, guided not by ideas but by repeated images, often amazing, and almost always destructive to the personality.*

*Three minutes of television have a thousand times more impact than a hundred objective studies by scholars or specialists. [ . . . ]*

*Television is the great poison of the century. It is enough that some of its broadcasters are installed in key positions by well-placed political personalities or by money manipulators, juggling the millions that regulate the life of television channels. These donors of illusions make opinion, dominate opinion, confuse opinion, and by what right? What remains of "democracy" at the end of such gawking by the caged multitudes?*

*In spite of everything, a young man has to assume this new world as it is, without feeling sorry about it. Assume it with its defects, but also with what he might be able to take advantage of: these infinitely elongated horizons; these sports, often disfigured by the use of drugs, but regenerated by the discipline and harmony that come from emulation; the possibilities of new knowledge gathered thanks to easy travel; its more accurate and more widespread culture, even if it is sometimes interspersed in a hodgepodge or in the absurd.*

*Reformers of genius will come on the scene in the twenty-first century, but they will not be able to prevent huge economic and social problems from hounding a world already weighed down by political, social, and racial complications.*

*These complications, if Europe wants to survive, whatever the cost, must be overcome. Such is today's challenge, the crude challenge that the weak fear, but that should also stimulate the hearts of the strong.*

*A challenge that not only reveals the circumstances of a day or a time but extends to everything that is deepest and most permanent within the human being, whatever it may be.[172]*

8)  *Souls Returning to a Spiritual Life*

*[...] The human being of our time has cast to the side a thousand years of Christianity and religion. Everyone wants to "live," to superabundantly enjoy the joys and pleasures. It has become, without even realizing it, a slave to mediocre pleasures, limited to a superficial welfare. It raises itself no higher than ground level.*

*How do you revive a spiritual life whose flames are almost extinguished, whose flame rises no more, smothered under ashes that are cooling little by little? Who will revive it? Who will bring back to life these embers turning to ash, giving inspiration from which the spiritual flame can spring back to life?*

*Without it everything is lost. It is necessary that the gift, generosity, love for mankind, the will to give and the sacred fervor of an ideal brimming with truth renew the inner life of each person. The heart of man is not just a receptacle of passing pleasures. It is an enchanted garden with its colors and perfumes. It wants to rise up out of the confused groves of existence. Political revolution? Yes. Economic and technological revolution? Yes. Social? Yes. Above all, we must dominate the energies of these revolutions with a spiritual revolution!*

*Happiness today is nothing more than a night club by-product. Man must first become a spiritual being again, oriented toward everything that raises him and ennobles him. Otherwise, however pleasant the scenery is, life is nothing more than a trough to feed at, where what is essential does not exist.*

9)  *The Century of the Elites*

*There is the soul.*

*There is also intelligence.*

*A revolution is not made with fanfare, and even less with hollow words, which can be pretty, but with the hollow ring of a tin bowl. Every enriching revolution is the fruit of a long intellectual preparation. More than ever, the future century will*

---

[172] Nothing was included from the seventh panel.

be the century of elites and the coordination of their discoveries. They will be the best, the most capable. They alone will bring in, will lead, and will change society. The time has ended when a human being could prepare his future while taking his time in ease, in ignorance, or in laziness.

The worker himself must cease to be, as he was for a long time, an ignorant laborer. He must be transformed through work and intellectual preparation into a highly qualified technician.

Modern industry, more costly, will recruit only well-selected collaborators. In tomorrow's world, there will be no more room for the mediocre. The mediocre will only help fill the huge trash bag of the miserable and parasitic; for them, the doors to any promising future are closed.

In the next century, you will have to raise yourselves on the basis of work, consistency, flexibility of spirit, and strength of character, on the intellectual level and in technical knowledge that will unfailingly mark the future drivers of men and nations.

Young people should get it into their heads that to the extent that they use their brains, or they increase their know-how, that they will become a living part of the elite and that is when they can undertake the renewal of society.

From new times will emerge the great work of renewal of an exorbitant society, to the extent that you, boys and girls of the twenty-first century who are already at the threshold, engage with their new methods and ideas, but also with a passionate ideal like that of your older brothers of heroic times.

Young comrades in Europe, your time has come.

Materially, of course, but above all spiritually and intellectually, you are prepared, ready for any sacrifice, the brain perfectly ready and structured, the body's strength ready for the hardest duels, the soul illuminating your trajectory.

Then, those who have prepared themselves for the rough struggle will be able to use their strong arms to raise their shields in this victory that the weak believe to be inaccessible.

Only those who have faith move and challenge destiny!

Believe! Fight!

Either you take the world, or you lose it. Take it!

In this human wilderness, where so many lambs are bleating, be the lions!

Strong like lions! Fearless like lions!

And may God help you!

Greetings, comrades!

On September 18th, 1992, Léon Degrelle again presented me with a copy of his work *La Cohue de 1940* (*The Mob of 1940*), given as a kind of culmination, a synthesis, to the recent "Manifesto," with the following dedication: "To my dear friend and comrade José Luis Jerez Riesco, thinking, both of us, of the immortal faith that animates and gives meaning to our lives; with fraternal affection, Léon Degrelle. Malaga, September 18th, 1992."

### Tintin, Mon Copain

Shortly before his death, Degrelle wrote a unique book called *Tintin, Mon Copain* (*Tintin, My Buddy*).

The vignettes of the young reporter Tintin and his fox terrier, Snowy, were read with joy and pleasure by several generations in many countries of the world since the cartoonist Hergé—the pseudonym of Georges Remi—a good friend and comrade of Léon Degrelle, first brought the character to life on January 10th, 1929, in a Catholic magazine. Degrelle, with his unique wit and the strength of his unusual and unforgettable personality, had served as an inspiration for Tintin.

Georges Remi, whose initials in reverse, R.G., make up the pseudonym *Hergé*, was born in 1907. He died on March 3rd, 1983.

Hergé had been trained and educated by Father Norbert Wallez. According to what Degrelle has shared, the famous character Tintin had several major influences: Father Wallez; the genius of Hergé, with his original art; and Léon himself, indirectly. Father Wallez was an exceptional man, who, according to Hergé, "had an enormous influence on me. He made me aware of myself, he made me see myself." The priest ran a newspaper that was initially called *Le XXéme Siècle*; later Hergé adjusted the title name orthographically to read *Le Vingtième Siècle*.[173] It was the second Catholic daily newspaper in Belgium. At that time Father Wallez decided to insert a supplement into his newspaper for the younger children, entitled *Le Petit Vingtième* which appeared every Thursday. It was illustrated by Georges Remi. His skills as a cartoonist allowed him to leave the accounting department, and to focus on the youth supplement. Sometime later he married Germaine Kieckens, a secretary at the newspaper.

Both Hergé and Léon were about the same age. Georges was born in Etterbeek, a village outside Brussels and Léon was a native of Bouillon. When they met, they

---

[173] [French for *The Twentieth Century*.]

were both roughly twenty years old, and they were both the same zodiac sign of Gemini. Hergé and Léon were immediately on familiar terms.[174]

Tintin, this European "B.D." *(Bande Dessinée)*,[175] was actually born in Mexico. In 1929, the enterprising Father Wallez had encouraged young Degrelle to go to Mexico to show solidarity in the struggle that Los Cristeros were facing at the time. As a Catholic journalist, he went there in order to bear witness to the world of the massacre that was being committed against the Christians of Mexico in that atrocious war unleashed by the enemies of Christ. When Degrelle returned home, he brought back something very unique: cartoon strips, unknown in Europe at that time, which had started becoming popular throughout the Americas, especially in the United States. Thus, Tintin came out of this interesting discovery. Snowy, Tintin's faithful canine companion, was inspired by the dog that accompanied Hitler during the First World War and with whom Corporal Hitler had been photographed on several occasions.

Pierre Ajame, editor of *Nouvel Observateur* and author of a book on Hergé (published by Gallimard in 1991), confirmed that Tintin's inspiration goes back to the Mexican newspapers that special envoy Léon Degrelle sent back to *Le Vingtième Siècle*. The Universal Encyclopedia *Quid* recognizes, without hesitation, that "Léon Degrelle inspired Hergé's Tintin character" and Bucquoy admits that Hergé "was fascinated above all by the uniforms that the Nazi Army wore."

In the culture section of the daily *El Mundo* in Madrid, dated Wednesday, December 24th, 1997, Borja Hermoso reported that Pierre Assouline, director of the French literary magazine *Lire*, had written a broad biography of Hergé, some four hundred pages, with revelations drawn directly from his personal files and from private correspondence with Hergé. Assouline obtained access to a lot of documentation from Hergé's second wife and widow Fanny Rodwell, who granted him permission to look through thousands of unpublished letters. In the *El Mundo* article, entitled "*Hergé fue Siempre un Hombre de Extrema Derecha*" ("Hergé was Always a Man of the Extreme Right"), Hermoso remarks on the great friendship of Hergé and Léon Degrelle. The publishing house Destino had just published the Spanish edition of Pierre Assouline's work on Hergé. He quite clearly brushed aside "his accommodation—if not connivance—with the German occupation during the Second World War," where we read that Tintin's creator was "one of those Belgians who was more comfortable during the occupation than during the liberation."

---

[174] [In the Spanish original: *Hergé y León se tuteaban*. The verb *tutear* here means to use the *tú* form with someone, which is the familiar form of 'you,' as opposed to the more formal *usted*. In the French context, this mirrors the verb *tutoyer*, meaning to use *tu*, instead of the more formal *vous*.]

[175] [French for cartoon strip.]

Assouline highlighted Hergé's relationship with Degrelle from their meeting when Hergé was editing *Le Vingtième Siècle*, the visceral anti-communism enclosed in the pages of Hergé's first volume *Tintin in the Land of the Soviets*, and the anti-Semitic tones in other works, such as *The Black Island*.

The main thesis of Pierre Assouline's book is that "Tintin saved Hergé from being burned at the stake." After the Allied victory over Germany, the witch hunts for collaborationists started and there were many Belgian citizens who were executed or sentenced to life imprisonment on account of their approval or, at least, their accommodation, of the German occupation of Belgium. Hergé was, in theory, a clear target since he had published his drawings in the Brussels newspaper *Le Soir*, a newspaper whose position was openly tolerant toward the National Socialists. At that time, Hergé had already published eleven volumes of the Tintin comics, including some comic masterpieces, such as *Cigars of Pharaoh*, *The Broken Ear,* and *The Secret of the Unicorn*. Tintin and Snowy had gone beyond just being for children and were now a piece of Belgian national heritage. Pierre Assouline explains this:

> *Yes, I think Tintin saved Hergé; many of Hergé's friends had a multitude of problems after the "Liberation" but he did not. Why? It would have been very embarrassing to condemn the father of Tintin; first, because he was a symbol of childhood, and second, because of his power as a national symbol. He was, and still is today, the only Belgian national symbol.*

Tintin had two main characteristics that set him apart: his rolled trousers and his unmistakable cowlick, which he had for fifty years. At that time, it was typical of the clothing worn by Léon Degrelle, but unusual as ordinary clothing for the youth. There are multiple photographs of Léon wearing the same style trousers, who was identified by this look so much that the cartoonist Paul Wellens, who illustrated Degrelle's 1933 book *Mes Aventures au Mexique* (*My Adventures in Mexico*), drew him wearing that style. As for the up-turned cowlick, that was the young Léon Degrelle's normal look, and it was how he appeared in the portrait that Albert Ratí made of him in 1927 and in all the photographs taken of Degrelle during those years. In addition to serving as inspiration for Tintin, he gave the cartoonist Hergé the inspiration to become the leading exponent of the so-called "clear line" in Europe.

It was Hergé himself who illustrated *Histoire de la Guerre Scolaire* (*History of the School of War*), written and published by Léon Degrelle in 1931. He was a frequent contributor to the Rex publications, even designing the covers for some of the books in the publisher's collection, such as *Le Carnaval de Binche* (*The Carnival of Binche*), by Alfred Labrique.

At the beginning of the war, Hergé aligned himself with the positions of rexism and of King Leopold III on neutrality. His drawings from those years have been censored for the sake of self-interest by the powerful Hergé Foundation because they have been deemed compromising or "politically incorrect."

During the war, while Degrelle was fighting on the Eastern Front, Hergé worked as a cartoonist and caricaturist at *Le Soir*, the most important newspaper published during the German occupation in Belgium. It was during those years that Hergé's genius really came out. *Le Soir*, leaning in favor of National Socialism, launched Hergé to universal fame. His work at *Le Vingtième Siècle* enjoyed the circulation of fifteen thousand copies, but with *Le Soir*, that jumped to more than three hundred thousand copies during the period of 1940-1944. The cartoonist would not be forgiven for his illustrations of "*Les Deux Juifs et Leur Pari*" ("The Two Jews and Their Wager") in *Fables*, a book by Robert du Bois de Vroylande, where he stereotypically caricaturized the Semitic race.

Tintin, according to the impressions of his creator, represented the search for perfection and an eternal, youthful eagerness for heroism. The defects and miseries that the protagonist was free from were reserved for the characters around him: the mischievous Snowy, the alcoholic Captain Haddock, or the clueless Professor Cuthbert Calculus.

On July 10th, 1942, León Degrelle dedicated the cover of the Rex Movement's political magazine *Voilà*, the successor to *Pourquoi Pas?* to Hergé.

Amidst the atmosphere of hatred unleashed by the pluto-communist Allies, the creator of Tintin was arrested on September 3rd, 1944. A stage of absolute intolerance began. Hergé witnessed scenes of torture and humiliation while in prison. He was about to be sentenced to death, but he had the good fortune to be released when a magistrate, who was a great follower and admirer of his fictional character's adventures, recognized him as "the cartoonist of Tintin." He was released but was prohibited from drawing from 1944 until September 1946. He resumed publication of his Tintin comic strip on September 26th, 1946, and it appeared in the news kiosks that Thursday. Tintin began to achieve global success and brought Hergé great fame.

In spite of everything, in the Résistance Museum in Brussels, the exhibit on Hergé appears in the gallery of "Traitors," with this comment: "According to certain information obtained, he was a rexist, although we cannot confirm this."

On several occasions during his exile in Spain, Degrelle received visits from Germaine Kieckens, Hergé's first wife, at his home in Constantina. During one of those visits, he gave her a flamenco costume as a memento of the stay.

The French historian Alain Guionnet wrote in the monthly magazine *Forces Nouvelles* two extensive articles on the subject of Tintin and Hergé. At the beginning of one of the articles, he stated:

> For Tintin, [Hergé] *had taken as a model the former chief of the Rexist Party, and why is that? Are they not strange, these coincidences that Hergé uses to represent his hero in various situations, which history undoubtedly attributes to Léon Degrelle's life? This is not the only convincing fact, but take the example of Toulouse, where Degrelle's painful journey concludes towards the end of summer 1940, when Hergé, on the occasion of his return to the newspapers, makes Tintin return, on the cover of Le Soir Jeunesse in its autumn 1940 issue. Or even Degrelle's silhouette, sketched since 1933, with that of "Jam" ("Alidor") in an old "Quick et Flupke" edition.*

For his part, "C. A. Hugins," pseudonym of one of the best Flemish cartoonists of today, wrote in *Forces Nouvelles* an article in which he shared the previous theses as well.

Germaine Kieckens also revealed a little secret:

> *Hergé wanted to draw Tintin in America first (from where Léon Degrelle returned in 1929 after walking the frontlines with the Cristeros) before drawing Tintin in the Congo. It was in 1932 that Degrelle published, in his Rex publishing house, the booklet The School War, with a foreword by Monsignor Picard. It was profusely illustrated with drawings by Hergé, which reached a circulation of six hundred thousand copies.*

On Thursday, October 17th, 1940, *Le Soir Jeunesse*, a supplement of *Le Soir*, announced on its cover: "Tintin and Snowy are Back!" A railway ticket revealed that they had returned from Toulouse and were heading to Brussels. Tintin was dressed in a shirt and tie, with sleeves rolled up. Léon Degrelle, from May 10th to July 29th, 1940, had been interned in nineteen prisons along a 2,600-kilometer (1,615 miles) route. He finished his "Via Dolorosa," by chance, in Toulouse. Tintin was returning to Brussels, and it was none other than Léon Degrelle.

The relationship between Degrelle and Hergé continued throughout the war. Léon ordered that two resplendent images of Tintin and Hergé be published on the cover of the July 10th, 1942, edition of the widely read rexist weekly *Voilà*. It was a fitting tribute to the great master of cartoons.

When Tintin found refuge in "Moulinsart," the name of the place was nothing more than an invented reference to the land of Spain. The connection between Tintin and Degrelle was extremely strong.

Another famous cartoonist, Paul Jamin, better known by his pseudonyms, "Alidor" and "Jam," had been associated with Hergé since 1925. In 1930, Alidor also began working at *Le Petit Vingtième*, collaborating with Hergé until 1936. He was the one who created a character that Hergé took up under the name "Seraphim Lampion." Degrelle recounted how Hergé hesitated, before the war, to accept being the official cartoonist of the Rexist Movement, since his direct competitor for that position was Alidor.

For his part, the writer Benoit Peeters, who dedicated a book to the brilliant cartoonist, entitled *Le Monde d'Hergé* (*The World of Hergé*), acknowledged that it was "through Mexican newspapers sent to Brussels by a correspondent (Léon Degrelle), of *Le Vingtième Siècle* (directed by Paul Werrie), when Hergé..." began to publish his first drawings of Tintin. Later, in 1934, it was Father Norbert Wallez who suggested to Hergé that he put Tintin's adventures in monographic volumes. Both Léon Degrelle and Hergé worked directly with Father Wallez, creating between them a community of spirit in organizations such as the Scouts. It is no surprise that Hergé was inspired by the young and fearless Léon, so bold and full of life. For them, the Scouts, the Catholic Church, work, and right-wing and anti-communist ideas were their common ground.

Hergé himself, on December 30th, 1975, declared in *La Libre Belgique*: "I discovered cartoons thanks to Léon Degrelle."

A reader of the newspaper *Forces Nouvelles* wrote into the publication, and his comments were put into the October 1989 issue:

> It was Léon Degrelle, sent as a reporter to Mexico by the Catholic daily Le Vingtième Siecle, who served as a model to Hergé for Tintin. Also, there are numerous photographs of Degrelle from that time wearing trousers like those of Tintin.

Olivier Mathieu was another close friend of Hergé. They had known each other since childhood, and Mathieu was passionate about Tintin. Mathieu had met Hergé on Avenue Louise de Ixelles, in Brussels, on February 25th, 1969. He was barely ten years old and was introduced to him by his mother.

On Friday, October 26th, 1990, Olivier Mathieu delivered a lecture with the title "From Léon Degrelle to Tintin" in the auditorium on Boulevard Bockstael, number 104, in Brussels for the opening of the Circle of Revisionist Students. Mathieu, born in 1960, was a great connoisseur of Hergé.

At the lecture, Mathieu posited:

*We are living in the time of absolute reversal of all values. We live in an age of total and permanent lies, camouflaged under the great statement of "freedom of thought."*

*Sometimes Hergé has to be interpreted in secret codes. For example, in his work Le Septre d'Ottokar (The Scepter of Ottokar) he speaks of "Müstler." This is a contraction of Muss(olini) and (Hi)tler."*

After Olivier Mathieu's brilliant dissertation, he closed his lecture with the blunt statement: "Yes, Tintin was, is, and always will be Léon Degrelle!" The lecture was later published as a brochure including unpublished, censored illustrations by Hergé.

### The Weekly *O Independente* in Lisbon Publishes an Interview with Léon Degrelle about Tintin

The subject of Tintin was again addressed by journalist Sarah Adamopoulos in the journal *Viver*, number 98, dated June 26th, 1992, which was part of the Portuguese publication *O Independente*. The article was entitled "*Eu, SS Tintin,*"[176] and was on a subject as controversial, and at the same time as exciting, as the man who inspired Tintin's adventures ("Tintin is me").

Adamopoulos expressly recognized that:

*Physiognomically, you can certainly see the resemblance, beyond the detail of the golf pants that Degrelle claims as his own. If Tintin had aged, he might well look like him. This is the story that begins and ends with the century: two men, Degrelle and de Gaulle, united by the single character of Tintin.*

*That Hergé was obviously and inevitably influenced by the current times is a natural fact not to mention simple common sense itself. Hergé is said to have been anti-communist (Tintin in the Land of the Soviets), anti-American (Tintin in America), and colonialist (Tintin in the Congo).*

In 2007, when the comic strip *Tintin in the United Kingdom* was first edited in color, *Tintin in the Congo* was removed from bookstores at the request of the Commission on Racial Equality, arguing that in it "the native savages look like monkeys and speak

---

[176] [Portuguese for "Me, the SS Tintin."]

like imbeciles," and also because, among other passages, there was a scene they deemed offensive in which the famous reporter was proclaimed chief of an African village for being "a good White man."

During the interview, Adamopoulos asked the following question: "Would the creator of Tintin have been a collaborationist?"

This was asked due to Degrelle's book *Tintín, Mon Copain* having been completed a few months prior. It was about to be published, and in it, across more than two-hundred pages, Degrelle tells how he served as a model for Hergé to create Tintin.

The manuscript was sent to Stéphane Steeman, president of the Association of Friends of Hergé. Steeman lived in Brussels in a house that, over time, was transformed into the Museum of Hergé. The museum housed hundreds of original documents, and all kinds of objects related to Tintin. In the summer of 1991, Steeman traveled to Spain to meet Léon and on October 3rd began negotiations on a definitive text. The meeting was front page news in many Belgian newspapers, and Steeman, by the mere fact of having met Degrelle, was described as a "collaborationist and traitor." Bloodthirsty journalists brought to light that Stéphane's father was the author Stanislas-André Steeman, and that he wrote, among other works, *Quai des Orfèvres* and *L'Assassin Habite au 21*.[177] He had published some of his literary work before the war, in the Rex publishing house founded by Léon Degrelle.

The meeting of Steeman and Degrelle in Malaga revived suspicions, however unfounded, that Hergé had been a collaborationist and Tintin a "fascist character."

Adamopoulos opened the interview with a direct question about the book:

> SA: *Is Tintin, Mon Copain the true story of the young reporter of "Le Petit Vingtième" or your own?*
>
> LD: *My book Tintin, Mon Copain will make public not only the true story of Hergé, but of both our lives, for they would coincide like fraternal twins, always meeting together, both in the immensity of the Americas, along thousands of kilometers of the Eastern Front, or in bitter Spanish exile. It is not, therefore, the life of one of the two characters, but the life of two accomplices, one created from the imagination and the other built from reality, both moved throughout the most unpredictable circumstances by identical enthusiasm and reactions.*

---

[177] Stanislas-André Steeman (1908–1970) was a Belgian author who wrote primarily French-language detective or mystery novels, including *L'Assassin Habite au Vingt et Un* (*The Murderer Lives at Number Twenty-One*). *Quai des Orfèvres* (*Goldsmiths' Quay*), however, is the name of a movie made in 1947 that was based on S.A. Steeman's novel *Légitime Défense* (*Self-Defense*).

*SA: You had to make some modifications to the original manuscript of your book; what were they and why did you agree to make them?*

*LD: It is normal for a writer to edit his text many times, correcting expressions, expanding forgotten scenes. Boileau explained this process with great expertise: "Throughout your task, you question, if necessary, your work twenty times; file and sand the edges as many times as necessary." You want to make people believe that they forced me to modify my book. Between you and me, it is by no means my style to let myself be intimidated. I have, in contrast, a taste for accuracy. Before I sent my manuscript to my editor, I reread it and improved it half a dozen times. Then, I submitted it to the best connoisseur of Hergé and Tintin on earth, Mr. Stéphane Steeman. We did not know each other, but Steeman is a lovely person. He made the trip from Brussels to Malaga by plane (a circumstance he loathes) in order to reread my manuscript with me. We had an absolutely magnificent three days as Steeman is fun, has a sense of humor, and a heart as big as the world. It is true that he pointed out a correction here or there in the narrative, an inaccurate date here or there, or a dubious interpretation of events. Small things. One of the chapter titles in my book bothered him from the beginning of the story (that is, in 1929), about half of my prose, at the time Hitler occupied Belgium. When I titled the chapter "Tintin at Hitler's House," I did not in any way mean to imply that Hergé had traveled to meet the Führer (he never saw him in his life, neither up close, nor far away). The chapter was titled that way because it happened during the occupation of Belgium by the Germans. To be more precise, and to please my wonderful guest Steeman, I replaced my "Tintin at Hitler's House" with "Tintin in Hitler's Time." This did not prevent the most important "big-brains" of the great left-wing press (who had not read a single line of my book, unknown to everyone except Steeman) from touting that the modifications were supposedly made under threat. You yourself, who are not familiar with the work I am going to publish, insist on this small perfidious question. Frankly, is this serious? I myself consulted Steeman to avoid publishing any inaccuracies, however minimal they might be. We polished my text together on my sunny terrace facing the great sea. Together, in a very cordial climate, we dined on delicious fine pasta and some old wines from my wine cellar. So, what is the reason for this mania of always wanting people to fight tooth and nail over things? A conversation is, first and foremost, something pleasurable, not a battle. The most heated adversaries, whenever they are honest, will always be welcome to me. It would be a diabolical work indeed, if in an experience of divergent ideas there were no point in common: painting, music, poetry, or philosophy. This was precisely what happened to me, and that is certainly true of you too. When you are upright and well educated, you do not turn dragonflies into fighter planes; any human contact is possible, and most of the time it is interesting and always enriching.*

*SA: Tintin is a young adventurer, determined, bold, and very charming. Is your personality recognized in these attributes?*

*LD: I would not risk attributing to myself the term "very charming." For that, it would be necessary to ask my wife. She certainly knows the proverb that "like attracts like." From the beginning of our youth, Hergé and I were a pair. Even in exile, as you will see in my book, Hergé was an admirable companion, not only to me, but also to all our fellow countrymen persecuted after 1945. He even had the courage to tell the press very bluntly: "Degrelle was a hero!" However, in these times of almost demonic hatred, it was virtually obligatory to publicly, and maliciously, assert that I had been a war criminal! Hergé had the extreme courage to confront the lowest insults about me.*

*SA: Is there a moral in Tintin or not? If so, which one?*

*LD: Of course, there is. Tintin is the symbol of courage, bravery, audacity, but also loyalty, fidelity and, above all, generosity, dedication, good deeds daily. Always generous. Always upright. Many young people today would gain a lot if they followed his example, instead of packing into the night clubs or snatching handbags from defenseless old women from the top of their noisy cars.*

*SA: If you are Tintin, who is Haddock?*

*LD: Captain Haddock was one of the twenty characters Hergé introduced over time into his fantasy world. Haddock was, as everyone knows, a firm and insatiable guy even in drink. He is an imaginary character; I do not know very well whom he might resemble. Perhaps Churchill, a real sponge of champagne and whiskey. In a short smock, his rear end gleaming white, with a glass of Dom Perignon in hand, Churchill drank abundantly starting in the morning. I met him personally, he also invited me one day to lunch with him in the restaurant of the House of Commons. That time, I can assure you, he was in shirt sleeves and that the alcohol did not stop. You wanted to know who resembled Haddock; there you have it. I hope you are satisfied.*

*SA: Hergé stated that he had never in his life been a rexist and even added that he had a deep aversion for the party you founded. Do you want to comment on that?*

*LD: Where did you dig up such nonsense!? Can you tell me a couple sentences by him that contain such a statement? Miserable stories that journalists tell. In my book, on the contrary, you will find quite a few poignant examples of sentiments that united him to me, even dozens of years after 1945, when I was in the depths of my exile. There, once again, I tell and bring the truth, not some kind of press sensationalism, simply tossed about without tone or sound, devoid of any scruples, in the midst of the great journalistic salad.*

*SA: What were your relations with Hergé when he refused to collaborate as a cartoonist for the Führer's propaganda in Belgium?*

*LD: Once again, how is it possible that you keep pulling out such foolishness?! After Belgium's defeat in the spring of 1940, when Hergé resumed publishing his comic strips, I had no contact whatsoever with him, for the simple reason that everyone thought I was dead as of May 21st, 1940! On that day, in fact, a war crime happened that is never mentioned: twenty-one of my poor colleagues in the prison transport truck, who were only accused, like me, of defending Belgian neutrality, were handed over by the Belgian police to the deranged French and murdered with great cruelty, specifically with bayonets, near a kiosk in the French city of Abbeville. Among the unrecognizable bodies, they thought they identified me. It was front page news all over the press. What kind of relationship could Hergé have had with that hastily identified body? As for Hergé's alleged collaboration "as an illustrator of the Führer's propaganda in Belgium," this exceeds the boundaries of nonsense. Hergé was never a propagandist, in any way, of "Adolf the Victorious." Such an opportunity was never even suggested, neither to him nor to any other Belgian citizen. Hitler did not need propagandists in those countries. His fabulous victories, achieved in a snap of the fingers, in Poland, Denmark, Norway, the Netherlands, in Belgium and France, between 1939 and 1940, saved him from having to turn to the Tintin comic book for propaganda. Moreover, who was Tintin at that time, practically unknown, to pretend to play the role of Hitler's pied piper, at a time when the immense wave of his armies had just flooded almost the entire European continent?*

*SA: Which Tintin story do you like most?*

*LD: It would be, indisputably, Tintin in the Land of the Soviets because Hergé, especially with this volume, was a precursor, denouncing Stalin as the most savage murderer of the century. Others presented him as a messiah and about whom the poet Aragón proclaimed: "Oh great Stalin. You who make man reborn, you who make spring bloom..." In 1975, Mitterrand was still singing the glories of the USSR: "It is especially because his revolution was made on the basis of an analysis that is of our own." Hergé's Tintin, for his part, since 1929, has unmasked the communist disgrace. It now lies in tatters, but unhappily, it was ripped up too late, after the damage was already done, unfortunately.*

*It was following Tintin's example that we left, in 1941, to go to the Soviet Union with the aim of annihilating that diabolical regime and bringing twenty admirable nations back to a European community. In 1942 everything was possible.*

*Our effort to liberate those countries was overthrown, not by communism, which by itself would have been inevitably swept away, but by Roosevelt's absurd fanaticism, who, before Stalingrad, was the great supplier of weapons and war material to the Soviets. It was even the Americans who took Stalin to Berlin, handing over to him one hundred million Eastern Europeans as slaves. From 1945 to 1990, Americans have paid the price for that absurdity, which cost them hundreds of millions of dollars in nuclear weapons before they got to see the fall of the now disfigured USSR, which will undoubtedly be unrecoverable for a long time.*

*SA: Hergé is said to be a colonialist, an anti-Semite, and a Nazi; what do you think of all this?*

*LD: Hergé was already a colonialist before 1940, like everyone else. In other words, he was sensitive to the role of Europe among peoples in need of material relief, of order, of a principle, of culture. All this in an atmosphere of good will. There is not a single word in Hergé's thousands of drawings that would be hurtful to or disparage people of color. The war, to the contrary, did not get rid of colonialism. The American victors merely changed the direction of a colonial order that should have continued for another fifty years, until the elites capable of succeeding it had been formed. The Americans ruined this world order to subdue fifty countries who suddenly became leaderless, and to secure huge economic gains, at any price. This is seen later in the massacre of women and children in Vietnam with napalm or in the huge slaughter of civilians in Iraq, perpetrated under the hypocritical mantle of "democracy" in order to ensure that the control of eastern oil and the maintenance of world dictatorship by the United States be respected, disregarding all fundamental, international laws.*

*As for Hergé's anti-Semitism, I can only say that in all of his work there are only five or six hooked noses. Is there any anti-Semitism in this? So, are we no longer allowed to laugh at funny stereotypes? It is true that Hergé had some fun, a time or two, with his Blumenstein. Has the Jew been transformed into a sacred creature? Untouchable? What is profaned by committing the crime of laughing because of a nose? This sensitivity borders on the ridiculous. Jews should have fun with Hergé's drawings, rather than dramatically confronting them. The day the painter Labisse made a portrait of me, particularly scathing, I rushed to get a copy to keep for my collection. I look at it from time to time, always smiling. So, tell your Israelites to do the same.*

*Finally, was Tintin a Nazi? I do not answer this question. There is no other option for you but to wait for the publication of my book. The surprise lies there, within its pages. Are you disappointed? You will not be for much longer."*

Degrelle ended the interview by saying:

> *My book* Tintin, Mon Copain *is a story yoking together the creator of an imaginary personality and that of a man of action, still alive, very alive, who together wanted to create a new Europe, which fifty years ago could have been saved. One day, perhaps, we will bitterly regret, in 1945, our banners were not triumphant!*

The last interview that Léon Degrelle gave at his home in Malaga was on November 20th, 1993, to Alejandro Nantón. Degrelle again addressed the topic of Tintin, when the interviewer asked him, "To what extent can we see Tintin as a National Socialist and why does this comic hero support that system?"

Degrelle was again blunt with his reply:

> *The Tintin subject is but a detail, but it has its humor. Everyone knows that I was the one who got Hergé going as the creator of Tintin. He himself explains this. This is not my statement; it is what Hergé said. Hergé was born almost the same year I was. We had the same conception of social obligation, the same conception of the state, the same conception of Europe. The proof is that his first book, which was inspired by me, was entitled Tintin in the Land of the Soviets. He wrote this first comic book against the Soviets because the Soviets were the contradiction to our civilization, they were the contradiction to Europe. They wanted to eliminate her, reduce her to a slave status, and Hergé, at that time, was a personal and spiritual friend. Then the war came. He participated in his way as a cartoonist, illustrating vignettes in the large newspaper Le Soir. Later, of course, he became a man of Europe and of the world, but after suffering, being imprisoned, seeing his best friends and my best friends shot, only because they were Europeans and anti-communists. To sum up, despite only making comics, Tintin and Hergé have been an important element in the creation of Europe, and we also see him realizing a vision of the future world.*
>
> *Hergé, always treated me as his friend, and do not forget that even in my exile, he sent his wife to see me to reiterate his friendship. In 1945, when Hergé was in jail, when they were shooting our anti-communist friends, Germany was not the one who lost the war, but Europe; the Europe of 1940 was forever dead…the Europe of today is morally weak. She is facing a very difficult future ahead of her, and if she is unable to overcome these obstacles, it is clear that in the great struggle of the next century, she will not be able to play an important role. Any young man who has faith in the future must also have willpower and courage. Without great effort*

*nothing will be done. Europe's effort can only be made on the basis of generosity and service to others."*

A few months before his death, on May 25th, 1993, Léon Degrelle sent a dedication to Stéphane Steeman with the following text: "To my dear Stéphane Steeman, a colorful, brilliant friend among all and so affectionate! Saluting him with a very affectionate greeting, Léon Degrelle."

On February 1st, 1991, the socialist newspaper *El País* published a series of vicious vignettes by the cartoonist Bucquoy in a campaign to discredit Hergé, under the title "Tintin, Sex and the Nazis: Ferocious Comics about the Cartoonist Hergé and His Creature." They even went so far as to allude to homosexuality in Hergé just because of his long-held friendship with Degrelle.

Hergé married his second wife, Fanny Vlamynck, in 1977. Hergé died in 1983 of leukemia at the age of seventy-six, well-known throughout Europe and around the world. Interestingly, in Spain his work was published somewhat later than in other European countries. His first two volumes did not appear in Spain until 1958, when they were published by the Juventud publishing house. In view of the success achieved by the adventures of Tintin, who encouraged the hopes and dreams of young generations, Hergé continued to publish some twenty titles. The Spanish translation of the adventures of Tintin, of whom Charles de Gaulle came to say, "that he was the only one who shadowed him on the world stage," was done by Concepción Zendrera, daughter of the owner of Juventud.

## Nostalgia and Longing

On January 25th, 1993, at the age of ninety-two, Léon Degrelle wrote and signed the following note in a folder:

*In exile, January 25th, 1993*

*Behold, sixty years ago, I was then in full action. I have seen fit to gather the first issues of the publications that marked my youth. I look at them now with emotion. I am reminded that, from the beginning of my career, my life has been an impulse of faith, an explosion of my ideal. I have lived no more than to create greatness, to give the multitudes the means to become ennobled and to overcome. At the end of my life, I have nothing to regret. The same convictions still burn within me. If I were twenty years old again, I would take the same road, however hard it has been;*

*even if coping with it were a thousand times more painful, I would climb again the rough ascent to the summits. Believe, fight, conquer or die; that was my life!*

*Léon Degrelle*

Despite his advanced age, Degrelle had the strength to go to the Faculty of Law of the Complutense University of Madrid on April 23rd to participate in a conference, which was also attended by a very young and courageous Ricardo Sáenz de Ynestrillas. Degrelle's participation at this academic event was reported in the Madrid press including *El País*. In its April 24th edition, it reported:

> *A lecture by Sáenz de Ynestrillas provoked a fight at Complutense, in the Faculty of Law. The lawyer Angel López Montero was going to give a talk, and Sáenz de Ynestrillas was going to speak at the lecture, organized by the group DISPAR as a result of the acquittal of the murder of Muguruza in the Alcalá hotel. The dean Mr. Iturmendi was about to be attacked....Even the presence of former SS officer Léon Degrelle was allowed at the university.*

At the end of the talks, Degrelle signed copies of *The Burning Souls* for numerous faculty and alumni. This amazing work was in its fifth edition, published by the Fuerza Nueva publishing house. Like the trees of Miguel Delibes,[178] he was willing to die standing with his boots on.

On June 15th, 1993, Degrelle spent his birthday in Malaga in the company of his family, friends and some comrades. He went to congratulate Mariano Bolaño Lozano, one of his best and most faithful comrades. I was even invited to the celebration, and Degrelle presented me with *L'Ordre SS* (*The SS Order*), in which he wrote "To my dear friend and comrade José Luis Jerez Riesco, the splendid gentleman of our ideal, with the brotherly affection and admiration of Léon Degrelle. June 15th, 1993. I am ninety-three years old today."

### The Last Interview

In Malaga, on November 20th, 1993, Alejandro Nantón, a national-revolutionary activist from the Canary Islands, conducted the last interview with

---

[178] Miguel Delibes Setién (1920–2010) was a Spanish novelist and member of the Royal Spanish Academy.

Degrelle. It was entitled *"Wallonien"* ("Wallonia"), and it toured a number of issues which Degrelle had often previously spoken about to the press, such as: "What did the person of Adolf Hitler represent in your life?" "How would you define the idea of 'Blood and Soil'?" or, taking as reference the concept of tradition in political thought, as did Julius Evola, René Guénon, or Miguel Serrano, "How did you live out your traditionalist Catholicism, your warrior and Nordic Christianity?" To this latter question Degrelle answered extensively as follows:

*Christianity is exactly in line with this tradition. For two thousand years Europe has lived within Christianity, whether in the countries of the Mediterranean or in the countries of the North. Charlemagne carried Catholicism throughout the different regions. The Nordic people,[179] like those in the south, have had the same spiritual life, and it is the very basis of our personality. There are obviously other religions, which may have their nobility, but the religion of Europe is precisely Catholicism, which is not the same as clericalism or the Bible. It is the life of Christ, the life of Christ renewed by Greek classicism and Roman civilization, which the Renaissance and the revolution brought to us after the Middle Ages. It is not just a tradition; it is a way of living and that is why it is so important. We talk about tradition, and it is the Christian religion that has maintained the great virtues in Europe, the life of the family; for example, public morality and private morality are two characteristics of Christian Europe. The man who has his very rich ideal, that is, the man who follows the law of his conscience is typically Christian. When we see the scandals of today, the incredible political corruption at all levels, even in countries that were a foundation of Catholicism, like Italy; how hundreds of politicians live from passive and active corruption, receiving money to which they are not entitled and forcing industrialists to hand it over; the immorality of youth, the desire to live, to enjoy everything, the existing hedonism, this true madness of well-being... well, all these things go against the very basis of Christianity. There will be no moral resurrection of Europe without a deep spiritual life, so much so that, being Catholic, I have always felt perfectly at ease in a future with National Socialism. Now, they will tell me that there were National Socialists who were pagan. In all governments there are people who are not Christian, and they must be endured. Even the Church admitted the French Republic, which had expelled the clergy. In the background, the Hitlerite system was deeply religious. Hitler always spoke of the Almighty and was not scandalized in any way when he saw me take*

---

[179] By *Nordic*, Degrelle understands northern Europe more broadly, contrasting it with Mediterranean, and not simply Scandinavian people.

*communion in his own house. It was clear that he hated some political clerics, and he was right to do so. The clergy are not intended to deal in politics, trade unions, or to even hold a job as priests. The priest should guide us to heaven, and the political man should guide us to public order. These are two separate missions. He respected these two missions. Catholicism, as I lived it, corresponded to the two thousand years of deep spiritual tradition in Europe.*

The interview dealt with questions related to the European community as the upper body, the State and regions as the lower body. He was also presented with questions related to his similarity to the famous cartoon character Tintin and on Islam as an emerging force against globalism.

The last question asked was: "What advice or guidance would you give to young National Socialists, whose souls are burning in these times of total struggle against globalism, the only enemy?"

Degrelle stated:

*We are facing globalism. The Asian world and the Yankee, above all, want to impose their implacable laws on the universe, and only with an entirely united Europe, from Dunkirk to Vladivostok, by uniting all her forces and raising an unparalleled faith, will we be able to resist and make of Europe a common unity the likes of which we have never known. With all our forces united, despite all the difficulties, we will be able to realize the next century.*

### A Foreword for a Bachelor's Thesis

January 30th had always been a very special date on Léon's calendar. It was a day of triumph, commemorating Adolf Hitler's rise to the Reich Chancellery. For many years, he had personally participated in those anniversaries, giving speeches and attending events to commemorate and remember that historic day in 1933. On that day of commemoration in 1993, he received an old friend and Falangist comrade from Barcelona, Luis Antonio García Rodríguez, at his home on Paseo Marítimo, in the city of Melilla, in Malaga. They both spent the morning talking under the war banners of Burgundy that formed the Red Cross of St. Andrew. These had once fluttered high in Russia as the advance battalion banners for the rexist volunteers on the Eastern Front, but on this occasion, they decorated the hall of the room in which they spoke together. Several photographs of the visit were taken. In one of them, Léon appears seated, conversing with his guest, under the beautiful picture *The Descent*, the scene in which Christ lies at the foot of the cross in the lap of his mother, the Virgin Mary, underneath her sad and compassionate gaze. It is an image of great expressive beauty. In the second photograph, the two speakers are between two gigantic golden Solomonic columns with vine leaves climbing up them. Luis Antonio, sitting on an adjoining sofa, under a large picture inspired by Franciscan life, is attentively listening to Léon's emphatic words. Luis Antonio, Léon, and his wife Jeanne had lunch together at a restaurant near the house.

Léon wrote Luis Antonio a prologue, the last one he would write in his life, for a book that Luis Antonio was finishing in Barcelona, with the title *Reflexiones de la Historia del III Reich* (*Reflections of the History of the Third Reich*), which he planned to publish soon.

The full text of the prologue is reproduced here, since the intended book has remained unpublished, and thus unknown until now:

*The twentieth century has witnessed two great social revolutions: communism and National Socialism. Compared to these, other social phenomena are but transitional stages.*

*Socialism, for example. It was certainly useful and even necessary in its time, but it was based on a mortal heresy: class struggle. Since that time, devoid of any ideal, it has diluted itself in corruption, with countless and endless scandals. From now on, it will only be sick and bedridden.*

*In France in 1993, tainted by several financial disgraces that were never punished, it has collapsed into a rambling electoral disaster. A few months later, a similar failure happened in Italy, where, at other times, it had been so sure of itself. Only rotten vestiges of local socialism have remained, after the regional elections, floating here and there on a new Dead Sea. In Milan, the great red metropolis of former times, the total votes for the Socialist Party did not exceed 2 percent.*

*What can be said of the two great social revolutions that marked the twentieth century?*

*Arguably, the first was the Bolshevik revolution unleashed in Russia by Lenin in 1917. It was a revolution of intellectuals, quite a few of them of withered spirit, mostly Jews. With a calculating brain and a frozen heart, when the occasion presented itself, they knew how to use the extreme misery of a massive, but exhausted, people (who lost four million men during the First World War). They fomented the most horrible revolution that Europe has ever known throughout her twenty-five centuries of history. For Lenin and his acolytes, democracy, freedom, and human rights were nonsense. They and their successors, led by Stalin, imposed, by terror, a doctrine of despair that annihilated in man any spirit of initiative, any desire to overcome oneself, and the necessary collaboration and emulation between the various* social strata. The latter, moreover, had been eliminated in bloodshed. Morally and intellectually, "homo sovieticus" had become a robot, and soon the robots became slaves. Millions of them fell beneath the discharges of firing squads, or in massive and desperate crowds, went to perish in hellish gulags.

Such was the Soviet Union, the absolute master of four hundred million human beings for three-quarters of the twentieth century, but that Soviet Union has disappeared. This does not mean that the pseudo-democracies, by dedicating themselves to virtue, eliminated it. It was the countries dominated by communism that had to assume their own liberation by themselves in 1989, even though Western democracies, without great effort, could have annihilated the Leninism of 1918.

By contrast, these "democracies," during the Second World War, ensured the survival of Stalin, that tragic and ruthless tyrant. He received everything he lacked from the Westerners like thousands and thousands of battle tanks (especially in late 1942, at the crucial time of the Battle of Stalingrad, he received seven hundred fifty Sherman tanks, the most powerful American tanks); Roosevelt, moreover, provided four hundred ninety thousand trucks, with which the Soviets were able to transport their troops, who until then had to trudge through the heavy snow of their country. Swarms of aircraft, vast amounts of raw materials, and even factories fully assembled to the last bolt also arrived. Without Roosevelt's help, Stalin would have never succeeded; he would not have even survived.

That alleged goddess of freedom, America, not only allowed the Soviets to win the final victory in 1945, but it also awarded them another hundred million slaves, handing over to Stalinist despotism all of Eastern Europe, from Berlin and Warsaw to Bucharest and Sofia. These one hundred million Europeans had to suffer for almost half a century under the Soviets' political domination and economic annihilation.

These have not in any way been eliminated by a reaction of virtuous Western democracies. None of them, between 1917 and 1987, stood up to this gigantic barbarism and none of them intervened to end it. It was those same subjugated peoples who, at the limit of suffering, rebelled and liberated themselves one after the other, from Soviet domination and arrogance, first in Eastern Europe, and then in the various states of Russia and Northwest Asia. Only then, in the face of total passivity of the regimes of Western Europe and the United States, did communism collapse. This huge societal scam was imposed upon three hundred million Russians for seventy-three years and, from 1945 onward, upon one hundred million unfortunate Eastern Europeans, handed over as cattle to Stalin, the all-powerful slave driver.

*Of the other experience of the century, which is to say, the immense social reform that Hitler carried out in Germany, between 1933 and 1939, almost nothing is known, since it was buried under millions of relentless assaults and low blows.*

*For the vast majority of the world's inhabitants, starting with the Germans themselves, Hitler is regarded only as the monster who turned some six million Jews into human "burgers" or soap. Is this figure true? No one doubts it, without any evidence to confirm such an exaggerated statement. Did the gas chambers eliminate twenty-four thousand Jews a day? Or, more modestly, twenty-four? Or maybe none, as is argued by Leuchter, the great American specialist in gas chambers? For decent people, as for him, the case is already closed, but we must believe in it unrelentingly, lest we face courts of exceptional jurisdiction, long prison sentences, and colossal fines of hundreds of thousands of francs! According to what we are supposed to believe, Hitler—such is dogma—not only fumigated the children of Torah like termites, but that is the only thing to which he dedicated himself. It is forbidden to even question this!*

*Who would dare even ask today what that cursed Hitler managed to achieve for his people?*

*Certainly, this they admit with a painful sigh, Hitler became Reich Chancellor in 1933 in a totally democratic way. He was brought to power through the undisputed will of the people, but what about later? Later, we hear nothing of it!*

*A defiant Spaniard, Luis Antonio García Rodríguez, has had the rare idea of examining this period in order to clarify the mystery.*

*In 1933, Hitler had to carry on his shoulders and assume six million unemployed in a half-ruined Germany. Luis Antonio García Rodríguez asks this question: How did Hitler, in two years, manage to create jobs for all those unemployed, when in the other countries, without exception, the rulers were absolutely unable to remedy the disaster of unemployment? The European community now has seventeen million unemployed, which will undoubtedly rise to twenty-four million in a few years' time, and this crisis is met with total powerlessness on the part of politicians.*

*So how did this wretched Hitler succeed in bring the disaster to an end? How did he ensure the welfare of the country's workers? How did he manage to impose upon big employers a respect for the worker? How, in the face of Marxism and communism, did he succeed in peacefully putting class struggle to an end?*

*How was he able to convey an irresistible dynamism to millions of young people in his country? How did he restore physical health to an entire people? Some sources point out that, under his leadership, the Germans produced one million six hundred* thousand children each year, while the French had a million fewer. What machinery did he invent to achieve large families? All these questions have been raised by García Rodríguez. First of all, he wanted to know the effective dimensions of the social revolution devised by Hitler, whose name is still being scorned today.

The Spanish author has a resolute will. For many years he has surveyed, researched, and analyzed, with a commendable tenacity, everything that has been published on the subject, despite the fanaticism of our day. He was astonished to discover the wealth of the social revolution that the creator of the Third Reich carried out for his people and that he would have undoubtedly stabilized Europe for centuries if, by 1945, the Americans and Soviets together had not pulverized that massive work.

Luis Antonio García Rodríguez was not satisfied to study this problem thoroughly for himself. He decided to submit his findings, in the form of a thesis, to the judgment of a university court, essentially impartial. As incredible as it may seem, it was truly impartial. It was in Barcelona that García Rodríguez aspired to a degree in social sciences. Under the direction of Professor Dr. D. Alberto J. Carro Iguelmo, he had the audacity to present to the Catalan university court his voluminous thesis on "The Social History of the Third Reich." Was it rejected by the instructors? Was it simply tolerated? We must keep in mind that this Hitler that he is dealing with is a monster, a sadist, a destroyer of Jews, etc. Well, it must be noted that the thesis was accepted by the committee and obtained the mention of outstanding.

A scandal? Yes, of course! In spite of the phenomenal campaigns that aim to stifle forever all of Hitler's societal achievement, even today, an academic thesis is devoted to his social revolution, and, at the height of paradox, it gets a mention of outstanding in the only European country that unites under the chairmanship of a socialist government.

In the face of this enormous work by García Rodríguez, which materially has the breadth of a dictionary, one wonders whether everything is laudable, or, more simply, acceptable.

Personally, I would have dealt with the first part (the story from chapter one to four), giving further nuance to the trials and pruning certain accusations that seem too sharp to me. The whole of the work, however, constitutes an imposing fresco, sometimes arduous but of great interest, on the characteristics of the social problems and social legislation of the Third Reich, on the National Socialist economy, on the Labor Front and its pedagogical organization, about the producer community, about enterprise, safety, health care, legal protection, the common good, popular tourism, and even the creation of the Volkswagen.

*Naturally, to assimilate such a compact social encyclopedia (two million printed characters), you have to have a stomach capable of digesting a Carrara marble mine or a cave full of stalactites. In any case, here is the instrumental work, with some imperfections, but also with its thousands of revealing facts.*

*It was awarded by a thesis committee.*

*Therefore, you readers no longer have any excuse to continue ignoring the existence of the greatest social revolution of the twentieth century. Read this study from cover to cover. As you finish the last page of the book, seemingly inexhaustible, you will be grateful to this tenacious Spaniard who, wishing to inform you, bled ink for several years in research and study so that people could realize what Hitler achieved, this man who is still repudiated in the social field, although this will certainly no longer be the case in the near future.*

## The Last Letter to Olivier Mathieu

On February 7th, 1994, Léon wrote a letter to Olivier Mathieu after having received the manuscript of his book *Léon Degrelle, as I Knew Him*. He told Mathieu:

*You will find, attached, the carefully revised text of your book. It is a text of high literary value. This is not only my opinion but also the opinion of Jeanne, who has read it with great care....Do you still keep in touch with the widow of the surrealist painter René Magritte? I would very much like to know where the original of Magritte's ad against me is located, it was an interesting document from before the war, and, if possible, I would like to buy it. Good luck to all and to all my great affection.*

*Léon Degrelle*

## Farewell Message to His Soldiers

On February 18th, 1994, on the occasion of the fiftieth anniversary of the Battle of Cherkassy, when he had but forty-one days left in his life, Léon Degrelle wrote an exciting and final farewell message to his legionaries, his brave soldiers, as a political testament:

*February 18th, 1994, at 7:00 p.m.*

My dear ones, my dear comrades!

Confined in the depths of my exile, I have never been closer to you than on this fiftieth anniversary of Cherkassy.

Those days, by dint of courage, renunciation, and sacrifice, you delivered the last great victory in the east to the armies of new Europe.

Remember with pride, in today's rotten world, only the virtues of heroes still shine.

Tomorrow, it will be they and the heroes now who will be gathered in glory. You are great and only this counts in life.

To you, my dear comrades, with the last beats of my heart, I kiss you,
*Léon Degrelle*
*February 18th, 1994*

### The Solemn Will

On February 25th, 1994, in Malaga, facing the Mediterranean Sea, Léon Degrelle wrote and signed his will on a sheet of paper with a small oak leaf above his name, in which he named his wife Juana "Jeanne" Brevet de Degrelle, as the sole heir:

*Solemn Will*

On February 25th, 1994, I, the signatory, Léon Degrelle, also acting under the name of León José de Ramírez y Reina, having been adopted in Cazalla de la Sierra by Mrs. de Ramírez Reina, of Constantina;

Living in Madrid, at calle Santa Engracia, number 37, or in Malaga, at Paseo Marítimo de Melilla, number 23, I bequeath to my wife, Mrs. Jeanne Brevet-Degrelle, all my personal goods and real estate, both in Madrid, at García Morato 37, and in Malaga, Paseo Marítimo, number 23, floor sixteen, as well as all the liquid money that I have that day, all without any condition, and without proviso, in its entirety.

Written by my hand, in complete freedom, and dominating all my faculties, in Malaga, on February 25th, 1994.

Likewise for all my assets of the "Caleta Real S.A." in Salobreña (Granada).
Signed and initialed: Léon Degrelle.
National Identity Number 27.761.932.

The will would be notarized by the notary of Malaga, D. Cayetano Utrera Ravassa.

### Mission Accomplished; My Honor is Called Loyalty!

A few weeks later, on March 10th, 1994, Léon was urgently admitted to the sanatorium Parque de San Antonio hospital in Malaga, suffering from heart failure.

On March 31st, 1994, Holy Thursday, at 11:10 p.m. at night, with echoes of the Passion procession made by the Malagueña Brotherhood on calle Larios wafting through the window of room number 225, next to the city's cathedral, Léon Degrelle serenely gave up his soul to God. Like a warrior-monk, he was able to say, "Mission fulfilled, O Lord" or perhaps he was singing *Non nobis Domine*.[180] So many times, he had told us, "If death comes, we will see it arrive without blinking; we will go with a light step and a sad smile for the memories that resurrect in the last few seconds." To paraphrase Francisco de Otazú:

> *Gold defeated steel, but no metal shines as bright as the stars. The stars shine their brightest while announcing the dawn, so if I had to name three stars, I would choose those of José Antonio, Codreanu, and León Degrelle, three stars for Europe.*

His death came the year he was to turn eighty-eight (8-8, H-H).[181] He had been born six years after crossing over to the twentieth century and died six years before its end.

The coffin containing Degrelle's body remained in room number 11 of Cemetery Park throughout the day on Good Friday, watched over by those closest to him. As was arranged, his mortal remains were incinerated at 11:30 p.m. on Friday, April 1st. His comrade in the Walloon Legion, Jean Vermeire, took charge of the ashes.

April 1st is also a memorable historical date. It is the "Day of Victory" of the National Forces of Spain, a glorious date on which Generalissimo Francisco Franco, in 1939, signed, in Burgos, the last war report, announcing urbi et orbe[182] "The war is over!" The era of peace began. Degrelle's life thus culminated victoriously in his transit to life eternal.

---

[180] [A short Latin hymn used as a prayer of thanksgiving and expression of humility. The Latin motto of the Knights Templar is "Non nobis Domine, non nobis, sed nomini tuo da gloriam," meaning "Not to us Lord, not to us, but to Your Name give the glory" in English.]

[181] In some National Socialist circles, 88—with "H" being the eighth letter in the alphabet—stands for "HH," interpreted as "Heil Hitler."

[182] [Latin for "to the city and to the world."]

The first Mass for his soul was officiated by Reverend Father Victoriano, who, in his youth, had studied in Belgium and knew and loved Degrelle. The Mass was celebrated in the small, secluded chapel of the sanatorium where his passing occurred.

Léon wanted his ashes to be spread in one of the four places he considered magical and geomantic, according to the wishes he had made known, in confidence, on some occasion, to his interior "hermetic" circle. Among the people with whom he had maintained these confidences were Mariano Sánchez Covisa and Jean Vermeire. I also had the privilege of being counted among them. When he conveyed to me these intimate and posthumous desires, the places chosen by him for his eternal rest were Mount Abantos, next to the Royal Monastery of San Lorenzo de El Escorial; Toledo, next to the walls of the fortress of El Alcázar, near the monument with the standing angel looking toward the sky, perched on a rock over the Valley of the Tagus River, while offering the sword of the victors to God; his hometown, Bouillon, in the vicinity of the castle of the first crusader of faith, Godfrey, in whose shadow he saw the years of his childhood and youth go by; and in Hitler's Eagle's Nest, in Berchtesgaden, Bavaria, between the snow-capped peaks and the whistle of the wind, amid the silence of the summits and the murmur of the springs, the thick forests and the snow-capped mountains where the flower of the Edelweiss is born.

## The First Reactions

When the news broke, the students were returning from their holidays during Holy Week. A huge poster was put up in the lobby of the Faculty of Law of the Complutense University of Madrid, sponsored by the university associations of Dispar, Nuevo Cauce, and Vanguardia Universitaria. It read:

> *At the end of March, coinciding with dates of mourning and remembrance, as if asking permission of the Most High to appear before His unappealable judgment, which will surely be merciful, the last man of integrity who survived the misfortunes and injustices of contemporary history has left us. He left us as he came: proud to have lived confronting lies and injustice. Not only has the man died, but the example has died. A blessed example you leave with us, Léon, with your prolific life and with your gallant death.*
>
> *Separated from your homeland, your life and your death are subjects of reflection for both the young and the old. Your ancient youth is an example for those who are dead in life.*

*Patriot, warrior, anti-Bolshevik, and Christian, one of those who deserves to be called so, who wears it proudly upon the chest, who stands up for it chivalrously when the hour comes.*

*Rest in peace, comrade and brother. May your example remain alive and serve for us as a stamp and mold. May it teach your great deed to us all, to all of us who still believe in a better world, in honest men, and in gallant lives. Let your image shine upon us to keep us encouraged, to give us nimble jumps and manly advances, without retreating, delivering blows that seek the cowardly enemy and the one disguised as a friend, and may your death, Léon, harangue us, all of us who saw in you more than a man, but also the commander.*

*Rest in peace, comrade.*

On April 8th, Blas Piñar was in Rome, at the restaurant Picar on Via Artegianato six. He was paying tribute to Gianfranco Fini, promoted by Flavio Palumbo, for having obtained the largest number of votes in that city, a constituency for whom he was elected representative. He was also there to attend a dinner organized by Renzo Lodoli to commemorate, with Italian veterans, as they did every year, the victory of the National Forces in Spain, on April 1st, 1939. During his stay in Rome, he could see that the streets were flooded with posters in memory of Léon Degrelle, as he relates in his memoirs "*Escrito Para la Historia*" ("*Written for History*"), in the volume entitled *La Pura Verdad* (*The Pure Truth*).

One of Léon's granddaughters, Elena Balaguer Degrelle, published the following letter on April 12th, 1994, in the newspaper *El Mundo*:

*Léon Degrelle, my grandfather.*

Mr. Director:

*It is difficult to summarize such a long and intense life in just a few lines. Léon Degrelle founded the "Rex" Party (short for Christus Rex, not referring to monarchy), won twenty-one deputies in the 1936 elections, created several newspapers and publishing outlets, and dedicated his years of exile in Spain to writing numerous works, including* The Burning Souls, *translated, with a foreword, by Dr. Gregorio Marañón. Above all, he was a beloved man as a father and grandfather.*

*I fail to understand why people like Gabriel Albiac have waited for his death, frivolously and senselessly, to call him a "murderer," thereby causing immense pain to his family and friends. I want to believe that this is due to ignorance.*

*Léon Degrelle, my grandfather, was never accused or convicted of murder. I attach a certificate signed by the Belgian Ambassador that he was sentenced to death on December 27th, 1944, for "infractions committed against State security," with a statute of limitations set for February 5th, 1969, and that "he was not prosecuted at Nuremberg." It is clear that his only crime was having fought on the losing side of a war and, as you know, vae victis![183]*

*Do you think, Mr. Albiac, that a man as liberal and democratic as Dr. Marañón, who devoted part of his life to studying history, would be an intimate friend and admirer of a "murderer"? Did you know that in one of Belgium's extradition claims, my grandfather hid in the home of a communist veteran whose life he had saved from prison? Would you be interested to know that he had Jewish coworkers on his newspapers and in his party, and one of them became a rexist deputy? I studied Information Science and am a strong supporter of freedom of expression, but reading articles like those of Mr. Albiac, I doubt whether I chose the right profession.*

*Elena Balaguer Degrelle*

In number 1,095 of the weekly *Fuerza Nueva*, dated April 14th, 1994, a heartfelt and moving article that I wrote *in memoriam* for my great and irreplaceable friend, entitled "*Léon Degrelle, the Heroic Sense of Life*," was published. It began like this:

*Léon Degrelle belongs to that lineage of guides and leaders of peoples who fill the history of humanity. His words were alive, burning, like his soul. He made his existence the ideal and of his ideal, honor. He resisted like a firm rock. Léon was that eagle that set his gaze upon the sun, and never blinked. He was convinced of the greatness that lies within every man when he uses his energies to joyfully pursue the superior. His existence was exaltation. He disdained the easy and loved virtue and will.*

### The Funeral Services

In Benalmádena (in Malaga), in the parish of the Virgin del Carmen, a Mass was celebrated in his memory, requested by "his comrades and friends," with this notice: "Join in the mourning of his family and pray for the eternal rest of his soul, a Mass to be held in the parish Virgin del Carmen (Sol y Mar, Benalmádena-Costa) on Friday, April 15th, at 8.30 p.m." Among those attending the funeral mass were, in the midst of a large group of loyal friends, Mariano Bolaño Lozano and General Remer.

---

[183] [Latin for "woe to the vanquished."]

In the memorial, these three phrases extracted from his work *The Burning Souls* were transcribed:

*If death comes, we will see it arrive without blinking; we will go with a light step and the sad smile for the memories that resurrect in the last few seconds. If we return then, when life, lukewarm, has made us forget this icy wind, our hearts will now recover forever the balance of life that knew not how to tremble before death. May fate always find us worthy and strong!*

*Once we have fulfilled our duties, what does it matter if death comes at the age of thirty or one hundred years? Short or long, life is only worth something if in the moment we must hand it over, we have nothing to blush about it.*

*The ideal will live to the extent that we give ourselves to it until we die. What a drama, indeed, that of an upright life!*

A Mass was held in Barcelona on Thursday, April 14th, at 8:30 p.m. in the church of San Félix Africana, on calle Francisco Arande twenty-one, near the Olympic village. Announcing the religious service, an obituary commissioned by "his comrades and those who see in his life an example of fidelity to an ideal," appeared in the press with these words: "Léon Degrelle. Founder of the Rex Movement. General of the Waffen SS. Hero of the West." The Mass was officiated in the Spanish language. The first pews were occupied by his friends and comrades from CEDADE: Jorge Mota, María Infiesta, Ramón Bau, Pedro Varela, Joaquín Bochaca, Agustín Vargas, Ángel Ricote Zumalla, etc. The church lights that lit up the space and dozens of small, thick candles tucked into their red glass holders gave the event a warm and intimate feeling. More than two hundred young people attended the religious service. In the courtyard of the parish, memorials were distributed with the name of Léon Degrelle under an Iron Cross with Oak Leaves. The priest, during the Mass, read a few paragraphs from *The Burning Souls*. At the door of the church, all the attendees, arms raised, sang in a compassionate but firm tone the hymn "*I Had a Comrade...*"[184]

The monarchist newspaper *ABC* in its Thursday, April 21st, 1994 edition, published this obituary:

---

[184] The original song is *Ich hatt'einen Kameraden*, also known as *Der Gute Kamerad*, written in 1809 by German poet Ludwig Uhland, and put to music in 1825. The song is used by many armies today for military funerals, including Germany, Austria, Spain, Chile, Colombia, as well as the French Foreign Legion.

*Léon Degrelle, founder and head of the Belgian Rex Party, head of the Walloon Division on the Eastern Front. Knight of the Iron Cross, Oak Leaves, passed away in Malaga on March 31st, 1994 at eighty-seven years of age. His wife, daughters, sons-in-law, grandchildren and great-grandchildren report that next Saturday, April 23rd, at 12:30 a.m., a Mass will be celebrated for the eternal repose of his soul in the Parish of San Fermín de los Navarros (calle Eduardo Dato, number 10, in Madrid).*

An impressive crowd attended the funeral Mass. The church proved insufficient to hold so many people who it wanted to pay tribute and respect to the leader of Europe. At the helm of the religious service was his widow, Mrs. Juana "Jeanne" Brevet de Degrelle, and his daughters, sons-in-law, grandchildren, and great-grandchildren, who were surrounded by the three hundred friends and comrades who filled the naves of the church. At the door of the church a memorial was distributed that showed an image of a cross upon which was placed a steel military helmet with SS runes and the caption *Victi invictis victuri*,[185] along with all the division insignia of the Waffen SS with the phrase *"Meine Ehre heißt Treue"* ("My Honor is called Loyalty") which had been commissioned by Bernardo Gil Mugarza and myself.

## The Posthumous Letter from His Daughter Anne

Léon's daughter, Anne Degrelle, published a letter entitled "Léon Degrelle, My Father" on April 20th, 1994, in the Madrid weekly *La Nación*, stating the following:

*He left at the age of eighty-seven, without ever abandoning his struggle. He never surrendered, fought like a lion to defend his ideals against a pack of false "historians," distorters of history, victors of a war where the best of European youth gave their lives. Since his early days at the University of Louvain, on the pages of the student newspaper he founded, he began to fight political corruption. His "Rex" Party served as a platform to project himself outside the limits of his native Belgium and to approach the larger political currents of the time: the falange of José Antonio; the fascism of Mussolini; the National Socialism of Hitler. Like them, he wanted to end the rotten democracies of old Europe. He tried to erase the privileges of an anti-social bourgeoisie. He gave his support to an oppressed working class and deprived*

---

[185] [Latin for "The defeated shall live unconquered."]

Marxism of its influence in the factories. His pen, his oratory, earned him the appreciation and respect of hundreds of thousands of compatriots who voted for Rex in 1936.

If he was a political fighter, he soon wanted to be one on the battlefield as well. In 1941, he formed his legion, the "Wallonie" (Walloon), which fought side by side with Spaniards (Blue Division), French (Charlemagne Division), Italian, Swedish, Danish, and even British. Almost three years of glory, starting as a simple soldier and winning the highest decorations, among them the great Iron Cross with Oak Leaves. Years of fierce war in a Russia that closed in on them like a huge trap, tied down on all fronts, from the Atlantic to the Urals, having to fight against the real criminals of humanity: the Allies and their incendiary bombs that ravaged Germany and its civilian population.

Now in exile, in this Spain that welcomed him when his plane fell on the beach of San Sebastián in 1945, he dedicated the last forty-eight years of his life to writing, to defending against hatred, slander, and insults; defending the memory of his comrades killed on the front; and putting into historical books what the "great adventure" of our century was, the last epic of certain crusaders who wanted to save a Europe—now only of the "common market"—that has lost all manner of Christian, spiritual, and patriotic values.

At this time of his life, I was his intimate collaborator; with his second wife, Jeanne Brevet, we were the first readers of his manuscripts and took turns typing them. He published, against all odds, more than twenty titles, with publishers who gambled everything just so that a different voice than the sacrosanct "holders of truth," the historians of falsehood, could be heard. One day this voice, together with those of the increasingly numerous "revisionists," will open the eyes of new generations. Anxious to hear him, that youth, which he loved, came to see him from the four corners of the earth, and returned home excited by his words and ideas.

He is gone. He left his life in Spain, the homeland of his friend and comrade José Antonio; the great nation that he studied and admired so much, in which his grandchildren and great-grandchildren were born (how he enjoyed when one of them, my son, volunteered for the Legion!); the Spain that gave him shelter thanks to Caudillo Franco, for which we, his family, will forever be eternally grateful; the Spain that he praised in his book The Burning Souls, translated, with a foreword, by Dr. Gregorio Marañón.

THANK YOU, SPAIN!

## In Memoriam

In J. Cuyás Rigau's article simply titled "Degrelle," published in the weekly *La Nación*, he highlighted as an essential feature of Léon's personality the fact that he was "a true crusader of incredible feats who, despite having been sentenced to death in his country, was never considered a war criminal," and was also always "a place of pilgrimage for French and Belgian youths, eager to meet the one who had been presented as Lucifer and was really a knight-errant with a glorious record" and all this because of constant disinformation.

For his part, the Aviation Colonel Armando Sánchez Oliva, in the same publication, wrote an eminently militaristic article titled "Léon Degrelle," in which he highlighted his exemplary service record, his bravery, his combat wounds, his distinctions, meritorious mentions, and his lofty decorations out in front of his volunteer unit. To paraphrase Hitler, he added:

> *I too would have liked to have had a son like him, and even to have been able to be like him, five times wounded, and twenty-two times decorated on campaign, fighting for Europe from the Ardennes to the Caucasus, in a fantastic cavalcade that took him from the rank of corporal to the head of a division, in front of the purest of Belgian youth at that time.*

Feeling true pride, he wrote:

> *I am honored to have his friendship and that of his children and grandchildren and I took part in campaigns that were organized in 1969–70 to oppose the danger of extradition. The last time I was with him was when we went up to the communion rail together at the funeral mass for the soul of Mariano Sánchez Covisa.*

For his part, the professor and historian from Murcia, Francisco Torres García, in an emotional article entitled "Degrelle: The Last Volksführer," recalled that "the last Volksführer appointed by Hitler, the last living division commander of the mythical Waffen SS" has died, and pointed out that "his life was possibly closer to the script of a good action movie than to that of a mere mortal of our time," who always fought to "secure for his homeland a position in the new Europe."

On April 28th, Blas Piñar recalled in his memoirs:

*We celebrated at our headquarters a posthumous tribute to Léon Degrelle, who had died in Malaga on March 31st. Chief in attendance was his widow Jeanne Brevet. José Luis Jerez Riesco and I spoke. The speech by José Luis Jerez was entitled "Léon Degrelle; the Man, the Christian, the Politician." Anne, one of Degrelle's daughters, thanked him.*

*Bernardo Gil Mugarza, the author of the book España en llamas (Spain in Flames), published a beautiful article in our magazine (number 1,096, April 30th to May 17th) about Léon Degrelle entitled "Requiem for a Great European."*

Miguel Serrano, the brilliant Chilean diplomat and good friend of Léon, gave an emotional funeral prayer in his country, offering the following words:

*Very recently, on a day of darkness, at the feast of the Light of Ostara,[186] in Holy Week, my beloved friend and Belgian comrade, Léon Degrelle, left this world. For those of us who knew him and for his own wife, this seems incredible. He was immortal, and he even said, "The lion will never die!" So did his comrades in arms of the Walloon Division on the Eastern Front during the Second World War. In exile, in Spain, he just died, in the week of the hero's resurrection. After the nigredo and the albedo, he resurrects on the rubedo,[187] on Easter Sunday, Sontag,[188] the day of the Sun, and in a body of immortal red light.*

*Today we pay tribute to that hero, to that comrade, to that friend, a guide and example of the nationalistic and National Socialist youths of the world, who never yielded, but maintained, with loyalty identical to my own, his ideals until the last day, here in this poisoned land. In remembrance of him, we convey to his wife, Jeanne, our support and encouragement that she might overcome her pain and have the strength necessary to continue disseminating the books and work that Degrelle leaves to her care and the comrades who will help her.*

Three years after his death, a colloquium on Léon Degrelle was held at the headquarters of Fuerza Nueva on April 3rd, 1997. In the year 2000, in the restaurant Il Boccalino in Madrid's Plaza de España, at a Christmas dinner organized

---

[186] Miguel Serrano, being the esoteric that he was, blends both pagan and Christian themes in his "prayer" for Degrelle, thus the reference to the goddess Ostara, root of the English word *Easter*.

[187] [The medieval Latin terms *nigredo*, *albedo*, and *rubedo*—which loosely mean blackish, whitish, and redish—were terms in alchemy that refer to the various stages of development, ending in *rubedo*, the purest, most refined state.]

[188] [German for Sunday.]

by the Association of Friends of Léon Degrelle, presided over by his widow and me, Blas Piñar shared a few emotional words "remembering Léon Degrelle."

The socialist-leaning newspaper *El País*, in Madrid, on May 7th, 1994, published an article by Thierry Maliniak, entitled "Cenizas que Queman" ("Burning Ashes").

The nationalist information outlet *Jeune Nation*, in its April 1994 edition, published an article titled "La Muerte de un Gigante"[189] ("The Death of a Giant"), which took up the entire cover page, cheering on the Degrelle generation. The editor of the publication, Yvan Benedetti, who penned the article began like this:

> *Léon Degrelle is no longer with us. Across Europe, nationalists mourn the loss of their big brother. The big brother always there to advise you in difficult moments, who has lived before you and who recounts, in the evening, those glorious tales of great campaigns in the heroic age. The big brother who you admire, who you wait for, for he is of your race, of your blood. Our big brother is no longer; he has left, illustrious and solitary, though not without having marked the way beforehand.* [...]

> *His example remains. The example that all the misery of this world and the anxieties of life can achieve nothing against the man who believes. The example that military defeat, war wounds, physical suffering, the murder of a neighbor, torture, exile cannot undermine the will of a man animated by an ideal, by faith. You deliberately chose your camp, that of lions, and you have made the adage of Seneca your own: "The man who knows how to die will never be a slave." Not a single second of your life have you been a slave and therefore you have lived, a lover of life and men.*

> *Like a hero of Rostand[190] you have set off confronting death, sword in hand...*

> *Here we swear the oath, on the young nation of our ancestors and on the blood of our dead, to return you to your house, to the land of Bouillon, just as we transported the Marshal to be among his own, to Douaumont.*

> *You have given us hope again.*

> *You have given us the faith and energy to fight for victory.*

> *REX has died, long live rexism!*

> *To your health, comrade!*

---

[189] The outlet *Jeune Nation* was a French-language publication; the author has mistakenly given the title of its article in Spanish translation. The original title was "La mort d'un géant." https://www.le-livre.fr/livres/fiche-r240153055.html

[190] This is likely a reference to Edmond Eugène Alexis Rostand, best known for his 1897 play *Cyrano de Bergerac*, who was an acclaimed neo-Romantic poet and dramatist.

On April 30th, 1994, at his noble manor at San José, on Parada de Gonta, near Viseu, Portuguese poet Rodrigo Emilio wrote a piece in memory of Degrelle when he learned of his death. He titled it *Adagio Final*:[191]

| | |
|---|---|
| *Dizem-me que morreu Léon Degrelle,* | *They tell me that Léon Degrelle has died.* |
| *Morreu lá agora!* | *He just died!* |
| *Pode lá ser?!* | *Can it be?!* |
| *Nao morreu tal.* | *That cannot be how he died.* |
| *Morrer era a última das coisas que lhe poderían suceder.* | *Dying is the last thing that could happen to him.* |
| *Mais—digo mais: morrer* | *More than that, I say, not just that;* |
| *É justamente a única coisa que nao poderá* | *Dying is just the one thing that could never* |
| *Acontecer nunca a Degrelle, gatanto-lhes Eu.* | *Happen to Degrelle, I shout to them.* |
| *Vale uma aposta?!* | *Is it worth a bet?!* |
| *Por mim, arrisco—e arrisco ja.* | *I will take my chances and I will take them now.* |
| *Dobrado contra singelo.* | *Double or nothing.* |
| *Degrelle morreu, senhores!* | *Degrelle has died, gentlemen!* |
| *Viva Degrelle!* | *Long live Degrelle!* |

The distinguished professor of Philosophy of Law and prolific Portuguese writer Antonio José de Brito, referring to Léon Degrelle, considered him a "Master of Life" and stated:

> *I believe that there is no more fascinating figure in European fascism than Léon Degrelle...The day will come, however, when the spring and the name of Léon Degrelle will finally return as one of the glories of Europe, not of the Europe of busybodies and plutocrats, but the Europe of dignity and courage.*

The Chilean diplomat and writer Miguel Serrano, a good friend of Léon Degrelle, declared the news of his death, saying:

> *I admire Léon Degrelle because he continues in the trenches, together with his Führer, with an uncompromising loyalty and an unshakable courage. He is a poet*

---

[191] In Jerez Riesco's original work, this poem by Rodrigo Emilio is given in Emilio's original Portuguese without translation (most Spaniards would be able to read and understand this simple poem in its original), so we likewise offer it here in Portuguese. The English translation provided here is my own.

*and also a priest-warrior in the service of the myth of Führer Adolf Hitler, whom he*
*knew personally, saw him and touched him. I admire and love my comrade, the*
*minstrel Léon Degrelle, very much.*

In September 1995, the publishing house Les Editions de la Toison d'Or, in Paris, published a book titled *In Memoriam. Léon Degrelle et le Rexisme* (*In Memoriam. Léon Degrelle and Rexism*). It was a compilation containing an anthology of texts and documents written by Léon, together with articles and comments by his friends and comrades. Contributors included Paul Fassange, Jean-Robert Debbaud, Pierre Daye, Jacques Crokaert, Ives Bouillon, Raphael Syndic, José Streel, L. Scheppers, Guy de Liedekerke, and Frédéric Anciaux.

An old comrade, René-Gilles Henrotay, a volunteer of the Walloon Legion who had been awarded the Iron Cross, Second Class, the Badge of the Wounded, the Medal of the East, the Close Combat Badge, and the Meritorious Cross, wrote in his book *Chemin d'Idéal* (*Way of the Ideal*) that the day after Léon's death, on April 1st, Good Friday, in his home at Braine-l'Alleud, he wrote an extensive poem, entitled "Léon Degrelle has Died," with feelings of bitter pain. The first stanza is composed of these heartfelt words:

*You never promised us more than death.*
*Today, death has welcomed you.*
*You never promised us more than glory.*
*In our hearts, Chief, you have already achieved it.*

## Eternal Hatred Eats the Insides of His Enemies

If the persecution by rancorous Jews and leftists of all stripes during his long exile had been a constant, then their final act, where they displayed their supreme vileness, was consummated on April 18th, 1994. They published an account of the promulgation of a "Royal decree banning access to the Belgian territory of the mortal remains of Léon Degrelle," in the Belgian State Bulletin on April 23th, 1994, reference number F.94-1112 (C-Win-198). It is reproduced here in its entirety as proof of the shameful extent to which the sowers of perpetual hate will go:

*Albert II, King of the Belgians, to all, present and to come, greetings.*
*Regarding article one hundred eight of the Constitution.*

*Regarding the Law of March 6th, 1818, on penalties applicable to infringements of the rules of internal administration, as well as penalties which may be established by provincial or municipal authorities, in particular article one, as amended by the Act of June 5th, 1934.*

*Whereas the presence on Belgian territory of the mortal remains of Léon Degrelle is incontestably of such kind that it may cause ruptures in public order.*

*Considering, therefore, that it is urgent to take measures in view of maintaining public order.*

*With the proposal of the Minister of the Interior,*

*We have decreed and we now decree:*

*Article One. Access to Belgian territory and deposit of the mortal remains of Léon Degrelle is prohibited.*

*Article Two. The perpetrator, co-perpetrators, and accomplices of any infringement of article one shall be punished by imprisonment for eight to fourteen days and a fine of between twenty-six francs and two hundred francs, or one of these sentences alone.*

*Article Three. Pursuant to articles forty-two and forty-three of the Criminal Code, a special confiscation measure shall be pronounced in the event of a violation of article one of this Decree.*

*Article Four. In the event of confiscation, as provided for in article three of this Decree, the mortal remains shall be returned to the authorities of the country of death.*

*Article Five. This Decree shall enter into force on the day of its publication in the Official Gazette of the Belgian State.*

*Article Six. Our Minister of the Interior is responsible for implementing this Decree.*

*Given at Brussels, April 18th, 1994.*

*Albert*

*By the King:*

*The Minister of the Interior and Public Administration, L. Tobback.*

The stupid and the wicked can never impose their miserable will upon God's designs, and therefore the ashes of Léon Degrelle are under heaven and united with the earth in the places he chose to rest in peace for eternity.

After his death, Jean Vermeire, the Captain of the Waffen SS and Degrelle's comrade from the Walloons, took charge of the ashes of Léon Degrelle. When Léon died, his wife Jeanne was also very ill, suffering from broncho-pneumonia, which, thanks be to God, she was able to overcome. While he was still alive, Léon had entrusted to Vermeire, who visited him frequently, that among the places where he would like his ashes to be deposited was Botassart, very close to his hometown of Bouillon, in the place known as "The Tomb of the Giant." Likewise, the mountain of Obersalzberg, near the Führer's "Eagle's Nest" in Bavaria, received a portion of his mortal legacy.

On November 16th, 2000, the Flemish language television channel Canvas broadcast a report by Freddy Coppens called "Degrelle, the Führer of Bouillon," in which Jean Vermeire confirmed the dispersal of Degrelle's ashes, who in his day was appointed by Hitler as "Chief of the People." Jean Vermeire stated: "The ashes of Léon Degrelle rest in an absolutely fabulous place. No one can ever take them from there. It was the total and perfect fulfillment of a promise. No one can reproach me…"

## The Trail of Light

Otto Skorzeny wrote that Léon Degrelle was a "brave soldier, who was wounded at the head of his units and received with every right the highest German military distinctions." Former Minister General Secretary of the Movement José Utrera Molina recognized:

> *I confess that I have met very few men equipped with the intellectual and moral energy of Léon Degrelle. True to a code of honor, with an extraordinary capacity to resist, he has never known the reluctance for action, nor has he ever suffered the drama of losing hope…I believe him to be in possession of a soul invulnerable to holding grudges, unable to hate, passionate, but not violent, vehement, but not strained…he is one of the most important and suggestive personalities in Europe…he knew few periods of rest, few useless or empty moments, few hours devoted to meaningless leisure.*

Léon Degrelle shared the following on one occasion:

> *God dwells in me. If, by some miracle, fate was to warn me again, yes, I would still go to the appointment, but to the appointment of the forgers of peoples, of the masters of life, the only ones that interest me…. I wanted to fill my soul with greatness, and it is a food that costs dearly. I pay the bill, but the bliss I had following my vocation, and forging a lofty destiny, makes up for the most bitter of bitterness…. I see, with a clear vision, that this life has given me a maximum of*

*sorrows and joys. In short, it was worth it. I am happy.... We are only defeated when our soul is defeated. Misfortune is nothing more than an incident.*

*The true sacrifice of exile is not there. What is harder and crueler to me is the feeling that the decades in which I could have done something great have gone away in silence and uselessness. I was carrying tumultuous forces within me, which I can only imperfectly distinguish. They lie inert in the background of my solitude. What I could have achieved for myself, and especially for others, was forbidden to me. Exile buried me alive. Since 1945 I have only survived in hibernation.*

*This is the drama of my exile: holding against my heart glowing possibilities, suffocated by a layer of lead. I was made to create. My arms have hung limp for decades. Will I be only the end of the epic, whose tools are destroyed for eternity?*

*In the service of my faith, my life has been a sword. I remained steadfast both in luck and in misfortune.*

What he never doubted is that the salvation of the world lies in the will of the souls who believe.

It can be said that no one has suffered for his ideals like Rudolf Hess did, but likewise, no one has fought for them like Léon Degrelle did. He was right when he said, without boasting: "The heroic thing was not dying on the Eastern Front, but fighting, from 1946 onwards, without dying."

Andrés Izquierdo wrote a poem for him in 1998 that ended with these words:

*Léon Degrelle, Léon Degrelle, immortal spirit,*
*Your eternal flame will never go out.*

*Léon Degrelle in memorium March 31st, 1994:*
*"May fate always find us strong and worthy!"*

www.ingramcontent.com/pod-product-compliance
Lightning Source LLC
Chambersburg PA
CBHW021602120626
46545CB00001B/23